Hawaii Early Learning Profile® – HELP®

HELP When the Parent has Disabilities
(1999 Revision)

(Former Title: *HELP When the Parent is Handicapped*)

**Developed and Edited By
Stephanie Parks**

Contributors:
Joal S. Reed; Mona J. Denning, OTR;
Nancy H. Makala, RPT; Karen A. Harless, MS, CCC, S/L;
Nancy K. Seese, MA; Tamara G. Watkins, MSW

**VORT Corporation
Palo Alto, California 94306**

First published in 1984 by VORT® Corporation.
The first edition of this work was developed under Grant No. G008810024 from the U.S. Department of Education, Special Education Programs, Handicapped Children's Early Education Program. The contents, however, do not necessarily reflect the position or policy of that department, and no official endorsement should be inferred.

Revised Edition © 1984, 1999 VORT Corporation.
This document is copyrighted by VORT under the U.S. Copyright Act. No part of this book may be reproduced in any form or by any means, electronic or mechanical, without prior written permission from VORT Corporation.

Printed in the United States of America. All rights reserved.

ISBN-10: 0-89718-091-7   ISBN-13: 978-0-89718-091-7
Library of Congress Catalog Card No. 84-051947

Published by:
VORT Corporation
PO Box 60132
Palo Alto, CA 94306

Publisher's Note
We are pleased to have the opportunity to publish this important resource. It is concise and comprehensive, yet we cannot anticipate the circumstances under which a reader may apply its contents. Each child is unique and masters skills and develops at a rate and an age often different from other children. We therefore urge that you seek additional professional advice if you have any concerns about a child's health or development. We expressly decline liability for the techniques, activities, or results of conclusions you may reach about a child or parent after reading and applying the contents of this book.

For use by professionals
These materials are intended for use by professionals working with the child and the family. All activities must be reviewed/adapted by the professional consistent with the parent's abilities. The child's doctor must be consulted under all circumstances regarding the child's sleep position, if the child has special needs/health issues, or if there are any health or safety questions whatsoever.

Safety First (see also the Safety Notes on page xvi - xvii)
Although precaution and safety notes are included for many activities, there may be some activities which are not appropriate for some children or parents, and some which have the potential for misinterpretation. It is your professional responsibility to carefully review the appropriateness of the activities for each particular child and parent, and to alter the activity and/or add additional safety precautions as needed. It is extremely important to use caution with the child and to supervise him carefully around sharp objects and utensils, appliances, small objects, scissors, hot water, etc. Remind parents of these safety issues, and advise parents to always supervise their child when playing with strings, ribbons, balloons, etc. Since each child is unique, before implementing any activities or suggestions from the HELP activities, you may want to review the recommendations of the American Academy of Pediatrics. Parents should ask their baby's doctor about the appropriate sleeping position for their baby.

Important Reminders
• The age ranges reported in HELP are the ages at which a skill or behavior typically begins according to the literature. These age ranges are **not** when a skill begins and ends! Some skills are time-limited and emerge into more complex skills, while others are lifetime skills. Literature varies regarding the age at which a skill emerges, for example, one source may have reported 9 month, another source 10 months, and another source 12 months. HELP would list that skill at the 9-12 month age range.
• **HELP** is a curriculum-based assessment, **not** a standardized test. It will not yield a definitive single age level or score. The major purpose of HELP as a curriculum assessment is to identify curriculum outcomes, strategies and activities. See *Inside HELP* for instruction on using HELP as an assessment.

CONTENTS

	Page
ACKNOWLEDGMENTS	iv
INTRODUCTION	v
INSTRUCTIONS	viii
UPDATES to HELP SKILL TEXT AND AGE RANGES	xiii
DISABILITY SENSITIVE COURTESY GUIDELINES	xiv
SAFETY GUIDELINES AND CONCERNS	xvi
INDEX TO COMMON ISSUES	xviii
CURRICULUM ACTIVITIES	
1.0 Cognitive Development	1
2.0 Expressive Language Development	71
3.0 Gross Motor Development	111
4.0 Fine Motor Development	161
5.0 Social-Emotional Development	197
6.0 Self Help Development	231
PARENT SKILLS REFERENCE LISTING	259
GLOSSARY	271
MATERIALS REFERENCE LISTING	275
BIBLIOGRAPHY	277
HELP Products	278

Notes:

This book contains adapted curriculum (activities) for each HELP skill (0-2). <u>See *Inside HELP* for detailed instruction on how to conduct the assessment of each skill</u>. See page 278 for a listing and description of all HELP Products.

The HELP assessments, including the *HELP Strands*, are **not** norm-referenced or standardized, and will not yield a single age level or score. The major purpose of HELP as a curriculum assessment is to identify curriculum outcomes, goals, strategies and activities.

ACKNOWLEDGMENTS

To the Parents
with disabilities in Project TIMMI
who are not handicapped parents

A project of this scope and nature could not have been accomplished without the teamwork, assistance, and encouragement of many nationwide. My deepest appreciation and gratitude is extended to:
The District 19 Community Services Board; TIMMI's Advisory Board, Crater Child Development Clinic; and the Social Service and Health Departments in Petersburg, Virginia for providing the supportive environment which enabled TIMMI to grow and flourish.

Diane M. Kline, Gail Martinez, and Ruth Moscowitz, original staff at this project's inception, who helped lay the groundwork for alternative thinking and creative thought.

Kathie Smith, Steve and Sherry Delany, and Mike Trent, who contributed numerous innovative parent activity suggestions arising from their own experiences as parents with disabilities.

Karen Harless for switching "hats" to illustrate our activities; Carol Fishwick, Elizabeth Denton, Pat Gallagher, Elisabeth D'Abruzzo, Nancy Costello, and Kim Jones for their expertise, direct consultation, and ideas relating to adult handicapping conditions.

Winifred Northcott, Yvonne Hazel, Linda Sherman, and Kay Ferrell for their well thought out reviews, and valued suggestions relating to many of the parent training activities in this book.

Stewart Gabel, Ginny Proud, Mike Whitner, and Liz Astin for their medical direction, support, and personal commitment.

The more than 100 "relatives" who participated nationally in TIMMI's *Problem of the Month* and provided us with fresh ideas.

Joan Danaher from the Technical Assistance Development System, who always provided immediate reinforcement and pragmatic advice; and Bob Joseph whose persistence stimulated much thought.

Denise Marks, Janice Jones, and Jeanne Trudo for their seemingly endless typing, proofreading, and retyping from barely legible drafts for this manuscript; and to,

The Prince William County Parent-Infant Education Program staff who enthusiastically supported the completion of this book when the demonstration phase of TIMMI ended but my writing had not!

Obviously, this book could not have been developed without the eagerness and commitment of the families enrolled in the project; the expertise, sensitivity, flexibility, and commitment of project staff; the patience and enthusiasm of Tom Holt, our publisher; the support of the Handicapped Children's Early Education Program; and the willingness of Setsu Furuno and associates and the University of Hawaii who allowed us to adapt their already superior program.

And finally, to my daughter, Kim, who will finally be getting her mother back!

S.P.

INTRODUCTION

HELP When the Parent has Disabilities is an infant/toddler (birth-two) curriculum designed to be used by professionals who are working with parents who have disabilities. It is a direct adaptation of the HELP Activity Guide*, an early intervention curriculum developed for infants and toddlers who have or are at-risk for developmental disabilities. *HELP When the Parent has Disabilities* was developed to help ensure that parents with disabilities are afforded the same opportunities as parents without disabilities to facilitate and participate in their child's developmental growth.

Most programs involved with parents and young children realize the vital role parents play in their children's learning and development. Active parent participation and involvement is thus emphasized throughout early intervention programs, parent training manuals, and early childhood curricula.

Most parent training manuals and early childhood curricula, however, do not tell us:
• How to involve a parent without hearing in her child's language program at home,
• How to explain to a mother who is mentally retarded a behavioral management program for her child,
• How to teach a parent who is blind to encourage her child to attend to and track objects, nor,
• How to enable a parent who uses a wheelchair to carry out therapeutic exercises with her child.

Consequently, parents with disabilities have often been left out of or inadequately served by traditional parent training programs. *HELP When the Parent has Disabilities* is intended to help close this critical gap and ameliorate the parent training barriers which arise as a result of the parent's disability or our own lack of knowledge and understanding.

Population for Whom this Guide is Intended

Alternative parent training activities are included for parents who are mentally retarded, deaf, blind, and physically disabled. The activities for mentally retarded parents are intended for parents who function within the upper moderate to mild range of mental retardation, or who function within the borderline range of intelligence. The activities for deaf parents are intended for parents with severe, profound, or total hearing loss. Suggested activities for blind parents are intended for parents without, or with minimal, functional vision. Most of the activities suggested for physically disabled parents are for parents who are non-ambulatory or who have limited control of their hands and arms.

Parent training activities are included to facilitate the development of children who are developmentally within the birth to twenty-four month age range. The activities were developed for children who are developmentally delayed, are considered "at risk," or have neuromotor impairments. They are also useful for disabled parents whose children are developmentally normal.

This guide is for use with mothers *and* fathers who have children who are boys *and* girls. For clarity, however, parents are referred to in the feminine gender, and children in the male gender. No sexual bias has been intended.

Development of this Work

This guide was developed from our experiences and insights gained through Project TIMMI, an acronym for Training and Intervention for Multihandicapped Mothers and Infants. Project TIMMI was funded as a demonstration project by the U.S. Department of Education's Handicapped Children's Early Education Program, now called the Office of Special Education Program. The Virginia Department of Mental Health and Mental Retardation and the United Way of Southside Virginia provided matching funds to support this project. The project was conducted by the District 19, Mental Health and Mental Retardation Services Board in Petersburg, Virginia from 1981 to 1984.

-----

*Setsu Furuno, Ph.D., Psychologist; Takayo Inatsuka, OTR; Katherine O'Reilly, RPT, MPH; Carol Hosaka, MA, Educator; Barbara Zeisloft, MS, Speech Pathologist; Toney Allman, MA, Psychologist: *Hawaii Early Learning Profile (HELP) Activity Guide*, Palo Alto, California, VORT Corporation, 1979.

A major mission of the project was to provide intervention which would facilitate the disabled parent's active participation in his or her child's development. To do this, we developed alternative service delivery strategies, teaching techniques, and materials to recognize and accommodate the needs of disabled parents and their children. Many of these adaptations were developed through trial and error in our work with Project families and from disabled parents who taught us as much as we taught them. Additional adaptations were developed by combining what we know about infants, parents, and handicapping conditions with available research and literature.

Adaptation of the Hawaii Early Learning Profile (HELP) Activity Guide

The *HELP Activity Guide* was chosen as the core curriculum to be modified for use with handicapped parents because of its widespread use, large number of "teachable" early childhood developmental skills, and the abundance of practical "fun" activities.

More than four hundred sequential developmental skills within six developmental areas, from birth to twenty-four months, were directly extracted from the *HELP Activity Guide*. Since our guide is parent-training oriented, we also developed a parent skill to parallel each developmental skill for the child. The parent skills were derived by simply asking, "What role does the parent play to encourage, facilitate, or maintain the particular child skill in question?" Parent and child skills are numbered in sequence within each developmental area. These numbers correspond with the *HELP Activity Guide's* numbering system to facilitate the reader's cross-reference between HELP manuals.

General guidelines have also been included for most of the parent and child skills. These guidelines define the child skill, explain the significance of that skill, and often include basic general activities and parent interactions to facilitate that child skill.

For each child skill we asked, "If a parent has a disability, could her disability interfere with her or our ability to implement the HELP activities suggested to facilitate the listed child skill?" If so, a need statement is defined and alternative parent training strategies are suggested. If the parent's disability did not appear to affect her or our ability to implement activities for a particular skill with her child, parent training activities were not included. This would have been a duplication of HELP activities and numerous curricula already available. For example, most of the developmental skill activities in the language section have been adapted for parents who are deaf, but none were adapted in the gross motor section because the parent's inability to hear does not interfere with her ability to implement gross motor activities with her child.

Since the developmental skills that we used for devising alternative parent training activities are taken directly from the *HELP Activity Guide*, their explanation regarding the child's developmental skill sequence and accomplishment is also relevant to this guide:

"The age references provided for the skills…are based on a synthesis of research and project data. These age references represent "approximations" since each child is unique and differs in his or her ability to demonstrate specific skills. Your child may successfully display skills before or after the indicated age range. Since each child is unique, you should not be concerned if your child does not display skills exactly within the specified age range. The skills detailed…are not necessarily all critical to the child's development. Many are included because of their teachability and amenability to intervention. It is assumed that a child will not necessarily accomplish all skills listed. A normal child may very well omit some skills and these omissions will not necessarily affect the course of his development. A child may very well complete a skill out of sequence… There was not always agreement in growth and development literature as to when a skill begins. We used our best judgment in determining the placement of the skills…"*

-----
*Furuno, S., et al.: *Hawaii Early Learning Profile (HELP) Activity Guide.* Palo Alto, California VORT Corporation, 1979, p. ix-xi.

The child skills are listed according to the age *range* in which they typically begin. The age range listed is not intended to connote that the skill has an *"end."* Some skills are time-limited and emerge into more complex skills, while others are lifetime skills. Also, in harmony with HELP, the language section is limited to expressive language skills because receptive language skills are incorporated into the cognitive section.

Direct therapy interventions for young children with motor impairments are highly specialized and individualized according to the child's particular needs. The gross motor section, therefore, is *not* intended to provide the reader with specific therapy techniques to carry out with the child. Instead the parent-training activities are to be used as guidelines to be kept in mind *if* special positioning or handling techniques have been prescribed by a physical or occupational therapist.

Limitations of this Guide

This activity guide is intended to be just that, a guide, not a definitive curriculum during your interventions with parents and children. Each parent and child has unique abilities and disabilities within a broad range of functional levels. We have tried to keep the adapted activities general, meaningful, and relevant to natural daily experiences for the parent and child.

The suggested activities are not universal nor exhaustive. Instead, they are intended to act as a springboard which will stimulate your own ideas to meet the particular needs of the parents and children with whom you are involved. This guide is not intended to replace aggressive intervention for the parent or child, nor to replace other early childhood curricula, such as the *HELP Activity Guide*. The purpose is to facilitate intervention and act as a supplement to other curricula.

This guide is not intended to be a parenting guide to teach parents to bathe and dress their child or to respond to illness. Our focus is to train parents to facilitate their child's mental, motor, and emotional development. If the parents you are working with are mentally retarded, general parenting skills are likely to be a necessary component to your interventions.

1999 Revisions

This edition of *HELP When the Parent has Disabilities* has been updated to include:
• Expanded Instructions for using *HELP When the Parent has Disabilities* as a curriculum guide
• Latest additional HELP materials which can be used to maximize and compliment *HELP When the Parent has Disabilities*
• General *"disability sensitive"* courtesy guidelines when working with parents who have disabilities
• Updated reference lists for finding materials and organizations related to adult disabilities
• Additional safety guidelines
• Developmental age range adjustments which reflect current literature.

Personal Reflections about working with Parents with Disabilities

Project TIMMI has enlightened and expanded our understanding and respect for parents with disabilities enormously. We have learned that the barriers to active parent participation in early intervention were often imposed by us, not the parent's disability. We had not offered the parents an alternative strategy when their disabilities appeared to interfere with traditional parent-training techniques.

We have also learned that there are more parent training similarities than there are differences. That is why this guide is intended to be a supplement to your regular parent-training program. The abilities of the parents that we work with far outweigh their disabilities.

The development of this guide is also a reflection of my sensitive and dedicated colleagues, who never stopped asking, "How can *my* interventions change to meet the needs of the parent and child?"

Stephanie Parks

INSTRUCTIONS

How to Use *HELP When the Parent has Disabilities*

I. First, take a quick tour of *HELP When the Parent has Disabilities*

[If you are new to HELP, be sure to review the summaries of the various other HELP materials described on page 278. HELP When the Parent has Disabilities is cross-referenced to all HELP materials. In order to realize maximum benefits of this book, it is recommended that it be used in conjunction with Inside HELP and the HELP Strands.]

1. ***HELP When the Parent has Disabilities* is divided into six major developmental domains.** Each domain is assigned a Domain ID # for easy cross-reference among all HELP materials.

    ### *Tips and Examples*
    Domain ID #
    1.0 Cognitive
    2.0 Language
    3.0 Gross Motor
    4.0 Fine Motor
    5.0 Social Emotional
    6.0 Self-Help

2. **HELP Child Skills are ordered according to age within each domain.** Each skill is assigned a Skill ID # which matches the skill numbers in all HELP materials. Each listed child skill is not necessarily pertinent or necessary for every child.

    The skill typically emerges at any time within the age range in months listed in parentheses. This age range does not signify when a skill begins and ends.

    A separate listing of the HELP child skills is available in assessment format via the HELP Checklist, HELP Strands and HELP Charts.

    Example: **Child skills within a domain**

    1.0 Cognitive
    1.01 Quiets when picked up (0-1 mo.)
    1.02 Shows pleasure when touched or handled (0-6 mo.)
    1.03 Responds to Sound (0-2 mo.)

3. **Parent Skills which parallel the child skill are listed directly below the child skill.** The listed parent skills are general skills directly related to the specific child skill or behavior. Each listed parent skill is not necessarily pertinent or necessary for all parents.

    HELP parent skills are sequentially listed in an appendix on page 259.

    Example: Parent skills parallel child skills

    1.01 <u>Child:</u> Quiets when picked up (0-1 mo.)
    <u>Parent:</u> Helps quiet child by picking up...

4. **A General Guidelines section follows each child and parent skill.** *These guidelines provide a brief definition and general information about the skill. It may also summarize general activities which support and maximize development of that skill.*

    Refer to *Inside HELP* for more specific definitions and assessment criteria for each child skill.

5. **A potential parent "Needs" statement** follows the general guidelines section for various parental disabilities. The need statement, highlighted by italics print, identifies potential barriers or needs which may be associated with a parent's disability. The need statements are directly related to the listed child/parent skill. They were derived from parents and Project staff from their experiences. The need statements are not exhaustive, and may not apply to all parents.

6. **Several curriculum activities** are listed after each need statement for each applicable parent disability. The activities have been adapted to address the *"potential parent need statement"* described in #5 above.

7. **A Glossary** is available on page 271. Definitions are listed for therapeutic terms and materials used through this guide.

8. **A Materials Reference Listing** is available on page 275. This list provides Company or manufacture names and ordering information for various adaptive equipment and assistive technology referred to in this guide.

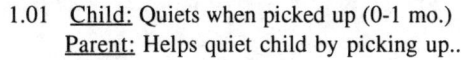

Example: **Parent needs in italics**

1.01 <u>Child:</u> Quiets when picked up (0-1 mo.)
   <u>Parent:</u> Helps quiet child by picking up...

Deaf Parent
May not hear and thus not respond to her child's fussing

If adaptations are not necessary, refer to *HELP at Home* and *HELP Activity Guide* for additional curriculum activities.

This list has been updated from the original *HELP When the Parent is Handicapped* publication to include updated companies, addresses, toll free numbers, and more recent technology for adults with disabilities.

INSTRUCTIONS (continued)

II. Using *HELP When the Parent has Disabilities* as a Curriculum Guide

Step 1 - Assessment: Determining where to begin

*Refer to **Inside HELP** for comprehensive information concerning assessment of the child's development, assessment adaptations, interpretations, transactional assessment (caregiver interactions, supportive environments), and criterion for crediting HELP child skills.*

    A. Assessment of Child's Development

        1. If the child is at risk for, or has a disability or developmental delay, a thorough initial and ongoing multidisciplinary assessment by pediatric specialists should be conducted with appropriate referrals to a local early intervention program. For these children early intervention professionals can use *Inside HELP* with the *HELP Strands* or other appropriate infant assessment instruments prior to using *HELP When the Parent has Disabilities*.

        2. If the child does *not* evidence delays or disabilities, curriculum plans can be developed from this Guide by going directly to the skills which approximate the child's age in each developmental area. In addition, review child skills below and above the child's current age to identify skills which may be emerging or which need continuing support. It can be useful to use the HELP Checklist as planning and monitoring tool with this Guide.

    B. Assessment of Parent Concerns, Priorities and resources

        1. Conduct one or more family centered interviews which focus upon the family's concerns and priorities related to the development of their child, as well as the resources they have available to address their concerns and priorities. The *HELP Family-Centered Interview* is available as resource to help structure this family-centered assessment, building on key daily activities relevant to the child and family.

        2. Assess the unique needs and abilities of the parent as it relates to the parent's disability and caregiving activities. Information about the parent's disability can be collected through parent interviews, observations, and medical and educational records which the parent may choose to share. Examples of general disability specific information which is useful to assess include:

           a. Parents who are *mentally retarded*: general reading level, ability to remember and follow directions (simple and more complex), time concepts, expressive and receptive language abilities.

           b. Parents who are *deaf or hard of hearing*: degree of hearing loss with or without amplification; age of onset; adaptive equipment used at home; and methods of communication.

           c. Parents who are *blind*: preferred methods for receiving print information (e.g., reader, audio tape, and/or Braille); orientation and mobility skills; use of residual vision; use of gestural communication; degree and age of onset of disability. If the parent is congenitally blind, the parent will not have a visual experiential basis for abstract visual concepts such as object permanence or visually directed reach.

           d. Parents who have *physical disabilities*: level of independence in daily living skills; degree of mobility; manipulative skills; strength; lifting, bending, and weight lifting abilities; adaptive equipment used for mobility and daily living.

C. Transactional Assessment
   It can be helpful to gather information about the following general environmental factors and caregiver interactions to assist in curriculum planning. More detailed transactional assessment information for each developmental area is available in *Inside HELP*.
   1. Environment:
      a. Availability of and roles of family, friend and religious support systems.
      b. Availability and accessibility of transportation and recreation facilities.
      c. Availability of developmentally appropriate and safe play materials and equipment.
      d. Child-proofed sleep and play areas.
   2. Caregiver interactions:
      a. Communication style with child: e.g., use of facial and vocal expressions; verbal descriptions.
      b. Ability to "read" and interpret child's cues and signals.
      c. Style of discipline, use of reinforcement.
      d. Involvement in developmentally appropriate activities.
      e. Understanding of child's developmental abilities and needs.
      f. Positioning in relation to child, and, positioning child in relation to play materials.

D. Identification of Medical Needs
   It is important to review the child's and when applicable the parent's medical history and current medical status carefully including vision and hearing if available before intervention and assessment. Some conditions may require a medical clearance from the family's physician prior to any intervention.

   If the child or parent has poor strength and endurance, limit the number of activities addressed at any one time. Watch carefully for any signs of fatigue, and discontinue or modify the intervention at the first sign of physiological distress, e.g., shortness of breath, rapid breathing, changes in behavior.

Step 2 - Develop a Curriculum Plan

A. Develop objectives and /or outcome statements expected to be achieved for the family and or child. These will be based upon the developmental needs of the child and, family concerns, priorities and resources.

B. Identify which child and parent skills from *HELP When the Parent has Disabilities* are most relevant for achieving the outcome statements, and or objectives developed above. These may include skills which the parent or child have not yet achieved, and, skills which may have been achieved but continue to need strengthening. Be sure to integrate skills from all areas of development.

C. Review the general guidelines and parent "need statement" for the appropriate parental disability listed for each of the targeted HELP skills.
   1. If the parent's needs are reflected in the "need statement," review and select appropriate adapted curriculum activities listed for the skill.
   2. If the parent "need statement," is not a need for the parent you are working with, traditional parent training curricula such as *HELP at Home* or the *Help Activity Guide* can be used.

Step 3 - Implement activities

A. All interventions and contacts should be conducted in a manner which reflects trust and respect for the parent as a parent and individual foremost, who secondarily has a disability. See page xiv for "Disability Sensitive Courtesy Guidelines."

B. When a parent training activity says to "explain" or to "relate to the parent" it is assumed that you will "explain" using the parent's preferred method for receiving information, e.g. print, interpreter, speech, and or demonstration.

C. All suggested therapeutic positioning and handing techniques for children who have atypical motor development should be prescribed and supervised by a pediatric therapist.

D. The suggested adapted parent training activities are not definitive nor exhaustive. Each parent is unique and may or may not need adaptations or may need additional supports. Parents will be your best resource for identifying adaptations and interventions to address the unique needs for themselves and their children.

E. **Safety First** (see also Safety Guidelines on pages xvi - xvii).
Although precaution and safety notes are included for many activities, there may be some activities which are not appropriate for some children, which need additional adaptations *to accommodate parent/caregiver disabilities*, and some which have the potential for misinterpretation. It is your professional responsibility to carefully review the appropriateness of the activities for each particular child and caregiver, and to omit, alter the activity, and/or add additional safety precautions as needed.

It is extremely important to use and demonstrate caution with the child and to supervise him carefully around materials listed in this guide. Training parents on these safety issues takes priority. If you believe any listed activity poses a safety hazard which would be difficult for the parent to remember or supervise, omit that activity. Parents should ask their baby's doctor about the appropriate sleeping position for their baby.

F. Keep interventions **culturally relevant.** Some skills and activities listed in the HELP may not be culturally relevant for every family. It is important to assess and adjust activities when appropriate to reflect the family and child's relevant cultural and environmental experiences. Interventions should occur using the child's primary native language, both verbal and non-verbal. Use toys and materials which are culturally meaningful to the child and family.

Important Reminders

• The age ranges reported in HELP are the ages at which a skill or behavior <u>typically begins</u> according to the literature. These age ranges are **not** when a skill begins and ends! Some skills are time-limited and emerge into more complex skills, while others are lifetime skills. Literature varies regarding the age at which a skill emerges, for example, one source may have reported 9 month, another source 10 months, and another source 12 months. HELP would list that skill at the 9-12 month age range.

• *HELP When the Parent has Disabilities* is a curriculum guide of parent training activities to maximize development for birth-two years. It is **not** a standardized test. It will not yield a definitive single age level or score.

• No child is expected to display all skills listed in this guide, nor achieve skills in an exact timetable.

• No parent is expected to display nor achieve all parent skills listed in this guide.

UPDATES TO HELP

Inside HELP (©1992, 1997) was developed by Stephanie Parks to provide a comprehensive Administration and Reference Manual for using HELP. *Inside HELP* provides: (1) flexible, clear, and valid definitions, (2) credit criteria, and (3) assessment procedures for each of the 685 core HELP skills and behaviors. It is intended to promote consistency and a common framework of reference among multidisciplinary professionals using HELP as a curriculum assessment for planning comprehensive programs for infants and toddlers with special needs and their families. *Inside HELP* and the *HELP Strands* were purposefully built upon the core original HELP skills to provide consistency and easy cross-referencing between all the HELP materials.

As a result of literature searches during the development of *Inside HELP*, some minor revisions were identified as necessary for some of the original HELP skill age ranges and text in HELP products printed prior to 1994 (copyright © prior to 1994.) These changes have been made in *Inside HELP* and products revised since 1994 to reflect current literature and trends in the field.

The changes are listed below, but have **not** been made in the body of this book. Refer to the list below when using information from *HELP When the Parent has Disabilities*.

Revised Age Ranges of HELP skills:

Skill#	New Age Range	Skill#	New Age Range
1.23	7-9	3.39	4-6
1.43	7-12	3.40	7-8
1.52	8-10	3.50	9-12
1.64	13-15	3.55	7-8
1.74	9-12	3.57	6-10
2.08	2-7	3.66	13-15
3.07	3-5	4.17	2-3
3.13	1-2	4.19	2-3
3.19	4-6	4.20	4-6
3.24	5-6	4.47	8.5-12
3.25	4-7	4.50	9-10
3.29	5-6	4.56	10-11
3.30	6-7	5.21	5-9
3.32	4-5	5.25	6-10
		6.19	8-10

Revised wording of HELP skills:
5.21 Lifts arms to parent
5.24 Distinguishes self as separate from parent
5.35 Engages in simple relational play
5.60 Enjoys solitary play for a few minutes
6.17 Mouths and munches solid foods
6.24 Chews food with coordinated movements

DISABILITY-SENSITIVE COURTESY GUIDELINES

Collaborating with parents who have disabilities

General

1. Call parents by their first name only with permission and only when extending that familiarity to others present.
2. Speak directly to the parent, not to the parent's companion.
3. Ask parents if they need assistance before you help them.
4. Be careful of your voice tone and style. Never patronize. If a parent needs you to speak in a louder voice they will tell you.
5. Treat parents as your equal in parent training and as the experts they are in knowing themselves and their baby best.
6. Schedule additional time that may be needed to accommodate the extra time parents may need to communicate and participate.
7. Refer to the parent's disability only when necessary and appropriate.
8. Respect all assistive devices as personal property. Do not lean on, move, play with or use them without specific permission.
9. Avoid terms that imply that parents with disabilities are overly special, brave or "superhuman."
10. If you have difficulty understanding a parent, do not pretend you understood. Rephrase and clarify whenever needed. Parents will not get upset if you are honest and in time your ability to understand the parent will improve.
11. Relax, be yourself. Offer an apology if you omit a courtesy, anyone can make a mistake. Treat all parents as you would like to be treated.
12. Do not make any assumptions. Each parent is unique. Remember, parents who have disabilities have more similarities with parents who do not have disabilities than differences.

Visually Impaired and Blind

1. Always speak directly to the parent rather than asking others what the parent can answer. You don't need to raise your voice.
2. The parent may use a long white cane or a guide dog to walk independently, or, may ask to take your arm. Let the parent decide. Do not grab the parent's arm but offer to let the parent take yours. The parent will keep a half-step behind to anticipate curbs and steps.
3. If the parent uses a guide dog, do not pet or distract the dog. It is not a pet.
4. The parent will want to know who is in the room with her. Speak when you enter and introduce the parent to the others including children if the parent is at your program center. Excuse yourself before leaving the room.
5. Be sure to keep doors and cabinets closed. The door to a room or cabinet or to a car that is left partially open is a hazard to people who are blind.
6. Don't worry about using words such as "see" People who are blind use them too. Feel free to say, e.g., "I'm glad to see you."
7. Don't talk about the "wonderful benefits or compensations" of blindness. The parent's sense of smell, taste, touch or hearing did not improve when he or she became blind. The parent may rely on them more and, therefore, may get more information through those senses than people who are not blind.
8. Be specific when describing the location of materials or objects, e.g., "There is a door six feet from you at two o'clock."

Hearing Impaired and Deaf

1. Use the parent's preferred method of communication. Be aware that the preferred method of communication may change according to the situation.
2. Use an interpreter whenever possible if this is the parent's preferred method.
3. Expect a slower pace of conversation regardless of the communication method used.
4. Always look directly at the parent during communication.
5. Speak clearly and evenly. Do not shout or exaggerate your speech. Avoid covering your face and mouth with your hands, facial hair or other distractions.
6. If needed, gently touch the parent on the arm or shoulder to get attention.
7. Always refer to the parent in the first person tense when using an interpreter or relay operator, e.g., do not say "Tell her to…"
8. If you are having difficulty communicating something, do not say, "Oh never mind it's not important;" try other methods to communicate your message, e.g., pen and paper.
9. Remember that a parent's lack of competency in English usage is not a measure of intellectual competency. English is a second language to parents who lost their hearing before language was acquired.

Physical Disabilities

1. Always ask the parent for permission before touching any assistive devices or equipment. Consider assistive devices as the parent's "personal space."
2. Always ask the parent if you can offer assistance before you provide it. If help is accepted or requested, ask for instructions.
3. If the parent uses a wheelchair, avoid touching the parent on the back or head. Sit down at the parent's eye level during communication whenever possible.

Mental Retardation

1. Talk clearly using concrete specific language, e.g., if you suggest that the parent take her child outside everyday, clarify the conditions (e.g., not raining).
2. Avoid clichés unless you are certain the parent understands your meaning.
3. Demonstrate and break instructions into small steps and invite the parent to try the instruction in your presence.
4. Use concrete markers to set appointment days and times, e.g. mark on a calendar, associate visit with a television show or other regular appointment.
5. Ask parents their preferred method for receiving print information, e.g., adding pictures, have it read to them.

SAFETY GUIDELINES

Sleep Position for Infants
The American Academy of Pediatrics recommends that healthy babies be placed on their back for sleeping in order to reduce the incidence of Sudden Infant Death Syndrome (SIDS). However, the Academy states that some babies may need to be placed on their stomach (prone) for sleep, e.g., premature infants with respiratory distress, infants with gastroesophageal reflux or with certain upper airway anomalies. Confirm with parents which sleep position is recommended for the child.

Remember that infants should spend some time playing on their stomach during awake times (unless instructed otherwise by the child's doctor).

Sleeping in a Crib
Review crib safety with parents. If the crib is older check that railings are spaced properly and that there is no peeling paint. Crib toys should not have buttons or other small pieces, sharp edges, or long ribbons or strings. Parents should also avoid large stuffed animals or toys that their child could use to climb out of the crib. Suggest a night light so their child can see clearly in the room. (This is essential for children with hearing impairments.)

Sleeping in a Bed
When the child is older and sleeps in a bed, the entire room must by safety-proofed. Help parents as needed to ensure that all toys in the child's room are safe. Put dangerous toys and items out of reach or in another room. Put safety covers on all electrical outlets. Use bed rails, if needed, and continue to use a night light.

Choking/Food Safety
The child is at highest risk for choking on food from birth until three years of age and remains at high risk until he is about four years of age. Choking can occur anywhere and anytime there is food. Inform parents to: avoid offering foods that can cause choking (or modify them to make them safer), always supervise their child when eating, encourage their child to sit in an upright position, and to eat slowly. Review potential consequences if their is unsupervised during snack and mealtimes, e.g., their could choke, fall out of his chair, or hurt himself by putting a spoon handle down his throat or up his nose. Some foods are easier than others to choke on. A food's potential to cause choking is often related to its size, shape, and/or consistency. Review the following guidelines with parents:
   Size: Avoid nuts and seeds unless they are finely ground. All pits and seeds from fruits and bones from fish, chicken, and meat should be removed. Large pieces of food may be harder to chew and are more likely to block the airway if inhaled. Food should be cut into bite-size pieces or thin slices that the child can safely and easily chew.
   Shape: Round foods can cause choking because they are more likely to block the child's airway completely than other shapes. Round foods, such as hot-dogs and carrots should be cut into short strips rather than round pieces. Grapes should be cut into quarters. Popcorn and round candies such as gumdrops or sour balls should be avoided.
   Consistency: Foods that are sticky or tough may be hard to remove from the child's airway. Advise parents not to serve their child peanut butter until at least developmentally one year old, and then spread it very thinly. Tough foods, such as meats and vegetables, should be cooked until they are soft enough to pierce with a fork. Raisins or other dried fruit and candy such as caramel should be avoided. Foods that are firm, smooth, or slick may slip down the child's throat and cause choking. Avoid large pieces of fruit with skin or raw peas. Consistency is another reason for avoiding grapes, peanuts, hard candy, and products like hot-dogs, the precautions mentioned above are followed.

Ensure that parents are trained in the signs of choking and when/how to call for emergency help i.e.: coughing, making high-pitched noises, inability to speak or cry, and/or have trouble breathing. Check with the local chapters of the American Heart Association, American Lung Association, or American Red Cross for pamphlets and accessible classes on preventing and treating choking. The American Red Cross Cardiopulmonary Resuscitation (CPR) course for infants and children includes a lesson on the emergency techniques for choking.

Safety Concerns to Teach and Demonstrate to Caregivers

Note: Direct therapy interventions for young children with motor impairments are highly specialized and individualized according to the child's particular needs. The gross motor section, therefore, is *not* intended to provide the reader with specific therapy techniques to carry out with the child. Instead the <u>parent-training activities are to be used as guidelines to be kept in mind *if* special positioning or handling techniques have been prescribed by a physical or occupational therapist.</u>

This is a partial list of basic **safety concerns to teach and demonstrate to caregivers. Always put the child's safety first!** Add to and modify this list as required for each family.

1. Things to lock up or move to high, out of sight, inaccessible places: insect killers, cleaning materials, shampoos, medicines, alcohol, aspirin, lighter fluid, cigarettes, matches, lighters, plastic bags, *Styrofoam* packing pieces.
2. Toys: Read all labels and instructions carefully. Remove all wrappings, pins, and staples. Check and remove any small parts. Routinely check the child's toys for broken pieces which can be dangerous. Blocks should be at least one-inch (1.25" on a side).
3. Keep electrical cords to small appliances out of the child's reach; adjust lamp cords so that the cord is not easily accessible; hide or tape them to the wall. Repair any frayed cords. Keep appliances flush against the wall.
4. Cap all electrical outlets not in use.
5. Add stickers or decals or a masking tape X to sliding glass doors, set low at the child's eye level.
6. Keep pot handles turned inwards on the stove. You may want to use a plastic guard to prevent the child from reaching the stove knobs or remove the stove knobs when not in use.
7. Remove breakable and valuable objects from your child's reaching and climbing range.
8. Place good books on high shelves or jam them in tight. Keep old magazines or children's books on accessible bookshelves.
9. Place and use protective gates at all stairways. They will be useless unless all family members latch them securely, always.
10. Keep off limit rooms latched. Tie a warning bell onto closed doors.
11. Tie cabinet doors securely shut (strings or rubber bands), or use special child-proof locks.
12. Remove poisonous plants; check before purchasing plants to make sure they are safe.
13. Remove or replace slippery throw rugs with non-skid rugs.
14. Caution all family members to keep the toilet lid closed or bathroom door shut; never leave any water in the bathtub, and never leave water-filled buckets out where the child may be.
15. Keep the child from wet slippery floors and freshly shampooed carpets until completely dry.
16. Store or repair unsteady or splintered furniture.
17. Examine play, sleep and living areas daily for sharp, dangerous, or tiny objects; remove pencils, scissors, knives, razors, popsicle sticks, pins, forks, nuts, popcorn, small hard objects, etc.
18. Tie cord blinds so that they are high and out of the child's reach.
19. Lower the thermostat on the water heater to ensure that the child can not burn himself.
20. Take caution when leaving windows open, especially those above the first floor. If the child push hard enough, the child can fall through the screen.
21. Once the child can open and close doors, using the knob, ensure that there is a dead bolt or chain on the front door.
22. Pad sharp corners of furnishings which the child may pull up to or bump into.

INDEX TO COMMON ISSUES
ISSUES NOT READILY IDENTIFIABLE FROM REVIEWING PARENT AND/OR CHILD SKILLS

Issues	Skill Numbers
MENTALLY RETARDED PARENT	
ABRUPT/ROUGH HANDLING	1.18; 3.44; 5.18
AFFECTIONATE BEHAVIORS WITH CHILD	5.51; 5.53
BEHAVIOR MANAGEMENT	1.51; 1.55; 5.39; 5.40; 5.41; 5.42; 5.48
FEEDING	
Choking	6.17
Food Safety	6.02; 6.18; 6.24
Introducing Foods	6.08; 6.11; 6.17; 6.19; 6.21; 6.24
Positioning	6.01; 6.08; 6.20
Scheduling	6.01
HYPERTONICITY, explaining about	3.39
INTERPRETING CHILD'S CUES	1.01; 1.06; 1.08; 1.21; 5.04; 5.05; 5.08; 5.15; 5.17; 5.50; 6.01
OVER-CONTROL, of activity	1.30; 1.35; 1.63; 4.51; 5.26
OVER-STIMULATION	1.02; 1.22; 2.06; 2.08; 5.07
SAFETY	1.13 (toys); 1.15 (mouthing); 3.17 (when rolling); 3.47 (standing); 4.40; 4.51; 4.66 (small objects and opening things); 5.36 (general environment); 5.45 (from imitating adults); 6.03 (sleeping); 6.17 (choking); 6.43 (toxic substances)
SHOES, selecting	3.47
STANDING, premature	3.23
TEASING	1.08; 1.20; 1.25; 1.26; 5.38; 6.02
TOILET TRAINING; premature	6.34
TOYS, lack of developmentally appropriate	1.13; 1.59; 1.74; 3.87; 4.41; 4.57; 4.58; 4.67
UNDER-STIMULATION	1.05; 1.22; 3.02
DEAF PARENT	
ENVIRONMENTAL SOUNDS, identifying for child	1.54
RECOGNIZING CHILD'S CRY, out of sight	1.01
BLIND PARENT	
ENVIRONMENTAL ORDER, considerations for parent's mobility	1.51; 5.49
GESTURES, explaining significance for child	1.39; 1.42; 1.47; 1.55; 1.59; 1.73; 2.24; 2.30; 4.57; 5.04
SAFETY	1.15 (mouthing); 3.79 (walking); 5.36 (general environment); 6.17 (choking); 6.43 (identifying toxic substances)
VISUAL CUES, providing child	1.06; 1.08; 2.07; 2.11; 4.27; 6.24; 6.29; 6.30
VISUAL CUES, recognizing child's	1.04; 1.06; 1.48; 1.55; 4.57; 5.04; 5.15; 5.17; 5.26; 5.32
VISUALLY DIRECTED REACH, explaining	1.11; 4.07; 4.16; 4.57
VISUAL PREFERENCES, NEEDS, AND CAPABILITIES, explaining child's	1.05; 1.06; 1.13; 1.35; 1.70; 1.85; 3.02; 4.01; 4.05; 4.06; 5.47
VISUAL PURSUIT AND OBJECT PERMANENCE,	
explaining — sounds	1.10; 1.16; 1.41
— objects	1.09; 1.20; 1.31; 1.33
PHYSICALLY DISABLED PARENT	
SAFETY, when child is out of reach	5.36
WHEELCHAIR HEIGHT, adapting child's equipment	1.01; 3.03

COGNITIVE DEVELOPMENT

1.01 Child: QUIETS WHEN PICKED UP (0-1 mo.)
Parent: Helps quiet child by picking up and responding to any of the child's needs

GENERAL GUIDELINES

Most newborns stop crying when they are picked up. They can be easily soothed with quiet talking, gentle rocking, feeding, or cuddling. Some infants, however, need additional calming techniques such as swaddling, pacifiers, or continuous motion.

Parents provide the trust and security their children require when they respond to their hunger and comfort needs. Parental tension can add to the duration and intensity of the child's crying. Thus, the parent's own comfort and confidence during his crying periods, as difficult as this may be at times, can be calming in itself to the child.

MENTALLY RETARDED PARENT

May interpret her child's crying as "mean" or "bad," think she will spoil her child if he is picked up too often, and/or be too rough or abrupt when picking him up.

1. Explain to the parent in concrete terms why young children cry and why they need to be picked up when they cry. For example, "At this age children:
   a. Cry as a way of talking to us. When your child cries, he is not being mean or bad. It's the only way he can tell you he needs something.
   b. Do not know the difference between day and night. Your child will probably need you in the middle of the night and cry to let you know he needs you.
   c. Are not spoiled when they are picked up. Instead, your child learns that you love him and are there for him."
2. Help the parent to think of things her child may be saying when he cries or "fusses." Relate these to daily activities. For example, "If it's been a long time since your child has eaten, when he cries he is saying 'I'm hungry'."
3. Continue to explore with the parent additional things her child is telling us when he cries, e.g., "I'm sick," "I'm scared," "I need a diaper change," "I just need a hug," "I need to know you are nearby," or "I just feel like crying for no reason; thanks for checking up on me."
4. If the parent does not respond to or misinterprets her child's crying or fussing, interpret aloud what her child may be saying, and praise the parent's positive responses as each situation occurs during your intervention.
5. Explore, demonstrate, and let the parent practice calming techniques which help soothe her child:
   a. Try holding the child molded in your body gently, but securely; gently rubbing or patting his back; or soft talking or humming while gently rocking him. If appropriate, demonstrate using a pacifier and/or swaddling the child in a security blanket.
   b. Point out which calming techniques seem to work best for her child.
6. When the situation arises, encourage the parent to practice calming her child with your assurance:
   a. Praise the parent, and interpret her child's positive responses and feelings, e.g., "Your baby feels safer now" or "That feels good to your baby."
   b. If the parent is too abrupt or rough with her child, explain and demonstrate that children like it when we are gentle, move slowly, and talk softly.
7. If a pacifier is used during the child's first months, caution the parent about over-use:
   a. Explain that when her child spits it out, he's probably had enough.
   b. Stress that the pacifier should never be forced into her child's mouth.
   c. Monitor and tell the parent when her child is ready to stop using the pacifier.
8. Help the parent anticipate and be prepared for her child's physical needs, e.g., always having an extra bottle prepared and a dry, clean diaper ready. Rehearse problem-solving situations, such as "If your child is hungry and a bottle is not ready, what will happen?"

DEAF PARENT

May not hear and thus not respond to her child's "fussing" sounds.

1. A sound *sensitive receiver box** can be placed next to the child's sleep area and connected to the parent's bedroom lamp. The lamp will blink in response to sound and thus alert the parent when her child is crying.
2. The parent can discriminate her child's physical behaviors which indicate that he is "fussy" and wants to be picked up, e.g., red face, waving arms, frown, etc.
3. Mirrors can be arranged throughout the family's living areas to help keep the child in easy view from different rooms. For example, place a concave mirror in the upper corner of a kitchen wall adjoining the living room.
4. Siblings and others in the household can alert the parent when her child is crying.
5. If the parent is non-vocal or has difficulty regulating her voice tone to a soothing level, a music box which plays soft music may be soothing to the child. Help the parent select soothing music boxes. Demonstrate suitable distances to place the music box in relation to her child.

PHYSICALLY DISABLED PARENT

Who uses a wheelchair or has limited mobility; may have difficulty bending over and/or lifting her child to help quiet him.

1. If the parent has difficulty bending over to pick her child up, adapt the child's sleeping surface:
   a. Adjust the height of the crib mattress to the parent's waist level.

---
*See Glossary.

1.01

  b. If the mattress cannot be adjusted high enough, the crib can be placed on pieces of wood.
  c. Crib leg extenders found in local hardware stores can also be used.
  d. A table top bassinet can also be fabricated to the parent's waist level for diaper changing.
3. Crib mattresses should be lowered to lap level if a parent uses a wheelchair. The parent can then lift her child from his crib to her lap. The parent can put a pillow on her lap to prevent her child from bumping on the wheelchair's arm.

3. If the parent has upper extremity coordination and strength difficulties, adapt crib railings so that they can be easily raised and lowered. There are many types of crib railings and thus adaptations are also varied:
   a. One common example is to drill or solder wide metal (extension) bars or rods to the existing rail lever mechanism. Parents can then manipulate the rail by pressing a knee against the bar or stepping down on a lever.
   b. Handles can also be added to the top or side of the rail for an easier grip.
   c. Consult local hardware stores about specific adaptation needs.
4. The child can be routinely placed on a blanket in his crib. The parent can then move her child closer by grabbing the blanket from the opposite side and rolling her child toward her, or by rolling up the side of blanket closest to the parent and pulling her child closer.
5. The parent may be able to gently roll her child on his tummy and slide one arm under her child's chest to facilitate lifting.
6. If the parent is unable to pick her child up from his crib, a "snuggly vest" can be fabricated for the child to wear to facilitate lifting. If a commercial vest is unavailable or unsuitable, use a towel or other soft heavyweight material to make a vest. Fold the material in thirds to make a wide band and cut off the length so that ends overlap in front, dependent upon the size of the child. Large secure fasteners can be sewn on the overlapping edge. The type of fastener should accommodate the parent's manipulative abilities. The child can be picked up from or lowered to the crib by sliding an arm or hand between the child's back and vest. Always raise and lower the child with his stomach facing down.
7. Refer to activities for 3.03 (Lifts head in prone) for suggestions to help parents life their child from the floor.
8. Anticipatory Guidance: Children learn quickly to "help" when being lifted by parents. They grab the parent's clothing and mold their bodies to facilitate lifting.
9. NOTE: These activities should initially be closely supervised until the parent is proficient and feels comfortable with them.

1.02 Child: SHOWS PLEASURE WHEN TOUCHED OR HANDLED (0-6 mos.)
Parent: Handles and interacts with child in a mutually satisfying manner

GENERAL GUIDELINES

The child responds to gentle handling and touch by molding his body to the adult's and, later, by cooing and smiling.

Children who have muscle tone abnormalities or are hypersensitive to their environment may require special handling techniques to facilitate optimal comfort and satisfaction for both parent and child. Consult a physical or occupational therapist for individual recommendations according to the child's needs.

Parents promote their child's pleasurable responses by touching and handling him with gentle patting, stroking, rocking, and smooth movements. Singing, humming, playing music, or talking to the child can make handling experiences even more pleasurable for him. This also helps him associate pleasant experiences with sound awareness.

MENTALLY RETARDED PARENT

May over- or under-stimulate her child when interacting with him.

1. Help the parent identify sights, sounds, and tactual experiences which seem to make her child happy.
2. Model and encourage the parent's positive interactions with her child during all of your interventions:
   a. Include face-to-face contact, responsive facial expressions, affection, talking, singing, humming, rocking, patting, and gently stroking and holding.
   b. Describe the child's positive response to interactions as they occur, and relate the interaction which caused it, e.g., "See how he looked at you and cooed when you smiled at him!"
   c. Interpret to the parent her child's physical signs which indicate he has had enough of or does not like a particular interaction. General signs to point out are gaze aversion, arching of back, or active physical resistance.
   d. If the parent is too rough or abrupt in her handling; provide physical prompting, demonstration, and monitoring.

1.03

1.0 COGNITIVE

3. During your visits, frequently prompt the parent to initiate positive interactions with her child. Use phrases such as: "He's looking for a kiss from you" or "He's upset; he'll feel better if you hold him."
4. Specifically caution the parent never to throw her child up in the air and catch him or to shake him real hard, even if he seems to like it. Explain that this can cause tiny blood vessels to break and cause brain damage.
5. If specific handling techniques are prescribed by a physical or occupational therapist:
   a. Demonstrate prescribed handling with a large rag doll and then the child.
   b. Let the parent practice with the doll and then her child.
   c. Take Polaroid pictures of correct and incorrect handling techniques as a reminder at home. This should include picking up, holding, feeding, sitting, etc.
6. Caution the parent not to present too many toys, sounds, or movements at one time. Describe specific examples of over-stimulation and relate why these situations are "too much" for her child.

DEAF PARENT

May not vocalize to her child during her interactions and handling.

1. Help select soothing music boxes or records, marking the appropriate volume on the player for the parent to play while rocking, smiling, stroking, and kissing her child.
2. If the parent uses sign language, encourage her to begin signing and speaking, when possible, somewhat slower than average, while a musical toy radio plays simple nursery rhymes.
3. Encourage and reinforce the parent's use of natural, inviting facial expressions during her interactions with her child.

PHYSICALLY DISABLED PARENT

Who is severely restricted in movement; may "miss" routine handling activities with her child.

1. Encourage household members and others who may help out in the home to frequently place the child in his parent's lap, in her same bed, etc., to maintain closeness.
2. If the parent cannot hold her child, she can nuzzle, provide face-to-face contact, and provide him important social and communication interactions by smiling, talking, and singing to him.

1.03 **Child: RESPONDS TO SOUND (0-2 mo.)**
Parent: Provides controlled opportunities for child to respond to sound

GENERAL GUIDELINES

The child's first responses to sound are at an awareness/reflexive level and are unintentional. He may startle, become still, increase his activity, widen or shift his eyes, blink, raise his eyebrows, cry, frown, tense his entire body, or change his respiration. These responses are usually to harsh or very loud sounds such as a telephone ring, door slam, or vacuum cleaner. These responses diminish within a few moments as the child gets used to or adjusts to hearing the sound. This ability to adjust to sounds is also termed habituation.

If a child does not consistently respond to sounds or if his responses are minimal, he should be referred for an audiological evaluation. Children who have auditory impairments should have auditory awareness training and controlled listening experiences.

A child may also display hypersensitivity to sounds. He may startle, blink, or cry, even to softer or more subtle sounds, or he may not habituate to sounds. This child may need a controlled sound environment where sounds are introduced more gradually with less intensity.

Parents can maximize their child's optimal sound awareness by exposing him to sounds according to his individual needs and responses. Parents can also capitalize on naturally occurring environmental sounds which have potential interest to the child by calling special attention to them.

If a child is extra sensitive to sounds, parents can introduce sound toys slowly and try to buffer environmental sounds when possible. For example, parents can oil squeaky oven doors, hold him securely when outside, and provide soothing voice tones during interactions.

MENTALLY RETARDED PARENT

May have difficulty judging suitable sound experiences, distances, and volumes for her child.

1. Ask the parent to name the different sources of sound to which her child likes to listen. If needed, help identify additional toys or household objects which make sounds that interest her child, e.g., rattles, crackling paper, squeak toys, humming, or talking.
2. Point out to the parent her child's vocal and bodily changes in response to sound as they occur. Describe responses such as her child's changes in breathing, vocalizations, and activity level.
3. Ask the parent to name some sounds which her child doesn't seem to like or that may be too loud and ask how she can tell he doesn't like them. Demonstrate ways to protect her child from overly harsh sounds.
4. Demonstrate to the parent appropriate distances to activate sound toys from her child's ear. Explain and demonstrate that some toys make sounds which are too loud, especially if held too close to her child. Let the parent squeak a loud toy next to your ear and vice versa. Emphasize how this hurts your ear and for children it's even worse.
5. Explain to the parent her child's startle reflect as an indication that a sound is too loud for him, e.g., "He sort of jumps or jerks his arms and blinks when a sound is too loud." Ask her if she's ever seen him do that to a loud sound:
   a. Demonstrate your own startle reflex to a loud sound.
   b. Ask the parent if she remembers startling to loud sounds, such as a car horn.

1.03

DEAF PARENT

May be unaware of many environmental sounds, and thus unintentional auditory deprivation or overload may occur for her child.

1. Relate to the parent her child's hearing abilities and preferences as outlined in the general guidelines. Point out the child's physical responses to various sounds.
2. "Sound" toys can be tested in the presence of a person with hearing to eliminate toys which are too loud for the child.
3. Mark toys which make sounds that attract the child, such as rattles and squeak toys with tape, stickers, and non-toxic markers.
4. Demonstrate to the parent how to activate the sound for each type of toy, and the appropriate distance to place it in relation to her child. Stress that the toy does *not* need to be next to her child's ear.
5. Provide musical toys, and relate to the parent the name of the tune and words.
6. Mark television, radio, and record player knobs so they can be set at appropriate volumes for her child.
7. Alert the parent of environmental sounds (e.g., vacuum cleaner, metal pans, crib railing rising and lowering, etc.) which may be too harsh if her child is hypersensitive to sounds. If needed, mark with special ALERT stickers.
8. Demonstrate the child's startle response to abrupt or loud sounds. The child's startle can help alert the parent when sounds may be too loud.
9. Explain to the parent her child's "habituation" to sound, i.e., if he gets used to hearing the sound he may stop actively responding. Demonstrate continuous rattle shaking, and point out her child's signs of habituation, e.g., he stops searching, brightening, etc.
10. Explain to the parent that her child will be able to sleep through most sounds, even if she takes him to a noisy store!

BLIND PARENT

May be unaware of her child's non-vocal responses to sound.

1. Describe for the parent her child's changes in facial expression, bodily movement, and respiration in response to activating different sound stimuli, e.g., soft rattle, ringing bell, squeak toy, or clap.
2. The parent can practice tactually discriminating her child's physical responses to sound while you activate different sound stimuli and describe his responses.
3. Try closing your own eyes to practice tactually discriminating the child's subtle bodily and vocal changes in response to sound.
4. Explain and demonstrate the concept of habituation, while the parent holds her child and feels his decrease in activity.
5. Explain the initial developmental sequence of auditory localization and concurrent visual orienting for young children. Relate to the parent that during her child's first month or two, his eyes may brighten, move, or blink, but he probably will not actually look for the sound; at around two to four months, his eyes will move to search for sounds held eight to ten inches from the side of each ear, but he may not actually find them.
6. The parent can use her outstretched hand as a concrete marker to help determine suitable distance from which to activate sound toys from the side of child's head or chest.

1.04 Child: RESPONDS TO VOICE (0-2½ mo.)
Parent: Provides adequate vocal stimulation to child

GENERAL GUIDELINES

The child demonstrates his awareness of voice by brightening his face, quieting, or slowly turning, and by two months, smiling. He may also respond by frowning or displaying a sober intense look as if trying to understand everything that is being said! By two months, he may recognize his parent's voice even in a crowded room and will respond to her voice more quickly than to an environmental stimulus. He is beginning to attach meaning to voices and associates his parent's voice with comfort and feeding.

Parents encourage their child's listening to voices by talking to him in a soothing manner when he is upset, and by using varying intonations and facial expressions when he is alert and playful.

MENTALLY RETARDED PARENT

May not spontaneously talk to her child.

1. Explain to the parent in concrete terms the importance of talking to children even though they do not understand our words yet. Include the following concepts:
   a. Children learn to listen when we talk to them.
   b. Listening to people talk now will help him learn to understand words during the next year.
   c. Children like it and feel important when we talk to them.
   d. It's not the words we say that are important to the child at this age, but *how* we say them, which makes him feel good. Using a soft voice, smiling, and looking at children when we talk make them feel good.
2. Model talking to the child frequently, describing what the child is doing, or commenting on what he is looking at. Model a soft voice tone, animated expression, and eye contact. Direct the parent's attention to her child's signs of listening and comfort.
3. Reinforce the parent's talking with her child. Stress and describe her child's positive responses when she talks to him. Remind her how she is helping him learn to understand and talk as he gets older.
4. If needed, suggest specific phrases for the parent to say to her child during daily activities, e.g., "It's time to eat, Johnny" or "What a nice shirt you have on."
5. While you are with the parent and child, remind her to tell her child what she or the child is doing, e.g., "I'm

putting on your diaper" or "You're looking at the window."
6. Refer to 2.13 (Babbles consonant chains "bababa").

DEAF PARENT

May not vocalize to her child or has difficulty pacing her vocalizations contingent to the child's response.

1. Point out to the parent her child's behavioral responses to your voice, e.g., alerting, brightening, turning toward you, or softening of facial features. Encourage the parent to use whatever expressive speech she may have, and point out her child's behavioral responses as she talks, hums, etc.
2. Capitalize on the parent's use of facial expressions as a means for communicating with her child:
    a. Explain to the parent that facial expression, touching, and gestures are just as much a part of communication as words are to young children.
    b. Ask the parent to watch for her child's behavioral responses which indicate he is attending.
3. Point out to the parent her child's physical cues which indicate when to start and stop her communication:
    a. When the child looks toward his parent, encourage her to communicate via voice and/or gestures.
    b. Demonstrate and let the parent practice communicating with gestures and voice, and then stopping and waiting for her child to respond. Point out her child's responses, and resume this turn-taking communication.
4. If the parent is non-verbal, suggest and demonstrate non-verbal facial sounds paired with facial gestures which elicit a response from her child. These could include smacking lips, tongue, clicking, making "raspberries" with tongue, or patting inflated cheek:
    a. Monitor the child's positive and negative responses to these sounds, and point them out to the parent as needed.
    b. If necessary, remind the parent to pause and watch for her child's responses before continuing.

BLIND PARENT

May be unaware of her child's non-vocal responses to voices.

1. Explain to the parent the non-vocal signals young children often use to communicate and those they rely upon from others to help them understand the meaning of things. Relate the following concepts:
    a. During the first few months, children may blink, smile, frown, and/or look at you when he hears voices.
    b. In addition to listening to voice and voice tone, the young child listens and learns the meaning of words by watching people's facial expressions and gestures and by looking at the context of the situation.
2. Describe the child's facial expressions in response to the parent's voice.
3. The parent can tactually discriminate her child's bodily changes in response to her voice by feeling his muscle tone, movement, and increased respiration.

4. Watch for and describe patterns of the child's non-vocal communicative signs which accompany his vocalizations. For example, the child's coo may be accompanied with a smile, and his lip smacking may be accompanied with raised eyebrows.
5. Explain to the parent the importance of giving her child time to respond, vocally and non-vocally, to her conversations with him. She can pause between her phrases and wait to hear his vocal responses and feel his bodily changes before resuming her conversation with him.
6. If the parent does not provide a face-to-face orientation while talking to her child, refer to 5.02 (Regards face).

1.05   Child: INSPECTS SURROUNDINGS (1-2 mo.)
         Parent: Provides adequate opportunities for child to visually explore his environment

GENERAL GUIDELINES

The child visually inspects his environment. During alert periods, he may spend up to 10 minutes looking around if attractive visual stimuli are within his visual field. He usually attends for a few seconds, rests, and then starts looking again several times during this period.

He can focus well at things 8-12" from his face, and at two months, can see large and moving objects from a few feet away. By four months, children can see as well as an adult at any distance.

Objects and toys which are colorful, have faces, have contrasting color patterns such as black and white checkerboards, or reflect light are especially attractive to the child during his first few months.

Parents help encourage their child's early "looking" by providing a visually attracting environment according to the child's individual needs and preferences. They can vary their child's visual experiences by placing their child in different places and positions during daily activities, and showing him interesting things to look at within his visual field.

MENTALLY RETARDED PARENT.

May unintentionally restrict her child's exploration needs by leaving him in a crib or in one position for long periods of time.

1. Ask the parent to show you the different things at which her child seems to like to look:
    a. Explain that children, even from birth, can see quite well and learn from looking at things. Point out the discriminating characteristics which make the toy or object attractive to her child, e.g., color, shape, size, sounds, patterns, and reflective ability.
    b. Suggest and encourage the parent to think of household objects and places around their home at which her child might like to look.
    c. Interpret the child's signs of visual interest, such as facial brightening or tensing, smiling, and vocalizing when he is looking at these things.

1.05

2. Verbally prompt the parent to name things to her child when he is looking at them, e.g., "Tell him what he's looking at."
3. Name specific daily activities when the parent can show her child something interesting at which to look. For example, tell the parent to show her child a baby jar picture during feeding, a colorful picture in a magazine she's reading, or the pretty picture hanging up. Suggest looking out of the window with her child so he can see the cars, trees, and people.
4. Discuss how boring it would be if we could only look at one thing for a long time, like when we're sick and have to stay in bed. Compare that feeling to a child's who stays in one place or position too long. Relate that since young children can't move themselves or get their own toys, we have to do it for them:
   a. Show the parent where to place interesting visual targets near her child's crib.
   b. Help the parent find various safe places around the home for her child to be during daily household activities.
   c. Demonstrate and make a pictorial chart of safe positions for her child to experience during the day, e.g., carried at parent's shoulder, prone on the floor with towel or blanket, and sitting in an infant seat.

BLIND PARENT

May be unaware of her child's visual capabilities, preferences, and stimulation needs at this age.

1. Describe children's general visual capabilities and preferences at this age to the parent as outlined in the general guidelines, assuming the child is not visually impaired.
2. Screen the child's vision to assess his visual preferences, the best distance to hold objects, how long he looks at things, and his tracking field. Describe the child's responses, preferences, and visual field to the parent.
3. Help the parent locate interesting visual targets around the home to direct her child's attention to during daily activities, e.g., looking out of windows or at shiny toasters.
4. Assist the parent with placing visually attracting mobiles and special pictures near her child's sleep and play areas within his visual field. Point out barriers which can restrict her child's vision, such as crib rail pads.
5. Recommend to the parent to change her child's position and the position of visual targets in his crib to provide him with varied visual experiences.
6. Comment upon the importance of adequate lighting during the child's waking hours, if needed:
   a. Suggest opening blinds and curtains during the day, and remind the parent to turn lights on in the evening.
   b. Help the parent identify which lights may be too adversive to her child, e.g., a light which is too bright directly over her child's crib.
   c. Explain that bright lights should be turned off and curtains closed during the child's sleeping times. Help identify suitable nightlights for the child.
7. Explain that looking out of windows will provide her child interesting learning experiences throughout his early childhood years.

1.06 Child: SHOWS ACTIVE INTEREST IN PERSON FOR AT LEAST ONE MINUTE (1-6 mo.)
Parent: Encourages child to become actively interested in object or person for at least one minute

MENTALLY RETARDED PARENT

May not recognize when her child is interested in something or may expect him to maintain his interest beyond his developmental level.

1. Teach the parent to recognize her child's behavioral signs of interest:
   a. When presenting an attractive object or talking face-to-face with the child, describe his responses which indicate interest, e.g., face brightening or intensing, eye contact, body stilling or becoming more active, making vocal sounds, and smiling.
   b. Explain how these changes tell us her child is interested in something. Relate that since he can't tell us with words yet, he uses his body a lot to talk.
   c. Ask the parent to carry her child around the room and stop to show him a picture or look out of the window. Let her name the ways her child tells her he's interested in looking at something.
2. Explain to the parent that when children look at something, they are often telling us that they want us to tell them what it is:
   a. Model short labeling phrases to the child when he is looking at something, e.g., "See your bear; you are looking at your bear!"
   b. Reinforce all of the parent's labeling when her child looks at something. Refer to Activity No. 2, 1.07 (Listens to voice).
3. Explain to the parent that at this age, children do not usually look at people or things very long:
   a. Relate that after about a minute, her child may want to take a break from looking at something to look at something different or just rest; after a short break, he may want to go back and look again. Demonstrate this concept using a favorite toy.
   b. Help the parent identify her child's disinterest cues as they occur. Describe his gaze aversion, turning body, or closing eyes. Tell the parent not to try to make her child look at something when he's doing these things.
4. Review interesting visual targets with the parent for her child to look at as suggested in 1.05 (Inspects surroundings).
5. Demonstrate to the parent how things that make sounds help attract her child's attention.

6. Model and explain to the parent how exaggerated facial expressions and talking are especially fun and interesting to young children:
   a. Encourage the parent to make silly, fun faces with her child.
   b. Name specific daily activities for the parent to remember at which to provide extra facial expressions and talking, e.g., during feeding, in front of a mirror, and while dressing him.

DEAF PARENT

May be unaware that sounds help attract and maintain children's interest in people and objects.

1. Explain that toys and objects which make sounds are more interesting to children and thus help them attend and learn:
   a. Refer to 1.03 (Responds to sounds) activities to help the parent identify appropriate sound toys.
   b. Explain and help select roly-poly toys which chime or jingle when pushed, and mobiles which make sounds when activated.
2. Reinforce the parent's use of facial gestures which help attract and maintain her child's attention. Point out her child's attending cues:
   a. If the parent is non-verbal, encourage her to begin using sign language along with her use of facial and gestural communication.
   b. Reinforce the use of any verbal skills the parent may have.
   c. The parent can hum, click her tongue, and make lip smacking sounds to help attract her child's attention.

BLIND PARENT

May need information and orientation assistance to assure visual stimuli are interesting and within her child's visual field.

1. If not previously done, refer to 1.05 (Inspects surroundings) to provide information regarding her child's visual capabilities, preferences, and needs.
2. If a mobile is used over the child's crib or playpen, help secure it to a location which is within the child's visual and reaching range:
   a. Explain the importance of using mobiles which have visual targets that face the child when he is looking up from a supine position.
   b. If a mobile is suspended from the ceiling or wall, attach a piece of bathtub skid tape to the crib or playpen rail as a quick locator for the parent to assure she places her child within the mobile's range.
3. Explain to the parent that in addition to hearing people talk, children are attracted to various facial expressions and often exaggerated silly faces:
   a. If the parent is interested in practicing various facial expressions with her child, describe various facial movements which attract her child's attention. Use descriptions, such as "Change your mouth into an exaggerated 'oh' while raising your eyebrows high and dropping your chin."
   b. Describe the child's facial expressions and other non-vocal signs of interest and delight when the parent makes exaggerated expressions.
   c. Explain that her child may be interested in seeing his own facial expressions. Help attach safe mirrors to sides of her child's crib and playpen within his visual field.
4. Explain that when children look at something, they often are communicating that they want us to tell them about it or to bring it closer. The parent can rely upon changes in her child's physical and vocal patterns to help discern when her child is looking at something.

1.07 Child: LISTENS TO VOICE FOR 30 SECONDS (1-3 mo.)
Parent: Talks to child using modified "child-sized" language during daily activities

GENERAL GUIDELINES

The child attends and listens to voices with increasing duration and responsivity each month. At one month of age, he may listen for up to two minutes, half a dozen times a day during his alert periods. By three months, he turns and will listen to speaking or singing voices for up to forty-five minutes, with a few breaks in between. He may even stop sucking during feeding to listen to a voice. He is especially responsive to voices after feeding and changing when he is comfortable and alert.

Parents encourage their child's listening and awareness of voice by talking to him in synchrony with the child's moods and alert states, using inviting facial expressions and varied intonation.

Children who are less responsive to voice or who have auditory impairments may need extra visual and tactual stimulation to help foster his auditory awareness. For example, before talking to their child the parent could attract his attention and then provide extra facial expression during conversation.

MENTALLY RETARDED PARENT

May use limited speech with her child and may not use a variety of vocal intonations.

1. Anticipatory Guidance: As the child gets older, the parent may over-use imperatives and commands, such as "Do this," "Don't do that," "Get that," etc., with her child. Over-use does not facilitate language and learning. Encourage the parent to begin using alternative descriptive phrases with her child early in his development.

   Activity Nos. 2-6 address five different expressive language skills for helping parents talk in meaningful ways to their child. Only one skill should be introduced and emphasized to the parent at one time; introduce others as the parent demonstrates proficiency.
2. Explain to the parent that children learn to listen when we tell them about things at which they are looking. Relate that when she sees him looking at a toy, a person,

1.07

or other object, she should tell him what it is and say something nice about it:
  a. Model short repetitive phrases which describe what the child is looking at, e.g., "That's a doll; see the pretty doll." Point out her child's listening signs.
  b. After modeling, ask the parent to tell her child what he is looking at or to say the same phrase you modeled. Point out how her child is looking and listening to her.
  c. Rehearse saying descriptive phrases about various meaningful toys and objects with the parent.
  d. Frequently prompt the parent during your sessions to tell her child what he is looking at, e.g., "He's looking at his rattle; what can you say?"
3. Explain to the parent that children also learn about things when we tell them what is happening around them or tell them what they are doing; therefore, it's good to tell her child what he is doing or what you are doing. Give two examples:
  a. Frequently model short repetitive phrases to the child which describe what you are doing, or what the child or the parent is doing, e.g., "You're smiling; you like that" or "You're looking at the bottle; I'm going to feed you the bottle."
  b. Prompt the parent to tell her child what she or her child is doing, suggesting a simple phrase as needed.
  c. List with the parent various daily activities when she can tell her child what he or she is doing; include playing, dressing, feeding, changing, and bathing. Role-play short descriptive phrases to say during these activities.
  d. During all future visits with parent and child, reinforce continuation and carryover with prompts, such as "You're playing so nicely with Jimmy; tell him what you are doing."
4. Explain that even though at this age children can't answer, they sometimes like to be asked questions. Relate that since her child cannot answer questions yet, we also have to tell him an answer:
  a. Help the parent think of questions and answers to tell her child, e.g., "How are you? You look tired!"
  b. Frequently model asking questions to the child, using exaggerated intonation and stress, e.g., "What's that, a ball? Yes, that's a ball."
5. Explain and demonstrate for the parent how children like to listen to voices that are higher pitched than usual:
  a. Practice using high pitched voices within a fun role-playing situation with the parent.
  b. Say a simple phrase to the child, first without intonation or stress, and then with lots of intonation and stress. Point out and describe her child's positive responses to the inflectional phrase.
  c. The parent may be interested in practicing voice tones and inflections on a tape recorder.

DEAF PARENT

May be non-verbal or have non-standard inflectional patterns.

1. Anticipatory Guidance: Although the parent's speech may have substitutions, omissions, and lack intonation and stress, her child in time will become familiar with and understand his parent's individual distinctive way of speaking.
2. Encourage the parent to use whatever verbal skills she has to describe her child's activities to him during the day.
3. Point out the child's physical signs of listening for longer periods of time to the parent.
4. Refer to 1.04 (Responds to voice).

BLIND PARENT

May be unaware of her child's non-vocal signs of listening and his needs for visual cues to help understand the meaning of language.

1. Describe the child's facial expressions as the parent talks to him. Explain to the parent that although her child may not be vocalizing to let us know he is listening, he is learning to listen for longer periods of time everyday.
2. Discuss how children rely upon gestures and facial expressions, as well as words, to help them understand their meaning and keep their listening attention. Refer to Activity No. 3, 1.06 (Shows active interest in person or object for at least one minute.)

1.08 Child: **SHOWS ANTICIPATORY EXCITEMENT (1½-4 mo.)**
Parent: Recognizes and provides opportunities which facilitate child's anticipatory excitement

GENERAL GUIDELINES

The child begins to associate certain sights, sounds, smells, and touch with an event that is likely to occur. When he sees his bottle, hears his mother's voice, or smells her cologne, he may brighten, arch forward, kick, wave his hands, or vocalize.

Parents help encourage their child's anticipatory excitement by giving him adequate time to look, listen, smell, and touch before providing the child the end result. For example, parents can call to their child before entering his room, show him his bottle before feeding, and show him is toy before squeaking it.

MENTALLY RETARDED PARENT

May misinterpret her child's anticipatory behaviors and may tease her child.

1. Describe to the parent in concrete terms the meaning of her child's anticipatory excitement:
  a. Explain that "at this age children begin to show us they can remember things that have happened before. Certain sights, sounds, and smells help them remember."

b. Give specific examples that may relate directly to the parent's child, such as "When Sammy sees his bottle, he may get all excited and wave his arms or stop crying because he remembers that bottles help make him stop feeling hungry."
c. Ask the parent if she can think of times when he waved his arms and got excited. If needed, prompt with "When he sees you come in his room?", "When he hears his music box?" etc.
2. Before the parent presents a bottle to her child, interpret and point out her child's behaviors which tell us he remembers what's going to happen next, e.g., kicking, heavy breathing, vocalizing, or quieting. Stress the importance of giving her child his bottle as soon as possible because he's telling us with these signs he wants it now; explain he will feel teased if she doesn't give it to him.
3. Model and suggest activities which promote the child's anticipatory excitement and explain the "clue" that made the child excited. Use situations, such as winding up a favorite toy — her child remembers that the winding sound will start the music, or "I'm going to tickle you!" — her child remembers that a high voice, big smile, and pointed finger leads to the feeling of being gently tickled.
4. Stress to the parent the importance of giving her child his bottle after showing it to him, picking him up after putting her arms out to pick up, and giving him his toy after she has shown it to him so her child doesn't get confused or feel teased.

DEAF PARENT

May be unaware of sounds which may precipitate her child's anticipatory excitement. She may thus misinterpret these behaviors or miss the opportunities to encourage them.

1. Explain to the parent that her child is learning to anticipate what is going to happen next by seeing and hearing familiar events. Provide an example, such as a bottle means it's time to eat to her child:
   a. Relate daily environmental sounds which may elicit her child's anticipatory excitement, e.g., footsteps, opening of doors, running water, opening curtains, or fixing breakfast.
   b. Alert the parent when you hear environmental sounds, and point out her child's reactions and his signs of anticipatory excitement.

BLIND PARENT

May not provide extra visual cues which facilitate her child's anticipatory excitement.

1. Explain to the parent that her child is learning to anticipate what's going to happen next by seeing and hearing familiar events first:
   a. Provide a familiar auditory example, e.g., "When we hear a car drive up, we expect that someone may knock on the door soon."
   b. Relate the example to her child's ability to anticipate an event by seeing a visual cue first, e.g., "When your child sees his bottle, he knows this means it's time to eat."
   c. Discuss the value of showing her child the toy, bottle, etc., before actually giving it to him.
2. Explain that just as it helps the parent to have someone tell her when something is going to happen, her child also needs these verbal cues. Provide examples, such as "We're going to take a bath" or "I'm going to tickle you."
3. Help the parent recognize her child's anticipatory excitement by pointing out his non-visual excitement cues such as increased vocalizations, breathing, kicking, and/or tensing his body.

1.09 Child: REACTS TO DISAPPEARANCE OF SLOWLY MOVING OBJECT (2-3 mo.)
Parent: Sets up opportunities for child to react to the disappearance of slowly moving objects, if recommended

GENERAL GUIDELINES

Thie child is beginning to remember that an object still exists although he can no longer see it. At this age, his memory of the object is only a few seconds. He reacts by looking at the place where he saw it disappear.

When testing for this reaction, an object is moved slowly across the child's visual field and hidden behind a barrier while the child watches; he should search for it with his eyes for a few moments at the place of disappearance.

Naturally occurring situations provide the child with experiences to develop his skill, e.g., his toys rolling out of sight, people leaving a room, and the parent moving behind the child's crib.

Controlled disappearance games may be recommended if the child needs extra help with visual memory and object permanence skills. The following activities may help parents encourage their child to follow and react momentarily to a disappearing object:
   a. Move their face slowly behind a barrier (their hands, paper, book, or crib).
   b. Activate a large attractive wind-up toy and let it move behind the screen.
   c. Pull toys on a string slowly under a cloth.

Disappearance games should be played when the child is alert, and for no longer than two or three minutes. The hidden object or person should continue to make sounds when hidden, and be brought back into sight after a few seconds. Sound cues should be withdrawn as the child begins to react.

The following parent training activities assume controlled disappearance games have been recommended.

MENTALLY RETARDED PARENT

May not interpret her child's lingering gaze as a signal to return the object back to his visual field; may also have difficulty judging appropriate speeds and distances to move an object from her child.

1. Explain this skill and the suggested activities to the parent as a way to help her child's memory, e.g., "We are helping Sally remember that even though she can't see a toy for a few seconds, it is still around." Further explain that at

1.09

this age we don't expect a child to move around to find something but, instead, we watch to see if he stares at the place where a toy used to be.

2. Model moving and returning a toy back to the child's visual field several times, saying each time, "I showed it to him again when his eyes kept looking at where it went away."
3. Let the parent practice moving the toy as modeled in Activity No. 2. If the toy is not returned promptly, according to the child's lingering gaze, physically or verbally prompt the parent. Explain the importance of returning the toy, not only to help her child's memory, but also to help keep him from feeling teased.
4. If the parent has difficulty judging how far away to move the object, roll it across a small table or lap board placed in front of the child.
5. If the parent moves or rolls objects too fast, use objects which roll more slowly, such as a weighted can or wind-up toy.
6. Demonstrate and suggest that the parent toss a balloon, or blow a tissue or a leaf near her child during daily activities and to watch for her child to stare at the place it went away. Remind the parent to show it to him again.
7. Demonstrate, and let the parent practice, slowly moving her face while talking behind a barrier, such as her hands or a box, and then returning it with a big smile and friendly "Hi."
8. Explain that if her child can hear a toy that is out of sight, it gives him a reminder that it is still there. Demonstrate and let the parent practice moving a musical toy out of sight and watching for her child's lingering gaze before returning it back to his sight.

DEAF PARENT

May be unaware that sounds from hidden or disappearing objects help remind her child they are still there.

1. Explain and demonstrate for the parent how the sound from a toy that her child cannot see helps him remember it's still there.
2. Suggest sound toys for the parent to use when moving toys out of sight. Refer to 1.03 (Responds to sounds).

BLIND PARENT

May have difficulty recognizing when an object is within her child's visual field, and may be unaware that her child reacts when objects are moved out of sight.

1. Explain this visual skill as it relates to the child's developmental stage, e.g., "At this stage, your child is learning to follow objects with his eyes. When an object moves out of sight, he will keep looking for a few seconds at the last place he saw it."
2. If the parent is congenitally blind, it may be helpful to explain the underlying cognitive concept of her child reacting to the disappearance of visual stimuli via a perceptual analogy: "When you were a baby, you may have needed to hold or hear a rattle to know it was there. At that age, if someone took it away or you dropped it, you might search for it for a few seconds with your hands or body. Then you would forget it was there unless you touched it or heard it again soon. As you got older, even if you could not touch it, you knew it was still around. Your child is learning this, not only by touching, but also by seeing."
3. Point out naturally occurring situations to the parent which provide the opportunity for her child to react to disappearing objects, e.g., when the parent walks out of the room, behind her child's crib, or other barrier; moving a bottle behind her back; and when his toy rolls under a blanket.
4. If the child needs specific extra opportunities to practice tracking and experiencing the disappearance of objects, help orient the parent to appropriate positions and distances to move objects within her child's visual field. Refer to 4.06 (Follows with eyes to midline).

PHYSICALLY DISABLED PARENT

Who has limited hand use; may have difficulty holding and moving stimulus slowly across her child's visual field.

1. A toy on a string can be easily attached to a velcor wrist band on the parent. If the parent has limited shoulder or elbow movement, a velcro leg band could be used for the parent to pull the toy slowly.
2. Demonstrate and/or suggest visual pursuit activities which require little or no fine motor control. For example, the parent could:
   a. Nudge a rolling toy or ball.
   b. Use her face as the moving visual target, slowly moving it behind a nearby barrier, such as a box.
   c. Blow light objects off a table, such as feather, tissue, or light ball, while you return it back to the child's gaze.
   d. Slide her hand under a bright cloth and move her whole hand across her child's visual field and out of sight.
   e. Slide objects across a *port-a-play gym.**

1.10   Child: **SEARCHES WITH EYES FOR SOUND** (2-3½ mo.)
       Parent: Encourages child to search for sounds with eyes. Sets up controlled sound stimulation activities, if prescribed by educator or therapist

GENERAL GUIDELINES

The child's responses to sounds becomes less reflexive and more purposeful. At this level, he searches with his eyes in response to sounds rather than only showing a bodily response. He is not yet able to actually locate the sound source when it is out of his direct visual field.

---

*See Glossary.

MENTALLY RETARDED PARENT

May have difficulty judging suitable distances, durations, and volumes of sound stimuli for her child.

1. Relate to the parent that her child is learning about sounds and becoming curious about from where they are coming.
2. Prompt the parent to think of and name different household and toy sounds that her child listens to each day:
    a. If parent has difficulty, prompt with running water, door bell, T.V., stereo, rattle, squeak toy, etc.
    b. Discuss how curious her child may be about where those sounds are coming from and prompt her to think of ways she can help him figure this out.
    c. Model, and let the parent practice, naming the source of sound and pointing toward it for her child. Emphasize that we don't expect him to find the sound all by himself yet; we have to show him from where the sound is coming.
3. Activate a sound and point out the child's behaviors which indicate he is looking for it; stress watching for the child's eye movements.
4. If the child needs additional controlled sound stimulation activities as recommended by a teacher or therapist:
    a. Help the parent choose and discriminate toys or objects that make attracting sounds which are not too loud or too soft, e.g., squeak toys, rattles, two spoons banging, or crumpling cellophane.
    b. Demonstrate the appropriate distance from the child to activate sounds using a concrete marking, such as two hand spreads from the child's shoulder. Let the parent practice with your prompts until proficient.
    c. Demonstrate, and let the parent practice, activating the sound from different locations around her child, e.g., each side of her child's head and then at midline.
    d. Stress that you do not expect her child to actually find the sound with his eyes, only to "look for it."
    e. Show the parent how to activate the sound for a count of three and then stop for a count of three to watch for her child's response.
    f. Explain that, at this age, children get tired of this game after hearing the sound two or three times.

DEAF PARENT

May be unaware of her child's bilateral sound localization abilities or learning needs.

1. If not previously explained, describe the developmental sequence for auditory localization and auditory habituation responses; point out toys which make sounds. Refer to 1.03 (Responds to sound).
2. If the child needs specific controlled sound stimulation and localization activities, explain and demonstrate the following points:
    a. Do not activate the sound directly in front of her child's eyes; we want him to look for the sound with his eyes.
    b. The sound stimulus should be presented to each side of her child's head.
    c. The appropriate distance and duration of sound stimuli for her child, e.g., shake the rattle two times, 7 to 15 inches to the side of his ear.
    d. The child's physical responses to sound by brightening, searching, and vocalizing.
    e. At this age we don't expect her child to find the sound source, just to look for it.
    f. The importance of pausing when her child responds, bringing the sound source to his visual field, and then reactivating the sound two more times.
3. Point out various environmental sounds to the parent that she can watch for that her child may respond to, such as electrical appliances, doors opening, footsteps, and barking dogs.

BLIND PARENT

May be unaware of her child's visual responses to sounds.

1. If not previously explained, describe the child's initial developmental sequence of auditory localization and concurrent visual skills. Refer to Activity No. 5, 1.03 (Responds to sound).
2. Describe a perceptual analogy to help the parent understand her child's searching for sounds. For example, explain that just as she may search for a sound through touch or turning toward the sound, at this age a child searches for sounds by moving his eyes.
3. Explain that since her child's eyes sometimes move independently of his head, his head position will not always indicate whether he has localized a sound.
4. If controlled sound-localization activities are prescribed for her child:
    a. Help the parent position sound stimuli at an appropriate distance from her child, within and outside of his visual field.
    b. If needed, suggest a concrete physical market to help assure the sound source is at a proper distance and within her child's visual field, e.g., an armspread from her child's tummy is within his visual field but not from the side of his shoulder.
    c. Monitor and describe her child's eye movements to the parent as she activates the sound.

PHYSICALLY DISABLED PARENT

Who has a poor grasp or limited upper extremity control; may have difficulty activating sound stimulus toys.

1. Naturally occurring sound stimuli, such as doorbells, cars honking, appliances running, and footsteps can be pointed out and named for the child.
2. The parent can use rattle toys which roll and elicit a sound. Attach small pieces of velcro to different rattles and sound making toys. The parent, using a velcro wrist cuff, can easily attach, shake, and move the toy into the child's visual field.
3. The parent can direct her child's attention to tape recorded music or animal sounds.
4. The parent can make tongue click or "raspberry" sounds to the side of her child and watch for and prompt his searching.

1.10

5. If the parent has limited mobility, she can keep several sound stimulus toys attached to strings and tied to her wheelchair, the child's crib, basinette, etc. This will avoid having toys being dropped out of reach.

1.11 Child: INSPECTS OWN HANDS (2-3 mo.)
Parent: Encourages child to look at own hands; facilitates when recommended

GENERAL GUIDELINES

The child looks at his hands and watches what he can do with them for several minutes at a time. He may watch his fingers move slowly, glance from hand to hand, and wave them to create an interesting visual spectacle against light.

The child learns about depth perception as he practices moving his hands close to and then away from his face. This skill also helps the child to have a more defined awareness of his body and uses.

If a child has increased or decreased muscle tone, he may have difficulty bringing his hands within visual range. Side-lying and supine cradling positions may be prescribed to facilitate this skill.

MENTALLY RETARDED PARENT

May have difficulty remembering prescribed positioning techniques and activities which help her child look at his hands.

1. Interpret for the parent how this skill is a learning experience for her child. Use a concrete explanation, such as "As your child begins to look at his hands he is learning about his body parts and what they do. Since his hands are the easiest part for him to see, he learns about them first. He will soon realize he can reach for things with them."
2. Demonstrate and have the parent practice fun activities which attract her child's attention to his hands:
   a. Gently bring the child's hands to your mouth and kiss.
   b. Bring the child's hand in view when washing them.
   c. Softly tap or rub the top of the child's hand when in prone.
3. If special positioning techniques are recommended for the child, such as side-lying:
   a. Demonstrate, and let the parent practice, the position with her child while you monitor and reinforce.
   b. Take a Polaroid picture of her child in the proper position for the parent to keep at home.
   c. Name specific times of the day to place her child in side-lying, such as after eating.
   d. Demonstrate and tell the parent to lie her child on alternate sides after each diaper changing.

BLIND PARENT

May be unable to visually monitor or understand her child's hand-watching behavior.

1. Describe this skill and its importance as a prerequisite for visually directed reach through auditory and tactual comparison. For example, explain that just as the parent learns about her environment through her hands, so does her child. However, instead of using auditory and tactile cues to reach for something, her child uses his eyes to help direct his hands. Before children do this, however, they need to spend time looking at and learning about their hands.
2. Place wrist bands with bells on each of the child's hands. Each wrist band bell could have a different tone to help the parent differentiate the child's left and right hand movements.
3. Monitor and describe the child's hand-watching behaviors to the parent.
4. Encourage the parent to "nibble" on her child's fingers, blow and kiss his palms, and place her child's hands on the parent's cheeks.
5. If special positioning techniques are prescribed:
   a. Clearly describe the position.
   b. Let the parent experience the position herself.
   c. Let the parent practice while you monitor and prompt as needed until she is comfortable implementing this independently.

PHYSICALLY DISABLED PARENT

With upper extremity weakness or control deficits; may have difficulty carrying out positioning techniques which help her child look at his hands.

1. If a side-lying position is prescribed to help the child inspect his hands, the parent may be unable to physically hold her child in this position; a firm pillow or blanket roll, the length of the child, can be placed behind the child's head and back to prop him during side-lying.

1.12 Child: WATCHES SPEAKER'S EYES AND MOUTH (2-3 mo.)
Parent: Frequently assumes face-to-face positions with child when talking

MENTALLY RETARDED PARENT

May avoid or not spontaneously assume face-to-face positions.

1. Relate how a small child likes to look at his parent's face often during each day. Include the following points:
   a. Children feel loved and cared for when parents look at them and smile.
   b. Since children can't understand words, they watch our facial movements when we talk to help them understand what we say. Refer to 1.39 (Responds to facial expressions).
2. Model and prompt the parent to practice saying simple meaningful phrases while holding her child in a face to face position:
   a. Describe the child's positive responses to his parent's vocalizations and eye contact, e.g., brightening, smiling, vocalizing, and watching her.

b. Point out when the child has had enough face-to-face talking and needs a break, e.g., head turning, gaze aversion, and body twisting.
c. Demonstrate a conducive distance for an adult's face from her child's face.
3. Name specific daily activities to talk face-to-face with her child, e.g., diapering, feeding, before picking up, etc. Suggest phrases to say to coincide with each activity.

DEAF PARENT

May be non-verbal.

1. The parent can hum, make tongue clicks, and make inviting facial expressions to encourage her child's face-to-face contact.
2. Encourage any speech the parent may have.

BLIND PARENT

May not engage in or has minimal face-to-face interactions with her child.

1. Anticipatory Guidance: Parents who have been blind all or most of their lives may develop alternative interactive strategies with their children. They may position themselves with their children facing out or in parallel fashion. Children appear to quickly adjust their own interaction styles to their parents', while continuing to seek and receive communicative facial cues from other various adults and children around them. Parents should thus be encouraged to interact in ways that are comfortable for them and their child. The parent's confidence and sense of competence will be transmitted to the child, and that is the most critical element.
2. Parents who become blind in their teens or adult life often continue face-to-face interactions. These can be encouraged by explaining the communicative value of parents' facial expressions to their children. Describe the child's face-to-face expressions during these interactions, e.g., "He's really watching your mouth and smiling!"
3. The parent may be able to recognize when her child is looking at her by discriminating her child's breathing patterns.

1.13 Child: BEGINS PLAY WITH RATTLE
(2½-4 mo.)
Parent: Places appropriate rattle toys in child's hand and encourages play

GENERAL GUIDELINES

The child may mouth, wave, and shake a rattle for a minute before dropping it. The child's reach and grasp is not mature enough to attain the rattle independently. Rattles provide a child visual, auditory, and purposeful movement experiences.

Parents can encourage their child's rattle play by placing easy to grasp rattles in his hand and with gentleness, physically prompting him to shake it. The child should experience rattle play at midline, with each hand, and in different positions, such as sitting, supine, and side-lying.

MENTALLY RETARDED PARENT

May select inappropriate sized rattles and/or expect developmentally higher rattle play skills.

1. Help the parent select appropriate rattles for her child:
    a. Remind her that her child's hand is very small at this age, so the handle portion of her rattle should not be much bigger than a pencil.
    b. Demonstrate inspecting toys to assure they are safe. Point out that safe rattles have no sharp edges, do not break easily, and do not have particles which can fall out.
    c. Have the parent test various rattles by dropping them on the floor, shaking them, and feeling for sharp edges.
    d. Ask, and explain if needed, what could happen if her child had an unsafe rattle.
2. Explain that at this age children cannot pick up rattles by themselves, so the parent needs to help by placing it in her child's hand.
3. If the child does not spontaneously regard or play with the rattle, demonstrate placing the rattle in the child's hand and prompting him to shake it by *gently* moving the child's arm at his elbow. Let the parent practice with your positive reinforcement.
4. Discuss the "okayness" of young children mouthing rattles.
5. If needed, suggest short phrases for the parent to say while engaging her child in rattle play, e.g., "Shake, shake, shake" and "See the pretty rattle?"

DEAF PARENT

May be unaware of rattle sounds.

1. Explain to the parent that the sounds of some toys encourage her child to shake them. Identify small toys which make a rattle sound when shaken or waved. Mark them with a permanent non-toxic marker for the parent's future reference.
2. Use or make rattles which are clear to provide the parent visual cues. Clear safety capped plastic medicine bottles or test tubes with colored rice, corn kernels, or aquarium stones work well.
3. The parent can tactually discriminate some rattle toys, depending upon the toy's vibro-tactile intensity.

BLIND PARENT

May not be able to visually check rattles for visual attractiveness, size, and safety.

1. Discuss the properties (size, shapes, colors) of rattles which are visually attracting in order for her child to play with it.
2. Describe the safety factors to be aware of when choosing rattles, e.g., check that they do not break easily, do not have particles which fall out, and are unpainted. The parent may be interested in tactually screening rattles with your monitoring.
3. Give a box containing suitable and unsuitable rattle toys to help the parent tactually discriminate safe, appropriately

sized and shaped rattles from unsafe and/or inappropriate rattles.
4. Explain that although her child can see the rattle, at this age he may not be able to reach for it to play, so she needs to help by placing it in his hand.
5. The parent can easily monitor her child's rattle play by listening to the rattle sounds, child's vocal expressions, and body movements.
6. Orient the parent to present rattles at her child's midline eight to fifteen inches from her child's chest to encourage his reaching.

PHYSICALLY DISABLED PARENT

Who has a limited grasp; may have difficulty holding, shaking, and placing a rattle in her child's hand.

1. The parent can place rattles in her child's hand by using her mouth, nudging the rattle into her child's hand when he's in a side-lying position, or using a velcro wrist cuff to shake and guide the rattle to her child's hand. Refer to 1.10 (Searches with eyes for sound).

1.14 Child: ENJOYS REPEATING NEWLY LEARNED ACTIVITY (3-4 mo.)
Parent: Provides opportunities for child to repeat newly learned activities

GENERAL GUIDELINES

The child begins to act purposely in an effort to recreate an interesting sound or visual spectacle. At first, he may bump into a roly-poly toy with his fist accidentally or kick his mobile unintentionally. As he recognizes he "caused something to happen," he repeats the same movement several times to make it happen again.

MENTALLY RETARDED PARENT

May not allow the needed response time for her child to repeat an activity.

1. Present a roly-poly toy and ask the parent what would happen if we hit or pushed it. Comment that she knew the toy would make a sound and move before actually hitting it because she had already learned that would happen. Relate how her child is learning he can make things happen, too. Include the following concepts:
   a. At this age, children like to keep hitting it three or four times to keep the toy moving; in this way, he learns that he can make something happen.
   b. He learns to keep the toy moving by kicking his feet, hitting it with his feet, or bumping it with his arm.
   c. If the toy is too far away, his hands and feet cannot reach it, so he wouldn't be able to practice making it move.
2. Model, and let the parent practice, introducing a roly-poly toy for her child to hit in various positions. Stress:
   a. Showing him how to "make it work."
   b. Keeping the toy within her child's reach.
   c. Giving him time to try it himself.

   d. Smiling and nodding, but not interrupting, while her child is hitting it.
   e. He may get tired of doing this after three or four times. Don't try to make him do it again; he can practice later.
3. Help the parent select additional toys which create an interesting visual or auditory spectacle for her child, demonstrating what the child may do to keep it going. Adjust mobiles or crib gyms within the child's reaching and kicking movements.

DEAF PARENT

May not be aware that sound toys encourage her child to purposely hit or move it repeatedly.

1. Explain that when children purposely hit or move toys, they are learning that they have the power to make things move *and* make sounds.
2. Help the parent identify roly-poly toys, mobiles, wrist bands, or booties with bells which create interesting sounds. Use roly-poly toys which create an interesting visual spectacle and sound when hit.

BLIND PARENT

May not be able to visually recognize if or when her child repeats an activity.

1. The parent can use toys which provide audible cues when her child repeats the activity, e.g., child shaking or kicking wrist band with bells, ankle bands with bells, mobiles, or toys which make sounds when hit.
2. Help orient the parent to the appropriate distance of an object or activity from her child, if needed.
3. Describe to the parent her child's facial expressions and the visual spectacles he produced with the toy. For example, some roly-poly toys have transparent coverings; when pushed, little animals or people rock back and forth.

1.15 Child: USES HANDS AND MOUTH FOR SENSORY EXPLORATION OF OBJECTS (3-6 mo.)
Parent: Allows, and facilitates if necessary, child's safe exploration of toys with hands and mouth

GENERAL GUIDELINES

The child may put objects in his mouth, bang them against his crib or floor, and pat, shake, or wave them. These actions are the child's first interactions in learning to relate to objects. He applies these actions to all graspable objects, without differentiating at this point what is the object's true function.

These actions teach the child how things feel, taste, and look when moved in different ways. He is learning that objects remain stable and their shapes remain the same, even though it may look different when he waves it in the air.

Parents facilitate their child's exploration of objects by giving them ample opportunities to hold and mouth a variety of safe graspable objects in his environment. Textured teethers, noise makers, paper, rubber toys, cold things, colored things, and plastic key-chain toys provide the child with varied visual, tactile, and auditory experiences.

MENTALLY RETARDED PARENT

May interpret her child's mouthing as "bad" or may have difficulty anticipating safety concerns when her child mouthes objects.

1. Show the parent pictures of young children exploring toys with their mouths. Explain that children learn about things at this age by feeling with their hands *and* mouth. Reinforce that this is okay and a good thing to do.
2. Discuss the pros and cons of mouthing objects and the safety factors involved within the support of a parent group setting.
3. Ask the parent to name things she needs to think about before letting her child mouth a toy to make sure that it is safe. Emphasize screening for *non*-toxic substances and objects which break off, splinter, are small enough to swallow, or are too heavy:
   a. Help the parent discriminate and select safe toys and objects for her child from a box of appropriate and inappropriate items. Specify what makes each a "good" or "bad" toy to mouth.
   b. Wash and rinse toys thoroughly with the parent, discussing the need to do this at least once a week because of germs. Name a specific day of the week to wash toys, if needed.
4. Stress that since her child is learning to put things in his mouth and he does not know yet which things are okay to mouth, she must check everyday to make sure there are no unsafe things in his sleep and play areas.
5. If the child is not exploring toys with his mouth, model gently guiding the child's hand to his mouth with an appropriate toy:
   a. Stress the importance of never "pushing" a toy in the child's mouth or removing a toy too quickly.
   b. Demonstrate removing physical assistance to the child after the toy has been guided to his mouth so he can explore it all by himself.
   c. Have the parent practice guiding her child's hand with a toy in it to his mouth with your verbal prompts and reinforcement.
6. Explain that at this age, no matter what we give to her child to play with, he may shake, mouth, wave, or bang the toy. This helps him learn how it tastes, feels, and looks:
   a. Demonstrate various actions children employ when playing with toys.
   b. Show the parent additional objects, such as a spoon and cup. Ask her to show you the different ways her child may play with them.
   c. Stress that even though we know cups are for drinking and spoons are for eating, her child is not ready to learn this.
7. Help the parent collect various household objects with which to let her child play. Put them in special boxes next to his sleep or play areas. Make a picture list of appropriate toys and objects with which her child can play.
8. Discuss the importance of providing times when the child has only one object or toy at a time. Explain that if he has too many things to look at all at one time, he may be too busy looking at them to learn about them from mouthing, shaking, waving, or banging them.
9. Demonstrate and caution the parent against giving her child toys which are too heavy for him to hold. Explain that he may accidentally hit himself in the face with it.

DEAF PARENT

May be unaware of the auditory reinforcement her child receives when he shakes, waves, or bangs objects.

1. Refer to 4.39 (Bangs objects on table).

BLIND PARENT

May not be able to visually monitor if her child is mouthing unsafe objects.

1. Provide the parent anticipatory guidance regarding mouthing safely at this developmental stage for her child:
   a. Offer to help the parent baby-proof her child's sleep and play areas for small or hidden objects that could be dangerous.
   b. The parent will learn to discriminate her child's mouthing sounds and be able to tactually check the object for safety.
2. Refer to 6.07 (Brings hand to mouth) and 6.09 (Brings hand to mouth with toy or object) for suggestions to help the parent encourage and detect her child's mouthing.
3. Describe the various actions her child uses with toys and his concurrent facial expressions and visual attending.

PHYSICALLY DISABLED PARENT

With limited mobility; may benefit from adaptations which help keep toys within her easy reach.

1. Small toys suitable for the child's mouthing and explorations often tumble to the floor or out of reach. They can be attached to strings and tied to the parent's wheelchair, child's highchair, etc. CAUTION: The child should never be left unsupervised with strings.

1.16 Child: TURNS EYES AND HEAD TO SOUND OF HIDDEN VOICE (3-7 mo.)
Parent: Talks to child from various locations during daily activities

GENERAL GUIDELINES

The child's auditory localization abilities are gradually maturing. He turns his eyes and head to find a speaker who is located toward either side of him. This localization ability helps him learn that different people have different voices.

1.16

MENTALLY RETARDED PARENT

May not talk to her child during daily activities, especially if he is out of sight.

1. Refer to 1.07 (Listens to voice for 30 seconds).
2. Explain to the parent that her child likes to hear people talk, even when he cannot see them. It helps him know people are nearby and lets him know when people are approaching him.
3. Praise how her child is learning to figure out from where voices are coming. Have parent call her child's name while you are holding him. Point out his responses that indicate he knew from where the voice was coming.
4. Name times when the parent is not in her child's immediate visual range for her to talk to him: as she enters his room; while cooking; cleaning house, etc. If needed, suggest short meaningful phrases to say according to the situation, such as "I'm fixing your bottle" or "I'm going to pick you up."

DEAF PARENT

May be unaware of her child's auditory localization skills.

1. Interpret for the parent this sound localization skill in relation to developmental stages, e.g., first her child only changed his expression when he heard a sound or voice, then he learned to look for it by moving his eyes. Now he is learning, or is ready to learn, to find where sounds and voices are coming from by moving both his eyes *and* head to find them when he cannot see from where the sound is coming.
2. Demonstrate talking and making vocal sounds from different locations out of her child's sight while the parent watches her child's head turning and eye movements.
3. Encourage the parent to vocalize and/or make other sounds, such as humming or tongue clicking, to her child when she is out of his direct sight. If her child does not look at her, suggest a way to vary the sound or suggest moving closer.

BLIND PARENT

May not be able to recognize when her child turns his head to locate voices.

1. The parent could position her child so she can feel when he turns his head to search for another person's voice, e.g., on her lap facing her while his head is propped on her bent knees, or on her lap facing out with his head supported against her chest.
2. Although the parent may be unable to visually monitor if her child turns his head to a voice when she is not holding him, she should be alerted to situations which naturally provide the child with this opportunity, e.g., talking before entering a room or when someone else calls from another room.

1.17 **Child: PLAYS WITH OWN HANDS, FEET, FINGERS, TOES (3-5 mo.)**
Parent: Encourages child to play with his hands, feet, fingers, toes

GENERAL GUIDELINES

The child becomes aware that his feet and toes are part of his body and that he can control their movements and feeling sensations. He may touch, clasp, or reach for his feet with his hands.

Parents encourage their child's awareness of his hands and feet by playing simple movement games with them, "nibbling on his toes," and bringing the child's hands to his feet when he is in a cradled position. Colorful stickers, small rolled up pieces of masking tape, ribbons, mittens with bells, or bracelets can be put on the child's hands and feet if the child needs extra help to attract his attention and increase his awareness of his hands and feet.

MENTALLY RETARDED PARENT

May be too rough during hand and feet games with her child.

1. Demonstrate two or three simple hand and foot movement games for the parent, such as "This Little Piggy," "Itsy Bitsy Spider," or an on the spot made-up game:
   a. Stress the importance of moving their child's hands, fingers, feet, and toes very gently. Explain that it hurts her child if we move him too fast or pull too hard.
   b. Use lots of facial expressions and voice inflections.
2. Let the parent practice hand and foot games with her child, choosing the game she likes best:
   a. Monitor and praise her gentle handling.
   b. If the parent is too rough, give verbal prompts explaining how to improve her handling, e.g., "Hold his foot lightly," or
   c. Talk for the child to relay his feelings, "Mom, that is a little too rough for my small hands!"
   d. Reinforce all of parent's verbal interactions with her child during this game.
3. Explore specific times during the day which lend themselves well for the parent to play these games with her child, e.g., drying after a bath, after diapering, and before putting on socks.
4. Refer to 1.11 (Inspects own hands), modifying explanations to include feet and toes.

BLIND PARENT

May not be able to visually monitor her child's hand and foot play.

1. Alert the parent of this developmental stage so she can tactually inspect her child's shoes and booties for unsafe or loose decor, such as sequines and buttons.
2. If the parent is unaware of gesture games and songs involving hand and foot movements to play with her child, demonstrate them with her, or provide clear verbal prompts while the parent plays them with her child.

3. Refer to activities for 1.11 (Inspects own hands) and adapt to include feet.

PHYSICALLY DISABLED PARENT

With congenital sensory deficit's or severe motor limitations; may be unaware of the sensory learning benefits for her child when he plays with his hands and feet.

1. Before suggesting hand and foot games, explain to the parent the sensory motor benefits to her child from these activities, i.e., he is learning body awareness and coordinated muscle control.
2. Discourage long periods of immobilization in highchairs, strollers, or infant seats, which may be over-used by parents with physical disabilities, to insure a "safe" playtime. Help set up unrestricting play areas, such as free time for the child on a blanket on the floor.
3. If the parent cannot play hand and foot games with her child, use ribbons, bells well secured on elastic wrist bands, or non-toxic faces drawn on her child's hands and feet to help encourage him to play with his hands and feet. The parent can provide her child special verbal prompts and praise.

1.18 Child: AWAKENS OR QUIETS TO MOTHER'S VOICE (3-6 mo.)
Parent: Uses a soothing voice to quiet or awaken child

MENTALLY RETARDED PARENT

May use loud or abrupt vocalizations which frighten her child upon awakening or when trying to calm him down; may also feel angry when her child cries.

1. Stress that all children cry when upset, hungry, not feeling good, or tired:
   a. Empathize how frustrating it is when children cry so much, but never hit or yell at the child. Explain "This will not help, but can hurt. Children don't learn to stop crying by hitting."
   b. Explain that soft voices help quiet a child, but loud voices can scare him.
   c. Demonstrate soothing and calming voice tones when her child's crying spells occur.
   d. Model specific phrases to say, such as "It's okay, I'm here; I know you're upset."
2. Let the parent practice using a soothing voice on a tape recorder.
3. Model and help the parent learn, if needed, to sing a lullabye to help awaken or quiet her child.
4. Discuss how it feels to wake up to loud voices.
5. If it is apparent that the parent cannot use a soothing voice to help quiet or awaken her child, demonstrate calming or awakening her child with a soft music box, or a stuffed animal with a music box coupled with humming.

DEAF PARENT

May be unintentionally too loud or abrupt in her speech to soothe her child.

1. Check with the parent to determine if she can monitor the volume of her voice. If so, explain that a low voice tone is more soothing to her child when first awakening or when trying to quiet. Let the parent practice low soothing speech with your cueing.
2. If the parent cannot regulate her voice volume, show her how to use a soft musical toy or a song to soothe her child when awakening or quieting him. If a record player or tape recorder is used, remember to mark the knobs at an appropriate volume for future setting by parent.
3. The parent may be able to hum soothing sounds to her child.

1.19 Child: LOCALIZES SOUND WITH EYES (3½-5 mo.)
Parent: Plays structured sound localization games with child when recommended

GENERAL GUIDELINES

The child searches and finds the source of distinctive sounds to the left, right, above, and below his eyes.

Naturally occurring environmental sound stimuli encourage the child to develop his sound localization abilities. Parents can facilitate their child's sound awareness and localization skills by capitalizing upon naturally occurring environmental sounds of potential interest. The parent can call her child's attention to sounds by showing and telling him where the sound is coming from. Telephones, doors closing, doorbells, electrical appliances, and alarm clocks are examples of sounds which parents can draw their child's attention toward.

If the child has a gross motor delay or motor impairment, the sound source and child should be positioned to facilitate his response to sound. Individualized positions can be recommended by an occupational or physical therapist.

Children who are less responsive to sounds or who have a hearing impairment may need controlled sound localization activities. Squeak toys, bells, and rattles can be used as the sound stimulus and should be held 7-15" from the child, to the left or right of his face, and then 7-15" above or below his eyeline, at gradually increasing distances. The sound should be activated three to four times and then stopped and wait for the child's response. If he cannot find the toy, it can be slowly brought into his line of vision and activated to make a sound until he finds it. Touching the side of the child's face closest to the sound provides him with an additional cue for finding the sound. The parent's expressions of delight and interest in the sound also helps the child appreciate and look for sounds.

1.19

MENTALLY RETARDED PARENT

May have difficulty judging appropriate distances, intensities, and durations of sounds during prescribed localization games with her child.

1. Identify with the parent specific sound toys and objects to use when playing localization games, e.g., bells, rattles, squeak toys, or spoons.
2. Model, and let the parent practice with your physical and verbal prompts, how to play sound localization games with her child. Stress the following concepts:
   a. Hold the sound toy 7-15" from the child's face, to the left of his eyes. The parent can use her forearm as a concrete marker to help judge distance.
   b. Activate the sound three or four times. The parent can count aloud softly or tap her foot as a reminder to stop.
   c. Reactivate the sound and bring it closer to the child until he locates the source.
   d. Give the toy to the child and praise him when he finds it.
   e. Repeat the procedure to the child's right, and then above and below his eyes.
3. Refer to 1.10 (Searches with eyes for sound).

DEAF PARENT

May benefit from sound toys which provide visual or tactile cues during sound localization games with child.

1. Use sound producing toys which the parent can hold in her hand to feel the vibrations, such as a wind-up alarm clock bell. Screen the toy's or object's sound to assure it is not too loud and frightening for the child.
2. Select toys with a noise mechanism which the parent can see, such as clear rattles that produce sound when shaken or music boxes with transparent clear cases.
3. Refer to 1.03 (Responds to sound) for additional material adaptations, and 1.10 (Searches with eyes for sound).

BLIND PARENT

May not be able to visually monitor when her child has localized a sound.

1. Describe to the parent her child's new or emerging visual abilities to search for sounds. See activities for 1.10 (Searches with eyes for sound).
2. The parent can position her child so that she can feel his subtle head movements to localize sounds. Refer to 1.16 (Turns eyes and head to sound of hidden voice).
3. Describe the child's visual responses for the parent as she plays sound localization games. If necessary, provide initial physical assistance to help determine an appropriate distance to activate the sound from her child.
4. Explain habituation, i.e., her child may stop looking for a sound after he has heard it several times.

PHYSICALLY DISABLED PARENT

Who has poor grasp or upper extremity control; may have difficulty operating a sound stimulus toy.

1. Refer to 1.10 (Searches with eyes for sound).

1.20 Child: FINDS A PARTIALLY HIDDEN OBJECT (4-6 mo.)
Parent: Encourages child to find partially hidden objects

GENERAL GUIDELINES

The child displays his understanding of part-whole relationships and recognition that whole objects still exist, even if he cannot see the whole object when he uncovers a partially covered familiar object. Naturally occurring situations, such as his bottle or toy being accidentally covered partially by a blanket, help the child learn these concepts.

If the child is having difficulty with visual memory and object permanence skills, special hiding games may be recommended. 1.09 (Reacts to the disappearance of slowly moving objects) is a prerequisite to this skill.

Introduce the following concepts to parent if this skill has been recommended for the child:

1. Start with familiar uniform objects or toys which are attractive to the child, such as a ball or cup; when the child is able to find those, use familiar non-symmetrical objects, such as a toy car or doll.
2. Covers should not be more attractive than the partially hidden object. Start with covers which are somewhat transparent, such as nylon netting from produce bags, and then switch to solid cloths.
3. Hide objects which make sounds (toy radio) or move (wind-up toy) to provide additional cues as needed.
4. Capitalize on naturalistic settings during daily activities: show the child an object sticking out of a pocket, purse, or grocery bag, or help him find his bottle or toy under his blanket.

MENTALLY RETARDED PARENT

May tease her child during hiding games.

1. If structured hiding games are recommended for the child, model partially hiding a toy or object, and describe the activity as a "Peek-a-boo game" with toys.
2. Point out for the parent several daily situations that naturally hide objects partially, e.g., a toy under a blanket, hanging out of mother's pocketbook, or partly under a couch, and a cookie under a napkin. Demonstrate showing a partially covered object to her child using verbal and physical prompts, and letting him have it if he does not uncover it.
3. Model, and let the parent practice, playing "Peek-a-boo" with a teddy bear or doll and encourage the child to pull a washcloth off the bear's or doll's head. To prevent

teasing or frustrating the child, emphasize the following points:
a. Do not cover the entire toy.
b. Let the child hold the toy after he has uncovered it.
c. If the child has difficulty pulling off the cover, help him.

DEAF PARENT

May be unaware that sounds of toys can assist her child in his search for them.

1. Demonstrate how the child may be able to find a hidden toy which makes a sound more easily than toys which do not make sounds. Explain that the sound offers the child an additional cue that the whole toy continues to exist even though he cannot see the whole thing.
2. Help select toys which continue to make sound for a few minutes after the parent has activated them. Stuffed animals with music boxes and toy radios are good choices.
3. As the child becomes proficient in finding the hidden toys which make sounds, the parent can begin hiding toys which do not make sounds.

BLIND PARENT

May not be able to visually monitor when her child has retrieved a partially hidden toy.

1. Describe this task using a meaningful analogy for the parent. Use an analogy, such as "Just as you are able to identify familiar objects by touching only part of it, your child is learning to identify familiar objects by seeing only part of it."
2. Use a large toy with a string attached and a towel for a cover. The parent can partially cover the toy and leave the string in her hand. When the child retrieves the toy, the string's movement will alert the parent.
3. The parent can partially cover rattles, a roly-poly, or other toy which will make a sound when her child has retrieved it.
4. The parent can put a large toy halfway in her apron pocket and encourage her child to find it. She can then feel when her child is attempting to find it.
5. Point out naturally occurring environmental situations which partially hide objects.

PHYSICALLY DISABLED PARENT

Who has limited hand control; may have difficulty manipulating covers if structured hiding activities are recommended for her child.

1. Attach loops to containers, such as cardboard boxes or plastic bowls, and cloths to be used as screens for hiding toys. The parent can slip her finger, wrist, or arm under the loop to control her covering or uncovering of the hidden object.
2. The parent can verbally prompt her child to find partially hidden objects in naturally occurring situations, such as toys covered by bubbles in the tub or by grass and leaves outside.

1.21 **Child:** CONTINUES A FAMILIAR ACTIVITY BY INITIATING MOVEMENTS INVOLVED (4-5 mo.)
Parent: Starts then stops activities with child and waits for his indication to continue

GENERAL GUIDELINES

The child indicates, by a consistent change in behavior, that he wants an action to restart after it stops. He may make a consistent sound, kick, wave, or wiggle.

Suggested toys and activities include wind-up cars, animals, and musical radios; gentle bouncing; rocking; and "Ah boo!" games.

MENTALLY RETARDED PARENT

May not allow her child response time before restarting an activity.

1. Concretely interpret the meaning of this child skill:
a. Use an explanation, such as "When we like an activity and want more after it stops, we can say we want more or make it happen again by ourselves; for example, if you're watching a good T.V. show and someone turns it off, you can either say 'turn it back on' or you can get up and turn it back on yourself."
b. Compare and contrast this idea in relationship to her child. Probe with questions, such as "If Johnny likes something, such as his musical radio, and it stops, can he tell you to turn it back on? Can he turn it on again?"
c. Name various ways that children may let us know they want more of something, e.g., kick, fuss, wave, and grunt. Prompt the parent to think of additional ways her child tells her he wants more of something.
2. Explore with parent action toys (wind-up toys, cars) and movement games ("Pat-A-Cake," "I'm gonna get you") which her child might like.
3. Model initiating the action of the toy or activity with the child, stopping the action, and then waiting for his response:
a. Point out and describe the child's behaviors which say "I want more."
b. Stress how we must wait and look for the child to kick, wave, etc., before we start the toy or activity again. Tell the parent to silently count to five to make sure child has enough time to respond.
c. Restart the activity.
4. Let the parent practice Activity No. 3 with her child, using a different action toy and movement game. "Coach from the sidelines" as needed to point out her child's responses and insure the parent allows enough time before restarting the activity or toy.

1.21

DEAF PARENT

May be unaware that her child "reacts" to restart a sound, or may have difficulty pacing a sound activity to her child's cues.

1. Identify action toys which make sounds for the parent. Encourage the parent to hum during movement games with her child.
2. Point out the child's behavioral responses and vocalizations in response to the cessation of the sound.
3. Emphasize waiting and watching for five seconds before restarting sound toys.

BLIND PARENT

May not be able to visually discriminate her child's non-audible cues to restart an activity.

1. Use battery-operated action toys with simple switches or buttons.
2. The parent may be able to "jiggle" or rock her child's stroller, carriage, or infant swing, stop, and then wait for her child's response.
3. The parent could hold her child in a rocking chair, rock, stop, and wait for her child's response.
4. While lying on her bed with the child on her chest, the parent could exaggerate her breathing and facial expressions and stop suddenly to watch for her child's responses.

1.22 Child: LOCALIZES TACTILE STIMULATION BY TOUCHING THE SAME SPOT OR SEARCHING FOR OBJECT THAT TOUCHED BODY (4-6 mo.)
Parent: Provides appropriate tactile stimulation to child; encourages child to localize if recommended

MENTALLY RETARDED PARENT

May provide too much or too little tactile stimulation to child.

1. Select two or three different textures and have the parent touch and describe what she feels. Show the parent how to let her child "feel" each texture, while modeling and verbally describing what you are doing and what the child is feeling. Explain that he likes to feel with his legs, arms, back, and cheeks, as well as his hands.
2. Let the parent practice gently rubbing her child with various textures, one at a time:
   a. Ask the parent to describe her child's reaction after she helped him feel each texture.
   b. Ask the parent which body parts her child seems to like having the different textures rubbed on best.
   c. Directly point out the child's signals which indicate he does not like the texture or wants you to stop, e.g., child twists, whines, and tries to move away.
3. Suggest to the parent times during the day which would be "good" times to provide special tactile stimulation to her child and demonstrate. For example, when bathing, model using a sponge or cloth and gently rubbing the child's arm and then leg while verbalizing to the child what you are doing.
4. Caution the parent not to "tickle" her child because small children cannot tell us when they have had enough, and tickling can end up hurting.

BLIND PARENT

May be unaware of her child's searching responses to tactile stimulation.

1. Explain that children look for the place on their bodies where they were touched. This helps them associate various body parts as part of themselves.
2. Monitor and describe to the parent her child's facial expressions and visual searching in response to tactile stimulation.

PHYSICALLY DISABLED PARENT

Who has limited hand or upper extremity control; may have difficulty holding or controlling a stimulus to encourage her child's tactile localization.

1. The parent could gently blow or lick her child's tummy, foot, hand, or leg.
2. The parent could hold a stimulus in her mouth to play tactile localization games.
3. Empty paper towel rolls covered with various textures may be easier for the parent to manipulate and control.

1.23 Child: PLAYS WITH PAPER (4½-7 mo.)
Parent: Provides safe opportunities for child to play with paper

GENERAL GUIDELINES

The child experiments with the various properties of paper by waving, shaking, crumpling, or tearing it. He is learning he can change the visual appearance of it and make special sounds. Paper-play provides the child opportunities to learn additional ways for interacting with objects.

The child's paper-play should be supervised. Recommended types of paper include foil bags from cookies, construction paper, wax paper, colorful tissue paper that doesn't fade when wet, magazine pages, and napkins. *Never* let the child play with plastic wrap or bags. Newspapers are not recommended because of their bleeding print.

MENTALLY RETARDED PARENT

May not generalize that paper can be used for play; may thus prevent her child's paper-play.

1. Name reasons why playing with paper is important and fun for the child. Include: children learn to use their hands, learn they can make something happen when they tear it, like to listen to the different sounds paper makes, and learn how different papers feel different.
2. Demonstrate and name the different qualities of various types of paper. Stress which paper with which her child must not play.

3. Supply a bagful of various papers. Have the parent sort through it and identify which papers are okay for her child to play with and which are *not* okay.
4. Make a special box with the parent for various papers which are good for her child's paper-play. Each week the parent can add a different type.
5. Name times during daily activities to let her child play with paper, for example, prior to mealtime when the parent discards the wrapper from a food item.
6. Discuss the importance of parent supervision during paper-play activities. Ask the parent to think of what could happen if she was not watching her child while he was playing with paper.
7. Assure the parent that it's okay if her child wants to taste the paper, and if he eats a little bit, he'll be all right. Explain she must, however, take big pieces out of his mouth.

DEAF PARENT

May be unaware of the variety of sounds paper can produce which help make paper-play interesting and educational for her child.

1. Explain that one of the reasons a child enjoys and learns from playing with paper is that it can produce many different sounds depending upon the type of paper:
   a. Provide various kinds and weights of paper for the parent to experience through tactile sensation. Relate that not only do they look and feel different, but each makes a different sound.
   b. Point out which types of paper makes attracting or crackling sounds (e.g., stiff cellophane, wax paper) and which paper makes little or no sound (e.g., Kleenex, napkins). Compare the soft sounds with the soft feeling and the stiffer papers with the louder sounds.

BLIND PARENT

May not be able to see when her child is mouthing paper.

1. Provide anticipatory guidance regarding the benefits of paper-play, precautions regarding mouthing, and plastic bags.
2. Help the parent identify which paper is safe for her child to play with and mouth. Generally, paper which is resistant to water is preferable to paper that becomes soggy when wet. Braille paper is suitable for the child to play with and mouth.
3. Explain that small bits of paper eating usually cannot be avoided and that's okay. The parent can listen for her child's mouthing sounds to help insure he is not mouthing too much.

1.24 Child: **TOUCHES TOY OR ADULT'S HAND TO RESTART AN ACTIVITY**
(5-9 mo.)
Parent: Restarts toy or activity when child touches her hand or toy

GENERAL GUIDELINES

The child is learning that objects produce actions independent of his own behaviors. After watching an action toy stop, he will try to make it start again by touching it or the hand of the adult who started the action. He has learned that his prior actions to recreate spectacles (waving, kicking, vocalizing) are not always enough to "make something happen again." Therefore, a prerequisite to this skill is 1.21 (Continues a familiar activity by initiating movements).

Parents encourage this skill by initiating simple action games and waiting for their child to respond before reinitiating it. The parent should leave her hand within easy reach of her child's hand to keep it readily available. Spinning a top; operating knobs on busy boxes or toy radios; activating action toys, such as wind-up animals, choo-choo trains, and cars; and playing "Peek-a-boo" or "Pat-A-Cake" are sample action toys and games parents can initiate with their child.

MENTALLY RETARDED PARENT

May restart a toy without giving her child enough response time to touch the toy or her hand in an effort to restart it himself.

1. Concretely interpret to the parent what it means when her child touches a toy or an adult's hand to restart an activity. Refer to Activity No. 1, 1.21 (Continues a familiar activity by initiating movements involved), and adapt according to the child's new signals of touching an adult's hand or toy.
2. Help the parent select an action toy and a movement game to play with her child. After the toy or game stops, explain how important it is to let her child have time to look at the toy, and touch it or her hand:
   a. Tell the parent to wait and watch what her child does with the action toy after it stops. Make a comment, such as "Let's see what Jimmy will do."
   b. Describe the child's reactions to the stopped activity, e.g., "Jimmy is really looking at the toy to see how it works," "Jimmy is banging on the toy to get more," or "Jimmy is looking at you for help."
   c. Verbally or gesturally prompt the parent when to restart the activity.
   d. "Fade out" prompts when the parent can "read" and respond to her child's cues independently.
3. If the parent has difficulty judging how much response time to give her child before reactivating a toy or activity, demonstrate silently counting to five as a concrete reminder.

1.24

DEAF PARENT

May be unaware that the cessation of sound prompts her child to touch her hand to reactivate a toy.

1. Refer to 1.21 (Continues a familiar activity by initiating movement involved).

BLIND PARENT

May not be able to visually monitor if or when her child touches a toy in an attempt to make it reactivate.

1. Describe to the parent her child's possible interactions with a toy as he attempts to restart it. The parent will be able to listen for her child's interactions with a toy if they are in close proximity to her.
2. Use roly-poly and action toys which activate or make a sound when touched. Some wind-up toys will also partially move and make a sound upon touch.

PHYSICALLY DISABLED PARENT

Who has limited use of her hands; may have difficulty manipulating wind-up toys or initiating movement games with her child.

1. Use toys that can be punched, leaned on, or pulled by a *wrist cuff** to initiate sound, movement, or other actions.
2. Refer to suggested adaptations for 1.21 (Continues a familiar activity by initiating movements involved).

1.25 Child: REACHES FOR SECOND OBJECT PURPOSEFULLY (5-6½ mo.)
Parent: Provides opportunities and encouragement for child to purposefully reach for a second object

GENERAL GUIDELINES

The child purposefully reaches for a second object while he is already holding a small object in his hand. He is learning that even though he is already holding something, there is still a possibility of holding something else. He does not need to actually attain the second object; his reaching efforts signal his purposeful intentions.

Parents can encourage their child to reach for a second toy by holding it within the child's reach and attracting his attention with verbal encouragement and gentle shaking of the toy. Sound producing objects are especially attracting. The second object should be more attractive than the one the child is holding. If the child does not respond, the parent can physically prompt him by tapping his empty palm or helping him reach by gently bringing his arm forward, holding it just above his elbow. All of the child's reaching attempts should be reinforced with praise, and by giving him the toy he has worked so hard to get. Rattles, squeak toys, measuring spoons, and plastic keys on chain are often good toys to encourage the child to reach.

*See Glossary.

MENTALLY RETARDED PARENT

May "tease" her child by holding the toy out of reach or taking it away before he has had enough time to try reaching.

1. Demonstrate, and have the parent practice, presenting a second toy to her child:
   a. Ask the parent to choose small attractive toys she thinks for which her child would reach.
   b. Point out which behaviors indicate her child is attending and purposefully reaching.
   c. Remind her, if necessary, to praise her child's reaching attempts; model the praise words, as needed.
   d. Stress that while her child is learning to reach for a second object, it is okay for him to drop the first object and it's okay if he cannot actually get the second object. Explain that this happens later, after lots of practice.
   e. Stress the importance of letting her child hold the toy he has reached for even if he cannot actually obtain it. Explain that if she doesn't give it to him, he may stop trying to reach for things.
   f. Monitor the distance the parent holds a toy away from her child, and physically prompt as needed. Explain and demonstrate that her child will not try to reach if he sees that the toy is too far away.
2. Demonstrate positions with the child which facilitate his reaching, such as in supported sitting or supine.
3. Encourage the parent to talk about what she is doing with her child and to use praise words. Model specific phrases for the parent to say as needed.

DEAF PARENT

May be unaware that sound toys can encourage her child to reach.

1. Explain and demonstrate how toys which make sounds help attract her child's attention and encourage him to reach toward them.
2. Assist parent in choosing attractive sound toys as suggested in 1.03 (Responds to sounds).
3. Encourage the parent to talk about and/or gesture to her child to reach for a toy.

BLIND PARENT

May not be able to visually monitor when her child has reached for a second object.

1. When the parent holds a second object out to her child, she can "feel" when he reaches for it if it is obtained.
2. Use sound making dangle toys, such as rattles or wrist bells on a string which will make sounds when the child's hand touches them. The parent can then monitor and thus reinforce her child's reaching, even if the toy is not secured.
3. Use squeak toys or other ones which will make sounds when the child reaches for them on a table.
4. The child could wear wrist bands which have one subtle bell attached to each band.

PHYSICALLY DISABLED PARENT

With upper extremity limitations; may have difficulty holding a toy to encourage her child to reach.

1. The parent can present the second object to her child by dangling it from her teeth:
   a. If the child does not attempt to reach, the parent can move the dangled object to gently tap the child's hand.
   b. Although the parent cannot provide verbal encouragement during this activity, she can use reinforcing facial expressions.
2. Colorful strings of plastic beads can dangle around the parent's arm. Be sure they dangle loosely enough so they can be knocked or swiped off her arm.

1.26 **Child:** WORKS FOR DESIRED, OUT OF REACH OBJECT (5-9 mo.)
Parent: Encourages child to "work" for toy out of reach

GENERAL GUIDELINES

The child's purposeful intentions expand as he realizes he can obtain objects that are out of his immediate reach. He purposefully pivots on his tummy, squirms, wiggles, rolls, or crawls to get a desired object. He does not have to actually attain the object; it is his purposeful intentions that are important.

Parents encourage this skill by giving their child the opportunity to "work" for toys by himself before giving it to him. Parents can also help motivate their child to want to "work" for a toy by making the toy especially attractive and providing him with verbal encouragement and praise. The child should always be given the toy after a few attempts so he realizes his "work" is worth it!

MENTALLY RETARDED PARENT

May tease her child by presenting an object too far out of reach, by not letting him have it after a few attempts, or by moving it further away as the child gets closer.

1. Concretely explain the purpose of this skill. For example, tell the parent, "Jimmy has learned he can get a toy that is near him by reaching his arm out for it. Now he is ready to learn how to get a toy that is even further away by moving his whole body."
2. Ask the parent to name the different ways her child moves his whole body around. If needed, probe with "rolling?", "crawling?", "pushing around on his tummy?", or "pulling up to stand at a chair?"
3. Help the parent estimate the distance her child usually moves when rolling, pivoting, etc. Use a concrete marker from the child's initial position to help determine how far away to place the toy, e.g., the parent's outstretched arm from her child's initial position.
4. Place an attractive toy at a location the parent has suggested in Activity No. 3, just out of her child's reach. Model verbalizing and shaking the toy to encourage her child to move to get it:
   a. If the child moves to obtain the toy, model praising the child and reinforce the parent for picking "just the right place!"
   b. Count the child's attempts to obtain the toy aloud, praising the child after each attempt. After the third attempt, if the child hasn't reached it, explain to the parent that we have placed it too far away, so now it is important to give it to him so he does not get mad.
   c. Say, "If I don't give it to him after he has worked so hard to get it, I would be teasing him. Teasing can make him angry and he will stop trying to learn to reach for things."
   d. Have the parent practice this activity with her child. Provide reinforcement and verbal prompts as needed.
5. Model, and let the parent practice, placing toys out of her child's reach from various positions, i.e., toward his right side, left side, and then in front.

BLIND PARENT

Can use auditory cues to help monitor when her child is "working" for a toy out of reach.

1. Attach wrist bands to the child which have well-secured small bells. The parent can attract her child toward a squeak toy. As the child "works" toward the toy, the parent can monitor his movements.
2. Point out the differences in the child's vocalizations, noting when his sounds indicate "working," as opposed to fussing in frustration. Describe to the parent her child's method of locomotion to obtain objects.
3. If the parent puts toys on a towel or small blanket that the child is on, she will have a concrete marker to help insure toys are placed within the child's reaching range.

PHYSICALLY DISABLED PARENT

May have difficulty moving toys within her child's reaching range if they roll or drop out of the parent's reach.

1. Toys can be tied to strings to help the parent retrieve them if they fall out of her, or her child's, reach.
2. The parent can use a *reacher** to obtain toys or move them closer.

1.27 **Child:** DISTINGUISHES BETWEEN ANGRY AND FRIENDLY VOICES (5-6½ mo.)
Parent: Understands that child can distinguish between friendly and angry voices; avoids strong negative inflections

GENERAL GUIDELINES

The child begins to interpret the speaker's meaning of words by discriminating the speaker's voice quality, facial expressions, and tone.

He associates soothing voices and varied inflectional happy voices with good feelings, and loud angry voices with unpleasant or less friendly situations.

---

*See Glossary.

1.27

MENTALLY RETARDED PARENT

May not realize that different voice tones affect her child differently.

1. Explain to the parent that although her child may not understand words, he is learning to understand what we mean by the way we say them:
   a. Play a game with the parent using nonsense language and angry and friendly voice tones. Ask parent to guess what you are saying by your tone of voice, facial expressions, and gestures.
   b. Stress that angry voices make her child feel afraid and friendly voices make him feel good. Ask the parent to think of times someone yelled or talked with an angry voice to her; what were her feelings?
   c. Tell the parent that it is important to use more friendly voice tones than angry ones with her child.
2. Point out the child's responses to angry and friendly voices as the situation arises.

DEAF PARENT

May be unaware that her child differentiates various voice tones.

1. Explain to the parent that just as she can interpret when someone is angry or friendly by their facial expressions, her child is learning to interpret when people are angry or friendly, even if he can't see them, by hearing the way their voices sound.
2. As the situation arises, e.g., child hears older sister yell at the dog, point out the child's responses to the angry voice.
3. Remind the parent that if her child becomes upset unexplainably, he may have heard a loud angry voice on T.V. or around the house.

BLIND PARENT

May be unaware of her child's facial responses to angry and friendly voices.

1. Explain that children at this age show us they understand the difference between angry and friendly voices by their facial expressions and body movements. As friendly and angry voice situations occur, describe to the parent her child's responsive expressions.

1.28 **Child: HAND REGARD NO LONGER PRESENT (5-6 mo.)**
    Parent: Recognizes excessive hand regard and provides an alternative interesting visual target

GENERAL GUIDELINES

As the child expands his interactions with his environment he relinquishes an old favorite past-time, looking at his hands. He should be much too busy for this. If hand-watching consumes much of the child's activity, professional consultation is advised. Interventions should be geared toward helping the child interact and enjoy his environment. Refer to 1.05 (Inspects surroundings), 1.04 (Shows active interest in person or object for at least one minute), 5.15 (Enjoys social play), and 5.18 (Enjoys frolic play) for parent activities to encourage their child's positive interactions with the environment. Parents should continue to monitor their child's hand-watching and divert his attention when it is excessive.

MENTALLY RETARDED PARENT

May continue to think hand-watching is okay if she was instructed to encourage hand-watching at an earlier age via activities for 1.11 (Inspects own hands).

1. Explain that since her child is older now, he should not spend lots of time looking at his hands; there are too many other things for him to be learning about, e.g., "If he looks at his hands a lot, he may be telling us he's bored, so you need to check that he has other toys and people nearby."

BLIND PARENT

May be unable to visually monitor if her child has excessive hand regard.

1. Monitor if the child regards hand and advise the parent accordingly if excessive.

1.29 **Child: BRINGS FEET TO MOUTH (5-6 mo.)**
    Parent: Plays "footsie" games while encouraging child to bring feet to mouth and explore

GENERAL GUIDELINES

If the child is delayed in bringing his feet to his mouth, parents can play "footsie" games to encourage this skill. Fun "footsie" games include "This Little Piggy Went to Market," "nibbling" and kissing toes, and playing "Peek-a-boo" with the child's feet over an adult eyes. Parents will have additional fun games.

The child with a gross motor impairment may need special positioning prescribed by an occupational or physical therapist to encourage this skill.

MENTALLY RETARDED PARENT

May prevent the child from putting his feet to mouth because she interprets mouthing as "bad."

1. Explain to the parent the learning benefits for her child when he explores his feet and brings them to his mouth, e.g., "He is learning to control his muscles; he is learning about body parts; and children at this age learn by looking, touching, listening, and mouthing."
2. Demonstrate, and let the parent practice, a "footsie" game of her choice with her child. Emphasize and monitor the following:
   a. Gentle movements and talking to her child with lots of vocal and facial expression.
   b. Never force her child's legs to bend.

c. Showing and naming her child's feet while playing, e.g., "See your feet? Pretty little feet."
3. Warn the parent not to tickle her child's feet because at this age it sometimes hurts. Remind her to always make sure there is nothing on her child's feet that he could mouth and swallow. Provide concrete examples.
4. Name specific daily activity times that the parent can play "footsie" games with her child, e.g., after diapering, after removing his socks, and before putting on his socks.

BLIND PARENT

May not be able to see if or when her child brings his feet to mouth.

1. Describe the positions and movements involved, and their developmental significance, when the child brings his feet to mouth, e.g., "Bringing his feet to his mouth promotes her child's body awareness and control; he lifts and bends his legs and wiggles his toes with his hands before putting them in his mouth."
2. Caution the parent not to use booties with bells, sequins, or other objects which the child may mouth and swallow when he brings his feet to his mouth.
3. If the child spontaneously brings or attempts to bring his feet to his mouth during a session or visit, alert the parent so she can become tactually familiar with this position.
4. If needed, help orient the parent to positions with her child which facilitate playing "footsie games" and encourages him to bring his feet to his mouth.
5. Describe the movements involved in playing various "footsie" games, e.g., "Gently wiggle each toe with each verse of the song and move onto his next toe."
6. Describe the child's facial reactions to "footsie" games, emphasizing his sounds of delight.
7. If the child needs physical prompting to help bring his feet to his mouth, describe the positions clearly and provide the parent physical assistance as needed.

PHYSICALLY DISABLED PARENT

With upper extremity limitations; may have difficulty carrying out the movements involved for "footsie" games.

1. The parent can "nibble," blow, and kiss her child's toes and feet. Help position the parent and child in accommodating positions if needed. For example, the child can lie supine in the parent's lap with his head against her knees and legs raised on parent's trunk.
2. Refer to 1.17 (Plays with own hands, feet, fingers, toes).

1.30 Child: SHOWS INTEREST IN SOUNDS OF OBJECTS (5½-8 mo.)
     Parent: Demonstrates making different sounds with a single toy; encourages child to imitate

GENERAL GUIDELINES

The child is interested in the sounds he can make with various objects. He purposely hits, shakes, or bangs an object to make a sound. He is also learning that he can make different sounds with the same object if he treats it differently. For example, his block sounds different when he bangs it on his highchair tray and then bangs it against a can, or paper sounds different if he waves it and then crumples it.

Parents can foster their child's interest and awareness of sound variety by enthusiastically calling his attention to various sounds as they occur in his environment, and by demonstrating and letting him try to make various sounds with objects, e.g., rattles, squeaking toys, banging spoons, blocks, and balls.

MENTALLY RETARDED PARENT

May expect her child to use a toy or an object in only one way; her child may thus be prevented from experimenting with toys or objects to make different sounds.

1. Demonstrate with the parent how one toy or object can make various sounds, depending upon what you do to it:
   a. Initially, use objects which do not have specific play functions, such as a top to a baby food jar rather than a block.
   b. Hit and slide the object against different surfaces. Point out the different sounds produced.
   c. Switch to demonstrating various sounds with toys and objects which have specific functions associated with them, such as spoons or cups. Hit, bang, or slide them. Explain that although we usually don't do these things with these objects, her child likes to because he can make different sounds with them and that's great learning!
2. Advise the parent to let her child have time to explore a toy before she shows him what to do with it. Relate that it's good to let him mouth, hit, or bang safe toys so he can learn how they look, feel, taste, and sound.
3. Help the parent identify several household objects and toys that she can use to make different sounds in front of her child.
4. As situations arise, point out to the parent and praise her child's purposeful interactions with objects to make different sounds.
5. During play sessions with the parent and child, verbally prompt the parent as needed to wait and watch to see how her child explores a toy all by himself.

1.30

DEAF PARENT

May not realize that different actions on a single object can produce different interesting sounds for her child.

1. Explain that one toy or object can make many different sounds, depending upon how you use the toy or object:
   a. Demonstrate various actions which produce different sounds, e.g., banging, hitting, and sliding.
   b. Point out the qualities of surfaces and objects which make loud versus softer sounds.
2. Discuss the importance of watching for and not interrupting her child's experimentations and explorations with objects when he is trying to make different sounds.

1.31 Child: ANTICIPATES VISUALLY THE TRAJECTORY OF SLOWLY MOVING OBJECT (5½-7½ mo.)
Parent: Sets up "disappearance games" which encourage child to anticipate where the object will reappear, if recommended

GENERAL GUIDELINES

The child correctly switches his glance from the place where an object disappeared behind a screen or barrier to the place he expects it to reappear. For example, if the child sees a ball roll behind his box of blocks, he looks to the other side, expecting it to reappear. Skill 1.09 (Reacts to disappearance of slowly moving object) is a prerequisite to this behavior.

Controlled disappearance situations do not need to be set up unless recommended to improve the child's object permanence and visual pursuit skills. People, sound toys, bubbles, and visually attracting toys are recommended as things to move and hide. Barriers or screens should not be initially more than twelve inches wide, and should not be more attracting than the object. Barriers which are opaque provide an extra cue for the child if needed. In controlled situations, as the child is learning, he needs to experience where the object reappears a few times before he can be expected to spontaneously look toward the correct reappearance site.

The following activities assume structured visual pursuit activities have been recommended.

MENTALLY RETARDED PARENT

May not attract her child's attention to the object before making it disappear.

1. Explain and demonstrate this skill in concrete meaningful terminology:
   a. Use an explanation, such as "We are teaching Danny to figure out where things go when he can't see them anymore."
   b. Let the parent experience the meaning of this skill by moving several different objects behind various barriers with the parent, asking her to guess where the object will show up again.
2. Stress to the parent the importance of attracting her child's attention to the object before hiding it:
   a. Point out her child's attending signals, such as eye-contact and reaching.
   b. Demonstrate ways to encourage her child's attention, such as shaking the toy, calling his name, and squeaking it if it is a sound toy.
   c. Tell the parent that if her child does not look at the object after trying this game three times, to stop the activity and try doing it another time with a different toy. Ask her which toy she could try next time.
3. Help the parent select attracting toys and suitable barriers or screens. Point out the discriminating features which make the toys attractive and the barriers suitable.
4. Model, and let parent practice until proficient, playing "disappear-reappear" games with her child. Stress the following:
   a. Attract her child's attention to the object before moving it.
   b. Move it behind a barrier no wider than twelve inches.
   c. Make it reappear on the other side, and attract her child's attention to it if needed by squeaking it and/or calling his name.
   d. Give her child the object to play with after it has reappeared.

DEAF PARENT

May be unaware that sounds from hidden or disappearing objects help remind her child they are still there.

1. Explain and demonstrate how musical and squeak toys help attract her child's attention and help him remember it's still there when it's hidden, and thus help him figure out to where it is moving.

BLIND PARENT

May need a conceptual basis to help understand the visual memory concepts associated with "disappearance-reappearance" games.

1. Describe a meaningful perceptual analogy to the parent to help explain the cognitive concepts underlying visual "disappearance-reappearance" games, e.g., "When you are walking barefoot across a cold floor and come across a throw rug, you know that the cold floor is still there and, if you keep on walking, you will feel it again. At this age, your child is learning that when something he was watching moves behind a cover and he can't see it anymore, he knows it is still there even if he cannot see it. Furthermore, he is learning that if it is a moving object, he will see it again on the other side of the cover." Follow this explanation with an example of daily events which cause objects to visually disappear and reappear, such as a ball rolling behind a chair or the parent walking behind his highchair.
2. Help identify suitable barriers or covers to move objects behind. The parent can move or pull toys on a string behind the barrier while you describe the child's shifting gaze to the point of the object's reappearance.

3. Rolling balls through open-ended boxes help the parent confine the area in which the ball can roll while providing a visual barrier for child.
4. Name various environmental events which expose her child to visual disappearance experiences, e.g., people, when they bend down to pick something up; small animals, when they run behind a couch; and faces, when we pull a sweater over our heads.

PHYSICALLY DISABLED PARENT

With upper extremity limitations; may have difficulty holding or controlling toys for "disappearance games."

1. Refer to 1.09 (Reacts to disappearance of slowly moving object).
2. The parent can attract her child's attention to naturally occurring events which make things disappear and reappear.

1.32 Child: FINDS HIDDEN OBJECT USING 1 SCREEN, 2 SCREENS, THEN 3 SCREENS (6-9 mo.)

Parent: If recommended, hides attractive object under 1 screen and encourages child to find it; then hides object using 2 and then 3 screens as child's ability dictates.

GENERAL GUIDELINES

When the child sees an object he wants being covered up, he removes the cover to find it. This skill demonstrates the child's understanding that objects still exist, even when he cannot see them. Finding a partially hidden object is a prerequisite to this skill.

Once he has mastered the skill of finding an object under one screen, he learns to find a toy he sees hidden when there are two (and later three) screens available from which to choose.

Contrived hiding games usually do not need to be set up for a child to learn this skill. He learns by naturally occurring situations, such as his bottle rolling under his blanket or his leg obscuring a toy from his vision.

If a child needs extra help with visual memory and pursuit, or object permanence skills specific hiding games may be recommended. The parent training activities for this skill assume controlled activities have been recommended. The following guidelines should be considered as the child is learning this skill.

1. Do not use two or three covers until the child is proficient at finding an object under one.
2. When using more than one cover, always place the object under the same cover.
3. Screens and hidden objects should be stationary; do *not* move them around after placement.
4. The child should watch the object being hidden.
5. Provide covers with extra cues as needed (transparent, free-forming to shape with the covered object).
6. Covers should not be more attracting than the hidden object. Covers can be plastic cups, napkins, hands, part of a blanket, or washcloths.
7. Hidden objects must be attractive to child; sound and action wind-up toys provide additional cues to help the child locate them.

MENTALLY RETARDED PARENT

May "tease" her child when hiding objects.

1. Refer to 1.20 (Finds a partially hidden object), adapting to cover the entire object.
2. Stress, through demonstration and parent practice, the following concepts:
   a. Allow her child time to explore and find the object.
   b. Let him have the toy after he's found it or tried to find it.
   c. Getting the child's attention before hiding it.
   d. Providing verbal prompts and praise the child.
   e. Using covers that the child is able to manipulate according to his motor ability.

DEAF PARENT

May be unaware that sound toys are easier for her child to locate in hiding games, and that the sound is muffled somewhat by the cover.

1. Refer to 1.20 (Finds a partially hidden object).
2. Explain that the sounds of toys will not be as loud when they are covered by thick screens.

BLIND PARENT

May not be able to visually discern when her child has found the hidden toy, or if he has become more interested in the screen than the object.

1. If the visual concept of object permanence has not been explained, refer to Activity 1.09 (Reacts to the disappearance of a slowly moving object) and concretely describe this hiding activity.
2. Use toys which make sounds when retrieved. Refer to 1.20 (Finds a partially hidden object). Adapt activities so that the entire object is hidden under the cloth or in an apron pocket. The parent can tactually assure the toy is completely hidden.
3. The parent can hide pieces of cereal or cookies in the palm of her loosely closed hand. She will then easily be able to monitor when her child opens her hand and takes it out, and the child will have an immediate reinforcement.
4. The parent can wear a solid apron with three big pockets of different colors. When a toy is hidden, the parent can monitor her child's searching. If the child is having difficulty, the parent can leave a part of the toy showing.

PHYSICALLY DISABLED PARENT

Who has limited hand control; may have difficulty manipulating screens for hiding objects.

1. Refer to activity adaptations for 1.20 (Finds a partially hidden object).

1.33 Child: PLAYS PEEK-A-BOO (6-10 mo.)
Parent: Initiates "Peek-a-boo" games in playful manner with the child

GENERAL GUIDELINES

When the child's or parent's face is covered and then uncovered quickly during "Peek-a-boo" games, the child responds with delight. He may chuckle, squeal, or laugh.

The social, cognitive, and language value of "Peek-a-boo" games for children are intermeshed. Socially the child enjoys positive give-and-take interactions with people, while beginning to realize the humor of situations. He may even feel he is "tricking" people when his head is covered, thinking they can't see him at all!

Cognitively, the child is beginning to understand "people permanence," that is, they still exist even if he can't see them. The words "Peek-a-boo" also have a consistent rhyme and inflection of voice. The child can thus learn to understand the meaning of the verbal phrase "Peek-a-boo" without actually needing to understand the words.

MENTALLY RETARDED PARENT

May not play "Peek-a-boo" with her child, or may be too abrupt during the game.

1. Model, and let the parent practice, playing "Peek-a-boo" with her child, covering and uncovering your face quickly with your hands or a cover:
   a. If the parent is too close (child "winches" or startles) or too far away (child doesn't notice), point out these behaviors and suggest positions which help assure an appropriate distance, e.g., on the parent's lap or over the rail of a crib. Demonstrate using an "armspread" as a concrete distance marker for playing "Peek-a-boo."
   b. If the parent leaves the cover on too long, help the parent judge how long to keep her face or the child's face covered, e.g., remove cover or hands as soon as she says "peek."
   c. Emphasize and model saying "Peek-a-boo" with an animated voice tone and calling her child's name.
2. Help the parent select various covers which are suitable to cover the child's face with during "Peek-a-boo" games, e.g., child's tee-shirt, washcloth, and extra diaper. Caution the parent never to use plastic bags; explain that her child wouldn't be able to breathe.
3. Suggest and explore with the parent daily activities which are good times to initiate "Peek-a-boo" games, such as when washing her child's face with a cloth or when pulling her child's shirt over his head.
4. If the parent has difficulty pacing herself with her child's attention during "Peek-a-boo" games:
   a. Tell the parent to call her child's name and wait for him to look at her before she covers his face.
   b. Use a perforated cover which allows the parent to see when she has her child's attention when covering her own face.
5. Post a picture of playing "Peek-a-boo" near the child's crib as a reminder to the parent to play this fun game with her child.

DEAF PARENT

May be unable to vocalize or say "Peek-a-boo" with inflection.

1. Show the parent how to use non-vocal sounds such as lip smacking or "raspberries" to help attract her child's interest in "Peek-a-boo."
2. Relate how the parent's use of exaggerated facial expressions during "Peek-a-boo" will encourage her child's attention.
3. When the parent covers her own face, she may be unable to hear her child's responses. Suggest using perforated covers so she can watch her child's expressions when her face is covered.

BLIND PARENT

May not be aware of the visual surprise element and learning benefits of this activity.

1. Describe the interactions and movements involved in "Peek-a-boo." Explain to the parent the cognitive learning benefits for her child which underlie "Peek-a-boo" games, e.g., "Children begin to learn that you are still there even when they cannot see you during 'Peek-a-boo.' What a surprise this is for them to see someone's face hide and then reappear!"
2. Identify natural daily activities that obscure the child's vision during which the parent can say "Peek-a-boo" in a playful manner, e.g., pulling a shirt over her child's head, the parent leaving her child's room and quickly returning, and washing her child's face with a cloth.
3. Play "Peek-a-boo" with the child while he is on his parent's lap:
   a. The parent can listen to her child's change in vocalizations and feel his movement changes which indicate excitement.
   b. Describe the child's facial expressions during the game.
4. Sew a bell securely on a cloth to cover the child's face during "Peek-a-boo." The parent can quickly discriminate when her child has removed the cloth and say "Peek-a-boo" in pace with her child.
5. If the parent does not use face-to-face positions with the child, plaing "Peek-a-boo" in a parallel position may be effective. The parent can also play "Peek-a-boo" with stuffed animals and jack-in-the-box toys.

PHYSICALLY DISABLED PARENT

With upper extremity impairments; may not be able to cover her own or her child's face for "Peek-a-boo" games.

1. Suggest playing "Peek-a-boo" behind already existing structures, such as a wall, door, or table.
2. The parent can encourage her child to cover and uncover her face and his own with a cloth to play "Peek-a-boo."
3. Suggest to the parent nuzzling her face against her child's tummy to hide her face for "Peek-a-boo."

1.34 Child: **SMELLS DIFFERENT THINGS**
              (6-12 mo.)
      Parent: Encourages child to smell different
              things in the environment

MENTALLY RETARDED PARENT

May limit child's experiences to smell various things, or may select inappropriate noxious stimuli for her child to smell.

1. Explain to the parent that just as we enjoy smelling nice fragrances and know what they are by their smell, her child likes to smell different things and is learning what they are by the way they smell. Provide concrete examples, such as walking into a kitchen and knowing what is cooking.
2. Help identify environmental objects for the parent to let her child smell, e.g., flowers, food, aftershave lotion, baby lotions, and her perfume (not out of the bottle though!).
3. Identify strong odors, or dangerous things that her child should *not* smell or taste, such as fingernail polish remover, Drano, bleach, etc. Mark these items with Mr. Yuk stickers. (Remind the parent that the stickers are to remind *her* to keep her child away from them. They are *not* to remind her child because he does not know what the stickers mean.)
4. Model and encourage the parent to use the words "ohh!" and "m-m-m!" or "yuk!" whem smelling pleasing and unpleasing fragrances.

1.35 Child: **PLAYS 2 TO 3 MINUTES WITH**
              SINGLE TOY (6-9 mo.)
      Parent: Provides toys appropriate to child's
              developmental level and interests

GENERAL GUIDELINES

The child's interactions with toys become more refined and differentiated as he realizes different objects are better for different things. For example, he is learning that rattles are most interesting if he shakes them, blocks are good for banging, and paper is good to crumple or tear. He continues to explore and test most objects and toys, especially new ones, by going through a number of taste, touch, shake, wave, or banging procedures before settling down to a favorite interaction with the toy. At this age, the child's interaction should last at least two to three minutes. Too many other toys or other excessive environmental stimuli may distract the child.

Recommended toys and objects for play at this age include rattles, roly-polys, empty paper towel rolls, washable unbreakable dolls, paper, squeaky toys, spoons, plastic cups, small balls, unbreakable small mirrors, and busy boxes.

MENTALLY RETARDED PARENT

May select developmentally inappropriate toys for her child, and may over-control or interfere with her child's exploratory behaviors.

1. Help the parent select developmentally appropriate toys during each stage of the child's development. Remember to tell her when her child has "outgrown" the toy:
   a. Provide picture lists at each stage.
   b. Identify characteristics of suitable toys at each stage, e.g., during first two months, things he can look at; later months, things he can hold, shake, "bat" at, and squeak, etc.
2. Each time the parent gives her child a toy, help prevent interference with her child's exploratory play, and her expectation that a toy must be played with in only one way:
   a. Interject remarks, such as "Let's give Lisa time to try the toy out, all by herself!"
   b. Suggest various things her child may want to try with the toy before giving it to him, e.g., bang, hit, mouth, roll, and comment how good this is because he is learning about all the things he can do with one toy.
   c. Avoid telling the parent specific objectives you may have in mind for the child with a toy. She may try to make her child interact with the toy "just right" without exploratory play.
3. Point out and help adjust, when possible, distracting things in the child's environment which decrease his attention, e.g., a bright light shining in the child's face, loud stereo, and too many toys or objects.
4. Model, and let the parent practice, telling her child what he is doing while playing, but not physically interfering, e.g., "I see you squeaking that toy; good boy!"
5. Model, and have the parent practice, demonstrating to her child a few things that he can do with the toy before giving it to him.
6. Emphasize how hard it is sometimes to sit back and watch children play, especially when we want them to play with a toy in a certain way. Praise the parent for her patience.

BLIND PARENT

May not be able to visually monitor her child's play.

1. Relate to the parent potential visual distractions in her child's play areas which could prevent sustained play.
2. The parent can monitor her child's play by listening to his differentiated vocalizations and the various sounds toys make during play.
3. Describe the visual qualities of toys which make them interesting to her child at this age, e.g., bright colors, toys which make a visual spectacle when moved (such as chime bells with transparent covers which allow the child to see moving objects when pushed), and toys with faces.

1.36 Child: SLIDES TOY OR OBJECT ON SMOOTH SURFACE (6-11 mo.)
Parent: Demonstrates sliding different toys and objects on a variety of surfaces to child; encourages child to practice

GENERAL GUIDELINES

The child learns to slide objects or toys across surfaces as an additional means to interact with things around him. He also learns he can produce various sounds depending upon the properties of the object and the surfaces he slides them on.

Parents can encourage their child to try "sliding" actions with sponges, toy cars, blocks, butter tubs, or any type of graspable objects. They can demonstrate and call their child's attention to the interesting sounds these objects make when they slide. Various surfaces such as rugs, linoleum, bumpy cement, or a washtub with sand provide the child with various sound, vibro-tactile, and visual experiences.

MENTALLY RETARDED PARENT

May not generalize that a variety of toys and objects, i.e., not just toy cars and balls, are appropriate for her child to roll or slide.

1. Explain and demonstrate to the parent how sometimes it is fun for children to roll or slide things that we usually do not think of as good for sliding or rolling:
    a. Explore the environment with the parent to select several toys and objects suitable for her child to practice rolling and sliding, e.g., a smooth plastic cup, toilet paper rolls, tennis ball can, Quaker Oats box, or butter tubs.
    b. As objects are selected, demonstrate and let the parent check to see if the toy or object rolls or slides well, is safe, and is easy for the child to handle.
2. Demonstrate to the parent and describe how rolling and sliding objects on different surfaces produce different effects, e.g., when an object rolls on the rug, it is quiet; but when it rolls on the kitchen floor, it makes sounds. Ask parent to show you various additional surfaces that would be interesting for her child to roll or slide objects across.
3. Model, and let the parent practice, demonstrating to her child how to roll and slide objects on different surfaces. Stress the following concepts:
    a. Attract her child's attention to the activity.
    b. Provide a verbal description of "what's happening," e.g., "Look, I'm sliding the keys," "See the keys move?", or "Listen to the sound."
    c. Pace the movement of the sliding object to her child's tracking abilities.
4. Name daily situations and activities for the parent to encourage her child's rolling or sliding of objects. For example, when the parent is wiping the table, she can give her child a cloth to help wipe; or before she gives him a toy, she can slide it to him rather than just handing it to him.

DEAF PARENT

May be unaware that various toys produce different sounds when they roll or slide.

1. Relate to the parent that objects and toys make different sounds if they roll or slide. These sounds help encourage her child to practice rolling and sliding objects.
2. Identify the various properties which affect the object's sound:
    a. Containers with a few hard things in them make more sound when rolled than empty containers or ones with soft things in them, e.g., tennis ball can with pebbles versus empty can.
    b. Metal objects make louder sounds than soft plastic or cardboard objects.
    c. Rolling or sliding objects on bumpy surfaces sound different than on smooth surfaces.
    d. Carpeting muffles sound when objects roll.

BLIND PARENT

Cannot visually monitor when and if her child is sliding or rolling toys.

1. Advise the parent of her child's sliding schemes when he begins to incorporate them. She can then use auditory cues to help discriminate when her child is rolling or sliding objects or toys and provide concurrent verbal encouragement:
    a. Different surfaces produce distinct sounds to help the parent discern where her child is rolling a toy.
    b. Various toys and objects produce distinct sounds to help the parent recognize which toy or object her child is sliding.
    c. Balls with bells, chime balls, toy cars with squeaky wheels, and Quaker Oats boxes filled with a handful of beans (top securely taped) provide excellent auditory cues for the parent while simultaneously reinforcing the child.

PHYSICALLY DISABLED PARENT

Who uses a wheelchair; may have difficulty finding accessible surfaces to help her child slide toys.

1. Small toys or objects can be placed on a smooth board or lap tray across the armrests of the parent's wheelchair while the child sits on her lap facing the tray.
2. The parent can push her wheelchair to a table with the child in her lap. The table must have adequate clearance to allow the wheelchair to get close enough and be at a suitable height for the child.
3. If the parent has limited hand control, she can demonstrate sliding or rolling objects with her forearm or foot if the toy is on the floor.

1.37 Child: FOLLOWS TRAJECTORY OF FAST MOVING OBJECT (6-8 mo.)
Parent: "Sets up" or uses naturally occurring experiences to encourage child to follow and find a rapidly moving or falling object after it passes behind obstacles

GENERAL GUIDELINES

The child watches and follows a rapidly moving object, such as a ball, roll behind a barrier. He anticipates the ball's appearance on the other side of the barrier and looks to that spot.

Naturally occurring situations include watching a pet run behind a couch, cars pass by a tree, toy cars quickly move behind the child's stuffed animal, or a toy roll and fall off of his highchair tray, and bending forward to find it.

Refer to the guidelines and activities for 1.31 (Anticipates visually the trajectory of slowly moving object), adapting to include fast moving objects.

1.38 Child: LOOKS FOR FAMILY MEMBERS OR PETS WHEN NAMED (6-8 mo.)
Parent: Offers ample opportunity for child to hear names of family members, pets, and friends

MENTALLY RETARDED PARENT

May not use consistent names for family members, pets, or friends.

1. Discuss with the parent how difficult it could be to figure out what someone's name was if we heard that person called three or four different names:
   a. Provide an example using your own or another's name, e.g., "My name is Barbara, but if every time you came to our center you heard one person call me Barbara, another call me Barb, another call me Barbi, another call me Bobbi, and finally another call me Mrs. Jones, how would you know which name to call me!?"
   b. Relate how this would be even more confusing for her child since he is just learning to understand words.
2. List all of the significant people and pets in the household. Explore the different names that might be used for each, including nicknames and special descriptors such as "cutie pie." Include the names the child may be called:
   a. Have a special photo session and family meeting. Family members can decide upon one or two names to consistently use when calling each other. Explain to the family members how this will help the child learn his own and their names more easily.
   b. Let family members take individual pictures of each other. Make a poster with the pictures and label respective names under each as a reminder to call each person by only one or two names.
   c. The parent can also use the poster in the future with her child when he is learning to identify pictures.

DEAF PARENT

May not verbalize names.

1. Encourage the parent's use of any speech she may have to name family members to her child when possible. Family member names which are long or more difficult to say may be able to be shortened. If the parent's speech is distorted, her child will learn to understand her over time.
2. The parent can sign family member names and direct her child's attention to them while the family member says his own name using speech.
3. Refer to 2.16 (Look and vocalizes to own name).

BLIND PARENT

May not direct her child's visual attention toward named family members.

1. Discuss how children learn to associate names of people by looking toward them when their names are called:
   a. Suggest gesturing with an extended arm toward family members and pets when calling their names during the day.
   b. Point out that if the parent carriers her child over her shoulder when talking to others, he cannot see to whom she is talking. Suggest carrying her child so he can face people during conversations.
2. The parent can discriminate when her child turns to look toward, or respond to, named family members by feeling her child's head turn or bodily changes such as reaching or waving arms when she is holding him.

1.39 Child: RESPONDS TO FACIAL EXPRESSIONS (6-7 mo.)
Parent: Uses a variety of facial expressions which *match* emotions or situations in front of the child

GENERAL GUIDELINES

The child learns the meaning of words and situations by watching other's facial expressions that accompany them. For example, his mother's smile and animated facial expression during "Peek-a-boo" assures him this game is fun and safe; in turn, he will smile and laugh. The parent's expression of tension or worry with the child is a signal to him that something is not right; in response, the child may fret or display a worried expression. The parent's facial expression is a powerful tool for encouraging or discouraging her child's exploration. The parent's reassuring smile and head nodding encourages the child to explore and experience new tastes, textures, and toys.

MENTALLY RETARDED PARENT

May display a "flat affect" or her facial expressions may not match the intent of the situation.

1. Play a game with the parent to guess angry, sad, and happy feelings by only looking at facial expressions:
   a. Let the parent guess the feelings behind your facial expressions, asking her what facial features let her

1.39

know how you feel, e.g., smile indicated you were happy, and eyebrows furrowed indicated you were angry.
  b. Let the parent practice angry, sad, and happy feelings using facial expressions, as you guess the feeling and describe her distinctive features that let you know. Give specific hypothetical situations for her to practice these facial expressions, e.g., "Your bag of groceries just dropped and the food went rolling everywhere!"
  c. Relate that just as we can figure out people's feelings by looking at their faces, her child is learning to do this, too.
  d. Review the importance of matching facial expressions to the feeling of a verbal statement. Demonstrate how confusing it would be if our facial expressions do not match our feelings, for example, say a firm "no" with a smile; then, say "no" with furrowed eyebrows.
2. Model and let the parent practice making animated facial expressions with her child. Point out her child's changes in facial expressions, bodily movements, and vocalizations.
3. Demonstrate and encourage the parent to practice making animated facial expressions with her child in front of a mirror with simple nursery games, e.g., "Peek-a-boo," and "Hi baby."
4. Caution the parent *not* to make faces which are frightening, and not to move in *too* quickly or closely to her child's face. If you see this occur, "talk" for the child from the sidelines, e.g., "Mommy, you are too close; that's why I'm blinking."
5. If the parent has difficulty using facial expressions consistently, practice only one at a time. Add new ones as the parent seems comfortable.

DEAF PARENT

Can use her facial expressions to communicate intent to her child regardless of her verbal abilities.

1. Reinforce the parent's use of facial expressions with her child. Explain that just as she relies upon watching others' facial expressions to help interpret the meaning or intent of the communication, so does her child at a very early age.
2. If the parent uses sign language, encourage her use of matching facial expressions and accompanying speech, when possible, with her child.

BLIND PARENT

May use limited facial expressions during interactions and may not have experienced the effect of facial expressions for communication.

1. If needed, explain how young children who have not learned the meaning of words often rely upon facial expressions of others to help them figure out what they are saying.
2. Describe different facial expressions and their meanings, e.g., raised eyebrows and open mouth is an expression of surprise.

3. If the parent is interested in using increased facial expressions with her child, provide clear verbal descriptions of the various expressions and their meanings, and let her practice with your prompts.
4. Describe for the parent her child's facial expressions and his apparent communicative intent. Also describe his expressions which are signs that he is understanding the parent's or others' facial expressions.
5. If the parent does not provide face-to-face positioning or facial expressions with her child, he can learn expressions from the many other people he is likely to encounter.
6. Help the parent hang a safe mirror in her child's crib or play area within his visual field so he can watch and experiment with his own facial expressions.

1.40 Child: **RETAINS TWO OF THREE OBJECTS OFFERED (6½-7½ mo.)**
Parent: Encourages child to obtain a third object while holding two

GENERAL GUIDELINES

When the child is offered two objects, one at a time, he retains both. When a third is offered he'll reach and retain it, but drops one of the objects he's already holding. The child may begin to "figure out" that he can still take another object if his hands are full by combining two in one hand. The objects should be small and easy to grasp. Small blocks, cookies, or rattles may be attractive and suitable.

MENTALLY RETARDED PARENT

May think that her child does not want an object when she offers a third if he does not immediately reach for it.

1. Demonstrate this skill with the parent, i.e., while she is holding an object in each hand, tell her to take a third:
   a. Comment how she quickly knew that since her hands were full she needed to move an object from one hand to the next, or let go of one so she could have a free hand to take something else.
   b. Relate this skill to her child, explaining that he is learning to do this, too, but at this age he needs more time and sometimes help to figure it out.
2. Demonstrate the various ways her child might try to figure this task out, e.g., dropping one object or transferring one to the other hand, while the parent offers you three objects.
3. Model, and let the parent practice, offering her child three interesting small objects, one at a time. Stress the following concepts during demonstration and parent practice:
   a. Attract her child's attention to the third object by calling his name and letting him see the object.
   b. Give her child enough response time; count silently to five before giving him the object.
   c. Provide the child verbal encouragement; suggest specific phrases to say as needed.
   d. Provide gentle physical prompting to the child as needed.
   e. Hold objects within her child's reach.

4. Name, and ask the parent to help think of, daily activities to teach her child this skill, e.g., offering a cookie when he is already holding something in each hand, and letting her child hold one sock in each hand and then offering him a more interesting toy when she is dressing him.

BLIND PARENT

May not be able to visually discriminate when, if, or how her child retains two of three objects offered.

1. Suggest offering small objects which provide auditory cues, such as rattles and squeak toys, to the child. The parent can then monitor the sounds to help recognize if her child is transferring or dropping the toy.
2. Provide anticipatory guidance for safety regarding the child's possible use of his mouth as a "tool" to hold an object in order to obtain a third.
3. If the child needs extra help with learning to transfer objects from one hand to the other, refer to 4.38 (Transfers objects).

1.41 Child: TURNS HEAD AND SHOULDERS TO FIND HIDDEN SOUND (7-10 mo.)
Parent: Points out hidden sounds in the environment to child; sets up situations which encourage him to turn head to sounds if recommended

GENERAL GUIDELINES

The child looks for sounds that suddenly occur by turning his head and shoulders to look for it. He can immediately find the sound if it occurs on a lateral plane to either side of his head. If the sound occurs to his side on a lower plane (e.g., a spoon drops to the floor), he turns his head and then looks downward.

Parents can continue to help their child visually link sounds to their source by calling his attention enthusiastically to the object or event which produced the sound.

MENTALLY RETARDED PARENT

May not label and call her child's attention to a sound.

1. Role-play guessing sounds while eyes are closed with the parent:
   a. Drop spoons, plastic cups, and tin cans; squeak toys; rattle spoons and pans; shut doors; walk with high heels and then rubber soles on the floor, etc.
   b. Guess what object or activity made the sound and from where the sound was coming.
   c. Relate that her child is learning to figure out from where sounds are coming. Since he is still learning, she can help teach him about sounds by showing him where they are coming from and by saying the name of the object or activity that caused the sound.
2. Name several common daily events which make interesting sounds for her child to learn about, e.g., doorbell ringing, someone knocking at the door, and bath water running:
   a. Help the parent think of specific phrases she can say about each sound event to her child, such as "Hear the doorbell? Let's go see!"
   b. Ask the parent how she can show her child from where the sound is coming. Demonstrate pointing or taking her child to the sound source if needed.
3. If specific sound localization games have been prescribed, demonstrate specific distances, locations, and sound toys to use:
   a. Stress the importance of giving her child the sound toy after she makes the sound.
   b. Name specific times to play these games in association with daily activities.

DEAF PARENT

May be unaware of her child's expanding auditory localization abilities and stimulation needs.

1. Explain and demonstrate to the parent her child's new or emerging auditory localization capabilities as described under the general guidelines.
2. Describe distant or hidden environmental sounds which may attract her child's attention, e.g., airplane overhead, car honking outside, and dog barking in the next room.
3. If controlled sound localization activities are recommended, refer to 1.19 (Localizes sound with eyes).
4. Suggest clapping, snapping fingers, or making tongue clicks when the parent is out of her child's sight as a method to help him localize sound.

BLIND PARENT

May not see her child's emerging localization responses to distance sounds and thus may not reinforce or encourage them.

1. Contrast for the parent her child's new or emerging auditory localization and concurrent visual orienting skills to his earlier skills, e.g., "When your child was younger, he let us know he could localize sounds by turning his eyes and head to find the sound source if it was nearby; now, he is learning to locate sounds even if they are out of sight and at a distance. He lets us know he's located them by turning his head and shoulders toward the sound."
2. Name sounds which are visually hidden in the environment that her child may respond to so the parent can be sure to verbally comment about them, e.g., washing machine in a closet, doorbell, and dog barking behind a couch or in another room.
3. Suggest taking her child to the window to look for sudden sounds outdoors, such as cars honking or children's loud play.
4. If the child needs special practice in localizing hidden sounds, suggest positions which help her recognize when her child has responded to a hidden sound, e.g., holding her child on her lap facing out so she can feel his movements as he orients to sound.

1.42 Child: IMITATES FAMILIAR, THEN NEW GESTURES (7-11 mo.)
Parent: Plays imitation games with gestures

GENERAL GUIDELINES

Imitation plays a critical role in all of the child's future learning. Imitation will be the basis for learning to wash, dress, toilet, and speak.

Children usually learn to imitate gestures in a sequential order, according to difficulty. At this stage, they first learn to imitate familiar and then "new" visible gestures. Familiar visible gestures are actions which the child uses often during play *and* those which he can see himself perform. Banging, waving, and sliding objects are typical familiar visible gestures at this age. "New" gestures are actions which the child does not use often during play. The "new" gesture should also be an action that the child can see himself perform. "Patting" and "rubbing" are developmentally appropriate "new" visible gestures.

Parents can encourage their child to imitate gestures within their natural familiar daily activities. When the parent feeds her child, she can give him a spoon and let him feed her; when she washes his face, she can give him a washcloth and let him pat his or her face; and when she's wiping kitchen counters, she can give her child an extra sponge to wipe his highchair tray. He should not be expected to copy gestures exactly.

MENTALLY RETARDED PARENT

May expect her child to imitate gestures which are too difficult for him to copy.

1. Explain that children learn how to do things by watching and copying other people's actions. Stress:
   a. At this age, her child can only learn to copy things for which his muscles are ready. For example, he can't copy us snapping our fingers because his muscles just are not ready to do that, but he can learn to copy us patting or banging on a table because we have seen him do this already.
   b. It helps her child learn to copy when he can see himself make the actions. For example, he can't see himself wiggle his own nose, so that would be harder for him to copy; but he can see himself pat the table, so that is a good action for him to copy.
   c. The child does not have to copy the action exactly; that takes time and practice.
2. Prompt the parent to name other actions that her child could learn to copy; review these with the parent to insure they are visible and within her child's gesture repertoire.
3. Choose one or two familiar gestures with the parent which would be good to encourage her child to copy. Model, and let the parent practice, encouraging her child to imitate. Stress:
   a. Getting the child's attention.
   b. Keeping it fun.
   c. Providing verbal prompts and praising all of the child's attempts.
   d. Providing gentle physical prompts if needed.
   e. Stopping, if the child is not interested at that time.

BLIND PARENT

May have difficulty identifying which gestures her child uses, and have difficulty recognizing if or when he imitates gestures.

1. If the parent is congenitally blind, she will not have experienced learning through visual imitation. If appropriate, give the parent a perceptual analogy to facilitate her understanding of the rationale for imitation games, e.g., "Children learn new things by copying or imitating what others do or say. As you know, at this age, your child is learning to imitate sounds of people by listening to them and practicing making the sounds himself. He knows he has done a good job when his vocalizations sound like yours. Your child is also learning to imitate the actions or movements people make. But, instead of learning through hearing, he learns to copy by watching the movements of others *and* then watching his own to make sure they are the same."
2. Explain that the easiest actions for children to learn to copy are those which they can already do and those that they can see themselves do. Provide specific examples of each and contrast these gestures to invisible unfamiliar gestures, e.g., patting his hand on a table is easier to imitate than snapping his finger because he can already "pat" things. Patting his hand is easier to copy than wiggling his nose because he can see his hand, but not his nose.
3. The parent can discern which familiar gestures to encourage her child to imitate by listening to and discriminating the sounds produced by toys during play, e.g., *banging* bells on a table versus *shaking* them in the air. The parent can in turn model these gestures for her child to imitate.
4. When the child is ready to learn new gestures, the parent can demonstrate new sound producing gestures, such as patting the refrigerator and then listening for her child's imitative response.

1.43 Child: RESPONDS TO SIMPLE REQUESTS WITH GESTURES (7-9 mo.)
Parent: Gives simple requests with gestures to child; encourages his gestural responses

GENERAL GUIDELINES

The child lets us know he understands our simple requests by using a consistent gesture. Simple requests include phrases such as "Up," "Come here," "Take your (ball)," "Dance," "What's that?" The child's responsive gestures could include: raising arms, to "Up"; moving toward you, to "Come"; taking the object, to "Take"; moving, to "Dance"; and giving you, showing you, or looking at something he is holding when you say "What's that?" The context of the situation and adult gestures provide cues to the child which help him learn the meaning of the actual words.

MENTALLY RETARDED PARENT

May not use gestures when giving a verbal request, and may expect her child to respond to requests which are beyond his developmental abilities.

1. Explain to the parent that, at this age, her child cannot understand many words yet, but he can figure out some of the things we say or ask by watching our gestures:
   a. Demonstrate a gesture without words and let the parent figure out what you are asking, e.g., motion "good-bye."
   b. Ask the parent how she could gesture to convey the meaning of "come here," "get the ball," and "come up."
   c. Model, and let the parent practice, saying short inflectional phrases to match the gesture.
2. Explain that many of the questions we ask children at this age help them learn and we should keep asking questions, but at this age, children cannot answer them with words and cannot actually do many of the things we ask. Therefore, she needs to tell her child the answer so he can learn what is the answer.
3. Tell the parent which requests she can expect her child to begin learning and responding to at this age if she uses corresponding gestures, i.e., "Up, "Come," "Bye-bye," and "Take the _____." Suggest additional familiar requests dependent upon the environment, such as "dance" or "boogie." Ask the parent to show you which gestures she can use with each of these requests.
4. Demonstrate the gestures we can expect and encourage from her child to these simple requests.
5. Let the parent practice giving simple requests using gestures to her child with your reinforcement. Interpret her child's responses aloud.
6. If you hear the parent make a request to her child which is too difficult, talk for the child in a friendly manner, e.g., "Mom, I can't do that; I don't know what you mean!" Remind the parent of the specific simple requests we can expect her child to understand at this age.

DEAF PARENT

Will often have developed an excellent gestural communication system with her child.

1. If needed, point out gestural requests the child should developmentally be ready to learn or has learned. Reinforce the parent's use of speech to supplement her gestural requests.
2. Parent and child positioning to ensure maximal eye-contact should always be encouraged.

BLIND PARENT

May be unaware of her child's gestures in response to requests.

1. A person who is congenitally blind may be unaware of the role gestures play when a child is learning the meaning of words. If appropriate, explain the functions of gestures as they relate to learning language. Provide the parent with an explanation, such as: "Just as spoken words carry messages between people, so do gestures or body movements. Children learn to understand the meaning of many gestures before they learn the meaning of words. Gestures help them learn the meaning of words. For example, when you say 'Come here' to your child and move your hands toward him, it helps him know what you are saying because he can see what you are saying as well as hear it. Soon he understands the word meaning without seeing any gesture cues."
2. Describe the body movements involved for gestures which are developmentally appropriate to her child's level of understanding. Physically assist the parent to "go through the motions" of the gestures if needed.
3. Explain that children use gestures to communicate their feelings, indicate what they want, and let us know they understand what we have said.
4. Describe and interpret the child's responsive gestures to the parent's simple requests.
5. The parent can learn to discriminate, and thus reinforce, many of her child's responsive gestures through auditory and movement cues which occur simultaneously with child's gestures. For example, when the parent holds her child and says, "Say bye-bye" she can feel his response; when music is playing and the parent says, "Dance Mike!" she can hear his movements if he is on a plastic mat or is wearing a wrist band with bells.

1.44 Child: LOOKS AT PICTURES ONE MINUTE WHEN NAMED (8-9 mo.)
Parent: Shows, and talks about, a variety of interesting pictures to child

MENTALLY RETARDED PARENT

May not show and name pictures to her child.

1. Help the parent select or make suitable picture books for her child. Explain that children at this age learn from and like to look at pictures of things they see around the house:
   a. Prompt the parent to name different foods, people, clothing, animals, utensils, and toys that her child would recognize and like to see pictures of in a book.
   b. Help find pictures of things the parent named in magazines and on food wrappers.
   c. Make a simple picture book using clear contact paper or a magnetic photo album. Print short descriptive phrases under each picture. Prompt the parent to help make up the phrases after you have demonstrated a few.
   d. Help select picture books for her child at the library or store.
   e. Take a few Polaroid pictures of meaningful people or objects and make a picture book or poster with the parent for her child to look at.
2. Give the parent clear guidelines regarding what we can expect from her child at this age when he looks at a book. Include:
   a. At first, we should let her child play with the book all by himself.

1.44

    b. Children usually mouth, try to tear, or bang on the book before they are ready to look at it.
    c. Do not give the child any books that can be easily torn if the book is an important one that the parent wants to keep.
    d. Children cannot turn pages of the book alone at this age.
    e. Children sometimes look at books upside down or sideways and that is okay.
3. Model, and let the parent practice, showing and naming pictures in a book to her child. Stress the following concepts:
    a. Point to the picture so her child can see it.
    b. Talk about the picture using short inflectional phrases with facial expressions.
    c. Show pictures at her child's pace, i.e., *don't* turn the page if her child is still looking; *do* turn pages when her child stops looking.
    d. Stop the activity when her child is distracted or not interested at that time.
4. Show the parent how to point out and name pictures that are hanging up in her house to her child when she is carrying him around.
5. Lend the parent a *Magic Wand Reader.** These "talking" books will provide the parent with a model for phrases to say with her child each time they look at the book.

DEAF PARENT

Who does not use, or has distorted, speech; may not verbally name pictures when looking at them with her child.

1. If the parent uses sign language, encourage her to begin signing to her child when labeling pictures.
2. Encourage the parent to use speech, if possible, when showing her child pictures.
3. If the parent has a metered tape recorder available, tape recordings of short descriptive phrases can be made and played to coincide with picture books. Be sure to mark the volume knobs so the parent can adjust them accordingly. Give the parent a matching written script.
4. The parent can use "See and Say" toys, i.e., toys which talk and name a picture when you turn a knob to the picture and pull a string:
    a. Write out the script to identify what each picture says when the parent pulls the string.
    b. Explain that the toy does not "talk" until the string is pulled completely out and then is let go.
    c. Advise the parent to wait and watch her child's responses before reactivating the toy.
5. Lend the parent a *Magic Wand Reader** which labels pictures with computerized speech. Give the parent a matching written script.

BLIND PARENT

May need tactile cues to discriminate the location, content, top, bottom, front, and back of pictures.

1. Utilize uniform braille or other tactual marking system for pictures according to the parent's system for identifying pictures or written words:
    a. For single pictures and photographs, always braille directly on the lower righthand corner.
    b. If using pictures from magazines or other lightweight paper, mount them on *braille paper** to insure they are sturdy enough to braille.
2. Help the parent locate pictures on the page so she can point to them with her child:
    a. Outline the pictures with Elmer's Glue which, when dried, will leave a raised transparent surface; or
    b. Apply transparent brailled dymo tape labels directly on top of the picture.
3. NOTE: Many blind parents have their own equipment for producing braille. They can take the responsibility for adapting the pictures. Each parent may want to design her own marking system according to her own level of sophistication in braille use.
4. The parent can use *"twin vision"** books with her child.
5. Help the parent hang pictures or posters in her child's room which are within his visual field from his crib:
    a. Thoroughly describe the visual content and qualities to the parent so she can describe them to her child, e.g., red dog with big brown eyes.
    b. Use pictures with textures such as children's hanging rugs.
6. Make "feely" and "scratch and sniff" books which have pictures with various textures and smells.
7. Use commercial books which squeak when the picture is pushed. This can help the parent locate and attract her child's attention to the pictures.

PHYSICALLY DISABLED PARENT

Who has a limited grasp or upper extremity control; may have difficulty turning pages in picture books.

1. The parent may be able to use her elbow to turn the pages of a book.
2. Try children's books which have thicker, cardboard pages.
3. The parent could use commercial or homemade adaptive equipment specifically made to help physically disabled adults use and turn pages of a book, e.g., *book holders,* *page turning sticks.**
4. Pictures can be mounted separately on cardboard pieces.
5. The parent can point out and describe pictures in the environment to her child.

---

*See Materials Reference Listing.

*See Glossary.

1.45 Child: RETAINS TWO AND REACHES FOR THIRD OBJECT (8-10 mo.)
Parent: Provides opportunities for child to attain a third object while holding two

GENERAL GUIDELINES

This skill is very similar to 1.40 (Retains two of three objects offered). At this level, however, the child displays more purposeful thought. He does *not* incidentally drop a toy to attain the third, but instead either purposely puts one down, transfers one to the other hand, or puts on in his mouth or under his arm. Parent training activities outlined under 1.40 are applicable to this skill.

1.46 Child: OVERCOMES OBSTACLE TO OBTAIN OBJECT (8-11 mo.)
Parent: Provides opportunities for child to successfully figure out how to overcome an obstacle

GENERAL GUIDELINES

The child figures out how to obtain a toy behind a barrier by reaching over, going around, or removing the obstacle. For example, a child may crawl around an adult to get a toy behind her, or may move his pillow to get his toy. Barriers naturally occur in the environment that children learn to overcome. If, however, controlled situations are recommended to promote this skill, initially use transparent or perforated partial barriers before moving on to barriers which completely hide the object. Barriers could be an acrylic cookbook holder, clothesbasket, boxes, pillows, or an adult. The object must be attracting to the child and within reach according to his motoric abilities.

MENTALLY RETARDED PARENT

May place the toy out of her child's motoric reach, use obstacles that are too difficult for her child to overcome, or not let her child have the object after he has "worked" to get it.

1. Illustrate the cognitive concept of this skill in a meaningful way to the parent:
   a. Set up a simple obstacle situation in which the parent needs to move the barrier to obtain an object.
   b. Remark how she knew that she needed to move the obstacle to make it easier for her to reach the object.
   c. Compare how her child is now learning how to figure out how to get things that are behind obstacles.
2. Point out two things in the environment which are suitable and two things which are *not* suitable to use as obstacles with her child:
   a. Name specific characteristics which make the suitable barrier good to use with the child, e.g., low height, within her child's motoric ability, and not too interesting to distract her child.
   b. Point out the characteristics which make barriers unsuitable, e.g., too high, out of reach, dangerous, etc.
   c. Ask the parent to select another barrier which would be good to use as an obstacle.
3. Demonstrate, and let the parent practice, setting up an attractive toy behind a barrier and encouraging her child to attain it. Stress the following concepts:
   a. Attract her child's attention to the toy by shaking or squeaking the toy and using verbal prompts.
   b. Make sure the toy and obstacle are within her child's reach or motoric capabilities.
   c. Let her child have the toy to play with after attaining it, or making purposeful attempts.
4. If the child does not overcome the obstacle, problem-solve aloud with the parent, e.g., Was it too far away? Not interesting? or Was her child tired? Adjust methods and try again.
5. List daily situations that may arise for the parent to encourage her child to overcome an obstacle and obtain an object, e.g., getting his toy when it's fallen behind a chair and getting his bottle if it rolls behind a cushion.

BLIND PARENT

May be unaware of the visual cues which help her child learn to overcome obstacles.

1. Describe how transparent, perforated, and partial barriers allow her child to still see the object. This helps him problem-solve how to "get to it."
2. The parent can use her own body as an obstacle to help recognize when and how her child obtains an object behind her.

PHYSICALLY DISABLED PARENT

Who has limited mobility; may have difficulty setting up controlled obstacle situations for her child.

1. The parent may be able to use a *reacher** to place a barrier in front of the object.
2. If the parent uses a wheelchair, she can use it as an obstacle to a toy on the floor. She can monitor and respond to the difficulty of the obstacle for her child by moving her wheelchair according to her child's ability, e.g., partially or completely in front of a toy.

1.47 Child: RETRIEVES OBJECT USING OTHER MATERIAL (8-10 mo.)
Parent: Provides opportunities for child to successfully figure out how to obtain an object by pulling the support it is on

GENERAL GUIDELINES

This skill recognizes the child's ability to problem-solve. He understands that if he pulls a support, such as a blanket, toward himself, he can obtain an object more easily than moving to get it. Supports should not be more attractive than the object. Napkins, diapers, pillows, and blankets are common daily objects which are suitable to use as supports.

---

*See Glossary.

1.47

MENTALLY RETARDED PARENT

May not understand and thus not prompt her child's attempts to obtain objects on supports.

1. Demonstrate, and let the parent experience, obtaining several objects by pulling the supports they are on:
   a. Let the parent think of and set up another "object on a support" situation.
   b. Relate how her child is learning, or ready to learn, how to do this, too.
2. Model, and then let the parent practice, encouraging her child to obtain objects on a support. Stress the following concepts:
   a. Get the child's attention by shaking or squeaking the toy or object.
   b. Provide her child verbal encouragement and descriptions. Suggest specific phrases to say if needed.
   c. Make sure that the child can pull the support, i.e., it is within his manipulative ability.
   d. Appropriate placement of object on the support, i.e., not within her child's reaching range.
   e. Provide gentle physical prompting to help the child, as needed.
3. Name natural daily situations during which the parent can encourage her child to pull supports to obtain objects, e.g., pulling a small blanket to reach his bottle or pulling a napkin to reach his cookie.

BLIND PARENT

May be unaware of the visual-motor process her child uses to learn this problem-solving skill.

1. If needed, help the parent understand the visual-motor processes her child uses to obtain an object by pulling its support:
   a. Provide an auditory-motor analogy, e.g., when the parent hears her alarm clock go off in the morning, instead of getting out of bed to shut it off, she may pull its cord or the placemat on her nightstand to bring it closer to her.
   b. Relate this analogy to her child seeing an object resting on a support, e.g., "He learns he can bring it closer by pulling the cloth because he can see it moving closer to him as he pulls the support."
2. Name various daily situations which frequently provide her child with this visual-motor, problem-solving experience, such as her child pulling his placemat to reach his cookie.
3. The parent can aurally monitor her child's attempts at pulling supports to obtain sound toys, such as a chime bell.

1.48 Child: LISTENS SELECTIVELY TO FAMILIAR WORDS (8-12 mo.)
Parent: Emphasizes labels for familiar words to the child during daily activities

GENERAL GUIDELINES

The child begins to understand the meaning of familiar words within sentences, without relying upon gestures. He first learns words which are meaningful to him and which he hears often. Meaningful words at this age include names of family members, pets, labels for games or social rituals (e.g., bye-bye, "Pat-A-Cake"), familiar objects (bottle, ball), body parts (hair, nose), and common foods (cookie, juice). He learns these word labels from hearing others say them frequently, using repetition and paraphrasing within a meaningful context.

The child shows that he understands the meaning of a word by looking at, moving toward, or touching the named object or person; displaying anticipatory excitement; gesturing; and/or changing his facial expression.

MENTALLY RETARDED PARENT

May not talk about meaningful things to her child during daily activities, and may not interpret her child's signs of understanding.

1. Explain the child's level of receptive language using concrete terminology:
   a. Relate that even though her child does not say many words yet, he is learning to understand what lots of words mean when he hears others say them.
   b. At this age, he can only learn to understand words which he hears often, and which in some way are important to him, such as bottle, or "Go bye-bye."
2. Ask the parent to name words that she thinks are important to her child at this age:
   a. Help elicit parent responses by naming categories, i.e., ask what are important toy words for him to learn? What are important food words?, etc.
   b. If the parent names a word which may not actually be meaningful to her child (e.g., baseball glove), help clarify by asking if her child sees (or eats, touches, plays with) it often *and* hears it said everyday.
3. Make a word list with the parent from Activity No. 2, with pictures if needed, of words which her child is likely to understand or is ready to learn to understand. Add a new word to this list each week. Post the list on the refrigerator.
4. Stress that her child will not learn to understand the words on his word list unless he hears them said often:
   a. Demonstrate saying three or four words on the word list using paraphrasing and repetition, and naming the daily situation. For example, for the word "bottle," model the phrase "Here's your bottle, see your bottle," explaining to say this before giving her child his bottle. Ask the parent what she could say to her child when he's finished drinking his bottle.
   b. Review the remaining words on the child's word list and let the parent think of phrases to say for each word, suggesting when to say them each day to her child.

5. Remind the parent to say familiar meaningful phrases about the objects on her child's word list to her child during all of your interventions with the parent and child. Point out her child's behavioral responses which indicate he is understanding some of the words.
6. Refer to 2.26 (Shows understanding of words by appropriate behavior or gesture) to help teach the parent to recognize her child's responses and gestures which indicate his understanding of words.

DEAF PARENT

May not verbalize familiar words to her child, and may be unaware of his receptive speech vocabulary.

1. Describe the child's receptive language capabilities at this age, explaining that he understands words before he can say them:
   a. Generate a list of words to emphasize which are meaningful to her child at this age.
   b. Encourage the parent to use any speech she may have which may be coupled with signing to emphasize important words to her child during daily activities.
2. Suggest and demonstrate using "See-n-Say" toys and picture books which have matching words on a tape recorder. Code the picture book to indicate when to turn the page according to the recorder's counter.
3. Explain to household members and friends the importance of using verbal labels in full sentences coupled with, and without, sign to help insure the child learns to understand and say words without gesture cues.
4. Anticipatory Guidance: A child can learn to understand his parent's non-standard speech through daily exposure which may or may not be coupled with signs; he also needs, however, an abundant exposure to standard verbal communication.

BLIND PARENT

May be unaware of her child's non-verbal signs of understanding words, such as glancing at named objects or brightening as if he understands.

1. Explain that children tell us they understand what we are saying by looking at or moving toward the named object or person, using gestures, and/or changing facial expression. Describe the specific movements involved for each of these responses.
2. Help the parent discriminate her child's non-verbal responses which indicate he understands the words we say:
   a. Describe the child's non-verbal responses to familiar words as they occur.
   b. The parent can concurrently listen for her child's "stilling," change in respiration or vocalizations, and when possible, feel her child's subtle movements or gestures.

1.49 Child: FINDS HIDDEN OBJECT UNDER THREE SUPERIMPOSED SCREENS (9-10 mo.)
Parent: Encourages child to find an object he's seen hidden under three layers of screens placed one at a time

GENERAL GUIDELINES

The child finds an object which he has seen hidden under three covers, each on top of the other. This is a testing item to evaluate the child's maturing level of visual pursuit, memory, object permanence, and persistence. Contrived hiding games do not need to be set up for the child unless recommended to improve these visual pursuit skills. The following guidelines and activities assume contrived hiding games have been recommended for the child.

Screens should be easily handled by the child according to his fine motor abilities and should not be more attractive than the hidden object. Screens should be arranged so they can only be removed one at a time, e.g., cookie under a small box with a bowl and cloth on top of the box. Free-form, transparent, or perforated screens can provide extra visual cues for the child if needed. Objects which move or make sounds (such as wind-up toy or musical radio) provide additional cues to help the child remember an object is still there. Initiate this activity using only one, then two, and finally three screens as the child demonstrates proficiency.

Refer to activities for 1.20 (Finds a partially hidden object) and 1.32 (Finds hidden object using one screen, two screens, then three screens) for adapted materials and methods which are also applicable to this skill. Additional activities, specific to this skill only, follow.

MENTALLY RETARDED PARENT

May tease her child during hiding games.

1. Demonstrate to the parent hiding an object under three layers of screens, and explain how this "game" helps her child remember where something is.
2. Prompt and help the parent to think of additional screens and objects to hide:
   a. As screens and objects are selected, describe the properties which make them suitable, e.g., her child can easily pick up the screen, the toy is her child's favorite, or the screen is just the right size.
   b. If inappropriate objects or screens are selected, describe what makes it unsuitable, e.g., the object is too dangerous, or the screen is too hard for her child to pick up.
3. Demonstrate, and let the parent practice, hiding a toy under two and then three screens with her child. Stress the following concepts:
   a. Properly positioning her child in relation to the screens so he can reach them.
   b. Do not hide the toy until she sees her child is looking at it.
   c. Let her child have the toy or object after he finds it or has tried to find it.

1.49

d. Provide verbal and physical prompts to her child as needed.
e. Describe the activity in short inviting phrases.

4. If parental teasing remained a problem during previous hiding activities, do not introduce this activity to the parent. The child will encounter natural situations to help him learn this skill. If you need to introduce this activity to the child for testing or learning purposes, wait until the parent is involved with another activity to prevent frustration for both parent and child.

BLIND PARENT

May be unaware of her child's expanded or emerging visual memory skills.

1. Describe for the parent her child's new or emerging visual memory skills in relation to his previously learned visually memory and object performance skills as described in 1.20 (Finds partially hidden object) and 1.32 (Finds hidden object using 1 screen . . .).
2. Let the parent tactually experience the cognitive concept underlying this hiding game:
   a. Give the parent a towel, small box with a top which contains cotton, and a cookie.
   b. Direct the parent to put the cookie under the cotton in the box, put the top on it, and then cover it up. Then let the parent find the cookie.
   c. Relate this to her child's new visual memory skills, i.e., just as the parent knew where to find the cookie because she remembered putting it there, her child is learning to remember where objects are by watching them being covered up.
3. Use screens which produce auditory cues for the parent to monitor her child's searching efforts. For example, wrap an object in wax paper and put it in a small paper bag.

1.50 Child: GUIDES ACTION ON TOY MANUALLY (9-12 mo.)
Parent: Demonstrates action toy for child and encourages him to manually guide the toy when it has stopped

GENERAL GUIDELINES

After watching an action toy stop, the child tries to figure out how to recreate the action by manually putting it through its actions. Parents can use a variety of mechanical, wind-up, and friction toys to encourage their child to reactivate them.

MENTALLY RETARDED PARENT

May restart the toy without giving her child a chance to try and figure out how to restart it, or may expect her child to restart it by adult methods.

1. Select several safe action toys with the parent. Explain that, at this age, her child is learning to make different action toys start up again after she shows him how they move and then they stop:
   a. Relate that her child is *not* ready to learn to restart the toy in the same way we do; instead he tries to push it to make it go. Demonstrate a few ways her child may try to manually guide several action toys.
   b. Stress that after we start the toy and it stops, we have to let her child have time to play with the toy all by himself.
2. Model, and let the parent practice, pacing her activating action toys with her child's responses:
   a. Give the parent clear verbal prompts as needed to insure her pacing is proper with her child, e.g., "He's still playing with it; wait until he takes his hand off the toy or looks at you before restarting it for him."
   b. Use a variety of action toys on several occasions to insure generalization.

BLIND PARENT

May be unaware of her child's non-audible attempts to manually restart action toys.

1. Describe the visual characteristics and movements of various action toys.
2. Use action toys which make sounds when manually put through their actions.
3. The parent can recognize when to reactivate the toy by listening to her child's verbal distress cues, or lack of sound from the action toy.

PHYSICALLY DISABLED PARENT

Who has use of only one hand, or limited grasping abilities; may have difficulty activating wind-up toys.

1. The parent can use toys which do not require fine motor manipulation to activate:
   a. A tether ball, balloon, or other toy on a string attached to the ceiling can be activated without extensive fine motor control, with the parent's head, elbow, or shoulder.
   b. Use roly-poly toys.
   c. Use mechanical toys which activate easily with a button. If needed, the parent could use a *pointer** in a *universal cuff** to press the button.
   d. Some commercial wind-up toys have large keys which the parent may be able to manipulate.
2. If needed, the parent can stabilize the mechanical toy using *dycem** or putting it between her knees while winding it up.

---

*See Glossary.

1.51 Child: **THROWS OBJECTS (9-12 mo.)**
Parent: Understands child's developmentally appropriate "throwing" of objects. Provides experiences for suitable throwing activities

GENERAL GUIDELINES

Throwing objects which are not typically meant for throwing is a normal developmental stage for children toward learning to play and interact with objects. When the child throws objects, he realizes he can make interesting visual and sound effects. The child's throwing of objects will decrease as he learns new ways to play with and manipulate things and, if the child does not receive too much attention either negative or positive, when he throws.

In the meantime, parents can set up safe, appropriate throwing experiences to help her child move on to new interactions with toys. Appropriate items to throw could include leaves outdoors, cloth blocks, and different sized and textured balls or bean bags. Suitable throwing places could include in laundry baskets, trash cans, and boxes, or on the ground outdoors.

MENTALLY RETARDED PARENT

May interpret her child's throwing or systematic dropping of objects as "bad."

1. As the child begins to learn voluntary release, provide anticipatory guidance to the parent that her child may start throwing and/or dropping things on purpose:
   a. Explain that when he does this, he is practicing how to let things go, make things happen, and make sounds.
   b. Empathize how frustrating it can be to have to keep picking up all the things her child has thrown or dropped, but her child is not trying to be bad.
2. Help the parent identify safe items and places which would be suitable for her child to drop or throw things.
3. Ask the parent to name items and situations in which her child should *not* be allowed to throw:
   a. If the parent has difficulty identifying objects, prompt with identifying foods, utensils, and specific breakable items around the home.
   b. If not named by the parent, stress that her child should not be allowed to throw things at people or at breakable items, such as televisions, lamps, etc.
   c. Demonstrate how to stop her child from inappropriately throwing, using role-play situations with the parent and, as the occasion arises, with the child.
4. Explain that at first her child does not know which things are okay to throw or drop and which things are not okay. Emphasize that at this age her child does not do this to be mean.
5. Show the parent how to teach her child the difference between "good" throwing or dropping and "bad" throwing:
   a. Model and/or discuss reinforcing her child's appropriate dropping or throwing by smiling and making exclamations, such as "Look! See it fall."
   b. Model and/or discuss the importance of not smiling and firmly saying "no" when inappropriate throwing occurs, e.g., "No, food is for eating. No throwing food." If the child continues, tell the parent to take away the food, again saying "Food is NOT for throwing."
   (CAUTION: Clarify as needed that the parent should *not* stop feeding her child altogether, just remove the particular food he keeps throwing.)
   c. Role-play various situations with you portraying the child and letting the parent practice saying "no" firmly.

DEAF PARENT

May be unaware of the reinforcing sounds produced when her child throws objects.

1. Explain to the parent that when her child throws objects, in addition to seeing interesting movements of the object, he likes to listen to the various sounds he can produce.
2. Identify the properties of various objects which produce sounds when thrown. For example, metal objects, such as spoons, make louder higher pitch sounds than soft stuffed animals.
3. Point out various surfaces which change the sound of an object when it is thrown and hits the surface. Examples can include carpeting muffles the sound, but hard floors amplify it; and the ground outside muffles sound, but throwing objects in metal trash cans outside amplifies the sound.

BLIND PARENT

May be unaware of the reinforcing visual effects her child receives when he throws or drops objects and may have realistic concerns regarding safety since she may be unable to visually monitor thrown objects.

1. Explain that when her child throws something, in addition to listening to its sound, he likes watching it move, bounce, and roll; different objects create different visual experiences, e.g., napkins move slowly and sway, rubber toys bounce, and plastic cups bounce and roll.
2. The parent can participate in appropriate throwing games and monitor her child's inappropriate throwing using auditory and tactile cues:
   a. Bean bags don't roll and can thus be easily located when dropped or thrown.
   b. Use soft blocks or balls which chime or ring.
   c. Throw leaves or grass on each other's feet outdoors.
3. The parent can restrict her child's play area from hard or breakable objects which may be potentially thrown during this stage.
4. Explain that during this "throwing stage," the parent should anticipate possible unexpected obstacles on the floor that her child has thrown. She can check the floor after each meal for dropped or thrown food, and check the floor near her child's crib and playpen for thrown toys which do not produce audible cues.

1.51

PHYSICALLY DISABLED PARENT

Who has difficulty bending or getting to the floor; may become understandably frustrated by her child's throwing or dropping of objects.

1. Explain the child's throwing as developmentally appropriate, agreeing how frustrating this can be for all parents.
2. If the parent has adequate upper extremity control, she could use a *reacher** to help retrieve objects her child has thrown.
3. Favorite toys can be tied with ribbons or strings to the child's highchair, playpen rails, or parent's wheelchair; when thrown, the parent can then easily retrieve them.

1.52   Child: **DROPS OBJECTS SYSTEMATICALLY (9-12 mo.)**
Parent: Understands child's developmentally appropriate behavior of dropping objects systematically; provides appropriate opportunities for child to practice

GENERAL GUIDELINES

The child intentionally drops various objects one-by-one. General guidelines and activities for parents during this stage are similar to 1.51 (Throws objects), which in most cases developmentally coincides with this skill.

1.53   Child: **USES LOCOMOTION TO REGAIN OBJECT AND RESUMES PLAY (9-12 mo.)**
Parent: Encourages child to obtain an object moved out of reach

GENERAL GUIDELINES

If a toy has at least two parts necessary to play, and one part rolls or falls out of the child's reach, he figures out how to bring it back. He may drag, pull, or carry the part back to his original play position. Suitable two-part toy examples include xylophone or drum with stick, blocks and a cup, or a coffee can with spools. The part that has moved out of reach should be within easy access and visible to the child. If the child becomes distracted when retrieving the needed part, parents can provide him gestural and verbal reminders.

MENTALLY RETARDED PARENT

May expect her child to retrieve the object when it is developmentally unaccessible, or may not give her child the time he needs to figure out how to get it because she retrieves it too quickly for him.

1. Concretely explain to the parent how her child is learning to get a part of a toy which has moved out of reach so he can resume play with the other piece:
   a. Explain through demonstration with the parent.
   b. Stress the importance of being able to see the object, and it being accessible to her child's level of locomotion.
   c. Help the parent think of places the toy could roll where her child could not reach it and she should help him.
   d. Demonstrate situations where her child can be expected to get the object all by himself.
2. Point out during naturally occurring situations where the child needs to retrieve a toy to continue play. Provide verbal prompts, such as:
   a. "Let him try to get it all by himself."
   b. "See how he's trying to figure how to get it back!"
   c. "He can't reach that; bring it a little closer."
   d. "Tell him what a nice job he did getting the toy."
3. If the child needs additional practice in learning to move to retrieve an object, demonstrate, and let the parent practice, setting up contrived situations for her child:
   a. Show the parent appropriate two-part toys.
   b. Demonstrate calling her child's attention to the out-of-reach object.
   c. Stress *not* taking an object out of her child's hand to move it out of reach.
   d. Show the parent how to place one part of the toy in an accessible place according to her child's level of motor development.
   e. Model phrases to say which provide her child verbal prompts and reminders to retrieve the object and bring it back to the other "part" to resume play.

BLIND PARENT

May be unable to visually monitor when, or where, a toy part has moved out of her child's reach.

1. The parent can detect subtle auditory cues when toy parts move out of her child's reach, and encourage him to retrieve it.
2. Sound toys and hard surfaces provide extra auditory cues to help the parent monitor her child's retrieval process.
3. Describe for the parent her child's method of locomotion and facial expressions when he is retrieving or trying to obtain an object.

1.54   Child: **LISTENS TO SPEECH WITHOUT BEING DISTRACTED BY OTHER SOURCES (9-11 mo.)**
Parent: Provides child adequate opportunities to listen to speech without an excessively competing sound environment

GENERAL GUIDELINES

Children learn to screen out natural environmental sounds in order to focus upon a speaker or a specific activity. Sudden or excessive environmental sounds will continue to interfere with his attending. If a child is easily distracted by everyday environmental sounds, such as background music, footsteps, or water running, provide controlled gradually increasing exposure to extraneous sounds while he is attending to speech or an activity.

---

*See Glossary.

MENTALLY RETARDED PARENT

May expect her child to attend to an activity or speech during excessive environmental sounds.

1. Demonstrate how excessive environmental sounds can interfere with our ability to attend to an activity or speech:
   a. Turn a stereo or radio on at a high volume and let the parent experience trying to understand your talking with loud sound interference.
   b. Talk again with the music at a softer level and comment how much easier it is to understand and attend to speech.
   c. Relate how it is also too difficult for her child to listen to us when sounds are too loud.
   d. Identify additional potential sources of distracting environmental sounds which can interfere with her child's ability to attend. Examples can include vacuum cleaner, television, loud action toys, and too many people talking at one time.
2. Point out and describe to the parent her child's signs of listening as they occur, e.g., eye contact, facial expression, and gestures.
3. Point out and describe the child's behaviors which let us know he is distracted, or is trying to "shut-out" external stimuli as they occur. These signs may include gaze aversion, inappropriate head shaking, body rocking, or gesturing which does *not* match the situation.
4. If the child is frequently distracted by everyday sounds demonstrate helping the child attend by:
   a. Directing speech to her child after obtaining his eye contact.
   b. Identifying and reducing when possible, the source of sound distraction.

DEAF PARENT

May be unaware of excessive sound distractions in the environment.

1. Help explain the child's selective listening skills using a selective-vision analogy with the parent, e.g., "Just as you can attend to print words on a page which have pictures, your child can attend to people's speech when other sounds, such as soft music, are also occurring." Compare being distracted by excessive sound to being distracted by excessive visual stimuli, e.g., "If there are too many interesting pictures, we might not bother to look at the fine print!"
2. Identify typical daily sounds which usually do not distract her child from listening to speech or attending to his parent's signs and gestures. Explain how these help her child learn to use selective listening and attending.
3. Point out sounds and their situations in child's environment which can distract her child from attending to speech or gestures. These may include vacuum cleaners, loud furnace motors, alarm and stove timers, loud action toys, and television and radios with the volume turned up too high.

4. Help the parent learn to "read" her child's gestural, facial, and bodily signs of attention and distraction. This can help alert her to check for, and adjust when possible, obstrusive environmental sounds.

BLIND PARENT

May have difficulty monitoring her child's non-vocal signals of listening or distraction when she is speaking to him.

1. Describe for the parent her child's non-verbal signals which indicate he is attending to other's speech or is distracted by environmental sounds. The parent may be able to associate her child's subtle auditory or movement responses which indicate he is attending or distracted during speech.

1.55 Child: KNOWS WHAT "NO-NO" MEANS AND REACTS (9-12 mo.)
Parent: Says "no-no" to child using congruent facial and vocal expressions at appropriate times

GENERAL GUIDELINES

The child understands the meaning of "no-no" and will react by briefly pausing his activity and/or looking at the adult. At this age, he usually does not have the control to stop his activity; an adult usually must intervene to stop and redirect the child.

MENTALLY RETARDED PARENT

May over-use saying "no" to her child, and expect him to stop his activity without additional prompts.

1. Clearly explain to the parent her child's new or emerging abilities and limits, as he is learning to understand the meaning of "no-no." Stress and illustrate several concrete examples for each of the following concepts:
   a. If her child hears "no" everytime he does something, he learns to ignore it.
   b. Saying "no" should be reserved for hazardous situations.
   c. The parent needs to help her child stop what he is doing when she says "no." At this age, he cannot always stop what he is doing by himself.
   d. The parent should redirect her child to an acceptable activity after saying "no," e.g., if her child starts to touch a hot oven, say "no" and move him to his highchair to play with some spoons.
   e. Use appropriate gestures, facial expressions, and intonations when saying "no," e.g., don't say "no" with a smile.
2. Role-play specific situations which illustrate Activity No. 1. If possible:
   a. Set up role-play situations within a parent group setting.
   b. Illustrate, via video, typical child situations which warrant a firm "no" and then discuss possible ways to handle the situation.

1.55

    c. Show a follow-up video which depicts ineffective and then effective adult responses to a "no" situation. Have the parent name which parent behaviors were effective and which were ineffective.
3. When natural situations arise, model and encourage the parent to say "no" effectively with her child. Stress and coach as needed, each concept listed under Activity No. 1.
4. Help the parent anticipate and discriminate possible daily situations in which to say "no" to her child and those which do not warrant a "no." An example could be "When your child puts a dangerous item in his mouth, say 'no,' but when your child is having trouble with a particular toy, show him how it works and say 'try it this way' instead of saying 'no'."
5. If not previously done, help the parent adequately "child-proof" her home to prevent excessive "no-nos" with her child.
6. Refer to Activity No. 2.c under 5.39 (Displays independent behavior).

DEAF PARENT

May not use speech to say "no-no" to her child, or her speech may be unintelligible or lack the typical intonation needed to stress the meaning of "no."

1. The parent can make an alternative vocalization within her verbal repertoire (e.g., "eh" or "ut"), using accompanying facial expressions and gestures to help get the meaning across to her child. Cue the parent during practice when her "no-no" is transmitted with adequate volume and intonation.
2. The non-verbal parent can clap her hands with emphasis to attract her child's attention to her head shaking, facial expressions, and sign for "no-no."

BLIND PARENT

May be unaware of distinctive facial expressions and gestures which help her child understand the meaning of "no."

1. Describe the various facial expressions and gestures (head shaking, furrowed eyebrows, finger pointing) which help her child understand the meaning of "no."
2. If the parent does not feel comfortable using gesture cues when she says "no," she can capitalize upon her vocal intonations to help get the meaning across to her child.
3. Describe the child's non-verbal reactions to "no-no" as they occur. The parent can listen for her child's momentary decrease in activity when he hears "no."
4. Help child-proof the environment, if needed, to prevent over-use of "no-no."

PHYSICALLY DISABLED PARENT

With limited mobility; may not be able to quickly respond to redirect or stop her child's dangerous activity.

1. Anticipatory Guidance: There may be unavoidable dangerous situations that arise which require the parent's quick response to intervene. At this age, the child may pause only momentarily to "no" before continuing a potentially dangerous situation (e.g., he suddenly learns to unlatch a safety gate, he starts to stick a nail file into a plug, or he starts moving quickly toward a hot oven). Parents who use a wheelchair, crutches, braces, etc. cannot run to prevent these situations:
    a. The parent can keep a loud whistle around her neck to reserve for using when her child is approaching hazardous situations. The shock of the whistle may distract her child and provide the parent with the extra few critical seconds to respond to the situation.
    b. CAUTION: If the child is too close to the dangerous situation (i.e., he already has his hand on a grease pan handle, or he has already unlatched the safety gate and is at the edge of the steps), the shock of a loud whistle may accentuate the problem. In this case, the parent could make a non-shocking but attracting noise, such as using her mouth to whistle, or making a loud "raspberry" sound to help distract him.

1.56   Child: RESPONDS TO SIMPLE VERBAL REQUESTS (9-14 mo.)
    Parent: Gives child simple verbal requests, within context

GENERAL GUIDELINES

In contrast to child skill 1.43 (Responds to simple requests with gestures), the child is learning to understand simple requests *without* gestures. Simple requests must be meaningful to the child and be given in context. A meaningful request in context involves what the child is doing, looking at, or holding.

MENTALLY RETARDED PARENT

May make too many verbal requests, may make requests beyond child's developmental abilities, and may make requests out of context.

1. Review specific simple requests with the parent which her child seems to understand at this age.
2. Concretely explain to the parent with examples that her child will not need as many gesture cues at this age but still needs context cues and meaningful requests:
    a. Illustrate how confusing it would be if her child was holding a ball and we said, "Give me the car."
    b. Tell the parent not to make requests to her child if the object or activity is not in her child's sight.
3. Refer to 1.43 (Responds to simple requests with gestures).

DEAF PARENT

May be unaware of her child's increasing receptive language abilities, and may be unable to provide simple verbal requests.

1. Explain to the parent her child's new or emerging receptive language ability to understand simple verbal requests without relying upon gestures. List specific simple requests the child appears to understand.
2. Encourage the parent to make these simple requests to her child using her own form of communication:
    a. Spoken language, "homemade gestures," sign language, or any combination thereof, should be encouraged.

b. When possible, reinforce these with the aid of a hearing person who can provide the *verbal* component of the request.
3. Make a book with simple action pictures to match a cassette recording of simple verbal requests. For example, have a picture of a parent giving a baby a kiss with a cassette-recorded voice saying, "Give me a kiss":
   a. Place only one action picture to a page with the verbal request printed below.
   b. Mark the appropriate volume level on the tape recorder.
   c. Following each recorded verbal request, provide the parent with a signal, such as a bell which is within her hearing range, or a numerical marking on the page to match the meter on the recorder to cue the parent when to turn the page.
   d. Each verbal request can be simultaneously carried out by the parent and child together until the child masters the request without assistance.
4. The parent can reinforce her child's correct response to simple requests with gestural, physical, or verbal when possible, reinforcements.

BLIND PARENT

May be unaware of visual contexts which assure her simple requests to her child are in context; and may be unable to visually monitor her child's non-verbal response to the request.

1. Explain the child's increasing receptive language capabilities and decreased reliance upon watching gestures to figure out word meanings. Name simple requests her child can now understand without gestures and those requests he continues to need gestures to help him understand.
2. Explain that although her child does not need to rely upon seeing as many gestures to help him understand a request, the request needs to be in context and meaningful:
   a. The parent can aurally monitor her child's activity to assure her requests are within context. For example, when she no longer hears her child drinking his juice or hears him banging his cup on the tray, she can say, "Give me your cup."
   b. The parent can tactually monitor her child's activities when he is in her lap to help assure her verbal requests are in context.
3. The parent can discriminate her child's non-verbal responses to simple requests through auditory and gestural cues. Refer to Activities No. 3 and 5, 1.43 (Responds to simple requests with gestures).

1.57 Child: REMOVES ROUND PIECE FROM FORMBOARD (10-11 mo.)
Parent: Encourages child to remove round piece from a shape puzzle

GENERAL GUIDELINES

A circle is the easiest piece to remove from a formboard. Children learn to remove puzzle pieces before being able to put them back in. If a child has difficulty or fine motor impairments, try: positioning the puzzle-board on an incline; using shape puzzles which have knobs; using 3-dimensional round objects to remove from the round space, such as a roll of tape, small paper cup, or cylindrical block; providing physical assistance; or building up the hole with putty to raise the circle piece above the surface.

MENTALLY RETARDED PARENT

May interfere with her child's exploratory play, and may expect developmentally higher formboard skills.

1. Before introducing formboards or shape puzzles to the child, explain and demonstrate the following concepts to the parent:
   a. We need to let her child try to figure out what he can do with the puzzle all by himself; he may mouth, bang, or hit the puzzle pieces, and that's okay.
   b. The circle is the easiest piece for him to take out at this age.
   c. The child's muscles are *not* ready to take out the other shapes yet.
   d. The child's eyes and muscles are not ready to work together yet to put the puzzle pieces back into their places.
   e. The child needs to be in a position where he can see and reach the puzzle pieces easily.
2. Demonstrate, and let the parent practice, showing her child how to take out the round puzzle piece. Model and stress the following concepts:
   a. Use verbal phrases, prompts, and reinforcement with her child, e.g., "See the circle," and "Take the circle out; good, you're trying!"
   b. Give her child time to practice without interfering.
   c. Provide unobtrusive physical assistance, as needed.
   d. Stop the activity when her child is no longer interested. Describe her child's disinterest cues aloud.

BLIND PARENT

May not be able to visually monitor her child's interactions with the formboard.

1. Before introducing a formboard to the child, let the parent become tactually familiar with its parts.
2. Describe any distinctive visual features of the formboard, such as the colors of the various shapes and the color of the puzzle base.
3. If needed, orient the parent to suitable positions for the board within her child's visual field and easy reach to facilitate manipulation.
4. After demonstrating to her child how to remove the circle, the parent can leave her hand near the circle's location to monitor her child's attempts to remove the circle and physically assist him if necessary.
5. Describe the child's facial expressions and other pertinent inaudible signs of frustration, curiosity, or accomplishment.

1.57

PHYSICALLY DISABLED PARENT

With limited hand or upper extremity control; may be unable to manipulate formboard pieces for demonstration or assistance to her child.

1. Use formboards which have large knobbed handles on the shape pieces.
2. Put a small strip of velcro on each puzzle piece. The parent can use a velcro wrist cuff to remove and insert the pieces.

1.58   Child: **TAKES RING STACK APART (10-11 mo.)**
      Parent: Demonstrates and encourages child to take rings off a ring stack toy

GENERAL GUIDELINES

The child takes rings off a stick on a base. He is learning the relationship between "parts" of a whole as he sees that toys can be taken apart and their spatial relationships. As he is learning these concepts and practicing his manipulative control, the base can lie horizontally or be tilted. He should be presented with only two to five rings, according to his individual persistence and attention level.

MENTALLY RETARDED PARENT

May expect her child to put the rings back on the stack, and may interfere with her child's explorations with the toy.

1. Before introducing a ring stack toy to the child, review the following concepts with the parent:
   a. Her child's eyes and muscles are not ready to be able to put rings on the stick, but he is ready to learn to take them off.
   b. Her child may take them off by pulling, sliding, or putting the stack on its side and pushing them off.
   c. Her child learns how to take them off, first by watching an adult take them off and then practicing all by himself.
2. Avoid ring stacks which have a graduated base or rings. The parent may spend too much time focusing upon placing the rings on the stick "just right."
3. Name specific places and positions which are suitable for her child to play with the ring stack.
   a. Place a ring stack too high or out of the parent's visual field and let her experience trying to take the rings off when they are in awkward positions.
   b. Relate the importance of proper positioning for her child.
4. Demonstrate, and let the parent practice, taking rings off the stack and encouraging her child to copy. Emphasize during demonstration and parent practice:
   a. Giving her child plenty of exploratory time.
   b. Giving her child appropriate verbal prompts and encouragement.
   c. Stopping the activity when her child shows signs of frustration or disinterest. Specifically describe these signs aloud to the parent as they occur, e.g., "Johnny's tired of this now; he's starting to throw the rings and look toward his 'See-n-Say toy'."

BLIND PARENT

May not be able to visually monitor her child's attempts, success, or frustrations when removing rings from a stack.

1. Let the parent become tactually familiar with the rings, the ring stack, and the various graduated ring sizes.
2. Describe any distinctive visual features of the ring stack, such as the various colors of the rings or pictures on the base. The colors can be marked with tactile cues to facilitate the parent's verbal descriptions and reinforcements to her child when he is playing with the ring stack.
3. Describe the child's inaudible attending behaviors, such as smiling, looking, and reaching while the parent is demonstrating to her child how to take the rings off.
4. Facilitate and describe proper positioning as needed to insure the ring stack is at a good height for her child's hands and within his visual field.
5. Describe her child's inaudible interactions with the ring stack, e.g., "He's pulling the rings off two at a time! What a proud smile he has!"

PHYSICALLY DISABLED PARENT

Who has limited hand or upper extremity control; may have difficulty holding and/or pulling off the rings to demonstrate this skill for her child.

1. Use rings with larger holes to make pulling them off easier.
2. The parent may be able to lie the ring stack on its side and slide the rings off without using a grasp.
3. Small velcro strips can be applied to the top edges or sides of the rings. The parent can use a velcro wrist cuff to pull them off and then return them again.
4. If the parent cannot stabilize the stacking base, she could hold it between her knees, use *dycem** under the stack, or glue or velcro the stacking base to a firmer support.

1.59   Child: **DEMONSTRATES DRINKING FROM A CUP (10-15 mo.)**
      Parent: Gives child cups to play with; encourages "pretend" drinking games

GENERAL GUIDELINES

The child's interactions with objects are becoming differentiated in accordance with the function of the object. Earlier, he would bang, shake, mouth, or wave all objects without regard to function. Instead, he now hugs dolls, drops blocks into a container, shakes a rattle, and pretends to drink from a cup during play.

---

*See Glossary.

MENTALLY RETARDED PARENT

May assume that since cups are not toys, her child should not play with them.

1. If the parent does not offer a cup to her child during feeding, refer to 6.20 (Drinks from cup held for him).
2. Explain that children usually like to play with empty cups just as much as with toys, and that's just fine.
3. Point out the advantages of letting her child play with empty cups, e.g., they can practice cup drinking skills, they begin to learn pretend play, and the parent doesn't have to buy so many toys.
4. Ask the parent to show you small, non-breakable cups with which it would be suitable for her child to play.
5. Model, and encourage the parent to participate in, pretend play using cups and spoons with her child. Demonstrate stirring, drinking, feeding dolls, and pantomining drinking sounds.
6. Name specific daily activities during which to remember to let her child play with a cup, e.g., when he is playing with a doll or at the table after he has finished his drink.

BLIND PARENT

May be unaware of her child's pretend gestures with objects, and their cognitive meaning.

1. If the parent is unaware of the relationship between pretend gestures and their cognitive function, explain this skill in relation to her child's other cognitive skills, e.g., "When your child was younger, he used to treat all objects alike during play. Just like his interactions with other objects, he would roll, bang, or wave an empty plastic cup as his way to play with it. At this age, he is learning to discriminate the appropriate social functions of different objects and interacts with them according to their functions. Since cups are for drinking, your child is learning to pretend he is drinking from them during play even when there is no liquid in it. When he sees other similar containers, he may pretend they are cups and pretend to drink from them, too."
2. Describe the child's interactions with cups during pretend play in front of a mirror or with a doll.
3. The parent can pair a vocalization, such as "Mm," when demonstrating pretend cup play and handing her child the cup. As he begins to associate and verbalize "Mm" during cup play, the parent can aurally monitor his activity.

PHYSICALLY DISABLED PARENT

With limited hand control or weakness; may have difficulty holding a cup during pretend cup drinking games with her child.

1. The parent may be able to use an *adapted cup holder** designed for compensatory grasps.
2. The parent can participate in pretend cup play with her child by letting him hold the cup while she enthusiastically verbalizes, e.g., "Mm, that looks good! Can I have some? Give mommy a drink" or "Great! Now give Tommy a drink; now give Teddy Bear a drink!"

1.60 **Child:** ENJOYS LOOKING AT PICTURES IN BOOKS (10-14 mo.)
Parent: Provides child with interesting picture books

GENERAL GUIDELINES

The guidelines and activities suggested for each parent disability under 1.44 (Looks at pictures one minute when named) are applicable to this skill.

At this age the child begins to look at books without as much parent direction. When appropriate, help the parent "update" her child's picture book collection according to his new interests.

1.61 **Child:** UNWRAPS A TOY (10½-12 mo.)
Parent: Provides opportunities for child to obtain safe objects wrapped loosely in paper

GENERAL GUIDELINES

The child unwraps a loosely wrapped object by tearing, shaking, or pulling the paper off. He knows something is hidden in the wrap through his expanding awareness of object permanence. The child should see the object being wrapped up at first, and then offered opportunities to unwrap things in which he does not know the contents. Parents should supervise their child's unwrapping activities.

Suitable wraps include waxed paper, commercial wrapping paper, paper bags, sturdy cellophane, tissue paper of various colors, napkins, and washcloths. Inedible objects should be larger than three square inches and, at first, smooth so that the paper slides off easily; edible objects should be at least the size of a cookie. Transparent and opaque wraps provide the child with extra visual cues to let him know there is something special inside. The wrap can be secured around the object by folding or slightly twisting.

MENTALLY RETARDED PARENT

May not provide opportunities for her child to unwrap objects, may intrude on child's attempts to unwrap a toy, and may not anticipate safety concerns.

1. Before giving the child a toy wrapped in paper, help the parent anticipate and prepare for safety concerns:
   a. Sort suitable from unsuitable wraps with the parent into two piles from a box containing various types of paper. Name the specific quality which makes the paper suitable or unsuitable, e.g., newspapers are not good to use as wraps because the child can get newsprint all over his hands, and soft cellophane should not be used because the child could choke on it.
   b. Sort with the parent into two piles suitable and unsuitable objects to wrap. Again, specifically name what

---

*See Glossary.

1.61

makes it suitable or not, e.g., if the object is too small, he may swallow it; and if the object has sharp edges, he could cut himself.
2. Contrast for the parent, through demonstration, various loosely wrapped toys with toys which are wrapped too tightly:
   a. Explain that, at this age, her child's finger muscles are not ready to open things which are tightly wrapped. We need to start opening those things for him.
   b. Explain that her child is ready to figure out how to unwrap the loosely wrapped toys, but he needs extra time to explore and figure it out.
3. Model, and let parent practice, encouraging her child to unwrap a toy. Stress and help the parent, as needed, to:
   a. Attract her child's attention to the task.
   b. Give her child verbal descriptions, prompts, and praise.
   c. Give her child enough time to try it by himself.
   d. Discourage mouthing of paper without punishment.
   e. Unobstrusively make the task easier if her child is having difficulty.
   f. Let the child keep the object after unwrapping it.
   g. Stop the activity when her child loses interest, naming his disinterest cues, e.g., "Okay, I see you looking at that toy now; you are finished with this."
4. Name naturally occurring situations during which the parent may let her child unwrap things, e.g., unwrapping store wraps after the parent opens it partially or wrapping her child's cookie in a napkin before giving it to him.

BLIND PARENT

May be unaware of the visual cues various papers provide to her child.

1. Point out that wax paper, sturdy cellophanes, and some types of tissue paper allow her child to see the object through the wrappings. Relate that this helps encourage him to open it.
2. Point out which papers have undesirable dyes or prints which rub off, especially when damp if her child mouths them, e.g., newspaper, crepe paper, and some colored tissue papers.

1.62 Child: FINDS OBJECT HIDDEN BY ONE SCREEN DISPLACEMENT (11-13 mo.)
Parent: Hides object from child with one displacement if recommended

GENERAL GUIDELINES

This item is used as an evaluation item to assess the child's maturing visual pursuit, memory, and intuitive thought processes. Contrived situations do not need to be set up unless recommended to improve the child's visual pursuit, memory, or intuitive thought process skills. 1.49 (Finds hidden object under three superimposed screens) is a prerequisite skill for this item.

The process for hiding an object by one screen displacement is:

1. A small object is put in a container while the child watches and sees the object in the container, e.g., a cookie in a small open box.
2. The container holding the object is covered by a screen, e.g., the small box with a cookie in it is covered with a dishcloth.
3. The object is removed from the first container without the child being able to see it, e.g., the box is turned over while it is covered by the dishcloth.
4. The container, now empty, is placed next to the cover which is hiding the object, e.g., the empty box is put next to the dishcloth which is on top of the cookie.
5. The child looks first into the container where he initially saw the object; when he cannot find it, he figures out it must be under the screen and finds it, e.g., the child looks into the empty box and then under the dishcloth to find the cookie.
6. If the child does not find the object, the adult should lift the screen and let him peek.

Containers to initially place the object in for displacement could be an adult hand, small jewelry boxes, or an empty toilet tissue roll. Suitable covers to act as the screen can be washcloths, cloth diapers, or a napkin. Hidden objects should be safe and attracting to the child. Hiding small music boxes provide the child with an extra sound cue to help him find it.

MENTALLY RETARDED PARENT

May "tease" her child during the displacement process or may become confused.

1. Demonstrate this activity with the parent in a game-like situation:
   a. Hide a cookie in your hand, cover your hand with a towel, and then show her the same hand empty while the cookie remains on a table under the towel.
   b. Ask the parent to find the cookie and then question how she knew where it was.
   c. Relate how her child is now learning to do this.
2. Demonstrate playing this game with her child, and let the parent practice. Stress and coach parent, as needed, to:
   a. Attract her child's attention and show him the cookie before hiding it.
   b. Show her child her empty hand.
   c. Provide verbal descriptions, prompts, and praise to her child.
   d. Let her child eat the cookie after he finds it, or makes attempts to find it.
   e. Let her child try to find it all by himself unless he becomes frustrated or distracted. Describe the child's signs of frustration or distraction.
3. If parental teasing remained a problem during previous hiding games, or if the displacement process from your experience would be too confusing for the parent, do not introduce this activity to the parent. If you need to introduce this activity to the child for testing or learning purposes, wait until the parent is involved with another activity to prevent misinterpretation and frustration for both parent and child.

DEAF PARENT

May be unaware of auditory cues which help her child locate a displaced hidden object.

1. After demonstrating the displacement process, refer to 1.20 (Finds partially hidden object).

BLIND PARENT

May be unaware of her child's expanded or emerging visual memory skills and their relationship to logical thinking.

1. Concretely describe how this higher visual memory skill relates to her child's logical thinking. Use an explanation, such as: "Now that your child knows that objects still exist, even when he can't see them, he is beginning to use logical thinking to find them. When he can't find an object in the place where he first saw it hidden, he will systematically look in other possible places until he finds it, even though he didn't see it placed there."
2. Explain, and let the parent tactually experience, the hidden displacement process. Have the parent put a cookie in a small box and place it on the table next to a napkin. The facilitator can then put the cookie under the napkin and let the parent find the cookie.
3. Stress that the objects need to be visually hidden from her child during the displacement process. The parent can hide the object in her fist and empty it after she covers her fist with a cloth.
4. Describe her child's attending and searching behaviors as the parent hides the object. The parent can lightly rest her hand next to the cover and tactually discern her child's attempts.

1.63 Child: PLACES CYLINDERS IN MATCHING HOLES IN CONTAINER (11-12 mo.)
Parent: Demonstrates putting cylinders in matching holes of containers; encourages child to try

GENERAL GUIDELINES

A cylinder is the easiest three-dimensional shape for the child to match to a round hole in a container.

Cylinders can be thick pegs, thread spools, empty medicine bottles, small juice cans, or commercial cylindrical blocks. Containers can be boxes or coffee cans with holes cut out in their lids. If commercial shape boxes are used, cover the non-circle shapes with solid contact paper. Outlining the hole with a marker emphasizes the circle shape.

The container should be positioned within easy visual and manipulative reach of the child, such as between his thighs when he is sitting on the floor. The child may need to be provided support in sitting, dependent upon his motor abilities.

Parents encourage this skill through demonstration, and by providing suitable materials and unobstrusive physical prompting according to the child's individual needs. He should never be physically forced to complete the task. Parents should praise all of their child's attempts, and stop the activity as the child's attention or frustration level demands.

MENTALLY RETARDED PARENT

May expect and physically manipulate her child to insert various shapes correctly into traditional shape boxes.

1. Before introducing shape boxes to the child, explain to the parent that her child is learning to match circle shapes to the circle holes. But, at this age, his eyes and hands are *not* ready to match square or triangle shapes.
2. Make homemade circle shape boxes with the parent using cardboard boxes and coffee cans with plastic lids. Let the parent check the can for sharp edges, tape seams with sturdy plastic tape, and help collect various cylinders for matching.
3. Demonstrate encouraging the child to put cylinders into the shape box, and then let the parent practice. Stress the following concepts and prompt the parent, as needed:
   a. The child should be positioned so he can reach and manipulate the box. Let the parent experience how difficult it would be to put the cylinder in the box if it was up too high.
   b. Attract her child's attention by tapping the box with the cylinder before demonstrating the task.
   c. Provide clear verbal descriptions of the task, and give verbal prompts and praise to the child. Ask the parent to think of appropriate phrases to say before introducing the activity to her child.
   d. If the child becomes distracted, help focus his attention by calling his name and tapping the shape box again with the cylinder. If he moves away, fusses, or twists his body, stop the activity for now.
   e. Do not interfere with her child's attempts; let him explore and practice.
   f. If her child needs help, do not take away the cylinder he is holding. Instead, either demonstrate with a different cylinder, gently tap the back of his hand to help him release it, and/or gently place his hand over the hole.

BLIND PARENT

May be unaware of the visual matching purpose for introducing this task to her child.

1. After letting the parent become tactually familiar with the shape box, explain the visual matching learning process involved for her child in this task. Explain that just as she recognizes which shape goes into which hole by matching their similar shapes through touch, her child is learning to match by seeing and feeling their similar shapes.
2. Describe additional distinctive visual cues which may help her child match shapes, such as outlining the circular hole of shape box with a bright color and using solid colored shapes.
3. Monitor and assist the parent, as needed, to assure her child and the shape box are positioned so he can adequately see and manipulate it. Describe the specific positions which help facilitate her child's matching.
4. The parent can monitor her child's success and attempts with the shape box by listening to the sounds the shapes make when he drops them into their container.

1.63

PHYSICALLY DISABLED PARENT

Who has mild upper extremity tremors; may be unable to accurately align the cylinder in the hole to model for her child.

1. Use small shape containers so the parent does not have to reach above her elbow level to insert the shape.
2. The parent may be able to decrease her tremors by holding her upper arm close and tight to her body while her forearms and elbow rest on the table.
3. The parent may have wrist weights previously prescribed by a therapist to help reduce tremor.

1.64 Child: STACKS RINGS (11-12 mo.)
Parent: Demonstrates and encourages child to put rings on a stick

GENERAL GUIDELINES

The child is able to put rings back on an upright stick with a base. The stick should be uniform in width and the base should be flat. This activity helps the child learn that he can put parts of a toy back together in a systematic way to make them whole again.

Parents encourage this skill by keeping the activity fun and adapting for any of the child's motor disabilities through positioning and with gentle physical prompting as needed.

1.58 (Takes ring stack apart) is a prerequisite to this skill.

MENTALLY RETARDED PARENT

May interfere with her child's exploration of ring stack toys, or may physically try to make him place the rings on a stick. If the rings are graduated, may expect his ring placement to be graduated.

1. Before and during demonstration of this task to the child, stress to the parent that her child:
   a. Does *not* need to put the rings on the stick in any particular order.
   b. Does *not* need to put all of the rings back on the stick.
   c. Often likes to explore the rings before trying to put them back on the stick; it's okay if he rolls, slides, or bangs them.
   d. Learns how to put the rings on the stick by first watching an adult and then trying it all by himself without help.
2. Refer to Activity Nos. 2-4, 1.58 (Takes ring stack apart) to teach the parent proper positioning and teaching techniques for her child.

BLIND PARENT

May be unable to visually monitor her child's attempts, successes, or frustration when trying to put rings on a stick.

1. Refer to 1.58 (Takes ring stack apart).

PHYSICALLY DISABLED PARENT

Who has limited hand control; may have difficulty manipulating rings and stabilizing the ring base.

1. If the parent has tremor, she may be able to stabilize her hand with the adaptations described in 1.63 (Places cylinders in matching holes). Use a short ring stack so the parent does not have to raise her forearms from the table surface.
2. Refer to 1.58 (Takes ring stack apart).

1.65 Child: MOVES TO RHYTHMS (11-12 mo.)
Parent: Provides opportunities for child to hear music and encourages him to move to rhythms

GENERAL GUIDELINES

The child delights in moving his body rhythmically to music. His "dancing" may or may not be in time with the beat of the music. He is displaying his ability to associate the rhythm of music with the rhythm of his body, just as he is learning to associate the melodic rhythm of his vocalizations to express various meanings.

DEAF PARENT

May not have experienced auditory rhythms, and may be unaware of her child's enjoyment of music.

1. Help the parent select musical toys, a radio, a tape recorder, record player, and records for her child.
2. Mark the appropriate setting for volume control to the child's listening comfort on record and cassette players and radios.
3. Model rocking and dancing with the child to music and encourage the parent to take the lead role. Point out the child's distinctive visual cues and movements used during various types of music.
4. Put different markers on the records or cassette tapes as visual cues to indicate fast, medium, or slow rhythms for the parent.
5. Suggest T.V. shows, such as teen-age dance programs and exercise shows which provide good visual cues of rhythms for the parent.
6. The parent can feel rhythm vibrations when touching the tape recorder, record player, and stereo speakers. Some tape recorders have needles which move to particular rhythms. The parent can use both as cues for moving to rhythms with her child.
7. Stereo speakers placed on uncarpeted floors help the parent feel vibrations when barefoot. She can then "dance" with her child.
8. The parent can make her own rhythms to dance with her child using a toy drum, tamborine, shake toys, or household items, such as spoons and pots, or by tapping on tables:
   a. Encourage the parent to model movements with her child when making rhythms.

b. If necessary help the parent identify various sound producing objects and actions, and monitor them for sounds which are too loud for her child.

BLIND PARENT

May be unable to visually monitor her child's movements to rhythms.

1. The parent can play lots of body-on-body rhythmic games, such as swaying and gently bouncing to music while her child is on her lap.
2. The parent can hear her child's rhythmic sounds if he wears tightly secured bells on his belt or on a wrist band.

1.66 Child: IMITATES SEVERAL NEW GESTURES (11-14 mo.)
   Parent: Models and encourages child to imitate combining two familiar gestures

GENERAL GUIDELINES

When two gestures which are familiar to the child are combined, they become a "new" gesture. These combined gestures are called "complex gestures." For example, if the child stirs a spoon in a cup and at other times pretends to drink from a cup, these two actions (stirring, then drinking) can be combined for the child to copy.

Parents can provide verbal prompts and modeling of the combined actions simultaneously with her child to help him during the learning process. Singing games with repetitive gestures, such as "Pat-A-Cake," "Wheels on the Bus," and "This Is the Way We . . ." help their child learn complex gestures in a fun way. Refer to 1.42 (Imitates familiar, then new gestures) which is a prerequisite to this skill.

MENTALLY RETARDED PARENT

May expect her child to imitate gestures which are too difficult.

1. Clearly explain to the parent which gestures her child can learn to copy. The explanation and activities for 1.42 (Imitates familiar, then new gestures) can be expanded to combining two simple gestures.
2. Demonstrate several singing gesture games and let the parent select one or two she already knows or wants to learn to play with her child:
   a. If the song's traditional gestures are too difficult for the child, replace them with simpler ones.
   b. Coincide the song with a musical rhyme radio, if available.
3. Stress and model for the parent gentle handling and movements when playing gesture song games with her child.
4. Refer to 5.19 (Repeats enjoyable activities).

DEAF PARENT

May use an abundance of gestures for sign language, however, may be unaware of fun children's gestural games; may also be unaware that gestures can activate sounds which help her child associate and remember them during imitation games.

1. Explain how gestural games with accompanying songs such as "Pat-A-Cake," "Row, Row, Row Your Boat," and "Wheels on the Bus" help her child learn to imitate new gestures; hearing the words and the tune helps him remember what gestures to make:
   a. Write out the words for several singing gesture games of parent's choice and child's level of gestures.
   b. Teach the parent the matching gestures.
   c. If the parent is non-verbal, a verbal sibling or adult can sing during these games, or provide cassettes, records, or a musical radio with rhymes which match the gestures.
2. Demonstrate and explain that banging, hitting, or shaking gestures make sounds which help her child learn to imitate the gestures and the sound.
3. If the parent uses sign language, she can select and teach her child a few simple signs to imitate. Help the parent select signs which match her child's receptive and fine motor development, explaining that some signs would be too difficult to copy at this age.

BLIND PARENT

May have difficulty identifying which gestures her child uses, and may be unable to recognize if or when the gesture is imitated.

1. Refer to 1.42 (Imitates familiar, then new gestures) if the parent has not been introduced to how her child learns to imitate gestures.
2. The parent can sing gestural games with her child, especially those involving clapping, stomping, or other "noisy" gestures which provide auditory cues for her to monitor her child's gestures.

PHYSICALLY DISABLED PARENT

With limited upper extremity control; may have difficulty modeling gestures for her child to imitate.

1. Refer to 1.42 (Imitates familiar, then new gestures).

1.67 Child: HANDS TOY BACK TO ADULT (12-15 mo.)
   Parent: Activates action toy and encourages child to give it back after it stops to reactivate

GENERAL GUIDELINES

The child has learned that since an adult has caused an action toy to activate, she is the best person to restart the toy. He purposefully hands it back to the adult, using her as a resource after determining that the task is too difficult to do alone. Parents can use a variety of mechanical wind-up toys, friction toys, bubbles to blow, and pop-up toys with their child to encourage this skill.

1.67

MENTALLY RETARDED PARENT

May restart the toy before her child has had a chance to hand it to her, or may expect him to be able to restart it independently.

1. Explain to the parent that, at this age, her child is still not ready to start most action toys by himself and he knows it. But, he has learned or is learning that an adult can, so he hands it back:
   a. Praise how "smart" he is to be learning to figure out that this is the easiest way to re-start the toy.
   b. Stress that when her child hands a toy back to the parent, he is saying, "Start it again!"
2. Model activating a toy, stopping it or waiting for it to stop, and then waiting for her child to hand it back:
   a. Emphasize giving the child enough time before restarting the toy so he can try to do it himself and/or give it back to the adult. Stress never to take the toy away while he's trying to figure it out.
   b. Demonstrate verbal and gestural prompts to encourage her child to hand the toy back if he seems confused or ready to "give up." Describe aloud the child's signals which tell us to help, e.g., "He's just looking at the toy and then at me; it's time for me to show him what to do."
3. Let the parent practice activating a toy and waiting for her child to hand it back. Provide verbal prompts as needed to insure proper pacing.

BLIND PARENT

May be unaware of her child's non-verbal signs of confusion if he is unsure of how to restart the toy.

1. If the parent does not feel her child handing the toy back to her, or does not hear his manual guiding of the toy, explain that her outstretched hand, coupled with a verbal prompt, helps him know to give it back to her.

PHYSICALLY DISABLED PARENT

With upper extremity limitations; may have difficulty activating and reactivating toys.

1. Refer to 1.50 (Guides action on toy manually).

1.68   Child: ENJOYS MESSY ACTIVITIES SUCH AS FINGERPAINTING (12-18 mo.)
Parent: Understands the importance of, and provides opportunities for, child to play with messy activities, such as fingerpainting

MENTALLY RETARDED PARENT

May restrict, or become frustrated with, play activities which are messy for her child.

1. Introduce messy play activities, such as fingerpainting, with the parent and child in a fun relaxing environment. A small parent-child group setting is recommended:
   a. Make clear comments about how much fun the activity is and that it's okay to be messy sometimes.
   b. Point out the child's behaviors which indicate he is learning from and enjoying the activity, e.g., "He's learning about color, seeing he can make pictures, and learning how paints can feel."
   c. Gradually encourage the parent to participate in messy activities with her child. Reinforce all parent participation and remark how her child especially likes it when she fingerpaints with him.
2. Provide or help the parent find materials, such as plastic sheets, for the floor at home to facilitate easy clean up. If necessary, teach parent how to wipe it off, fold, and store safely when not in use.
3. Provide or help the parent find old shirts for herself and the child.
4. Suggest places at home which facilitate easy clean up, e.g., fingerpainting with soap suds or shaving cream in the tub, outside, on the porch, or in a small rubber pool.
5. Remind and help the parent select, if necessary, *only* non-toxic paints, fingerpaints, etc. Explain why she must supervise these types of activities.

BLIND PARENT

May not understand the benefits of messy play for her child as may have learned to highly value environmental order to facilitate mobility.

1. Discuss the learning benefits of messy play for young children, e.g., increases tactile awareness, encourages use of hands, etc.
2. Help the parent identify ways to accommodate her child's messy play activities:
   a. Suggest places in or out of the home where messy play activities would be easiest to clean up, such as the kitchen table, bathtub, back patio, porch, or an empty baby pool.
   b. Help the parent select "old clothes" for herself and her child which would be suitable for messy play. Weather permitting, suggest allowing her child to play with paints while he is only wearing diapers.
3. Suggest parent and child positions which facilitate positive interactions, parent demonstration, and parental monitoring during messy activities. The parent could sit directly next to the child, or directly behind him with the child sitting between the parent's legs.
4. Help the parent select suitable and safe non-toxic materials for messy play:
   a. The colors of paints or dough could be brailled on the labels of the jars, or another coding system devised by the parent, to aid in the identification of the containers, e.g., one rubber band = red and 2 = blue.
   b. Use pudding, unsweetened Jello, or Cool Whip for "painting" alternatives to help the parent who cannot visually monitor her child's mouthing or clean up. These materials are very tactile when the parent is washing up. Explain which colors (flavors) are the messiest, advising vanilla pudding or lemon or lime

Jello, rather than chocolate pudding or strawberry Jello which may stain.
5. Relate the child's facial expressions and hand motions during fingerpainting and describe what he has "painted."

1.69 Child: REACTS TO VARIOUS SENSATIONS SUCH AS EXTREMES IN TEMPERATURE AND TASTE (12-18 mo.)
Parent: Exposes, and remarks to child about various temperature and taste sensations; recognizes his reaction responses

GENERAL GUIDELINES

The child clearly displays his likes and dislikes to tastes and extremes in temperature using exaggerated adult facial expressions.

Children should not be forced to eat foods with new tastes or dishes with mixed flavors, or long term feeding problems can occur. Instead, parents can introduce new and varied tastes by letting the child lick the spoon while she's cooking and offering small amounts in his dish to experiment with during mealtime.

The child is also learning the concepts of hot, cold, sweet, and bitter. Parents can describe these temperature and taste adjectives to help him attach verbal meaning to his perceptions during daily activities.

MENTALLY RETARDED PARENT

May not interpret her child's reactions to various sensations, and may not vary her child's taste or temperature experiences.

1. Explore with the parent, yours and the parent's own feelings and reactions to extreme temperatures and taste. Prompt with questions, such as "How does it feel if you walk outside barefoot and it's snowing?" and "What's it like when you taste a lemon?":
   a. Help describe the specific feeling or sensation, e.g., "It feels cold," "I tingle inside," or "It tastes sour; my mouth feels puckery."
   b. Role-play the facial expressions or bodily reactions we may have to these specific situations, e.g., raised eyebrows and mouth opened wide to sudden cold.
2. Relate that children at this age also experience many feelings and sensations to different temperatures and tastes, and they react with many of the same facial expressions and body movements that we use:
   a. Ask the parent if she can think of times when she has seen her child react to the taste or temperature of something.
   b. Ask how she knew her child liked it or did not like the taste or temperature.
3. Name specific situations during which the parent can provide her child with extra sensation experiences, e.g.:
   a. Touching snow, ice, and warm clothes out of a dryer (being cautious to check that clothes do not have any metal, such as zippers or snaps, which can burn him).
   b. Tasting sweet and sour food, such as pineapple chunks and lemons.
4. Explain that when she tells him the word for how things taste or feel to him, she is teaching him to understand what these words mean:
   a. Help the parent think of times she can tell her child "Oh, that's cold!" and "Ow, that's hot!"
   b. Help the parent think of foods or drinks the child has about which she can say "Mm, that's sweet," or "That's sour!"
5. Clearly describe the child's bodily and facial reactions to temperature and taste sensations as they occur. Ask the parent to tell you what he is "saying" when her child gasps, spits out the food, or smiles.

BLIND PARENT

May be unaware of her child's facial reactions to various sensations.

1. Explain that young children display facial expression changes similar to adults as a reaction to extremes in temperature and tastes. Concretely describe the various common facial expressions used with extreme sensations, e.g., wrinkled up nose and furrowed eyebrows to distasteful foods, or raised eyebrows and open mouth to hot or cold temperatures.
2. Describe to the parent her child's facial expression reactions as they occur to various sensations. The parent can recognize her child's concurrent audible and bodily responses and label the corresponding taste or temperature descriptions for her child, e.g., "You really shivered; it's so cold!"

PHYSICALLY DISABLED PARENT

Who has impaired sensory input; may have difficulty recognizing which temperatures are too extreme for her child.

1. The parent can practice the same methods with her child that she uses to protect herself against extreme temperature exposures, e.g., knowing that ovens, curling irons, etc. should not be touched; using a submersible thermometer to test bath water.

1.70 Child: SHOWS UNDERSTANDING OF COLOR AND SIZE (12-18 mo.)
Parent: Emphasizes primary colors and contrasting size during daily activities

GENERAL GUIDELINES

The child explores the relationship between sizes and shapes of objects and becomes more aware of their colors. He tries to place rings on a stick from largest to smallest and practices nesting cans. He may play with his red ball, but ignore his blue one. He looks at shape boxes curiously and tries to match the various shape blocks in their respective holes, even though he may only be successful with the cylindrical ones at first.

1.70

Parents help foster their child's size, shape, and color awareness by pointing out and providing him with the word labels that describe these properties of familiar objects during daily activities.

MENTALLY RETARDED PARENT

May not use color or size descriptors in her conversation during daily activities.

1. Explain to the parent that, around this age, children begin to have favorite colors:
   a. Tell the parent your favorite color(s), ask if she has favorite colors, and then ask if she thinks her child has favorite colors.
   b. Explain that although her child likes different colors, he does not know what their names are yet.
2. Tell the parent that she can teach her child to learn the names of different colors by telling him the name of colors:
   a. Model, and encourage the parent to think of, specific short phrases to say which use a color name for familiar toys, food, and clothing, e.g., "See your red ball," or "Look at your blue shirt."
   b. Name specific daily situations for the parent to name the colors of things within phrases she says to her child, e.g., when dressing her child, she can tell him the colors of his clothing; or when eating, she can name the colors of his food.
3. During your intervention sessions with the parent and child:
   a. Verbally prompt the parent to name the colors of various toys or materials with which she and her child are involved.
   b. Praise all of the parent's spontaneous color labeling to her child, remarking how she is teaching him the names of colors.
4. Make a different color box each week with the parent:
   a. Label the box as red (or blue, yellow, etc.) using a red marker or red square of construction paper.
   b. Select various household objects or pictures of objects to keep in the box.
   c. The parent can use the color boxes during special play times with her child to name the colors for him.
5. Introduce incorporating the size labels of "big" and "little" into the parent's descriptions as you see her incorporating colors into her daily conversations with her child:
   a. Adapt Activity Nos. 2 and 3, substituting the labels of "big" and "little."
   b. Give the parent a concrete reference for which things to call "big" and which things to call "little." Relate that things which are bigger than her child should be called "big" and things which are smaller than her hand can be called "little."

BLIND PARENT

May not be able to visually discriminate color, and may be unaware of her child's color preferences.

1. Anticipatory Guidance: People who are blind usually have been exposed to the concept of colors and their role as an important descriptive property, and will have developed tactile marking systems for identifying colors.
2. Explain the child's expanding interest and understanding of colors, sizes, and shapes. Monitor and describe her child's color preferences with toys and food:
   a. Relate how the parent's naming of colors during daily activities for her child helps him learn to attach the name label with his visual impression of the color.
   b. Discuss various household items, toys, things outside the window, etc., which are meaningful to the child and identify their colors as needed.

1.71 Child: PLACES ROUND PIECE IN FORMBOARD (12-15 mo.)
Parent: Encourages child to place round piece in a formboard

GENERAL GUIDELINES

A circle is the easiest piece for the child to place in a formboard or shape puzzle because there are no angles to match. When children place or attempt to place circle pieces in their corresponding places, they are demonstrating cognitive matching skills. If a child has fine-motor impairments or difficulties, adapt the board, pieces, or positioning of the board and child as prescribed by a therapist; refer to general guidelines for 1.57 (Removes round piece from formboard); and praise the child for his matching intent regardless of his exact placement of the circle. Matching colors of shapes to the color of their place of insertion provides the child with extra matching cues.

MENTALLY RETARDED PARENT

May expect her child to insert all shapes into the formboard.

1. Introduce formboard activities to the parent as described in 1.57 (Removes round piece from formboard), adapting for the circle's insertion rather than removal.
2. Show the parent why round objects are the easiest to insert:
   a. Demonstrate with a formboard that there is only one possible rotation to match a circle to a circle, but there are a few possible rotations with a triangle, and the triangle corners are more difficult to fit.
   b. Let the parent experience the difference between inserting a circle and a more complicated shape (e.g., star, octagon) in a more complicated commercial shape box.
3. Help the parent select various household items which are suitable for shape matching activities, e.g., putting spools or baby food jar lids into cut out round holes on milk cartons or coffee cans.
4. Model, and let the parent practice, encouraging her child to match circles in formboard toys. Stress, through demonstration and prompts to the parent, the following concepts:
   a. Let her child try to figure it out all by himself.
   b. Give her child verbal descriptions, prompts, and praise.

c. It's okay if her child does not let go of the piece after matching it to the hole.
d. Only give her child the circle pieces for matching; the other shapes may frustrate him.
e. Position the board within her child's easy reach and visual field.
f. Change the activity when her child stops playing with the formboard, looks toward and whines for other toys, or moves away from the activity.

BLIND PARENT

May be unable to visually monitor her child's interactions with the formboard.

1. Refer to 1.57 (Removes round piece from formboard).
2. Relate how just as it is tactually easier to match a round piece in a formboard, circles are easier for her child to match visually. First he learns through tactual trial and error, but soon he learns to recognize where a shape goes by matching their visual cues.

PHYSICALLY DISABLED PARENT

With limited hand or upper extremity control; may be unable to manipulate formboard pieces for demonstration.

1. Refer to 1.57 (Removes round piece from formboard) to adapt materials.
2. The child's receptive language abilities at this developmental age may enable the parent to omit demonstration and rely upon her verbal encouragement and directions.

1.72 Child: NESTS TWO THEN THREE CANS (12-19 mo.)
Parent: Provides various sized round containers, and encourages child to "nest" them: first two, then three containers

GENERAL GUIDELINES

Nesting involves putting a smaller container into a larger one. Nesting fosters the child's understanding of spatial and size-relationship concepts. Round containers are easier to nest than square ones, such as boxes, because the child does not have to negotiate rotations to make them "fit." Various sized cans, plastic cups, and aerosol spray can covers are suitable for nesting. The greater the contrast in size between the two containers, the easier it is for the child.

MENTALLY RETARDED PARENT

May interfere with her child's trial and error attempts while learning to nest cans.

1. Demonstrate, and let the parent, "nest" cans while explaining the skills involved. Stress during demonstration and explanation:
a. Her child is learning that small containers fit into larger containers.
b. He learns this by giving him the right kind of containers, showing him how to do it, and then by letting him practice it all by himself.
c. It's okay to make mistakes; sometimes he may try to put the big can into the little can, and when it doesn't fit, it helps him learn to try it other ways.
d. He should only be given two cans at a time to nest until he puts them together easily; then he'll be ready for three.
2. Help the parent select safe nesting cups and cans among household objects. Point out the discriminating features which make them suitable for nesting: cylindrical shape, no sharp edges, contrasting sizes, and unbreakable.
3. Let the parent introduce a nesting activity with her child using two nesting cups. Provide the parent reinforcement and prompts to assure she:
a. Does not interrupt her child's attempts.
b. Describes the activity to her child and gives him verbal reinforcement and praise. If needed, suggest specific phrases to say.
c. Provides additional demonstration when her child signals he wants help. Describe her child's signals as they occur, e.g., "He's handing it to you," or "He's looking at you for help."
d. Stops the activity when the child has had enough.
4. As the child becomes proficient with nesting two cans, show the parent how to introduce a third can following the same guidelines already suggested. Help her anticipate additional problems her child may encounter, e.g., "If her child puts the second can in the first can backwards, he can't fit the third one in, but that's okay; don't do it for him until he has tried to fix it two times."

BLIND PARENT

May benefit from tactual cues to help her quickly determine graduated order of containers for nesting.

1. Suggest various household items which are suitable for nesting, but not typically found nested by the parent, e.g., aerosol spray can covers, cups, bowls, etc. of various sizes.
2. Ask the parent to suggest a "Marking" method to help her quickly identify subtle size differences in commercial nesting cups, e.g., she could make identifying notches with a nailfile on the rims of 3 various sized round plastic containers: one notch = largest, 2 notches = middle sized, and 3 = smallest.
3. Use various sized containers which are tactually different, e.g., plastic cup (largest), styrofoam (middle sized), and paper cup (smallest).

1.73 Child: UNDERSTANDS POINTING (12-14 mo.)
Parent: Points to objects and interprets child's pointing

GENERAL GUIDELINES

The child interprets other people's pointing gestures as meaning he should look toward something. He also uses the pointing gesture himself as a means for communicating "Look," "What's that?", "I want that!", or in response to a question, such as "Where is your ball?"

1.73

MENTALLY RETARDED PARENT

May not point, or may point in an ambiguous manner without clear verbal direction to her child.

1. Role-play with the parent ambiguous and unambiguous pointing situations. First, point using a "flick of the hand" which scans a large area saying, "See that," and ask the parent at what she thinks you wanted her to look. Next, point directly at something saying, "See the pretty curtains":
    a. Discuss with the parent the reasons why the second statement was easier to understand.
    b. Relate how confusing it must be for her child if we don't point clearly, and name the object.
2. Name daily situations which are good times for the parent to point things out and name them to her child. Examples include point to pictures in a book, point to and describe animals and big trucks when you are out for a walk, and point to and name people when they come inside. Ask the parent to think of some more good things to point out and name for her child.
3. Explain that as soon as her child learns what pointing means, he may start pointing, too:
    a. Demonstrate the ways her child may point according to his motoric abilities.
    b. Tell the parent to name the things he's pointing at since he can't always say the word by himself yet.
4. Explain that sometimes it's hard, at this age, for children to stick only one finger out to point. Demonstrate specific activities which help her child's finger muscles learn to point, e.g., poking his index finger in plastic soda bottles, empty egg cartons, or your gently closed fist. Caution the parent never to "make" her child's finger point.
5. Interpret for the parent the different things her child may be saying when he points, e.g., "I want something" or "Look at that, Dad!"

DEAF PARENT

May misinterpret her child's pointing gestures if she cannot hear his accompanying vocal inflections.

1. Explain to the parent that her child uses pointing to say, "What's that?", "Look at that!", and "I want that," and he may vocalize using different inflections to help define what he means.
2. Help the parent interpret her child's pointing intentions when he spontaneously points. The parent can then watch for her child's discriminatory facial expressions, dependent upon his pointing intentions.

BLIND PARENT

May not use pointing as a communicative gesture, and may be unaware of her child's pointing gestures.

1. If the parent is not observed to use pointing gestures, explain the communicative power of pointing to children at this age. If she is interested in using this gesture with her child, concretely describe or physically assist the parent with the pointing posture:
    a. The parent can use contextual and auditory cues as guides for out-of-reach objects toward which to point.
    b. She could touch objects close at hand with a pointed finger.
    c. Name various things that can be seen from different windows in her home, so the parent can point and name them with her child.
2. Describe and interpret for the parent her child's pointing gestures as they occur.
3. NOTE: The child will probably learn to use his own alternative methods for calling his parent's attention to an event. He can still learn his "pointing power" with others in the environment.

1.74 Child: PULLS STRING HORIZONTALLY TO OBTAIN TOY (12-13 mo.)
Parent: Demonstrates, and provides opportunities for child to obtain objects and toys by pulling a string horizontally

GENERAL GUIDELINES

The child purposefully pulls a string attached to a toy horizontally to obtain a toy which is out of reach. This skill demonstrates the child's ability to problem-solve; he is using the string as a "means" to attain a goal, in this case a desired object. If the child has limited fine motor control or grasp, large beads should be tied on the end of the string, or large loops can be slipped over his hand.

There are many commercial pull-toys which parents can use to demonstrate and encourage their child to pull. Various ribbons and thick strings or cords which are 15-24" long can also be tied to the child's existing toys or interesting objects around the home. Toys which make sounds or visual spectacles (e.g., toy dogs which wiggle, toy birds which flap their wings when pulled) provide the child additional encouragement to learn this skill.

MENTALLY RETARDED PARENT

May not have toys with strings attached.

1. As the child approaches this cognitive developmental age, explain to the parent that children at this stage like toys which have strings attached. Ask her to select a few of her child's favorite toys on which to tie ribbons or heavy strings:
    a. Help the parent judge an appropriate length for the string.
    b. Caution the parent never to let her child sleep with these toys because he could get tangled up in them and possibly choke.
    c. Let the child watch his parent tie the strings on a few of his toys.
2. Explain to the parent that her child is learning that he can get the toy more easily if he pulls the string rather than moving to get it. Demonstrate this concept by placing an object at the end of a table with an attached string near the parent's hand and let her retrieve it.

3. Demonstrate the appropriate placement of the toy and string in relation to her child, and how to attract his attention to pull it. If the child does not pull the toy toward himself:
   a. Probe with the parent the possible reasons and adjust as appropriate.
   b. Probing questions can include: Is the toy out of sight? Is the string out of reach for her child? Is her child distracted? Is the string too difficult for him to pick up? Does her child like the toy? Is the string more interesting than the toy right now?
   c. Explain not to physically make her child pull the string; he'll do it when he's ready.
4. Stress to the parent that it is very important to let her child have the toy to play with after he's worked so hard to try to get it. Explain that he'll feel teased and won't want to try anymore if he doesn't get to play with it.

BLIND PARENT

May not be able to visually monitor her child's attempts or successes in securing an object by pulling its string.

1. If the parent is unaware of the visual-motor process underlying this problem-solving skill, refer to Activity No. 1, 1.47 (Retrieves object using other materials).
2. Use noise-making toys with strings attached. The parent can aurally monitor her child's successes and attempts after placing the string in his hand.
3. The parent can position her child on her lap and tactually monitor his arm movements during his attempts to pull a string to reach his toy.
4. Attach beads to the string or use heavier cord to help the parent locate them when they are dropped.
5. Describe the child's facial expressions and gestures which signal his interest, frustration, and delight during his learning process.

PHYSICALLY DISABLED PARENT

Who has difficulty grasping; may not be able to grasp a string to demonstrate obtaining a toy.

1. Put loops at the end of thick strings. The parent can slip her thumb, finger, or entire hand through to demonstrate pulling the toy on a string for her child.
2. Attach a large bead on the end of the string.

1.75 Child: MAKES DETOURS TO RETRIEVE OBJECTS (12-18 mo.)
Parent: Sets up situations, and encourages child to make detours to retrieve objects

GENERAL GUIDELINES

The child figures out the easiest route to obtain a toy that has moved behind an obstacle. For example, if a ball rolls under a chair and out the back, he goes around the chair rather than trying to crawl under it.

MENTALLY RETARDED PARENT

May retrieve the object for her child before he has had a chance to problem-solve.

1. Role-play situations with the parent where a ball has rolled under a coffee table or chair. After the parent retrieves it, ask why she didn't crawl under the table or chair to get it? Relate how her child is learning to figure out that this is the simplest way.
2. Set up a similar situation with the child. Demonstrate and stress the importance of:
   a. Verbally encouraging her child to "go get it!"
   b. Redirecting her child's attention to the task if he becomes distracted.
   c. Letting her child play with the object after he's worked so hard to get it.
3. Help the parent anticipate and discriminate specific daily situations which give her child the opportunity to practice figuring out detours, and those which are too difficult or dangerous at this time. For example, if his toy car rolls under and out from the child's playpen or if his cookie drops and rolls under his highchair, she should let him try to get it. But, if the toy rolls behind the wood stove, or a couch that he cannot fit behind, she must get it.
4. As natural "detour" situations arise in your presence, point them out to the parent and remark, "Let's see how he figures this out all by himself." If, however, the detour is obviously too difficult or dangerous, specifically describe the problem and tell the parent to get it for him.

BLIND PARENT

May not be able to visually monitor the path a rolling object takes and thus not discriminate obstacle situations that arise.

1. Describe and explain to the parent the visual-planning skills her child is learning in detour situations.
2. The parent can play a "come and get me" game with her child which sets up a detour situation and allows her to monitor her child's path for getting to her. For example, the parent could crawl under a table and wait on the other side with a favorite toy, encouraging her child to come and get it.
3. Look around the home and name examples of several detour situations that could arise for her child during the day. Describe them as they occur in your presence.
4. Help the parent set up simple detour situations and describe her child's visual planning attempts.

PHYSICALLY DISABLED PARENT

Who uses a wheelchair; can set up obstacle situations using her wheelchair as the obstacle for her child to make a detour around.

1. The parent can push or prop a ball under her wheelchair, and move her wheelchair until the ball is on the other side. She can then verbally and gesturally encourage her child to obtain it by moving around the wheelchair rather than under it.

1.76 Child: LOOKS AT PLACE WHERE BALL ROLLS OUT OF SIGHT (12-13 mo.)
Parent: Encourages child to look for the ball in the place it rolled out of sight; helps him obtain it if needed

GENERAL GUIDELINES

The child observes a ball roll out of sight, and if it does not reappear on the opposite side of a barrier where he has learned to expect it to reappear, or if there is no open side for it to roll out from, he continues to look for at at the point of disappearance. The child is not expected to obtain the object. Example situations include ball rolls under a couch, a bed with a dust ruffle, or between a couch and a wall, but it stops before reaching the other side.

Contrived situations do not need to be set up unless recommended to improve the child's visual pursuit skills. Musical balls and audible wind-up toys provide the child with auditory cues during his searching process.

MENTALLY RETARDED PARENT

May not encourage her child to look for a ball which has rolled out of sight.

1. Demonstrate to the parent rolling ball under a couch or other low barrier, so it stops at some point under the couch and is hidden. Explain that her child is learning to find things that have rolled away and he cannot see them anymore. Emphasize:
   a. Sometimes the ball or toy may be too hard for her child to reach, but she should give him time to look for it before she gets it for him.
   b. If her child did not watch the ball roll under the couch, he will not know it is there; therefore, he will not look for it.
2. Let the parent set up a "ball rolling under the couch situation" with her child, while providing the parent verbal prompts as needed. Demonstrate the importance of verbal praise and gestures to help attract her child's attention to look in the right place.
3. Help the parent think of natural situations which may occur that she can encourage her child to search for the object. Examples may include her child's shoe getting pushed under the bed during dressing, or his cup dropping behind the couch and getting stuck.

DEAF PARENT

May be unaware that sounds from hidden objects rolled out of sight help her child find them.

1. If the child is having difficulty looking toward the place where a ball has rolled out of sight, explain and demonstrate to the parent that a toy which makes sound helps her child recognize where it is.

BLIND PARENT

May be unaware of this visual pursuit skill, and may have difficulty locating the ball after it has moved behind an obstacle.

1. Concretely describe and explain the meaning of this visual pursuit skill as described in the general guidelines.
2. Name natural situations which may arise where something rolls out of her child's sight.
3. The parent can use a *beeper ball** for contrived hiding situations so she can easily retrieve it after she has felt or heard her child's attempts to find it.

PHYSICALLY DISABLED PARENT

With mobility limitations; may have difficulty retrieving hidden objects for her child after he has searched but cannot retrieve it.

1. The parent can set up situations which hide the object, however, the barrier is not too low for her child to crawl under. For example, a ball could roll under a table with a tablecloth which hides the ball. If the child does not search for it, the parent can adjust the cloth momentarily so he can see it.
2. If a toy rolls out of reach for both child and parent during daily activities, the parent can praise her child's searching attempts and remark, "Oh well, we'll wait for Daddy to get it later; let's play with something else."

1.77 Child: RECOGNIZES SEVERAL PEOPLE IN ADDITION TO IMMEDIATE FAMILY (12-18 mo.)
Parent: Facilitates positive interaction between child and other adults beyond the immediate family

GENERAL GUIDELINES

The child indicates his recognition of others by looking toward them, pointing toward them when their name is called, or by their willingness to interact with them with little or no stranger anxiety. Parents should introduce unfamiliar people to their child in a supporting and gradual manner.

MENTALLY RETARDED PARENT

May expect her child to interact with people he does not recognize.

1. Explore with the parent the various people outside of their family that her child seems to know well. Ask the parent how she can tell he knows or recognizes them. Help list the various behaviors her child displays to let us know he recognizes other people, e.g., he looks toward them when their name is called, he likes to play with them, it's okay to let them hold him, etc.
2. Discuss your own and the parent's feelings when meeting someone new for the first time. Relate how her child also has these same feelings, but "having mom around" helps. Tell the parent never to make her child go to a person he doesn't know yet.
3. If the parent is socially isolated, explore community supports to expand the child's and parent's social contacts.

---

*See Glossary.

1.78 Child: FINDS OBJECT HIDDEN BY DISPLACEMENT WHEN TWO SCREENS ARE USED (13-14 mo.)
Parent: Hides object from child by displacement using two screens, if recommended

GENERAL GUIDELINES

The displacement process and guidelines for this skill are identical to 1.62 (Finds object hidden by one screen displacement), except there is now an additional screen available. This screen is not used in any way; it only lays next to the first screen. This additional screen poses higher visual pursuit and memory skills for the child as he now has an extra screen with which to contend. This skill item is usually for evaluation purposes only.

If contrived hidden displacement games have been recommended to encourage this skill, refer to 1.62, modifying the activities to include two screens. Do not move the object from screen to screen, and do not introduce the second screen until the child has mastered the displacement process with one screen.

1.79 Child: PULLS STRING VERTICALLY TO OBTAIN OBJECT (13-15 mo.)
Parent: Demonstrates and encourages child to pull string vertically to obtain a toy

GENERAL GUIDELINES

This problem-solving skill is similar to 1.74 (Pulls string horizontally) in that the child realizes that he can obtain a toy by pulling a string. This time, however, he is expected to pull the string vertically to obtain a toy that has dropped below a barrier and is now out of sight. Thus, he must combine his problem-solving and object permanence skills. For example, the child retrieves a toy which has dropped down from his stroller or highchair by pulling the string to which it is attached.

Toys should be light and easy to pull. Balloons are very attracting for this activity. Parents can bring the toy within the child's sight if he is having difficulty.

Teaching process and methods for parents with disabilities for this skill are similar to 1.74. Refer to those activities and modify so the string is vertical.

1.80 Child: HIDDEN DISPLACEMENT THREE SCREENS (14-15 mo.)
Parent: Hides object from child by displacement using three screens, if recommended

GENERAL GUIDELINES

The displacement process and guidelines for this skill are similar to 1.62 (Finds object hidden by one screen displacement), however, there are now two additional screens available. These additional screens are not used in any way; they only lay next to the first screen which is hiding the object from displacement. The additional screens require higher visual pursuit and memory skills, for the child must contend with two additional screens. This skill item is for evaluation purposes.

If contrived hidden displacement games have been recommended for the child, refer to 1.62, modifying the activities to include three screens. Do not move the object from screen to screen.

Do not attempt this activity until the child has mastered 1.78 (Finds object hidden by displacement when two screens are used).

1.81 Child: HIDDEN DISPLACEMENT TWO SCREENS ALTERNATELY (14-15 mo.)
Parent: Hides an object by displacement, randomly under one of two screens, if recommended

GENERAL GUIDELINES

This skill is similar to 1.78 (Finds object hidden by displacement when two screens are used). There are two screens available, however, this time the parent randomly hides the object under either screen. The child at first may search under each screen. When he consistently uncovers the correct screen first, he is demonstrating the higher visual pursuit process defined for this skill. This skill is for evaluation purposes.

If contrived hidden displacement games have been recommended for the child, refer to 1.62 (Finds object hidden by one screen displacement) for a description of displacement and modify the parent training activities by using two screens alternately.

Do not attempt this activity until the child has mastered 1.80 (Hidden displacement, three screens).

1.82 Child: PATS PICTURES (14-15 mo.)
Parent: Encourages child to pat pictures

GENERAL GUIDELINES

The child becomes more actively involved with pictures and begins to pat them. This is in contrast to previous picture skills where he interacted primarily by looking at them. Parents encourage this skill by providing interesting picture books for her child, and by periodically pointing to and patting the pictures while describing them in meaningful terms for their child. Textured pictures and pictures which squeak if pushed help encourage the child to pat them. At this age, children continue to need to have opportunities to look at or explore books independently.

Refer to 1.44 (Looks at pictures one minute when named) for adaptive materials and methods to use with disabled parents. When appropriate, help the parent update her child's picture book collection according to his new interests and the book's "wear and tear."

1.83 Child: HELPS TURN PAGES (14-15 mo.)
Parent: Encourages child to assist while turning pages of a book

MENTALLY RETARDED PARENT

May inhibit her child's efforts to help turn pages because she thinks he will tear them, or may interpret her child's attempts as meaning he is ready to turn pages independently.

1. Explain to the parent that her child is learning to help turn pages of a book. Stress the following concepts during your explanation:
   a. He can't do it all by himself yet.
   b. Helping us turn pages now helps him learn to turn them by himself later.
   c. If he tears the page by accident, that's okay; we can tape it.
   d. If he tears the page on purpose, he's interested in what he can do with paper. Take the book away and give him some paper to play with.
2. Demonstrate, and let parent practice, encouraging her child to assist with page turning. Emphasize:
   a. Slowly separating and lifting the page halfway.
   b. Waiting until the child is ready to turn the page; if he is still looking at a picture, we must wait.
   c. Gently prompting her child's hand to help turn the page if he doesn't try after saying, "Turn the page, Susie; help turn the page." (This gives the parent a concrete time guide to help determine how long she should wait.)
3. Use books with pages which do not tear if the parent continues to prevent her child's attempts to help turn pages.
4. Refer to 1.44 (Looks at pictures one minute when named).

PHYSICALLY DISABLED PARENT

Who has limited grasp or upper extremity control; may have difficulty helping her child turn pages.

1. Refer to 1.44 (Looks at pictures one minute when named).

1.84 Child: IMITATES "INVISIBLE" GESTURE (14-17 mo.)
Parent: Imitates one of child's invisible gestures, encouraging him to imitate it again

GENERAL GUIDELINES

An "invisible" gesture is one that the child cannot see himself make. Head shaking, nose wrinkling, eye blinking, and various mouth movements are examples of invisible gestures. These are usually more difficult to imitate than gestures the child can see himself perform.

The invisible gestures chosen for imitation activities should at first be those which the child has already been observed to use during play or communication. The activities should be fun and spontaneous.

Imitating in front of a mirror, using exaggerated gestures, and pairing gestures with simple singing movement games may facilitate the child's imitation attempts.

MENTALLY RETARDED PARENT

May confuse invisible with visible gestures.

1. After explaining that an invisible gesture is one that her child cannot see himself perform, demonstrate an example. Ask the parent to think of more, prompting as needed.
2. If the parent confuses visible from invisible gestures, this will not interfere with her child's learning; he will just have experiences with both. Do not force the issue; the important thing will be to keep imitation games fun.
3. Refer to 1.42 (Imitates familiar, then new gestures) for imitation teaching strategies with parent.

BLIND PARENT

May not be able to visually monitor her child's gestures.

1. Refer to 1.42 (Imitates familiar, then new gestures) if the rationale and explanation of imitating gestures has not been reviewed with the parent.
2. Name the invisible gestures her child uses during play and communication. The parent can select her child's audible invisible gestures to imitate and monitor for imitation games, e.g., lip smacking, sniffing nose, and coughing.

1.85 Child: MATCHES OBJECTS (15-19 mo.)
Parent: Points out familiar objects in the environment which match to the child

GENERAL GUIDELINES

The child is able to identify which object from two or three different ones is identical to the object he is holding. For example, if the child is holding a spoon and there is a spoon and a napkin in front of him, he selects the spoon when asked to "get another one." He may pick the matching spoon up, or put his spoon on top of the other one.

The matching objects should be simple and familiar to the child and be identical in size, shape, and color.

The contrasting objects, which he is choosing from, should at first be different in size, shape, color, and function from the matching objects. These contrasts can be gradually reduced.

Children learn about matching concepts when others point out meaningful matching objects in their environment and describe them. Contrived matching situations do not need to be set up unless recommended to improve the child's matching concepts.

MENTALLY RETARDED PARENT

May become too task-oriented during matching exercises, which may lead to the parent's and child's frustration.

1. If the parent has demonstrated rigid task-focused interactions during previous sessions, do not introduce this activity within a controlled learning situation. Instead, explain that her child likes to find things that look just alike:
   a. Give examples of things that are the "same," e.g., "He likes to see that one of his shoes looks just like his other one," and "His spoon looks like mom's spoon."

b. Ask the parent to think of other things that are the same that her child likes to see. Prompt the parent to think of matching objects using toy, food, utensil, and clothing categories as a framework for discussion.
c. Demonstrate and encourage the parent to show and describe various things around their home that are just alike to her child.

BLIND PARENT

May have difficulty selecting objects for matching games which are visually the same, e.g., same color and same print; may not be able to visually monitor if her child has selected the matching object when asked.

1. Explain that her child is learning to match objects by comparing how they look. Use a tactual analogy, such as "Just as you can recognize when objects are the same by feeling and comparing their texture, shape, weight, and size, your child is learning to compare things that are the same. In addition to feeling them, he is learning to compare and match objects in size, shape, and color by only looking at them."
2. If needed, monitor objects selected for matching activities to assure they are visually identical in color or other visual design.
3. The parent can recognize if her child has selected the correct matching object by feeling which object is left, or by requesting that her child give it to her.
4. The parent can recognize and help her child as needed to match body parts with each other. She can touch his hand and say, "Find Mommy's hand."

1.86 Child: PLACES SQUARE PIECE IN FORMBOARD (15-21 mo.)
  Parent: Encourages child to place square pieces in formboard

GENERAL GUIDELINES

The child displays his maturing spatial awareness and shape discrimination abilities as he is able to place a square piece in a shape puzzle. He learns proper placement through trial and error as he learns to negotiate fitting the corners of the square into the board.

The child should be able to remove the circle and square pieces from the formboard, and be able to insert the circle piece before expecting him to place the square piece in the board. The circle and square board openings and pieces should be the only ones available to the child while he is learning these shapes.

Circle and square formboards can be made out of sturdy cardboard, or commercial formboards can be covered so only the circle and square pieces are available.

Refer to 1.57 (Removes round piece from formboard) and 1.71 (Places round piece in formboard) for guidelines and activities to accommodate parental disabilities, adapting to teach their child to place squares in the formboard.

1.87 Child: INDICATES TWO OBJECTS FROM GROUP OF FAMILIAR OBJECTS (15-18 mo.)
  Parent: Asks child to select two objects from a group of three to five familiar objects during daily activities

GENERAL GUIDELINES

The child is able to point to, pick up, or give two named objects from a group of five. He demonstrates not only his receptive understanding of the word labels, but also his ability to remember two labels.

The objects must be familiar and already within his receptive vocabulary. The child should initially be presented with only two or three objects before expanding his choices to five. Asking for related objects helps the child remember which ones were requested, e.g., a cup and spoon, or his shoes and socks.

Parents can request two objects during their child's daily activities without setting up contrived situations. If the child does not respond, the parent can pick up both objects and name them for him.

MENTALLY RETARDED PARENT

May expect her child to select objects which are not in his receptive vocabulary.

1. Review and explain the child's current receptive vocabulary. Refer to Activity Nos. 1-3, 1.48 (Listens selectively to familiar words) and update the child's "word list" with the parent.
2. Explain that her child is learning to remember two objects from his word lists if we ask him to show us two. Stress that if we ask her child to select two objects, he must understand what they are and be able to see them.
3. Demonstrate playing a "give-me" game with the child:
  a. Have the parent gather five objects from her child's word list.
  b. Start out presenting her child with two objects and asking him to "give me" one of them. Gradually introduce the remaining objects asking him to give you two at a time.
  c. Model short clear requests and praise.
  d. Model showing the child the correct objects if he does not respond, or gives you an incorrect object.
  e. Describe her child's behaviors which indicate whether he is confused or understands, e.g., eye pointing, or looking in another direction.
4. Let the parent practice the "give-me" game with her child as you provide verbal prompts and reinforcement to the parent.
5. Name specific daily activities that the parent can ask her child to give her two familiar objects, such as after eating she can say, "Give me your cup and spoon." Role-play this specific situation with the parent. Stress that if he does not give them to her, she should:
  a. Point to the cup and spoon and put her hand out.
  b. Then pick up the cup and spoon and say, "Here's your cup and spoon," and try again at the next meal.

1.87

DEAF PARENT

May be unaware of her child's expanding receptive verbal vocabulary.

1. Update the child's "word list" generated in 1.48 (Listens selectively to familiar words) to include his new receptive vocabulary. If the parent uses sign language, let her circle the words her child can understand in sign language.
2. Relate that her child is learning to remember two of the objects on his word list at a time, providing concrete examples.
3. If the parent uses sign language she can begin to sign two objects at a time within a request from her child's list. Encourage the parent to couple any speech she may have with the signs.

BLIND PARENT

May be unaware of her child's non-verbal signs for indicating two objects.

1. Describe to the parent her child's physical indicators of understanding two object requests, e.g., shifting his eye gaze, pointing, or touching.
2. The parent can determine her child's responses to two object requests when she asks her child to give them to her.
3. Explain that, at this age, it is important that her child can see both objects that the parent names and that the two objects should not be with more than three other objects at a time.

1.88 Child: **BRINGS OBJECTS FROM ANOTHER ROOM ON REQUEST (15-18 mo.)**
Parent: Asks child to get a familiar object from another room

GENERAL GUIDELINES

The child's increasing memory and object permanence skills enable him to bring familiar objects from another room on request. The child should be able to bring a requested object that is in the same room before he can be expected to get an object from another room. The object must be familiar and kept in a familiar place of the room within easy reach of the child. If the child becomes distracted "en route," the parent can repeat the request and follow it up with physical guidance to the child as needed.

MENTALLY RETARDED PARENT

May expect her child to carry out requests which are developmentally too difficult.

1. Explain to the parent that her child is ready to learn to get one thing at a time from another room when asked, but there are three important things she must remember before asking him to do that: he must know what the object is, he must know where it is usually kept, and he must be able to reach it:

   a. Review the objects that her child understands the meaning for from the child's "word list," and refer to 1.48 (Listens selectively to familiar words).
   b. Circle the objects on the list which are kept in a typical place, and which the child can reach.
   c. Make a new list (using picture cues as needed) of the objects her child can learn to get from another room.

2. Model, and let the parent practice, asking her child to get an object on the new word list from another room. Stress the following concepts during demonstration and parent practice:
   a. Use short direct phrases.
   b. Provide her child gesture cues and verbal encouragement.
   c. Praise her child if he gets it.
   d. Help her child if he does not get it.

3. Emphasize to the parent that she should never scold her child if he does not get the named object. Explore the possible reasons why her child did not follow through with the request. Use question probes, such as "Did he forget because he started playing with something else?" "Did he hear you say it?" "Was the object in a place that he could find and reach it?"

DEAF PARENT

May be unable to make a clear verbal request.

1. The parent can request objects in her child's receptive sign language vocabulary using signs and gestures coupled with any speech she may have.
2. The parent can play a game of showing her child a picture of a familiar object in another room and gesturing to her child to go get it.

BLIND PARENT

Can auditorily "track" her child's movement to carry out a request.

1. Review objects which are within the child's reach, as needed.

1.89 Child: **TURNS TWO OR THREE PAGES AT A TIME (15-18 mo.)**
Parent: Encourages child to turn pages of a book using his own methods

GENERAL GUIDELINES

The child may push pages of a book a few at a time, go backwards when flipping pages, and not stop to look at the pictures; he is too busy experimenting with how to turn pages than to worry about how to turn them correctly. He also usually does not have the fine motor control needed to turn pages one at a time.

Parents encourage their child to turn pages of a book by providing him with ample exposure to books, and by accepting and praising his own methods of learning. Large books with worn pages and loose bindings are easier for the child to practice.

MENTALLY RETARDED PARENT

May physically manipulate her child to turn pages of a book "just right."

1. Demonstrate for the parent the various methods her child may use when he is first learning to turn pages of a book. Remark that it's okay if he spends more time practicing this than looking at the pictures. Explain that his finger muscles are not ready to turn the pages one at a time yet but this helps him learn.
2. Model, and let the parent practice, giving her child a book to practice turning pages without physically interfering. Let the parent demonstrate for her child how to turn pages with a different book. Suggest short verbal phrases to say to her child, e.g., "Turn the pages; see?" and "Good turning."

1.90 Child: IDENTIFIES SELF IN MIRROR (15-16 mo.)
Parent: Provides numerous opportunities for child to look at self and others playfully in a mirror

GENERAL GUIDELINES

The child has developed an understanding that mirrors reflect exact images but are not the real thing! Several months ago, when he looked into a mirror and saw a toy, he'd reach to the mirror in an attempt to get it. Now when he sees images, he quickly responds by turning to look for them.

With his realization that mirror images are only reflections of what is in front of them, he realizes that the child he sees is himself. He may point to the mirror when asked, "Where's Billy?", or experiment with various bodily gestures.

Parents help their child recognize his mirror image as himself by giving him plenty of opportunities to see himself in mirrors, and by saying his name while pointing to his reflection and then touching the child. "Peek-a-boo" games help make mirror play and identification of self more fun for the child.

MENTALLY RETARDED PARENT

May not recognize mirrors as a "play" vehicle for her child.

1. Describe to the parent the learning benefits and fun her child can have by looking into mirrors, i.e., he learns what he looks like, learns he can make himself look different when he makes silly faces, and he learns that mirrors reflect things he sees.
2. Identify where mirrors are located in the child's house:
   a. Discriminate whether her child can see the mirrors by himself or whether the parent needs to pick him up to see them.
   b. Remind the parent that since she is bigger than he is, she needs to be certain he is lifted high enough to see himself. Demonstrate suitable positions to hold her child in front of the mirror.
   c. Help discriminate which hand-held mirrors are safe for the child to play with alone.
3. Name places at stores the parent goes to which may have mirrors for her to show her child, e.g., meat departments at grocery stores, and dressing rooms at clothing stores.
4. Demonstrate games to play in front of the mirror: "Peek-a-boo," "Kiss the baby," and making silly faces.
5. Stress and model the importance of saying her child's name to him and pointing to his reflection during mirror games so he can learn that the reflection he sees is himself.
6. Ask the parent to think of, and help her find, other household objects which are not mirrors, but will reflect her child's image, such as cookie or pie pans, a spatula, or the bottom of a coffee can.
7. Name specific fun times to let her child look in the mirror to see himself, e.g., when he has a messy face, is wearing mommy's hat, etc.

DEAF PARENT

May not vocalize to her child during mirror activities to promote identification.

1. Encourage the parent to sign her child's name in front of a mirror with him, and then to point to, touch, and hug her child.
2. Suggest signing her child's name within simple phrases, such as "Hi John," and "See John."
3. As the child touches his or the parent's mirror reflection, the parent can reinforce his interest with funny faces, signs, and smiling.

BLIND PARENT

May be unaware of the learning benefits of mirror-play for her child.

1. If the parent is congenitally blind, she may benefit from an explanation regarding the function of mirrors in her child's learning process as described in the general guidelines.
2. If the home does not have mirrors which are accessible to her child, help the parent relocate them if possible in areas which are easily accessible to her child. Full length mirrors could be provided and placed from the floor up.
3. Help orient the parent to positions which assure her child is in view of mirrors hanging in the home.
4. Assist the parent with hanging safe mirrors at her child's eye level in his crib and playpen.
5. Help the parent identify safe toys which have mirrors. Orient the parent to the appropriate distance from her child within his eye level to hold mirrored toys.
6. Name environmental objects which are not mirrors, but reflect images such as toasters, cookie pans, and windows at night.
7. Describe her child's silly faces and gestures he displays when in front of a mirror.

1.91 Child: IDENTIFIES ONE BODY PART (15-19 mo.)
Parent: Emphasizes "important" body parts for child on self, child, dolls, and others during daily activities

GENERAL GUIDELINES

The child indicates he understands a named body part by touching it, looking directly at it, or by moving it.

Body parts which are frequently named during the day and those which are easy to see are usually the easiest body parts for which a child learns the names. Some children can point to body parts on a doll or other people before they point to them on themselves.

MENTALLY RETARDED PARENT

May not discriminate which body parts are meaningful to her child at this age, and may name too many body parts at one time.

1. Help clarify for the parent which body parts are appropriate for her child to learn the names for at this age:
   a. Specify that they should be body parts her child can see on himself or in a mirror, and those that he hears the names for said often during the day.
   b. Give examples of an appropriate and an inappropriate body part for her child to learn its name, explaining why, e.g., "Not elbow because he rarely looks at elbows and people rarely talk about elbows. Mouth is a good body part to learn the name for because he can see it in a mirror and we talk about mouths all of the time, such as 'Take it out of your mouth'."
2. Generate a list with the parent of four meaningful body parts that she can begin teaching her child:
   a. Name daily activities for the parent to name, touch, rub, show, or talk about each body part.
   b. Model specific phrases she can say to help emphasize the part.
   c. Stress only talking about one body part at a time.
   d. Cut out magazine pictures of these important parts and tape a different one on various mirrors as a reminder to emphasize it in the mirror with her child.
   e. Make up simple finger-play songs to play with her child using one body part at a time.
   f. Tell the parent to talk about and point out these parts on herself and on her child.
   g. Demonstrate naming these parts on dolls and animals.
3. Help generate a list of simple requests to ask her child for each of the selected body parts, e.g., "Brush your hair," "Wipe your nose," and "Shake your hands."

DEAF PARENT

May not verbally label body parts to her child.

1. Anticipatory Guidance: Parents who use sign language provide ample experiences for their children to recognize body parts because the sign for body parts is the gesture of touching the body part.
2. Relate to the parent that she can expect her child to begin touching or signing his own body parts and those on a doll in response to her sign.
3. Encourage the parent to couple whatever speech she may have with her sign for meaningful body parts to her child.
4. If the parent does not use speech, tape record simple songs which emphasize different body parts, one body part per song on each cassette side; give the parent the corresponding script. She can initially sign the body part during the song but should gradually withdraw the sign to help assure her child understands the verbal label.

BLIND PARENT

May not be able to visually determine when her child has correctly identified his own body parts, body parts of dolls, or body parts in pictures.

1. For large body parts (arms and legs), put wrist or ankle bands on the child with bells attached which produce distinctively different tones. The parent can then aurally discriminate her child's response to instructions, such as "Shake your leg" or "Shake your arm" during gesture songs and games with her child.
2. When teaching body parts of a doll, the parent could position the doll on her lap. When she gives directions, such as "Touch baby's leg," she can tactually determine if her child has correctly responded by feeling his finger and where it is on the doll.
3. If the child follows commands well, he may be able to guide the parent's finger to the correct body part on the doll, e.g., the parent could say, "Touch the baby's eye with my finger," while offering her pointed finger to the child.
4. When using pictures to teach body parts to her child, the parent may be able to recognize if her child has responded correctly by feeling where his finger is on a raised surface picture. The child may also be able to guide his parent's finger to the raised surface picture in response to her simple command.
5. When teaching the child to identify his own body parts, the parent can feel if her child has touched the correct part after giving him ample response time. She can also offer the child her own open hand or gently closed fist and say, "Show me your nose," "... foot," etc.

1.92 Child: RECOGNIZES AND POINTS TO FOUR ANIMAL PICTURES (16-21 mo.)
Parent: Provides sufficient opportunities for child to see animals and animal pictures; emphasizes labeling animals when pointing them out to child

MENTALLY RETARDED PARENT

May not have opportunities to expose her child to a variety of animals.

1. When possible, plan field trips with the parent and child to visit the zoo, county fair, or a farm.

2. Visit local pet shops and parks with the parent and child. Model and encourage the parent to name and point out the various animals and their animal sounds to her child.
3. Take photos of the animals while on field trips and cut out animal pictures from magazines to make a special animal picture book.
4. Refer to Activity No. 3, 1.44 (Looks at pictures one minute when named).

DEAF PARENT

May not use speech to label animals and may be unaware of animal sounds.

1. Trips to local parks, zoos, and fairs expose the child to actual animal sounds and other people who will be naming the various animals.
2. Encourage the parent to use any speech she has to name animals coupled with the sign for a particular animal when looking at animal pictures.
3. Use animal "See-N-Say" toys and *Magic Wand Readers** which emphasize animals.
4. Make animal picture books and pair with a tape recording of names and sounds of animals.
5. As the child becomes familiar with his parent's sign for animals, she can ask him to find pictures of various animals using sign language.

BLIND PARENT

May be unaware of the coloring and other visual markings of unfamiliar animals.

1. Describe the coloring and markings of various unfamiliar animals, e.g., spots, stripes, or long haired when visiting zoos and parks, going for walks, and when selecting animal pictures.
2. The parent can tactually mark animal pictures and books as described in 1.44 (Looks at pictures one minute when named).
3. Point out animal pictures which may be on her child's clothing, cereal boxes, and cookie packages so the parent can point them out and talk about them to her child.

1.93 Child: UNDERSTANDS MOST NOUN OBJECTS (16-19 mo.)
Parent: Labels many noun objects for child throughout daily activities

GENERAL GUIDELINES

The child understands the meaning of the word labels for most common objects in his environment, such as foods, toys, clothing, pets, utensils, and other common household items, such as radios, lights, telephones, and televisions.

He indicates his understanding by looking toward, getting, touching, or giving the named object.

MENTALLY RETARDED PARENT

May not routinely talk to her child about objects in his environment, or may only name objects with imperative statements.

1. Prompting and reinforcing the parent's expressive language with her child about things that are meaningful to him is stressed throughout this curriculum for most activities:
    a. Continue to model talking about things that are meaningful to her child, i.e., what he is looking at, what he's eating, what he is playing with, etc., using frequent repetition and paraphrasing.
    b. Verbally prompt the parent when appropriate to remind her to talk to her child, e.g., "Tell him what he's looking at," "What is he eating?", "Tell Jimmy what's he's eating," or "What can you say before you give him the ball?"
    c. Reinforce to parent how her child likes to hear her tell him things, e.g., "See how he smiles at you!", "See how he looked at what you talked about!", or "You are really helping him understand the meaning of words when you talk to him!"

DEAF PARENT

May not use speech to label objects for her child during daily activities.

1. List for the parent her child's expanding receptive speech vocabulary.
2. Continue to encourage the parent's use of speech, if possible, during daily activities and in conjunction with her gestural and/or sign language.
3. If the child is isolated from speech many hours during the day, discuss the value of neighborhood play groups, church toddler programs, and public library story telling times to help expand her child's receptive and expressive speech.

BLIND PARENT

May be unaware of her child's non-vocal communicative responses which indicate he understands what she has said.

1. Describe and interpret her child's expanding gestural repertoire which he is using to initiate and respond to communication, e.g., visually directed point, reaching, showing, giving, finger pointing, and head shaking.
2. Name these gestures as they occur during the child's and parent's communication efforts. The parent can learn to associate the subtle verbal, auditory, and movement changes which accompany her child's gestures and verbally respond accordingly.

---

*See Materials Reference Listing.

1.94 Child: **SERIES OF HIDDEN DISPLACEMENTS: OBJECT UNDER LAST SCREEN (17-18 mo.)**
Parent: Hides object by displacement under the third screen, if recommended

GENERAL GUIDELINES

This skill item is usually for evaluation purposes only, to assess the child's maturing visual pursuit and memory skills. There are three screens in front of the child. The evaluator shows the child a small object, hides it in her hand, and systematically puts her hand under each screen from left to right. She does not empty her hand until it is under the third screen, and then shows the child her empty hand. When the child has found the object several times, the order should be reversed, moving the evaluator's hand from right to left. If the child does not find the object, the evaluator can let the child "peek" under the correct screen and recover.

If contrived "hidden displacement games" have been recommended, do not attempt this activity until the child has mastered 1.81 (Hidden displacement two screens). Refer to 1.62 (Finds object hidden by one screen displacement) for displacement guidelines and parent activities, modifying for three screens.

1.95 Child: **SOLVES SIMPLE PROBLEMS USING TOOLS (17-24 mo.)**
Parent: Sets up or uses naturally occurring situations which encourage her child to solve simple problems by using an unrelated object

GENERAL GUIDELINES

The child demonstrates his expanded problem-solving skills when he purposely uses an unrelated object to "act upon" another. Examples of his goal directed behaviors using other objects may include pulling toys around using a support, such as a blanket or wheeled toy; carrying many toys around using a bag, box, or his own clothing; knocking down milk carton bowling pins with a ball; hitting a balloon with a paddle; obtaining an out-of-reach toy using a stick-like object to bring the object closer; or using a stool to bring himself closer to an object out of reach.

Parents help their child learn to solve the simple problems by demonstrating various methods of solving them with "tools" when their child appears "stuck."

MENTALLY RETARDED PARENT

May not recognize developmentally appropriate situations to encourage her child to solve simple problems using tools.

1. Role-play several problem-solving situations with parent:
   a. Place fifteen blocks on a table next to an empty box. Ask the parent how she would move all of the blocks to her child's room.
   b. Wedge a small object between the refrigerator and kitchen cabinet or out of reach under a couch; ask the parent how she could get it.
   c. Point out something that is out of reach on a high shelf, and ask the parent how she gets it.
   d. Interpret how the parent knew she could not get these things without help from a box, stick, or stool (or whatever "tools" she used).
   e. Relate that her child is now learning to solve these types of problems.
2. Name situations which may occur for the parent to encourage her child's problem-solving. Help the parent select safe "stick-like" tools to help her child bring toys closer, such as paper towel roll tubes or plastic spatulas.
3. Describe several situations in which her child will *not* be able to use a tool to obtain an object, demonstrating and explaining why for each situation; tell the parent she will need to get the object for him.
4. Demonstrate, and then let the parent practice, similar problem-solving situations with her child. Stress:
   a. Giving her child verbal directions, encouragement, and praise.
   b. Making sure a "tool" is nearby.
   c. Showing the child how to solve the problem if he does not figure it out, and then letting him try again.
5. Help the parent anticipate additional "child-proofing" needs at home as her child becomes more proficient in obtaining out-of-reach objects.

1.96 Child: **IMITATES SEVERAL "INVISIBLE" GESTURES (17-20 mo.)**
Parent: Imitates several of the child's invisible gestures on separate occasions, encouraging him to imitate them back

GENERAL GUIDELINES

Refer to 1.84 (Imitates "invisible" gesture), gradually increasing the number of invisible gestures for imitation.

1.97 Child: **POINTS TO DISTANT OBJECTS OUTDOORS (17½-18½ mo.)**
Parent: Models pointing and calling child's attention to distant objects; acknowledges child's pointing by talking about the object pointed toward

MENTALLY RETARDED PARENT

May not point to or describe distant objects outdoors with her child, or may not respond to her child's pointing.

1. Take a walk outdoors with the parent and child:
   a. Discuss how her child learns by being able to look at the many things outside, such as birds, cars, trucks, different buildings, and flowers; but, since there are so many things for him to see, he may miss looking at some things or may not know their names. She can teach him by pointing to and talking about them.
   b. Model pointing and talking about different objects to the child, reminding the parent how important it is to

first get her child's attention by calling his name and slowly moving a pointed finger toward the object while he watches.
  c. Explain that when her child points, he is saying, "Look, Mom" and "Tell me about that."
2. Ask the parent what she can point to and name to her child when they are looking out of windows at home.
3. Encourage the parent to take her child out for a walk everyday. Explain how she is helping him learn so many things when they go for walks:
  a. Name times when she should not take him out for walks, e.g., when he is sick or when it is storming.
  b. Discuss safety considerations when she is taking a walk with her child.

BLIND PARENT

May not be aware of distant objects that exist in the environment and thus be unable to name or point to them.

1. If the parent does not use or is not aware of the pointing gesture as a communicative tool for her child, refer to 1.73 (Understands pointing).
2. Describe to the parent distant objects that can be seen outdoors from various windows in the home. The parent can then point outdoors and label different objects for her child, e.g., "See the car?" or "Look at the big tree."
3. Encourage the parent to point toward and label environmental sounds she hears when outside, e.g., airplanes, dogs, birds, fire engines, etc.
4. Take a walk outdoors, shop, or go to the park with the parent and child:
  a. Before going out, describe to the parent various distant objects by which they will be walking.
  b. During the outing, quietly cue the parent when she and her child are in view of various interesting objects and their approximate location, e.g., "The big tree is 50 feet away at 3 o'clock." The parent can then point out and label distant objects for her child.
  c. Identify at what her child is looking or pointing. The parent can then reinforce her child's pointing by commenting about the object.

1.98 **Child: ATTEMPTS AND THEN SUCCEEDS IN ACTIVATING MECHANICAL TOY (18-22 mo.)**
   Parent: Activates a mechanical toy and encourages child to restart it after the action stops

GENERAL GUIDELINES

The child is learning how to make things "work" without help. He may turn on televisions and radios, turn handles on "Jack-in-the-box" toys, try out light switches, and figure out how to activate mechanical toys. Earlier, he knew these tasks were beyond his abilities and he called for adult help. The child's maturing eye-hand coordination and his experiences with watching other people making things happen provide him with the motivation and power to do things for himself.

Parents can facilitate their child's interest and skill toward turning things on and making them work by showing the child how to activate and turn things on, and by giving him opportunities and time to practice with various objects. Wind-up toys with large keys, mechanical toys with switches, musical toys with knobs, and pop-up boxes which activate with buttons, knobs, and dials help the child practice these skills. If the child has limited fine motor control, mechanical toys which activate with simple buttons could be used.

MENTALLY RETARDED PARENT

May restart the toy before her child has had a chance to restart it by himself, or may continue to expect him to give her the toy to restart it.

1. Explain that her child is now ready to try and start action toys all by himself, thus:
  a. The parent should not hold her hand out anymore for her child to give it back to her to restart it.
  b. The parent should let him try it all by himself, and not restart it for him until he has tried two times unsuccessfully and hands it to her.
2. Model, and let the parent practice, giving her child an action toy after showing him how it works. Emphasize and encourage the parent's verbal prompts without interfering, and waiting to show her child how to activate the toy until he has tried two times unsuccessfully to start it by himself.
3. Help the parent select and test various toys suitable for this activity which are appropriate to her child's fine motor abilities. If an action toy's switch or key is too difficult, explain why and help find alternatives.
4. Help the parent anticipate safety concerns which may arise now that her child is learning to turn things on. Refer to Activity No. 2, 4.66 (Inverts small container spontaneously to obtain tiny object).

BLIND PARENT

May be unable to visually monitor her child's attempts at activating action toys.

1. Describe, demonstrate, and let the parent become tactually familiar with the various actions her child may use or try to make several action toys start, e.g., hit it, turn it, or pull a switch. The parent can associate her child's audible cues with the various methods he uses to "make toys work."
2. Provide the parent with developmental anticipatory guidance regarding her child's safety now that he can turn things on. Relate how he may begin turning on the stove, heaters, and curling irons, and figuring out how to open safety gates. Help the parent child-proof the home, as needed.

1.99 Child: USES PLAYDOUGH AND PAINTS (18-24 mo.)
Parent: Provides opportunities for child to explore and manipulate playdough, and experience various painting activities

GENERAL GUIDELINES

Playdough and paints allow the child to experiment with a variety of tactual and visual experiences. He learns he can change the shape and color of things as he pats, pokes, hits, and squeezes dough, and dabs, strokes, and dribbles paints.

Playdough can be homemade with three cups of flour, one cup of salt, three-fourths cup of water, a teaspoon of oil, and food coloring if desired. The dough can be stored in plastic bags. Parents encourage their child's play by demonstrating rolling, poking, pulling, squeezing, and pounding dough, and encouraging him to copy, using both hands.

Paints can be commercial tempera or watercolor. The child can use cut-up sponges, potato slices, blocks, his hands, and various brushes with paint. Parents can paint with their child on large newsprint or butcher block paper, covering a large area. The parent will need to control the paint containers for her child at this age. Pages from "Paint with Water" books can be used with little mess and interesting visual effects for the child. The child can use Q-Tips, sponge pieces, or brushes according to his ability.

To facilitate easy clean up, the parent and child can wear old shirts, cover tables and the floor with large sheets of plastic or newspaper, and keep paints in weighted cups.

The child may periodically taste playdough and paints. Parents must assure that these materials are non-toxic.

MENTALLY RETARDED PARENT

May not provide playdough or paints for her child's play, or may expect her child to use dough or paint beyond his developmental abilities.

1. Refer to 1.68 (Enjoys messy activities, such as finger-painting).
2. Teach the parent the playdough recipe in the general guidelines and help as needed to make a batch.
3. Demonstrate various methods for playing with playdough and paints with the child. Provide clear (age-appropriate) guidelines for her child's dough and paint play; include the following concepts:
   a. Her child cannot make actual things with the dough, but the parent can pretend that his shapes are balls, plates, etc.
   b. Her child cannot paint actual pictures yet, but the parent can pretend they are beautiful pictures.
   c. Her child cannot always paint within the limits of paper; always use large pieces of paper.
   d. Do not scold the child if he tastes playdough or paints; instead, make a face and say, "Yuk." Gently redirect his hand back to the table.

BLIND PARENT

May not be able to visually monitor her child's interactions with paints and dough, and may be unaware of the materials' colors.

1. Identify the colors of various non-toxic paints and playdoughs. The parent can color-code the individual containers using her own tactual marking system.
2. Describe color changes that occur for her child when they are mixed.
3. Add sand to finger and tempera paints. The parent can feel her child's beautiful impression paintings more easily, and the child will enjoy feeling and seeing this interesting texture.
4. Describe the child's inaudible signs of delight and interactions with the materials.

PHYSICALLY DISABLED PARENT

Who has a limited grasp; may have difficulty manipulating tools for painting and playdough.

1. The parent could use a *universal cuff** to hold brushes and sponges for painting with her child.
2. The parent will probably have adaptive equipment to help open paint jars. If paint jars have narrow openings, transfer paints into separate wide-mouth cups.
3. The parent can use her fist and forearm for pounding and rolling playdough with her child.

1.100 Child: PASTES ON ONE SIDE (18-24 mo.)
Parent: Teaches child to apply paste on one side of shape and turn it over to stick on paper

MENTALLY RETARDED PARENT

May not provide her child with pasting experiences, or may physically manipulate materials with her child during pasting.

1. Help the parent select and discriminate suitable pastes and paper for her child to use:
   a. Caution *never* to use cement or commercial permanent bonding glues, such as "Krazy Glue." Explain their dangers and name places to keep these out of her child's reach.
   b. Make a homemade paste mixture using flour and water.
   c. Cut out three-inch shapes from paper scraps, greeting cards, or construction paper with parent.
   d. Use large paper bags or construction paper on which to paste the shapes.
   e. Explain that her child should not have the entire jar of paste; help the parent think of disposable things to put a portion of paste on, such as butter tubs, small paper plates, and coffee can lids.
2. Before introducing pasting materials to the child, demonstrate the various things he may do with it. For example,

---

*See Glossary.

he may taste the paste, put too much or too little paste on the paper, forget to turn the piece over, or paste on both sides. Explain that is just fine and helps him learn better pasting as he gets older.
3. Participate in pasting activities with the parent and child:
   a. If the parent tries to "make" her child paste in a certain way, remind her that his finger muscles are not ready for perfect pasting yet; he needs lots of practice trying to do it by himself.
   b. Model and reinforce the parent's verbal descriptions of the pasting activity and praise her child's hard work.
   c. Tape the final products on the refrigerator.

BLIND PARENT

May benefit from an orderly arrangement of the various materials used during pasting, and from help in selecting visually attractive papers for her child to paste.

1. Help select and describe the various visual qualities of papers used during pasting, e.g., colorful, shiny, reflective, and opaque.
2. The cut-out scraps for pasting can be kept in boxes and the paste in a pie-tin or butter cup for the parent's easy location.
3. As her child masters pasting skills and is ready for pasting simple designs, such as eyes on an outlined animal picture, tactually mark the positions on the paper to help the parent direct her child's attention to the proper location.

EXPRESSIVE LANGUAGE DEVELOPMENT

2.01   Child: **CRY IS MONOTONOUS, NASAL, ONE BREATH LONG (0-1½ mo.)**
2.02   Child: **CRIES WHEN HUNGRY OR UNCOMFORTABLE (0-1 mo.)**
    Parent: Interprets child's cry as his means of communicating his needs

GENERAL GUIDELINES

During the first few weeks, the child's crying sounds are undifferentiated. He cries with his whole body, often trembling, trashing about, and stiffening.

He may have long spells of crying, for up to thirty or forty minutes, several times a day. On some days, his cry may last from one to three yours. The child's cry is his first social communication to alert others that he is tired, hungry, wet, or frustrated. Environmental tension can add to the intensity and duration of the child's cry.

Parents help develop their child's sense of security when his cries are attended to promptly. He learns that crying helps produce the comfort he cannot provide himself.

MENTALLY RETARDED PARENT

May not interpret her child's cries as meaning he is hungry, tired, needs a diaper change, or needs to be held.

1. Help make a list with the parent of all the things her child may be saying when he is crying. Use this list as a problem-solving vehicle for discussion. For example, ask the parent, "If you just fed him and changed his diapers, and he starts crying, what may he be telling you with his cry?" Continue problem-solving to exhaust possibilities and corresponding parental responses.
2. Model responding to the child's cries calmly. Interpret the child's feelings aloud when he cries, e.g., "Oh you're lonely; you're telling us you want Mom to hold and kiss you."
3. Emphasize how important the parent is to her child. Relate how he needs her to help him feel good because he can't help himself at this age. Ask the parent if she can remember times when she cried and someone came to help her.
4. Follow parent training activities for 1.01 (Quiets when picked up).

DEAF PARENT

May not hear and thus be unable to respond to her child's crying when he is out of her sight, and may be unaware of harsh auditory stimuli which may precipitate her child's crying.

1. Explain the child's crying sound to the parent, i.e., "high pitched, loud, long in duration, and very unpleasant!"
2. If the child is hypersensitive, various environmental sounds may precipitate his crying, e.g., winding up infant swings or pulling up his crib railing. Explain and demonstrate the child's startle reflex. The parent can use this as a cue that sounds may be too adversive for her child, especially if it is followed by a cry.
3. Point out various auditory stimuli that help calm her child, i.e., humming, soft voice, and music boxes.
4. Refer to 1.01 (Quiets when picked up).

BLIND PARENT

May be interested in knowing how her child's appearance changes when he cries.

1. Provide clear verbal descriptions of the child's appearance when he cries, e.g., "At first, he only wrinkles his nose and opens his mouth a little; as you feel his body stiffen, he turns red and his eyes shut; all babies look like that when they cry hard."
2. If the child is hypersensitive, sudden harsh lighting may precipitate his crying. If this is observed, alert the parent and help adapt lighting by changing the light's position, using shades, or using lower watt bulbs.

2.03   Child: **MAKES COMFORT SOUNDS – REFLEXIVE (0-2½ mo.)**
    Parent: Reinforces child's vocal sounds of comfort

GENERAL GUIDELINES

The child's first sounds are throaty. At first, they are reflexive, occurring automatically as a result of changes in the tension of his vocal cords. They occur when he is relaxed and feeling good.

From the child's birth, parents can begin establishing a rich and responsive language environment. When parents respond to their child's sounds by talking, cooing, and smiling, he learns his sounds bring rewarding results.

MENTALLY RETARDED PARENT

May not talk to her child or respond to his sounds.

1. Encourage parent to begin talking to her child right away:
    a. Model nodding, smiling, and saying short inflectional phrases to the child frequently.
    b. Explain that, even though he can't understand our words, he can understand our feelings, i.e., "When we talk to him, he feels good and loved."
    c. Explain that talking to him now helps him learn to talk later.
    d. If the parent cannot think of anything to say to her child, suggest and model short phrases, such as "Hi there," "I love you," or "You're so pretty."
    e. Whenever the parent talks to her child, remark how he really likes that, i.e., "See how he looks at you!"
2. When the child makes comfort sounds, interpret them to the parent, i.e., "He's telling us with those sounds that he feels good."

2.03

3. Tell the parent that when she smiles and talks to her child when she hears his sounds, she is teaching him that talking is a good thing to do.

DEAF PARENT

May be unaware that her child makes reflexive comfort sounds and thus not reinforce them.

1. Explain that the child's first vocal sounds happen when he is feeling good, and often occur by accident when his muscles used for speech relax.
2. Demonstrate saying some of the early comfort sounds, such as "mm," "ooh," and "k" as the parent watches your mouth.
3. When the child vocalizes comfort sounds, cue the parent and help point out changes in her child's facial and bodily movements. Explain the importance of attending, but not interrupting, him at this time.
4. Explain that when we respond to her child's sounds by smiling and talking back, her child learns that vocalizing is a good way to get our attention and may thus continue to make more sounds.
5. If the parent is non-verbal, she can talk back to her child using facial expressions, head nodding, and patting.

BLIND PARENT

May be unaware of her child's communicative facial expressions.

1. Describe the child's facial expressions when he makes comfort sounds and when the parent talks to him, e.g., "His face looks so relaxed now; he keeps his mouth slightly open the whole time he makes those sounds" or "His eyes are open wide when you talk to him."

2.04 Child: MAKES SUCKING SOUNDS (½-3 mo.)
Parent: Recognizes the differences in child's nutritive and non-nutritive need for sucking

GENERAL GUIDELINES

The child's sucking sounds are reflexive at this age. They are the result of changes in tension of the muscles used for sucking and may occur when the child is comfortable and relaxed.

Sucking also helps quiet infants, as it reduces hunger pains and relieves muscle tension. Sucking on his fingers may help satisfy the child's sucking needs and act as a calming technique.

MENTALLY RETARDED PARENT

May interpret her child's sucking sounds as always meaning he is hungry.

1. Explain that when her child makes sucking sounds, it does not always mean he wants to eat, i.e., "When he makes these sounds he is telling us he feels good." Provide the following guidelines to help the parent discriminate if her child is sucking for comfort or because of hunger:
   a. The parent can check the time to see if it is near his feeding time to help her know when his sucking is for comfort or hunger.
   b. If her child's sucking is followed by a cry, he may be hungry; check the time.
   c. If it is not time to eat, her child is probably sucking for pleasure.
2. Model looking, smiling, and making soft tongue click sounds at the child. Encourage the parent to try doing this, explaining this is another way of talking to her child.
3. If the child sucks his fingers, assure the parent that this is okay and a great way for her child to help himself feel good.

DEAF PARENT

May be unaware that he child's sucking produces sounds.

1. Tell the parent that when her child sucks, with or without a bottle, he makes short "tongue click-like" sounds.

BLIND PARENT

May be interested in the relationship between her child's sucking and looking.

1. Explain the relationship between children's sucking and looking, and its developmental progression. That is:
   a. During the first few days of life, children shut their eyes when they suck because they cannot handle more than one activity at a time and looking is a big activity! When they look at something, they may stop sucking.
   b. In contrast, when children are a few weeks old, their sucking during non-feeding times may help quiet their active body and let them concentrate on looking at things better.
   c. Around two or three months, when children suck with bursts and pauses during feeding, they often look during their pauses.
   d. Around three or four months, children seem to be able to look and suck during feeding at the same time.

2.05 Child: CRY VARIES IN PITCH, LENGTH AND VOLUME TO INDICATE NEEDS SUCH AS HUNGER, PAIN (1-5 mo.)
Parent: Differentiates and responds appropriately to child's different cries

MENTALLY RETARDED PARENT

May not differentiate her child's cries.

1. Ask the parent if she notices any differences in her child's crying sounds. Explain he is beginning to tell us his different needs with different cries.
2. Point out concrete discriminating features of her child's cry and relate them to his apparent intent, e.g., "His sudden high shrilling cry with lip quivering means something hurts" or "He really shakes his arms while crying when he is hungry."

DEAF PARENT

May not be able to aurally discriminate the changes in her child's cries.

1. Explain that as her child is developing, the sound of his cry changes. He makes different crying sounds to tell us his different needs.
2. The parent may be able to recognize specific patterns of physical changes in her child which indicate what the problem is, e.g., her child turns bright red if his stomach hurts, or he brings his hand to mouth when hungry.
3. Relate that when he's crying, he might stop momentarily to listen for her footstep or voice.

2.06   Child: LAUGHS (1½-4 mo.)
Parent: Initiates social interactions with child which encourages him to laugh

GENERAL GUIDELINES

The child communicates his delight and pleasure through chuckling and laughing. Parents foster their child's laughter by providing compatible doses of interactive stimulation, such as smiling, nuzzling, making silly faces, and making silly sounds coupled with exaggerated facial expressions.

MENTALLY RETARDED PARENT

May over-stimulate her child in an effort to make him laugh or keep him laughing.

1. If the parent is observed to intrusively poke, tickle, shake, or jiggle her child in an effort to make him laugh, explain:
   a. These things don't feel good to children.
   b. Children don't laugh at the same things adults do at this age.
   c. Name and demonstrate several things that children at this age often laugh at, e.g., nuzzling tummy or making tongue click sounds.
2. When you see the child laugh, relate to the parent the preceding event that seemed to cause him to laugh.
3. Demonstrate, and let the parent practice, nuzzling gently at her child's belly and then looking and smiling at him. Emphasize the following as you demonstrate this "game":
   a. Wait for her child to respond before nuzzling again; describe his responses.
   b. Her child tells us it's time to stop by turning his head, twisting, or crying.
   c. Keeping her face at a conducive distance from the child's face after the nuzzle.
4. Comment how sometimes children just don't feel like laughing, even when we do things they like. Help the parent think of times when her child won't feel like laughing, e.g., he is tired, hungry, sick, or just not in the "mood."

DEAF PARENT

May not hear her child's laughing sounds.

1. As the child begins to incorporate laughing, the parent can recognize the changes in his facial and bodily movements.
2. Point out various sounds which may precipitate her child's laughter, e.g., squeak toys or adult's silly sounds.

BLIND PARENT

May be unaware of visual stimuli which precipitates her child's laughter.

1. Describe to the parent the various facial expressions, toys, and visual spectacles which seem to precipitate her child's laughter, e.g., "when we make a funny face, or move his favorite bright stuffed animal up and down in a playful way."

2.07   Child: COOS OPEN VOWELS (AAH), CLOSED VOWELS (EE), DIPTHONGS (OY AS IN BOY) (2-7 mo.)
Parent: Reinforces child's coos

GENERAL GUIDELINES

The child begins cooing one syllable vowel-like sounds to express sheer contentment and as a means to initiate or respond to interactions with adults.

Parents encourage their child's vowel sounds when they respond to his sounds with smiling and by repeating his sounds back to him. They can also encourage his sounds by providing interesting toys for him to "coo" to, and by initiating conversations to their child with short inflectional phrases.

MENTALLY RETARDED PARENT

May not interpret her child's cooing as a means for communicating.

1. Interpret the child's coos as they occur to the parent, e.g., "When he makes those sounds, he's saying 'I'm happy', 'Look at me', 'Talk to me'."
2. Tell the parent if she makes the same sounds her child does, or smiles when he coos, he's learning that what he says is important.
3. Teach the parent a "Copy Sound" game to play with her child:
   a. Introduce the game as a way to show her child she thinks he is wonderful and likes the sounds he makes.
   b. Explain the rules of the game, i.e., "When you hear your child make a sound, smile and copy the exact sound; then wait for him to make another sound and copy it again. Stop playing when he stops making a sound."
   c. Role-play this game with the parent, as you initiate a vowel sound and cue her to copy.
   d. Demonstrate the "Copy Sound" game with the child and then let the parent practice.
   e. Emphasize face-to-face positioning and exaggerated facial expressions.
   f. Suggest specific times to play this game, e.g., during diapering or before picking him up from his crib.

2.07

DEAF PARENT

May be unaware of her child's cooing sounds.

1. Explain to the parent the production of her child's cooing. For example, cooing sounds:
   a. Are soft in nature and pleasant to hear.
   b. Are no longer throaty sounding; they arise from the nasal area.
   c. Progress from simple open vowel sounds where his mouth is open, to closed vowel sounds where his mouth is almost closed, and then he combines two vowel sounds.
2. Explain the function and meaning of her child's cooing for the parent. He coos:
   a. When he's feeling happy and content.
   b. To communicate to others.
   c. In response to various enjoyable activities (cuddling, rocking, light tickling, etc.).
   d. In response to various visual and sound stimuli (seeing someone smile, hearing them talk, hearing soft music, seeing favorite toys).
3. Make a chart or cards of faces with mouth positions and corresponding vowel sounds. Fingerspell the vowel sounds and demonstrate with your mouth.

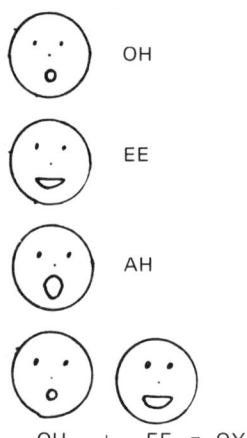

4. As you hear the child coo, cue the parent and fingerspell his vowel sound.
5. Encourage the parent to watch for her child's various facial or mouth movements before she vocalizes or increases her facial expressions. Explain that children often stop cooing to watch and listen to others.
6. If the parent uses speech, encourage her to say vowel sounds to her child.
7. The parent can gently place her fingertips on her child's throat to feel is cooing vibrations.

BLIND PARENT

May be unaware of visual stimuli which precipitate her child's cooing.

1. Point out and describe the particular toys and other visual stimuli her child is looking at when he coos. Describe his communicative facial expressions which accompany his cooing sounds.
2. Explain that, in addition to hearing the way words sound, children watch mouth movements and facial expressions when others talk as a way of learning speech and understanding what we are saying.

2.08 Child: DISASSOCIATES VOCALIZATIONS FROM BODILY MOVEMENT (2-3 mo.)
Parent: Encourages and reinforces child's vocalizations

GENERAL GUIDELINES

During his first few months, the child's whole body often moved when he vocalized. His maturing body control enables him to vocalize now without bodily movement. He will lie quietly and coo in response to stimulation.

Gentle handling and "quiet" times facilitate the child's ability to disassociate his vocalizations from bodily movements.

MENTALLY RETARDED PARENT

May over-stimulate her child with quick movements, bouncing, or tickling when he's vocalizing.

1. Model gentle handling and soft vocalizations with the child. If you observe rough handling, interject non-judgmental comments such as "He likes it when you move slowly and when you talk softly."
2. Teach the parent a few simple lullabies to sing to her child, such as "Rock-A-Bye Baby," while rocking him gently.
3. Help the parent think of "greetings" to say before she picks her child up from his crib, e.g., "How nice to see you" and "What are you doing?":
   a. Model saying these short phrases, leaning over his crib rail for a minute or two before picking him up.
   b. When you notice the parent going to pick her child up, remind her how he likes to hear her talk to him first.

DEAF PARENT

Will not always be able to rely upon watching her child's bodily movements as a cue that he is vocalizing.

1. Explain that her child's maturing body control now allows him to make his sounds without moving the rest of his body. She can continue to watch the changes in his facial expressions and lip movements during his vocalizations.
2. Relate that her child may be cooing during times when there is no adult stimulation. He may coo while watching a mobile in his crib or while looking at a stuffed animal placed nearby.

2.09 Child: CRIES MORE RHYTHMICALLY WITH MOUTH OPENING AND CLOSING (2½-4½ mo.)
Parent: Differentiates and responds appropriately to child's different cries

GENERAL GUIDELINES

As the child matures, he has better coordination of his respiration and phonation muscles. This coordination is demonstrated when the child opens and closes his mouth rhythmically with concurrent rhythmic crying sounds.

DEAF PARENT

May be unaware of her child's new rhythmic crying sounds.

1. Explain her child's maturing coordination and its effect on his rhythmic crying sound. Point out the child's concurrent rhythmic mouth movements as they occur.

2.10 Child: SQUEALS (2½-5½ mo.)
Parent: Encourages child's squealing

GENERAL GUIDELINES

Squealing is a vocal expression of the child's delight, happiness, and excitement. Squealing is produced by the child as a loud sudden burst of high-pitched vowel sounds.

Parents can encourage their child's squealing by gently tickling him, making silly faces, moving him up and down in the air, and playing "I'm gonna get you" games with their fingers on his tummy. Each parent will learn their own individual interactions which delight their child.

MENTALLY RETARDED PARENT

May not be able to discriminate or choose games which make her child happy.

1. Teach parent a few simple games or activities which seems to make her child excited, such as making funny faces and playing "Itsy-Bitsy Spider" on his tummy:
   a. Teach songs and games in which the parent enjoys and feels comfortable. Show her several and let her select the ones she wants to learn.
   b. Avoid tickle games and "swinging in the air" activities if you have observed the parent over-stimulating her child or handling him abruptly.
2. Point out and describe to the parent her child's behaviors which indicate he has had enough of, or does not want to participate in, the game, e.g., gaze aversion, crying, or turning away. Have parent practice discriminating these cues as she plays with her child.
3. Model exaggerated facial expressions when playing games with the child. Point out how her child watches and likes to see them, i.e., "Look how he's watching my face!"

DEAF PARENT

May be unaware of her child's squealing, and may not be familiar with the term.

1. Explain that squealing is a loud, sudden burst of high-pitched vowel sounds her child produces vocally when he is happy and excited.
2. Cue parent when her child is squealing during games so she can associate his corresponding facial and physical movements.

2.11 Child: RESPONDS TO SOUND STIMULATION OR SPEECH BY VOCALIZING (3-6 mo.)
Parent: Provides controlled sound and vocal stimulation to child

GENERAL GUIDELINES

The child vocalizes in response to his own sounds, to the speech of others around him, and to sound stimulation. This is the beginning of his own vocal and interactive play which appears to have communicative intent.

MENTALLY RETARDED PARENT

May not talk to her child or respond to his vocalizations.

1. Stress that all of the child's vocal sounds and facial expressions at this age are his ways of talking:
   a. Ask the parent which sounds she's heard her child make; add the sounds you've also heard him say.
   b. Ask her to make facial expressions she has seen her child make or, if hesitant, imitate them yourself; explore what he may be saying when he uses those expressions.
   c. Explain that when we talk to him, he is learning to talk back with his sounds and facial expressions.
2. Teach the parent a "Tell Me a Story" game to play with her child. This game is played as follows: When the parent sees her child look at her she says, "Tell me a story." She then waits for him to respond with a sound or change in facial expression and in turn says, "Oh, really? Tell me some more" or "I like that." She again waits for a vocal or facial response from her child and says one of the same phrases again. This game is continued until the child twists his body, fusses, or looks away:
   a. Explain the rules of this game and role-play with the parent several times.
   b. Demonstrate this game with the child, stressing en face positioning.
   c. Have the parent practice this game with her child, providing verbal prompts, as needed.
   d. Name times during the day to play this game which are associated with typical daily activities.
   e. Post note cards or pictures of the child with the phrase "Tell Me a Story" in applicable areas, such as over the child's crib or changing area.

2.0 EXPRESSIVE LANGUAGE

2.11

f. During your sessions, when you see the child looking at his parent, point that out and suggest that she "tell him a story."
g. Encourage the parent to think of new phrases she can add to the game.

DEAF PARENT

May not be able to hear her child's responses to sound or speech, and may have difficulty pacing her interactions contingent to her child's vocalizations.

1. Point out the child's facial and bodily changes as they occur when vocalizing. Family members with hearing can be enlisted to draw attention to the child's vocalizations as they occur so the parent can watch his bodily responses to sound and vocal stimulation.
2. Encourage the parent who is comfortable using her voice to vocalize and hum to her child, but to pause periodically to watch for his response.
3. List the sounds her child is making to help increase the parent's awareness of his vocal abilities at this age. This can be done through fingerspelling the sounds or writing them down.
4. See activity adaptations for 1.03 (Responds to sound) to help parent identify sources of sound.
5. Show the parent facial activities which are non-verbal, but still provide auditory stimulation for her child, i.e., kissing, smacking lips, clicking tongue, raspberry with lips, and running index finger over lips while blowing air.
6. If the parent can recognize (through lipreading) her child's vocalizations, demonstrate how to play the game of "facial activity — vocalization — facial activity" with her child. Cue the parent as needed to insure her contingent pacing with her child, i.e., she withholds her increased facial expressions and other lip sounds until she sees her child's signs of vocalizing stop.

BLIND PARENT

May be unaware of the visual attributes of stimuli which elicit her child's vocalizations.

1. Describe the visual attributes of various meaningful stimuli in the child's environment so that the parent can describe them verbally during conversations with her child.
2. Describe the child's eye contact, eye pointing, and facial expressions which accompany his vocalizations. Explain he uses these gestures as a means to start and keep conversations going. The parent can begin to associate her child's subtle movements and audible sounds which indicate he wants to initiate or keep the conversation going.
3. Help the parent present sound toys within her child's visual field, as needed.
4. Describe positions which help insure the parent is in her child's visual field when she is talking to him, e.g., leaning over his crib or leaning down if he is playing on the floor.

2.12 Child: LAUGHS WHEN HEAD IS COVERED WITH A CLOTH (3¼-4½ mo.)
Parent: Briefly and playfully covers child's head with a cloth

GENERAL GUIDELINES

When a child's head is briefly covered with a cloth, he excites at the reappearance of his parent and laughs. The parent communicates that, although she is out of sight, she is still there. This game helps the child learn this concept in a supportive and fun way.

To keep the game fun, parents can use increased vocal inflection and facial expressions, and verbalize short phrases, such as "Where's baby?", "I see you," and "Peek-a-boo."

Not all children go through this stage. If the child does not delight in this activity, parents can play other games which foster delight and laughter.

MENTALLY RETARDED PARENT

May unintentionally frighten or frustrate her child by leaving the cloth on his head too long or playing too roughly.

1. Include the following concepts through discussion with the parent as you introduce this "Peek-a-boo" game:
    a. At first, her child might be frightened when his head is covered because he can't see anything; soon he learns this is quite funny.
    b. Cover his face for only two seconds; she can count aloud to help determine how long to keep his head covered.
    c. He cannot pull the cloth off yet by himself or tell us with words when he wants it removed; we have to take it off for him.
    d. He tells us he doesn't want to play this game by fussing.
    e. When we uncover his face, we have to say "Peek-a-boo" with a big smile, but not too loudly or he will be frightened.
2. Role-play this "Peek-a-boo" game with the parent:
    a. Let the parent experience inappropriate interactions which prevent the game from being fun: keeping the cloth on too long, saying "Peek-a-boo" too loud or too close to the child, and pulling the cloth off too quickly.
    b. Ask her if she can think of ways to make the game more fun for her child.
    c. Repeat this activity with an inflected but gentle voice and appropriate pacing.

DEAF PARENT

May not have been exposed to language oriented "Peek-a-boo" games.

1. Demonstrate this "Peek-a-boo" game and explain its interactive language aspects which keep it fun for the child. Include:
    a. Since her child can't see anything for a few seconds, he is both scared and excited.
    b. If he hears that we are still there, he's not so scared.

c. When we pull the cloth off, he's thrilled to see us again and learns this is a great trick to do.
d. When an adult says "Peek-a-boo" with lots of smiling, he knows that we are sharing in this excitement.
2. If the parent is comfortable with using speech, encourage her to call his name or hum while his face is covered.
3. If the parent is non-verbal, she can touch him, gently pat him, or make non-verbal sounds, such as kissing or tongue clicking, while her child's head is covered.
4. When the cloth is removed, the parent can express a special surprised facial expression, coupled with a vocalization, if possible, or a big kiss.

BLIND PARENT

May not be aware of the visual surprise elements in disappearance games which elicit her child's laughter.

1. Describe this activity and explain the visual delight and surprise elements which precipitate her child's laughter.
2. If the parent is interested in playing "Peek-a-boo" games with her child:
   a. Advise approaching her child with the cloth from behind his head. (Parent sites en face with child, while her hand is behind his back with cloth.)
   b. Describe her child's facial expressions during the game.
3. Name naturally occurring situations which hide the child's face that the parent can accompany with "delight" phrases, e.g., when she pulls his shirt off, washes his face, nuzzles his face in her chest, etc.
4. Anticipatory Guidance: If parent and child do not assume en face positions, the parent will have discovered many other interactive games which encourage his laughter.

2.13 Child: BABBLES CONSONANT CHAINS "BABA-BABA" (4-6½ mo.)
Parent: Provides a meaningful and responsive language environment for child

GENERAL GUIDELINES

As the child discovers he can purposely produce sounds, he practices them over and over again. His initial accidental combination of vowel sounds with a few consonants (d, b, m are often the first) lead to long strings of consonant-vowel combinations.

Although a child's vocalizations are not typically thought of as true purposeful communication at this age, adults usually interpret and assign communicative intentions to his sounds. This helps create a basis for his later purposeful communication through vocalizations.

Parents can encourage their child's babbling of consonant chains and future expressive language skills by providing a sensitive and responsive language environment. Parent strategies which facilitate a positive language environment include:
1. Attracting the child's attention and eye contact before talking to him by making an attracting sound or visual spectacle, such as an exaggerated facial expression.
2. Talking to the child about things that are meaningful to him: what he is looking at, what he is doing, and what the parent is doing.
3. Using child-size language: slower paced, shorter utterances, repetition of important words, exaggerated intonation and stress, saying words in special and simple ways (e.g., doggie instead of German Shephard), and saying her child's own sounds back to him.
4. Assigning communicative intent to the child's sounds and gestures, and responding by talking back and doing what the child seems to want. For example, if the child is babbling and looking at a distinct object, the parent can get it for him and talk about it.
5. Taking turns during communication; letting the child initiate and finish his own vocalizations before talking back.

The child does not always need people to encourage him to babble because his sounds are often reinforcing in themselves. If a child does not babble, or his sounds decrease, he may have hearing problems and should be referred for an audiological evaluation.

MENTALLY RETARDED PARENT

May not reinforce her child's babbling.

1. Help the parent understand the communicative significance of her child's babbling sounds:
   a. Review the various expressive sounds her child is making.
   b. Explain that although her child doesn't say words yet, he uses these sounds as words; he needs to practice making them to help him learn how to talk later.
   c. Describe several example situations of her child babbling and help the parent think of what he might be saying if he could really talk, e.g., when her child is looking at a toy and babbling "bababba," he might be saying "I like that; tell me about it" or "I wonder what that toy does." If her child is babbling "mamama" and reaching toward a toy, he might be saying "Give me the toy."
   d. During your sessions, frequently ask the parent what her child might be saying if he had words, when you observe him babbling.
2. Teach parent ways to respond to her child's babbling:
   a. Explain that if we talk back to children when they stop "talking," we let him know we're trying to understand him; this will make him want to talk more.
   b. Ask parent to think of things she could say back to her child, using example situations in Activity No. 1c., such as "You're talking to your toy bear," "That's a bear you're talking to," or "Here's the rattle."
   c. Tell the parent how much her child likes it when we talk like him; when he says "dadada," she can say "dadada" back to him.
   d. Ask the parent frequently what she can say back to her child, when you observe him babbling.
   e. During your sessions, model talking back to the child using exaggerated inflection and stress.
3. Encourage the parent to incorporate child-size meaningful language directed toward her child during daily activities:
   a. Explain that, although her child can't understand what we are saying yet, he won't learn what words mean unless he hears us talk a lot.

2.13

b. Tell the parent that, at this age, it is good to talk about what we are doing, what the child is doing, and what the child is looking at. Give several examples of each.

c. Review typical daily child and parent activities, such as waking up, dressing, changing, eating, and playing. Help the parent think of phrases she can say to her child during each activity, e.g., "What can you talk about when he's eating or when you are changing his diaper?"

d. Name various objects and toys which are meaningful to the child. Help the parent think of things to say when he's looking at each, such as "You are looking at your mobile; see the birds; see them move."

e. Verbally prompt the parent frequently during your sessions to talk about what she is doing, what her child is doing, and what her child is looking at, e.g., "Tell Bobby what you're doing."

f. Praise all of the parent's verbal interactions with her child, telling her she is a good teacher.

DEAF PARENT

May be unaware of her child's babbling sounds and thus may interrupt or not reinforce them.

1. Relate to the parent the meaning and intent of her child's babbling: "He is beginning to put his single sounds together and this is called babbling. He repeats one sound over and over again in a series, such as 'baba-baba' or says a vowel sound, such as 'ooo' a lot longer. He is playing with his sounds and likes to listen to himself. He also enjoys hearing others make his sounds back to him; this becomes a game for him."

2. Relate that a child's first consonant sounds are often the b, m, and d sounds, and the first vowel sounds are the "oo," "ah," "ee," and "uh" sounds. Explain that babbling incorporates these sounds in isolation and in repeated consonant-vowel combinations, such as "bababa," "mama-mama," and "dada-dada."

3. Assist the parent to recognize, through lipreading, her child's babbling chains. Model the child's typical sounds, pairing the oral production with the written or finger-spelled symbols. Identify the child's babbling chain as he is engaged in vocal play. The parent can feel the vibrations from her child's babbling by gently placing one or two fingers on his throat for "oo," "ah," "ee," "uh," "ba-ba," and "da-da" sounds, and at the side of his nose for his nasal produced sounds, such as "ma-ma" and "na-na."

4. Emphasize to the parent that it is important not to disturb her child's vocal play because he will stop vocalizing if interrupted to listen to her or watch her signing. Assist the parent with watching and waiting for a lull in her child's vocal play. She can then respond and reinforce his sounds by smiling, kissing, and using facial activities which the child enjoys, such as lip smacking, tongue clicks, etc.

5. Encourage the parent to reinforce her child's vocal productions with whatever vocal abilities she may have. Emphasize it is not important *what* she says, but *how* she says it, so her child learns talking is a good thing to do.

6. Explain and demonstrate that her signs, gestures, and spoken words should be transmitted slower than usual when communicating with her child.

7. Suggest one or two children's television shows which provide language experiences to which her child can listen.

BLIND PARENT

May have difficulty assigning communicative intentions to her child's babbling if she is unaware of his non-verbal signs of communication.

1. Name the child's non-verbal communication signs at this age, i.e., his eye pointing and reaching gestures. The parent can then know to:
   a. Feel for his reaching gestures and head turning when she is near him to help determine what to talk about or give him.
   b. Periodically ask others who have vision what he is looking at or reaching toward.

2.14 Child: VOCALIZES ATTITUDES OTHER THAN CRYING – JOY, DISPLEASURE (5-6 mo.)
Parent: Differentiates child's vocalized attitudes; responds accordingly

GENERAL GUIDELINES

The child communicates his feelings during all of his daily activities and interactions with people.

He communicates his feelings of discontent with grunts and complaining sounds, and his feelings of excitement and pleasure with coos, gurgles, chortles, belly laughs, and squeals. These vocalizations carry corresponding voice qualities, tone, and inflections.

Parents encourage their child's vocalized attitudes by responding to their communicative intent. For example, when the child grunts in frustration to reach a toy and the parent responds by giving it to him, he learns his vocalized attitude was helpful! When a parent also verbalizes the child's feeling for him, using matching inflection and tone, she communicates she understands him.

MENTALLY RETARDED PARENT

May not discriminate or respond differentially to her child's vocalized attitudes.

1. Facilitate a discussion of children's expressions for various feelings, using a variety of pictures with children's expressions:
   a. Ask what the pictured child's expression is saying to us. Supply "feeling" words as needed for the parent to choose from. Ask the parent if she has seen her child making these feeling expressions?
   b. Ask what sounds the pictured child might be making if we could hear him; ask if she has heard her child making these sounds and in what situations.
2. Use the pictures from Activity No. 1 to facilitate rehearsing various parent responses (what she can say and do) dependent upon her child's vocalized attitudes:
   a. When he's making happy sounds what can you say? For example, "You're happy" or "This is fun."
   b. When he's making happy sounds what can you do? For example, smile, laugh, and make the same sound.

c. Repeat Activity Nos. 2a and 2b with several possible child attitudes.
d. Explain when she responds to his feelings, she makes him feel loved and understood.
3. Monitor the parent's interpretations of her child's vocalized attitudes as they occur:
a. If she "misses" his cues, interpret aloud the child's feeling, e.g., "He doesn't want to sit in his seat anymore; see how he's fussing and wrinkling his nose."
b. Prompt the parent to respond to his vocalized attitudes as they occur, i.e., "What can you say to him to tell him you know he's feeling sad?"

DEAF PARENT

May be unaware of her child's expanding vocal abilities to express attitudes.

1. Anticipatory Guidance: The deaf parent is likely to be very sensitive to her child's facial and bodily expressions of feelings. People without hearing often depend upon animation in their communicative modes to emphasize degree of feeling or attitude. For example, the sign for happy is open hands patting the chest several times with a slight upward motion. However, the person's facial expressions qualify *how* happy or *what kind* of happy. For example, if one is conveying a sarcastic happy, the sign is coupled with raised eyebrows and a smirk.

   Although the parent may be very sensitive to her child's expressions of attitudes, his expression may at times be more subtle or confusing, and the parent may be interested in knowing his new varied sounds.
2. Explain that her child's vocalizations vary according to his feelings and attitudes, and that hearing persons can usually tell how he is feeling (angry, frustrated, tired, excited, happy, content) by listening to these sounds.
3. Help the parent understand what her child's "attitude" sounds are through fingerspelling and written words. Explain:
a. "Whining" is a high-pitched sound, such as "wawawa," and means "I want something."
b. "Grunting" is a deep sound from his throat and chest, such as "ahahah," and means "I'm frustrated" or "I'm angry."
c. "Gurgling" is a pleasant back-tongue sound, such as "gago," and means "I'm happy" or "This is fun."
4. As the child vocalizes attitudes during your sessions, cue the parent as to which sounds he is making:
a. The parent can discriminate her child's various gestural and facial expressions which accompany his vocalized attitudes.
b. Encourage the parent to vocalize, talk, and/or use signs to communicate in response to his vocalized attitudes. Explain that this helps her child learn that his sounds are useful, which will help make him want to continue to use them.
5. Explain that her child responds when he hears others vocalize various attitudes. He may show a frightened expression or cry if he hears shouting or angry voices, even if he can't see the person. When he hears other people laughing and using high-pitched silly sounds, he may laugh or coo in enjoyment!

BLIND PARENT

May be unaware of her child's facial and gestural expressions which accompany his vocalized attitudes.

1. Clearly describe the child's facial and gestural expressions as they occur when he vocalizes his various feelings, e.g., furrowed eyebrows, puckered lips, legs kicking when fussing, arms waving, chest shaking from breathing hard, and raised eyebrows when squealing.
2. When the parent holds her child, she can note his variation in muscle tone and bodily movements as he vocalizes attitudes.
3. Explain that her child watches others' facial and gestural expressions when they communicate various attitudes; when he watches expressions, it helps him figure out the meaning of what people are saying.

2.15 Child: **REACTS TO MUSIC BY COOING** (5-6 mo.)
Parent: Provides musical experiences which are pleasing to the child

MENTALLY RETARDED PARENT

May be unaware of musical experiences which are pleasing to young children.

1. Discuss the parent's interest in music, for example, when does she listen to it? What are her favorite types? etc. Ask if her child likes music and how can she tell? Does he seem to like certain types?
2. Encourage the parent to sing her favorite songs to her child. Include the following concepts:
a. A good singing voice is not important; he just likes to hear her voice.
b. Music makes him feel good.
c. He learns that words are fun to hear in music.
3. Help select or lend children's records and musical toys. Name children television shows which play music he might light to hear.
4. Explain if he hears loud music on radios or stereos all day, he stops listening to it because it is too much.

DEAF PARENT

May be unaware of appropriate musical experiences for her child, and of their type or volume.

1. Relate to the parent that children usually enjoy the sound of soft music and will often coo (a melodic soft vowel sound — "oo," "aah," "ee") as if he is singing alone. If the child coos to music during your presence, identify his cooing sounds for the parent (written or fingerspelled).
2. Show the parent commercial toys which play songs, e.g., music boxes and wind-up stuffed toys which play lullabies. Explain that these toys are usually at a comfortable volume and can be placed near the child. Demonstrate the appropriate distance for each toy.
3. If a television is present, assist the parent in marking knobs to insure the sound is at a comfortable level for her child and help identify shows which play music:
a. Point out which exercise shows often have music. The parent can watch the exercise for rhythm cues, and move or rock her child to the rhythm of the music.

b. Music dance shows can provide music for the child and rhythm cues for the parent through the dancers' movements.
c. The parent can feel music vibrations through the television speaker.
4. Mark the appropriate volume on radio or stereo system volume controls. Point out easy listening music stations.
5. The car radio and button can be set by the facilitator for selection of easy listening music. Mark the dial for volume and encourage the parent to turn the radio on for her child while driving.
6. Encourage parent to hum her own songs to her child while rocking, feeding, or playing with him.

BLIND PARENT

May be unaware of her child's non-audible responses to music.

1. Describe the child's silent responses to music, e.g., stilling or increased movement, smiles, facial brightening, and searching for the source with his eyes.

2.16 Child: LOOKS AND VOCALIZES TO OWN NAME (5-7 mo.)
Parent: Vocalizes the child's name often during daily activities; reinforces his positive responses

GENERAL GUIDELINES

The child will look toward the speaker and sometimes coo when his name is called.

Parents can help teach their child his name by saying it often during play and daily activities. They also help him learn his name by using a consistent name for him rather than several nicknames which could confuse him. Touching the child, attracting his attention, and "Peek-a-boo" games while saying the child's name help him learn to associate his name label with himself.

MENTALLY RETARDED PARENT

May not say her child's name often or consistently, and may not interpret or recognize her child's acknowledging responses.

1. Emphasize the importance of consistently referring to the child by the same name — preferably something short and simple. Refer to 1.38 (Looks for family members or pets when named).
2. Model saying the child's name frequently during sessions. Explain touching him and looking at him while saying his name teaches him what his name is.
3. Verbally prompt the parent to say her child's name often during daily activities, e.g., "Call his name before you give him that toy."
4. Praise the parent when she says her child's name during activities; point out how she is helping him to learn his name, and that she is a good teacher.

5. Show the parent how to reinforce her child when he responds to his name by attending to him when he looks or vocalizes, and by praising him. Explain that her child will not always look or vocalize when she calls his name, especially while he is just learning what his name is, or when he is busy playing.
6. If the parent pokes at her child's face when calling his name:
   a. Directly demonstrate how to point to the child *without* touching him when calling his name. Explain that poking at the child's face can scare him.
   b. Demonstrate gently touching the child's tummy when saying his name.

DEAF PARENT

May not use speech to say her child's name.

1. The parent should create and use a name sign for her child and use it often during daily activities, if speech is not her primary communication mode:
   a. A comprehensive signing dictionary could be consulted before adapting a name sign to avoid a sign that means something else or has a negative connotation.
   b. Encourage the parent to say her child's name along with his name sign. The child will learn to recognize his verbal name over time, even if it is somewhat distorted.
   c. Hearing adults, siblings, and friends should also be encouraged to say the child's name and use his name sign during their interactions with him.
2. When the child is first learning his name sign, adults should sign his name with their hand on his body while they say his name.
3. Alert the parent to watch for her child's indications of vocalizing when his name is signed or spoken.

BLIND PARENT

May be unaware of her child's non-vocal responses to his name.

1. Describe the child's facial and gestural responses to his name, such as eye contact, head turning, stopping his activity, etc. The parent can listen for her child's pauses in play to help recognize when he is responding.

2.17 Child: BABBLES DOUBLE CONSONANTS "BABA" (5-8 mo.)
Parent: Includes double consonant words in her child's language environment

GENERAL GUIDELINES

The child's maturing coordination of lips, tongue, and jaw enable him to progress from producing strings of consonant-vowel chains (babababa) to more controlled "couplets" of double syllables, such as "baba," "mama," and "gaga."

Although these "couplets" are not intentional word labels, parents may interpret and respond to them as meaningful words; this helps the child learn the power of his sounds and leads to his understanding of their communicative purpose in the near future.

In addition to providing an overall meaningful and sensitive language environment for their child as outlined in 2.13 (Babbles consonant chains "bababab"), parents can encourage their child's double consonant babbling by using double consonant words (mama, dada, byebye, oh-oh) with the child and repeating his sounds back to him.

MENTALLY RETARDED PARENT

May not reinforce her child's babbling.

1. Continue with activities outlined under 2.13 (Babbles consonant chains).
2. Name double consonant words the parent could use when talking to her child.
3. Explain that her child is still practicing his sounds and learning that they mean something. When he says "dada," "mama," or "baba," he does not always mean daddy, mommy, or bottle. Help the parent think of the other things her child may be saying when he babbles double consonants.

DEAF PARENT

May be unaware that her child's babbling sounds have become more refined.

1. Relate that her child is now beginning to produce some vocalizations which sound more like words because he can put just two of his sounds together now, rather than repeating the sound over and over again. Explain that this takes more vocal control. Relate that these sounds are still called babbling.
2. During vocal play, assist the parent in recognizing the child's babbling couplets (fingerspelled or written, and lipreading). The parent can feel the vibrations of the produced sounds as you imitate her child's sounds. She can also feel her child's vibrations by gently touching his throat for vowels and most consonant sounds (b, d) and his nose for the m and n sounds.
3. Remind the parent to watch for her child's signs of babbling before interacting. While he is babbling, she can respond by smiling, raising eyebrows (as if to understand), or slightly nodding her head. Stress, however, that too much stimuli will cause her head to stop his sounds so he can listen and watch her.
4. Encourage the parent to vocalize, if comfortable, double consonant words in conjunction with her signs (mama, dada, oh-oh). Relate to her that the word "bye" is typically said for the child as a double consonant word "bye-bye." Explain this is much easier for her children to say.

BLIND PARENT

May be unaware of her child's non-verbal gestures which accompany his double consonants.

1. Refer to 2.13 (Babbles consonant chains "bababab").
2. Explain that children watch our mouths to help them learn how to form their own sounds.

2.18 Child: **BABBLES TO PEOPLE (5½-6½ mo.)**
Parent: Provides a meaningful and responsive language environment for child

GENERAL GUIDELINES

As the child learns his babbling brings him attention, he has learned that he can participate in communication interchanges with adults. He may even try to interrupt his parent's conversations with others by suddenly increasing his babbling to say "Talk to me!"

Parental facilitation techniques and activities for encouraging their child's babbling to people are identical to those described in the general guidelines and activities for 2.13 (Babbles consonant chains "bababab").

2.19 Child: **WAVES OR RESPONDS TO BYE-BYE (6-9 mo.)**
Parent: Encourages child to notice and respond to others' waves for "bye-bye," in context, during daily experiences

GENERAL GUIDELINES

The child is beginning to associate the waving gesture to the word "bye-bye." At this age, he needs to see the gestures from others to help him with this association and produce his own wave. At first his wave may be backwards (so he sees his own palm), or very subtle with his hands only slightly moving, or he may move his entire arm somewhat without moving his fingers. The child often delays his "waving" until the person has left!

Parents help their child learn to wave by modeling the waving gesture and physically prompting him to do the same as they say "bye-bye." Parents should avoid confusing the child by saying "bye-bye" only within the appropriate context.

MENTALLY RETARDED PARENT

May not interpret her child's subtle waving movements as prerequisites to waving.

1. Model and encourage the parent to wave and say "bye-bye" as people or pets leave the room in front of the child. Describe her child's responses, such as face brightening, arm movements, etc.:
   a. Explain that, at this age, this is the way he waves because his arms aren't ready to wave the way we do.
   b. Demonstrate the various movements her child may use as he learns to wave like us.
2. Ask the parent to think of times she can say "bye-bye" and help her child wave so he learns what the word "bye-bye" means:
   a. Verbally prompt, as needed, including when pets or family members leave a room or the house, at stores when they leave the check-out lines, etc.
   b. Explain not to encourage her child to wave unless he or someone else is leaving, or he will be confused and not learn what the word "bye-bye" means.

2.0 EXPRESSIVE LANGUAGE

2.19

DEAF PARENT

May not be aware that children usually learn "bye" as a double consonant word "bye-bye."

1. Anticipatory Guidance: The "bye" and "hi" signs are the same as the waving gesture for those with hearing.
2. Relate to the parent that, since her child is still babbling and using double consonant words at this stage, it is easier for him to say the same sound over rather than to say a single sound; therefore, it is easier for him to understand and say "bye-bye" instead of the single word "bye." Encourage the parent when vocalizing and modeling "bye" to say it as a double word.

BLIND PARENT

May be unaware of her child's inaudible responses to "bye-bye."

1. If the parent does not wave "bye-bye" with her child, describe the gesture and how it helps her child learn the meaning of the word "bye-bye."
2. The parent may be able to monitor the movement of her child's arm and hand as he waves when she is holding him. Describe her child's more subtle responses as indicated, and the typical developmental progression of children's waving gestures.

2.20 Child: SAYS "DADA" OR "MAMA" NONSPECIFICALLY (6½-11½ mo.)
Parent: Helps child associate his "dada" and "mama" vocalizations with the corresponding parent

GENERAL GUIDELINES

The child usually says "mama" and "dada" with greater frequency than his other double consonant sounds because they usually have been the sounds which have been reinforced most by his parents. At this age, however, when the child says "mama" or "dada," he may say them randomly without attaching specific meaning.

As parents continue to respond to these sounds, they help their child learn to differentiate and attach "mama" for mother and "dada" for father. To help their child attach specific meanings for "mama" and "dada," parents can:
1. Call themselves "Mama" and "Dada" appropriate in front of their child, i.e., "See Mama!" "Here's Dada."
2. Say "Mama" and point to themselves if the child says "Dada" to mother.
3. Respond with delight and attention to the child's "Mama" or "Dada" by the respective parent.

MENTALLY RETARDED PARENT

May feel upset if her child only says "dada" (or "mama" when parent is the father).

1. Provide anticipatory guidance that her child says "dada" (or "mama") because it is easier for her child to say; when he says the wrong name, he is not really calling mother or father yet; he's just practicing his sounds and beginning to learn what they mean.
2. Tell the parent she can help her child know who mama and dada are by saying the words while pointing to mama and dada during the day:
    a. Suggest various situations in which the parent can point to herself and say "mama" (or "dada").
    b. Model phrases to say to her child, e.g., "Mama's hair," "Come to Mama," and "I'm Mama" (when child says dada to mother).
3. During your sessions with the parent:
    a. Verbally prompt the parent to tell her child she's Mama (or Dada if it is the father).
    b. If the child says "dada" to mother (or the reverse), remind the parent he is still learning and doesn't really think her name is "dada," and he is not calling for daddy.

DEAF PARENT

May not be able to recognize or reinforce her child's nonspecific productions of "dada" or "mama."

1. Refer to 2.17 (Babbles double consonants "baba") to assist the parent with recognizing when her child produces "mama" and/or "dada." Explain he has not attached specific meanings yet, but she can help him learn the meaning by signing or saying "mama" when she refers to herself and when he says "mama."
2. Encourage the parent to use "mama" and "dada" as titles for mother and father when communicating with the child, pairing vocalizations with sign.
3. Family members and other people present should alert the parent when her child vocalizes "mama." She can then immediately reinforce his productions by saying or signing, "Here's Mama."

2.21 Child: SHOUTS FOR ATTENTION (6½-8 mo.)
Parent: Attends when child shouts for attention

MENTALLY RETARDED PARENT

May not interpret her child's shouts for attention.

1. Discuss and prompt the parent to think of various reasons why people shout, e.g., when angry, to call someone's attention, and when happy:
    a. Relate how children shout to get attention; when her child shouts, he is saying "I want you," "Come talk to me," or "Something is wrong."
    b. Point out that when we want someone who is in another room, we can go get them or call their name, but a child at this age cannot do this, so he shouts instead.
2. Help the parent interpret what her child is saying when he shouts, depending upon the situation and place:
    a. Give several example situations (feeding, crib, playpen, getting into danger) and ask the parent what her child

is saying when he shouts, e.g., "During feeding, the phone rings and while you are talking, he starts shouting."
b. Interpret the child's shouting when it occurs to the parent and prompt her corresponding response, as needed.

DEAF PARENT

May be unable to hear her child's shouts for attention.

1. Explain children's shouting sounds (e.g., loud short bursts of babble sounds) and their intent for attention. Highlight her child's discriminating facial and body movements when he shouts.
2. Hearing persons in the household can alert the parent when he is shouting out of her sight. Older siblings can be quite helpful with this!
3. See activity adaptations for 1.01 (Quiets when picked up) for additional suggestions to increase parent's awareness of times when her child is shouting.

2.22 Child: **PRODUCES THESE SOUNDS FREQUENTLY IN BABBLING: B, M, P, D, T, N, G, K, W, H, F, V, TH, S, Z, L, R (7-15 mo.)**
Parent: Provides adequate vocal stimulation for child; reinforces child's vocalizations throughout the day

GENERAL GUIDELINES

The child uses all of these consonant sounds during his babbling and vocal play. They are listed in the order which most children acquire them. Although children will not use all of these sounds as they begin to say single words, they often follow the same sequence in using the sounds they do incorporate to say words. For example, the child is likely to say "ball" before he can articulate "shoe."

Parents encourage these sounds by continuing to provide their child with a reinforcing and meaningful language environment. Refer to 2.13 (Babbles consonant chains "bababba") general guidelines and continue parent activities.

DEAF PARENT

May not be aware of the developmental sequence of sounds, and may have difficulty recognizing and reinforcing her child's expanding vocalizations.

1. Relate to the parent the general developmental order of children's sound production, i.e.:
   a. Vowels first.
   b. Bilabial m, b, and p sounds produced by using both lips next. These may be heard during feeding and appear as if her child is smacking his lips.
   c. Then d and t with the remaining consonants usually appearing in the above given order.
2. Assist the parent in identifying the sounds her child makes as they occur. Use fingerspelling or written letters to list the child's vocalizations.

2.23 Child: **VOCALIZES IN INTERJECTIONAL MANNER (7½-9 mo.)**
Parent: Exposes child to vocal interjectional patterns; reinforces child's interjections

GENERAL GUIDELINES

Many of the child's sounds resemble exclamations as he is able to alter his pitch, loudness, and stress.

Parents encourage their child's use of exclamation sounds by modeling a variety of inflections in appropriate contexts. "Uh-oh," "oops," "wow," "boom," and "oh" are favorites for the child to hear and learn.

Parents can reinforce their child's own use of exclamatory sounds by sharing in the excitement of his sound through repetition and expansion into a meaningful sentence. For example, when she hears her child inflect a sound similar to uh-oh, the parent can say, "Uh-oh! The cup fell!"

MENTALLY RETARDED PARENT

May not model or reinforce interjectional speech sounds with her child.

1. If you do not observe the parent using exclamations, explain and demonstrate how exclamatory inflection helps us figure out the meaning and feeling of the speaker:
   a. Model saying "Wow!", "Uh-oh!", "Ah!", and "Oops!" in a short phrase with emphasis and a high-pitched tone. Contrast this by saying each exclamation in a phrase without inflection or emphasis, one at a time.
   b. With each modeling, ask the parent to pick which way the word sounded more exciting and let her know how you were feeling.
   c. Relate that her child learns to understand words by the "feeling" with which they are said.
2. Encourage the parent to practice exclamatory phrases:
   a. Give example situations which warrant exclamations, e.g., juice spills, a dog runs through the room quickly, or the child has a very messy face.
   b. Model corresponding short phrases for her to select. Encourage her to come up with her own phrase.
   c. Use tape recorders to practice for fun.
3. Model, and let the parent practice, playing an "Uh-oh" game with her child using a busy box or similar pop-up toy. Each time a different animal pops up, use a different exclamation.
4. As the child vocalizes interjections, help the parent repeat and expand it into a meaningful sentence for her child:
   a. Model and encourage the parent to copy her child's exclamations exactly the way he says them.
   b. Give several example situations in context, e.g., child interjects "Ut!" as he drops his toy. Prompt the parent to think of what to say to tell him she understands what he's saying, e.g., "Uh-oh! The toy dropped."
5. Point out the child's expressions which indicate he likes it when his parent uses exclamations, i.e., "See how he laughed" or "He heard you say that; now he's trying."

2.23

DEAF PARENT

May not expose her child to vocal interjectional patterns, and may not recognize her child's interjections.

1. Explain that young children enjoy hearing and watching adult's exclamations. They quickly learn the meaning of a situation by listening to the tone of voice and animated manner associated with the exclamation. Relate that when her child or objects topple over, "boom," "oops," "uh-oh" are commonly used expressions.
2. Encourage the parent to use a variety of exclamatory expressions while playing with her child. Have the parent use the expressive mode which is most comfortable for her. Many of these exclamations are represented in sign language. Encourage the parent to use her voice, if comfortable in association with the sign.
3. Name the exclamations her child is using as they occur. The parent can associate her child's accompanying facial and bodily gestures for reinforcement.
4. Help select children's records which provide a variety of interjectional tones.

BLIND PARENT

May be unaware of the visual spectacle which prompted her child to use an exclamation.

1. Some of the child's interjectional vocalizations may be accompanied by auditory cues which can help the parent determine their meaning and thus reinforce her child. For example, "Uh-oh!" accompanied by the sound of a block hitting the floor may be reinforced by the parent saying, "Uh-oh, you dropped a block!"
2. If there are no auditory cues to help assign meaning to the child's exclamations, the parent may respond, "Oh, my! What happened? You must have seen something neat!"
3. Describe the various visual spectacles as they occur to which the child vocalizes exclamations.

2.24 Child: BABBLES WITH INFLECTION SIMILAR TO ADULT SPEECH (7½-12 mo.)
Parent: Exposes child to speech with varied inflection; reinforces child's inflectional babbling

GENERAL GUIDELINES

The child's babbling begins to take on patterns of intonation, stress, and speech which is similar to adult sentences. In addition to using interjections for exclamations, he places stress on his final syllables during babbling phrases.

Parents encourage their child to babble with inflection by speaking with extra emphasis, stress, and interjections during their interactions with the child. They can help reinforce their child's use of babbling with inflection by interpreting what he may be saying and use the interpretation to talk back to him using the same types of inflection, or by answering his inflections which sound like questions.

If the child's babbling decreases or is observed to lack a variety of intonations and inflection, he should be referred for a hearing evaluation to rule out hearing loss.

MENTALLY RETARDED PARENT

May not speak to her child with varied inflections.

1. Review how children learn to understand what we are saying by the way we say it:
   a. Demonstrate saying the same phrase as a question, an imperative, and as an exclamation, e.g., "That is great?", "That is great," and "That is great!"
   b. Give examples of common phrases said to children, and let the parent practice saying them as a question and then with excitement, e.g., "Do you want to get up?", and "You want to get up!"
2. Anticipatory Guidance: Parents who do not incorporate inflectional patterns into their speech may be able to use inflections more comfortably through songs and rhymes which can provide the child exposure to inflections:
   a. Teach simple inflectional songs and rhymes for the parent to sing or say during various activities, e.g., "This is the way we put on your clothes" (sung to the tune of "Mulberry Bush").
   b. Make up simple tunes or rhymes with specific intonation patterns.
   c. Lend children's records or rhyme song toy radios, or make jingle-type songs on cassette tapes, for the parent to play and sing with her child.
3. Help the parent interpret and respond to what her child is saying when he babbles with inflection. Point out the child's discriminating intonations and accompanying gestures which help tell us what he is saying, e.g., "He made his voice sound like he's asking a question and is reaching and looking toward his toy." Ask the parent what she can say and do to let him know she understands what he is trying to say.

DEAF PARENT

May not provide inflectional variety in her speech, and may be unaware of her child's inflectional patterns in speech.

1. Anticipatory Guidance: If the child is observed to lack intonation and stress in his babbling, he may have a hearing loss or may lack sufficient opportunities to hear normal speech patterns. Professional consultation is advised to rule out hearing loss if there are ample language models in the home.

   If there do not appear to be opportunities for the child to hear normal speech, explore community resources to help expand the child's hearing exercises, such as neighborhood play groups, foster grandparents, or church nursery programs.

   Suggest taking the child on various outings to playgrounds and stores on a regular basis.
2. Explain the child's babbling with inflection to the parent, i.e., "He is trying to talk like adults; his babbling is beginning to sound like sentences even though he is not saying words; he likes to listen for the inflection or melody of adult speech."

3. When you observe the child babbling with inflection, cue the parent to his inflectional patterns:
   a. Thumb up means high inflection; thumb down means lower inflection.
   b. Move your hand in an up and down horizontal wave-like fashion to help the parent understand his speech rhythms.
   c. The parent can watch for her child's corresponding expressions and gestures to help determine his intent, e.g., visual regard, reaching, and showing.
4. Help select musical rhyme toy radios and records, or make cassette tapes with rhymes and songs, which contain a variety of inflections.
5. Remind the parent to watch for her child's babbling to finish before responding with her gestures or speech.
6. Suggest children's television shows which provide lots of inflections, such as "Sesame Street" or "Captain Kangaroo."

BLIND PARENT

May be unaware of her child's increasing gestural usage which accompanies his babbling with inflection.

1. Describe each of the child's new gestures and patterns which accompany his babbling inflections, e.g., "When he babbles and sounds like he's asking a question, he always raises his eyebrows and tilts his head."
2. Name the child's accompanying gestures to babbling which help explain his communicative intent, e.g., showing a toy by holding it out, reaching toward objects, looking toward objects, and waving.

2.25 Child: BABBLES SINGLE CONSTANT "BA" (8-12 mo.)
Parent: Reinforces and interprets child's single consonant vocalizations

GENERAL GUIDELINES

As the child develops more control over his speech production, he is able to break down his babbling strings and "couplets" to produce only one consonant sound. After much practice and differential reinforcement by adults for certain one-syllable consonant sounds, the child begins to use and attach various meanings to each. For example, he may say "ba" for "bye, bottle, certain toys, or a name for a sibling; and "da" to mean "I want that," "Look at that," or "What's that?"

Parents help foster these "pre-words" by interpreting their meaning for the child, even before he has a meaning associated to them. Parents reinforce their child's continued use of "pre-words" by investigating and responding to the child's intent, dependent upon contextual and gestural cues. The parent also teaches and prepares her child for future true word use by interpreting and repeating his "pre-word" as a true word. For example, when child says "da?" the parent helps by saying, "What's that? That's a ball!"

MENTALLY RETARDED PARENT

May not interpret or reinforce her child's single consonant sounds.

1. Anticipatory Guidance: If you have encouraged the parent to reinforce her child's babbling sounds by repeating them back, it is time to reorient the parent to reinforce his sounds *not* by saying them back, but by saying the true words. Illustrate with several examples.
2. Help identify and interpret the single syllable sounds her child is now making and anticipate a few he may start saying soon:
   a. Tell the parent to stop saying them back to him the same way he says them; instead, say them back as a real word.
   b. Interpret the various meanings her child may have when he says single consonant sounds.
   c. Give example situations within context and ask the parent to think of things he may be saying when he says "ba," "da," etc.
   d. Help identify several words the parent could say back for each child utterance.
3. Demonstrate games to play with the child which emphasize one-syllable words for the parent to say, e.g.:
   a. Peek-a-boo, say "boo".
   b. Parent blowing bubbles, say "pop" with each bubble popping.
   c. Jack-in-the-box and other pop-up toys, say "pop" and "bye" when closing.
4. When you observe the child's single consonant sounds, remind the parent to "tell him the right word in a sentence," prompting as needed. Praise the parent for being such a good teacher in helping her child learn to talk.

DEAF PARENT

May not be able to recognize or reinforce her child's single consonant productions.

1. Explain single consonants as the next step after producing "couplets" of consonant-vowel combinations as outlined in the general guidelines. Refer to 2.13 (Babbles consonant chains "bababab") for assistance in identifying the child's sounds for the parent and activities to encourage his vocal productions.
2. Demonstrate playing "Peek-a-boo" games with the child, emphasizing the production of "boo."
   a. If the parent feels comfortable vocalizing "boo," she may be assisted in her production by imitating your modeled "boo" (a mirror can help parent check proper lip placement), and feeling the sound production at your throat.
   b. If the parent is not comfortable vocalizing, she can emphasize the visual production of "boo" on her lips.
   c. Other members of the family or friends who use speech can play "Peek-a-boo" games with the child so he can see and hear single vocalizations from those who are oral, while seeing the proper production from parent.
   d. Refer to 2.12 (Laughs when head is covered with a cloth) for suggestions to explain and teach "Peek-a-boo" games.

2.25

BLIND PARENT

May have difficulty interpreting her child's communicative intent if she cannot see his gestures, facial expressions, or context of the situation which accompanies his single consonant "pre-words."

1. Anticipatory Guidance: The child may begin to develop adaptive strategies to help the parent determine the context of the situation and the meaning of his "pre-word." For example, the child may hand an object to his parent rather than pointing toward it or only showing it to her.
2. Help the parent interpret her child's communicative intent when he babbles single consonant sounds by describing his gestures and the context of the situation. The parent can then become familiar with and associate the particular inflection, stress, and tone her child uses to help attach meaning to his intent.
3. Remind the parent, as necessary, that it helps her child learn to say single syllables by watching her mouth movements.

2.26 Child: SHOWS UNDERSTANDING OF WORDS BY APPROPRIATE BEHAVIOR OR GESTURES (9-14 mo.)
Parent: Interprets which words her child understands

GENERAL GUIDELINES

The child begins to understand and respond to the meaning of one or two words within adult sentences and verbal requests. He shows us he understands what we are saying by:
1. Looking at or moving toward the named object.
2. Displaying anticipatory excitement gestures.
3. Changing his facial expressions.
4. Carrying out a simple request appropriately.

Parents help their child understand and respond to their spoken words by:
1. Emphasizing words in sentences which are meaningful to the child.
2. Talking to their child within the context of the immediate situation, i.e., the referred to object or activity is present or currently happening.
3. Using gestures, as needed, to help clarify their statements or requests.

The following activities supplement those outlined for 1.48 (Listens selectively to familiar words) and assume they have been, or are being, implemented.

MENTALLY RETARDED PARENT

May not discriminate her child's behaviors which indicate he understands, from those which indicate he needs more help to understand.

1. Teach the parent to identify her child's behaviors which indicate he understands what we've said:
    a. Review with the parent several words from her child's word list (developed in 1.48) and help think of action phrases to say them in, e.g., "It's time to *eat*" or "Get your *ball*."
    b. Model a phrase and discuss the various ways her child tells us he understands the phrase. For example, if we said, "Do you want your *bottle*?" her child may smile, start tugging on you, fuss if he's impatient, or go to get it.
    c. Ask the parent to name some things her child might do to let us know he understands what we have said, using additional example phrases.
    d. Model saying some phrases to the child, and let the parent watch him and name the ways he shows us he understands the phrase.
2. Help the parent recognize when her child does not understand something we've said:
    a. Ask her to think of a word that is not on her child's word list and use it in a sentence with her child, prompting as needed.
    b. When the parent says the phrase to her child, point out her child's behaviors that show us he doesn't understand, e.g., he brings the wrong thing, he stares at her with a confused look, etc.
    c. Ask if she can think of ways to help him understand what she said. Suggest and model, as appropriate, gesturing and pointing, showing the child, and carrying out the request.
3. Discuss, and help the parent think of, times her child may not show us he understands, even though at other times he does, e.g., he's tired, he's busy, he didn't hear what we said, we said it too fast, he needed a gesture, the object talked about was not in sight, etc.
4. Role-play child actions which illustrate understanding phrases and not understanding phrases:
    a. Let the parent say the phrase and you act as the child.
    b. After displaying signals of understanding or not understanding, ask the parent to guess if you understood.
    c. Say a phrase in a foreign language to let the parent experience how confusing a request or statement could be if you don't understand the words.
    d. Tell the parent a statement and ask her to tell you she understands without using any words.

DEAF PARENT

May not say phrases to her child without using gestures.

1. List the child's words and action phrases he seems to understand.
2. Explain that, as her child is learning the meaning of words, it is good to use lots of gestures, but as he becomes familiar with them, he should learn to understand them by only hearing the word without help of gestures. If the parent cannot communicate without gestures:
    a. The parent can ask others who use spoken language in the household to talk to her child without gestures.
    b. Use action pictures with taped cassette recordings with her child; refer to Activity No. 3, 1.56 (Responds to simple verbal requests).

BLIND PARENT

May not be able to visually monitor her child's behaviors which indicate he understands what she said.

1. Describe the gestures and behaviors her child displays which tell us he understands what we have said. The parent can pay special attention to her child's audible and movement response cues of understanding.
2. Review the child's receptive vocabulary pointing out words for which he still relies upon gestures.
3. The parent can make requests or statements to her child which provide her tactual and sound cues, e.g., "Give me your _____," "Drink your juice," "Get with your ball," or "Dance."

2.27 Child: BABBLES IN RESPONSE TO HUMAN VOICE (11-15 mo.)
Parent: "Talks" to child meaningfully throughout day; reinforces child's vocal responses

GENERAL GUIDELINES

The child babbles purposefully in response to other's talking to him. His varied intonations and inflections help him to further express his meaning and let the receiver know his reciprocal communicative intent.

Parents encourage their child's mutual babbling dialogue by talking to the child about things that are meaningful to him, giving him a turn to respond, listening to his responsive babbling, and assigning meaning to his apparent conversations.

The activities for 2.13 (Babbles consonant chains "babababa") are prerequisite and complement the suggested activities for this skill.

MENTALLY RETARDED PARENT

May not talk meaningfully to her child; may not interpret her child's responsive babbling as his attempt to "talk back."

1. Review the previous ways her child has "talked back" to the parent when she talks to him, i.e., looked at her, smiled, squealed, and cooed:
   a. Explain that although her child may still not talk back to her with words, now that he makes lots of babble sounds, he is ready to "talk back" to her by using them.
   b. Ask the parent to name the babble sounds she hears her child using.
2. Demonstrate how her child may begin to talk back to the parent with babbling through role-play. Play the part of the child and have the parent talk about what she is going to do today. Suggest specific phrases to say, as needed.
3. Demonstrate, and let the parent practice, talking to her child while he is playing, waiting for his response, and then continuing the dialogue:
   a. Suggest something meaningful to talk to the child about, such as describing with what he is playing.
   b. Stress waiting five seconds before talking again, and waiting for him to finish talking.
   c. Interpret what the child may be using with his babbling and gestures.
4. Use two toy telephones as a vehicle for the parent and child to hold responsive conversations.

DEAF PARENT

May not hear her child's responsive babbling and may thus interrupt him or not allow him enough response time.

1. Explain that her child is beginning to talk back to others using his elaborate babbling skills. Compare this with his earlier skills, i.e., he responded to others by only making a sound or changing his vocal expressions:
   a. Explain that his language is still made up of mostly babbling sounds, but he is beginning to make them sound like speech sentences and using them for conversations to talk back to people.
   b. Demonstrate and point out that she may need to wait longer when he babbles back to her before talking or gesturing back.
   c. Fingerspell or write out examples of her child's babbles sentences.
2. If the parent is non-verbal, she can begin to cue her child to "talk back" to her signs and gestures using his "words," e.g., gesturing by pointing to the child and tapping his lips, or signing "Use your voice" by placing her index and third fingers in a V at her throat and drawing them up toward her chin.

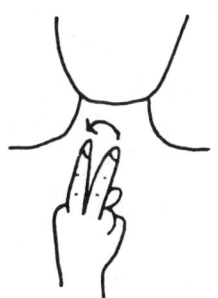

Place tips of "V" at the throat and draw up to chin

3. The parent can use "See-N-Say" toys, talking telephones, and talking dolls with her child during play and encourage him to talk back. Relate to the parent what each of the talking toys says.
4. Check local libraries for children's story telling times which incorporate total communication. The storytellers and interpreters are usually quite vocally animated.

BLIND PARENT

May be unaware of her child's communicative gestures which accompany his responsive babbling to her talking.

1. Describe any of the child's responsive gestures which accompany his responsive babbling. The child's increasing conventional use of inflection often match his gestures, which will help the parent recognize which gestures he may be using and interpret his intent. For example, a rising intonation may be accompanied by the child's head tilting to the side, signifying a questioning response.

2.28

2.28 Child: BABBLES MONOLOGUE WHEN LEFT ALONE (11-12 mo.)
Parent: Provides time alone for child to babble to self and interesting toys

GENERAL GUIDELINES

The child babbles to himself and toys when he is alone. He practices babbling new and old sound combinations, and delights in hearing his own voice and his ability to control it.

Parents can encourage their child's babbling when alone by providing him interesting things to "talk to" (mirrors, dolls, stuffed animals) and by not interrupting him when they hear him practicing.

MENTALLY RETARDED PARENT

May interrupt her child's solitary monologues.

1. Explain how sometimes children talk to themselves so they can practice saying their sounds. Point out the child's concrete behaviors which differentiate when he is looking for a parental response from when he talks to himself or his toys for practice:
    a. When the child is looking at us while talking or is shouting from far away, he probably wants us to talk back to him.
    b. When he is looking at or playing with a toy *without* looking for someone, he is probably practicing his sounds, so we should not interrupt him.
2. Ask the parent if she has seen her child talk to any particular toys or pictures. Help identify other toys or books to which he may like to talk:
    a. Explore times when her child is alone (nap time, while parent is showering or cooking, etc.) that she can make sure he has one or two of his toys or books to keep him company.
    b. Stress that he likes talking to her more than his toys because she listens and can talk back.

DEAF PARENT

May be unaware that her child babbles when he is alone.

1. Relate to the parent that, just as her child at an earlier age cooed when left alone, he now will babble to himself or toys because he likes to hear and practice his sounds.
2. Encourage parent to watch her child through lipreading and watching his gestures before intervening to see if he is babbling. Explain that, if she disturbs him, he will stop babbling to watch and listen to her.
3. Hearing adults and siblings can let the parent know when they hear her child babbling in his crib or while playing out of sight. Relate the sounds her child is saying while babbling alone and interpret what he may be saying.
4. Explain that, when he is alone, he also likes to talk to toys, books, and mirrors. Parent can watch to see if he seems to babble to some toys more than others.

BLIND PARENT

May have difficulty discriminating when her child is talking to toys, himself, or other people if she cannot see his body orientation or at what he is looking.

1. Provide anticipatory guidance that children talk to themselves and toys.
2. Advise the parent whenever you observe her child directing his babbling to toys or himself. The parent may then be able to attach her child's special babbling intonations and volume with specific toys and situations.
3. Describe the toys, pictures, and objects to which her child seems to babble the most.

2.29 Child: SAYS "DADA" OR "MAMA" SPECIFICALLY (11-14 mo.)
Parent: Says "dada" or "mama" in meaningful contexts with child, and interprets his expanded meaning when he says "mama" or "dada"

GENERAL GUIDELINES

In contrast to the child's earlier non-specific productions of "mama" and "dada," the child says them to specifically mean mother or father.

Earlier, when the child was practicing his single and double syllable consonant-vowel combinations, his "mamas" and "dadas" were probably reinforced most by his parents. As the child realizes through experience that these couplets produce the best results, he begins to attach meaning to them and use "ma-ma" and "da-da" discriminately and purposefully.

Some children will say "dada" specifically for mother and father because "dada" is often an easier sound for the child to produce.

At first, his specific productions of "mama" and "dada" will represent entire sentences for him. For example, "mama" or "dada" may mean "I want you," "I'm hungry," "I need help," or "There's Mom." His gestures, intonation, and context of the situation help his parents interpret his meaning.

Parents can encourage their child to say "mama" and "dada" specifically, by continuing to provide differential reinforcement and by providing ample opportunities for him to hear and attach specific meanings to each. For example, they can point to their own photographs and label them, identify themselves in front of mirrors with the child, and incorporate "mama" and "dada" throughout daily conversations and meaningful contexts ("Give Mama the ball," "There's Dada") with gestures.

MENTALLY RETARDED PARENT

May not provide ample opportunities for her child to hear and attach different meanings to "mama" and "dada," and may not interpret her child's communicative intent when he says "mama" or "dada."

1. Demonstrate and encourage activities which enable the child to hear and attach meaning to "mama" and "dada":

a. The parent can point to her clothing and say, "Mama's shirt; Mama's pants," when her child is looking at her.
b. Take pictures of each parent for them to point to and say "Here's Mama" and "Here's Dada."
c. Play "Peek-a-boo" saying "Where's Mama? Here's Mama."
d. Ask the parent to think of additional times she can say "Mama" and "Dada" specifically.
2. Help the parent interpret what her child may be saying when he says "mama" or "dada":
  a. Explain that, since he doesn't have very many words yet, her child says "mama" and "dada" to mean different things. Illustrate using examples, such as mama may mean "Come here," "Help," or "I want to get up."
  b. Name example situations which provide the context to help interpret what the child means when he says "mama," e.g., ask the parent what her child is saying when he's yelling "mama" from his crib, pointing to a toy and saying "mama," or pointing to the car and saying "dada."
  c. Ask the parent what her child may be saying when you hear him say "mama" or "dada" during your presence.
3. If the child is calling his mother "Dada," explain that he really means "Mama," but the tongue movements to say Dada are easier for him to make. Model responsive phrases and gestures for the parent to use if her child calls her "dada," e.g., "I'm Mama; soon you'll be able to say Mama."

DEAF PARENT

May not be aware that her child's vocalized "mama" or "dada" is now specific and may have various communicative meanings.

1. Encourage the parent to refer to herself and other family members using appropriate role titles, e.g., Mama, Dada, and Grandma:
  a. The parent should couple her speech, if possible, with the sign for mama and other family titles.
  b. If the parent is non-verbal, she can imitate the lip movements to couple with her signs.
  c. Verbal adults can say the role title without using sign.
2. Help the parent recognize when her child begins to say "mama" and "dada" specifically, by point out his gestural indicators.
3. Explain that when children say "mama" or "dada," they are often trying to communicate a whole phrase or sentence with the one word. Provide examples with context situations and possible accompanying gestures her child may use. The parent can respond to her child's "mamas" by watching for contexts, facial expressions, and gestures.

BLIND PARENT

May not use pointing or "showing" gestures to help her child attach meaning to his "mama" and "dada" utterances, and may have difficulty interpreting her child's meaning if she cannot see his gestures or the contextual situation.

1. If you do not observe the parent using personal reference gestures when using role-titles, such as "Mama" and "Dada":
  a. Describe the gestures, i.e., extending arm and finger toward named person, or patting chest when referring to self.
  b. Explain how these gestures encourage her child to look toward the person being pointed out, which helps him attach meaning to the word label.
2. Describe the child's non-verbal signs which tell us he receptively understands "Mama" and "Dada," e.g., "When I said, 'Where is Mama?' he smiled and looked right at you!"
3. Describe the context and child's gestures when he says "Mama" or "Dada." The parent can learn to interpret her child's expanded meaning by listening to his varied vocal changes when saying "Mama" or "Dada, dependent upon the situation.

2.30 Child: REPEATS SOUNDS OR GESTURES IF LAUGHED AT (11-12 mo.)
Parent: Laughs when appropriate at child's silly sounds or gestures

GENERAL GUIDELINES

When the child realizes that his vocalizations or gestures prompted laughter and attention from others, he repeats them in an effort to maintain and attract additional attention. He may even add an additional "extra" gestures, such as a coy smile, clapping, or tilting his head.

Positive attention from others increases the child's self-esteem, and helps him recognize the social and communicative power of his vocalizations and gestures.

MENTALLY RETARDED PARENT

May not realize that positive attention can encourage her child to repeat his behaviors.

1. Model laughing, applauding, and cheering the child for his new or silly sounds and gestures during intervention sessions with the parent and child. Describe and point out the child's positive responses, explaining he feels important and special when we give him attention.
2. Name a few ways we can tell children we like what they did or think they are fun and silly, e.g., smiling, laughing, patting, nodding, and saying "Great," "Good job," "Silly goose," or "Terrific!" Encourage the parent to name additional ways. Post a list of "Things that make me feel good" on the wall under a picture of the child smiling.
3. Play a game of making silly sounds into paper towel-roll tubes or coffee cans. Model laughing at the child's funny sounds and faces.
4. Caution the parent that, if she laughs at her child when he misbehaves, he will probably misbehave again because he likes to see his parent laugh:
  a. Provide concrete examples, such as "If you laugh when he hits another child, he will think hitting is funny and will keep on doing it."

2.30

b. Name additional undesirable behaviors and ask the parent what will happen if she laughs, e.g., "If he throws food and you laugh, what will he think? Then what will he do?"

DEAF PARENT

May be unaware that her child makes and repeats silly sounds if laughed at.

1. Relate through comparison that, just as her child repeats a silly gesture or facial expression if we laugh at them, he may also repeat a vocal sound if he sees it makes us laugh.
2. The parent can watch for her child's accompanying lip movements when she sees her child make silly gestures. Fingerspell or write the silly sounds her child is making, cueing the parent if he is also using exaggerated intonations to be silly. The child's accompanying facial expressions will also provide the parent excellent visual cues, so she can laugh with her child.
3. Encourage the non-verbal parent to engage her child in silly sound-play by making kissing, tongue clicking, and "raspberry" sounds.

BLIND PARENT

May not be aware of her child's silly gestures.

1. Anticipatory Guidance: The child will probably have developed adaptive strategies to gain attention for his silly behaviors by this developmental age. He may rely upon silly sounds or gestures which provide tactile or auditory feedback from his parent.
2. Explain that children make and repeat silly gestures if they are laughed at; he may tilt his head and squint his eyes, and make a silly face by wrinkling his nose and sticking out his tongue, or wiggle his body to dance:
    a. Describe the child's silly gestures which do not produce audible cues and facial expressions as you observe them. Explain their context, if needed.
    b. The parent can associate her child's silly sounds which often accompany his gestures.

2.31 Child: **SPEECH MAY PLATEAU AS CHILD LEARNS TO WALK (11½-15 mo.)**
2.32 Child: **UNABLE TO TALK WHILE WALKING**
Parent: Understands that child's speech may plateau as he begins to learn to walk; continues appropriate vocal stimulation

GENERAL GUIDELINES

As the child begins to place enormous thought and energy into initiating and coordinating walking, he may put his talking "on hold." He may babble less and not acquire new words or new babble combinations until he has mastered the art of walking and can redirect his energies back into talking.

Parents should continue to provide a rich language environment because their child's receptive language skills continue to expand daily. Trying to "make" a child talk could become a frustrating experience for both parent and child and thus should be avoided.

All children do not stop or reduce their talking during this period. If the child's speech has been observed to plateau, all parents may benefit from anticipatory guidance to prevent their undue concern and frustration.

MENTALLY RETARDED PARENT

May try to make her child talk, or may stop talking to him if she is not reinforced by his responsive vocalizations.

1. If you observe the child's speech to plateau, explain to the parent that, just like a lot of children, while her child is learning to walk, it is hard for him to think about walking and talking at the same time so he talks less:
    a. Assure the parent that after he starts walking well, he will start talking again because then he will not have to think so hard about how to walk.
    b. Relate an analogy to help the parent understand her child's reduction in speech, e.g., "If you were learning to walk on a tightrope, imagine how hard it would be to talk to someone when you were trying with all your might to balance yourself!"
2. Stress that although her child may talk less, he still listens to what people are saying so he can learn the meaning of words:
    a. Empathize how frustrating it can be to talk to her child and not hear him talk back, but stress it is still very important to keep talking to him so he can learn words.
    b. If the parent appears frustrated when her child does not talk back to her, talk for the child with phrases, such as "Gosh, Mom, I am thinking so hard about walking and not falling, I can't talk. But, I still love to hear you talk!"
3. Model, and let the parent practice, saying encouraging phrases to her child while he is practicing walking, e.g., "There you go! Look at what a big boy you are!"

2.33 Child: **OMITS FINAL AND SOME INITIAL CONSONANTS (12-17 mo.)**
Parent: Understands child's developmentally appropriate omission of initial and/or final consonants; vocalizes correct speech to child in response

GENERAL GUIDELINES

The child often omits or distorts the initial and final consonant sounds in his "words." For example, he may say "poon" for spoon, "gie" for doggie, or "tup" for cup.

Parents may benefit from anticipatory guidance to prevent undue concern about their child's misarticulations. They can help him use clearer speech as he experiments and practices his words by modeling the correct pronunciation of his words or phrases when they hear them. The temptation to laugh at or repeat his "cute" mispronunciations should be avoided to prevent reinforcement and confusion.

MENTALLY RETARDED PARENT

May expect her child to say words correctly, or may reinforce his mispronunciations by laughing at or repeating them.

1. Advise the parent that all children mispronounce words when they are leaning to talk because their mouth movements and muscles are not ready to say words exactly right:
   a. Illustrate common misarticulations with a few examples.
   b. Ask the parent if she can think of words her child can say, but not exactly like an adult.
2. Emphasize how tempting it is to laugh at or repeat words the way small children say them because it sometimes sounds so cute. Stress, however, if we laugh at his words or say them the way he does, he will *not* want to learn to say them correctly.
3. Model examples of ways to respond to a few of the child's misarticulations. Role-play additional situations with the parent. For example, say "key" while pointing to the kitty cat and help the parent think of a phrase, such as "Yes, that's a kitty cat."
4. When the child says word approximations during your sessions with the parent, prompt her, as needed, to say his words correctly within a descriptive phrase. Use verbal prompts to the parent, such as "What did he just say? Tell him about it."

DEAF PARENT

May be unaware that children omit or distort initial and final consonants when they are first learning to talk, and may not be able to model the correct pronunciation of her child's "words."

1. Explain the child's misarticulations are normal in developmental progression toward learning to say words:
   a. Fingerspell or write the phonetic spellings of her child's word approximations that you observe.
   b. Explain that her child will learn to say the words correctly as his muscles involved in speaking mature and as he has more practice speaking.
   c. The parent can depend upon hearing family members and friends to monitor and report her child's improved articulation skills.
2. Inform others in the home who use speech about the importance of saying the child's mispronunciations correctly for him.
3. Encourage the parent to provide as many opportunities as possible for her child to hear good speech models. Record with stories, children's books, visits to the park, radios, and neighborhood toddler groups can help provide speech models.

BLIND PARENT

May have difficulty discriminating her child's word approximations if she cannot see the context in which they are being used.

1. Help interpret for the parent her child's word approximations, as needed, so that she can recognize them at other times during the day. The child may provide inflectional and tactual gesture cues, such as tugging or "giving," to help her interpret his new or multiple meaning word approximations.
2. Explain that children learn to pronounce their words better as they mature and by watching the speaker's mouth because he tries to copy the same mouth movements.

2.34 Child: BABBLES INTRICATE INFLECTION (12-18 mo.)
Parent: Reinforces and responds to child's intricate vocal inflectional patterns

GENERAL GUIDELINES

The child's babbling becomes more conversational in structure as he includes an intricate variety of intonations and inflectional patterns used by mature speakers. He may express delight, scold, ask questions, relate stories, or even sound quite serious as if he was reading the daily news! Although he does not use words, his communicative intent is usually quite clear.

Children learn to use and attach meaning to various inflectional patterns by hearing others use them in association with specific gestures and context. For example, although he may not understand the words in "Don't you ever do that again!" he learns that the intonational pattern expresses anger.

Parents can thus encourage their child to incorporate conversational inflectional patterns by using them themselves during daily conversation as the particular situation demands. Parents can also show their child that his inflectional babbling is useful by interpreting his communicative intent effectively, e.g., "Oh, you are so angry at that toy!" or "You are really telling me a great story!"

Although the child's inflectional patterns at this developmental age are more sophisticated than in the past, the parent activities for 2.24 (Babbles with inflection similar to adult speech) are applicable to this skill.

2.35 Child: EXPERIMENTS WITH COMMUNICATION – NOT FRUSTRATED WHEN MISUNDERSTOOD (12-17½ mo.)
Parent: Recognizes child's experimentation with communication; interprets and replies when appropriate

GENERAL GUIDELINES

The child usually does not become frustrated or show concern if his babbling, words, and word approximations do not receive a reply from others. He is much too busy testing his expressive ability to form new sounds, words, and babbling phrases. He may carry on a monologue to his toys, family members, and pets, or himself.

2.35

MENTALLY RETARDED PARENT

May think her child should only talk to people, not toys or himself.

1. Explain that children like to talk to toys, pets, and themselves as a way to practice new sounds and make new words. Reinforce the importance of not interrupting her child when he is "talking."
2. When you observe the child "talking" to a toy, animal, or himself, ask the parent what she thinks he might be saying.
3. Praise all of the parent's spontaneous responses to her child's vocalizations. Point out the child's gestural cues and the parent's corresponding response, e.g., "Timmy held his arms out and babbled to say he wanted the ball; even though he did not say that with words, you knew what he was telling you!"

DEAF PARENT

May be unaware that children experiment with "talking" and may have an undirected monologue.

1. Relate the child's vocal play at this developmental age, explaining he is not always interested in receiving a reply.
2. Alert the parent to watch to see if her child is talking to himself, toys, or pets before changing or interrupting his activity.

BLIND PARENT

May be unaware of her child's gestures and the context in which he is "talking"; she may thus be unable to discriminate when his talking is non-directed.

1. Provide anticipatory guidance regarding children's experimenting with communication and non-directed babbling:
    a. Name the toys and pets to which you observe her child "talking."
    b. The parent may be able to discriminate subtle differences in her child's voice tone and inflectional pattern when he is involved in non-directed experimental "talking."

2.36 Child: **USES SINGLE WORD SENTENCES (12-14 mo.)**
Parent: Interprets and expands child's one word sentence into a complete sentence

GENERAL GUIDELINES

The child says one word utterances to communicate a complete sentence. His single words may be conventional true words ("hot," "ball," "more") or sound combinations which are not true words, but are used consistently as words. For example, the child may consistently call his stuffed animal "boo-boo."

The child's single word can have a variety of meanings. When he says "ball," he may be saying "I want to play ball," "That's a ball," "Where is the ball?", "Look at my ball," or "I'm holding a ball." The context of the situation, the child's particular intonational pattern, and his accompanying gestures help the listener decide which sentence he may be saying.

Parents encourage their child's one word sentences by modeling the correct pronunciation of the child's word, and interpreting and expanding it into a more complete thought aloud to their child.

MENTALLY RETARDED PARENT

May not interpret or expand her child's single word sentences.

1. Start a list of each of the child's expressive words, word approximations, and his consistent sound combinations used as words. Draw simple pictures next to each word, as needed:
    a. Title the list "Words I Can Say" and draw a mouth on top of the list. Compare and contrast this list to the child's receptive vocabulary list (refer to Activity Nos. 2-4, 1.48), drawing an ear on the top of that list and titling it "Words I Can Understand."
    b. Ask the parent to listen to her child's new words each day, and add them to the list every week together.
2. Explain to the parent that, since her child cannot say whole sentences yet, he will say one word to mean a whole sentence. Provide several examples using words from the child's expressive word list.
3. Role-play guessing what the whole sentence is, using the same single word in different contexts with corresponding intonations and gestures. Tell the parent her child likes to hear her guess his whole sentence when he says one word because that way he knows he was understood.
4. Verbally prompt the parent during your sessions to tell her child what sentences he is saying using only one word. Describe his gesture and context cues, as needed, to help her think of the sentence.
5. Remind the parent to say her child's word approximations correctly so that he can learn to say them the right way. Review the child's word approximations on his expressive word list. Help the parent think of simple phrases to say which have the word pronounced correctly to her child.

DEAF PARENT

May be unaware that children use single spoken words to express an entire thought or sentence.

1. Relate to the parent how children use single spoken words to communicate an entire message as outlined in the general guidelines. Review each of her child's spoken "words" and give examples of messages he may be saying, using the appropriate "point," "show," or "question" gestures as cues.
2. Alert the parent when you hear her child saying single words so she can watch his lip movements, corresponding gestures, and facial expressions. Help interpret the child's "sentence," as needed, and encourage the parent to sign, gesture, or use her speech to tell him his complete sentence.
3. If sign language is used in the home, the child may be using single signs to communicate an entire message. The

parent and hearing adults should encourage the child to couple his voice with his signs. The non-verbal parent can use the "Use your voice" sign as illustrated in 2.27 (Babbles in response to voice).

BLIND PARENT

May have difficulty interpreting her child's one word sentences if she is unaware of his gestural cues and the situational cues.

1. Describe the child's accompanying gestures and facial expressions which help to interpret the meaning of his single word sentences. The parent can learn to associate and discern her child's intent, dependent upon the particular intonation, inflection, or pitch used when he says it.
2. If the child's single word sentence is unclear, the parent could explore his communicative intent through trial and error. She can probe with statements such as "Ball? Do you want to play ball? Bring me the ball," or "Ball? Your'e looking at your ball," and wait for the child to make another utterance or tactual gesture, such as giving her the ball.

2.37 Child: USES EXPRESSIVE VOCABULARY ONE-THREE WORDS (12-15 mo.)
Parent: Exposes child to adequate speech and language activities; fosters and reinforces child's expressive vocabulary

GENERAL GUIDELINES

The child may have one to three words (in addition to Mama and Dada) in his spontaneous expressive vocabulary. He may imitate many more words that he hears others say, but he does not use these in his spontaneous verbal repertoire. His first words are ones which he has heard often and are meaningful to him. "Cup," "ball," "hot," "car," and "doggie" are examples of common first words in addition to "Mama" and "Dada." He uses his words to connote a wide range of intentions. "Cup" may mean he is thirsty, sees his cup, or wants to give his cup to his mother. "Mama" may mean "Help," "There is Mother," or "Come here."

The child's single word can also have a variety of meanings because he is likely to over-generalize word labels. For example, all men may be "daddy" and all large animals may be "cows" or "doggies."

Parents encourage their child's expressive words by providing him with a rich language environment for understanding the meaning of words and by modeling how words are produced. This is an important time for parents to label actions and objects in the child's immediate environment, using repetition and slow, clear enunciation of words. "Baby-talk" and continually asking "What's that?" should be avoided.

Parents can also encourage their child's expressive speech by emending and expanding his single words into a complete sentence to let the child know his speech is understood and useful. Refer to 2.36 (Uses single word sentences).

MENTALLY RETARDED PARENT

May over-use "What's that?" with her child, without providing him the answer, or may not spontaneously label and describe things, actions, or events.

1. Refer to activities for 1.07 (Listens to voice for 30 seconds) if the parent does not talk about meaningful things to her child.
2. If the parent continuously asks her child, "What's that?" discourage this practice, explaining that he still needs a lot more practice hearing the names of objects:
   a. Illustrate changing a "What's that" question to a "That is" statement, e.g., "Instead of saying 'What's that?' and pointing to the picture of a baby, say, 'That's a baby'."
   b. Demonstrate additional "What's that" questions and let the parent practice changing them into "That is" statements.
   c. Let the parent show her child an alphabet picture book using "That is" statements.

DEAF PARENT

May be unaware of her child's expressive vocabulary.

1. Relate to the parent the words which are in her child's spontaneous spoken vocabulary. Explain the various meanings her child may use for each of them:
   a. Explain the difference between imitating words versus saying words spontaneously, relating that her child's imitative vocabulary has many more words.
   b. Cue the parent when you hear her child use his words so she can watch his lip movements, facial expressions, and note the context in which he says them.
   c. Start a list for the parent of the child's expressive vocabulary and add to it as the child's words increase.
   d. The parent can then encourage her child to "use his words" on his expressive vocabulary list rather than over-anticipating his needs.
2. If the parent uses speech, review the importance of repeating word labels and using them in a variety of short phrases, i.e., "Daddy's cup," "red cup," and "You're drinking from your cup."

2.38 Child: VOCALIZES OR GESTURES SPONTANEOUSLY TO INDICATE NEEDS (12-19 mo.)
Parent: Correctly interprets child's vocalizations and gestures which indicate wants, and responds accordingly

GENERAL GUIDELINES

The child becomes more efficient in communicating his needs as his combined gestural and vocal patterns become more consistent and conventional. He points and looks toward what he wants, nods his head for "yes" or "no," twists his wrist to say "all gone," holds things out to "show," and waves his hand for "bye."

2.38

In addition, he often accompanies his gestures with babbling or word approximations which have adult inflectional patterns that help the listener determine whether he is asking a question or making a request.

Parents can encourage their child to vocalize and gesture his needs by:
1. Modeling conventional gestures when talking to the child and other people.
2. Interpreting the meaning of the child's vocalizations and gestures and responding accordingly.
3. Verbalizing the child's complete message for him, i.e., "You want more milk? Okay!"
4. Giving him the opportunity to express his needs, rather than over-anticipating them before he has had a chance to vocalize or gesture.

Parents should not respond too quickly when the child indicates he wants something with only a grunt, whine, or gesture. If his needs are answered too quickly, he will not have a reason to vocalize. Parents can encourage their child to couple whatever verbal abilities the child may have with his gestures by waiting for and asking him to "use his words."

MENTALLY RETARDED PARENT

May misinterpret or not respond to her child's vocalizations and gestures used to indicate his needs.

1. Explain to the parent that since her child cannot tell us what he wants with full sentences, he tells us by his actions, babbling, and/or (if applicable) using one word:
   a. Demonstrate various conventional gestures young children make to indicate needs and have the parent guess what you are saying.
   b. Demonstrate coupling some of her child's vocalizations you have observed with gestures and let the parent guess what you are saying.
   c. Let the parent practice telling you something using only gestures and sounds she has heard her child make.
2. Help the parent interpret her child's gestures and vocalizations as natural situations arise:
   a. Describe the child's gestures and context aloud and ask the parent what he is telling us.
   b. Remind the parent to tell her child what he is saying with his sounds and gestures, and do what he is asking so he can know she understands what he is trying to say.
   c. If the child only grunts, demonstrate encouraging the child to "use his words," e.g., "Do you want a cookie? Say, 'Cookie'."

DEAF PARENT

May not encourage her child to vocalize to indicate his needs.

1. Anticipatory Guidance: If the parent uses sign language, the child will probably be using approximated signs and gestures to communicate with her. The preciseness of his signs and gestures will continue to develop as his fine motor coordination matures.

   Many of the gestures hearing people use are the same or similar to the gestures used by people without hearing,
with a few variations. For example, the look gesture in sign language is directing a manual V (index and third finger) from the speaker's eyes to the specific object, while the common gesture is pointing with an extended index finger.

   The child may rely only on his gestures and learned signs if his vocalizations have not produced desired results to get what he wants.
2. Encourage the parent to wait and watch to see if her child is vocalizing when he is gesturing to indicate his needs before giving him what he wants:
   a. Relate that if she always responds to his indicated needs when he only uses gestures, he will not see a reason to talk.
   b. The parent can cue her child to "use his words" by pointing to him and gently tapping his lips, or signing V at the throat as illustrated with 2.27 (Babbles in response to human voice).
3. Relate the vocalizations her child uses to indicate his needs:
   a. Explain that he may use only one spoken word or word-like vocalization (specify according to child's actual observed vocalizations) to mean a whole thought or sentence.
   b. Explain that children's inflections help hearing people recognize what they are requesting, even though they may not be vocalizing needs with true words.

BLIND PARENT

May not be aware of the gestures her child uses to indicate needs.

1. Anticipatory Guidance: The child will have probably begun to rely upon vocalizations and tactual gestures (e.g., tugging, pulling, giving) with his parent to indicate needs. The child's conventionalized intonation patterns and the context of the situation will also help the parent interpret his indicated needs.
2. Describe and interpret the gestures her child uses to express himself as you observe them.
3. The parent can ask her child to "bring it to me" or "take me to what you want" in situations where his message is unclear. She can also feel the direction of his pointing gesture to help interpret what he wants.

2.39 Child: GREETS WITH VERBAL CUES (12-15 mo.)
Parent: Exposes child to varied opportunities to hear verbal greetings from others; encourages child's verbal greetings within an appropriate context

GENERAL GUIDELINES

The child incorporates conventional waving into his spontaneous gestural communication repertoire to say "Hi" or "Bye." He may accompany his wave with a verbal "Hi" or "Bye." He no longer needs to rely upon seeing others wave, but does so with only verbal or contextual cues.

Parents help their child learn to understand and incorporate waving and verbal greetings into his communicative repertoire by modeling the wave gesture and verbal greetings in natural contexts. They can also take advantage of situations, such as waving to cars and animals passing by, and waving to him during "Peek-a-boo" games.

MENTALLY RETARDED PARENT

May not model greetings frequently in front of her child, or may confuse him by trying to make him say or wave "Bye-bye" out of context.

1. Suggest specific times during the parent and child's daily activities to wave and say "Hi" and "Bye," according to their individual routines:
   a. Examples may include arriving and leaving the doctor's office, friends coming over, mail carrier, or sitting on the porch waving to cars.
   b. Explain that when her child sees her wave and say "Hi" or "Bye," she's teaching him what that means.
   c. Caution parents not to say "Hi" or "Bye" unless she or someone else is coming or going somewhere.
   d. Ask the parent to imagine how confusing it might be to her child if she said "Bye" and did not go anywhere!
2. Demonstrate, and let the parent practice, playing "Peek-a-boo" with her child saying "Hi" and "Bye" instead of "Peek-a-boo."
3. Remind the parent to say "Bye" to you just before you leave so her child can hear her. Reinforce her efforts with a smile and nod, and point out child's waves or vocalizations.
4. Take a walk outside with the parent and child and play a game of saying "Bye" to animals and cars as they pass by.

DEAF PARENT

May be unaware that her child is able (or ready to learn) to greet people by only hearing the verbal greeting without gestures.

1. Refer to 2.19 (Waves or responds to "Bye-Bye").
2. Relate to the parent when her child is beginning to learn the meaning of the spoken words "Hi" and "Bye" without needing to see someone wave. Explain that he will continue to respond to hearing these words by waving, but may also start to say "Hi" or "Bye-bye."
3. Provide anticipatory guidance that children often delay their verbal greetings until the person is actually gone, so that the parent can continue to watch for his vocalizations after someone has left.
4. Inform the parent when her child is able to say or approximate verbal greetings. She can then encourage him to "say his words" when he waves by tapping his lips or signing a V at the throat, as illustrated in 2.27 (Babbles in response to human voice).
5. Encourage the parent to say "Hi" and "Bye-bye" in appropriate situations during the day using gestures and speech, when possible.
6. If the parent is non-verbal, she can ask other family members who have speech to periodically say "Hi" and "Bye-bye" to her child without gestures when they arrive or go somewhere.

BLIND PARENT

May be unaware of her child's spontaneous waving gestures to greet people.

1. If you do not observe the parent using a waving gesture for greetings, describe the gesture and how it helps her child understand the meaning of "Hi" and "Bye."
2. Suggest various times, in addition to people coming or going, when children like to wave and see others wave "Hi" and "Bye":
   a. The parent can hear cars and animals passing by at which to wave to with her child.
   b. She can listen to various pop-up toys her child is playing with at which to wave and say "Hi" and "Bye."
3. Describe the child's waving gesture when you observe it and any accompanying facial expressions. The parent will be able to recognize when her child is waving if she is holding him or if he is wearing a wrist band with a jingle bell.

2.40 **Child: USES EXCLAMATORY EXPRESSIONS — "OH-OH," "NO-NO"**
(12½-14½ mo.)
Parent: Uses exclamatory expressions with child

GENERAL GUIDELINES

The child begins to use exclamatory words meaningfully in appropriate situations. He may say "Oh!" when he is surprised or excited; "No-no!" when he does not want something or recognizes something is wrong or dangerous; and "Uh-oh!" when something goes wrong, such as dropping or breaking a toy.

Children learn to understand and use exclamatory expressions by hearing others use them during their daily activities. Exclamatory phrases have interesting inflectional patterns which are quite appealing to the child and help him to associate their meaning with the situation.

Parents can encourage their child to use exclamations by modeling them with matching inflection and facial expressions as various situations occur during the day. For example, if something spills, the parent can say, "Uh-oh!"; if there is something hot, she can point and say, "Hot!" or "No No!"; and say "Ah!" when opening a package. Parents can also use exclamations while reading a story, taking a walk, or playing with pop-up toys with her child.

MENTALLY RETARDED PARENT

May not use exclamatory expressions, or may not use them with varied inflection and facial expression.

1. Demonstrate saying "Oh!", "Uh-oh!", and "No-no!" with exaggerated inflection and facial expression. Use pictures of exclamatory situations to facilitate demonstration and discussion:

2.40

a. Encourage the parent to practice using exclamations and complete the sentence (e.g., "Uh-oh! I dropped my purse") according to the pictured situation.
b. Contrast saying the exclamation without facial or vocal expression and ask the parent which method got the message across the best.
c. Explain that her child learns to understand and say "Oh!", "Uh-oh!", and "No-no!" by hearing us say them to him with lots of expression.
d. Practice using these exclamations in front of a mirror or using a tape recorder with the parent.

2. Name common situations in which to say each exclamation. For example, each time the parent or child drops something, she can say, "Uh-oh!"; each time she or the child gets near something hot, she can say, "No-no!"; and each time she opens up a package or sees something special, she can say, "Oh!":
    a. Role-play various situations and ask the parent which exclamation "fits" best.
    b. Remind the parent, as needed, during your sessions to use exclamations when appropriate situations arise, e.g., "Bobby just spilled some food; what can you say?"
3. Select and demonstrate specific toys and books with which to use exclamatory expressions when playing with her child.
4. Remind the parent that, although her child may say "no-no" or may understand when she says "no-no," he cannot always stop himself from doing the "no-no!"; she needs to stop the situation. Give specific examples, such as pulling hair, going near a hot stove, or getting into Mommy's purse.

DEAF PARENT

May be unaware of some exclamatory expressions used in speech.

1. Explain to the parent that there are many exclamatory expressions which her child may hear and begin to use. They are easy for him to learn to say and understand because they are usually said with a lot of inflection, sounding quite musical. Point out:
    a. "No-no" is one exclamation in particular which is represented in sign language and is an early imitated sign.
    b. "Uh-oh!" is used when something spills or, like "boom," when something falls.
    c. "Oh!" is often said in surprise.
    d. "Yea!" is used in congratulations.
    e. Model the typical matching facial expression and gesture for each exclamation.
2. Have the parent show you any exclamatory expressions that she uses in communicating with her child. For example, "Wow!" in sign language is a shake sideways with a down turned hand, fingers pointed toward floor.
3. Encourage the parent and others in the home to use vocal exclamatory expressions during daily activities.
4. Identify the child's verbal exclamations as they occur. The paren can watch her child's vocalizations and facial expressions and respond accordingly.

5. If verbal, encourage the parent to use her voice with exclamatory expressions. She can be cued as to the high/low sound of "uh-oh" and feel "no-no" at the nose and throat. "Yea!", "Oh!", and "Wow!" are also felt at the throat and are very visual.

BLIND PARENT

May be unable to determine the visual events which precipitated her child's exclamations.

1. Provide anticipatory guidance, as needed, to explain which exclamations her child uses with various situations. For example:
    a. When the child says "Oh!", he has seen something special. The parent can then respond by saying "You must see something great!" and listen for further auditory cues about the situation.
    b. When the child says "No-no!", he may be approaching something dangerous; the parent can then know to intervene and find out what her child may be getting into.
2. Auditory cues will frequently accompany the child's "Uh-oh!", e.g., the sound of dropping, breaking, or spilling.
3. Name visually surprising events during which the parent can say "Oh!" to, e.g., opening packages, opening curtains on a bright day, showing the child his face in a mirror when he has pudding smeared all over it, etc.

2.41 Child: SAYS "NO" MEANINGFULLY (13-15 mo.)
Parent: Provides opportunities for child to say "no," abiding to his response when possible

GENERAL GUIDELINES

The child says "no" often and appropriately to requests and daily situations. He may also shake his head or turn away. At first, he may say "no" even when he means "yes" because he cannot say "yes" yet, but recognizes "no" as a response word. He may also say "no" to everything in order to test his power and limits with others.

Parents can help their child express the word "no" and foster his sense of independence by:

1. Saying his "no" response for him when he gestures "no," e.g., "No? You're not ready to get up?"
2. Respecting the child's "no's" when possible and, when not possible, letting him know they respect his feelings but he cannot always do as he pleases, e.g., "I know you don't want to put your coat on, but it is too cold outside; you need to wear your coat."
3. Giving the child opportunities to make "no" decisions, e.g., "Do you want to look at this book? Okay, find a book for us to look at."
4. Avoiding "Do you want. . ." questions, unless the child's possible "no" response can be respected, e.g., avoid "Do you want to go to bed now?"

MENTALLY RETARDED PARENT

May think her child is "bad" when he tests his power to say "no."

1. Explain the child's "no" expressions within a positive framework as they occur, e.g., "When he says 'no' he is telling us he feels big enough to make decisions; what a good job you've done to make him feel that way!"
2. Refer to the activities under 2 and 3, 5.39 (Displays independent behavior) to help the parent avoid her own "over-use" of "no" and respect her child's use of "no" within limits.
3. Point out the child's "no" gestures and model labeling them aloud to him as they occur. Later, ask the parent to "tell your child what he's saying when he shakes his head."

DEAF PARENT

May not recognize when her child uses speech to say "no."

1. Advise the parent when you observe her child incorporating "no" into his expressive vocabulary. She can encourage and watch for his verbal "no" which is usually quite visual and easily lipread.
2. Encourage the parent to say "no" according to her speech abilities, when possible. This can be combined with her head shake and sign for "no."

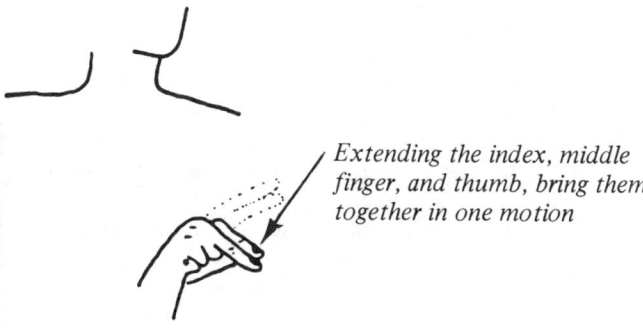

Extending the index, middle finger, and thumb, bring them together in one motion

3. If the child expresses "no" primarily through gestures, the parent can gesture for him to "use his words" as illustrated in 2.27 (Babbles in response to human voice).
4. Explain the importance of letting her child see, hear, and say "no" under various situations to help him learn that the word "no" has various meanings. Demonstrate contrasting gestures for saying "no" according to the situation, e.g.:
   a. Offering the child a choice to play with a toy and labeling his "no" response verbally and shaking your head slightly with questioning raised eyebrows.
   b. Telling the child "no" with furrowed eyebrows and a firmer head shake when he misbehaves.
5. The parent can provide her child opportunities to say "no" by gesturing questions in appropriate contexts. For example, she can gesture "Do you want more milk?" by holding out his cup and gesturing to him and then the cup, and watch for his verbal response.

6. Provide anticipatory guidance that her child will probably not be able to say or nod his head "yes" for awhile; he may say "no" to mean "yes," and may say "no" just to see how far he can go! The parent should continue to provice ample opportunities for her child to learn "yes" by modeling "yes" with gestures, signs, and vocalizations, when possible.

BLIND PARENT

May be unaware of her child's "no" gestures.

1. Describe the gestures the child uses to indicate "no." If he does not say "no," the parent can lightly place her hand on the side of her child's neck before asking him questions. She can then discern his response and label them for him to help him learn to say "no."

2.42 Child: NAMES ONE OR TWO FAMILIAR OBJECTS (13-18 mo.)
Parent: Models correct pronunciation of object child named within a complete phrase

GENERAL GUIDELINES

The child is able to spontaneously, or upon request, label one or two objects which he sees or is involved. He can only name objects which are familiar and meaningful to him. Familiar toys, utensils, and clothing items which he interacts with daily and which he hears named frequently are often the first objects named.

When the child begins to say the names for objects, he usually only says the word spontaneously if he can see the object or is interacting with it in some way. His initial word production are also often an approximation of the actual word. For example, he may say "ba" for ball or bottle, and "kuh" or "kuh-ee" for cookie or cup. He may name all round objects as "balls" or may only name his rubber blue ball as "ball."

To help encourage their child to name objects, parents can:
1. Name objects when the child is looking at or interacting with them.
2. Model the correct pronunciation within a complete phrase after the child has said a word label approximation. For example, when the child says "ba" and points to the ball, parents can say "Ball! Do you want to play ball?"
3. Encourage the child to use the "words" he has by asking him what he wants before giving it to him, *without* making too much of an issue or withholding the object as a punishment.
4. Help the child associate objects with the sounds he can already say. For example, when the child says "ba," the parent can give him a ball and say "ball."

MENTALLY RETARDED PARENT

May not emend and expand her child's words when he names objects.

1. If the parent does not talk about meaningful things to her child during daily activities, refer to 1.48 (Listens selectively to familiar words).

2.42

2. Help the parent discriminate which objects her child is learning to name:
   a. Review objects which are meaningful to her child from his receptive word list (Refer to Activity Nos. 2-4, 1.48). Ask the parent if she has heard her child say the names for any of these words.
   b. Review the child's expressive sounds which are not words. Give an example of matching one of his sounds with a word which has a similar sound from his receptive word list, e.g., "ka" for cup. Let the parent match the remaining sounds with objects on her child's word list as you make the sound.
3. List the words for objects identified in Activity No. 2 that the child is learning or ready to say. List the child's current sounds or word approximations next to each word:
   a. Help identify specific times at which the parent can say these words to her child, e.g., "Cup" during eating, "shoe" during dressing, and "ball" when playing ball.
   b. Help the parent to think of a phrase she can say for each word.
   c. Ask the parent to tell you how her child may try to say each word. Explain that when she hears him make that sound, she should name the object correctly and say it in a phrase; give specific examples.
4. Role-play emending and expanding the child's word approximations. Let the parents say the child's "words" as you model repeating the "word" with correct pronunciation and saying it within a phrase. Reverse roles.
5. Make a picture book with the parent of the objects her child is learning to name:
   a. Take Polaroid pictures of the objects or use magazine pictures.
   b. Write the "script" for each picture as the parent dictates the phrase.
   c. Model, and have the parent practice, pointing and saying the phrase to each picture with her child. Stress giving him ample opportunity to name the picture.
6. Stress with the parent that whenever she says "what's that?" to her child, she needs to tell him the answer if he does not say it after three seconds. Demonstrate, and let the parent practice with her child, providing verbal prompts, as needed.

DEAF PARENT

May be unaware of her child's speech labels for objects, and may not reinforce his verbal naming.

1. Identify and relate to the parent the speech labels for objects you observe her child to be using as they occur:
   a. Differentiate which words are approximations from the child's more exact productions, explaining how this is developmentally appropriate.
   b. Generate a written list of the child's expressive words and his current pronunciation. Review them with the parent as she watches their production on your lips.
   c. The parent can then gesture to her child to "use his words" when he is looking at or interacting with the objects on his expressive word list. Refer to 2.27 (Babbles in response to voice) for the illustrated "use your words" sign.
   d. Let the parent practice "reading" her child's speech productions with your clarification, as needed.
2. Review the child's expressive sounds which he is not yet using as word labels with the parent. Compare them to the speech labels he understands for objects so the parent can begin watching and reinforcing her child when he produces them in context. The parent can reinforce him by giving him the object and by using any speech he may have, coupled with a smile. Emphasize how this will help him realize his speech is worthwhile because it produces results.
3. Lend a *Magic Wand Reader** which names objects of pictures on each page aloud. The parent can encourage her child to "use his words" and reinforce them by activating the book's words with the magic wand when she sees him vocalize.

BLIND PARENT

May be unable to interpret her child's word approximations for objects he sees if she is unaware of what he is looking at.

1. Review with parent her child's expressive sounds, explaining how he is (or will be) using them to name objects which he sees or is interacting:
   a. The parent can discriminate which word approximations he child is using to name more than one object through physical and auditory context. For example, if she hears him say "ba" and he takes the ball she is holding, she will know his "ba" meant ball; but, if she gives him his bottle and he says "ba," she will know he meant bottle, not ball.
   b. Identify additional word approximations her child is using to label objects through his gestures or eye pointing that you observe, for the parent's future reference to model correct pronunciation and expanded phrases.
   c. With experience, the parent can associate the child's more subtle inflections and intonations included in his word approximations with his apparent meaning.
2. If the child appears to be "naming" an unidentified object, and there is no one available at the time to help interpret, the parent can still reinforce her child's sounds by saying something, such as "Yes, 'ba-ba'; you must see something with that sound; bring it to Mommy."

2.43 **Child:** **ATTEMPTS TO SING SONGS TO MUSIC (13-16 mo.)**
Parent: Sings simple repetitive songs with child

GENERAL GUIDELINES

The child "sings" to music using approximations of familiar words, or elaborate babbling or jabbering. He may sing "row-row," "be-be," or nonsensical sound combinations, such as "ba-ba-di-do." His "singing" is off-key and may sound more like talking, very quiet vocal play, or yelling!

Music provides the child pleasurable auditory experiences through its varied intonations, rhythms, and repetitive words.

---

*See Materials Reference Listing.

These musical qualities can encourage the child to participate, and practice his own sounds and imitation skills, in a fun and reinforcing way.

Parents encourage their child's vocal participation to music by providing him ample opportunities for him to listen to various types of music and songs sung by family members. Simple repetitive tunes are the easiest for the child to imitate.

MENTALLY RETARDED PARENT

May not know the "script" for children's songs to sing.

1. Anticipatory Guidance: Singing can be an excellent medium for parents who have limited expressive language. Parents who may have difficulty talking to their children may be able to sing various songs during daily activities. This could be encouraged to provide the child enjoyable interactions and good experiences with language.
2. Sing repetitive simple songs during group activities with parents and children:
   a. Sing "Good morning, good morning, how are you this morning?"; and "This is the way we drink our juice, drink our juice, drink our juice . . ." (sung to the tune of "Mulberry Bush"; replacing "drink our juice" with various other actions, such as "play with our blocks," "take off our shoes," etc.).
   b. Discuss times for parents to sing these songs at home during daily activities with their children.
   c. Ask different parents to choose a favorite song to sing as a group during "circle time."
3. Lend children's repetitive records or cassette tapes for the parent to play with her child. Suggest times to play the songs, e.g., while eating or while playing.
4. Interpret to the parent when the child's "singing" attempts are his way of "singing." Explain that, at this age, children cannot sing to the tune or say all of the song's words yet, but his practicing now helps him learn to sing better later.

DEAF PARENT

1. Refer to 1.65 (Moves to rhythms) and 2.15 (Reacts to music by cooing) to help the parent identify appropriate musical experiences for her child.
2. Provide anticipatory guidance that her child may begin to imitate "singing" the words to songs he hears. Explain that children's first attempts are not in tune to the beat of the music and sound more like talking or yelling.
3. Explain that songs with repetitive verses are the easiest for the child to learn:
   a. Identify which of the child's musical toys, records, and cassette tapes include singing voices to the music.
   b. Tape-record additional simple songs, such as "The Car Goes Beep Beep," "Happy Birthday," and "Row, Row, Row Your Boat" which are very visual when sung. Provide the written script and number code phrases according to tape recorder's number marking system. If the parent is non-verbal, she can hum and gesture to the words.
   c. Stress that a good singing voice is not important!
4. Relate to the parent the various sounds you observe her child to use for his "singing" attempts.

2.44 Child: **USES VOICE IN CONJUNCTION WITH POINTING OR GESTURING (14-20 mo.)**
Parent: Interprets and responds to child's vocalizations and gestures

GENERAL GUIDELINES

The child accompanies his gestures with "words," word approximations, or babbling sounds to help get his meaning across more clearly to the receiver. When he says "da," he may be saying "Daddy," "What's that?", "I want that," or "Look at that," but his pointing gesture, inflection, and the context of the situation help define his intent.

Parents encourage their child to accompany his gestures with vocalizations by letting him know they are understood and useful, and by not over-anticipating what her child is trying to say with isolated gestures.

Refer to the general guidelines and parent activities for 2.38 (Vocalizes or gestures spontaneously to indicate needs) which are also applicable to this skill.

2.45 Child: **USES TEN-FIFTEEN WORDS SPONTANEOUSLY (15-17½ mo.)**
Parent: Interprets and models correct pronunciation of words child says within a complete phrase

GENERAL GUIDELINES

The child's expressive single word vocabulary increases each week as he practices and is reinforced for associating his more refined vocalizations as meaningful symbols for actions, objects, people, pets, body parts, and adjectives. Examples of children's first "words" or their approximations include "mommy," "car," "ball," "milk," "juice," "go," "bye-bye," "up," "doggie," and "hot." He says his "word" or word approximations spontaneously to indicate needs, make a comment, or ask a question. His single word utterances, although expanded to include more words, continue to represent an entire thought and may have multiple meanings.

When parents interpret, model correctly, and then say the child's intentions in a more complete sentence, they reinforce their child's use of expressive words. They are letting him know his sounds are understood and produce results.

Although it is impossible to always accurately interpret the child's communicative intent, parents can observe the context of the situation and note any of the child's intonations, inflections, and gestures to interpret his intentions with relative confidence. For example, when the child lifts his arms from his highchair and says, "Ah!", parents can say, "Up? You want to get up; okay!" Refer to the parent training activities listed for 2.42 (Names one or two familiar objects) and include the child's new action, noun, people, pet, and adjective "words."

2.46 Child: VOCALIZES WISHES AND NEEDS AT THE TABLE; NAMES DESIRED ITEMS (15-17½ mo.)
Parent: Encourages child to vocalize needs at mealtime

GENERAL GUIDELINES

The child spontaneously requests things he wants during mealtime using single words, word approximations, and gestures. He may say "ju!" (juice), "mih" (milk), "mo" (more), or "kee" (cookie). At times, he may just point and grunt, especially if this "works" for him, i.e., he receives what he wants without having to "use his words." He is most likely to name a desired drink or food if it is visible, but out of reach, and if he is hungry or thirsty.

Food preparation and mealtime are excellent universal interactive activities for facilitating the child's receptive and expressive language. The child's usage for independence and food or drink can be just the impetus he needs to make his "words" useful.

Parents help expand their child's receptive vocabulary by talking about what they are doing during food preparation (e.g., "I'm stirring the pudding") and what everyone is eating at the table ("How about some more milk").

Parents can also help encourage their child to vocalize his wishes and needs at mealtime with the following guidelines:
1. Give the child opportunities to choose what he wants at the table, e.g., "Do you want juice or milk?"
2. Do not over-anticipate the child's needs, i.e., pretend not to see or hear the child's gestures or grunts; wait for a vocal response.
3. Interpret the child's word approximations and gestures for him. Model their correct pronunciation within a meaningful phrase, e.g., "More? You want more potatoes? Okay!"
4. Unobtrusively encourage the child to vocalize his wishes without turning it into an issue or pressuring him.

MENTALLY RETARDED PARENT

May not interpret her child's vocal and gestural requests during mealtime.

1. Plan several home or center sessions around mealtime. When possible, include simple food preparation at mealtimes or picnics within a parent-child group setting. Model descriptive phrases about food and encourage the parent to practice with your prompts, as needed. Use verbal prompt phrases, such as "Tell Kimmy what that is before you give it to her" or "Great, you told her what you are making; you have helped her learn the word for pudding!"
2. Interpret each of the child's "words" and gestures aloud for the parent during mealtime:
    a. Ask the parent to tell you what her child wants after your interpretation, e.g., "He's reaching for his cup and saying 'mo'; what does he want? What can you tell him to let him know you understand?"
    b. After the meal, write down the phonetic spellings for each of the child's word approximations used during mealtime with the parent. Draw or use pictures for the item next to each word approximation.
    c. Role-play emending and expanding phrases to say for each of the child's "meal-time" words.
    d. Post the child's mealtime word list in clear view of the family eating area, and let the parent proudly add (or let you add) new mealtime "words" each week.

DEAF PARENT

May be unaware of her child's words or word approximations during mealtime.

1. Plan a few sessions around a meal. Relate to the parent what vocalizations her child uses (with or without gesture) during the meal. The parent can then gesture to her child to "use his words" at future meals according to his expressive abilities. Refer to 2.27 (Babbles in response to voice) for the illustrated "use your words" sign.
2. Encourage the parent to use her speech, when possible, to tell her child what he is gesturing for, and to name various food items and utensils at the table. If the parent is non-verbal, she can capitalize upon watching for and praising her child's vocalizations at the table. Other family members who use speech can model "mealtime" words and interpret the child's vocalizations for the parent.
3. If mealtimes appear to be "silent," the parent can play a radio (marked for the appropriate volume), set at an "easy listening" music station, to provide a pleasant sound environment during mealtime for the child.

BLIND PARENT

May have difficulty interpreting her child's wishes during mealtime if she is unaware of his accompanying gestures.

1. Plan a session around mealtime with parent and child:
    a. Describe each of the gestures and signals the child is using to indicate his wishes, such as pointing, body twisting, and grimaces.
    b. Interpret the child's word approximations according to his gestural cues.
2. The parent can hold a food item in each hand, just out of her child's reach, and ask her child "do you want juice or a cookie" and listen for his vocal response. If his vocalization is unclear, she can bring the items within reach and determine which word he said.

2.47 Child: MAKES SOUNDS IN BABBLING, BUT OFTEN SUBSTITUTES THOSE SOUNDS IN WORDS (15½-21 mo.)
Parent: Does not expect child to pronounce his words perfectly; models correct pronunciation

GENERAL GUIDELINES

The child produces a variety of new speech sounds in his babbling repertoire, but cannot transfer his new sounds to form words. Instead, he continues to substitute his more familiar speech sounds in his "words." For example, although the child may say "sh" during babbling, he may not be able to say "shoe"; instead, he says "too."

The child's perfect articulation and incorporation of sounds into words takes years to develop. Babbling provides the child the practice needed to discover and learn about his potential for speech production. Through babbling, he is learning about sound relationships which will help him develop better word articulation skills during the next few years.

Parents continue to be their child's primary language model and language facilitator. Parents can repeat their child's misarticulations correctly to help him see and hear proper word formations, but should not try to make him say it "right" or tell him, "No, that is not how you say it." Over-correction can inhibit the child's interest and motivation to talk. Singing songs using sounds instead of words, and saying fun environmental sounds, such as "Choo choo choo" and "beep beep beep" during play, provide the child positive language experiences to hear and practice new speech sounds in a fun and supportive environment.

MENTALLY RETARDED PARENT

May try to make her child say words with correct articulation.

1. Observe the parent's responses to her child when he uses sound substitutions in his words. If she is telling him he is "wrong" or tries to make him say words exactly right:
   a. Explain that her child's tongue and lip muscles are not ready to say words exactly right.
   b. Relate that since her child's tongue and lip muscles just are not ready to say words exactly right, we cannot make him say words right; he will learn to do this with time and practice.
   c. Name examples of common sound substitutions or omissions that children often make at this age: "tup" for cup, "poon" for spoon, "dot" for that, and "too" for shoe.
   d. Ask the parent to name some words her child says, but cannot say exactly right.
   e. Explain that her child feels bad if we tell him he is saying his words wrong; he is so excited that he is learning to talk and he especially wants to please his parents.
   f. Relate an example of how you felt from your own experiences when you were trying to do something as well as you could, but someone kept telling you, you were wrong, e.g., trying to draw a picture or speak a foreign language.
   g. Ask the parent if she can remember a time when she was trying to do something, but someone kept telling her she was wrong; how did that feel?
2. Reinforce to the parent that she is her child's most important teacher. She teaches her child how to talk by letting him hear and see how words sound and look when she talks to him. Review several of the child's sounds and words. Praise the parent for teaching him all of these words and sounds.
3. Explain to the parent that she teaches her child how to say his words right by showing him how to say them correctly without telling him he is saying them wrong:
   a. Provide a few examples from the child's word approximation vocabulary, i.e., "If your child touches his spoon and says 'poon' you can say, 'Spoon; yes, that is a spoon!'."
   b. Ask the parent what she can say to her child when he points to his cup and says "tup," points to his hair and says "air," or looks at the kitty and says "keykey." (Use the child's word approximations which you have observed.)
4. Demonstrate bringing your face to the child's "face level" to talk to him, e.g., bending down, kneeling, and sitting him on your lap facing you:
   a. Point out how these positions let him see your mouth when you talk.
   b. Let the parent practice talking to her child at his eye level. Point out how he can watch her mouth when she talks at his level.
   c. Name naturally occurring activities which bring the parent's face to her child's eye level: When he is taking a bath and she is sitting on the floor next to him, when he is in his highchair and she is sitting in front of him, and when she is kneeling while picking up his pants.
   d. Help the parent think of phrases to say to her child during these daily activities, e.g., "Bubbles; see the bubbles from the soap?", "Mmm, it is time to eat, here is your banana," or "I am pulling up your pants."
5. Demonstrate to the parent a few fun sound-making activities she can play with her child:
   a. Push a train of cereal boxes saying "choo choo choo."
   b. Make silly sounds through paper towel tubes and into large coffee cans.
   c. Make up a finger-play song, such as singing "Diddle-de-do, diddle-de-di" as you alternate tapping fingers across the table with each hand.
6. Let the parent experience what it is like for her child to learn to say new words. Teach her to say a short phrase in a foreign language, such as "Bonjour, Marie," to say "Hello, Mary" in French:
   a. Model saying the phrase quickly and ask the parent to say it. Compare this with modeling the phrase very slowly and clearly. Ask the parent which method was easier for her to learn to say the phrase.
   b. Relate that since her child cannot speak English yet, his learning to talk is just like us learning to speak a new foreign language.
   c. Point out that, just as it was easier to learn to say it slowly and clearly, it is easier for her child to learn words when she says them slowly and clearly to him.

DEAF PARENT

May be unaware that her child makes sounds in babbling which he cannot use in words.

1. Fingerspell or write out for the parent the various sounds her child is observed to incorporate in his babbling:
   a. Relate that, although her child can say these sounds in babbling, he cannot use all of these sounds in his words yet.

2.47

    b. List the words her child says with substitutions using phonetic spellings.
    c. Explain this is a normal stage of development; it is easier to say sounds in babbling than in words because he repeats the same sound many times in a row; it is harder for him to combine single sounds to make a word.
    d. Relate that with more practice, maturation, and experience hearing the words sound correctly, his words will become more articulate.
    e. Review the words her child can say without substitutions or omissions.
2. Explain the importance for others to model the correct pronunciation of words to her child, rather than copying him because it sounds cute that way:
    a. Relate a few word approximations children say that adults sometimes think sound "cute," and thus reinforce them by laughing and saying them the same way, e.g., "keykey" for kitty cat or "tup" for cup.
    b. Leave a copy of the general guidelines for this skill with the parent to share with hearing family members.
3. Point out children's television programs which emphasize slow, clear, "child-size" speech: "Romper Room," "Captain Kangaroo," "Sesame Street," etc. Assist with marking volume knobs at a conducive level for her child. Explain that her child can hear the television from anywhere in the room; he should not sit right next to it.
4. Suggest additional vehicles the parent can use to provide her child ample opportunities to hear good speech models, if needed:
    a. List children's records and tapes which provide repetitive rhythmic songs.
    b. Investigate storytimes at local libraries. Some storytimes have the stories told in speech and sign.

2.48 Child: JABBERS TUNEFULLY AT PLAY (17-19 mo.)
Parent: Reinforces the value and usefulness of verbal communication with child

GENERAL GUIDELINES

The child jabbers strings of nonsensical sound repetitions that have inflectional patterns similar to adults. He jabbers to people, his pets, his toys, and himself as a means to carry on conversations, to practice this new skill, and for pure enjoyment. The child's adultlike gestures and intonations which accompany his jabber help the listener interpret what the child is talking about.

Parents can encourage their child's jabbering by enthusiastically listening and responding to his "conversations" when they are directed at them, and not interrupting him when he is jabbering just for the fun of it.

MENTALLY RETARDED PARENT

May not respond to her child's jabbering or may interrupt it.

1. Relate to the parent the importance and value of her child's jabbering in meaningful terms. If the child has already begun to jabber, use an example of his jabbering when it occurs as a beginning point for discussion. If the child is emerging into this stage, use tape recordings or group sessions of other children's jabbering as an initial discussion vehicle to help the parent anticipate this skill. The following concrete related ideas can be used during your explanation of jabbering:
    a. Her child hears other people talk in sentences and wants to, too.
    b. Even though he may say some real words, he is not ready to put words together to make sentences yet.
    c. Since he cannot put words together yet, and since he really wants to talk in sentences, sometimes he will put together his sounds that are not real words to make sentences.
    d. It is great when he puts his sounds together to make them sound like he is talking in sentences because this lets him practice getting ready to talk in sentences.
2. Teach the parent a few active listening skills to use with her child. Introduce this activity with a discussion about how just as we do not feel like talking to someone if they are not listening, children will not feel like "talking" (i.e., jabbering) if they think no one is listening. Include how frustrating it can be to want to talk to someone and realize they are not really listening:
    a. Point out that when you were talking to the parent, she was looking at you and nodding her head (plus any other listening behaviors you noticed) which let you know she was listening.
    b. Contrast listening behaviors with ones which would show we were not listening, e.g., "If you had been talking on the phone, looking out the window, or not answering any of my questions, it would have seemed to me that you were not listening!"
    c. Ask the parent what she can do to show her child she is listening to him.
    d. Demonstrate additional gestures and phrases which can tell her child we are listening to him: raised eyebrows, big smile, "Oh my!", "Oh, really," laughing, and "You are really telling me a great story!"
    e. Role-play the child's jabbering and let the parent practice these listening skills.
    f. When you observe the parent using active listening skills, tell her she is really showing her child how important she thinks he is by listening to him when he talks.
3. Help the parent interpret her child's jabbering by looking at his gestures and facial expressions, listening to his inflections, and looking at the context of the situation.
4. If the parent does not incorporate any varying intonations, refer to 2.23 (Vocalizes in interjectional manner).
5. If the parent is observed to interrupt her child's jabbering during play, refer to 2.28 (Babbles monologue when left alone).
6. Make pretend telephones with the parent using cups and thick strings. Demonstrate "talking" on the phone with with her child for fun:
    a. Model saying short inflectional phrases about the "here and now," such as "Hi, I see you are talking on the

phone," "You are wearing your pretty blue pants today!", or "I'm sitting on the chair talking; you are sitting on the floor."
  b. Stress giving her child ample response time and responding to any of his sounds, even if we cannot understand his meaning.
  c. Have a three-way "conversation" with the parent and child using the pretend telephones.
  d. If the child does not vocalize, stress that is okay, she can try again later; or if the child is listening, point out what a good time he is having just listening to her.

DEAF PARENT

May be unaware of her child's jabbering and how this relates to his later speech.

1. Define for the parent what children's jabber is and why this is an important skill as described in the general guidelines:
   a. Phonetically spell out and demonstrate some of the jabbering sounds her child is beginning to use as the parent watches your mouth.
   b. Relate how children's jabbering can sound just like an adult conversation and sometimes they seem to be telling a whole story.
   c. Relate that her child's jabbering has very few if any actual words; at this stage, he is practicing combining sounds he has, to make rhythmic combinations.
2. The parent can watch for her child's jabbering from his distinctive gestures, facial expressions, and lip movements:
   a. Encourage her to look to see if he is jabbering to his toys or to himself before interacting with him so she does not interrupt him.
   b. The parent can smile, nod her head, and raise her eyebrows when her child is looking at her and jabbering, to reinforce his sounds.

BLIND PARENT

May have difficulty discriminating when her child's jabbering is directed toward her.

1. Advise the parent when you observe her child jabbering to himself, his toys, and the parent:
   a. The parent may be able to use her sound localization skills to determine when her child is jabbering toward her and when he is turned jabbering to his toys.
   b. The child may demonstrate subtle or overt intonation pattern differences when he "talks" to toys, people, or himself.
2. Describe to the parent favorite toys, objects, and pictures to which her child seems to like jabbering.
3. Describe the child's new gestures and facial expressions which accompany his jabbering.

2.49 Child: ECHOES PROMINENT OR LAST WORD SPOKEN (17-19 mo.)
Parent: Understands child's echoing can be a natural stage in language development

GENERAL GUIDELINES

The child echoes or repeats the prominent or final word from an adult's question, direction, or comment to him. For example, if the parent says, "Get your shoes," the child may say "shoes"; or if the adult says, "Do you want to go bye-bye?" the child may say "bye-bye." When the child echoes the adult's last word, he does not necessarily understand what was said.

Echoing is not a language skill to be taught. Echoing is a frequently observed natural stage during language development, thought to help the child remember what was said to him. It should not, however, be the child's primary method for expressive speech.

MENTALLY RETARDED PARENT

May assume her child understands her directions when he echoes her final words.

1. If the child is observed to echo prominent or last words from adult directions or questions, explain to the parent that this is another way her child is learning to practice saying words:
   a. Stress that just because he says the word, it does *not* mean that he understands what she said.
   b. Provide concrete examples of situations that could arise, e.g., the parent tells her child to get his socks and he says "socks" but does not get them.

DEAF PARENT

May be unaware that child echoes the last spoken word and/or may not understand why.

1. Advise the parent if her child begins to repeat the last word that is spoken in a direction. Relate that this helps him to remember the direction given to him. It is a normal stage in language development. It only becomes a concern when he echoes all speech and does not say any words on his own.
2. Continue to identify the child's spontaneous and echoed words for the parent.

2.50 Child: USES EXPRESSIVE VOCABULARY OF FIFTEEN-TWENTY WORDS (17½-20½ mo.)
Parent: Provides child a meaningful and responsive language environment

GENERAL GUIDELINES

The child has a spontaneous expressive vocabulary of fifteen to twenty words. At this age, his "words" are often family member names; names of pets; labels for important objects, such as "ball," "bottle," "milk"; and action words, such as "up," "go," "look," and "bye-bye." He also begins

2.50

labeling body parts and incorporating modifiers, such as "hot," "dirty," "mine," and "big." Certainly, these first words are not universal for all children. Each child will have his own unique expressive vocabulary, dependent upon the words which are important in his individual environment.

The child uses his words to greet people, regulate their attention, reply to others, and request information. He also expresses words to imitate, repeat, and rehearse for practice. His single word utterances continue to function as his way to communicate an entire thought. When he says "milk," he may be saying "I want some milk," "There's the milk," or "You are drinking some milk." The child's accompanying intonational patterns, gestures, and the context of the situation enable the listener to interpret the child's intentions fairly accurately.

Parents encourage their child's expanded expressive word vocabulary by interpreting and expanding their child's one word utterances, and by providing him with a rich language environment to hear meaningful words which enable him to see their usefulness for communication.

MENTALLY RETARDED PARENT

May not expand or interpret her child's one word utterances, and may not provide a meaningful language environment.

1. Encourage the parent to talk to her child about meaningful things throughout the day. Stress her importance as her child's most important teacher who helps him learn to talk:
    a. Explain that, although her child can't say lots of words or sentences, he can understand many of the things we say to him.
    b. Relate that her child continues to learn how to say different new words by hearing her talk about what he is doing and what she is doing. Give specific examples for each, such as "You're eating your apple," "I'm brushing your hair," "The ice is cold," and "It's raining outside; see how wet it is!"
2. Review typical daily activities and help the parent think of meaningful phrases to say to her child. Use probing questions, such as:
    a. "What can you tell your child about the water when he's taking a bath?" (Dripping, wet, splash splash, warm)
    b. "What can you say when you're drying him off?" ("I'm drying your arms, your legs, and your hair.")
    c. "What can you say when you're pouring his milk?"
    d. "What can you tell your child about the blocks he's playing with?"
3. Discourage the parent from over-using "What's that?" commands, if necessary. Refer to 2.37 (Uses expressive vocabulary one-three words).
4. Review interpreting and expanding the child's one word utterances into a complete thought. Refer to 2.36 (Uses single word utterances).
5. Engage the parent and child in a playdough activity:
    a. Model and prompt the parent to describe how the dough looks, feels, and smells to her child.
    b. Demonstrate rolling, poking, squeezing, and patting the dough. Ask the parent what she can tell her child so he can hear the words which describe what you are doing.
    c. Praise the parent for saying all of these new words to her child.
6. Refer to 1.91 (Identifies one body part).

DEAF PARENT

May be unaware of her child's expanding speech vocabulary.

1. Refer to 2.36 (Uses single word sentences) and 2.45 (Uses ten-fifteen words spontaneously) to help the parent identify and reinforce her child's new words.
2. Continue to identify for the parent her child's new words as you observe them so the parent can encourage her child to use his words rather than over-anticipate his needs.

2.51 Child: **USES JARGON WITH GOOD INFLECTION AND RATE (18-22 mo.)**
Parent: Recognizes child's jargon as his way to practice sounds, inflections, and fluency

GENERAL GUIDELINES

The child practices his sounds, inflections, and fluency through jargon, especially during solitary play. His jargon is composed of nonsensical sound combinations, sometimes interspersed with true words. His inflections, fluency, and intonations resemble adult conversations and he appears to understand exactly what he is saying. In addition, he may laugh, gesture, and incorporate a variety of adult facial expressions which make his jargon look like he really is carrying on a conversation; it's just in a foreign language!

Some children do not go through the "jargon state." Instead, they progress directly into actual word phrases.

Parents should continue to provide adult models for speech rather than imitating their child's jargon.

MENTALLY RETARDED PARENT

May expect her child to talk in sentences since his jargon sounds like a true sentence.

1. Explain to the parent about the jargon stage if you observe it with the child during your intervention sessions. Stress that her child is not ready to talk in sentences; at this age, children practice making sentences with their sounds, not words. Assure the parent that his sentences will become clearer as he gets older.
2. If necessary, advise the parent not to imitate her child's jargon. Explain that since she is his most important teacher for teaching him how to talk, if she talks like him, he will think that's the right way to talk. Continue to reinforce the parent's labeling, parallel, and self-talk as outlined under previous language skills.

DEAF PARENT

May think her child is talking in sentences since his facial and gestural expressions mirror true sentences.

1. Provide the parent anticipatory guidance about her child's natural jargon stage, if applicable. Refer to the general guidelines to define jargon and its rationale.

2.52 Child: USES OWN NAME TO REFER TO SELF (18-24 mo.)
Parent: Uses child's name during interactions and encourages him to refer to himself by name

GENERAL GUIDELINES

The child refers to himself by his first name spontaneously or upon request. In addition to the implied language skill involved in saying his name, the child says his name as his affirmation that he is a separate, important, and independent person.

Parents can encourage their child to say his own name by modeling his name often during meaningful daily activities through conversations and descriptive phrases. For example, during dressing, parents can say, "Susie's shoes" or "Susie's pants"; during bathtime, parents can say, "I'm washing Jimmy's arm; Jimmy see your wet arm!" "Peek-a-boo" and hiding games are also fun activities in which the child can hear his name repetitively, e.g., "Where's Michael? Michael? Where are you? There's Michael!" Parents can also encourage their child to answer "Who's that?" in mirrors, and ask questions, such as, "Who wants a cookie?" If the child does not answer, the parent should supply the answer, e.g., "Sarah wants the cookie."

MENTALLY RETARDED PARENT

May not say her child's name during daily activities, and may expect him to always answer to "What's your name?"

1. Refer to 2.16 (Looks and vocalizes to own name) to encourage the parent to say her child's name during daily activities.
2. Refer to 1.38 (Looks for family members or pets when named), if the parent does not use a consistent name for her child.
3. Demonstrate an "I see (child's name)" game. Look into mirrors, pie pans, and a metal spatula and say, "I see Johnny! Who's that?" Model waiting for a response and answering if the child does not respond:
   a. Let the parent practice this game.
   b. Suggest playing this game after his bath in the bathroom mirror, and at department and grocery stores when they pass by a mirror.
   c. Stress that if her child does not answer, that's fine, answer for him; he needs to hear the answer many times before he can start answering.
4. Take pictures of the parent and child to make a special chart or book. Label the pictures according to the pictured action with the parent and child's names, e.g., "Jimmy's playing ball" or "Mommy is playing ball with Jimmy." Encourage the parent to read the "script" and point to the pictures with her child. Cover the pictures with clear contact paper to preserve them.
5. If you observe the parent trying to make her child say his name to you or others:
   a. Talk for the child, "Oh Mom, I don't always want to say my name when you ask me!"
   b. Stress that all children like to "be quiet" just when we're trying to show others all of their new words. Empathize how frustrating this can be for the parent, so it's probably best just to answer for him instead of trying to make him say it.
6. Demonstrate a "hide 'n' go seek" game with the child. Model enthusiastically saying the child's name while looking for him, and after finding him:
   a. Explain to the parent that she can play this game even when she really knows where her child is. The parent can just turn her head and pretend she doesn't see him!
   b. Suggest natural situations which may arise when the parent can say "Where's Jimmy? Jimmy, where are you?", e.g., when he's under his covers, before she enters his room, or when he is under the table or behind a couch.

DEAF PARENT

May not use speech to say her child's name.

1. Refer to 2.16 (Looks and vocalizes to own name).
2. Demonstrate saying "Who's that?" in the mirror and "Who's cookie (shoes, pants, ball, etc.)?" with the child. Encourage the parent to say these phrases to her child using gestures, and voice if she is comfortable using speech:
   a. The parent's raised eyebrows and shrugged shoulders, when she points or holds up something of the child's will provide her child ample cues of her intent.
   b. If the child responds by signing his name, the parent can use her "Use your voice" sign.
   c. The parent can sign and/or say her child's name, coupled with her "Use your voice" sign, if she does not see him respond to her questions.

2.53 Child: IMITATES ENVIRONMENTAL SOUNDS (18-21 mo.)
Parent: Models and encourages child to imitate environmental sounds

GENERAL GUIDELINES

The child imitates making animal, nature, or machine sounds. His imitations are usually the word labels for sound rather than the actual sound. He may say "beep beep" for a car horn, "ruff-ruff" for a dog barking, "boom" for the sound of thunder or an object falling, and "rhumm" for a car engine. He may even begin to label an object by its sound rather than its name. For example, he may call a dog, "ruff-ruff."

The unique and interesting intonational patterns offered by environmental sound labels are easy to remember and provide

2.53

the child excellent sound-play practice in a fun way. Parents encourage their child to imitate environmental sounds by pointing them out and modeling their sounds as they occur during play and daily activities. The child will enjoy and learn from hearing his parent say "ker-plunk" and "splish-splash" in the water; "rhumm-rumm," "beep," and a screeching halt sound when playing with cars; and animal sounds when looking at their pictures or actually seeing them. Sneezing, hiccups, choo-choo trains, raindrops, wind, and squeaking doors also provide fun opportunities to point out and make up special sound labels.

MENTALLY RETARDED PARENT

May not point out or imitate environmental sounds to her child.

1. Explain to the parent that children love to hear us tell them the sounds animals, cars, airplanes, squeaky doors, and water make:
    a. Demonstrate making a few sounds as you explain how they sound silly and interesting to her child.
    b. Relate that, since her child likes to hear these sounds so much, he may try to say them if he hears adults say them.
    c. Relate that, when her child practices making these sounds, it helps him learn to say new sounds which will help him learn to say new words.
2. Describe a few sounds you hear in the parent's home and encourage the parent to name some as you listen quietly together. These may include "tick-tock" for a clock, "chirp-chirp" for a bird, "rumble-rumble" for the washing machine, and "crackly-pop" from the fireplace.
3. Review daily activities with the parent and help identify sounds she can name for her child as they occur. These may include "drip-drip" from the water, "ah-choo" when someone sneezes, "knock-knock," "ding-dong" to the doorbell, or "rrripp" when paper tears.
4. Make a tape recording of various environmental and animal sounds for the parent to play with her child. Cut out pictures from magazines with the parent for pictures to match the various sounds.
5. Sing "Old MacDonald" and "The Car Goes Beep Beep" with the parent and child. This can be an excellent parent-child group activity. Model exaggerated facial and vocal expressions.

DEAF PARENT

May be unaware of environmental sounds and their sound word labels which encourage the child to imitate.

1. Relate to the parent various speech labels used to symbolize various environmental sounds, if needed. Point out that these sounds have special rhythms and interesting sound patterns which encourage her child to try to copy saying them. Relate that this will help him learn new sounds to use in his speech.
2. Show the parent how she can make various sounds for her child to associate with various environmental sounds, e.g., tongue click for a clock, blowing through lips to make them vibrate for the sound of a car or motorcycle, or a "raspberry" for the sound of a balloon deflating. Demonstrate these sounds with the parent in front of a mirror.
3. Suggest and demonstrate for the parent "See-N-Say" toys which have animal sounds.
4. Make a tape recording with various environmental sounds. Mark corresponding pictures with numbers to match the recorder's number tracking system.
5. Identify various sounds in the environment. The parents will be aware of vacuum cleaner, car, or dropping sounds because of the vibrations. Relate more subtle sounds, such as water dripping, clocks which have audible ticks, and the toilet flushing:
    a. The parent can then encourage her child to listen to the sounds through gestures and facial expressions.
    b. Orient the parent to conducive distances that her child can hear these sounds, e.g., a water next to his ear but a doorbell from across the room.

2.54 Child: IMITATES TWO WORD PHRASES (18-21 mo.)
Parent: Models "child-size" two-word phrases

GENERAL GUIDELINES

The child begins to combine two of his words to make a comment or ask a question. These usually include an action word and/or modifier. Initially, he can only say the phrase in imitation of model. Two-word phrase imitation usually does not occur until the child has an expressive single word vocabulary of at least thirty words.

Parents can model two-word phrases to their child which contain single words he can already say spontaneously. Saying short phrases, such as "Go bye bye," "More milk," and "Car go" with inflectional emphasis placed on each word, encourages the child's imitation. Story time is an excellent time for parents to stress two-word phrases.

MENTALLY RETARDED PARENT

May not incorporate or emphasize modifiers and action words when she talks to her child.

1. List five to ten of the child's expressive vocabulary words separately on index cards. Illustrate each word card with a simple picture. Use the word cards to introduce to the parent appropriate two-word phrases she can encourage her child to say:
    a. Explain that since her child can say so many single words now, he is ready to start saying two words at a time to make a short sentence. Give a concrete example, such as "When your child wants a cookie, he says one word 'kuh-key'; now he is ready to learn to say two words together, such as 'more kuh-key'."
    b. Explain that he must already be able to say each word separately before he can learn to say it in a two-word sentence. Give a concrete example, such as "Susie can already say the words 'more' and 'cookie'. But, since she cannot say chocolate, she is *not* ready to learn to say chocolate cookie."

c. Illustrate, using the child's word cards, several two-word combinations her child is ready to learn to say. Use one card as a core word and demonstrate making various word combinations by switching only one word. For example, if the core word is "Mommy," demonstrate "Mommy, shoe," "Bye, Mommy," and "Mommy, go."
d. Let the parent make several more two-word phrases with the word cards.
e. Stress that at this age her child may say his two words in any order. Illustrate this concept by reversing two word cards, e.g., "Mommy, go" and "Go, Mommy."
f. Cover the index cards with clear contact paper to make them indestructible. The parent can enjoy "reading" fun phrases to her child.
g. Stress that her child is not expected to say all of the phrases yet. Emphasize that, when the parent says the two-word phrase to her child, she is helping him get ready to learn to say them.
h. Combine meaningful words to say during daily activities, such as "More juice," "Eat cookie," and "Cookie all done" to model during mealtimes.
2. Demonstrate a "Whose Is It?" game for the parent to play with her child. The adult says "Whose pants? (pause) Susie's pants! Whose pants?" and waits for an imitative response. If the child does not imitate the two-word response, the parent answers the question and moves on to another "Whose Is It" question:
a. This game can be played with body parts, clothing, and toys.
b. The parent can collect a few of her own personal items and a few of the child's to put in a shopping bag. The parent and child can take turns pulling out the "surprise" while the parent says, "Whose brush?"
3. Show the parent how much fun it can be to sit at the window with her child and say "Bye" to moving things: "Bye, car!", "Bye, doggie!", and "Bye truck!"
4. Make a "feely" book with the parent for her child. Encourage her to help write the "script" with descriptive touch and feel words: "Soft cotton," "Scratchy sandpaper," "Sticky tape," and "Soft cloth."

DEAF PARENT

May not be able to verbally model two-word phrases for her child to encourage his imitation.

1. Relate to the parent about young children's two-word phrases as described in the general guidelines for 2.57 (Uses two-word sentences). Stress that her child's two-word phrases do not need to be in grammatical order, and his two-word combinations help the listener clarify her child's language intent.
2. Anticipatory Guidance: Nouns, verbs, and modifiers are used in sign language. Articles, such as "a," "an," and "the" are usually absent. In addition, one sign plus a body and facial expression can be used to symbolize an entire statement. Short sentences may also be presented in various word orders.

3. List the two-word phrases for the parent that you have observed her child saying or imitating:
a. Review the difference between imitated and spontaneous phrases.
b. List additional two-word phrases that her child may begin to imitate based upon his current single word vocabulary.
4. Encourage the parent to communicate the short phrase from Activity No. 3 to her child using gesture and speech, if possible.
5. The parent can encourage her child through her sign for "Use your voice" to say his two-word phrases.
6. Make special short phrase tape recordings to match pictures in one of the child's books. Label the script for the parent on the picture book and code where to turn the page using the meter numbers on the tape recorder.

2.55 Child: ATTEMPTS TO SING SONGS WITH WORDS (18-23 mo.)
Parent: Exposes child to simple songs and fingerplays

GENERAL GUIDELINES

The child begins to "sing" along with simple tunes and gesture songs. He uses a few words interspersed with hums and nonsensical sound combinations. His singing becomes more melodic in comparison to his earlier "shouts" for singing, but he cannot actually sing in tune with the melody.

Nursery rhymes, fingerplays, and children's songs offer the child an opportunity to practice various sound combinations and rhythms in a relaxed, interesting, and fun atmosphere. Simple repetitive songs with interesting inflections and gestures are usually favorites for children.

Parents can sing and encourage their child to participate in songs and fingerplays, such as "The Wheels on the Bus," "If You're Happy and You Know It Clap Your Hands," " Ring Around the Rosey," "Old MacDonald," or their own homemade songs. They can initiate singing activities spontaneously during playtime, while driving in a car, during the child's bath, or anytime the parent just feels like having a mutually enjoyable interaction with her child.

The parent activities for 2.43 (Attempts to sing songs to music) are applicable to this skill.

2.56 Child: NAMES TWO PICTURES (19-21½ mo.)
Parent: Exposes child to a variety of meaningful pictures; encourages him to name a few

GENERAL GUIDELINES

The child can name spontaneously, or upon request, at least two pictures of familiar people, toys, foods, or household objects.

Parents can show and describe to their child various types of pictures in his everyday environment. The child will enjoy looking at pictures in catalogs, magazines, advertisements, and

2.56

family photo albums. Parents can also point out and name pictures which are on cereal and other food boxes, on the child's sheets or clothing, and on posters and murals in stores. A special homemade book can also be made with pictures of the words or word approximations which the child already has in his expressive vocabulary.

MENTALLY RETARDED PARENT

May not point out or describe pictures to her child.

1. Explain to the parent that children at this age love to look at all sorts of pictures; looking at pictures helps him learn the meaning of new words, and encourages him to practice saying the words he already knows.
2. Show the parent various pictures that are available around the home for her to show her child. These could be the babies on the diaper box and baby food jar, animals on the cereal box, the cookie on the cookie box, and pictures from junk mail. Ask the parent if she can think of any other pictures around her house at which her child might like to look:
   a. Demonstrate for the parent how to attract her child's attention to look at one or two pictures, by pointing or tapping at the picture, calling his name, and using animated facial and vocal expressions.
   b. Ask the parent to show her child another picture. Provide the parent verbal prompts, as needed, to help her attract her child's attention to the picture and talk about the picture within a simple phrase.
3. Help the parent think of things she can say to her child when she shows him a picture. Explain that he likes to hear the name of the object in the picture and anything else she might want to say about it:
   a. Demonstrate this concept by labeling a picture and then modeling a short descriptive phrase, e.g., "Cookie! Mmm; cookies taste good!"
   b. Let the parent practice thinking of things she can tell her child about the picture of the baby on his cereal box, the pictures hanging up in his room, and the picture hanging on her living room wall.
   c. Stress waiting for her child to touch the picture and/or use his own words or sounds before taking one picture away.
4. Show the parent an example of a colorful advertising mailing that adults often throw away. Point out all of the pictures that would probably be interesting to her child. Discuss how wonderful these are to let her child look at and play with, because if he tears them, it doesn't matter.
5. Help make a picture book containing pictures of the words the child can say or is learning to say:
   a. Ask the parent to name several words that her child can say.
   b. Help select pictures from magazines and take Polaroid close-ups. Cover them with clear contact paper.
   c. Demonstrate, and let the parent practice, "reading" this book with her child.
6. Review with the parent "winning ways" to read books with her child. Stress talking in simple language about the picture and waiting for the child to respond before turning the page:
   a. Tell the parent *not* to turn the page if her child is still looking at, touching, or "talking" about the picture.
   b. Remind the parent that if she is holding the book to make sure her child can see the pictures, too. Demonstrate various positions, as needed.
   c. Discourage the parent's over-use of "What's that?" when she is showing her child pictures. Refer to 2.37 (Uses expressive vocabulary one-three words), if needed.
7. Help the parent think of things she can say or do to tell her child she is proud of him when he tries to name the pictures he sees, e.g., "That's right; that's a cat," "Great; you said cookie," or giving him a special smile, hug, or pat.
8. Take a trip to the local library with the parent and child. Help identify schedules for special storytelling times, how to check out books, and locations of suitable children's books.

DEAF PARENT

May not provide speech labels to her child when he looks at pictures, and may be unaware of his expressive speech picture labeling.

1. Relate to the parent when her child is ready to begin naming pictures he sees:
   a. Review the child's spontaneous expressive speech vocabulary. Explain that these will probably be the first words he will be able to say when he looks at pictures.
   b. Explain that children sometimes name pictures without any prompting and sometimes when they are asked "What's that?"
   c. If the parent does not use speech, encourage her to periodically sign "What's that?" and "Use your voice" to her child when she points out pictures to him.
   d. The parent can watch her child to see if he is labeling the picture in response to her prompts. If not, explain that she should say the name and/or provide the sign. Also, a family member with speech can be recruited to label the object.
2. Encourage the parent to use any speech she may have to label pictures in the child's environment. Remind the parent, with demonstration, that repetition of word labels are important for her child while he is learning their speech names.
3. Refer to 1.44 (Looks at pictures one minute when named).

BLIND PARENT

May be unaware of subtle pictures in the environment that she can point out and label for her child.

1. Refer to 1.44 (Looks at pictures one minute when named) for suggestions to help the parent identify pictures for her child.
2. Give the parent some old magazines or catalogs to let her child look at during play. Suggest letting her child have some of the advertising "junk" mail she receives. Explain that the shiny papered advertisements are usually colorful

pictures of clothing, cars, or department store items. This paper is also less likely to "bleed" than newsprint.
3. Point out and describe various subtle pictures that may be available in the environment, such as pictures on food cartons, the child's dish and cup, vitamin bottle, etc.

2.57 **Child: USES TWO-WORD SENTENCES**
(20½-24 mo.)
Parent: Encourages child to expand his single word sentences to two-word phrases

GENERAL GUIDELINES

The child initiates two-word phrases and sentences to communicate complete thoughts. His entry into spontaneous two-word phrases follows his spontaneous single word expressive vocabulary of at least thirty words, and his earlier practice with imitating others' two-word phrases.

The child's two-word combinations are not grammatically complete; however, his intentions are clear and the words have a definite relationship with each other. He may say two words to comment about a sequential event ("Car go"), or to qualify or quantify his topic ("More milk," "Milk a'gone," "Mommy shoe").

Parents can encourage their child's spontaneous two-word sentence productions by expanding their child's single words into short phrases and encouraging him to imitate. The parent training activities for 2.54 (Imitates two-word phrases) are applicable to this skill.

GROSS MOTOR DEVELOPMENT

3.01 Child: NECK RIGHTING REACTION (0-2 mo.)
Parent: Understands child's neck righting reaction if tested

GENERAL GUIDELINES

The child's neck righting reaction is tested as an evaluation of the child's motor functioning. The presence of this reaction is needed to help the child develop rolling skills in the future.

When a therapist or physician tests the child's neck righting reaction, she gently lifts the child's head while he's in supine and rotates it to the side. The child's shoulder, and then hips should follow in the same direction as the child's head.

MENTALLY RETARDED PARENT

May assume she should turn her child's head at home to make him roll if she sees a professional test her child's neck righting reaction.

1. To avoid misinterpretation, do not test the child's neck righting reactions in view of the parent unless you are certain she understands this procedure is for evaluation purposes only.

BLIND PARENT

May not be able to visually monitor her child's neck righting reactions when tested.

1. Describe the neck righting reaction and the procedure for evaluation before testing.
2. The parent can lightly touch her child's shoulders and feel his responses while the evaluator tests the child's reaction.

3.02 Child: TURNS HEAD TO BOTH SIDES IN SUPINE (0-2 mo.)
Parent: Alternates stimuli and positions which encourage child to turn head to both sides

GENERAL GUIDELINES

Prone positioning is the preferred position for children at this age. When in supine, however, the child should be able to move his head from side to side. If stimuli are present on only one side of his visual field, he may tend to keep his head turned only to that side.

It is important for the child to develop the symmetrical ability to turn his head to both sides. If a child is put in his crib in only one position, or carried in the same arm, muscle tightening could occur on one side of his neck. Positioning and carrying the child on alternating sides helps to encourage his symmetrical head turning.

MENTALLY RETARDED PARENT

May leave her child supine for long periods; visual stimuli may be minimal or presented to only one side for the child.

1. Explain to the parent the importance and reasons for not leaving her child lying on his back all day. Include:
   a. His neck muscles can get tight and he won't learn to use them as well.
   b. His head can flatten on one side if he doesn't move it around.
   c. At this age, he cannot move around by himself; we need to move him.
   d. He doesn't get to look at and learn about things if he lays in his crib all day.
2. Explain the importance of providing interesting things for her child to look at on each side of his head. Include:
   a. If he doesn't have anything to look at, he'll keep his head to one side because he won't have a reason to turn it.
   b. We should never physically move the child's head; that can hurt.
3. Help the parent remember to alternate her child's position in the crib frequently using a concrete guide. For example, tell the parent to put her child with his head toward one end when it is daytime, and at the other end when it is nighttime.
4. Help the parent set up interesting things for her child to look at on both sides of her child's crib and play areas within his visual field.
5. Demonstrate, and let the parent practice, carrying her child alternately on her left and then right shoulder; and feeding her child cradled in her left arm and then, when the bottle is half empty, switching to her right arm.
6. Demonstrate several safe places and positions to place her child during the day; associate these with specific daily activities, e.g., "When you're doing the dishes, he can lay on his tummy here"; "When you're watching T.V., he can sit in your lap"; etc.

BLIND PARENT

May be unaware of the effects of visual stimuli for encouraging her child to turn his head.

1. Describe the child's natural preference to keep his head turned to one side, and the importance of encouraging him to turn it to both sides by placing him in different positions during feeding, in his crib, and when she is carrying him.
2. Explain that her child will tend to keep his head turned toward things that are interesting to look at. Thus, if he only has things to look at on one side, he may prefer to keep his head only to that side.
3. Describe visual stimuli that are attracting to her child at this age, and help position them on both sides of the child's crib and playpen within his visual field. Refer to 1.05 (Inspects surroundings).

3.02

PHYSICALLY DISABLED PARENT

May have difficulty alternating arms when carrying her child to encourage his symmetrical head turning.

1. The parent can use a *Snuggly** or other carrying pouch. This helps discourage the child's asymmetry because his head can turn freely either way, and it also frees the parent's arms for other tasks. The carrying pouch can be adapted with velcro, draw strings, or elastic to help the parent manipulate the pouch independently, if needed.

3.03 Child: LIFTS HEAD IN PRONE (0-2 mo.)
  Parent: Provides ample opportunities for child to be on tummy; stimulates to lift head in prone

GENERAL GUIDELINES

The child's primary position during awake periods (when not held) should generally be spent in prone and side-lying.

During the first month or two, he should be able to briefly lift his head up from prone. His head should face forward, as he lifts it rather than holding it to one side.

Sound and visual stimuli encourage the child to lift his head in prone. If a child has difficulty lifting his head, a small roll or pillow may be prescribed by a therapist to place under his chest.

MENTALLY RETARDED PARENT

May place her child on his back for long periods, or may have difficulty remembering prescribed prone positioning and handling techniques.

1. Demonstrate and concretely explain the importance of prone positioning for the child. Include the following concepts:
    a. Her child gets to use his neck muscles more if he is on his tummy because he learns to pick his head up.
    b. After eating he might spit up and choke if he is on his back.
    c. It can get very boring for him to lay on his back all day; since he can't roll over by himself, we have to put him on his tummy.
2. Demonstrate and explain the importance of putting her child in prone only on firm surfaces:
    a. Caution the parent never to put a pillow under her child's face.
    b. Compare and contrast suitable firm places with places which are not firm enough for her child to lie in prone on, e.g., soft couch versus a firm mattress or the floor.
    c. Explain that it is too difficult for him to lift his head up if he is on a soft surface.
3. Have the parent identify three or four safe and firm places for her child to be on his tummy. If there are no suitable places, help the parent set up special areas:

    a. Basinettes can be homemade with large sturdy shallow boxes decorated with contact paper and visually attracting pictures. A mattress can be made with firm foam and covered with a king size pillowcase or cloth.
    b. Safe areas on the floor near corners and walls can be set up with a blanket and pictures taped to the wall.
    c. Large plastic clothes baskets or some baby bathtubs may be adapted if there are no safe alternatives.
    d. Help the parent think of various times during the day to place her child in prone in the identified safe areas.
4. Each time you visit and see the child on his tummy in safe areas, reinforce the parent.
5. Model, and have the parent practice, shaking a toy or talking to her child in prone to encourage him to lift his head.
6. If a towel-roll support has been recommended to facilitate her child's head lifting in prone:
    a. Make a towel-roll and secure it with plastic tape for long-term use.
    b. Demonstrate positioning the roll under his chest with his arms forward. Have the parent practice several times with your verbal and physical prompting, as needed.
    c. Leave Polaroid pictures of proper positioning taped to his crib and other identified play areas.
    d. Monitor the parent's positioning of her child frequently.
    e. If needed for emphasis, let the parent experience improper positioning. Demonstrate and encourage the parent to lay prone on the floor with a couch pillow under her face, neck, and then chest. Point out how difficult and uncomfortable it is to lift up her head in the first two positions.
    g. Suggest times within parent's and child's daily activities in which to position her child over the roll, e.g., after bath time or while the parent is washing the dishes.
    h. Tell the parent her child should not sleep on the towel-roll.

BLIND PARENT

May be unable to visually monitor her child's prone position and brief head lifting actions.

1. Anticipatory Guidance: The parent may be hesitant to position her child in prone. Fears of suffocation may be heightened if she cannot visually monitor his face. If the child has normal reactions in prone, he will naturally clear his nose. When applicable, assure the parent of his built-in capabilities to clear his nose in prone and encourage prone positions.
2. Demonstrate and explain that visual stimuli can encourage her child to briefly lift his head:
    a. Attract the child's attention to a bright squeak toy. The parent can lightly touch the back of her child's head to monitor his movement. Orient the parent to your placement of the toy within her child's visual field.
    b. The parent can position herself in prone on the floor directly in front of her child's head while he is in prone. She can monitor his head lifting, in response to her talking and/or presenting toys, by feeling the direction of his breathing.

---

*See Glossary.

c. If face-to-face positions are avoided, the parent can position herself straddled in a hand-knee position over her child, so that her chest is directly above his head. Her voice and toy presentation will attract him to lift his head.

3. The parent can lie in a supported supine (slightly inclined) position and hold her child prone on her chest when she talks or sings to him. This will encourage her child to lift his head while allowing the parent to easily monitor his movements.

4. If a towel-roll support has been prescribed to facilitate the child's head lifting in prone:
   a. Clearly describe the position of the roll in relation to the child's chest and arm position.
   b. Let the parent become tactually familiar with her child in this position, and then practice placing him over the roll.
   c. The parent can encourage her child to lift his head as described in Activity No. 2.
   d. The towel-roll should be monitored frequently to insure it is holding up to her child's weight and daily use.

PHYSICALLY DISABLED PARENT

Who uses a wheelchair or has limited mobility and bending abilities; may have difficulty placing her child in prone on the floor, playpen, or crib.

1. A parent who uses a wheelchair and has adequate upper extremity strength and control, can place her child in prone on a *wheelchair lap tray.* She can then hold her child with one hand on his buttocks while holding a toy in her other hand to stimulate his head raising.
2. Put a large piece of *tri-wall** on the parent's bed with a quilt on top for the parent to play with her child in prone. Tri-wall provides the firm surface necessary for the development of propping and weight-shifting skills in prone. The child should be closely supervised and not left unattended on a bed. The side of the bed could be pushed against a wall for safety.
3. If the parent has good upper extremity control and strength, she can use a canvas *log carrier** or securely attached receiving blanket around the child's abdomen to raise and lower him to and from the floor (tummy toward floor). The parent can dangle a toy from her wheelchair to the child to encourage his head raising.
4. A parent in a wheelchair may be able to transfer herself and her child to a couch and then lower herself to the floor. Once the parent is on the floor, she can transfer her child from the couch to the floor with her.
5. Use a standard-sized red wagon with a blanket folded for a bottom cushion. A wagon offers several benefits: adequate height for reaching from a wheelchair (larger tires can be added to raise height), high sides for safety, and it is large enough to allow a child up to 4 months in age to be active.
6. The parent should use proper lifting techniques if she is ambulatory but has back problems:
   a. She can place one knee on the floor beside her child, keeping her back straight, and slide her arms under the child to bring him close to her body. She should stand up keeping her back erect.
   b. Legs from a playpen can be removed so that the parent can step into the playpen after collapsing the side. She can then lift her child, rather than bending over the playpen edge.
7. Refer to 1.01 (Quiets when picked up) for crib adaptations.

3.04   **Child:** HOLDS HEAD UP 45 DEGREES IN PRONE (0-2½ mo.)
      Parent: Provides ample opportunities for child to be on tummy; stimulates to lift head in prone

GENERAL GUIDELINES

The child's increasing head control enables him to lift his head in prone to form an approximate 45° angle to his trunk. His head should continue to face forward at midline.

Guidelines regarding positioning activities and visual stimuli to encourage the child to lift his head can be followed as outlined under 3.03 (Lifts head in prone). Continue to monitor

---

*See Glossary.

3.04

and facilitate those activities, helping the parent to adjust presentation of visual stimuli slightly higher.

BLIND PARENT

May not be able to visually monitor her child's increasing head control.

1. When the child's head is at a 45° angle, the parent can gently touch the back of her child's neck to determine his angle. The wrinkles on his neck provide additional cues.
2. Explain and demonstrate to the parent about the importance of touching his neck gently:
   a. Excessive downward pressure on the child's neck will produce hyperextension; he cannot learn head control in that position.
   b. Let her feel the child's neck when it is in hyperextension.
3. Help the parent present toys at appropriate locations to prevent neck hyperextensions and assure the toy is in her child's visual field when he is prone:
   a. Adjust visual stimuli in the child's crib and play areas and at his eye level when his head is lifted 45°. Mark with tape on the child's crib where his eye level is. Adjust the tape higher as the child's head control increases.
   b. Suspend toys at correct heights from a *port-a-play gym.**
   c. The parent can monitor the proper height for presenting toys by gently keeping her hand on the back of her child's head.

3.05 Child: HOLDS HEAD TO ONE SIDE IN PRONE (0-2 mo.)
Parent: Provides ample opportunities for child to be on tummy with interesting visual targets on each side of his head

GENERAL GUIDELINES

When placed in prone, a child instinctively tries to clear his nose. He should be placed in prone only on firm surfaces, and he should be able to turn his head to both sides. Constant positioning with his head turned to one side can lead to neck asymmetries. Visual stimuli should be positioned near each side, or toward the nonfavored side, if applicable.

If the child cannot clear his nose in prone or cannot turn his head to each side, consult with the child's physician. This child should not be placed in prone until specific positioning and handling techniques have been prescribed by a physical or occupational therapist.

Follow the positioning guidelines and parent activities listed under 3.02 (Turns head to both sides in supine) and 3.03 (Lifts head in prone).

Provide parents anticipatory guidance that their child's head should never be physically forced to turn.

---

*See Glossary.

3.06 Child: LIFTS HEAD WHEN HELD AT SHOULDER (0-1 mo.)
Parent: Supports child's head when held at shoulder and encourages child to lift head

GENERAL GUIDELINES

When held upright at the parent's shoulder, the child may be able to lift his head up momentarily.

Parents need to provide adequate support to their child's head when holding him at their shoulder.

MENTALLY RETARDED PARENT

May not provide adequate support for her child's head when lifting or carrying.

1. Observe the parent lifting and carrying her child. If she is not providing adequate head support for her child, demonstrate and have the parent practice proper handling techniques:
   a. Explain that her child's neck muscles are not strong enough for him to hold his head up all by himself yet. Stress providing the child support with her hand at his head.
   b. Model, and let the parent practice, picking him up from various positions, such as his crib, infant seat, and playpen.
   c. Leave a Polaroid picture of proper positioning with head support as a reminder.
2. Model, and let the parent practice, showing things to her child, such as pictures and windows, while held at her shoulder.
3. Demonstrate and let the parent practice carrying her child in alternate positions, such as holding him at her waist. Stress making sure both her child's arms are forward and the parent's upper arm is supporting the back of her child's head.

PHYSICALLY DISABLED PARENT

May have difficulty providing adequate head support while carrying him or pushing a wheelchair.

1. The parent can use a *Snuggly** or other carrying pouch adapted with velcro, draw strings, or elastic to facilitate easy fastening.

3.07 Child: HOLDS HEAD UP 90 DEGREES IN PRONE (1-3 mo.)
Parent: Provides ample opportunities for child to be on tummy; stimulates to lift head in prone

GENERAL GUIDELINES

As the child's neck extensors develop, he begins to lift his head up high enough from prone to form an approximate 90° angle to his trunk. His chest remains close to the support.

The child's head should not be physically manipulated into this position. Attracting visual and sound stimuli help encourage the child to lift his head.

Guidelines, positioning, and activities can be followed as outlined under 3.03 (Lifts head in prone). Help parents adjust presentation of visual stimuli to his higher visual field in prone and continue to monitor proper positioning. The child should not be encouraged to look at things above his eye level. This could cause him to hyperextend his neck, which does not promote good head control.

3.08 Child: HOLDS HEAD IN SAME PLANE AS BODY WHEN HELD IN VERTICAL SUSPENSION (1½-2½ mo.)
Parent: Lifts and carries child in a manner which facilitates his head control

GENERAL GUIDELINES

This item is used as an evaluation of the child's motor functioning.

When held horizontally in mid-air with support provided at the child's abdomen, the child holds his head at the same level as his trunk, while his legs hang down.

Absence of this reaction may indicate the need for special handling and monitoring by a physical or occupational therapist to facilitate head control. Special activities do not need to be implemented if the child demonstrates this reaction.

Parents can facilitate their child's head control by placing their child in prone before picking him up, and sliding their arms under his chest and tummy to "scoop" him up to their arms and carry.

MENTALLY RETARDED PARENT

May not be able to safely implement some of the typically prescribed activities which encourage her child to hold his head up in vertical suspension.

---

*See Glossary.

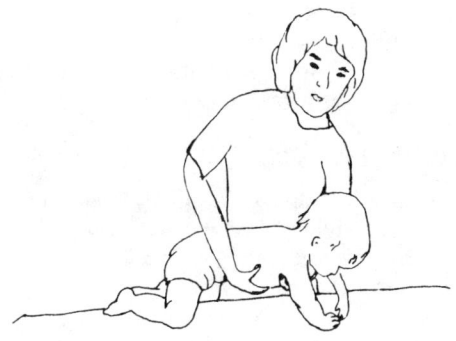

1. If indicated, introduce special handling and carrying techniques to the parent which encourage her child to hold his head up:
   a. Explain that her child needs to learn to use his neck muscles better by picking him up from his tummy.
   b. Explain that if we pick him up when he's lying on his back, he uses his neck muscles in the wrong way.
   c. Demonstrate lifting the child from his playpen, crib, and the floor by placing him in prone and "scooping him up" under his belly.
   d. Demonstrate holding the child in prone horizontally and walking him slowly around the room to look at the parent, pictures, or out a window.
   e. Do not advise the parent to hold her child and pretend he is an airplane or bird, as suggested in some activity guides.
2. Have the parent practice the demonstrated positioning and handling techniques with her child until she incorporates them spontaneously:
   a. Provide verbal and physical prompts, as needed.
   b. Leave Polaroid pictures posted above his crib and playpen.
   c. Remind the parent to talk to her child while she's picking him up from prone.

BLIND PARENT

May be unable to visually monitor her child's reactions and the therapist's testing procedures if evaluating this skill.

1. Describe the testing procedure and rationale before evaluating the child's reactions in ventral suspension.
2. The parent can gently touch her child's head or chin during the testing to monitor his head movement.
3. If horizontal prone picking-up and carrying positions are recommended, clearly describe the parent's hand and arm positions in relation to her child's chest and tummy. The parent may want to practice with a large doll until completely familiar with the technique.

PHYSICALLY DISABLED PARENT

May already incorporate picking her child up from prone in a horizontal position if activities for 3.03 (Lifts head in prone) and 1.01 (Quiets when picked up) have been implemented.

3.09 Child: EXTENDS BOTH LEGS (1½-2½ mo.)
Parent: Provides opportunities for child to move out of a totally flexed posture into a more extended posture

GENERAL GUIDELINES

This item is used to evaluate the child's level of motor functioning. At birth the child's active movements occur in a flexor pattern as he draws his legs and arms close to his body. During his second and third month, however, his movements are directed primarily in a more extended pattern. He should not, however, display a stiff extended pattern.

Prone positions facilitate the child's movement from flexion to extension. If the child remains in a totally flexed or stiff extended pattern, specific exercises may be recommended by a therapist. Physically manipulating the child's legs in or out of extension is not recommended unless supervised by a therapist. Refer to 3.03 (Lifts head in prone) to help parents position their child in prone.

MENTALLY RETARDED PARENT

May misinterpret a therapist's explanation and positioning techniques.

1. If special exercises or positioning have been prescribed for the child because of obligatory flexor patterns, explain their purpose in meaningful terms to the parent:
   a. Explain that since her child is older, he is ready to keep his body straighter. Ask the parent to tell you why his body doesn't look straight, or point out how his arms and legs look bent.
   b. Relate that the demonstrated exercises are to help her child learn to straighten out his body.
   c. Caution the parent never to pull her child's arms or legs out straight because it can hurt his muscles. Explain that he needs to move them all by himself.
   d. Tell the parent that keeping her child on his tummy helps him learn to straighten his legs out.
   e. Suggest specific times to carry out prescribed exercises, such as after diapering.
   f. Ask the parent to think of a song or special slow music box to play while she implements the exercise. This can help keep the activity fun, assure slow pacing, and help the parent judge the duration of the exercise.

BLIND PARENT

May not be able to visually monitor her child's flexion and extension patterns.

1. Describe the child's flexor and extensor postures, explaining their developmental progression. The parent can then become tactually familiar with her child's postures.
2. Demonstrate to the parent prescribed positioning and exercises with her child by using a hand-over-hand demonstration method, until she is comfortable and tactually familiar with the position and exercise movements.

3.10 Child: ROLLS SIDE TO SUPINE (1½-2 mo.)
Parent: Encourages child to roll from side to supine

GENERAL GUIDELINES

When placed in a side-lying position the child can roll to his back.

This skill can be encouraged by placing the child periodically in side-lying, and by moving a toy in a 180° arc within his field of vision to encourage him to follow the movement. The toy should be held below the child's eyeline (at his shoulder-neck area), 8 to 12 inches away. If toys are presented above or directly at eye level, his neck may hyperextend in order to see the toy which will promote an abnormal rolling pattern.

Parents should alternate sides when placing their child in side-lying to facilitate symmetrical neck and trunk alignment. The child should not be physically manipulated through rolling unless recommended and supervised by an occupational or physical therapist.

MENTALLY RETARDED PARENT

May not place her child in side-lying, and may have difficulty judging proper distance and pacing for moving toys.

1. Demonstrate, and let the parent practice, placing her child in side-lying. Emphasize keeping the child's arms forward. Explain:
   a. From this position her child is learning to roll to his back.
   b. He cannot roll to his back unless we help him lie on his side first.
   c. He cannot roll to his back from his tummy until he has lots of practice rolling from his side.
   d. He cannot roll from his back to his side because it is too hard for him; she will have to help him move back on his side or tummy.
2. Demonstrate, and let the parent practice, holding a toy 8 to 12 inches from her child's shoulders in side-lying, moving it in an arc to encourage him to roll to his back. Emphasize:
   a. Appropriate placement of the toy.
   b. Getting her child's attention by shaking the toy and calling his name.
   c. Slowly moving it at her child's pace.
3. If the parent demonstrates difficulty with judging proper tracking distance and placement of toys, and the child needs extra help with this skill, use a physical guide, such as a *port-a-play gym** or ribbon strung horizontally across crib rails. Use a large doll for initial positioning practice:
   a. Point out that the ribbon or gym bar is directly above the child's shoulders. Contrast this placement with placing the ribbon or gym bar above the child's head to demonstrate improper positioning.
   b. Let the parent practice placing her child in side-lying in the correct position in relation to the gym bar or ribbon.

---

*See Glossary.

   c. Loosely attach a toy on a string from the ribbon or gym bar, 8 to 12" from the child's shoulder, and demonstrate sliding it across slowly. Let the parent practice moving the toy while her child rolls to his back. Explain the importance of detaching the toy after he has rolled over and placing it on his hand.
4. If the child needs physical assistance to roll, tell the parent not to move his head, but rather demonstrate gently guiding his upper arm or hip.

BLIND PARENT

May be unable to visually monitor her child's rolling, and may have difficulty assuring that toys are presented at a proper distance within her child's lower line of vision.

1. The parent can lie on her side on the floor parallel to her child in a side-lying position (parent's chest toward child's back):
    a. The parent will be able to present toys to her child at a suitable distance and eye level placing her outstretched arm across her child's shoulder.
    b. She can pace her movement of the toy according to her child's movements against her chest.

2. The parent could use a *port-a-play gym** or ribbon strung across crib railings:
    a. The parent can tactually recognize where to place her child by noting a specific crib rail in relation to the crib gym and the child's shoulder in side-lying.
    b. The parent can gently touch the back of her child's head to monitor his movement and pace the toy movement accordingly.

PHYSICALLY DISABLED PARENT

Who uses a wheelchair or has limited mobility; can use adapted areas for her child to practice rolling skills as listed under 1.01 (Quiets when picked up) and 3.03 (Lifts head in prone).

1. If the parent lowers her child to prone on the floor with a *log carrier** or receiving blanket, she can gently pull up one side of the blanket or log carrier to position her child in side-lying. She could then dangle a toy on a string over and across her child's shoulders to encourage him to roll.

---

*See Glossary.

3.11 Child: KICKS RECIPROCALLY (1½-2½ mo.)
     Parent: Does not restrict child's leg movements; carries out prescribed positioning if child's muscle tone interferes with his reciprocal kicking

GENERAL GUIDELINES

The child, when lying supine, kicks his legs alternately when excited or just for fun.

This skill is used as an evaluation of the child's motor functioning. If he does not kick, or does not kick in a reciprocal pattern, it may be the result of muscle tone abnormalities or asymmetries of muscle function.

Positioning and handling to accommodate the underlying tone and asymmetries may be prescribed by a therapist. Kicking should not be physically taught; active kicking movements are facilitated through proper positioning. Refer to 3.03 (Lifts head in prone) and 3.12 (Extension thrust inhibited) if towel-rolls and side-lying have been prescribed to facilitate tone.

MENTALLY RETARDED PARENT

May unintentionally restrict her child's legs which prevent his reciprocal kicking.

1. Check the child's clothing:
    a. If footed pajama legs are too short, the feet can be cut off.
    b. If the parent swaddles her child in a blanket, explore if the parent provides ample opportunities for her child to be "unswaddled."
2. When the child kicks if he is excited or for fun, interpret his positive communicative sign: "He really likes it when you look at him and smile; see his legs kicking!"
3. Anticipatory Guidance: If a child does not kick excitedly, and there are no identifiable motoric causes, he may be showing initial signs of apathy and lack of interest in his environment. Interventions should focus on activities described in this Guide's cognitive and social-emotional sections during the first few months. Jingle bells loosely tied around his ankles may also help stimulate his interest and excitement in kicking.

BLIND PARENT

May be unable to visually detect her child's kicking when excited.

1. Bells or bands attached to child's ankles could provide the parent extra auditory cues which signal her child's excitement during play, when she approaches, and when he sees a favorite toy.

3.12 Child: EXTENSOR THRUST INHIBITED (2-4 mo.)
Parent: Positions child in prone and side-lying if prescribed to help inhibit child's extensor thrust

GENERAL GUIDELINES

Extensor thrust is a reflex normally present at birth. It usually begins to diminish during this period without specific intervention. This reflex is tested by placing the child in supine with his legs loosely flexed next to his chest. If the sole of one foot is scratched and sudden extension of the legs occur, then the reflex is present. This procedure is only for evaluation purposes by a physician or therapist. The child's soles should never be stimulated beyond testing as this may facilitate abnormal motor patterns.

If a child has prolonged extensor thrust, it may indicate muscle tone abnormalities. Prone and side-lying positions are usually recommended. Handling techniques should be carried out under the supervision of a physical or occupational therapist.

MENTALLY RETARDED PARENT

May have difficulty remembering prescribed positions for her child which inhibit extensor thrust.

1. Do not test this reflex in front of the parent unless you are certain she understands the procedure is for evaluation purposes only. She might model this procedure at home.
2. Caution the parent never to tickle the bottom of her child's feet because it is bad for his muscles at this age.
3. If special positioning has been prescribed because the child has increased tone, explain the rationale in concrete terminology:
   a. Demonstrate "tight muscles" by flexing your arm muscle tightly. Let the parent try this so she can experience how much more difficult it is to bend her arm when it is that tight.
   b. Explain, "Many of your child's muscles are too tight; it is hard for him to bend them. We can help him make them looser by laying him on his side and on his tummy."
   c. Caution the parent never to make her child's arms or legs bend by pulling them because that can hurt his muscles.
4. If side-lying positions have been recommended, demonstrate, and have the parent practice, placing her child in side-lying using a bolster or blanket roll at least the length of the child:
   a. If a blanket-roll is left with the parent, securely tape it for long-term use.
   b. Take Polaroid pictures of the child in side-lying with the blanket-roll, and post them above the child's playpen.
   c. Remind the parent to always make sure her child has a toy to look at in this position.
5. Demonstrate, and let the parent practice, changing her child's diaper in side-lying or supine on a bean bag chair.
6. Remind the parent to alternate sides when placing her child in side-lying. Alternate mirrors or pictures toward each end of the child's crib as reminders.
7. Refer to 3.03 (Lifts head in prone) for prone positioning.
8. Explain that her child should not lie only on his side or only on his stomach. If needed, identify and associate various ways to position her child in relation to the parent's and child's daily schedule. For example, he can play after bath time on his side and sit in his parent's lap after dinner.

BLIND PARENT

May need to become tactually familiar with prescribed positioning and handling techniques.

1. If the child's extensor thrust response is tested, describe the procedure and her child's response movements. Test the child on the parent's lap.
2. If the child has increased tone requiring intervention, let the parent feel the areas of her child's increased tone. Increased tone can be further described by using a rubber band (overstretched) for demonstration of hypertonicity or letting the parent tighten her own muscles.
3. If side-lying positions have been recommended, the parent can feel the positioning process for her child through your physical guidance and verbal descriptions. Let her practice with your monitoring until comfortable.

PHYSICALLY DISABLED PARENT

May have difficulty physically manipulating and maintaining her child in side-lying if recommended.

1. Construct a permanent blanket roll or provide a bolster to help the parent maintain her child in side-lying positions.

3.13 Child: FLEXOR WITHDRAWAL INHIBITED (2-4 mo.)
Parent: Positions child in prone and side-lying if prescribed to help inhibit flexor withdrawal

GENERAL GUIDELINES

Flexor withdrawal is a reflex normally present during the child's first two months. This reflex is tested to evaluate the child's level of motor functioning; it is not a motor skill to teach. Flexor withdrawal is tested by scratching the bottom of the child's foot while he is lying supine; if his leg draws quickly into flexion, the reflex is present. The child's soles should never be purposely stimulated beyond testing as this may facilitate abnormal motor patterns.

This reflex should begin to diminish after the child's second month. Prolonged presence may indicate tone abnormalities. Prone and side-lying positions are usually recommended if the child has a persistent flexor withdrawal reflex.

Refer to 3.03 (Lifts head in prone) and 3.12 (Extensor thrust inhibited) for parent training activities regarding prone and side-lying positions for the child.

3.14 Child: **ASSUMES WITHDRAWAL POSITION (2-3½ mo.)**
Parent: If prescribed, implements positioning techniques to help normalize muscle tone

GENERAL GUIDELINES

This item is used for evaluation purposes to test the child's level of motor function; it is not a motor skill to teach.

The child's withdrawal position is observed when he is lying on his back and he spontaneously flexes his arms and legs, bringing them close to his body.

A child with muscle tone abnormalities may be unable to assume this position or may not be able to move out of this position easily. If side-lying or prone positions have been prescribed for tone abnormalities, refer to 3.03 (Lifts head in prone) and 3.12 (Extensor thrust inhibited).

Gentle side-to-side rocking on the parent's lap in a semi-cradle position with the child's head and back against the parent's thighs (his hips flexed with his legs positioned on her stomach), may also be recommended.

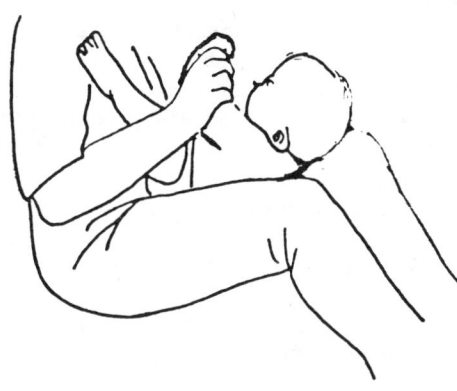

All handling techniques should be under the supervision of an occupational or physical therapist.

MENTALLY RETARDED PARENT

May display abrupt handling when implementing prescribed rocking techniques with her child.

1. If gentle rocking in cradled positions have been prescribed for the child, select a music box which plays soft slow music to demonstrate the activity:
   a. Demonstrate the positions and pace of rocking to music.
   b. Emphasize smiling and talking to the child during rocking.
   c. Let the parent practice with her child, with your prompts, and reinforcement until proficient before recommending this activity at home.
2. When the parent can demonstrate the prescribed rocking activity with her child:
   a. Leave a Polaroid picture of the parent and child positioned properly.
   b. Name specific times to implement the activity, such as before bedtime and naps.
   c. Dependent upon the therapist's recommendation, help the parent judge the duration of this activity, e.g., rocking her child through the completion of the music box song.
   d. Name the child's behaviors which tells her she should stop before the music stops, e.g., if he arches his back, twists his body, or cries.
3. Home use of hammocks or swinging in a blanket should not be prescribed unless the parent consistently demonstrates gentle handling with her child.

BLIND PARENT

Should become tactually familiar with prescribed rocking activities with her child.

1. Place the child in the recommended position on the parent's lap. She can become tactually familiar with her child's body position in relation to her own.

PHYSICALLY DISABLED PARENT

With limited lower extremity abilities; may be unable to rock her child on her thighs if recommended for her child's increased tone.

1. The parent may be able to gently rock her child while he lies in prone on a rocking chair.
2. If available, the child could be positioned in supine on a water bed, small partially deflated air mattress, or bean bag chair.
3. The child could be placed in a hammock suspended across his crib railings at the parent's wheelchair height for sleeping and gentle rocking.
4. The parent may be able to hold her child cradled in her arm while she rocks him in a rocking chair.

3.15 Child: **HOLDS CHEST UP IN PRONE — WEIGHT ON FOREARMS (2-4 mo.)**
Parent: Provides ample opportunities for child to play in prone; implements special positioning to help him lift his chest up and bear some weight on forearms if prescribed

GENERAL GUIDELINES

The child's head control is developing to the point where he can hold his head up with his chest off a surface, bearing partial weight on his forearms.

Toys, pictures, and people encourage him to lift his chest up in order to get a better look. Wedges and towel-rolls placed under his chest may also be recommended to facilitate weight-bearing on forearms and head control.

The following adaptations are additive to the guidelines and activities for 3.03 (Lifts head in prone) which include towel-roll use.

3.15

MENTALLY RETARDED PARENT

May not adjust visual stimuli according to her child's increased head control.

1. Help the parent discriminate her child's increasing head control. Explain, "Now that Jimmy's older, he's learning to push his chest off the floor; see how I can slip my hand under it! See how he leans on his arms and lifts his head higher? This shows us the muscles in his neck are getting stronger."
2. Let the parent present a toy while her child is in prone:
   a. If she does not adjust for his new height, demonstrate the proper distance and height to hold a toy.
   b. Caution her not to show her child the toy above his eyeline because "his head will lean too far back and he can't learn to use his neck muscles as well."
3. If a roll had been prescribed for earlier prone skills, and continues to be recommended, check to assure its size and condition continue to be suitable for the child's size. If not, reconstruct it to the recommended size.
4. Help the parent adjust any visual stimuli in her child's crib and play areas to a higher height, when appropriate.

BLIND PARENT

May have difficulty positioning stimuli within her child's increasing visual field in prone.

1. The parent can monitor her child's head position by lightly touching the back of his head. She can raise the toy accordingly and feel her child's head and chest lifting.
2. Help the parent adjust or position visual stimuli in her child's crib and play areas, as needed, to accommodate her child's higher visual field.

3.16 Child: **ROTATES AND EXTENDS HEAD** (2-3 mo.)
Parent: Encourages child to extend and rotate his head while in prone if recommended

GENERAL GUIDELINES

In prone, the child lifts his head and chest up, bearing partial weight on his forearms. He is able to turn his head to each side.

If the child prefers turning his head to only one side, parents can position stimuli toward his non-preferred side. The child's head should not be physically manipulated to turn.

The following activities are additive to the guidelines and activities in 3.03 (Lifts head in prone) and 3.15 (Holds chest up in prone — weight on forearms).

MENTALLY RETARDED PARENT

May not present stimuli to both sides of her child's head.

1. Check the child's sleep and play areas to assure visual stimuli are available on each side.
2. If the child needs extra help extending and rotating his head in prone:
   a. Demonstrate, and let the parent practice, sliding a toy across a *port-a-play gym** or ribbon strung across the crib bars perpendicular to the child.
   b. Demonstrate approaching the child from alternating sides when he is in his crib, playpen, and on the floor to say "Peek-a-boo."
3. If the child has neck asymmetries, help the parent remember which side of her child's head to present extra "stimuli":
   a. If the child has a physical marking, such as a birthmark or freckle on his non-preferred head turning side, use that as a reminder.
   b. Device a sticker system in the child's crib and play areas. The sticker can serve as a reminder to put his favorite toys on that side.

BLIND PARENT

May be unable to visually monitor her child's head extension and rotation as she presents toys to him.

1. Let the parent become tactually familiar with her child's head rotation and extension abilities by lightly touching the back of his neck while you attract his movement to each side.
2. Check to assure visual stimuli within the child's crib and play areas are available on both sides, at proper heights, and within the child's visual field.
3. Alert the parent if her child displays a head turning preference during solitary play. She can then:
   a. Tactually check her child's play area before leaving him alone to assure his favorite toys are toward his non-preferred side.
   b. Know to approach him toward his non-preferred side.
   c. Attach toys to a *port-a-play gym** or suspended from a ribbon strung across the child's crib toward her child's non-preferred side.

3.17 Child: **ROLLS PRONE TO SUPINE** (2-5 mo.)
Parent: Encourages child to roll from prone to supine, facilities through handling techniques if prescribed

GENERAL GUIDELINES

The child rolls from his stomach to his back moving his body segmentally. He may initiate the roll with his hip, head, or shoulder.

Parents can encourage their child to roll by moving an attractive toy across his line of vision in an arc toward his back and providing gentle physical prompting, as needed.

If the child consistently rolls by arching his head and hips and "flipping" over, it is not considered a true rolling pattern. Specific handling techniques to facilitate a segmental rolling pattern should be prescribed and supervised by an occupational or physical therapist.

---

*See Glossary.

MENTALLY RETARDED PARENT

May not anticipate safety concerns as her child begins to roll, and may be too abrupt or rough if implementing prescribed handling techniques.

1. Help the parent discriminate safe from unsafe areas to place her child around his home:
   a. Directly name areas never to leave her child alone, e.g., parent's bed, couch, chair, or table.
   b. Role-play "what-if" situations, i.e., "What if you are changing Jimmy on the table and the doorbell rings?" or "What if Jimmy is lying on the couth while you're watching T.V. and the phone rings?"
   c. Tell the parent to always check her child's crib and play areas for toys which have hard corners that could hurt him if he rolled on top of them.
2. If the child is rolling from his tummy to his back, tell the parent his muscles are not ready for him to roll back to his stomach again. She has to help him roll back over when he's tired of being on his back.
3. Anticipatory Guidance: The child may be delayed in rolling or may stop rolling without any apparent underlying motoric cause. Investigate whether the child has had ample experiences in prone, and explore the child's affective responses and experiences. If he has not experienced success in reaching objects or "making things happen," he may lack the motivation to roll. Intervention to increase the child's motivation and interest in his environment will become a priority.
4. Demonstrate, and let the parent practice, encouraging her child to roll using a moving toy as a motivator. Stress the importance of letting her child hold the toy since he worked so hard to get it.
5. If the child is exhibiting abnormal rolling patterns and special handling techniques have been prescribed:
   a. Demonstrate with a rag doll the difference between "flipping" and segmental rolling to illustrate why special handling techniques are being taught to the parent.
   b. Demonstrate the techniques which facilitate segmental rolling with a rag doll, and let the parent practice several times before she practices them with her child. Emphasize slow and gentle movements.
   c. Demonstrate the handling techniques with the child, and let the parent practice with your hands over the parent's hands. Fade your physical assistance, as appropriate. Emphasize slow, gentle movements *and* giving the child a "surprise" when he has completed his roll.
   d. Provide Polaroid pictures of the sequenced handling techniques in rolling. Attach them to a poster board in their sequential order, marking the steps with numbers.

BLIND PARENT

May not be able to visually monitor her child's rolling pattern, and may have difficulty presenting and moving toys within her child's visual field to encourage rolling.

1. Describe segmental rolling patterns and demonstrate them with a rag doll while the parent tactually monitors them:
   a. The parent can touch the doll's head, hips, and legs during your demonstration.
   b. Let the parent become familiar with positions which could hinder her child's rolling, such as having the doll's arms "stuck" under its chest.
   c. If the child is exhibiting a flipping pattern during rolling which warrants special handling, describe the pattern and demonstrate with a doll while the parent touches the doll's shoulders and hips.
2. Explain to the parent how moving a toy across her child's visual field toward his back encourages him to roll so he can keep watching the toy:
   a. Orient the parent to the toy's presentation distance and location tracking arc in relation to her child's shoulders. Explain that, if the toy is held too high, her child may tilt his head back too far to look for it and end up flipping over.
   b. She can monitor her child's tracking by gently touching the back of his head while she presents the toys.
3. If handling techniques have been prescribed to facilitate the child's rolling:
   a. Describe and demonstrate the techniques with your hand over the parent's hand.
   b. Continue practicing with the parent on various occasions, fading your physical guidance as the parent becomes tactually familiar and comfortable with the techniques, positions, and pacing.

PHYSICALLY DISABLED PARENT

Who uses a wheelchair; may have difficulty encouraging her child to roll when he is on the floor.

1. If the parent uses a wheelchair, she can dangle and move toys on strings from her child's perimeter of vision toward the back of his head to encourage him to roll when he is in prone on the floor.
2. If the child needs special handling techniques and positions to facilitate rolling:
   a. Refer to 1.01 (Quiets when picked up) and 3.03 (Lifts head in prone) to accommodate the child's rolling surface to the parent's disability.
   b. The parent can participate by being the "surprise" at the other end of the child's roll if her upper extremity abilities prevent proper handling techniques during the child's rolling process.

3.18 **Child: HOLDS HEAD BEYOND PLANE OF BODY WHEN HELD IN VENTRAL SUSPENSION (2½-3½ mo.)**
Parent: Lifts and carries child in a manner which facilitates his head control

GENERAL GUIDELINES

The child should raise his head above the level of his trunk when held horizontally in mid-air with support provided at his abdomen.

This skill is not taught. It is used as an evaluation of the child's motor functioning. Special activities do not need to be implemented if the child displays this reaction. Absence of this reaction, however, may indicate the need for special

3.18

handling and monitoring by a physical or occupational therapist to facilitate head control. Refer to 3.08 (Holds head in same plane as body when held in ventral suspension).

3.19 Child: ASYMMETRICAL TONIC NECK REFLEX INHIBITED (3-5 mo.)
Parent: Implements prescribed positioning techniques which help inhibit child's asymmetrical tonic reflex if indicated

GENERAL GUIDELINES

This item is used as an evaluation of the child's motor and neurological functioning. If the child has an *asymmetrical tonic neck reflex (ATNR)*,* he assumes a fencing position, i.e., his head is turned toward his extended arm while his other arm bends upward toward his head and close to his body.

The child's asymmetrical tonic reflex should diminish by the time he is three to five months of age, and should never be obligatory. Prolonged persistence of this reflex can interfere with the child's ability to roll and play with toys at midline. It can also cause neck and trunk asymmetries. Positioning the child in side-lying on his flexed arm side may be recommended to help inhibit this reflex pattern. Supine positions should also be avoided for these children.

The following activities assume the child has a persisting ATNR. Individualized seating, handling, and carrying techniques should be carried out under the supervision of an occupational or physical therapist.

MENTALLY RETARDED PARENT

May have difficulty understanding and implementing prescribed handling and positioning techniques.

1. Explain to the parent the rationale for implementing special handling and positioning techniques for her child in meaningful terms:
   a. Demonstrate the knee jerk reflex on yourself and the parent to help explain what is a reflex. Stress that it is something that happens automatically, and we really cannot control it very well.
   b. Relate how her child has a different reflex (demonstrating an ATNR on a rag doll or on yourself) that sometimes makes it hard for him to move his arms together.
   c. Explain that since her child has this reflex, we need to hold, carry, and lay him down in special ways.
   d. Relate that her child will have a hard time learning to roll, crawl, and bring his hands together to hold his bottle unless he is held, carried, and laid down in these special ways.
2. Refer to 3.12 (Extensor thrust inhibited) to teach the parent how to position her child in side-lying:
   a. Help the parent remember which side to position her child on in side-lying using an identifying mark on the child, such as birthmark or mole, or keep a special bracelet on the child's hand.
   b. Tell the parent not to place him on his back except when diapering.
3. Demonstrate, and let the parent practice, picking her child up using the prescribed techniques from his crib, the floor, his infant seat, and other play areas:
   a. Let the parent practice with a rag doll until proficient.
   b. Take Polaroid pictures of proper lifting techniques and post above these areas.
4. If special seating is prescribed, refer to Activity No. 2, 3.21 (Holds head steady in supported sitting).
5. Reinforce the parent's good handling techniques, specifically describing why they are good, e.g., "You carried him so well; you remembered to keep his arms forward."
6. Rough or abrupt handling should be commented upon if and when it occurs without over-correction, e.g., "Easy; he likes it when you move him slowly."

BLIND PARENT

May not be able to visually monitor her child's ATNR and prescribed positioning techniques.

1. If evaluated, describe the movements involved to test the child's asymmetrical tonic reflex. The parent can tactually monitor her child's response by lightly touching his shoulders during the testing and then feeling the positions of her child's arms.
2. If special positions and handling techniques are prescribed:
   a. Describe in detail for the parent the positioning and handling movements and her hand placements as they relate to the child's body and movements. Tape record these instructions for the parent's future use, as needed.
   b. Place the child in the prescribed positions and let the parent become tactually familiar with them.
   c. The parent can practice positioning and handling with your gradually fading hand-over-hand physical assistance and verbal direction until comfortable.
3. Review the importance of presenting visual stimuli to her child's non-preferred side when he is on his tummy.

PHYSICALLY DISABLED PARENT

May have difficulty bending, lifting, or positioning herself to carry out prescribed handling techniques with her child.

1. Construct a permanent blanket-roll or bolster to help the parent maintain the child in a side-lying position.
2. The parent can pick her child up from prone positions as outlined in 1.01 (Quiets when picked up) and 3.03 (Lifts head in prone).
3. If adaptive seating is prescribed for the child, make the inserts permanent.

---

*See Glossary.

3.20 Child: HOLDS HEAD IN LINE WITH BODY WHEN PULLED TO SITTING (3-6½ mo.)

Parent: Does not pull child up to sitting position, pulling his hands; implements prescribed handling techniques to accommodate poor head control, if indicated

GENERAL GUIDELINES

This item is for evaluation purposes only to assess the child's level of head control. The child should hold his head in line with his body when pulled slowly by his hands from his back to sitting. If the child's head lags during this "pull to sit" procedure, this may indicate poor head control.

Parents can encourage their child's increased head control by giving him ample opportunities to be in prone positions. They should *not* pull their child from supine to sitting with his hands because this method facilitates abnormal extensor patterns and does *not* encourage better head control. The child's transition to supported sitting should instead be achieved from a side-lying to sitting motion.

Special seating, carrying, and handling techniques may also be prescribed by a therapist to accommodate and improve the child's head control.

The following activities assume the child has poor head control. They supplement the activities for 3.03 (Lifts head in prone) which emphasize prone positions to develop head control.

MENTALLY RETARDED PARENT

May have difficulty remembering prescribed handling techniques if her child has poor head control.

1. Do not test "pulling-to-sit" in front of the parent unless you are certain she understands this is for evaluation purposes only; she may interpret this as the proper way to get her child into sitting.
2. If the child has poor head control, demonstrate to the parent with a rag doll how pulling her child up to sit by pulling his hands is not good:
   a. Point out how the doll's head flops back, and relate how this is not good for her child's muscles.
   b. Tell the parent *not* to pull her child to sitting in this manner because this can hurt her child's neck muscles.
   c. Post a drawing of a child being pulled to sit with an X marked over it.
   d. Proceed to Activity No. 3.
3. Demonstrate, and let the parent practice, bringing her child to supported sitting position from side-lying as prescribed by a therapist:
   a. Use a large rag doll for initial demonstration and practice.
   b. Post Polaroid pictures of this procedure next to the drawing of the incorrect method marked with an X in Activity No. 2.
4. Help the parent remember and generalize prescribed techniques for carrying and picking her child up to accommodate his poor head control. During the period of four to six training sessions:
   a. Demonstrate, and let the parent practice, picking her child up with head support from his crib, car seat, playpen, highchair, infant seat, and the floor.
   b. Demonstrate, and let the parent practice, carrying her child with head support from his crib to the living room, from the living room to the kitchen, and from the kitchen to his room.
   c. Name a few, and prompt the parent to think of, additional times to remember to carry her child with support to his head, e.g., when carrying him at the store, outdoors, at a friend's house, and at the doctor's office.
   d. Post Polaroid pictures of the parent picking her child up with head support over his crib, highchair, playpen, diaper changing area, and car seat.
5. Praise the parent when you observe her picking her child up and/or carrying him with appropriate head support. Specifically describe why her handling is good, e.g., "You are really holding Danny nicely; see how both of his arms are brought forward and his head is supported against your arm? Great!"
6. If rough or abrupt handling methods are observed do not over-correct the parent, but make comments, such as "Easy; he likes to be picked up very slowly to help his neck muscles."
7. Refer to Activity No. 2, 3.21 (Holds steady in supported sitting) if adapted seating is prescribed.

BLIND PARENT

May not be able to visually monitor her child's head control.

1. Let the parent monitor her child's head control response during the "pull-to-sit" testing procedure by placing her hand gently on the back of her child's head. Emphasize this procedure was for testing purposes only, letting her feel how this does not help her child's head control.
2. Describe the child's movements and adult hand placement involved to bring her child to supported sitting through side-lying:
   a. Demonstrate this procedure while the parent tactually monitors with one hand on the back of her child's head and her other hand on his hip.
   b. Let the parent practice this procedure with her child providing verbal and physical prompts, as needed, until the parent is comfortable with the technique.
   c. The parent will be able to tactually monitor her child's hand movements during his transition from side-lying to sitting.
3. Position the child in the parent's arms to demonstrate recommended carrying positions. Point out important contact points to remember. For example, when carrying the child in a cradled position, note which part of her child's head is positioned against which part of her arm and check that both of the child's arms are positioned forward.
4. Describe to the parent where to place her arms in relation to her child's body parts when picking him up from his

3.20

crib or the floor while he is in prone and he is in supine, and when lifting him from his infant seat. Provide verbal and physical prompts, as needed, during the process until the parent feels comfortable picking her child up using this technique.

PHYSICALLY DISABLED PARENT

With decreased mobility; may have difficulty implementing prescribed handling techniques to accommodate her child's head control.

1. The parent may be able to encourage prone positions and practice bringing her child to sit through side-lying and lifting him from prone through adaptations outlined under 1.01 (Quiets when picked up) and 3.03 (Lifts head in prone). Snuggly vest sizes may be needed to be changed to adapt for the child's growth and lack of head control.
2. Other adults in the home can be taught how to place the child properly in his parent's arms and lap.

3.21 Child: HOLDS HEAD STEADY IN SUPPORTED SITTING (3-5 mo.)
Parent: Provides necessary support and opportunities for child to develop head control in upright positions

GENERAL GUIDELINES

The child should be able to hold his head steady for a minute or two when he is placed in a sitting position with support provided at his hips and trunk. Parents can present and point out attractive toys, mirrors, and interesting spectacles in the room to encourage their child's head orientation while in supported sitting. They can also carry their child at their shoulder or in a backpack to provide opportunities for their child to develop steady head control in upright positions.

If the child's head is flopped forward or to the side when held in upright supported sitting positions, he should be seated in a supported semi-reclined position. Special adaptive seating may also be prescribed by a therapist.

Refer to 3.03 (Lifts head in prone) and 3.20 (Holds head in line with body when pulled to sitting) for additional activities to promote the child's head control. The following activities supplement those prerequisite adaptations.

MENTALLY RETARDED PARENT

May not accommodate the support she provides her child in sitting to his head control abilities.

1. If the child has *not* evidenced prior head control problems, advise the parent when she can begin providing less support to her child's head when carrying and putting him on her lap:
   a. Explain that since her child is getting older, his neck muscles are getting stronger.
   b. Demonstrate, and let the parent practice, carrying her child at her shoulder and holding him on her lap. Point out providing support initially only at his hips.
   c. Explain that her child can only hold his head up in these positions for a minute or two; she should provide more support when she sees his head flopping (demonstrate), because his neck gets tired.
2. If the child has poor head control and adaptive seating has been prescribed:
   a. Make inserts permanent with *tri-wall*,* foam pieces, or taped towel-rolls. Attach them with velcro to the child's seat or carrier.
   b. Affix color-coded stickers on seat inserts to match colored stickers on the infant seat if they are not permanent.
   c. Take a Polaroid picture of the child positioned in his seat. Cover it with clear contact paper and affix it to the back of his seat.

BLIND PARENT

May not be able to visually monitor her child's head position when supported upright.

1. Let the parent feel her child's entire body position while you support his hips in sitting. Explain that he cannot maintain a steady head position for more than a minute or two.
2. The parent can feel her child's body responses and head control while she carries him around the house, providing less support to his head and trunk.
3. Explain to the parent that when her child is interested in looking at an object held at his eye level, it helps encourage him to hold his head steady. To help insure toys are presented at a proper height and distance:
   a. The parent can place her child in sitting on the floor between her legs facing out, while supporting her child's hips with her inner thighs. She can use one hand to monitor her child's head movements, and the other hand to reach around and present toys in relation to his head position.
   b. The parent's outstretched, semi-flexed arm will probably be a suitable distance to present toys to her child when she is sitting behind him; if not, physically assist the parent to the proper distance.
   c. Point out visual stimuli in the environment that is at her child's eye level when he is carried upright at her chest facing out or at her shoulder.

PHYSICALLY DISABLED PARENT

Who uses a wheelchair; may have difficulty supporting her child in sitting when she is moving her wheelchair.

1. The child can sit in a reclining position facing out, against the parent's chest. When she uses her footrests, her thighs become somewhat inclined, providing suitable support.
2. If the child has significant tone abnormalities, she could carry him in a *snuggly vest** when moving in her wheelchair.

---

*See Glossary.

3.22 Child: SITS WITH SLIGHT SUPPORT (3-5 mo.)
Parent: Places child in sitting, providing slight support at hips

GENERAL GUIDELINES

The child is learning to sit briefly on firm surfaces if support is provided at his lower back. Brief periods in this position help the child develop trunk and head control. He is able to begin sitting for longer periods in a highchair and infant seats adjusted to an upright position.

A child with abnormal tone and subsequent poor head and trunk control will require adaptive seating under the supervision of a therapist. Refer to 3.21 (Holds head steady in supported sitting).

The following activities are for children who *do not* have tone abnormalities and are ready for sitting with support.

MENTALLY RETARDED PARENT

May provide too much support or not enough support for her child in relation to his emerging head and trunk control abilities.

1. Demonstrate, and let the parent practice, placing her child in sitting with support in various places, such as his highchair, infant seat, and on the parent's lap:
   a. Adjust the child's infant seat to a more upright position.
   b. Show the parent how to position her child in his highchair using towels as "stuffing" on the sides of his seat for support, if needed.
   c. Show the parent how she can hold her child on her lap facing out, without leaning against her chest if she holds him at his hips.
2. Emphasize to the parent that her child should not spend long periods of time in sitting positions:
   a. Explain that her child's back, chest, and neck muscles are not strong enough to keep his back and head straight.
   b. Relate that when her child is on his tummy it helps make his neck, chest, and back muscles stronger.
   c. Relate that her child should not sit in his highchair for longer than a meal, nor in his infant seat for longer than a half an hour or the length of a television show.
   d. Point out the child's physical signs as they occur which tell us he has been sitting too long, e.g., his body tilting to the sides or forward, head flopping forward, heavy breathing, or fussing.
   e. Ask the parent where she can put her child to change his position when he begins to tilt to the side or hang his head down.

3.23 Child: BEARS SOME WEIGHT ON LEGS (3-5 mo.)
Parent: Does not encourage child to stand

GENERAL GUIDELINES

This item is for evaluation purposes to help determine the child's level of maturation and motor reflexes. When the child is held upright on a firm surface, he should bear some weight on his legs.

This is not a skill to be taught nor is it an indicator that the child is ready to stand. Weight-bearing activities, such as standing the child, and using "walkers" or jolly jumpers, at this age, are discouraged. These activities can produce abnormal extensor patterns.

MENTALLY RETARDED PARENT

May interpret this reflex as meaning her child is ready to stand.

1. Do not test this reflex in front of the parent unless you are certain she understands the procedure is for evaluation purposes only.
2. If the parent is observed to "stand" her child up, or tells you he is standing:
   a. Explain that his leg and ankle muscles are not ready for standing yet because they are not strong enough to hold up his whole body.
   b. Caution the parent that if she keeps her child in standing before he is ready, this could cause his feet to turn in, demonstrating with your feet.
   c. Point out how her child slumps over when he is standing.
   d. Explain that he will not be ready for standing until he can crawl.
   e. Review the various appropriate positions and movements for her child at this age, e.g., rolling, on tummy, in infant seat, etc.

3.24 Child: MORO REFLEX INHIBITED (4-5 mo.)
Parent: Inhibits moro reflex with gentle handling and adequate head support

GENERAL GUIDELINES

The moro reflex may be tested as an evaluation of the child's neurological functioning by a physician or therapist. It is elicited by a sudden backward movement of the child's head, and is characterized by rapid extension and then return of the child's arms to flexion at his chest. The child may also suddenly cry in response to this movement. This reflex is normally present at birth, but should diminish by four or five months of age.

Special handling techniques emphasizing gentle movements and head support may be prescribed to help inhibit the child's moro reflex, if it has not diminished.

MENTALLY RETARDED PARENT

May assume that the procedure used by professionals to test a moro reflex is something she should do with her child at home.

1. Do not test this reflex in front of the parent unless you are certain she understands the procedure is for evaluation purposes only.
2. If the child's moro reflex is elicited by rough or abrupt handling, point out the child's sudden arm movements:
   a. Explain that these arm movements tell us that he needs to be handled more slowly with extra support to his head.
   b. Demonstrate, and let the parent practice, slow handling with extra head support. Compare how her child's arms do not jerk so much when she picks him up and moves him slowly.
   c. Provide periodic verbal reminders for the parent to "pick him up nice and easy" before she changes his position during your sessions.
3. Refer to 3.20 (Holds head in line with body when pulled to sitting), Activity No. 4, to help provide her child adequate head support when she picks him up and carries him.

BLIND PARENT

May not be able to see what is happening to her child if his moro reflex is tested.

1. Describe to the parent the procedure and reason for testing the moro reflex. Explain that although this will not hurt her child in any way, he may become momentarily frightened by this unfamiliar movement and cry. The parent can remain nearby to console her child, as needed.

3.25 **Child:** **PROTECTIVE EXTENSION OF ARMS AND LEGS DOWNWARD (4-6 mo.)**
Parent: Understands child's protective extension responses; facilitates child's prone propping positions if recommended

GENERAL GUIDELINES

This item is for evaluation purposes to test the child's maturing protective responses and neurological functioning. If the child is held in ventral suspension and then moved rapidly downward (head toward the floor), he should automatically quickly extend his arms and legs downward to protect himself.

Prone propping activities and lifting the child up in a prone position help him to develop protective extension. Refer to 3.03 (Lifts head in prone) and 3.08 (Holds head in same plane as body when held in ventral suspension) for activities relating to prone propping and lifting.

MENTALLY RETARDED PARENT

May misinterpret the testing procedure for protective extension.

1. Do not test the child's protective extension response in front of the parent unless you are certain she understands this procedure is for evaluation purposes only and should not be carried out at home.

3.26 **Child:** **BEARS WEIGHT ON HANDS IN PRONE (4-6 mo.)**
Parent: Provides ample opportunities for child to be on tummy; stimulates to lift head and chest in prone

GENERAL GUIDELINES

The child's head control is well-established. In prone, he should be able to lift his head and chest off a firm surface, pushing up with extended arms and supporting his weight on his hands.

If a child is delayed in motor skills or has tone abnormalities, a towel-roll may be recommended by a therapist to promote head control and weight-bearing on hands. Refer to 3.03 (Lifts head in prone) and 3.15 (Holds chest up in prone — weight on forearms).

3.27 **Child:** **EXTENDS HEAD, BACK, AND HIPS WHEN HELD IN VENTRAL SUSPENSION (4-6 mo.)**
Parent: Implements prescribed handling techniques if indicated to improve child's head and trunk control

GENERAL GUIDELINES

This item is for evaluation purposes only. It is tested by holding the child in mid-air supported under his trunk. In this position, he should lift his head above the level of his trunk and his back should remain straight. This reaction illustrates his maturing ability to overcome the influences of gravity. Special activities do not need to be implemented if the child demonstrates this reaction.

Absence of this reaction may indicate the need for special handling as prescribed by a physical or occupational therapist. Refer to activities outlined for 3.08 (Holds head in same plane as body when held in ventral suspension).

3.28 **Child:** **ROLLS SUPINE TO SIDE (4-5½ mo.)**
Parent: Encourages child to roll from supine to side

GENERAL GUIDELINES

The child usually learns to roll from his back to his side after he has learned to roll from his stomach to his back.

The child's body should move segmentally when he rolls. He may initiate this roll from his head or shoulders, or from his hip. Attractive toys and parent verbal encouragement help motivate the child to roll from his back to his side to reach the toy.

If the child consistently arches his back and "flips" to turn, this is an undesirable movement pattern and not considered a roll. Physical manipulation to help the child move segmentally may be prescribed for some children with tone abnormalities.

Parent training methods for 3.17 (Rolls prone to supine) can be implemented to facilitate the child's rolling from supine to side.

3.29 Child: SITS MOMENTARILY LEANING ON HANDS (4½-5½ mo.)
Parent: Positions child in a manner which facilitates his sitting momentarily while leaning on hands

GENERAL GUIDELINES

When placed in sitting on a firm surface, the child's trunk naturally leans forward. If his hands are placed on the floor or on his knees, he can maintain this sitting position without support for a few seconds. His legs should be slightly flexed.

Parents can encourage their child to practice this new or emerging skill by sitting on the floor with their child between their legs and gradually reducing their support at the child's hips and trunk. In this position, toys should be presented to the child on the floor. If the child looks at something that is placed too high, his neck could hyperextend.

MENTALLY RETARDED PARENT

May prop her child in unsuitable sitting positions.

1. Demonstrate to the parent sitting her child in an appropriate propped position on the floor. Point out providing the child initial support at his hip, as needed, and *gradually* releasing your hands:
   a. Tell the parent to check to make sure her child's legs are bent, not straight out (demonstrate), before she lets go of him.
   b. Show the parent how her child needs to put his hands on the floor or on his knees to hold himself up at this age.
   c. Relate that since her child needs his hands to hold himself up, he cannot play with a toy in this position.
   d. Emphasize that her child can only hold this position for a few seconds before we need to provide him support at his hips. Count aloud the number of seconds her child can maintain sitting without support.
   e. As the child loses control or becomes stressed, name his behaviors that tell us he needs to have more support or to have his position changed.
   f. Explain that her child should have something interesting to look at while he's sitting so he doesn't think sitting is boring. Demonstrate sitting the child in front of a floor length mirror, a picture placed at his propped sitting eye level, or with a favorite toy placed in front of him on the floor.

2. Let the parent practice the demonstrated sitting position with her child while you provide verbal and physical prompts, as needed, to remember the points stressed during your demonstration in Activity No. 1.
3. Take Polaroid pictures of the child in a proper and an improper sitting position. Post them above his play area with an X marked over the improper position. Let the parent tell you what is wrong with her child's position in the picture which has the X over it.
4. Caution the parent never to leave her child alone in a propped position because he can fall. Have the parent demonstrate what she would do if the phone rang or someone came to the door while her child was propped in sitting.

BLIND PARENT

Should become tactually familiar with her child's proper and improper propped sitting positions.

1. Describe the child's appropriate propped sitting position. Note the relationship of his hands relative to his legs. Describe his head position, his forward trunk position, and flexed knees. Explain he can only maintain this position a few seconds before he falls too far forward or off balance to the side.
2. The parent can become tactually familiar with the described propping position as her child sits between her legs on the floor.
3. Explain the importance of keeping visual stimuli at or below her child's propped eye level or on the floor. Refer to Activity No. 3, 3.21 (Holds head steady in supported sitting).

PHYSICALLY DISABLED PARENT

May be unable to place her child in a supported sitting position on the floor.

1. If the parent uses a wheelchair, alternatives to transferring herself to the floor include:
   a. Placing her child in a sitting position on a lap board while the parent provides him the needed support.
   b. Pushing her wheelchair up to a table and placing her child in sitting on the table.

3.30 Child: DEMONSTRATES BALANCE REACTIONS IN PRONE (5-6 mo.)
Parent: Provides opportunities for child to reach for toys in prone

GENERAL GUIDELINES

If the child is placed in prone on a surface which is slightly tilted, he responds by curving his body in the opposite direction of the tilt. This is a protective balance response which helps the child prevent a fall. This reaction may be tested by a therapist to evaluate the child's level of neuromotor functioning and readiness for additional weight-shifting skills.

Parents can encourage their child's balance responses by encouraging him to reach for objects with alternating hands

3.30

while he is in prone. Refer to the parent training activities for 3.43 (Holds weight on one hand in prone).

MENTALLY RETARDED PARENT

May assume she should tilt her child in prone at home if this skill is tested.

1. Do not test the child's balance reactions on a tilt board or therapy ball in front of the parent unless you are certain that she understands this procedure is for evaluation purposes only.

BLIND PARENT

May not be able to see her child's balance reactions in prone.

1. Clearly describe for the parent the evaluation procedure and her child's reactions if his balance reactions in prone are tested.
2. Let the parent feel her child's balance reactions in prone while she rocks him, or offers him a toy, while he is prone lying across her lap.

3.31 Child: **CIRCULAR PIVOTING IN PRONE (5-6 mo.)**
Parent: Provides ample opportunity for child to be in prone; encourages circular pivoting

GENERAL GUIDELINES

The child moves in a circular direction on his tummy by pushing his arms and legs in a haphazard manner. Although he does not actually move from one place to another, his circular pivoting prepares him for further crawling by giving him weight-shifting and movement experiences. The child should demonstrate balance reactions in prone (Refer to 3.30) before he can be expected to develop this skill.

Parents can encourage their child to pivot on his tummy by placing attractive toys just out of reach toward the side of his leg.

MENTALLY RETARDED PARENT

May expect her child to crawl when she sees him pivoting in prone.

1. As the child begins or is ready to learn to pivot, provide the parent anticipatory guidance regarding developmental prerequisites to crawling. Explain with meaningful statements, such as:
   a. "Before your child actually starts crawling, he may move around in a circle on his tummy without actually going anywhere. This is great because he's getting his muscles ready for crawling."
   b. "He can't learn to move around on his tummy unless he is put on his tummy lots of times during the day." (Explore how often the parent puts her child in prone, where she places him, and if toys are available.)

2. Demonstrate, and let the parent practice, putting a toy out of reach to the side of her child. Stress attracting her child's attention to the toy, providing him verbal prompting and praise, and giving him the toy if he tries to reach it but the placement was too difficult.

BLIND PARENT

May be unable to visually monitor her child's pivoting or pivoting attempts.

1. Describe to the parent her child's movements during pivoting. Explain that seeing a toy out of reach, a few inches away from his waist, encourages him to pivot.
2. Let the parent practice attracting her child's visual attention and toy placement to encourage his pivoting with your verbal prompting and descriptions.

3.32 Child: **MOVES HEAD ACTIVELY IN SUPPORTED SITTING (5-6 mo.)**
Parent: Assures adequate trunk support and environmental stimulation which encourages child to move his head actively in sitting

GENERAL GUIDELINES

The child, when sitting with appropriate trunk support, should be able to maintain good head control as he turns his head in all directions.

If adequate trunk support is not provided, the child may develop patterns of "fixing" to provide the stability he needs to look around. He should also not be encouraged to look up over his head, as this can facilitate hyperextension of his neck.

The child can be supported sitting in an infant seat, corner of a sofa, and the parent's lap. Interesting visual stimuli should be available at the child's eye level.

If the child is having difficulty actively moving his head in sitting, he may need extra support in his highchair. His feet should be supported and small pillows or towel-rolls should be placed at the sides of his trunk.

MENTALLY RETARDED PARENT

May not be aware of her child's trunk support needs in sitting.

1. Demonstrate various seating and positions which provide her child adequate trunk support to look around, e.g., highchair, car seat, infant seat, or corner of a couch. Point out the distinctive features of the seats, e.g., her child is not leaning to the sides or forward, he can rest his back on something, or he is able to move his head around.
2. Let the parent practice sitting her child in the various demonstrated places. Post Polaroid pictures of her child in sitting, as needed, which demonstrates adequate and inadequate support for his trunk. Mark an X over the picture with unsuitable positions.
3. If prolonged propping on a couch is observed, explain that her child is not learning to use his back and neck muscles

in that position. He still needs time on the floor to learn to roll and crawl.

4. Help the parent think of fun games to play while the child is sitting, e.g., blowing bubbles, "Peek-a-boo," and vocal play. Help select toys to let her child play with when he is sitting.
5. Ask the parent to show you good places for her child to sit supported so he can watch her when she's cooking, sweeping, visiting with friends, etc.

BLIND PARENT

May be unaware of her child's increasing visual field and stimuli which encourage him to move his head in supported sitting.

1. Describe the child's emerging sitting and head control skills. Explain the significance of this skill as it relates to his increased ability to look around the room in sitting.
2. Assist the parent in identifying good places for her child to sit which will allow him to watch her as she performs her daily activities.
3. Help adjust visual stimuli in his play areas which encourage him to look around while he is in his infant seat.

3.33 Child: HOLDS HEAD ERECT WHEN LEANING FORWARD (5-6 mo.)
Parent: Assures adequate trunk support for child to hold his head erect when sitting

GENERAL GUIDELINES

In addition to being able to move his head to look around, the child should be able to maintain his head in a fully erect position when placed in sitting if given adequate trunk support. Head bobbing will be decreased and head flopping should not be observed.

The general guidelines and activities for 3.32 (Moves head actively in supported sitting) apply to this skill.

3.34 Child: SITS INDEPENDENTLY INDEFINITELY BUT MAY USE HANDS (5-8 mo.)
Parent: Carries out activities which facilitate child's sitting independently in a variety of appropriate positions

GENERAL GUIDELINES

When placed in a sitting position, the child should be able to sit without support for at least five minutes. He may place his hands forward on the surface to help balance. The child's sitting positions can be varied: legs extended, crossed, or flexed to one side.

The child who demonstrates the following preferred or obligatory sitting positions should be evaluated by a physical or occupational therapist to determine special positioning and handling needs:

1. Reverse tailor ("W" sit)
2. Wide based (ring) sitting.
3. Asymmetries (more weight on one hip with trunk appearing shorter on one side and head tilted).
4. Head dropped back.
5. Knees locked with legs extended.
6. Inability to free hands.

If the child has difficulty keeping his back straight, gentle bouncing, tapping at the shoulders and/or rubbing and tapping at the base of the child's spine may be recommended under the supervision of a therapist.

MENTALLY RETARDED PARENT

May conclude that since the child can sit alone, his motor abilities are higher than his developmental level.

1. Explain to the parent that although her child can sit by himself, he is not old enough to catch himself if he falls off balance, thus, she must be very careful where she sits her child:
    a. Help the parent choose two safe places in the home for her child to practice sitting.
    b. Remind the parent never to leave her child alone in a room while seated until he is able to catch himself by putting his hands out.
2. Explain that even though her child is able to sit well, he is not able to get into this position all by himself; the parent needs to help. Have the parent name several times during the day that would be good times to place her child in sitting.
3. Point out how, at this age, since her child may need his hands to hold himself to sit, she will need to help him sit if he wants to play with a toy.
4. Tell the parent that her child should not sit in one position all of the time. It is important for him to be on his tummy, side, and back. Relate that since he cannot move out of sitting by himself, she needs to help him.
5. If the child needs special positioning as recommended by an occupational or physical therapist:
    a. Leave Polaroid pictures of her child's proper positioning for the parent.
    b. Demonstrate, and let the parent practice, with a large rag doll.
    c. Model and let the parent practice many times in your presence to prompt and reinforce until the parent is proficient.
6. If tapping or rubbing the child's back has been recommended, be sure the parent taps or rubs gently to the appropriate places on her child's back before recommending this activity independently at home.
7. After the child has been sitting for five minutes and is ready to change positions, ask the parent what her child is doing to tell us he wants to stop sitting, e.g., fussing, grunting, or certain worried facial expressions.

3.34

BLIND PARENT

Can become tactually familiar with her child's proper sitting positions and any recommended positioning or handling techniques.

1. If the child prefers undesirable sitting positions, such as "W-sitting," orient the parent tactually to the position, noting why it is undesirable:
   a. Reposition the child in a more desirable position, allowing the parent to tactually monitor the child's transitional movements.
   b. Assist the parent with repositioning her child to proper sitting positions with your hand over hers and "moving her through" the transitional movements with her child. Fade physical assistance and use verbal prompting until the parent is comfortable positioning her child in sitting independently.
2. If rubbing or tapping has been prescribed:
   a. Orient the parent to specific locations on her child's back, using specific bones on the child as reference points.
   b. Demonstrate the techniques on her so she feels the amount of pressure to apply.
   c. Demonstrate with the child as you place your hands over the parent's to tap or rub the child.
3. The parent can listen for her child's changes in vocalizations which indicate he is ready to change positions.

PHYSICALLY DISABLED PARENT

Who uses a wheelchair; may have difficulty placing her child in sitting on the floor.

1. The parent can place her child in sitting on a wheelchair lap tray, table, or bed mattress with tri-wall. The child must have constant supervision on these raised surfaces.
2. If the parent has fairly good trunk control, she will be able to help lower her child to sitting on the floor from her wheelchair:
   a. The child's increasing motor abilities allow him to "help" when his parent is lowering him to the floor.
   b. The parent can move her wheelchair next to a couch to use as a wedge when she lowers her child to the floor.

3.35 **Child: RAISES HIPS PUSHING WITH FEET IN SUPINE (5-6½ mo.)**
Parent: Helps discourage child's supine "bridging" if it is prolonged, used as a form of locomotion, or if the child has muscle tone abnormalities

GENERAL GUIDELINES

As the child explores the various ways he can move his body, he may raise his hips off a firm surface while lying supine. He does this by pushing up with his feet flat on the surface. This is not a skill which should be specifically taught or encouraged.

If the child arches his back or hyperextends his head, he is displaying undesirable motor patterns which should be discouraged. Children who have muscle tone abnormalities, or use this type of "bridging" for locomotion, should also be discouraged from this behavior by encouraging his rolling as a form of locomotion.

3.36 **Child: BEARS ALMOST ALL WEIGHT ON LEGS (5-6 mo.)**
Parent: Does not encourage child to stand prematurely

GENERAL GUIDELINES

When a child is placed in standing, he can hold most of his weight when lightly supported at his trunk.

This reaction is for evaluation purposes only to help determine the child's level and quality of motor development. It is not a skill to be taught or an indication that the child is ready for standing activities. Parents should be advised that standing, bouncing, or assisted walking activities do not aid in development of walking skills. A child with muscle tone abnormalities will be at risk of developing abnormal patterns of "fixing" or increased tone if encouraged to stand before he is motorically prepared. "Walkers" and Jolly Jumpers are discouraged.

Refer to 3.23 (Bears some weight on legs).

3.37 **Child: LIFTS HEAD AND ASSISTS WHEN PULLED TO SIT (5½-7½ mo.)**
Parent: Does not pull child up by his hands to sit

GENERAL GUIDELINES

This child skill is used for evaluation purposes only to assess the child's head and trunk control. When tested, the child's hands are held while he is in supine, and gently pulled into a sitting position. He should assist by lifting his head and actively pulling against the evaluator's grip. If the child's head lags, it is indicative of poor head control. A child does not learn better head control from this procedure.

Refer to 3.20 (Holds head in line with body when pulled to sitting).

3.38 **Child: ROLLS SUPINE TO PRONE (5½-7½ mo.)**
Parent: Encourages child to roll from supine to prone; facilitates segmental rolling when prescribed

GENERAL GUIDELINES

When a child rolls from his back to his stomach, his body should move segmentally.

Attractive toys and the parent's verbal encouragement help motivate the child to roll to reach the toy. If his arms get "stuck" under his chest, the parent can gently lift his corresponding shoulder to help him bring it out.

If a child consistently arches his back and "flips" to roll over, this is an undesirable movement pattern and not considered a roll. Physical manipulation to help the child move segmentally may be prescribed for some children with tone abnormalities.

Refer to 3.17 (Rolls prone to supine) and adapt parent training for helping the child learn to roll from his back to stomach accordingly.

3.39 Child: BODY RIGHTING ON BODY REACTION (6-8 mo.)
Parent: When indicated, carries out appropriate relaxation activities which promote child's body righting on body action

GENERAL GUIDELINES

If an evaluator turns the child's head to one side while he is in supine, his body should roll over segmentally with his shoulders turning first and then his legs following. This is a test procedure used to evaluate the child's level of motor functioning. A child's head should not be manipulated in this way except for evaluation purposes.

If the child "flips" stiffly as one piece, it may indicate increased muscle tone. Relaxation exercises on a therapy ball may be a prescribed treatment technique for the child's hypertonicity. The following parent training methods assume relaxation activities have been recommended and are supervised by a therapist.

MENTALLY RETARDED PARENT

May implement relaxation activities with her child in an abrupt or rough manner.

1. Do not test the child's body righting reaction in front of the parent unless you are certain she understands this is an evaluation procedure and should not be carried out at home.
2. If relaxation activities have been prescribed for the child's hypertonicity, explain the reason to the parent in meaningful terms:
   a. "Your child's muscles are too stiff; see how he holds his legs out straight and has difficulty bending them; the exercises I am going to teach you can help you help him to relax his muscles."
   b. Let the parent feel the difference in her child's muscle tone before and after exercises.
3. Demonstrate "tight" or "stiff" muscles by letting the parent squeeze a small rubber ball as hard as she can and then ask her to bend her arm while she is still squeezing:
   a. Let the parent contrast this activity with bending her arm while she is *not* squeezing the ball or tightening her muscles.
   b. Relate how the parent made her muscles tight on purpose, but her child does not make his muscles tight on purpose.
4. Demonstrate, and let the parent practice, rocking her child in a cradled position rather than recommending relaxation activities on a therapy ball:
   a. Encourage the parent to sing a lullaby while rocking her child.
   b. Take a Polaroid picture to help the parent remember proper positioning.
   c. Emphasize watching to see that her child's arms are forward and his chin is touching his neck.

PHYSICALLY DISABLED PARENT

Who uses a wheelchair; may have difficulty implementing prescribed relaxation activities with her child on a therapy ball.

1. The parent could gently rock her child in a cradle or reclining rocking chair.
2. The parent may be able to rock her child cradled in her lap if she has adequate trunk control.

3.40 Child: DEMONSTRATES BALANCE REACTIONS IN SUPINE (6-7 mo.)
Parent: Implements activities which encourage child's balance response in supine, if prescribed

GENERAL GUIDELINES

This item is for evaluation purposes to assess the child's balance responses and trunk control. If the child is placed supine on a surface which can be tilted, such as a tilt board, he should respond by curving his body in the opposite direction of the tilt. This automatic response helps the child prevent a fall.

If the child does not demonstrate a mature balance response in supine, gentle side-to-side rocking in supine on a tilt board or therapy ball may be prescribed by a therapist. The child can also be encouraged to reach for a suspended toy which is moved slowly across his midline while he is lying supine, to help facilitate his balance responses and trunk control.

MENTALLY RETARDED PARENT

May be too rough or abrupt when implementing prescribed activities to encourage her child's balance reactions in supine.

1. Do not test or encourage the child's balance reactions on a tilt board or therapy ball in front of the parent unless you are certain she understands that these activities are not to be implemented at home.
2. Demonstrate, and let the parent practice, encouraging her child's balance reactions in supine through reaching for toys rather than on a therapy ball or tilt board:
   a. Stress moving the toy slowly across the child's chest in pace with his reach and trunk rotation.
   b. Emphasize the importance of letting her child have the toy after he's worked so hard to reach for it.
   c. Let the parent choose two toys she thinks her child would like to reach for when she holds them in front of him.
   d. Suggest carrying out this activity after she has changed his diaper and he is still lying on his back.

3.40

BLIND PARENT

May not be able to see her child's balance reactions in supine.

1. Describe the evaluation procedure and purpose to the parent if you are testing her child's balance reactions in supine. She can lightly place her hand on the side of her child's trunk to feel his reactions. Describe her child's accompanying arm, leg, and head movements. If the child's balance reactions are absent or immature, describe the desired response.
2. If special activities have been prescribed to encourage the child's balance reactions on tilt boards or therapy balls:
   a. Orient the parent to the slow speed and direction of the tilt with the therapy ball and/or tilt board before placing the child on this equipment.
   b. The parent can practice tilting the board or ball with a large rag doll until she is comfortable implementing activities with her child.
   c. The parent can position her hands directly next to her child's trunk to monitor his movements.
3. Orient the parent to the position of a dangled toy in relation to her child's chest. She can lightly place one hand next to her child's shoulder to monitor his reach and move the toy in place with his movements.

3.41 Child: PROTECTIVE EXTENSION OF ARMS TO SIDE AND FRONT (6-8 mo.)
Parent: Carries out activities which promote child's protective extension of arms to side and front if prescribed

GENERAL GUIDELINES

The child extends his arms forward or to the side to protect himself if he loses his balance in sitting. This response is an automatic reaction to protect the child from a fall. An evaluator may test this reaction by purposefully pushing the child off balance to the side and then forward. The child should extend both arms forward, quickly and symmetrically, if he is pushed forward; he extends one arm out quickly to the side, toward the direction of the tilt, if he is pushed sideways.

Activities in prone which encourage balance reactions and weight-bearing on hands help develop the child's protective extension responses; refer to 3.43 (Holds weight on one hand in prone).

If the child does not display this protective response or if his response is delayed, additional activities may also be prescribed. These may include:

1. Gently pushing the child off balance in sitting while supporting him at his hips, forward and to the side.
2. Encouraging him to touch the floor and bear weight on his hands, while gently rocking him from side to side in sitting.
3. Placing the child in prone on a bolster and moving him forward while encouraging him to "reach" the floor.

MENTALLY RETARDED PARENT

May handle her child too roughly during activities designed to promote protective extension.

1. Explain that even though her child is learning to catch himself if he starts to fall over when he is sitting, he still *cannot* catch himself if he falls backwards. Relate that the parent must, therefore, quickly catch her child if she sees him start to fall backward:
   a. Demonstrate what protective extension is and then, if appropriate, demonstrate with the parent.
   b. Review with the parent safety concerns for 3.34 (Sits independently indefinitely, but may use hands), and find safe places for the child to sit.
   c. Demonstrate letting her child sit in front of a cushion or couch. Explain that, if he starts to fall backwards, he won't get hurt if there is something soft behind him to help catch him.
   d. Ask the parent what could happen if her child was sitting on a hard floor and started to fall backwards.
2. If rocking activities have been prescribed to promote the child's protective extension, stress smooth and gentle handling to the parent:
   a. Demonstrate, and let the parent practice, tilting activities with her child while singing a simple rhythmic song.
   b. Provide initial physical assistance to assure the parent's hands are supporting her child at his waist and hips.

BLIND PARENT

May be unable to visually monitor her child's protective extension responses.

1. Describe the child's arm movements and positions when he uses his protective extension responses.
2. If activities have been prescribed to encourage the child's protective extension in sitting, the parent can carry out activities with the child on her extended legs while she sits on the floor and tactually monitors.

3.42 Child: LIFTS HEAD IN SUPINE (6-8 mo.)
Parent: Recognizes child's ability to lift head in supine as an indication of increasing head control

GENERAL GUIDELINES

The child lifts or flexes his head when lying on his back. This behavior is observed for evaluation purposes to assess the child's head control. If the child cannot lift his head in supine, previously addressed activities which encourage head control in prone and during rolling are often recommended rather than encouraging him to lift his head in supine.

3.43 Child: HOLDS WEIGHT ON ONE HAND IN PRONE (6-7½ mo.)
Parent: Encourages child to reach for toys in prone

GENERAL GUIDELINES

The child lifts and bears his weight in prone on an extended arm and reaches for an object with his opposite arm. Initially, he may flex his non-reaching arm, bearing weight on his forearm rather than his hand.

Parents can encourage their child's reaching in prone by offering him attracting objects to reach for on each side alternately. Mobiles, port-a-play gyms, and placing him prone in front of a mirror can also encourage him to reach.

MENTALLY RETARDED PARENT

May have difficulty judging an appropriate distance to present toys to encourage her child's reach.

1. Explain to the parent that her child learns to balance when he is on his stomach and has to reach for something. Relate that this will help him learn to crawl and to move into a sitting position independently:
   a. Demonstrate reaching for something while you are prone on the floor. Describe how you really have to "hold" or balance yourself on the other side. Let the parent try this.
   b. Demonstrate this reaction with her child as the parent presents a toy just out of reach.
2. Demonstrate, and let the parent practice, where to place toys to encourage her child's reach and balance:
   a. Use the child's fingertips as a concrete marker and position the toy one handspread away.
   b. Show the parent what would happen if the toy was too far away or right next to his hand. Demonstrate with the child.
   c. Demonstrate placing a busy box upright in front of her child's fingertips to encourage him to reach.
   d. Help secure other toys or texture pictures to the sides of the child's crib or playpen.

BLIND PARENT

May have difficulty assuring toys are presented at an appropriate distance and height in relation to her child.

1. Orient the parent tactually to her child's movement during reaching in prone. Specifically note the position of his hands, elbows, and shoulders in relation to one another, and his proper head alignment by feeling his skin wrinkles on the back of his neck.
2. Help the parent suspend toys from her child's *port-a-play gym** or ribbon strung across his crib at the correct height and distance to encourage his reaching. After determining suitable distances and placement, the parent can become tactually familiar with the proper toy placements.

---
*See Glossary.

3. Toys, which rattle or jingle when reached for, will help alert the parent when her child successfully reaches for them.
4. Help adjust other stimuli attached to the child's crib or playpen sides to heights which encourage his reach.

PHYSICALLY DISABLED PARENT

Who uses a wheelchair; may have difficulty placing toys at just the right spot to encourage her child to reach when he is playing on the floor.

1. The parent can dangle toys on strings to her child on the floor to encourage reaching in prone.

3.44 Child: GETS TO SITTING WITHOUT ASSISTANCE (6-10 mo.)
Parent: Helps child move into a sitting position if he is having difficulty

GENERAL GUIDELINES

The child moves from a prone, supine, or side-lying position into sitting independently. He may use his crib railings or other support to assist him.

If the child needs help to attain a sitting position, moving him into a transitional side-lying position is recommended rather than pulling him to sit from supine with his hands.

The parent can help her child move into sitting by moving him into side-lying, sliding her hand under his chest at his armpit, and then slowly pulling him up while her other hand supports the child's opposite hip (see illustration). The child should assist in this process by using his hand, trunk, and arm. If he is moved too quickly, he will not have the opportunity to assist. As the child begins to initiate movements into a sitting position, the parent's physical assistance can be reduced to providing assistance only at his hip.

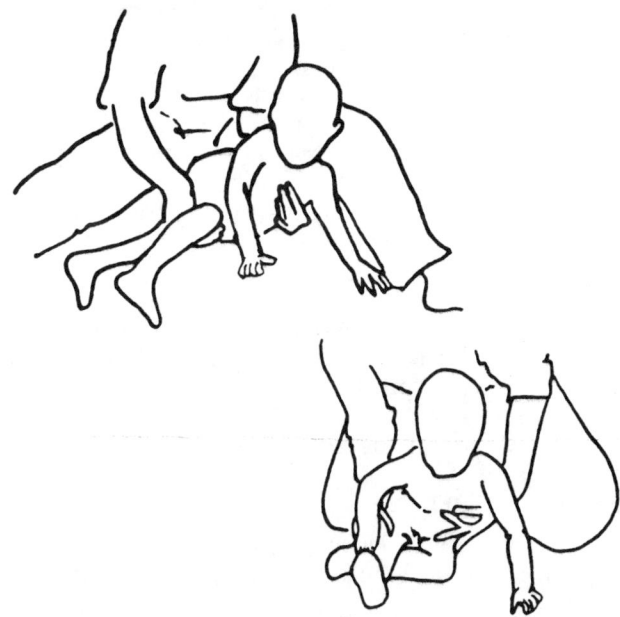

3.44

MENTALLY RETARDED PARENT

May abruptly pull her child to a sitting position.

1. If you observe the parent putting her child into a sitting position before he has had ample opportunity to try to sit independently, explain the importance of giving him time to try to sit up by himself.
2. If the parent pulls her child into sitting by pulling his arms abruptly, explain that this method does not let her child's head and back muscles work together in the right way. Relate that this can also hurt his shoulder joints.
3. Demonstrate, and then let the parent try, getting into a sitting position from supine in a straight sit-up fashion. Contrast this method with moving into sitting through a transitional side-lying position. Discuss how the second method is much easier.
4. Demonstrate bringing the child to a sitting position from side-lying from each side, emphasizing where your hands are in relation to the child's chest and hips, and moving him into sitting very slowly so he will have to use his head and trunk muscles to help.
5. Let the parent practice transitional side-lying to sitting movements with a rag doll:
   a. Provide physical prompting for the parent's hand placement and verbal prompting to reinforce slow movement.
   b. Practice bringing the doll to sitting from alternate sides.
6. Let the parent practice with her child while you provide physical and verbal assistance until she is proficient.
7. Leave sequenced diagrams or Polaroid pictures of the parent bringing her child to a sitting position from side-lying.

BLIND PARENT

May need to become tactually familiar with handling techniques to help her child move into a sitting position.

1. If the child needs facilitation to move into a sitting position, increase the parent's awareness of the transitional movements:
   a. Provide clear step by step descriptions as the parent moves her own body into sitting from lying on the floor.
   b. Demonstrate facilitation techniques with your hand over the parent's hand using a rag doll, and then with her child.
   c. The parent can note her proper hand placement in relation to her child's hip, chest, and armpit.

3.45 Child: BEARS LARGE FRACTION OF WEIGHT ON LEGS AND BOUNCES (6-7 mo.)
Parent: Does not over-use weight-bearing and bouncing activities with child

GENERAL GUIDELINES

When a child is placed in supported standing, he bounces slightly up and down, bending his knees and pushing up with his feet.

This reaction is tested to help determine the child's level and quality of motor development. Although limited bouncing activities are fun for the parent and child who does not have tone abnormalities, they should not be specifically encouraged. They are contraindicated for children with hypertonicity.

3.46 Child: STANDS, HOLDING ON (6-10½ mo.)
Parent: Helps child stand at appropriate furnishings for short periods

GENERAL GUIDELINES

The child can stand by holding onto a railing or low support when placed in that position. Children should, however, be able to pull themselves up to a standing position before it is appropriate for them to spend time standing.

The child continues to need ample opportunities for maturing balance and body righting reactions in creeping and sitting. Standing activities should, therefore, not take priority over other more important motor activities, such as creeping and sitting.

MENTALLY RETARDED PARENT

May leave her child standing at furniture, and may expect her child to walk now.

1. Tell the parent that although her child is learning to stand:
   a. He still needs to spend most of his time creeping and sitting to help develop his muscles.
   b. His muscles are not ready for walking.
   c. He cannot get down from standing by himself; she needs to help him.
   d. He should not be left alone when he's standing.
2. If lower extremity weight-bearing activities have been prescribed for the child:
   a. Help identify safe places for the child to stand; refer to 3.47 (Pulls to standing at furniture).
   b. Model and then demonstrate with your hands over the parent's hand appropriate hand placement on her child's hips and proper pacing for weight-shifting.
   c. Point out the distance between her child's feet and his slight knee flexion.
   d. The parent should demonstrate prescribed activities independently several times before recommending home carry-over.
   e. Name specific times of the day to implement the prescribed activities and suggest a concrete marker to help her judge the duration of the activity, e.g., a musical toy or egg timer.
   f. Ask the parent to think of a toy or picture book her child could look at while he is standing.
   g. Ask the parent to think of a song to sing or rhyme to tell her child during this activity.

3.47 Child: PULLS TO STANDING AT FURNITURE (6-10 mo.)
Parent: Encourages child to pull up to standing; helps when necessary

GENERAL GUIDELINES

The child pulls himself up to standing through a half-kneel position while holding onto furniture. His pull to stand movement may be so quick that his transitional half-kneel position goes unnoticed. At this stage, his arms do most of the work. The child should keep his feet flat on the floor most of the time when standing.

Parents can encourage their child to pull up to standing by placing attractive objects or toys on stable furnishings and providing physical assistance, as needed or prescribed.

This is a good time to address the issue of shoes with parents. Bare feet are recommended for children unless contraindicated by temperature or terrain. Bare feet allow more sensory feedback for motor development than feet restricted by shoes. Orthopedic or high-topped shoes are generally not indicated, unless prescribed for certain nonmuscle tone related orthopedic problems. In general, sneakers are a reasonable choice for footwear.

MENTALLY RETARDED PARENT

May "stand" her child up at furniture without allowing him opportunities to practice pulling up, and may not anticipate safety precautions.

1. Show the parent a concrete example of furniture which is sturdy and which is a suitable height for her child to pull up to at home. Ask the parent to identify other furnishing in the home which are:
   a. Okay for the child to pull up to because they are at the right height and are sturdy.
   b. Not okay because they are too high, have wheels, or could fall over on the child.
2. Help move throw rugs away from low tables at the parent's home. Demonstrate how her child could slip on the rug if he was pulling to stand.
3. Check low furnishings for sharp corners. Ask the parent what could happen if her child pulled himself up to stand at sharp corners. Show her how to pad the corners with foam rubber and masking tape.
4. Help the parent child-proof low tables at home to which the child may be learning to pull up.
5. Emphasize that, although it may be easier for us to stand the child directly at furniture, it is important for him to practice pulling up by himself.
6. Model encouraging the child to pull to standing with a toy placed on the furniture. Stress the importance of sitting behind him in case he falls, especially while he is learning.
7. Remind the parent that her child cannot get down from standing by himself; she has to help him. Name his physical cues that tell her to help him down, e.g., worried look on his face, red face, slumped over, and fussing.
8. Explain and demonstrate the child's footwear needs:
   a. Encourage the parent to let her child go barefoot when it is warm because he learns from feeling things with his feet.
   b. Show the parent various shoes available for children. Demonstrate how hard leather shoes and high-topped shoes do not bend very well and, therefore, do not let her child move his feet or ankles enough. Demonstrate the flexibility of "sneaker" type shoes and encourage her to buy that type for cold weather and outdoors.
   c. Demonstrate proper and improper shoe size, letting the parent feel her child's toe and foot width room.
   d. Ask the parent what she can do to know when to buy her child new shoes since he cannot tell her when his shoes are too tight.

BLIND PARENT

May not be able to visually monitor when or how her child pulls up to standing.

1. Describe to the parent her child's transitional movements as he pulls to stand at furniture. Describe his facial signs of accomplishment:
   a. Comment how her child is especially attracted to pulling up to furniture which provides him a better view of a toy, a window, and other various objects.
   b. Explain that he cannot get down from standing yet. If he does not vocalize when he is ready to get down from standing, she can check his positioning after a few minutes.
2. Tables, bookcases, or other unstable furnishings could be moved to unaccessible places.
3. Help child-proof, as needed, to insure unsafe and tiny objects are not accessible to the child's new heights.

PHYSICALLY DISABLED PARENT

Who uses a wheelchair; may be unable to help her child down from standing.

1. End tables, chairs, and bookcases should be moved to facilitate accessibility to the parent. For example, an end table next to a couch may have only one foot of space between the side of the table and the wall. The couch and table could be moved flush against the back and side wall so the child cannot squirm through.
2. The parent can move behind her child and either lean forward to help him down, or "break" his fall with her legs.
3. If the parent has sufficient trunk control, she can encourage her child to pull to standing at her wheelchair. To insure safety, the wheelchair footrests should be padded and the wheelchair locked. The child can also be encouraged to pull to standing at the side of her chair.
4. If the child's crib mattress has been raised to help the parent pick her child up when he was younger, it should be lowered to an appropriate position. When the child pulls to stand at the crib rail, he will be at a suitable wheelchair height for lifting.

3.48 Child: BRINGS ONE KNEE FORWARD BESIDE TRUNK IN PRONE (6-8 mo.)
Parent: Implements prescribed handling techniques to help discourage child's trunk asymmetry if indicated

GENERAL GUIDELINES

This item is for evaluation purposes. The child flexes his hip and knee in prone and brings his knee forward while his belly remains on the floor. This movement may occur spontaneously during play or elicited when an evaluator lifts the child's hip slightly on the side in which he brings his knee forward. This skill displays the ability to weight-shift and helps prepare him for crawling. Some children, however, do not display this skill and move directly into creeping on hands and knees.

If the child displays asymmetries of his trunk and extremities in this position, weight-shifting activities, such as reaching in prone, may be prescribed by a therapist. The child should be encouraged to reach for toys with the arm which is on the same side of his trunk shortening or flexed side. Positioning the child in side-lying on his flexed side during play may also be recommended.

The following parent training activities assume side-lying and reaching in prone have been prescribed to discourage the child's trunk asymmetries.

MENTALLY RETARDED PARENT

May have difficulty remembering prescribed handling and positioning techniques for her child.

1. Explain to the parent in meaningful terminology why special activities are recommended to help discourage her child's trunk asymmetry:
   a. Show the parent a picture or diagram of a young child who is symmetrical when lying in prone.
   b. Place the child in prone with his shirt off. Ask the parent if she can see which side of his back is shorter. Explain that his muscles on that side are not being used in the same way as his longer side.
   c. Explain that the prescribed activities will help him use the muscles on his shorter side better which will help him learn to crawl.
2. Demonstrate, and let the parent practice, encouraging her child to reach for a toy in prone using his arm on the side of his trunk shortening:
   a. Stress presenting the toy toward her child's arm which is on his shortened trunk side. If possible, use a physical marking on the child to help her remember (e.g., freckle, birth mark) toward which arm to present toys.
   b. Point out how the shortened side of her child's back gets longer, like his other side when he reaches for toys.
   c. Help the parent present toys at the proper height and distance from her child. Explain the toy should never be lower than her child's head and one of her hand-spreads away from the child's hand.
   d. Remind the parent how important it is to let her child play with the toy after reaching for it.
   e. Leave a Polaroid picture of presenting toys to the child toward his arm on his shortened trunk side in prone. Post it over the child's play area.
3. Demonstrate, and let the parent practice, placing her child in side-lying for play:
   a. Stress lying him on the side which is his shortest.
   b. Identify a physical marker, such as freckle on the child, if possible, to help the parent remember on which side to position her child.
   c. Help set up a busy box on the child's crib, playpen, or other play area for the child to play with in side-lying.

BLIND PARENT

May not be able to visually monitor her child's trunk asymmetry.

1. Describe the child's trunk asymmetries. The parent can feel the difference while her child is lying in prone if she slides both of her hands down the sides of her child's back. Note how the child's shortened side pulls his shoulder and arm down.
2. Let the parent feel the difference in her child's trunk when he reaches for a toy:
   a. Orient the parent to proper toy placement in relation to the child's hand on his shortened side to encourage reaching.
   b. The parent can keep one hand lightly positioned on her child's back as he reaches for toys to monitor his movements.
   c. Help adjust busy boxes and other toys attached to the child's crib and playpen to encourage his reaching in prone.
3. Let the parent become tactually familiar with her child's position in side-lying. Note proper toy placement to encourage his play in relation to the child's arm, hand, and head.

3.49 Child: CRAWLS BACKWARD (7-8 mo.)
Parent: Understands child may crawl backward as he experiments with moving

GENERAL GUIDELINES

Some children crawl backward before they crawl forward. Crawling backward should not be discouraged nor encouraged; it is simply the result of the child's experimentation with movement. Assure parents that this is a normal developmental milestone if indicated.

3.50 Child: DEMONSTRATES BALANCE REACTIONS ON HANDS AND KNEES (8-9 mo.)
Parent: Carries out activities which promote child's balance reactions on hands and knees if recommended

GENERAL GUIDELINES

After a child is able to assume a hand and knee position independently, he begins to develop balance reactions which help him maintain that position. If these reactions are tested, the child, when tilted on a board, should move his head, trunk, and extremities in the opposite direction of the tilt. The child spontaneously demonstrates his balance abilities when he is on his hands and knees and reaches for an object without collapsing. He develops this balance by rocking forward, backward, and to either side when he is on his hands and knees.

If the child's balance reactions on hands and knees are delayed, activities to improve balance may be prescribed. These may include encouraging the child to balance on hands and knees while he is tilted on a tilt board or therapy roll, and rocking him while in a hand-knee position on the floor. The following adapted parent training guidelines assume balance activities have been prescribed.

MENTALLY RETARDED PARENT

May carry out rocking activities with her child too roughly or abruptly.

1. If the parent has displayed rough or abrupt handling with her child, avoid hand-knee balance activities which involve tilt boards and therapy balls.
2. Teach the parent balancing activities for her child on the floor in safely supported positions:
   a. Demonstrate rocking the child from side-to-side while he is on his hands and knees on the floor.
   b. Demonstrate this position in front of a mirror, while you are sitting with your legs apart and the child between your legs facing the mirror.
   c. Stress how you are supporting the child with both of your hands around his waist while you gently move him from side-to-side.
   d. Sing a song or play a musical toy while talking to the child in the mirror.
   e. Let the parent practice with her child after your demonstration. Provide verbal and physical prompts, as needed, stressing appropriate pacing.
   f. Advise the parent to stop the activity when the musical toy stops or when she feels her child wanting to lie down. (To insure appropriate duration, tell the parent how many turns on the musical toy knob to make.)
   g. Repeat steps a-f to demonstrate, and let the parent practice rocking her child forward and backward on his hands and knees only when the parent has demonstrated proficiency with rocking her child from side-to-side.
   h. Name specific times for the parent to carry out this activity in association with particular daily activities.

BLIND PARENT

May not be able to visually monitor her child's balance reactions on hands and knees.

1. Describe to the parent her child's balance responses as they are observed or tested. The parent can assume a hand-knee position and experience the movements associated with the balance responses as you tilt her off balance.
2. If hand-knee balance activities have been recommended for the child:
   a. Describe adult hand placement in relation to the child's trunk and waist.
   b. Provide initial hand over the parent hand assistance while the parent is learning the appropriate pacing of rocking movements with her child.
3. Discuss carrying out prescribed balancing activities in front of a mirror or *port-a-play gym** to provide interesting visual stimuli for her child to look at during the activity. Orient the parent to appropriate distances and heights for toy placement, as needed.

PHYSICALLY DISABLED PARENT

May have difficulty carrying out balancing activities with her child on the floor or on equipment.

1. The parent may have a waterbed on which to tilt and rock her child.
2. The parent may be able to rock her child on his hands and knees on her bed, or while the child is in his crib.
3. If the parent is sitting in a chair or wheelchair, she can dangle toys on a string to her child while he is in hands and knees on the floor to encourage reaching.

3.51 Child: SITS WITHOUT HAND SUPPORT FOR TEN MINUTES (8-9 mo.)
Parent: Engages child in activities which encourage him to sit without hand support

GENERAL OUTLINES

After assuming a sitting position, the child should be able to sit independently without propping his hands on the floor for support. His back should be straight and head erect.

Parents can give their child activities to occupy his hands and encourage independent sitting balance. They can play "Pat-A-Cake," play ball, position busy boxes at an appropriate height in the child's play areas, and give him larger toys which require two hands to play, such as a doll or stuffed animal.

Refer to the general guidelines under 3.34 (Sits independently indefinitely, but may use hands) for undesirable sitting patterns and parent activities if the child needs extra help keeping his back straight.

---

*See Glossary.

3.51

MENTALLY RETARDED PARENT

May not provide activities to occupy child's hands as his sitting abilities increase.

1. Show the parent that we can tell her child is balancing himself better when he is sitting because he no longer needs to always put hands on the floor or on his knees:
   a. Relate that since her child does not need his hands to sit up, they are free to play with toys.
   b. Ask the parent to show you or think of some toys her child might like to play with in sitting now.
   c. Demonstrate games and gestures she can play with her child in sitting now that he can use his hands, e.g., "Pat-A-Cake," pushing a ball, the "up" gesture, and waving.
2. Stress to the parent that her child still cannot catch himself if he starts to fall backwards:
   a. Demonstrate how older children and adults catch themselves if they fall backwards. Explain that her child has not learned to put his hands behind himself yet.
   b. Ask the parent what could happen if her child was sitting in front of her low table and started to fall backwards.
   c. Let the parent show you two safe places for her child to sit.

3.52 Child: CRAWLS FORWARD (8-9½ mo.)
Parent: Provides ample opportunities for child in prone

GENERAL GUIDELINES

The child crawls forward bearing weight on his belly and extremities. His locomotion pattern to move forward may vary, but should include both arms and both legs. The child is not ready for crawling until he can bear weight on one hand in prone and demonstrate balance reactions on hands and knees.

Parents can encourage their child to crawl when developmentally ready by giving him ample opportunities in prone, providing motivating stimuli out of the child's reach, and gradually increasing the distance of the stimulus as he becomes more proficient.

The following parent training activities assume the child is developmentally ready for crawling.

MENTALLY RETARDED PARENT

May tease her child with a toy while encouraging him to crawl forward.

1. Explain to the parent the importance of placing toys or interesting objects near her child to help motivate him to crawl. Include and demonstrate the following concepts, as appropriate, to the situation and prompt the parent to complete the "therefores":
   a. Crawling is hard work at this age; if there isn't a toy or something fun to play with in front of him, he won't want to work hard to figure out how to get it; therefore, keep a toy nearby.
   b. If the toy is too far away, her child knows he can't get it, so he won't try; therefore, keep the toy near him.
   c. If the toy is taken away after her child has worked so hard to get it, he'll stop trying; therefore, never move a toy from him after he's gotten it.
   d. If her child tries hard and still can't get the toy, he may stop trying; therefore, give him the toy after he's tried.
2. Demonstrate, and let the parent practice, placing a toy in front of her child at a motivating distance:
   a. Let the parent select toys or other objects which she thinks would attract her child to move.
   b. If the child does not try to move forward, tell the parent to encourage him later and play a different game with him now.
3. If the parent confines her child to a playpen, an infant walker, or a highchair for long periods, stress how her child can't learn to crawl unless he has lots of time on his tummy on the floor.

BLIND PARENT

Can tactually and auditorily monitor her child's crawling progress to insure motivating toy placements.

PHYSICALLY DISABLED PARENT

Can use push and pull toys on sticks on strings if she has difficulty getting on the floor with her child.

3.53 Child: MAKES STEPPING MOVEMENTS (8-10 mo.)
Parent: Does not encourage child to walk prematurely

GENERAL GUIDELINES

The child makes stepping movements when he is supported in standing.

This reaction is tested to help determine the child's level and quality of motor development and weight-shifting abilities when held upright. This reaction is not taught and does not indicate that the child is ready to be "walked." Cruising around furniture is an effective activity for developing the child's weight-shifting skills.

Refer to 3.36 (Bears almost all weight on legs) and 3.61 (Walks holding onto furniture).

3.54 Child: ASSUMES HAND-KNEE POSITION (8-9 mo.)
Parent: Helps child assume a hand-knee position if prescribed

GENERAL GUIDELINES

The child practices lifting his belly off the floor in prone and maintaining a hand-knee position in preparation for creeping on his hands and knees. He may also rock himself to practice his balance in this new position which will also be important for creeping. He can usually only stay in a hand-knee position a few moments before he returns to belly-crawling.

If the child has gross motor delays, a therapist may prescribe helping the child assume a hand-knee position by placing him prone over a large roll until his balance returns. The roll should be thick enough to allow the child's arms to fully extend. Attractive toys and books should be available for the child to play with while he is in this position.

The following activities assume special positioning has been prescribed.

MENTALLY RETARDED PARENT

May have difficulty remembering prescribed positioning to help her child assume a hand-knee position.

1. Clarify for the parent the purpose of positioning her child over a roll in meaningful terms:
   a. Explain that this position helps her child use his arms, stomach, and leg muscles better so he can learn to crawl with his belly off the floor and later learn to walk.
   b. Demonstrate the difference between belly-crawling and creeping. Let the parent try each so she can feel the difference in how her muscles "work."
2. If towel, blanket, or pillow rolls are used, permanently secure them at the appropriate thickness for the parent's use at home.
3. Demonstrate, and let the parent practice with your assistance, placing her child over the roll:
   a. Point out the appropriate placement of the roll in relation to the child's chest and tummy.
   b. Give the parent a Polaroid picture of her child in this position to post on a wall next to the roll.
4. Use concrete markers to help the parent know when and how long to keep her child positioned over the roll:
   a. Specify how many times a day to place the child over the roll and associate them with mealtimes or television shows if the parent has difficulty telling time.
   b. Associate the duration to keep her child in this position with the length of a musical toy or parent activity (e.g., while you are eating dinner), depending upon the therapist's recommendations.
   c. Help the parent think of special toys or objects for her child to look at or play with in this position.
   d. Specifically tell the parent not to put her child to bed in this position.

BLIND PARENT

Will need to become tactually familiar with positioning her child over a roll to assure proper roll placement.

1. Orient the parent to her child's position in relation to the roll after you have positioned him properly over the roll. As the parent becomes tactually familiar with this position:
   a. Point out the position of her child's hands and extended elbows in relation to his shoulders, and the position of his knees in relation to his hips.
   b. Point out the position of the roll, noting its relationship to his chest and tummy.
   c. Explain that her child's head position is often dependent upon at what he is looking; the parent can feel the back of his neck to assure he is not hyperextending his head.
2. Help the parent select visually interesting toys and objects for her child to play with and look at when he is positioned over a roll. If he is positioned on the floor, describe her child's visual field at that level in terms of what is naturally visible to him. The parent may be interested in placing pictures, mirrors, or busy boxes at the child's eye level.

PHYSICALLY DISABLED PARENT

Who uses a wheelchair; may have difficulty positioning her child over a roll on the floor.

1. A table at suitable height for the parent in a wheelchair can be kept in the corner of a room on which the parent can position her child. Various toys on strings can be tied to the table legs to help the parent retrieve them if the child pushes them off the table during play.

3.55 **Child: DEMONSTRATES BALANCE REACTIONS IN SITTING (9-10 mo.)**
Parent: Implements balance activities with her child in sitting if prescribed

GENERAL GUIDELINES

If the child is tilted slightly off balance while he is sitting, his head, trunk, and extremities move in the opposite direction of the tilt. This balance reaction demonstrates the child's increasing trunk control which enables him to maintain an upright position and prevent falling.

If the child does not demonstrate balance reactions in sitting, special balance activities may be prescribed. These may include:

1. Swinging the child gently while he is sitting in a hammock.
2. Sitting the child on a large therapy ball, vestibular board, or bolster and gently moving it from side to side providing gradually reduced support at his hips.
3. Letting the child sit straddled on an adult's leg and encouraging him to pick up a toy from the floor on each side.
4. Bouncing the child on an adult's knees, face-to-face and providing gradually reduced support at his trunk or hips.

The following activities assume "balance in sitting" activities have been prescribed and are supervised by an occupational or physical therapist.

MENTALLY RETARDED PARENT

May be too rough or abrupt in balancing activities with her child in sitting.

1. Avoid hammocks, tilt boards, and therapy balls if the parent has demonstrated rough or abrupt handling with her child.

3.55

2. Explain why special balancing activities are being recommended in meaningful terms:
   a. Demonstrate balance reactions in sitting with yourself and the parent (i.e., let the parent push you off balance and then gently push the parent off balance). Stress how your trunk moved in the opposite direction to help keep you from falling, and this is called balancing.
   b. Relate that her child needs extra help with learning to balance so he will not fall when he is sitting.
   c. Emphasize *not* to purposely push her child off balance the way you demonstrated with each other because he could fall quickly and hurt himself.
3. Demonstrate sitting the child straddled across one of your legs while you are sitting on the floor with your back resting against a wall or couch. Show the parent how to encourage her child to pick up a toy from the floor on each side of your leg. During demonstration, stress gentle handling and support at the child's hip so he will not fall:
   a. Let the parent practice this activity several times with your verbal and physical prompting, as needed.
   b. Suggest times during the day to practice this activity, and specify how many times to encourage her child to pick up the toy.
   c. Ask the parent to think of additional toys or objects her child would enjoy picking up from the floor.
   d. Suggest short phrases to say to her child during this activity, e.g., "Great! You picked up the block."
4. Demonstrate, and let the parent practice, bouncing her child on her knees in a face-to-face position:
   a. Play a musical rhyme radio to help the parent know when to stop and to encourage gentle bouncing.
   b. Emphasize the parent's hand support at the child's trunk.
   c. Explain that her child should never have anything in his mouth when she is bouncing him on her knees because he could choke.
5. Help identify safe sitting places for her child at home. Stress that since her child cannot always keep himself balanced when he is sitting, he could fall over. Ask the parent what could happen if he was sitting on the floor next to a low table with a sharp corner and he fell off balance.

BLIND PARENT

May not be able to visually monitor her child's balance reactions in sitting.

1. Describe the bodily movements involved in balance reactions. Demonstrate with the parent by pushing her slightly off balance to let her experience this concept.
2. The parent can help facilitate and feel her child's balance reactions in sitting by rocking him gently back and forth while he is sitting on her lap as she supports him at his trunk. Encourage the parent to think of a favorite rhyme or song to sing during this activity to keep it fun.
3. The parent can implement other prescribed balancing activities with her child through verbal descriptions and initial hand-over-hand demonstrations.

3.56 Child: **PROTECTIVE EXTENSION OF ARMS TO BACK (9-11 mo.)**
Parent: Implements activities which help child develop backward protective extension if prescribed

GENERAL GUIDELINES

The child protects himself from falling backwards when he is sitting by automatically extending his arm out to the floor slightly behind him. This reaction may be tested by gently tipping the child backwards when he is sitting.

If the child does not display a backwards protective response in sitting, parents can encourage their child to pivot in sitting to help develop this response. Refer to 3.63 (Pivots in sitting — twists to pick up objects). In addition, activities which involve tilting the child off balance in sitting may be prescribed by a therapist.

MENTALLY RETARDED PARENT

May carry out prescribed tilting activities with her child in sitting too abruptly, and may not anticipate safety needs if her child does not have protective extension.

1. Do not test the child's protective reaction in sitting in front of the parent unless you are certain that she understands this is for evaluation purposes only.
2. If the child does not have backwards protective extension in sitting:
   a. Tell the parent her child cannot catch himself if he is sitting and starts to fall backwards.
   b. Ask the parent what could happen if her child was sitting in front of a low table with a sharp edge and he fell backwards, sitting on a hard floor and fell backwards, or sitting in front of a hard object and fell backwards.
   c. Help identify safe places in the home to let her child sit, e.g., carpeted areas, or next to a couch.
   d. Point out unsafe areas in the home where the parent should not let her child sit. Help the parent determine why these are unsuitable places.
3. If tilting activities in sitting have been prescribed, avoid using tilt boards or directly "pushing" the child off balance. Instead, demonstrate, and let the parent practice, rocking her child on her lap. The child can face out while the parent holds him by his hips and rocks him. Encourage her to rock him while she sings "Row Row Row Your Boat" or plays a musical toy.

BLIND PARENT

May be unable to visually monitor her child's backward protective responses in sitting.

1. Describe backward protective responses in sitting:
   a. If interested, let the parent experience this response as you describe it by gently pushing her off balance.
   b. Describe the child's reactions if tested. The parent can listen for his hand reaching backward if he is sitting on a plastic mat.

2. Let the parent sit behind her child during tilting activities if prescribed. She can provide slight support to her child's hips and tactually monitor his responses.

PHYSICALLY DISABLED PARENT

Who uses a wheelchair; may have difficulty implementing tilting activities with her child on the floor and with tilt boards.

1. The parent can rock her child on her lap or let him sit on a large mattress.

3.57 Child: GOES FROM SITTING TO PRONE (9-10 mo.)
Parent: Encourages child to go from sitting to prone; facilitates with positioning if prescribed

GENERAL GUIDELINES

The child moves independently from a sitting to a prone position by shifting his weight through a series of transitional movements. He shifts his weight first to one hip as he moves into side-sitting, and then to his forearm as he lowers himself and rotates his trunk to a prone position. The child should *not* move into prone from sitting by leaning forward between his legs.

Parents can encourage their child to move into prone from sitting by placing toys to the outside of his knees and encouraging him to reach with his opposite hand. Soft surfaces, such as carpeting or a bed are recommended to prevent injury if the child moves rapidly.

A series of hand placement techniques to help facilitate the child's weight-shifting and trunk rotation from sitting to prone may be prescribed if the child has tone abnormalities.

MENTALLY RETARDED PARENT

May have difficulty remembering prescribed positioning techniques.

1. Demonstrate encouraging the child to move from sitting to prone by placing an attractive object just out of reach:
   a. Demonstrate, and let the parent practice, lightly tapping the child's hand (opposite to the toy) with the toy to encourage him to reach with it.
   b. Show the parent where to place the toy after tapping his hand (approximately 12"-18" away from side of child's knee) using a concrete guide, e.g., placing the parent's elbow at the child's knee and placing the toy where her hand ends.
2. If specific handling techniques have been prescribed to help the child move from sitting to prone:
   a. Demonstrate the positioning techniques on the parent and then with the child while the parent is watching; have the parent practice on a rag doll, and then with her child, providing physical and verbal assistance until the parent can implement this independently.
   b. Emphasize proper hand placement on the child and gentle handling.
   c. Take a series of Polaroid pictures which illustrate the hand placement and child's positions during the transition from sitting to prone.
   d. Ask the parent to choose a good place to tape the pictures for her easy reference.
3. Help the parent identify safe, soft places in her home to practice these activities with her child. Ask her what could happen if she practiced these activities with her child on a hard floor.

BLIND PARENT

May not be able to visually monitor her child's movement from sitting to prone.

1. Describe to the parent the transitional movements her child uses to move from sitting to prone. The parent can move herself from sitting to prone to help her understand and experience the transitional series of weight-shifting movements.
2. Tactually orient the parent to her child's position in side sitting, noting the position of his legs in relation to each other, his hips, and the position of his trunk and head:
   a. Explain to measure approximately 12"-18" from her child's knee as a guide for placing toys to encourage him to move into prone.
   b. The parent can lightly support her child with her hand placed on his side opposite to the toy. She can then feel his rotational movement and encourage him, as needed, to reach for the toy.

PHYSICALLY DISABLED PARENT

Who uses a wheelchair; may have difficulty encouraging her child to move from sitting to prone when he is on the floor.

1. Parent can dangle a toy on a string to her child who is sitting on the floor. She can first tap his hand with the toy and then move it past his opposite knee to encourage him to retrieve it.
2. If the child needs special handling techniques, the parent can practice them on a bed or large table placed in the corner of a room.

3.58 Child: LOWERS TO SITTING FROM FURNITURE (9-10 mo.)
Parent: Encourages child to lower self safely to sitting from standing at furniture; assists as needed

GENERAL GUIDELINES

The child is able to lower himself to a sitting position on the floor from standing at a support. His transition from standing to sitting is smooth and controlled in contrast to his earlier falling or "plopping" down to sit.

Parents can help their child while he is learning to control his transition from standing to sitting by:
1. Using graduated pieces of furniture for support during his transition from standing to sitting (e.g., while the child is

3.58

standing at a low table, a toy could be placed on a lower stool next to him and then one on the floor).
2. Placing large pillows behind him until he can safely lower himself independently.

MENTALLY RETARDED PARENT

May have difficulty anticipating safety precautions when her child is learning to sit from standing at furniture.

1. Help the parent identify furnishings which are suitable and safe for her child to pull up to. Refer to 3.47 (Pulls to standing at furniture).
2. Remind the parent to always look behind her child when he is standing at furniture to see if there is anything he could fall back on:
   a. Ask the parent what could happen if her child was standing at her cocktail table and her ironing board (or an actual potentially dangerous object you see in the home) was behind him and he fell.
   b. Ask the parent what she should do when she sees something behind her child which he could fall on when he is standing at a piece of furniture.
   c. Assist the parent in identifying safe toys to put on the floor to encourage her child to go from standing to sitting.
3. Help the parent identify suitable cushions to place behind her child while he is learning to sit from a standing position:
   a. Demonstrate placement of the pillows in relation to the child.
   b. Demonstrate, and let the parent practice, providing support at her child's hips, if needed, while he is moving from standing to sitting.

BLIND PARENT

May not be able to visually monitor the method her child uses to sit from standing at furniture.

1. Describe to the parent her child's movements when he goes to sitting from standing at furniture.
2. Concretely identify with the parent where to place toys on the floor to encourage her child to sit from standing, e.g., one foot from the outside of the child's heel.
3. Refer to 3.47 (Pulls to standing at furniture).

PHYSICALLY DISABLED PARENT

Who uses a wheelchair; may have difficulty helping her child sit from a standing position.

1. The child could wear clothing with cross suspenders. This can help the parent guide his direction or "break" a fall as he is moving from standing to sitting.
2. The parent will need to check to insure her wheelchair is locked when her child starts to pull himself up and down at it.

3.59 Child: **CREEPS ON HANDS AND KNEES** (9-11 mo.)
Parent: Encourages child to creep on hands and knees; implements weight-shifting activities if prescribed

GENERAL GUIDELINES

The child moves forward on his hands and knees with his belly off the ground. His arms and legs should move in a reciprocal pattern. Initially, the child may rock or move backwards in this position in preparation for creeping forward.

Parents can encourage their child to move forward when he is on his hands and knees by placing favorite toys just out of reach, creeping next to him, or sitting on the floor facing him while providing enthusiastic verbal prompts.

If the child has motor delays, rocking the child at his hips while in a hand-knee position may be prescribed by a therapist to encourage his weight-shifting. The child should be encouraged to reach for a toy with his arm which is opposite to his shifted weight.

Refer to 3.52 (Crawls forward) for activities which help parents provide stimulus for their child to move forward. Refer to 3.54 (Assumes hand-knee position) if the child needs special positioning to assume a hand-knee position.

The following activities assume weight-shifting has been prescribed for the child in a hand-knee position.

MENTALLY RETARDED PARENT

May carry out prescribed weight-shifting activities with her child too roughly or abruptly.

1. Demonstrate prescribed rocking activities for the child while he is in a hand-knee position:
   a. Stress proper hand placement on the child's hips using his diaper or pants as a marker.
   b. Provide the parent physical assistance with your hand over hers; emphasize moving slowly and feeling her child's weight shift.
   c. Gradually fade physical assistance with the parent providing verbal cues, as needed.
   d. Review several times which hand to encourage her child to reach with, dependent upon his weight shift.
2. Sing "Row Row Row Your Boat" or play a rhythmic musical toy when the parent rocks her child on his hands and knees. A short song or tune can help the parent pace her movements smoothly and slowly. She will also know to stop the activity at the end of the song.
3. Suggest a specific time during the day to carry out this activity at home with her child when the parent demonstrates proficiency.

BLIND PARENT

May need tactual orientation to carry out weight-shifting activities with her child while he is in a hand-knee position.

1. Let the parent become tactually familiar with her child's hand-knee position, noting his tummy off the ground and extended arms.

2. Provide the parent hand-over-hand guidance as you demonstrate rocking her child from side to side. She can feel his weight-shifting and where to place her hands in relation to his trunk.
3. Provide initial guidance, as needed, to insure proper toy placement in front of her child during rocking activities and when she is encouraging him to creep forward.
4. A bell secured on the child's clothing can help the parent monitor his movements as he begins to creep quickly around the home. This may be especially helpful if the child does not vocalize a lot and if he likes to creep behind furnishings, doors, etc.
5. Suggest placing stickers or markings on sliding glass doors at the child's creeping and future walking heights.

PHYSICALLY DISABLED PARENT

Who uses a wheelchair; may be able to carry out weight-shifting activities with her child in a hand-knee position on raised surfaces.

1. If the child is not creeping yet, the parent can rock her child from side to side while in a hand-knee position on her bed. Use *tri-wall** to provide a firm surface.
2. If the child is beginning to creep around, but needs extra help with weight-shifting, the parent can transfer herself to the floor. She can sit in a corner of a room to provide trunk stability, if needed.

3.60 Child: STANDS MOMENTARILY (9½-11 mo.)
Parent: Provides opportunities for child to practice standing alone with an immediate support available

GENERAL GUIDELINES

The child stands alone for one or two seconds if he lets go of a support. Initially, he may stand alone by accident because he is distracted watching or manipulating a toy at a support.

Parents can provide their child opportunities to practice briefly standing alone by letting him stand at safe, sturdy furnishings. They can also periodically give him a toy to hold which requires two hands or play an adapted game of "Pat-A-Cake" by hitting the table together. The child should not be stood in the middle of the floor without a support immediately available. Refer to 3.47 (Pulls to standing at furniture) to help identify suitable furnishings at which the child can practice standing alone.

MENTALLY RETARDED PARENT

May interpret her child's momentary standing as meaning he can stand independently and that he is ready to walk

1. Provide anticipatory guidance that her child's momentary standing does not mean he is ready to stand alone nor ready to walk:

---
*See Glossary.

a. Explain that her child needs lots of practice standing and holding onto furniture or to her, before he is ready to stand or walk alone.
b. Discuss how frightened her child would feel if he was stood in the middle of the floor without anything to hold on to.
2. Help identify safe suitable furnishings to let her child pull up and stand at. Refer to 3.47 (Pulls to standing at furniture).

3.61 Child: WALKS HOLDING ON TO FURNITURE (9½-13 mo.)
Parent: Encourages child to cruise around furniture

GENERAL GUIDELINES

The child can take a few steps, or "cruise," sideways if he holds onto furniture for support. Furniture supports should be at the child's chest level to facilitate normal movement patterns.

Parents can encourage their child to cruise around low tables, chairs, or at his playpen railing by placing toys a few steps out of his reach on the support. They should encourage him to cruise to the left and to the right.

Refer to activities outlined for 3.47 (Pulls to standing at furniture) to help parents identify appropriate furnishings for their child to pull to and cruise around. Demonstrate motivating distances to place favorite toys, if needed.

3.62 Child: EXTENDS HEAD, BACK, HIPS AND LEGS IN VENTRAL SUSPENSION (10-11 mo.)
Parent: Implements prescribed handling techniques if prescribed to facilitate child's head and trunk control

GENERAL GUIDELINES

The child should automatically lift his head, hips, and legs in a controlled extensor pattern when held in mid-air in ventral suspension. This procedure is used for evaluation purposes to assess the child's level of neuromotor functioning and ability to overcome the influences of gravity.

Absence of this reaction may indicate the need for special handling prescribed by a therapist. Refer to 3.08 (Holds head in same plane as body when held in ventral suspension).

3.63 Child: PIVOTS IN SITTING (10-11 mo.)
Parent: Encourages child to pivot in sitting

GENERAL GUIDELINES

The child's maturing balance and protective responses in sitting enable him to twist his body and move in a circle while he is in a sitting position.

Parents can encourage their child to pivot by moving toys slowly out of reach so he must pivot to reach them. They can

3.63

also play "Peek-a-boo" behind the child with puppets or other toys to encourage him to pivot. Toys should be presented toward alternating sides.

If the child moves into prone from sitting rather than pivoting, the parent can provide "pelvic cueing," i.e., gently hold him at his hip to encourage him to maintain a sitting position as he pivots to obtain the toy.

MENTALLY RETARDED PARENT

May only sit her child in chairs or on couches which does not allow him to develop pivoting skills.

1. Demonstrate what pivoting in sitting is, explaining that her child needs to learn this to help his balance. Place an object out of reach and ask the parent to get it while she is sitting on the floor so she can experience this skill.
2. Help select safe areas with the parent at home for her child to practice sitting. Stress the importance of the area being free of obstacles. Tell the parent her child will not be able to twist his body and practice his balancing if he is on a couch or in a chair; ask her why.
3. Demonstrate, and let the parent practice, placing toys out of her child's reach to encourage him to pivot. Stress, and prompt the parent as needed, to:
   a. Choose a toy that is interesting to her child.
   b. Show it to him before moving it toward his back.
   c. Let her child play with the toy after he has obtained it, or tried to obtain it.
   d. Place the toy on alternate sides of her child.
   e. Hold her child gently at his hips if he moves into prone rather than pivots.

BLIND PARENT

May not be able to visually monitor her child's efforts or his movements involved in pivoting.

1. Describe the rotational movements and balancing skills involved for her child to pivot when he is sitting:
   a. Let the parent pivot while sitting on the floor so she can feel the balance reactions and rotational movement involved.
   b. Explain that just as she may pivot in sitting to reach something she knows or hears is behind her, her child is motivated to pivot when he sees a favorite toy moved behind him.
2. Demonstrate encouraging the child to pivot while the parent sits toward one side of her child with her hands lightly placed on his hips. Offer the child a toy on the opposite side:
   a. Stress the importance of showing her child the toy in front of him for a few seconds before moving it to his side toward his back.
   b. Describe the distance of the toy using a concrete reference point, e.g., "a forearm away from the side of his hip."
   c. The parent can feel her child's pivoting responses, providing stability at his hips, as needed.

PHYSICALLY DISABLED PARENT

Who uses a wheelchair; cannot provide her child stability at his hips, to discourage him from moving into prone to obtain a toy on the floor.

1. The parent can move her wheelchair toward the back of her child while he is sitting on the floor and hold toys out to him at a sitting height rather than placing them on the floor. Offering toys at this height may encourage the child to pivot rather than move into prone because he will not be able to obtain the toy in prone.

3.64 **Child:** CREEPS ON HANDS AND FEET (10-12 mo.)
     Parent: Understands that some children creep on their hands and feet before gaining balance in an upright position

GENERAL GUIDELINES

Some children who are learning to gain balance in an upright position begin to move forward by "walking" with both feet and hands flat on the floor; many children do not. It is not necessary for parents to encourage their child to creep on his hands and feet. Provide parents anticipatory guidance about this normal development progression, as needed.

3.65 **Child:** WALKS WITH BOTH HANDS HELD (10-12 mo.)
     Parent: Encourages child to walk three or four steps with adequate support

GENERAL GUIDELINES

This child is able to take three or four steps forward when an adult holds both of his hands or when he is holding onto and pushing a support, such as a small chair, weighted box, or "walker" without the seat.

The child's hands should be held by his sides, no higher than his shoulders, so his center of gravity is not altered. Taking three or four steps with support is plenty of practice at this stage in the child's development.

MENTALLY RETARDED PARENT

May try to make her child walk more than a few steps, and may "drag" him while walking by holding his hands above his head and walking him too quickly.

1. Clearly define developmental expectations for the child's walking at this age. Include:
   a. Her child's muscles are ready to walk three or four steps if he is holding onto something or his hands are held.
   b. Her child's muscles are *not* ready to walk more than three or four steps or they will become tired and not work as well, which will make her child move off balance.

c. "Walking" her child at this age is just for fun and practice; if she wants him to move across the room, or into another room, let him crawl.
d. If her child does not want to practice walking, we should not make him. He tells us he does not want to practice walking by bending his knees and trying to drop to the floor or (whatever individual behaviors you have observed, such as twisting or stiffening).
2. Demonstrate the proper height to hold the child's hands when helping him walk a few steps:
   a. Use a doll to illustrate how *not* to hold the child's hands. Tell the parent this hurts his arms and makes him fall off balance.
   b. Use a doll to illustrate holding its hands at shoulder height; let the parent practice.
   c. Demonstrate, and let the parent practice, helping the child walk holding his hands at a proper height by bending over or knee-walking at the child's height. Leave a Polaroid picture of this method.
3. Stress the importance of letting her child walk at his own pace:
   a. Demonstrate dragging a doll too quickly, pointing out how the doll's legs are not really stepping, just sliding.
   b. Demonstrate, and let the parent practice, "walking her child a few steps" watching his feet move so we walk *with* him.
   c. Suggest counting slowly to four to help insure proper pacing and duration.
4. Help the parent select suitable chairs, weight boxes, etc. at proper heights and weights for her child to push to practice walking a few steps.

PHYSICALLY DISABLED PARENT

Who uses a wheelchair; may have difficulty holding her child's hands to encourage him to walk.

1. If the parent has adequate trunk control, place the child in standing approximately two feet in front of the parent. She can lean forward, hold her child's hands, and encourage him to walk a few steps toward her while you sit behind the child (wheelchair footrests should be lifted and wheels locked).
2. The child can hold onto the seat of his parent's wheelchair while she slowly guides the chair backwards. The parent may need to move both legs to one footrest, and remove the other one.
3. The child can push weighted boxes, light chairs, or a block wagon.

3.66 Child: STOOPS AND RECOVERS
(10½-14 mo.)
Parent: Encourages child to stoop and pick up objects, insuring appropriate support as needed

GENERAL GUIDELINES

The child bends over and touches a large object on the floor without falling. Initially he may not be able to actually pick up the toy and will need to hold onto a stable support with one hand.

Parents can encourage their child to practice his "stooping" abilities during naturally occurring daily activities and play. For example, they can ask their child to pick up his toys from the floor, pick up the ball during ball play, or pick up trash and throw it away.

If the child is having difficulty balancing himself, parents can ask him to pick up items that are on the floor next to a couch, chair, or cocktail table to provide him support. The child can also be encouraged to bend forward and pick up a toy from the floor when he is sitting on a small stool.

MENTALLY RETARDED PARENT

May not encourage her child to stoop and recover objects from the floor.

1. Demonstrate stooping to pick up an object, while explaining to the parent that her child is learning to do this. Relate how this helps him learn to balance, which helps him with walking and his later running.
2. Help the parent identify safe furnishings for her child to use as a support, if needed, to pick up objects off the floor. Refer to 3.47 (Pulls to standing at furniture).
3. Name a few common daily occurrences in which the parent can ask her child to pick up things from the floor:
   a. Ask the parent to think of another situation where she can encourage her child to pick something up off the floor.
   b. Stress that her child will not always be able to actually pick the object up and that is okay; she should help him after she sees he is having a difficult time.
   c. Review the praise words to say which show him she is proud of him.
4. Demonstrate one or two activities which encourage the child to stoop and recover, such as ball play or picking up a favorite toy. Model encouraging phrases, praise, and physical assistance to her child, as needed. Let the parent practice with your prompting and encouragement.

BLIND PARENT

May not be able to visually monitor her child's stooping abilities.

1. Describe the child's movements when he attempts, or is able, to pick things up off the floor.
2. When the child is standing at a support, demonstrate the appropriate distance to place an object in relation to his foot to encourage him to retrieve it. The parent can lightly place a hand on his waist to feel his movements when stooping.

3.67 Child: STANDS BY LIFTING ONE FOOT
(11-12 mo.)
Parent: Provides safe opportunities for child to pull up to standing

GENERAL GUIDELINES

The child pulls himself up to stand at furniture through a half-kneel position. In contrast to his earlier pull to stand movements, the child uses less arm "work" to pull up and more weight-shifting with his legs. Refer to the parent training activities for 3.47 (Pulls to standing at furniture), which are applicable to this skill.

3.68 Child: STANDS A FEW SECONDS
(11-13 mo.)
Parent: Encourages child to stand alone 2-3 seconds after removing support

GENERAL GUIDELINES

The child is able to stand independently two or three seconds after a support (e.g., adult holding him at child's hips or the child letting go of a low table) has been removed.

Parents can initiate activities with their child when he is standing and gradually remove his support or distract him from his support for a few seconds. The child should always have a support immediately available. For example, the child can stand at a low table and play with a busy box, or stand in front of a floor length mirror or textured wall hanging, while the parent provides him support at his hips. The parent can slowly let go of the child's hips as she feels his stability and balance.

MENTALLY RETARDED PARENT

May expect her child to stand up without support nearby, or may hold her child in standing improperly.

1. Use a fairly sturdy cloth-type doll to demonstrate proper and improper adult support to promote the child's balance in standing:
   a. Hold the doll with its arms over the head and let the parent push the doll at its bottom to show how easily the doll can fall off balance.
   b. Let the parent hold the doll by its legs and point out how the doll flops forward because it cannot balance.
   c. Demonstrate holding the child at his hips to help him stand in front of a mirror or picture on the wall. Explain that holding him at his hips helps him keep his balance because he learns to balance right in the middle of his body.
2. Stress that her child's muscles and balance abilities at this age are only ready to let him stand up alone for three or four seconds:
   a. Let the parent count as she lets go of her child in standing.
   b. Ask her what would happen if she let go of him in standing and left him there alone.
3. Help identify toys for the child to play with at low tables or chairs.

BLIND PARENT

May be unaware of visual activities which encourage her child to stand alone for a few seconds.

1. Explain that children often learn to stand alone at first by accident because they are so busy looking at something, they don't even realize that they are not holding onto anything.
2. Help identify and describe interesting things around the home or at your center which are at the child's standing eye level (e.g., things on tables, low hanging mirrors, pictures, designs on wallpaper, and watching the fast and colorful movements on the "Sesame Street" television show). Demonstrate appropriate distances to position the child from each of these things.

PHYSICALLY DISABLED PARENT

Who uses a wheelchair; may have difficulty providing her child support when he is learning to balance in standing.

1. The parent can use her wheelchair or knees for the child's support (child facing parent):
   a. She can offer him a light toy, such as a small stuffed animal, while he is standing supported against the chair or parent's knees.
   b. A cushioned couch or another adult could be behind the child to help "break" his fall if he loses his balance and the parent cannot catch him.

3.69 Child: ASSUMES AND MAINTAINS KNEELING (11-13 mo.)
Parent: Helps child assume and maintain an appropriate kneeling position

GENERAL GUIDELINES

The child is able to move from a sitting position to kneeling and maintain his balance with his hips extended. He should not sit back on his feet.

Children with decreased muscle tone may be unable to maintain this kneeling position, and may fall back to a "W" sitting position, which should be discouraged.

Parents can facilitate their child's kneeling by letting him play at sturdy surfaces, such as a sofa, chair, or low table which are his chest height, and provide him support, as needed, at his hips.

MENTALLY RETARDED PARENT

May not recognize appropriate kneeling positions for her child.

1. If the child has low tone and been observed to sit on his heels or "W" sit during or after kneeling, demonstrate or point out these positions to the parent as they occur:
   a. Explain that these are *not* good positions because they make her child's muscles move in the wrong way.
   b. Post Polaroid pictures with a big "X" across them to help the parent remember to move her child out of these positions.

2. Demonstrate, and let the parent practice, letting her child knee-stand at a low table or couch:
   a. Point out how her child's bottom is not sitting on his feet; it is straight in line with his back, which helps his chest muscles develop.
   b. Provide gentle support at the child's hips, if needed.
   c. Ask the parent to select two toys for him to play with when he is kneeling at low tables.
   d. Explain that he may only want to stay kneeling in that position for a minute and that is okay.
3. Caution the parent that her child cannot catch himself if he starts to fall when he is kneeling; she needs to help him change positions.

BLIND PARENT

May be unaware of her child's kneeling patterns.

1. Describe and demonstrate, with a segmented doll, appropriate and inappropriate kneeling patterns.
2. Help identify furnishings in the home which are chest height to her child in kneeling.
3. The parent can tactually orient herself to her child's knee position and provide him physical assistance, as needed.

3.70 Child: WALKS WITH ONE HAND HELD (11-13 mo.)
Parent: Encourages child to walk a few steps while holding his hand

GENERAL GUIDELINES

The child is able to walk five or six steps while holding an adult's hand. His hand should be held by his side rather than overhead

MENTALLY RETARDED PARENT

May try to make her child walk more than a few steps, and may "drag" him by holding his hand overhead.

1. Refer to 3.65 (Walks with both hands held).

BLIND PARENT

May be unable to visually monitor her child's arm position when his hand is held or when he pushes a support during walking.

1. Tactually orient the parent to her child's proper arm height in relation to his chest and shoulder when he is holding her hand while learning to walk.
2. Help identify small chairs, stools, weighted boxes, doll carriages, etc. which enable her child to push with his arms at chest level.
3. Anticipatory Guidance: If the parent uses a cane while walking with her child in an unfamiliar place, the arc of the cane will be wide enough to accommodate the parent and child.
4. If the parent's present traveling techniques do not lend themselves well to traveling while holding her child's hand she may benefit from consultation with an orientation mobility specialist.

PHYSICALLY DISABLED PARENT

Who uses a wheelchair; may have difficulty holding her child's hand to encourage him to walk.

1. The arm of a wheelchair is usually at a suitable height for the child to hold on to. The parent can move her wheelchair slowly forward as her child holds on to its arm.

3.71 Child: STANDS ALONE WELL (11½-14 mo.)
Parent: Encourages child to stand alone; positions child in prone stander if prescribed

GENERAL GUIDELINES

The child stands independently for at least ten seconds when he is placed in a standing position. He may then become frightened, unsure of how to move from this position, as he loses his balance.

Parents should stay close at hand when their child is practicing his new standing skills. They can rescue him as he loses standing balance by helping him lower to the floor or initiate walking. Refer to 3.68 (Stands a few seconds) for parent training activities to help their child stand.

A *prone stander** may be prescribed by a physical therapist for some older children with gross motor impairments who cannot stand independently. The following activities assume a prone stander has been prescribed for the child.

MENTALLY RETARDED PARENT

May have difficulty remembering prescribed prone board activities for her child.

1. Explain to the parent that the prescribed prone board is to help her child's legs get stronger and to give him chances to see what it's like to stand up:
   a. Discuss how we might feel if we never got a chance to stand up.
   b. Interpret how proud her child must feel when he gets to stand up just like everyone else.
   c. Stress that her child is not ready to stand up without the board and is not ready to walk.
2. Demonstrate with concrete guides for the parent how the prone stander's strap should "fit" on her child. The strap should be positioned across her child's diaper and it should be tight enough that she cannot put her finger between the strap and her child's diaper.
3. Take a Polaroid picture of the child positioned properly in the prone board and affix it to the board to help the parent remember this position.
4. Make an outline of the child's body with tape on the board to provide the parent a visual image for positioning her child.
5. Give the parent a concrete timeframe to let her child stand in his standing board:

---

*See Glossary.

3.71

a. For example, tell the parent to let him stand at his board after each meal for the duration of a television program.
b. Tell her to take her child out of the board if his head slumps forward because this means his muscles are too tired. Demonstrate how her child would look.
6. Demonstrate several activities to engage her child in while he is in his standing board, such as showing him a book, playing "Peek-a-boo," or playing with his busy box.

3.72 Child: WALKS ALONE TWO TO THREE STEPS (11½–13½ mo.)
Parent: Encourages child to walk alone two or three steps, gradually reducing assistance as indicated

GENERAL GUIDELINES

The child takes a few steps independently. His gait is usually unsteady and he holds his arms up close to his chest.

Parents can encourage their child to practice his initial independent steps by: encouraging him to take a few steps alone between furnishings or two adults; letting him walk barefoot or with soft soled shoes, so his feet can move freely (unless special shoes have been prescribed); and *not* making him walk when he appears frightened.

MENTALLY RETARDED PARENT

May expect her child to walk more than a few steps.

1. Provide the parent with anticipatory guidance, i.e., we cannot expect her child to walk more than two or three steps alone yet; he needs to have more practice with balancing. Explain that when children are learning to walk alone, it is scary for them, so if an adult or a piece of furniture is about an arm's length away, he will feel safer.
2. Demonstrate, and let the parent practice, encouraging her child to take a few steps alone between you and her:
   a. Model saying praise words to the child. Ask the parent how she can let him know how proud she is of him.
   b. Point out and describe any of the child's signs of being frightened; tell the parent she needs to help him when he makes that face (or cries, whines, etc.).
3. Check the shoes the child is wearing. If they are high-topped and hard soled, discourage their use. Demonstrate by bending a shoe (not on the child) how difficult it is for her child to bend his foot in them. Suggest bare feet in the home, when appropriate, and sneakers outdoors. Demonstrate how sneakers are flexible.
4. Have the parent identify two safe places in her home where her child can practice walking between two pieces of furniture. If there are none available, help arrange an area to encourage his walking.

BLIND PARENT

May not be able to visually monitor her child's independent walking attempts, and may be concerned for his safety.

1. Encourage the child to take a few steps between you and the parent:
   a. Define the appropriate distance between two people or furnishings.
   b. Describe the child's gait, facial expressions, and arm placement as he takes a few steps.
2. Help the parent identify or set up furnishings for her child to walk between.
3. Provide anticipatory guidance that all children fall at this age when they are practicing their walking skills. Describe his protective responses which help protect him when he falls.

3.73 Child: DEMONSTRATES BALANCE REACTIONS IN KNEELING (12–15 mo.)
Parent: "Sets up" opportunities which encourage child to develop balance reactions in kneeling when prescribed

GENERAL GUIDELINES

The child's balance reactions when kneeling are tested by placing him in a kneeling position with his hips extended (i.e., not sitting back on his feet) on a surface which can be slightly tilted, such as a tilt board. When tilted, the child's head, trunk, and extremities should move in the opposite direction of the tilt to help him maintain an upright position.

If the child does not display these balance reactions, activities may be prescribed to help develop them. Activities may include encouraging the child to balance while kneeling when he is gently rocked from side to side to music; playing games which require him to weight-shift from knee to knee, such as throwing bean bags or balls into containers; or placing him on a tilt board and rocking him from side to side while providing some support at his hips.

The following parent training activities assume kneeling balance activities have been prescribed for their child.

MENTALLY RETARDED PARENT

May implement kneeling balance activities too abruptly or roughly with her child.

1. Avoid demonstrating kneeling balance activities on tilt boards.
2. Explain to the parent why special kneeling balance activities are being prescribed in meaningful terminology:
   a. Let the parent push you off balance while you are kneeling to demonstrate balance reactions. Let her experience these reactions if she is interested. Point out how your head, chest, and arms moved in the opposite direction so you would not fall down.
   b. Demonstrate the child's balance reactions by shifting him off balance while you provide support at his hips; contrast how he is not moving his body in the direction opposite of the tilt which means he can fall easily when he loses his balance.
   c. Relate that the prescribed activities will help her child learn to balance better, which will help him keep from falling in kneeling, walking, or crawling.

3. Demonstrate, and let the parent practice, kneeling balance activities on the floor:
   a. Provide hand-over-hand assistance to help the parent discriminate her proper hand placement on the child's hips, and the amount of support required.
   b. Help guide gentle side to side movement while singing "Row Row Row Your Boat" or use a slow rhythmic musical toy.
4. Leave pictures of the child's appropriate kneeling position emphasizing that his bottom should not be sitting on his feet, and highlight the parent's hand placement on her child s hips. Tell the parent how many times a day to practice Activity No. 3, associating it with specific daily activities. For example, she can help him balance on his knees after a certain television show or after his bath.

BLIND PARENT

May not be able to visually monitor her child's balance reactions in kneeling.

1. Describe how balance reactions are tested in kneeling and the bodily responses to help maintain an upright position:
   a. Let the parent experience these movements by pushing her slightly off balance at her hips while she is kneeling if she is interested.
   b. Let the parent lightly support her child at his hips while his balance reactions are being tested so she can feel his reactions.
2. Orient the parent tactually to her child's position in kneeling, noting extended hips and the distance between his knees. Provide her with hand-over-hand assistance as she is learning proper hand placement, amount of support, and the speed and direction of movement during kneeling balance activities with her child.

3.74 Child: **FALLS BY SITTING (12-14 mo.)**
 Parent: Provides safe opportunities for child to practice lowering himself from standing; responds positively when child falls to sitting

GENERAL GUIDELINES

The child initially falls into sitting when he no longer wants to stand or becomes tired. He may also lower himself to sitting by holding onto a support, if available. His fall into sitting will become less abrupt as he develops more balance and control.

Parents can help their child practice his transition from standing to sitting and lessen his "pain" by:
1. Gently and slowly guiding him through the motions from standing to sitting.
2. Clapping or saying "uh oh!" with a smile when he falls to help him feel proud and less worried.
3. Assuring there are no obstacles nearby that he can hurt himself on if he falls into a sit from standing.

MENTALLY RETARDED PARENT

May not let her child practice controlled sitting from standing because he will get hurt, or may not anticipate safety considerations during this stage.

1. Provide the parent with anticipatory guidance statements:
   a. Stress that all children initially fall into sitting from standing until they have had enough practice to get down from standing by moving slowly.
   b. Explain that even though it looks like it hurts when he falls on his bottom, it usually does not hurt him. If he cries, it is usually because his fall scared him, not because he got hurt.
   c. Stress, however, that if her child falls and hits his head, or falls into a toy or piece of furniture, this *does* hurt and she needs to help him.
2. Emphasize to the parent that her child will be more frightened when he falls into sitting if he sees we have a frightened look on our faces. Demonstrate assuring phrases to say to her child when he falls without really hurting himself.
3. Provide concrete guidelines to help the parent recognize when she only needs to say reassuring phrases to her child if he falls, and when she needs to provide him physical comfort:
   a. Explain, if her child falls into sitting and does not actually cry, the parent can smile and say, "Uh-oh, you went boom!"
   b. Explain, if the child cries, she can give him a hug and say, "It's okay, I know that scared you."
   c. Model these responses as natural situations arise.
   d. Verbally prompt the parent to respond according to the situation, as needed.
4. Ask the parent what could happen if her child was standing in front of a low table or in front of his toy metal cars and fell into sitting. Help the parent identify ways to prevent these situations from happening.
5. Help identify safe places in the home with the parent to let her child practice sitting from standing. Point out that hard flooring hurts more than carpeting when he falls.

BLIND PARENT

May have realistic concerns if she cannot visually monitor her child's falls from standing.

1. Provide the parent anticipatory guidance that children learn how to move from standing to sitting by falling. Explain that, even though this may cause a loud "thump" and crying from her child, these falls do not usually hurt because he falls on his bottom. Children often cry, not because it hurts, but because they are scared.
2. Explain that her child may look at her when he falls to see if she has a worried expression on her face. If he sees she is upset or worried, he is more likely to cry.
3. Assure the parent that occasional bumps and bruises are unavoidable with all children. The parent will be able to discriminate if her child really hurts himself by listening to the type of fall and the tone of her child's crying.

3.75 Child: STANDS FROM SUPINE BY TURNING ON ALL FOURS (12½-15 mo.)
Parent: Encourages child to stand up from supine independently

GENERAL GUIDELINES

The child stands up from lying on his back first by moving into a hand-knee position and then rising to stand without holding onto a support. He figures out how to get into standing independently through practice, opportunity, and motivation. If the child always has someone to help him stand up, or is always near a piece of furniture to use for help, he will not have an opportunity to practice.

Specific handling techniques may be prescribed to help the child through his transitional movements to standing if he has motor impairments.

MENTALLY RETARDED PARENT

May not provide her child the motivation or opportunity to encourage him to stand up independently.

1. Advise the parent when her child is developmentally ready to stand up by himself. Demonstrate, and let the parent experience, the transitional movements used to move into standing from lying on her back.
2. Help identify with the parent open areas in the home in which to let her child practice standing up by himself:
   a. Point out that if he is near a couch or chair he will not need to practice getting up by himself because it is easier for him to hold onto furniture.
   b Explain when he gets up by himself, it helps him develop his balance and muscles better.
   c. Discuss that, even if he looks like he is having trouble getting up, let him try to do this all by himself. Explain that, at first, he may look like he cannot do it because he is thinking real hard to figure out how to stand up; this is how he learns.
3. Suggest times when to encourage her child to stand up all by himself. For example, the parent could change his diapers on the floor and let him get up all by himself.
4. Help the parent think of motivating phrases to say which may encourage her child to stand up, e.g., "Stand up, let's play ball" or "Stand up, it's time to go out and play."
5. Describe the child's feelings aloud to the parent when you observe him trying to stand up, e.g., "You're working so hard" or "You're so proud trying to stand up by yourself!"
6. If specific handling techniques have been prescribed to help the child move into standing:
   a. Demonstrate the techniques on the parent.
   b Let the parent practice with a large rag doll.
   c. Take a series of Polaroid pictures of the parent and child, and label the order of the transitional steps from supine to standing. Highlight the parent's hand placement on the child by circling it with a marker.
   d. Stress slow and gentle handling.

BLIND PARENT

May not be able to visually monitor how her child moves from supine to standing.

1. Describe the child's movements and expressions as he moves from supine to standing. Explain that her child may grunt, sigh, or make other distress sounds while he is learning to stand up because this is hard work for him. Stress that she should not immediately help him if he sounds a little strained because he needs this opportunity to practice.
2. If special handling techniques have been prescribed:
   a. Demonstrate them on the parent first.
   b. Provide hand-over-hand physical assistance to the parent, noting her hand placement in relation to her child's body parts. She can feel the amount of support to apply with the appropriate speed of movement.
   c. Let the parent practice the techniques with her child while you provide verbal assistance, if necessary, until the parent feels comfortable to carry this out at home independently.

3.76 Child: WALKS BACKWARDS (12½-21 mo.)
Parent: Understands that some children like to practice walking backward

GENERAL GUIDELINES

The child may walk backwards up to six feet without support. His maturing balance and interest in movement enables him to test out his backward walking abilities. The child may enjoy walking backwards while pulling a toy on a string or helping his parents move a big box or chair.

Walking backwards is not a significant walking skill. If the child does not demonstrate this skill, there is little reason for concern or contrived efforts to try to make him do this.

Provide parents with anticipatory guidance regarding the "okayness" of their child walking backwards for fun or, if the child does not walk backwards, that this is no cause for alarm. Walking backwards in an infant walker should be discouraged, however, especially if the child has motor impairments. Walking backwards in a "walker" is likely to facilitate abnormal movement patterns.

3.77 Child: THROWS BALL UNDERHAND IN SITTING (13-16 mo.)
Parent: Models throwing balls underhand in play; provides child physical assistance if needed

GENERAL GUIDELINES

The child can throw and roll a ball when he is sitting. He usually does not have the balance or control at this age to throw a ball when he is standing without support.

He can push the ball to make it roll and can throw it using an underhand motion if he is sitting on a chair or other support off the floor, so his hand does not bump into the floor.

Balls of any size are suitable for rolling, however, the child will need smaller "graspable" balls for throwing. Bean bags, wads of paper, rubber balls, clutch bags, and tennis balls are appropriate for the child to throw.

Parents encourage their child's ball throwing by providing him opportunities to play with balls, demonstrating how to throw and roll balls, and providing him gentle physical assistance while he is learning, if needed. Children should be encouraged to throw balls with each hand. Knocking down targets, such as stacked milk cartons, can provide an additional incentive for him to throw.

MENTALLY RETARDED PARENT

May expect her child to engage in developmentally higher ball playing skills.

1. Demonstrate to the parent the various ways her child may throw and roll balls. Explain that, at this age, he needs to be sitting because he cannot balance and throw while he is standing yet.
2. Tell the parent to give her child the ball in a different hand each time so the muscles in both of his arms get exercise.
3. Refer to 5.46 (Plays ball cooperatively) to help the parent identify safe areas to play, suitable balls to use, and ways to keep the game fun.
4. If the child needs physical assistance to roll or throw balls:
   a. Demonstrate providing assistance to the parent so she can feel the gentle handling.
   b. Demonstrate, and let the parent practice, physically prompting her child as you verbally stress slow and gentle movements.
   c. Do not stress exact underhand motions, to prevent the parent from focusing upon making her child throw "just right."

BLIND PARENT

May not be able to visually monitor her child's method of throwing, and may have difficulty locating the ball during play.

1. The parent can present a small ball to her child with her hand covering the top of the ball. This will encourage him to grasp it underhand for throwing.
2. Bean bags may be easier for the parent to locate during throwing activities with her child.
3. Play ball with the parent and child. Describe his methods for throwing or rolling. If the child needs physical assistance, the parent will be able to help him with minimal orientation.
4. Orient the parent to suitable distances for targets to be placed from her child, depending upon your observations of how far and in what direction her child typically throws.

PHYSICALLY DISABLED PARENT

With limited mobility or upper extremity control; may have difficulty holding, retrieving, or throwing balls with her child.

1. Refer to adaptations for 5.46 (Plays ball cooperatively).

3.78 Child: CREEPS OR HITCHES UPSTAIRS (13½-15 mo.)
Parent: Encourages and facilitates child's creeping or hitching upstairs

GENERAL GUIDELINES

The child either creeps up a few stairs on his hands and knees (or feet), or "hitches" up by sitting backwards and pushing his bottom up to each step.

Parents must always closely supervise their child's initial stair-climbing activities. The following activities can help encourage him to learn to move up steps:

1. Let him practice climbing in areas where there is only one or two steps, such as a curb or entrance into the house.
2. Place a "goody" at the top of a few steps.
3. Let him try climbing on top of a sturdy box before climbing onto a low couch.
4. Provide him physical assistance and support, when needed.

Safety gates should continue to be used. The child's increasing interest in climbing, moving, and exploring his environment will likely be too tempting for him to resist climbing stairs when no one is looking.

MENTALLY RETARDED PARENT

May not anticipate safety concerns for her child on steps.

1. As the child begins to move around, make a home visit to help insure that all stairs in the child's environment are safe. Ask the parent to identify all stairs in the home and explore different ways to make steps safe via gates, keeping doors shut, or setting up barriers.
2. Identify steps in the home with the parent which are suitable for her child to practice climbing up. Stress she should only let him practice if she is right next to him, explaining he could lose his balance and fall.
3. Demonstrate, and let the parent practice, activities suggested in the general guidelines to encourage her child to creep up steps.
4. Provide anticipatory guidance that children should *not* be encouraged to crawl down steps until they can climb up them easily, and he is not ready to walk up steps yet.

PHYSICALLY DISABLED PARENT

May have difficulty maneuvering steps to safely guide her child when he practices climbing up them.

1. When a parent is non-ambulatory, rather than having the child learn climbing skills on stairs, set up a series of sturdy boxes or cushions which lead up to the parent's lap or couch.
2. If the parent is ambulatory but has difficulty maneuvering steps, she may be able to sit on the third or fourth step and encourage her child to climb up between the parent and the wall:
   a. The child should be within easy reach of the parent. She can slide back downstairs on her buttocks with her child on her lap to practice again or resume floor activities.
   b. Caution the parent to never "over-reach" in these activities.

3.79 Child: WALKS WITHOUT SUPPORT (13-15 mo.)
Parent: Provides child ample opportunities and encouragement to walk independently

GENERAL GUIDELINES

Children without motor impairments may begin to walk as early as nine months and as late as eighteen months.

When the child first starts to walk independently, he demonstrates an unsteady wide-legged gait and holds his arms up high for balance. He appears to walk in a side-to-side rocking manner. At this stage he can walk across an entire room. Crawling or creeping, however, remains his primary mode of locomotion for exploration and going from room to room. He will have difficulty walking on uneven surfaces and thick-piled carpet. He needs to grab a support to help himself stop.

As the child's walking balance improves with practice and maturation, he gradually lowers his arms, displays a smoother gait, and begins to walk as his primary means for locomotion. He learns to stop independently and can use his hands while he walks to carry small toys or wave.

MENTALLY RETARDED PARENT

May expect her child to use walking as his primary means of locomotion before he is ready, or may restrict his practice times by over-using playpens or highchairs.

1. Provide anticipatory guidance regarding the child's early walking abilities and needs. Include the following concepts:
   a. He cannot walk farther than the length of this room.
   b. He still needs to crawl around a lot.
   c. When he is walking, he cannot stop himself; if she calls his name and tells him "no" or "stop," she has to help him stop.
   d. He needs to practice walking; if he stays in his playpen or highchair all day, he will not be able to practice.
   e. He cannot carry things or talk when he is walking because he has to keep all of his attention on walking; do not ask him questions or ask him to carry things when he is practicing his walking.
   f. He needs to practice walking on smooth, hard, flat floors; it is too hard for him to walk on hills, bumpy ground, and thick carpet.
   g. He does not look at the floor when he is walking; if there are toys, throw rugs, shoes, or other things on the floor, he can fall; we need to make sure the floor is clear before he practices.
2. Make a "Do's and Don'ts" picture list for encouraging the child to walk. Use the concepts listed in Activity No. 1.
3. Help the parent identify suitable places in and outside of the home to let her child practice his walking. Stress why these are good places for him to practice (e.g., smooth, no obstacles, flat, etc.).
4. Model saying encouraging praise words to the child when he is practicing his walking.
5. Review daily activities and routine errands outside of the home. Help the parent discriminate according to the activity when she can let her child practice walking, from when she should carry him or use a stroller. For example, when the parent goes to a shopping center, her child needs a stroller or to be carried; at home when he goes into another room, he can crawl; and when she lets him down from his chair after eating, she can let him walk.

BLIND PARENT

May have realistic safety concerns as her child begins walking.

1. Describe children's early walking patterns and abilities as outlined in the general guidelines for this skill.
2. A jingle bell securely attached to the child's shoestring or waistband can help the parent keep accurate "tabs" of her child's location around the home.
3. The parent can use a stroller or a harness when walking outdoors or shopping. As the child becomes more independent with his walking, the parent can promote his habit of always holding her hand when outdoors.

3.80 Child: WALKS SIDEWAYS (14-15 mo.)
Parent: Sets up situations which encourage child to walk sideways

GENERAL GUIDELINES

The child walks sideways a few steps to his left and right without support. His feet should not cross over each other. He initially learns to shift his weight for "sideways walking" by cruising around furniture.

If the child needs extra help with learning to walk sideways, parents can:

1. Let their child play at low furnishings and encourage him to walk sideways to get a toy.
2. Play "Ring Around the Rosey."
3. Set up narrow corridors where the child can only "fit" sideways to get a toy, e.g., pull a sofa away from the wall a foot.
4. Demonstrate and encourage their child to walk sideways along a long carpet strip in a game-like situation.

MENTALLY RETARDED PARENT

May have difficulty with pacing when encouraging her child to walk sideways.

1. Explain to the parent that walking sideways helps her child learn to balance.
2. Review suitable furnishings to let her child walk around. Refer to 3.47 (Pulls to standing at furniture).
3. Play "Ring Around the Rosey" with the parent and child. Emphasize moving very slowly. Sing the words to the song slower than usual. Stress never pulling her child's arm because that can hurt and can make him fall off balance.
4. Make up a simple "side-step" dance with the parent to a musical toy. The parent can model this dance with her child to encourage him to move sideways.

3.81 Child: RUNS – HURRIED WALK (14-18 mo.)
Parent: Provides a safe environment which accommodates the child's early running

GENERAL GUIDELINES

The child's maturing walking abilities and his drive for increased mobility and independence encourage him to experiment with running. His running is actually a rapid walk, with his alternating feet remaining on the ground at all times. He moves his body stiffly and upright.

Parents usually do not need to encourage their child's "running" because once he has mastered walking, his contentment to sit for long periods or simply walk dwindles. Instead, parents may need to adapt the environment to allow him safe open areas to exercise his new-found powers.

If the child appears to lack motivation or interest in "running," parents can help "spark" his motivation, and help him learn the fun and benefits of "running," by playing chasing games or encouraging him to run after a ball or toy car during play.

Children who have abnormal movement patterns should not be encouraged to run without consultation from a physical therapist.

MENTALLY RETARDED PARENT

May not anticipate safety considerations when her child begins to run.

1. Praise the child's new motor abilities. Discuss how proud the parent must be, and emphasize how difficult it can also be to try and keep up with her child now that he is moving around so quickly:
   a. Explain that since her child can move more quickly, we have to move more quickly to make sure he does not get hurt.
   b. Tell the parent that when she is walking on sidewalks or in stores with her child, she needs to always hold his hand. Ask her what could happen if she was not holding his hand.
2. Make a home visit to assure the home is adequately child-proofed to accommodate the child's new running and climbing abilities:
   a. Suggest moving furnishings to provide open spaces for the child, if needed.
   b. Point out all furnishings that the child could climb up on. Let the parent check to see what he could get into at that new height.
   c. Look for obstacles the child could run into. Help move or pad them with foam rubber.
3. Emphasize the importance of letting her child play outside with the parent's supervision:
   a. Explore if there are safe areas to play outside, such as a front porch or backyard. Point out and fix, when possible, potentially hazardous situations (unsafe railings on the porch, large holes in the ground, broken or rusty fences, broken glass).
   b. Help the parent find a nearby playground to take her child.
   c. Suggest outdoor play toys (balls, boxes, tubs of water, bubbles).
   d. Encourage the parent to take her child out to play at least three times a week for an hour.
   e. Review weather conditions and clothing needs for the child. Relate to the parent how she can decide what type of outer clothing her child needs by thinking about her own. If she needs a coat, so does he; but if she does not need a coat, her child does not either.
   f. Inform the parent that cold weather does *not* cause children to get colds, so she can take him out in cold weather, but be sure he has on a hat and coat.
   g. Explain that when it is raining or thundering to stay inside for play.
4. Suggest chasing games cautiously. Chasing games have the potential to get out of hand for some parents who display rough or abrupt handling.

BLIND PARENT

May have realistic safety concerns as her child begins running and climbing.

1. Describe and explain the child's "running" movements. Help child-proof the home and backyard according to the child's new quick physical activities:
   a. Help anticipate furnishings her child may be able to climb up on so the parent can pay special attention when she hears her child approaching them.
   b. Explain that sometimes children do not watch where they are running because they are busy turning their heads to see if anyone is chasing them or looking too far ahead at what he is running toward. Falls, bumps, and bruises are inevitable for all children.
2. Refer to Activity Nos. 2 and 3 for 3.79 (Walks without support).

PHYSICALLY DISABLED PARENT

May have difficulty keeping up with her child as he begins to move quickly.

1. Parents can use safety gates and keep doors shut to rooms not being immediately used. This can help keep her child in sight and within easy access. Play areas outdoors should be securely fenced in.
2. If the parent is non-ambulatory and socially isolated, investigate volunteer groups for a companion to accompany the parent and child to playgrounds.

3.82 Child: BENDS OVER AND LOOKS THROUGH LEGS (14½-15½ mo.)
Parent: Recognizes child's ability to bend over and look through his legs as a fun position which promotes his balance and flexibility

GENERAL GUIDELINES

The child demonstrates his flexibility and balance when he bends down and looks backwards between his slightly flexed

3.82

legs. Children sometimes assume this position to challenge and practice their new movement abilities and to see their world upside down.

It is not necessary for parents to "teach" their child to bend down and look through his legs if he does not assume this position during play. They can, however, take advantage of this position, if their child assumes it, to play "Peek-a-boo," talk about how the world looks upside down, and let him see what he looks like in a mirror upside down.

Parents can also let their child bend over to get toys out of boxes, or play in a dishpan of water or sand, to encourage his trunk flexibility and balance.

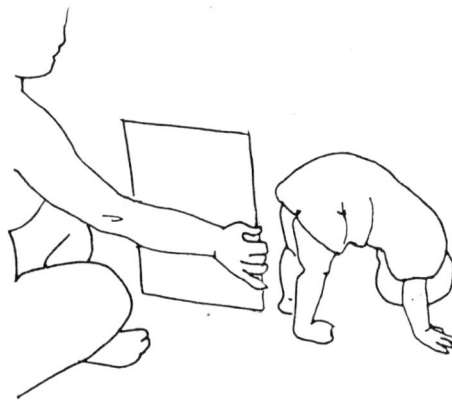

MENTALLY RETARDED PARENT

May not spontaneously play games with her child when he bends over and looks through his legs.

1. Praise and point out to the parent her child's increasing balance abilities if you observe him bending over and looking through his legs.
2. Discuss how different everything must look to her child when he is looking through his legs because everything is upside down:
   a. Explain that children sometimes like to bend over like that just to see how different everything can look.
   b. Spontaneously demonstrate, and let the parent practice, playing "Peek-a-boo" with her child if he assumes this position.
3. Take a dishpan of water and sponges outside on a warm day with the parent and child. Let the child bend over to pick up a sponge from the pan. Play a game of washing the house or fence with the sponge, going back frequently to dip the sponge in the pan for more water.

BLIND PARENT

May not be able to visually monitor when her child bends over and looks through his legs.

1. Describe the child's position when he bends over and looks through his legs. Relate how children like to do this because they see their environment upside down which may be a brand new experience for them:
   a. The parent can become tactually familiar with her child in this position when you notice him assuming it.
   b. Help the parent position herself or a toy in relation to the back of her child's legs to play "Peek-a-boo."

3.83 Child: **DEMONSTRATES BALANCE REACTIONS IN STANDING (15-18 mo.)**
Parent: Carries out activities which encourage child's balance reactions in standing if prescribed

GENERAL GUIDELINES

If the child is standing on a surface which is tilted, his head, trunk, and extremities should move in the opposite direction of the tilt. This automatic balance reaction helps him prevent a fall and maintain an upright position.

The child's balance reactions in standing are not expected to emerge until he has been walking independently long enough to narrow his base of support, i.e., he stops walking with his legs spread far apart.

Special activities to encourage the child's balance reactions in standing may be prescribed by a therapist if the child:
1. Demonstrates a consistent wide base of support in all directions.
2. Displays structural or functional asymmetry which results in his weight-shifting to one side only.
3. Does not have control to free his hands while walking.

Gently rocking the child from side to side in standing to music or on an unstable surface, such as a mattress or tilt board, are common activities which may be prescribed. Positioning and adult hand placement during this balance activities will vary for each child.

MENTALLY RETARDED PARENT

May be too rough or abrupt if balance in standing activities have been prescribed for her child.

1. Do not test the child's balance reactions in standing in front of the parent unless you are certain that she understands this is for testing purposes only. She may interpret that pushing her child off balance is something she should do at home.
2. If balancing activities have been prescribed, explain their purpose to the parent in meaningful terminology:
   a. Let the parent push you off balance at your hips. Point out how your head, chest, and arms moved against the push to keep you from falling. If interested, let the parent experience these reactions by pushing her gently off balance.
   b. Explain that we use these reactions automatically when we walk which keeps us from falling. Relate that her child needs extra help learning to balance when he is walking, so he will be able to learn to run and jump when he gets older and not fall so much now.
3. Avoid prescribing balance reaction activities on unstable surfaces.

4. Demonstrate, and let the parent practice, gently rocking her child from side to side when he is standing and she is kneeling face-to-face with him:
   a. Play a slow rhythmic musical toy or sing "Row Row Row Your Boat" to help the parent use slow pacing and judge how long to rock her child.
   b. Provide initial hand over parent hand assistance to help her discern proper hand placement on her child's hips, the amount of support to provide, and smooth side-to-side movement.
   c. Leave a Polaroid picture which highlights the proper positioning of the parent in relation to her child.

BLIND PARENT

May not be able to visually monitor her child's balance reactions in standing.

1. Before testing the child's balance reactions in standing, describe the testing procedure and the balance reactions that are being observed:
   a. Relate how these are similar to the reactions we have when we are driving a car around a sharp turn, and our bodies automatically move in the opposite direction to help us stay upright.
   b. Let the parent lightly place her hand on the side of her child's trunk opposite to the tilt, so she can monitor his movement when his balance reactions are tested.
2. If balancing in standing activities have been prescribed for the child, provide the parent initial hand-over-hand assistance until she is familiar with her proper hand placement, amount of support needed for her child, and the speed and direction of movement.

3.84 Child: WALKS INTO LARGE BALL WHILE TRYING TO KICK IT (15-18 mo.)
Parent: Demonstrates and encourages child to kick using any method

GENERAL GUIDELINES

The child walks or bumps into a large ball as his method for kicking it forward. He will not be able to actually kick the ball with his foot until his balance improves to the point where he can stand on one foot with help.

Parents can encourage their child's early kicking skills by providing him large lightweight balls (light rubber balls, beach balls, foam rubber balls) and by letting him play freely within open areas. Parents can demonstrate kicking balls during play and should praise all of their child's attempts without expecting a mature kick. The child can also be encouraged to kick a ball while he is seated in a chair so he does not have to balance his body while kicking.

MENTALLY RETARDED PARENT

May not have balls for her child to play with, or may expect him to kick the ball in a mature manner.

1. Ask the parent if her child has any balls to play with. If he has none or they are inappropriate (e.g., a baseball), help select appropriate inexpensive balls to purchase or lend one, if possible.
2. Demonstrate the various ways her child may try to kick a ball. Explain that he will not be able to kick it the way we do with our feet yet because he is not old enough to have enough balance.
3. Model, and let the parent practice, kicking the ball with her child very lightly. Tell her since the ball is so light, she should only tap the ball with her foot instead of a hard kick.
4. Help identify with the parent safe, open areas indoors and outdoors to play ball with her child.
5. Play ball with the parent and child. Stress keeping ball play fun and letting the child play with the ball the way he wants. Explain he is not ready to kick, throw, or catch balls like us or older children.

BLIND PARENT

May not be able to visually monitor how her child kicks, and may have difficulty locating the ball after it has been kicked.

1. Describe the child's early kicking attempts, how he approaches the ball, and his facial expressions during ball play.
2. The parent can kick the ball back and forth with her child in an unobstructed hallway to help confine the ball's travel.
3. Use balls which have bells in them when practicing kicking outdoors.
4. Balloons and punch balls are *not* recommended. They can break easily and the pieces may be difficult to find. Balloon pieces are dangerous for the child because he can put them in his mouth and easily inhale them.

PHYSICALLY DISABLED PARENT

Who is non-ambulatory; may not be able to demonstrate kicking a ball to encourage her child's kicking.

1. A parent who uses a wheelchair may be able to roll the wheelchair into the ball or bend over and push the ball to her child. She can provide her child verbal prompts and encouragement, i.e., "Kick the ball with your foot."
2. The parent may be able to passively move her leg to kick a ball while sitting if she has adequate upper extremity control and strength.

3.85 Child: THROWS BALL FORWARD (15-18 mo.)
Parent: Encourages child to throw balls while standing during play

GENERAL GUIDELINES

The child's maturing balance, control, and confidence enables him to throw a ball toward in standing. He may throw it overhand or underhand.

If the child has poor balance, parents can give him support at his trunk or hips to provide him extra stability. The child

3.85

could also stand against a couch or hold a table with one hand for support.

Adapted parent training activities for 3.77 (Throws ball underhand in sitting) and 5.46 (Plays ball cooperatively) are applicable for this skill. If needed, advise parents when their child is ready to practice throwing while standing.

3.86 Child: WALKS WITH ASSISTANCE OF EIGHT-INCH BOARD (15-17 mo.)
Parent: Helps child walk across an eight-inch board if recommended

GENERAL GUIDELINES

The child can walk at least three feet along an eight-inch wide board raised one or two inches off the floor, if he holds an adult hand. This skill may be tested to evaluate the child's ability to balance and walk with a narrow base of support. Specific balance beam activities do not need to be taught if the child's gross motor development is following along in an expected progression.

The following activities assume the child needs extra help with walking using a narrower base of support.

MENTALLY RETARDED PARENT

May not pace her walking with her child's when she is helping him walk across a beam.

1. Demonstrate, and let the parent practice, helping her child walk across a balance beam with the board directly on the floor:
   a. Emphasize holding the child's hand out to his side rather than pulled over his head.
   b. Show the parent how to knee-walk next to her child while he holds onto her shoulder if the parent has difficulty holding his hand to his side.
   c. Stress waiting to step until her child takes a step.
   d. Count aloud slowly to help the parent pace her movements with her child's.
2. Name ways in and around their home that the parent can encourage her child to walk with a narrower gait:
   a. These may include walking on sidewalk cracks, across a piece of masking tape on the floor, or along a line drawn in the dirt with a stick.
   b. Demonstrate how the child may walk on these lines, i.e., straddling them, or not walking in a perfectly straight line.

BLIND PARENT

May not be able to visually monitor her child's gait.

1. If the child needs practice to help narrow his gait, describe to the parent his current gait, e.g., "He walks with his feet more than a foot apart; these activities will help encourage him to walk keeping his feet less than six inches apart." The parent can knee-walk behind her child with her hands lightly placed on her child's hips to feel his current gait.
2. Orient the parent to the length, width, and height of the balance beam before she helps her child walk across it.

PHYSICALLY DISABLED PARENT

Who uses assistive devices to walk; may need an adapted method to help her child walk across balance beams.

1. If the parent uses a wheelchair, she can:
   a. Propel the wheelchair slowly next to the board as her child holds the armrest and walks on the board.
   b. Propel the wheelchair backwards, straddling the board, encouraging her child to follow.

3.87 Child: PULLS TOY BEHIND WHILE WALKING (15-18 mo.)
Parent: Demonstrates and encourages child to pull toys on strings while walking

GENERAL GUIDELINES

Note: Adult supervision is required at all times with these activities to ensure that the child does not accidentally become entangled in any strings.

The child pulls a toy attached to a string while walking independently. Children often are able to push toys while walking before they are able to pull them. The child's standing balance and confidence in walking enable him to carry out these purposeful activities. Earlier, he had difficulty using his hands and walking at the same time.

The child should have experiences pushing "push-toys" before he is expected to pull toys on strings. The strings on pull-toys should be long enough for the toy to reach the floor and provide a little extra slack. If the string is too long, it could tangle or the child could trip. Sturdy, fairly heavy, and wide toys are the easiest to pull. Toys which make sounds when pulled are motivating for the child and allow him to hear his pulling efforts when the toy is behind him.

In addition to using commercial ones, pull-toys can be made by stringing juice cans or shoes boxes together. Tie a large bead or loop on the end for the child's easy grasping. Parents can put a favorite doll or stuffed animal on the toy for more fun.

MENTALLY RETARDED PARENT

May not have push- or pull-toys for her child at home.

1. Demonstrate how children can use their strollers or old infant walkers as push-toys. Put stuffed animals or other toys in them for the child to push.
2. Help the parent select suitable commercial push- and pull-toys to purchase by giving her pictures from advertisements, or lend them from your toy lending library, if available.
3. Explain that children learn to push toys when walking before they can pull them. Clarify, if needed, the difference between push- and pull-toys (pull-toys usually have strings).
4. Make one or two pull-toys with the parent using shoeboxes and/or juice cans. Point out the length of the string in relation to the child's hand and the floor.
5. Help the parent anticipate situations when her child may need help from her, e.g., the toy gets stuck wrapped around a chair leg or his own leg.

BLIND PARENT

May not be able to visually monitor when her child pulls toys.

1. The parent can make or buy pull-toys which make sounds when pushed or pulled. Orient the parent to a suitable length for the strings in relation to her child.
2. Describe to the parent any visual spectacles the toy produces when her child pulls it, e.g., the toy dog's eyes move, head tilts, etc.

3.88 Child: THROWS BALL OVERHAND LANDING WITHIN THREE FEET OF TARGET (16-22 mo.)
Parent: Plays ball with child aiming at targets; encourages his overhand throw

GENERAL GUIDELINES

The child can throw a ball about three feet overhand while standing. He brings his hand up toward the side of his head and if aimed toward a target, throws the ball within three feet of it. This skill demonstrates the child's increasing control of his arm and hand movements in coordination with his release skills and balance in standing.

Throwing balls overhand or swatting tether balls overhead are excellent activities if the child has decreased shoulder mobility and control (provided he can raise his arm up without pain). However, passive elongation activities (such as gently rotating the child's upper trunk and shoulders) which have been prescribed by a therapist should precede this activity.

If parents present the ball to their child underhand, the child is more likely to grab the top of the ball for overhand throwing. Balls can be bean bags, tennis balls, wads of paper, or round sponges.

Targets should be large and gradually moved three feet away from the child. Boxes, laundry baskets, and plastic milk cartons for "bowling pins" make interesting targets.

MENTALLY RETARDED PARENT

May be too rough during ball play with her child, or expect him to be able to hit targets.

1. Model a calm approach during ball play. Too much clapping and excitement may encourage the parent to pace ball play too quickly or roughly.
2. Refer to 5.46 (Plays ball cooperatively) to help the parent identify safe areas to play ball, suitable balls to use, and ways to keep the game fun.
3. Help identify and set up fun targets for the child to throw toward. Stress that, at this age, her child is not expected to always hit the target, but just aim in that direction.
4. If passive elongation exercises have been prescribed:
   a. Demonstrate the exercise on the parent so she can experience the amount of hand pressure and gentle movements.
   b. Physically assist the parent to carry out the exercise with her child by placing your hands on top of hers.
   c. Let the parent practice the exercises several times with her child until proficient before recommending that she do this at home.
   d. Have the parent play a rhythmic musical toy to help her judge the duration of the exercise and to encourage slow and gentle handling.

BLIND PARENT

May not be able to visually monitor if her child uses an overhand movement when throwing balls or how close he came to the target.

1. The parent can hold the ball underhand when offering it to her child. He will be more likely to pick it up overhand and thus help encourage an overhand throw.
2. The parent can encourage her child to throw bean bags at large objects. Bean bags cannot roll away, thus helping the parent discern how close her child is throwing to the target.

PHYSICALLY DISABLED PARENT

With limited mobility or upper extremity control; may have difficulty playing ball with her child.

1. Refer to 5.46 (Plays ball cooperatively).

3.89 Child: STANDS ON ONE FOOT WITH HELP (16-17 mo.)
Parent: Provides support for child in situations which encourage him to stand on one foot

GENERAL GUIDELINES

The child demonstrates his ability to shift his weight partially to one side when he briefly stands on one foot. At this stage, he needs a support to help him bear weight on his standing foot. This skill can be observed when the child mounts a ride-on toy, steps into his pants, or steps over an obstacle as he holds onto the wall or an adult's hand.

Parents can provide their child opportunities to practice standing on one foot with help by:

1. Letting the child hold onto the parent's shoulders and encouraging him to pick his foot up to slip on a shoe or his shorts.
2. Holding his hand and letting him step over obstacles (e.g., puddle of water outside, rungs of a ladder on the floor, kiddy pool).
3. Holding his hand as he steps up on a small curb or step.

If the child has difficulty standing on one foot with help, activities may be prescribed by a therapist which facilitate the child's weight-shifting skills in standing. Activities may include cruising around furniture (refer to 3.61, Walks holding on to furniture) and ball play in standing (refer to 3.85, Throws ball forward).

3.89

MENTALLY RETARDED PARENT

May not realize her child needs support during activities which require him to briefly stand on one foot.

1. Demonstrate putting the child's shoe or shorts on while he is standing holding onto your shoulders:
   a. Point out how he has to stand on one foot when he lifts his other foot up.
   b. Explain he is too young to stand on one foot by himself, so he needs to hold onto something to help him, in this case your shoulders.
   c. Ask the parent to think of something else he could hold onto while she puts his shoes or shorts on, e.g., a table or bed.
2. Help the parent think of and anticipate other specific situations which require her child to briefly stand on one foot (stepping up to a curb, over an obstacle, stepping out of his pants, etc.). Ask what her child can hold onto for each of these situations to help him balance.
3. Tell the parent never to actually lift her child's foot off the floor to see if he can stand on one foot because he could fall. Explain he needs to learn how to lift it up by himself so his balance will get better.

3.90 Child: WALKS UPSTAIRS WITH ONE HAND HELD (17-19 mo.)
Parent: Holds child's hand and helps him walk upstairs

GENERAL GUIDELINES

The child can walk upstairs, placing both feet on the same step before moving up to the next step, if his hand is held.

Parents should hold their child's hand at his side, rather than overhead. The parent can stay one or two steps behind the child to catch a fall and to help hold his hand at an appropriate level.

A few smaller-sized steps are preferred to initiate stair climbing activities. Stepping up to curbs, on sturdy low boxes, and on stools can also help the child prepare for walking upstairs.

The child usually cannot walk down steps yet, but can creep down backwards or "hitch" down by sitting on his bottom; these activities should be closely supervised.

MENTALLY RETARDED PARENT

May pull her child upstairs by his arm, or may expect him to use alternating feet.

1. Demonstrate walking up a few steps, pointing out how you alternate feet. Explain that her child is not ready to walk upstairs like that because his legs are too short and he does not have enough balance. Model how young children initially walk upstairs.
2. Identify with the parent suitable steps in and around the home to help her child practice walking up with his hand held. Explain that her child is not ready to walk up more than six steps yet.
3. Review safety considerations addressed under 3.78 (Creeps or hitches upstairs).

4. Demonstrate, and let parent practice, holding her child's hand to walk up a few steps:
   a. Stress slow pacing. Have the parent count with each step her child makes.
   b. Emphasize standing one step below the child and holding his hand at his side.
5. Emphasize that her child is not ready to walk downstairs yet. Caution the parent to be within three steps of her child if he creeps or hitches down.

BLIND PARENT

May not be able to visually monitor her child's creeping or hitching down steps and be concerned for his safety.

1. The parent can sit beside her child on the steps as they "hitch" down the steps together. Later, when the child is learning to walk downstairs, the parent may feel more comfortable continuing to "hitch" down while holding her child's hand as he walks down.

PHYSICALLY DISABLED PARENT

Who is unable to ambulate steps; may have difficulty helping her child walk up.

1. The parent can sit on a short flight of steps and encourage her child to walk upstairs as he holds a railing and her hand. An ambulatory adult should be present while the child is initially learning to negotiate steps.
2. Small stools can be placed next to the sink, couch, bed, etc. for the child to practice stepping up on; the parent can hold one of his hands, if needed.

3.91 Child: CARRIES LARGE TOY WHILE WALKING (17-18½ mo.)
Parent: Encourages child to independently carry large safe objects while walking

GENERAL GUIDELINES

The child no longer needs to hold his hands out to his sides to help stabilize himself when he walks. He is thus able to carry large lightweight objects or toys without assistance.

Parents can encourage their child to carry large objects during daily activities and play. They can ask him to carry his various stuffed animals, large balls, pillows, small trash cans, etc. to help out around the house or ask him to get them from another room for play.

Objects should be comparatively light, not have any sharp edges, and not obstruct the child's view when walking. He should not be allowed to walk with long sticks or stick-like objects.

MENTALLY RETARDED PARENT

May not anticipate objects which are not suitable for her child to carry.

1. Compare and contrast objects which are suitable for the child to carry with objects which the parent should not let her child carry:

a. Show the parent several appropriate and then inappropriate objects for her child to carry. Point out the discriminating features, e.g., not too big or he will not be able to see where he is walking; and not too heavy or he can hit someone with it by mistake or fall and hurt himself.
b. Ask the parent to show you two more objects that would be good to let her child carry.
2. Name several specific situations that the parent can encourage her child to carry an object when he walks, e.g., put his teddy bear in the chair or bring his trash can in the kitchen so mommy can empty it. Ask the parent if she can think of ways to encourage him to carry a ball, a pillow, or his new box of blocks across the room.

BLIND PARENT

May need anticipatory guidance to assure objects the child carries do not obstruct his view.

1. Point out that her child should not try to carry objects which could be in front of his face and block his visual field e.g., large boxes, tall stuffed animals, or large foam pillows.

3.92 Child: PUSHES AND PULLS LARGE TOYS OR BOXES AROUND THE FLOOR (17-18½ mo.)
Parent: Sets up purposeful situations which encourage child to push and pull large toys or boxes around the floor

GENERAL GUIDELINES

The child's balance and control in walking enable him to push and pull large toys, boxes, and small furnishings around independently.

Parents can demonstrate and let their child push and pull child-size chairs, large boxes, wagons, or stools. They can also show him how to make pushing and pulling large objects purposeful by showing him how to take his toys for a ride, push a stool up to a sink, transfer several toys at one time to another room in his wagon, or move his chair over to a small table so he can color. Handles can be contrived with ropes or by cutting out a hole toward the top side of a box.

MENTALLY RETARDED PARENT

May not discriminate appropriate from inappropriate large objects for her child to push or pull around the house.

1. Encourage the child to push his toybox. Praise his emerging abilities to push and pull large objects, explaining to the parent how this is helping his muscles.
2. Suggest specific daily actvities to the parent which provide opportunities for her child to push or pull large objects, e.g., pushing his highchair to the table, pushing the laundry basket of clothes, and pulling his ride-on toy to the door before going outside.

3. Show the parent objects that her child should *not* be allowed to push or pull and name their discriminating features, e.g., vacuum cleaner — too heavy; unsturdy stool or chair — can tip over; or a chair without casters — can scrape the floor.
4. Point out obstacles which make it difficult for the child to push or pull large toys, e.g., narrow doorway or floor molding between rooms. Tell the parent she will need to help her child in these situations.
5. Bring the parent a large discarded box. Show her all the fun things her child can do with it, e.g., climb in and out, and push or pull his toys. Ask her if she has any other boxes with which to let her child play.

3.93 Child: WALKS INDEPENDENTLY ON EIGHT INCH BOARD (17½-19½ mo.)
Parent: Sets up situations which encourage child to walk with a narrow base of support if needed

GENERAL GUIDELINES

The child demonstrates his ability to balance while walking with a narrow base of support when he walks independently across a six-foot board, eight inches wide.

At home parents can encourage their child to walk with a narrower base of support by letting him practice walking between two obstacles, such as a sofa pulled one foot away from the wall, helping him walk along a curb, or holding his hand as he tries to negotiate the wide edge of a sand box. Parents can also draw parallel lines in the sand or dirt, or make lines on the floor with masking tape, to encourage their child to walk between them.

Help parents identify and set up these situations at home, as needed, stressing the importance of keeping the activity fun. If the child needs assistance, refer to 3.86 (Walks with assistance on eight-inch board).

3.94 Child: TRIES TO STAND ON TWO-INCH BALANCE BEAM (17½-18½ mo.)
Parent: Provides support, if needed, as child is learning to bear weight on one foot

GENERAL GUIDELINES

The child independently steps up on a two-inch wide beam, three to four inches off the floor, with one foot. This skill is tested to evaluate the child's balance in standing and ability to bear weight on one foot without support.

Refer to the general guidelines and activities for 3.89 (Stands on one foot with help) if the child has difficulty stepping up on a beam independently.

3.95

3.95 Child: BACKS INTO A SMALL CHAIR OR SLIDES SIDEWAYS (17½-19 mo.)
Parent: Provides opportunities for child to seat himself in small chairs

GENERAL GUIDELINES

The child climbs forward into a small chair and turns around to sit down, or he may back himself up to the chair to sit down and slide into it if it is low enough.

To encourage this motor planning skill, parents can:
1. Let their child have a special small chair or stool that is "his" to sit in and play, eat, watch television, listen to stories, etc.
2. Keep the chair pushed against a wall or hold it while the child is learning to climb in to prevent sliding.
3. Give him opportunities to try climbing in chairs, rather than lifting him into the chair.

Rocking chairs and chairs with wheels should be avoided until the child is proficient in negotiating small stable chairs.

MENTALLY RETARDED PARENT

May always lift her child into chairs, or may not anticipate safety needs as her child is learning to seat himself.

1. Help identify a special chair with the parent for her child to use:
   a. If a child-size chair is unavailable, look for foot stools, plastic milk crates, or double-strength small boxes.
   b. Name times and activities to encourage her child to climb in and sit on "his" chair all by himself.
   c. Identify walls or supports, such as a couch, to place the chair against so it will not slip away when he tries to sit down.
   d. Demonstrate the various ways her child may try to sit down in it.
2. Empathize with the parent how much easier it is to just put her child in a chair rather than waiting for him to climb into it by himself. Explain, however, if she keeps helping him, he cannot learn to do this by himself because he needs practice. Discuss how nice it will be when he can get into chairs without always having to be lifted into them.
3. Point out chairs in the home which she will need to help her child climb into, e.g., highchairs, rocking chairs. If you notice any unsturdy chairs, such as one with a wobbly leg tell the parent not to let her child try to sit in it because he can fall.

BLIND PARENT

May not be able to visually monitor when her child climbs into chairs.

1. The parent can remove low wobbly tables and chairs if she is concerned about her child falling. Small chairs can be placed against a wall or she can hold them while encouraging her child to sit down.

3.96 Child: KICKS BALL FORWARD (18-24½ mo)
Parent: Models, and encourages child to kick ball forward

GENERAL GUIDELINES

The child kicks a ball with his foot in standing without assistance. This skill requires the child to shift and bear weight on one foot momentarily.

Parents can offer their child balls that are light and about the size of a beach ball. The child should be encouraged to kick with each foot.

If the child cannot kick a ball because he cannot balance his weight on one foot, refer to 3.89 (Stands on one foot with help).

MENTALLY RETARDED PARENT

May not have appropriate balls with which her child can play.

1. Help parent select an appropriate ball to purchase for her child:
   a. Small beach balls can often be purchased for under one dollar at drug stores.
   b. Show her an example of an appropriate-sized ball and point out its light weight. Explain that this makes it easier for him to kick, and it is soft so no one gets hurt during play.
2. Play a simple game of ball with the parent and child. Model gentle kicking, throwing, and praising the child for all of his efforts.
3. Help the parent identify safe open areas to play ball with her child in or around her home.
4. Remind the parent that her child needs to wear shoes when he practices kicking balls. Ask her what could happen if he kicked a ball with bare feet.

BLIND PARENT

May not be able to visually monitor her child's kicking.

1. Kicking a ball produces a distinct sound which can be differentiated from throwing or walking into it.

PHYSICALLY DISABLED PARENT

Who uses assistive devices for mobility; may have difficulty modeling kicking balls for her child.

1. Refer to 3.84 (Walks into a large ball while trying to kick it).

FINE MOTOR DEVELOPMENT

4.01 Child: REGARDS COLORFUL OBJECT MOMENTARILY (0-1 mo.)
Parent: Provides colorful toys or objects for child to look at

GENERAL GUIDELINES

Children respond to the brightness value of colors at birth. They seem to look longer at colors of medium intensity (medium yellow, greens, pinks) than colors that are bright (reds, oranges, blue) or dim (gray, beige). The newborn will also respond to light intensities. He will squint or shut his eyes tightly if the light is too bright.

Children can usually look at an object for 4-10 seconds, especially if it has contrasting colors, such as black and white or green and yellow. They prefer patterns to solid colors. The optimal visual distance for focusing at this age is reportedly eight to twelve inches away from the child's eyes; beyond that, things are hazy.

Parents can place visually attracting mobiles, pictures, *stabiles*,* and toys in their child's crib and play areas within his line of vision to encourage visual attention. Visually attractive objects which produce soft rattle or jingle sounds and/or slightly move can also help encourage the child's visual attention.

The position in which a child is placed to look at stationary or moving visual stimuli is also important. Recommended positions include cradling in arms (as if to feed, semi-reclined in an infant seat or lap, and side-lying in his crib. Toys should be presented at, or below, the child's eye level to prevent hyperextension of his neck.

Attending can be hard work for a child. If controlled vision stimulation activities have been recommended, the child should be well-rested and the activity stopped when the child maintains gaze aversion, twists his body, or fusses.

Observe the child's sleep and play environments for visually attracting objects and their placement. In addition, observe the parent's method for showing her child toys in relation to the position of her child, the distance of the toy within his line of vision and the duration of presentation. If there are any needs, or if controlled vision stimulation has been recommended the following parent training activities can be implemented

MENTALLY RETARDED PARENT

May over- or under-stimulate her child's visual needs, and may have difficulty judging the appropriate distance and duration for presenting objects.

1. Ask the parent if she has noticed whether her child has favorite things at which to look. Discuss why he may like to look at those particular things. Help select additional various toys and objects which are likely to be visually attractive to the child:

---
*See Glossary.

   a. Point out how young children like to look at colorful, bright things, and toys with patterns and faces.
   b. Explain that, at this age, children get tired of looking after this amount of time.
   c. Point out the child's signals which indicate he doesn't want to look anymore, e.g., his eyes shut, body twists, or looks the other way.
   d. If the parent cannot imitate measuring the proper distance to hold toys from her child, measure the distance and then let the parent present the object at the correct spot. Remind her to count slowly to ten before taking the toy away even though at first her child may only glance at it briefly.
   e. If the parent consistently holds toys too close to her child's eyes, demonstrate how difficult it is to look at things too closely by holding an object too close to your eyes and then the parent's eyes.
   f. Explain that young children can only look at one thing at a time; therefore, she should only show him one toy at a time.
3. When using a dangling object, such as a toy on a string, remind the parent that the *object*, not the parent's *hand*, is held a handspread away from her child's chest. Do not use dangling objects if the parent has trouble with this concept and does not quickly adjust the distance.
4. Explain that children need to look at different things from different positions:
   a. Model specific positions which facilitate the child's attention as described in the general guidelines. It may be necessary to demonstrate only one position per session with the parent.
   b. Have the parent practice placing her child in various positions as they are demonstrated.
   c. Associate these various positions with specific daily activities at home, e.g., sidelying after feeding.
5. Tell the parent not to try to make her child look at things when he is sleepy, hungry, or needs a diaper change. Ask her when a good time would be to show him toys.

DEAF PARENT

May not be aware that auditory stimuli can help attract her child's visual attention.

1. Explain that different sounds can help attract her child to look at different things:
   a. Mark with stickers or permanent non-toxic markers squeak toys, rattles, and other toys according to the sounds they make. For example, mark squeak toys which make long sharp harsher tones with red, and squeak toys with softer short tones with green.
   b. Explain that toys marked with red may be too harsh for her child and cause him to cry or turn away.
2. Demonstrate activating the various sound stimulus toys (i.e., squeezing a squeak toy vs. shaking a rattle toy) two times and waiting for her child to look. Have the parent practice, cueing her when to start and stop the sound, as needed.

4.01

3. Encourage the parent to vocalize, call her child's name, and praise him during these activities according to her verbal abilities.

BLIND PARENT

May be unaware of her child's visual capabilities, preferences, and visual field, and may not be aware when her child is looking at something.

1. Explain children's visual capabilities, preferences, and visual fields at this age as outlined in the general guidelines. Screen the child's visual responses to various objects at various distances, and describe his individual preferences and responses.
2. Assist the parent with positioning mobiles, stabiles, and toys within her child's visual field in his crib and play areas:
   a. Describe the visual qualities of each stimuli.
   b. Provide a concrete guide for placing mobiles or other dangling toys, such as one or two handspreads from her child's chest.
   c. If crib rail pads are used, explain how they obstruct his line of vision and help attach interesting visual stimuli, if needed.
   d. Assist the parent with conducive room lighting, as needed.
3. Suggest wearing bright sweaters, necklaces, or scarfs.
4. Orient the parent to her child's visual field when he is sitting in her lap (cradled or facing out) and in his infant seat.
5. If the child and/or parent avoid face-to-face positions during feeding, construct a donut from cardboard which can be slipped over the end of his bottle (if bottle fed) to provide an interesting focal point for the child during feeding; paint the donut with a checkerboard pattern.
6. The parent may be able to discern when her child is looking at something by listening for his cessation of sucking during feeding and body quieting. NOTE: After one or two months, the child may provide additional excitement and attending cues, such as panting, vocalizing, or moving his arms and legs. At three months, he may begin to look and suck at the same time. Advise the parent accordingly.
7. Describe her child' facial expressions when he looks at things, e.g., eyes widening, squinting, etc.

PHYSICALLY DISABLED PARENT

With decreased coordination or grasp; may be unable to hold a colorful toy if controlled vision stimulation activities have been prescribed.

1. A *port-a-play gym** can be positioned over the child during prone play on the floor, or while he is in a semi-reclined infant seat. Toys can be suspended within the child's visual field.
2. Assist the parent in attaching mobiles and other visual stimuli to her child's sleep and play areas.

3. Some toys may be easier for the parent to hold than others, e.g., toys with larger handles or lightweight plastic toys.
4. The parent can wear colorful clothes and necklaces to attract her child's visual attention.

4.02 Child: MOVES ARMS SYMMETRICALLY (0-2 mo.)
Parent: Recognizes child's arm movements as a positive response to stimuli; implements special positioning if prescribed

GENERAL GUIDELINES

The child moves both arms at his sides in random smooth cycling patterns, especially when he sees a person or interesting visual stimuli. His whole body often moves when he moves his arms, his legs kick, and his head may turn. A premature infant may display a more jerky movement pattern; this usually "smooths out" with additional maturation time.

If the child's arms do not move symmetrically, side-lying positioning may be prescribed to encourage movement of the lesser-used arm. Wrist bands with bells placed on the child's asymmetrical arm may also encourage him to move it more. Refer to 3.12 (Extensor thrust inhibited) for activities which relate to helping parents position their child in side-lying, if applicable.

MENTALLY RETARDED PARENT

May not recognize her child's arm movements as a sign of excitement, or if the child has asymmetries, she may not understand why special positioning has been recommended.

1. Interpret for the parent the meaning of her child's waving arm movements when he sees her or interesting objects, e.g. "When he waves his arms and legs when he looks at you, he's telling us he likes to see you or likes looking at the toy you're showing him."
2. Let the parent present one or two toys to her child. Ask her if she can tell which toy he likes best by watching his arms and legs.
3. If special positioning has been recommended for the child, point out which arm is not moving as much. Explain that the recommended position will help him learn to move that arm more.
4. If a wrist band with bells has been recommended to encourage the child to move one arm more symmetrically:
   a. Point out a concrete marker on the child's arm to help the parent remember which arm to put the wrist band on, e.g., a birthmark, a freckle, or make a freckle with a non-toxic marker.
   b. Demonstrate testing the wrist band for safety and proper fit.
   c. Advise the parent not to let her child sleep with the wrist band.

---

*See Glossary.

BLIND PARENT

May be unaware of her child's arm movements as a response to visual stimuli.

1. Describe the child's arm movements, explaining that he often moves them when he is excited because he sees his parent or an interesting toy:
   a. Attach bells of different tones to each of the child's wrists so the parent can hear her child's excitement as you present and describe various stimuli.
   b. The parent can listen to her child's arms and legs move in excitement without bells when they hit the crib mattress.
   c. Describe which of her child's toys seem to make him most excited.
   d. Help the parent position toys and mobiles within the child's line of vision. Refer to 4.01 (Regards colorful toys momentarily).

4.03 Child: REGARDS COLORFUL OBJECT FOR A FEW SECONDS (½-2½ mo.)
  Parent: Provides colorful toys or objects for child to look at

GENERAL GUIDELINES

The child's visual capabilities and preferences expand greatly during his first three months. He will look at bright colorful objects for at least four or five seconds and by one month he may wave his arms, kick his legs, pant, or vocalize in response to visual stimuli. He also begins to make eye-to-eye contact with others and watch an adult smile.

When the child is around two months of age, he begins to show a preference toward looking at people rather than objects, if given a choice. Adult faces and bodies are complex, constantly moving and provide the child multisensory stimulation. By the time the child reaches his third month, he looks at things all around his room and sometimes seems to look or stare indefinitely at his surroundings.

Parents can encourage their child's visual attention by providing him with a variety of interesting things to look at from various positions, and by offering him an abundance of face-to-face contact. Refer to the general guidelines and activities for 4.01 (Regards colorful object momentarily) for specific recommended visual experiences, adjusting for the child's increasing visual field. Refer to 5.02 (Regards face) for activities relating to face-to-face contact.

4.04 Child: FOLLOWS WITH EYES MOVING PERSON WHILE IN SUPINE (½-1½ mo.)
  Parent: Provides opportunities for child to watch people during daily activities

GENERAL GUIDELINES

The child will stare at, or follow with his eyes, the contour and movement of a person from a few feet away.

Parents can talk to their child while moving toward and away from him, and wear bright colored clothing to help attract his attention. Parents should provide ample opportunities for their child to watch people around him during his awake periods.

MENTALLY RETARDED PARENT

May leave her child in his crib or in one position for long periods of time.

1. Discuss with the parent how boring it would be if we always had to stay in bed. Relate that, even at this age, her child gets bored quickly and wants to watch what other people are doing when he is awake.
2. Help the parent fix up safe areas in different rooms of the house for her child to be able to watch people when he is awake. Point out her child's eye movements when he follows people, commenting how he likes to look at what's going on around him.
3. Ask the parent to name safe places where her child could be to watch her when she washes dishes, cooks dinner, watches T.V., etc.
4. Help the parent think of short phrases she can say to her child when she walks by him, such as "Hi there!" or "How are you doing?"

BLIND PARENT

May be unaware of her child's visual tracking abilities.

1. Explain that young children are especially attracted to the contours and movement of people walking by them; if she wears red or yellow sweaters or scarfs, her child may be even more interested in watching her and her movements.
2. Help orient the parent to suitable places around the home and positions for her child which provide him a good view of people and daily activities during waking hours.

4.05 Child: STARES AND GAZES (1-2 mo.)
  Parent: Provides a visually stimulating environment for child

GENERAL GUIDELINES

The child displays a vague indirect regard and expression for much of his waking hours. He periodically interrupts his passive staring to intently look at interesting people and objects. When people interact with him, his active attention can be maintained for longer periods.

Refer to guidelines and activities for 4.01 (Regards colorful object momentarily) and 4.03 (Regards colorful object for a few seconds) to help parents provide a visually stimulating environment.

4.06 Child: FOLLOWS WITH EYES TO MIDLINE (1-3 mo.)
Parent: Engages child in tracking activities which facilitate following an object with eyes to midline if prescribed

GENERAL GUIDELINES

The child is able to follow a slowly moving object from the side he is facing, when he is lying on his back, to his midline. The child's head usually moves concurrently with his eye movement.

This skill may be tested to evaluate the child's visual functioning and stage of visual-motor coordination. Children develop tracking skills through their daily experiences in interacting with others and watching visual stimuli in their environment. Specific tracking activities are thus not necessary unless the child displays visual attending or tracking difficulties.

If tracking activities have been prescribed, the following guidelines should be kept in mind:
1. The child should be positioned so his head and body are stable. He can be positioned in supine, in the parent's lap, or well supported in a reclined infant seat.
2. The objects for tracking can be a person's face or a bright toy at least the size of a fist.
3. The object should be presented approximately eight to twelve inches from the child's eyes.
4. The object should be moved slowly at the child's pace, after attracting his attention to the object. If the child "loses" the object, bring it back to his line of vision and repeat.
5. Tracking activities can be hard work for a young child; they should not last more than a minute or two.
6. Toys which make sound may help attract and maintain the child's attention.

The following parent training activities assume specific tracking activities have been prescribed.

MENTALLY RETARDED PARENT

May have difficulty judging appropriate distances and pacing for tracking activities with her child.

1. Help the parent understand the purpose of tracking activities for her child:
   a. Present an object to the parent and tell her to follow it with her eyes. Comment how her eye muscles work together to help her follow the object.
   b. Explain that her child needs extra help she he can follow objects with his eyes and you will be showing her ways to help him use his eyes better.
2. Demonstrate for the parent how to encourage her child to track an object:
   a. Show the parent how to hold the object at the appropriate distance from her child's eyes; use your handspread from the child's chest as a concrete guide when initially positioning the toy. Since an adult handspread is approximately seven inches, explain to hold the toy "a little higher than your hand."
   b. Show the parent how to attract her child's attention by gently shaking the toy and calling his name. Point out her child's eye contact with the object as it occurs, e.g., "See how he is looking at the rattle; now I can slowly move it."
   c. Emphasize how we need to move the toy slowly, making sure her child's eyes are following it while we move the toy.
   d. Demonstrate bringing the toy back to where her child's eyes are looking if he stops tracking the toy.
   e. Illustrate tracking only two times on each side of the child and then stopping. Explain we need to stop because this is hard work for children at this age and they need to rest.
3. Let the parent practice tracking an object with you and then with her child:
   a. If the parent has difficulty pacing her movements with her child's eye movements, verbally prompt her to go slowly and to watch her child's eyes, or try having the parent tap her foot to help keep an even slow pace.
   b. If the parent has difficulty judging the correct distance to hold objects from her child, review using a handspread from her child's chest as a concrete guideline.
   c. Explain that if her child blinks, the object may be too close to his eyes; if his eyes do not follow it, the toy may be too far away.
   d. Remind the parent, if necessary, to stop the tracking activity after doing this two times to each side, and ask her if she remembers why.
4. Demonstrate, and let the parent practice, encouraging her child to track an adult face following the same guidelines in Activity No. 2. If the parent does not spontaneously vocalize during the activity, suggest a few short phrases to say. Explain that since her child loves to hear her voice so much, talking to him encourages him to look at her.
5. Name specific times for the parent to implement tracking activities with her child:
   a. Associate these times with daily activities, such as after feeding or bath time.
   b. Name times not to try these activities, e.g., when her child is crying, sleepy, or sick.
6. Ask the parent to find two toys about the size of her fist that her child seems to like to look at for tracking activities.

DEAF PARENT

May be unaware that sound toys or her voice helps her child track an object.

1. Explain to the parent that sounds can help attract her child to look at and watch objects move:
   a. Demonstrate the tracking process with and without the use of a sound toy (rattle, jingle bells).
   b. Identify suitable sound toys for the parent to use during tracking.
   c. Clearly demonstrate how often to activate the sound to prevent over-stimulation, e.g., first shake the rattle three times to attract her child's attention, then move the rattle without shaking it, and then shake it three more times at midline or when her child's eyes lose track of the toy.

2. Explain that people's voices help attract her child to look at and follow their faces:
   a. Demonstrate encouraging the child to track your face as you vocalize.
   b. Encourage the parent to use whatever speech she may have, or if non-verbal, suggest humming or making kissing sounds.

BLIND PARENT

May have difficulty assuring objects are presented within her child's visual field and moved in pace with his eye movements during tracking activities.

1. Clearly describe this tracking skill to the parent as outlined under the general guidelines.
2. Assist the parent in identifying her child's best distance to present objects for tracking activities. Help orient her to the appropriate distance using a concrete physical marker (e.g., a little more than a handspread from her child's chin or upper chest).
3. Have the parent position her child supine on her lap, with the child's head resting near her knees so he can face her. Use sound-making toys at first to help the parent monitor and get the "feel" of tracking activities:
   a. As the parent moves a toy or her face to encourage her child's tracking, she can monitor his tracking by feeling his head move against her knees.
   b. Verbally prompt or cue the parent regarding the tracking distance, speed, and when to stop, as needed. Describe her child's tracking responses.
   c. As the parent becomes proficient with tracking activities for her child, she can be encouraged to carry these out independently.
   d. The parent may need a reminder to carry out tracking activities from her child's right to left and left to right sides.
   e. Explain to the parent that her child is not expected to follow the object past his midline.
4. If necessary, encourage the parent to smile, nod, and talk while she is carrying out the tracking activity, explaining that her child is more likely to track with this type of encouragement.
5. Help the parent select visually attracting toys which encourage her child to track. Describe the toys to which her child seems especially attracted.
6. Use a *port-a-play gym** to help the parent insure a suitable tracking distance. Orient the parent to various positions for her child in relation to the gym, and distance of the dangling toy from the bar. Make tactual markings on the bar which indicate her child's visual tracking field.

7. Use the parent's own body parts as reference points for tracking activities with her child, e.g., "Move the toy horizontally from your left shoulder to your chin."

PHYSICALLY DISABLED PARENT

With decreased coordination or limited grasp; may have difficulty moving objects smoothly across her child's visual field.

1. Refer to 4.01 (Regards colorful object momentarily).
2. The parent may be able to slide toys slowly across a port-a-play gym to encourage her child's tracking.
3. A plastic toy with a handle can be slipped over the parent's hand. The parent can slowly move her arm across her child's field of vision.
4. The parent could use her face as an excellent stimulus for tracking.

4.07 Child: BRINGS HANDS TO MIDLINE IN SUPINE (1-3½ mo.)
Parent: Encourages child to bring hands to midline; facilitates through positioning when necessary

GENERAL GUIDELINES

The child is able to move his arms against gravity while lying in supine to bring them to his chest. His random arm movements help him to learn the needed shoulder control to bring his hands to midline and prepare him for reaching. The child may begin to reach up and swipe at objects held at midline by three months of age.

Parents can encourage their child to bring his hands to midline by gently clapping his hands together, encouraging and helping him to pat her face in a game-like way, helping him pat his bottle, and letting him wear wrist bands with bells.

If a child's muscle tone interferes with his ability to bring his hands to midline, side-lying and supine cradling positions can facilitate this skill. Refer to 3.12 (Extensor thrust inhibited) and 3.14 (Assumes withdrawal position) for parent training activities involving positioning the child in side-lying or supine cradling.

---

*See Glossary.

4.07

MENTALLY RETARDED PARENT

May place her child in positions which prevent him from bringing his hands to midline.

1. Use a rag doll lying in supine to demonstrate and contrast to the parent how her child's arm positions are changing as he gets older, i.e., during the first few weeks, he kept his arms to his sides; now he is bringing them forward to his chest.
2. Explain in meaningful terms why it is good for her child to bring his hands to midline:
   a. Relate that it helps her child's shoulder muscles get stronger when he brings his hands to his chest.
   b. Ask the parent to try bringing her hands to her chest and feel how her shoulder muscles work to do this.
   c. Relate how bringing his hands to his chest also helps get his muscles ready for reaching for things.
3. Demonstrate, and let the parent practice, encouraging her child to bring his hands to his chest by gently putting his hands on her cheeks and then gently playing a "Pat-A-Cake" game. Simplify the "Pat-A-Cake" rhyme to two short phrases. Emphasize using slow and gentle movements.
4. Demonstrate, and let the parent practice, holding and carrying her child in a cradled position:
   a. Stress to always check to make sure both of her child's arms are brought forward.
   b. Take Polaroid pictures, one depicting proper holding with the child's arms forward, and one demonstrating improper holding with one of the child's arms left behind toward the parent's back. Mark an X over the picture of poor positioning.
5. Help the parent make and adjust a mobile or crib gym to encourage her child's reaching:
   a. Demonstrate proper positioning and distance from the child.
   b. Explain, at this age, he may only wave his arms toward hanging objects; he is not ready for actually grabbing and holding him.
6. Demonstrate how placing the child in side-lying helps him keep his arms forward to reach for a toy. Refer to 3.12 (Extensor thrust inhibited) to help the parent position her child in side-lying, if needed.
7. Provide anticipatory guidance to the parent that her child cannot obtain toys to play with at this age by himself; she needs to put his toys in his hand for him.

BLIND PARENT

May be unaware of her child's midline hand placement as it relates to his later visually directed reach.

1. Describe the child's new or emerging abilities to bring his hands to his chest:
   a. Contrast how before he used to keep his hands at his side, but in that position he could not see them; when he brings them toward his chest, they are more accessible to look at.
   b. Explain that "looking" at his hands helps her child learn they are a part of his body and he can do things with them. Soon he will look at an object and then his empty hand and figure out he can reach for it. When he reaches for things now it may not be purposeful, but he can see his hands well in this position which helps him learn a more controlled and purposeful reach in the near future.
2. Let the parent become tactually familiar with the proper forward placement of her child's arms when she is carrying him, holding him, placing him in side-lying, and putting him in his infant seat.
3. The parent can play hand-at-midline games with her child through verbal descriptions of midline games and physical guidance, if needed.

4.08 Child: ACTIVATES ARMS ON SIGHT OF TOY (1-3 mo.)
Parent: Presents toy which encourages child to activate arms on sight; facilitates arm movement as necessary

GENERAL GUIDELINES

The child loves looking at visual stimuli. He moves his arms randomly and symmetrically when a toy or person appears as his way to show interest and excitement.

If the child has increased or decreased muscle tone, however, he may not move his arms in a smooth random fashion. This can interfere with later manipulative play and make it more difficult for parents to "read" his excitement cues. Special positioning, such as positioning the child in an infant seat or on the parent's lap with his hips flexed and arms brought forward and close to his body, may be prescribed by a therapist to help facilitate active arm movements.

Refer to 4.02 (Moves arms symmetrically) for parent activities relating to encouraging their child to activate his arms in response to people and objects. The following activities assume additional positioning activities have been prescribed by a therapist to facilitate the child's active arm movements.

MENTALLY RETARDED PARENT

May have difficulty remembering prescribed positioning techniques.

1. Explain and demonstrate for the parent the rationale for using special handling techniques with her child in meaningful terms:
   a. Introduce the positions with a statement, such as "These positions help Bobby learn to move his arms so he can learn to play with toys. When he is lying on his back his arm muscles cannot work as well."
   b. Have the parent present toys to her child while he is lying supine and then when he is in a recommended position. Contrast how special positioning encourages her child to move his arms.
2. Demonstrate, and let the parent practice, placing her child in an infant seat and presenting attractive objects to him:

a. If special seat inserts have been recommended, color code the inserts with stickers to match proper placement on the seat.
b. Help the parent identify several safe places in the home to let her child sit in his seat.
c. Ask the parent to select two or three favorite objects to show her child while he is sitting in his seat.
d. Stress showing the object to him nearby for a count of three before giving him one. Explain that this gives him time to move his arms. Review that he waves his arms to tell us he likes looking at the toy.
3. Demonstrate, and let the parent practice, holding her child in supine cradling. Provide the parent physical prompting, as needed:
   a. Take a Polaroid picture of the parent holding her child properly.
   b. Suggest special facial expressions and phrases to say with her child.
   c. Interpret for the parent her child's arm movements as his way of telling her he likes what she's saying.

BLIND PARENT

May need physical guidance to help orient her to prescribed positions which facilitate her child's active arm movements.

1. Let the parent become tactually familiar with her child in prescribed positions. Specifically point out the relationship and positioning of her child's trunk, arms, and head in relation to specific parts of the child's infant seat, and in relation to the parent's arms and chest when she is holding him. Help the parent present toys within her child's visual field, as needed.
2. Put wrist band bells on the child's wrists. The parent can listen to his increased active arm movements in prescribed positions as compared to a supine position.

4.09 Child: BLINKS AT SUDDEN VISUAL STIMULUS (2-3 mo.)
Parent: Recognizes that the child blinks at sudden visual stimuli

GENERAL GUIDELINES

The child blinks his eyes when a visual stimulus is too bright or is presented too closely or suddenly to the child. This item is for evaluation purposes to access the child's automatic visual responses. The child should not purposely be taught to blink.

Parents can use their child's blink response as a cue that visual or auditory stimuli are too harsh or too close.

MENTALLY RETARDED PARENT

May not interpret her child's blinking as cue that visual or sound stimuli are too close or harsh.

1. Do not overtly test the child's blink response in front of the parent unless you are certain that she understands that bringing an object to her child's face suddenly was for evaluation purposes only. The parent may think she should do this at home with her child.

2. Demonstrate blinking as a reaction to something too close, too sudden, or too loud by asking the parent to clap loudly in front of your face and automatically blinking. Explain that her child also blinks to let us know when something is too close, loud, or sudden.
3. Anticipatory Guidance: The parent may approach her child's face too quickly and too closely during interactions. She may also present toys too quickly and closely to his face. When these situations occur, point out her child's blinking response and interpret that this means he is telling us to move slower or that the toy or our face is too close to him.

BLIND PARENT

May be unaware of her child's blinking responses.

1. Explain to the parent that her child's blink response is an automatic protective response:
   a. "Just as you automatically pull back your hand if you touch something hot, your child automatically shuts his eyes quickly and briefly if a light is too bright, or if something moves toward his face too quickly or too close to his eyes."
   b. The parent can then know to approach her child's face slowly during interactions and may want to lead her hand approaches toward her child's face with the back of her hand.

4.10 Child: FOLLOWS WITH EYES PAST MIDLINE (2-3 mo.)
Parent: Engages child in tracking activities which encourage him to follow an object with eyes past midline if recommended

GENERAL GUIDELINES

The child's eyes follow a slowly moving visual stimulus horizontally from the side he is facing past his midline, while lying on his back; head movement often accompanies his eye movements. The child may visually "lose" the object shortly after he has followed it past his midline.

This behavior may be tested to evaluate the child's visual functioning and stage of eye-coordination. Formal tracking activities are not necessary unless recommended. If recommended, refer to tracking guidelines and activities for 4.06 (Follows with eyes to midline), adapting to track past midline.

4.11 Child: FOLLOWS WITH EYES DOWNWARD (2-3 mo.)
Parent: Engages child in tracking activities which encourages him to follow an object downward if recommended

GENERAL GUIDELINES

The child follows the movement of an object in a downward direction toward his chest. Head movement may

4.11

accompany his eye movement; however, his eye movements may *not* be smooth or consistent yet.

Positioning the child in an infant seat, talking to him while changing his diaper, and gently raising his legs up and tapping his feet together encourage him to look downward.

Formal tracking activities do not need to be implemented to teach the child to follow objects downward unless recommended. If tracking activities have been recommended, refer to 4.06 (Follows with eyes to midline) for general tracking guidelines and parent training activities.

4.12 Child: INDWELLING THUMB NO LONGER PRESENT (2-3 mo.)
Parent: When indicated, carries out activities and positioning techniques which discourage child's indwelling thumb

GENERAL GUIDELINES

During the first two or three months, the child's thumb remains close to his palm. As his nervous system matures through normal movement experiences, his thumb moves out of this "fixed" position which prepares him for later functional oppositional thumb-finger movements.

A prolonged indwelling thumb may be indicative of neurological dysfunction. "Hand opening" can be facilitated by gently stroking the back of the child's hand and by placing the child in a prone position. The child's hands should not be physically manipulated or pulled open.

Refer to 3.03 (Lifts head in prone) for parent activities to position their child in prone.

MENTALLY RETARDED PARENT

May be rough or manipulative with her child's hands.

1. If the child holds his hands tightly fisted with an indwelling thumb:
   a. Tell the parent not to try and open her child's hands by pulling his fingers. Explain that this can hurt his finger muscles.
   b. Relate that her child is not keeping his hands closed on purpose; that's just the way his muscles are working.
   c. Demonstrate, and let the parent practice, gently stroking the back of her child's hand with a finger and then a rattle, and letting him hold it as his hand opens.
2. If prone positioning is indicated to facilitate the child's hand opening, explain that being on his tummy helps him relax and open his hands. In addition to 3.03 (Lifts head in prone) activities, help the parent think of various areas to place her child in prone where he can feel different textures with his hands, such as on a rug, carpet, towel, or blanket.

4.13 Child: GRASPS TOY ACTIVELY (2-4 mo.)
Parent: Encourages child to actively grasp safe and appropriately-sized objects

GENERAL GUIDELINES

During the first month, the child may grasp an object reflexively, but usually quickly drops it. Around two or three months, although his grasp is still automatic, it becomes more voluntary and he holds the object actively for a few moments. His grasp is still quite strong in comparison to his later more voluntary grasp.

Parents encourage their child's grasping by placing their own finger or small toys (rattles, teethers, etc.) in their child's hands.

MENTALLY RETARDED PARENT

May use inappropriately-sized and shaped toys to encourage her child to grasp, and may expect developmentally higher grasping skills.

1. Help the parent choose toys which are an appropriate size and safe for her child to hold:
   a. Explain that the size of the toy she gives her child to hold needs to be small since his hand is small.
   b. Review appropriate grasping toys by sorting through a box of various objects.
   c. Describe the properties, such as size, safety, or texture, which make them suitable or unsuitable during the sorting process.
   d. Ask the parent to show you some of her child's toys which are good to let him hold.
2. Explain to the parent that her child is *not* ready to hand the toy back to her or pick it up himself; she must either place the toy in or very near his hand for him to be able to hold it. Demonstrate each of these concepts with the child and then let the parent practice giving her child toys.
3. Interpret for the parent her child's involuntary release when you see him drop a toy:
   a. Explain that when her child drops an object, it does not always mean he doesn't want to hold it anymore; he lets go of things by accident.
   b. Relate that since her child may let go of things that he still wants to hold she can go ahead and give it back to him.
4. Praise the parent when you see her give her child things to hold, e.g., "You're really helping him learn to hold things!" or "Look how he smiled when you gave him that toy!"

DEAF PARENT

May be unaware of small toys which make sounds.

1. Show the parent which of her child's "graspable" toys make sounds. Demonstrate which toys make sounds when they are squeezed and which toys make sounds when they are shaken. Explain that her child may shake or wave all toys at this age regardless of their sound because that's the way he plays with toys at this age.

BLIND PARENT

May not see when her child has dropped his toy.

1. The parent can use small sound toys to recognize when her child has dropped a toy he was holding. Explain that if her child's toy drops out of sight or touch, he will need help finding and holding it again.
2. Relate how her child brings the toy in front of his face to see what he is holding; this helps him realize his hands are part of himself and he begins to associate what he sees with what he feels.

4.14 Child: LOOKS FROM ONE OBJECT TO ANOTHER (2½-3½ mo.)
Parent: Encourages child to look from one object to another

GENERAL GUIDELINES

The child shifts his attention from one visual target to another when they are presented within his visual field, approximately eight inches apart. His eye movements are smooth and controlled.

The following activities may be recommended if the child is having difficulty shifting his gaze between two objects:

1. Present and attract the child's attention to one attractive object and then introduce a second object about eight inches away.
2. Present toys which have different sounds, such as a rattle and a squeak toy, to the child; activate them alternately.
3. Put a puppet on each hand and alternately shake each one.
4. Slowly move the first object next to the second one so the child tracks the first toy to find the second. The first toy can then be moved to its original position and squeaked.

Parents can play these games while their child is sitting on their lap, in a semi-reclined infant seat, or lying on his back after a diaper change.

MENTALLY RETARDED PARENT

May have difficulty judging appropriate distances to present objects, and may over- or under-stimulate her child with toys.

1. Demonstrate, and let the parent practice, holding two objects within her child's visual field:
   a. If the parent has difficulty positioning the toys at appropriate distances between each other, use a *port-a-play gym** with two dangling toys secured at correct distances, or use the width of the child's shoulders as a reference point between objects.
   b. If the parent has difficulty determining the correct distance from her child to hold the objects, use the distance from her fingertips on her child's chest to her elbow as a concrete guide.
   c. Stress the importance of letting her child hold one of the toys after he has looked at them.

---

*See Glossary.

2. If squeak toys or rattles are used to attract the child's attention, stress the importance of alternating the sounds slowly at the child's pace:
   a. Demonstrate only shaking or squeaking one toy at a time, two times.
   b. Explain and demonstrate waiting for a count of three before activating the second toy.
   c. Explain that if we squeak both toys at the same time or squeak them too much, her child will get confused because he won't know at which toy to look.
3. Ask the parent to show you two of her child's toys at which she thinks he would like to look:
   a. Help her think of a specific time during the day to encourage her child to look at them.
   b. Remind the parent not to make her child "play this game."
   c. Explain that if he looks the other way, fusses, or twists his body, she should stop the game and try it again another time.

DEAF PARENT

May be unaware that alternating sounds can help her child alternate his glances between objects.

1. If not previously explained, relate how sounds from toys help attract her child's attention, and mark appropriate sound toys as described in 4.01 (Regards colorful object momentarily).
2. Explain and demonstrate that when two sound toys are presented, it encourages her child to shift his eyes to look at each object because he is looking for the sound. Relate and demonstrate the following guidelines:
   a. Use sound toys which have different sounds (most rattle toys are plastic and most squeak toys are rubber to help the parent differentiate).
   b. Do not make the sound with the toy the child is looking at; after he has looked at the first toy a few seconds, she can make a sound twice with the second toy and wait to see if his eyes shift; after they have shifted to look at the second toy for a few seconds, she can make a sound with the first toy two times.
   c. Do not make sounds with both toys at the same time; this can confuse him because he doesn't know for which sound to look.

BLIND PARENT

May be unaware of her child's visual field for presenting two objects.

1. Explain to the parent her child's emerging ability to shift his gaze between objects if they are not more than eight inches apart from each other:
   a. Assess and describe to the parent her child's ability to shift his gaze between two objects.
   b. Relate approximately how many inches apart the objects are from each other and the distance from her child's face for presentation.
   c. Describe any extra encouragement her child needs to switch his gaze, e.g., shaking or squeaking the toy he is

4.0 FINE MOTOR

4.14

not looking at, and moving it toward the toy he is looking at.
2. Help the parent check mobiles to assure that the dangling objects are within her child's visual field and that the dangling objects' pictures, faces, or most attracting features are facing the child when he looks at them:
   a. Describe the child's ability to shift this attention between objects on the mobile.
   b. If there are too many dangling objects for the child, suggest removing a few according to the child's needs.
3. When the parent presents two objects to her child, she can use each of his shoulders as a reference point for positioning the objects within her child's visual field to insure an appropriate distance between them.
4. The parent can present two objects to her child while he is cradled supine facing her with this back against her thighs (the parent can sit on a couch with her feet on a footrest or table). In this position, the parent may be able to monitor her child's subtle head movements when looking between objects, and feel his arm movements to reach for the toys.
5. Help the parent select distinct attractive visual targets, as needed, describing each of their visual qualities. Relate how sound toys attract her child's visual attention.

4.15 Child: KEEPS HANDS OPEN FIFTY PERCENT OF THE TIME (2½-3½ mo.)
Parent: Positions child in prone or side-lying to facilitate hand opening if indicated

GENERAL GUIDELINES

During the first two months, the child's hands remain tightly fisted. Through normal movement, holding, reaching experiences, and maturation of the nervous system, the child's hands gradually open up. They remain open in a resting position approximately half of the time at this age.

Prolonged "fisting" is usually an indicator of muscle tone abnormalities. Prone and side-lying positions help facilitate the child's hands to open. The child's hands should never be pried open.

Refer to 3.03 (Lifts head in prone) and 3.12 (Extensor thrust inhibited) for activities to train parents to position their child in prone or side-lying, if indicated.

4.16 Child: REACHES TOWARD TOY WITHOUT GRASPING (2½-4½ mo.)
Parent: Encourages child to reach for toy

GENERAL GUIDELINES

The child's emerging eye-hand coordination and purposeful motor control are demonstrated when he reaches toward nearby objects. He may look from the object to his hand and then look at the object again to initiate his visually directed reach. He usually misses his target, however, and may reach below, beyond, or in front of the object. Initially, he may reach with one arm, swiping at objects with a closed fist. He soon begins to reach with his hands open.

The child's ability to discriminate depths and distances tell him when he has a chance of reaching something. He will only reach for objects which he knows he has a chance to obtain. For example, the child may reach for a dangling toy one foot away, but will not reach for it if the toy is four feet away.

Parents encourage their child's reaching by placing attractive toys and objects within the child's reaching range. One or two dangling toys or safe objects strung across the child's crib and play areas give him opportunities to practice. In addition, toys which rock and make reinforcing visual effects and sounds, such as roly-poly toys, encourage him to reach and bat at them. If the child does not reach toward an object, the parent can gently touch her child's hand with it and move it directly above his hand to help remind him of his eye-hand directed behaviors.

MENTALLY RETARDED PARENT

May have difficulty judging appropriate distances to place toys from her child to encourage his reaching.

1. Demonstrate to the parent the appropriate distance to place or present a toy so it is within reach of her child. Use the length of the child's arm as a concrete guide. Let the parent practice presenting toys at this distance.
2. Explain to the parent that her child may not be able to actually get the toy all by himself yet. Relate how important it is to let him touch or "bat" at it, and help him hold it after he's worked so hard to reach for it. Stress, if she holds the toy out of reach, her child will think she is teasing him and will stop wanting to reach for things.
3. Help the parent select safe interesting toys or household objects to string across her child's crib and play area.
4. Demonstrate, and let the parent practice, attracting her child's attention to a toy within his reach by calling his name, tapping his hand, and shaking or squeaking a toy. Comment that, if he is not looking at the toy, he will not reach for it.

DEAF PARENT

May be unaware of the reinforcing sounds objects make when her child swipes at them.

1. Point out toys and objects which produce sounds when her child swipes at them in contrast to having to squeeze or shake them to make a sound. For example, roly-poly toys, keys on a chain, measuring spoons on a ring and bells on a string produce reinforcing sounds to the child when he swipes or hits them.

BLIND PARENT

May be unaware of her child's visually-directed reaching abilities.

1. Describe and explain to the parent her child's visually directed reach. Compare and contrast that, just as she uses auditory and tactual cues when she reaches for an object, her child uses visual cues to reach for something. Include the following points:
   a. If her child sees that an object is much further than his reach, he probably won't bother reaching for it.

b. Her child is beginning to link what his eyes see with what his hands feel, and with what his arms can do to reach.
c. Children's initial reaching patterns are inaccurate until they have more practice with eye and hand coordination.

2. Explain to the parent that, since her child cannot see his hand if it is at his side, he may not reach for objects; at this age, he may need to see his hand to remember its reaching function. Relate that she can help him by gently bringing his arm forward so he can see it, or tap his hand with the toy, so he can feel it.
3. Help orient the parent to appropriate distances for suspending toys on crib gyms or a *port-a-play gym** to encourage her child's reaching. Use the child's chest and semi-flexed arm length as a concrete guide for presenting toys. The parent can monitor her child's batting and reaching movements if the toys make sounds when moved.
4. Describe the reinforcing visual effects her child produces and enjoys when he swipes or bats at mobiles or roly-poly toys.

PHYSICALLY DISABLED PARENT

With limited grasp or hand control; may have difficulty presenting toys to her child which encourage his reach.

1. The parent can encourage her child to reach for her face, hair, dangling necklace, or neck scarf.
2. The parent can present toys to her child in a fun way by holding them with her mouth.
3. The parent could slide her arm through colorful pop-bead rings or under colorful clothes to dangle in front of her child.
4. Mobiles and toys suspended on a *port-a-play gym** will encourage her child to reach, while the parent provides the important verbal praise and encouragement.

4.17 Child: FOLLOWS WITH EYES 180 DEGREES (3-5 mo.)
  Parent: Engages child in tracking activities which encourage him to follow an object 180 degrees if recommended

GENERAL GUIDELINES

As the child's visual-motor coordination abilities mature, he is able to follow an object from the side he is facing in supine, past his midline in an arc to his other side. His eye movements are becoming smoother; however, there will still be some head movement during tracking.

If tracking activities have been recommended to improve the child's visual-motor coordination, refer to the general guidelines and parent training activities for 4.06 (Follows with eyes to midline), adapting demonstration to a 180° arc.

---

*See Glossary.

4.18 Child: FOLLOWS WITH EYES, MOVING OBJECT IN SUPPORTED SITTING (3-4½ mo.)
  Parent: Provides opportunities for child to follow moving objects in supported sitting

GENERAL GUIDELINES

As the child's visual acuity and coordination mature, he is able to follow moving objects from a few feet away when held in a sitting position or placed in an infant seat.

Parents can place their child in an infant seat or other supported semi-reclined sitting positions during their daily activities to provide him ample opportunities to watch activities around him. His infant seat can also be positioned near his mobile so he can watch its movement.

Refer to 4.04 (Follows with eyes moving person) for parent activities which are applicable to this skill.

4.19 Child: FOLLOWS WITH EYES UPWARD (3-4 mo)
  Parent: Engages child in tracking activities which facilitate following objects upward with eyes if recommended

GENERAL GUIDELINES

The child is able to track the movement of an object upward, above his direct line of vision. Initially his upward gaze is brief.

Typical daily activities provide the child experiences for following objects upward. Mobiles, positioning toys within the child's reach, letting the child sit in an infant seat to watch his environment, and providing face-to-face contact while talking, singing, and moving your head back and forth, each encourage the child to follow objects and people.

If specific tracking activities have been recommended to encourage the child to follow an object upward, it is important not to move objects too high above his line of vision. This may cause his neck to hyperextend in his effort to look at the object. Refer to 4.06 (Follows with eyes to midline) for general tracking guidelines and activities, adapting to include vertical upward tracking.

If a child has visual problems, he may display a preferential upward gaze. Activities which promote an upward gaze should be discouraged.

4.20 Child: GRASP REFLEX INHIBITED (3-4 mo.)
  Parent: Provides ample opportunities for child to grasp objects; places child in positions which help inhibit his grasp reflex if recommended

GENERAL GUIDELINES

The child is born with a grasp reflex. If a toy or finger is placed against his palm, he automatically responds by closing his fingers around the stimulus with a tight grasp. The child's

4.20

grasp reflex should begin to diminish around three or four months of age and emerge into a more voluntary grasp.

A prolonged grasp reflex may be indicative of a child's increased muscle tone. Positions which help the child relax, such as side-lying, supine cradling, or prone, help inhibit his grasp reflex and allow him to play more purposefully with toys. Refer to 3.03 (Lifts head in prone) and 3.12 (Extensor thrust inhibited) for parent training activities involving these positions, if recommended.

Parents can encourage their child to reach for and grab a variety of graspable and varied textured objects. Small soft pliable squeak toys, rattles, and teethers, are suitable for the child to hold and feel. At this age, he may actively hold the toy for about a minute before dropping it. The child should have grasping experiences with each hand. If the child's grasp reflex makes it difficult for him to release toys, parents can gently shake his arm or rub the back of his hand to help facilitate his release.

MENTALLY RETARDED PARENT

May select inappropriately-sized toys for her child to hold and expect him to hold them for longer than a minute.

1. Help the parent select safe graspable objects for her child to hold. Refer to 4.13 (Grasps toy actively).
2. Demonstrate presenting a toy near the child's hand and encouraging him to purposely reach and grab it:
   a. Explain that the parent does not always need to place the toy in her child's hands now that he is learning to reach.
   b. Emphasize that when her child drops a toy, she needs to help him take it again because he cannot pick it up by himself yet.
3. As the child's grasp reflex diminishes, explain to the parent that her child will not hold toys for very long. Relate that this is because he is learning that he can use his muscles to open and close his hands and so he practices doing this a lot; when he practices, he drops toys by mistake.
4. If the child has a prolonged grasp reflex, caution the parent not to pry his fingers open to make him let go of his toy:
   a. Demonstrate, and let the parent practice, gently shaking her child's arm or rubbing the back of his hand.
   b. Stress that her child is not holding the object tightly on purpose; his hand muscles just have not learned to let go of objects easily.

BLIND PARENT

May be unable to visually monitor her child's voluntary grasping abilities.

1. The parent can feel the effect of her child's diminishing reflexive grasp when he holds her finger with a more voluntary grasp.
2. Use small pliable squeak toys to let the parent hear her child's voluntary grasping and toy dropping as it occurs.
3. Emphasize to the parent the importance of showing her child a toy before giving it to him to hold.

4. If special positioning has been prescribed, let the parent feel the effect of the position on her child's grasp as she puts her finger in his hand.

4.21 Child: CLASPS HANDS (3½-5 mo.)
   Parent: Encourages and facilitates child bringing hands to midline and clasping if needed

GENERAL GUIDELINES

As the child spends more time with his hands in midline, he discovers he has two hands and begins mutual fingering and clasping. This helps prepare him for later transferring of objects from hand to hand and playing with toys at midline.

Parents can encourage their child's hand-clasping by holding him in cradled positions and by playing "hand-games" which call attention to his two hands. For example, gently rubbing or patting the child's hands together and "nibbling" on his fingers while bringing them into his visual field encourage him to notice and clasp his hands.

If the child's muscle tone interferes with his ability to bring his hands together in midline, side-lying may be recommended. Refer to 3.12 (Extensor thrust inhibited) for parent activities to position to child in side-lying.

MENTALLY RETARDED PARENT

May be too rough during hand play with her child.

1. Explain mutual hand clasping and fingering as a good learning experience to help her child learn to use his hands in play. Demonstrate how young children finger and clasp their hands and ask the parent if she's seen her child playing with his hands.
2. Demonstrate encouraging her child's hand play by gently holding and bringing his forearms forward, rather than holding his wrists.
3. Observe how the parent carries and holds her child and sits him in his infant seat. If one of the child's arms is tucked behind him, point this out and explain he cannot bring both hands together in this position. Demonstrate, and let the parent practice, each of these positions with her child's arms positioned forward.

4.22 Child: USES ULNAR-PALMAR GRASP (3½-4½ mo.)
   Parent: Provides objects and toys for child to hold which encourage his ulnar-palmar grasp

GENERAL GUIDELINES

The child holds small objects against his palm with his little and ring fingers. Initially, the child's grasp on a toy will be somewhat weak and brief. At this age, the child is still unable to recover a dropped toy, so parents need to give it back to him when he accidentally lets go.

Rattles with slender handles, empty pill bottles filled with beans (secured tightly and covered with attractive contact paper), thick pegs, and teething rings are suitably-sized to accommodate the child's ulnar-palmar grasp. Large squeak toys, round toys, and rattles with thick handles are too difficult for the child to grasp.

Refer to guidelines and activities for 4.13 (Grasps toy actively) for activities to help parents encourage their child's grasp.

4.23 Child: LOOKS WITH HEAD IN MIDLINE (4-5 mo.)
Parent: Presents visual stimuli to child with his head in midline

GENERAL GUIDELINES

The child is able to look at objects while his head is in a midline position. His earlier *asymmetric tonic neck reflex (ATNR)** influenced him to look at things when his head was turned toward the side. If the child still exhibits an ATNR, refer to 3.19 (Asymmetrical tonic neck reflex inhibited) for positioning to help the child look at objects in midline.

MENTALLY RETARDED PARENT

May not present visual stimuli at her child's midline.

1. Point out to the parent how her child's neck muscles are working to help keep his head looking straight ahead. Ask what would happen if her child only had things to look at on the side of his crib. Help adjust mobiles and pictures, as needed.
2. Demonstrate and encourage the parent to say short inflectional phrases to her child in a face-to-face position while his head is in midline. Comment how his favorite thing to look at is her, especially when she smiles and talks to him.

BLIND PARENT

May be unaware of child's new resting visual field.

1. Describe the child's emerging ability to look at things with his head at midline. Help adjust mobiles, pictures, and toys in the child's crib and play areas to accommodate his new head position and visual field.

4.24 Child: FOLLOWS WITH EYES WITHOUT HEAD MOVEMENT (4-6 mo.)
Parent: Recognizes child can look at things in his visual field without turning his head

GENERAL GUIDELINES

The child is learning to coordinate his eye movements in isolation of his head or other bodily movement. He can track a slowly moving object within his visual field horizontally, vertically, and in a circle with little or no head movement.

This skill is tested as an evaluation of the child's visual-motor functioning. As with previous tracking skills, the child must have adequate head and trunk support. This skill is not specifically taught. If the child's tracking skills are delayed, however, special tracking activities may be prescribed. Refer to 4.06 (Follows with eyes to midline) for parent training guidelines which relate to tracking, if applicable.

BLIND PARENT

May rely upon monitoring her child's head movement to help determine at what he is looking.

1. Advise the parent when you observe that her child can look at and follow objects that are within his visual field without moving his head:
   a. Have the parent hold her child in her lap facing outward with his head resting against her chest.
   b. Provide verbal monitoring to advise the parent when her child is looking at the toy as she presents and moves it.
2. Explain to the parent that her child will continue to turn his head to look for hidden sounds and things outside of his visual field.
3. The parent can present and slowly move a toy in front of her child's face to help determine his field of vision without needing to turn his head.
4. The parent can determine if her child is looking at a toy she is showing him by recognizing when he reaches for it.

4.25 Child: KEEPS HANDS OPEN MOST OF THE TIME (4-8 mo.)
Parent: Positions child in prone or side-lying to facilitate hand opening if indicated

GENERAL GUIDELINES

The child moves out of his earlier fisted hand positions and holds them in a relaxed open position most of the time. Open hands enable the child to explore and touch his environment more freely.

If the child's hands remain fisted, he may have muscle tone abnormalities. Prone and side-lying positions help relax and facilitate the child's hand opening. Refer to 3.03 (Lifts head in prone) and 3.12 (Extensor thrust inhibited) for activities to help parents position their child in prone and side-lying, if indicated.

4.26 Child: REACHES FOR OBJECT BILATERALLY (4-5 mo.)
Parent: Encourages child to reach with both arms

GENERAL GUIDELINES

The child reaches for an object by moving both arms together as a unit. The inhibition of his asymmetrical tonic reflex enables him to demonstrate a more accurate directed reach toward objects than his earlier general reaching movements. He reaches with both arms before he learns to use his arms independently of each other.

If the child's reaching is asymmetrical, special positioning and handling may be prescribed to encourage the child's non-preferred arm to reach. For example, offering the child a toy while he is in a side-lying position on his preferred side can

---

*See Glossary.

4.26

encourage him to reach with his non-preferred arm. Holding the child cradled in supine with his shoulders rounded and brought forward may also facilitate reaching for his bottle or toys with both arms.

Refer to 4.16 (Reaches toward toy without grasping) for parent training activities to encourage reaching. The following activities assume special handling has been prescribed to discourage the child's asymmetries during reaching.

MENTALLY RETARDED PARENT

May have difficulty understanding why special activities have been prescribed to encourage her child's bilateral reach.

1. Let the parent hold something out to you and demonstrate a bilateral reach. Encourage her child to reach for a toy and point out how he is not using one arm as much as the other one. Explain that, at his age, it is important for her child to reach with both arms so he can learn to use the muscles in both arms.
2. Demonstrate, and let the parent practice, only one positioning technique per session:
    a. If side-lying has been prescribed, help the parent remember which side to lie her child on by using a concrete marker as a reference point, e.g., a certain freckle, or his head toward a specific end of his crib facing the door.
    b. Review how far away to present toys in relation to the child's chest.
    c. Tell the parent never to pull her child's arms to encourage him to reach.
    d. Stress letting him have the toy after he has reached for it.

BLIND PARENT

May not be able to visually monitor her child's bliateral reach.

1. Place a wrist band with a bell on the child's non-preferred arm. Hang sound-making toys with objects on the child's *port-a-play gym** or mobile. The parent will be able to hear when her child reaches with his non-preferred arm and when he is successful at swiping the hanging object.
2. Review the concept of visually directed reach and the importance of presenting attractive toys within the child's visual field and reach. Refer to 4.16 (Reaches toward toy without grasping).
3. Orient the parent to suitable distances and locations to present toys, bottles, her own face, etc. to her child which encourage him to reach with his non-preferred arm.

---

*See Glossary.

4.27 Child: REACHES FOR TOY FOLLOWED BY MOMENTARY GRASP (4-5 mo.)
Parent: Presents toys which encourage child to reach and grasp.

GENERAL GUIDELINES

The child is able to grasp a toy he has reached for. His arms will not be completely extended and his reach may sometimes overshoot the object until his eye-hand coordination becomes more controlled with maturation and experiences.

Parents can present easily graspable objects that are at least the size of a small block, to encourage their child to reach and grasp. Rattles with small handles, soft sculptured toys, small squeaky toys, teething rings, and plastic keys on a chain are examples of easy to grasp and attractive toys.

MENTALLY RETARDED PARENT

May pull toys further away from her child after he reaches for them, or may expect him to keep holding a toy after he has grasped it.

1. As you demonstrate encouraging the child to reach for and grasp a toy, point out to the parent how her child is now learning to hold onto toys all by himself. Explain, however, that since his muscles are not very strong yet, he will not hold onto the toy for long. Count aloud with the parent to see how long her child can hold a toy.
2. Stress to the parent that, everytime her child reaches and grasps or tries to grasp a toy, she should give it to him so he can hold it:
    a. Explain that, if she does not give it to him or moves it out of his reach, he will feel teased and learn real fast that if he cannot have the toy after all that work, there is no reason to keep learning to reach for things.
    b. Relate how her child will not be able to learn how to feed himself or learn to use his hands very well if he does not want to reach for things.
3. If the parent appears to want to force her child to keep holding a toy so she does not have to keep retrieving them, show her how to suspend toys within her child's reach so he can easily reach, grasp, drop, and retrieve them.
4. Help the parent select toys which are attracting for her child to reach, suitable for grasping, and safe:
    a. Use pictures from magazines or toy catalogues.
    b. Collect toys or construct homemade ones from empty pill bottles, empty spools of thread, hair rollers, etc.
    c. Show the parent a few inappropriate toys and help her determine why they are not good for her child at this age.
5. Demonstrate the various positions the child can be encouraged to reach and grasp from, e.g., supported sitting, side-lying, supine, and held at adult's chest facing outward to reach for mirror image. Explain that her child may not be able to pick up his arms and reach for toys while he is on his tummy.

BLIND PARENT

May not be able to visually monitor her child's reach and grasp attempts and successes.

1. Describe the child's visually directed reach and grasping skills at this age. Explain that, at first, he may sometimes reach too far and miss grasping the object; he needs more experience coordinating his vision with his hands.
2. The parent can hold sound toys (bells, rattles, etc.) for her child to practice reaching and grasping. She will feel when he reaches and grasps the toy she is holding and be able to monitor how long he holds it by listening to the sounds of the toy.
3. Compare how just as toys with interesting textures and sounds encourage her child to reach for and grasp them; the toy's appearance also motivates him. Describe the visual qualities of several of her child's toys.
4. Point out particular sides or angles of toys which are most attracting to her child when she presents them to him. For example, there are some commercially available squeak toys which are not sculptured to give tactual cues; one side may be white, while the other side has an interesting face imprinted on it. The blank side is where the squeaker is, which could be used as a tactual reference point for the parent.
5. Relate how slightly moving toys, such as mobiles, attract the child's attention and encourage him to reach toward the movement. Explain that the parent can shake a toy, even if it is not a "shake-toy," to also attract his attention and encourage him to reach and grasp.
6. Let the parent feel the size and shapes of toys which are easy for him to grasp.

4.28   Child: USES PALMAR GRASP (4-5 mo.)
  Parent: Provides graspable toys and objects within child's reach

GENERAL GUIDELINES

The child uses all of his fingers, except his thumb, to grasp and hold objects against his palm.

Parents can provide their child small cylindrical shaped objects, such as thick pegs, large thread spools, rattles, teething biscuits, and small blocks, to give him grasping experiences. The child will be unable to grasp large toys, such as balls, books, or stuffed animals.

Parents can let their older delayed child practice grasping objects, such as crayons, xylophone sticks, and small rolling pins, during play.

If the child has muscle tone abnormalities, side-lying or a semi-reclined supported position may be recommended.

MENTALLY RETARDED PARENT

May expect her child to hold toys which are too big.

1. Explain to the parent that, since her child's hands are small, the things he holds must be small:
   a. Demonstrate several safe toys and objects which are of a suitable size and shape for the child to grasp.

Describe the qualities which make them suitable, e.g., smooth, small, and interesting.
   b. Show the parent several toys and objects which are either too large, too small, and/or unsafe for her child to hold. Ask why she thinks each of these things are *not* good for letting her child practice his holding.
2. Refer to 3.12 (Extensor thrust inhibited) if side-lying positions have been recommended to facilitate the child's grasp.
3. Stress that her child cannot hold toys for very long at this age. Refer to Activity No. 1, 4.27 (Reaches for toy followed by momentary grasp).

BLIND PARENT

May not recognize when or how her child grasps toys.

1. Refer to 4.27 (Reaches for toy followed by momentary grasp).

4.29   Child: REACHES AND GRASPS OBJECT (4½-5½ mo.)
  Parent: Provides ample opportunities and materials which facilitate child's grasp

GENERAL GUIDELINES

The child is able to reach for, grasp, and maintain his grasp on an object for about a minute. The general guidelines and parent activities for 4.27 (Reaches for toy followed by momentary grasp) are applicable for this skill, adapting for the child's extended duration for grasping objects.

4.30   Child: USES RADIAL PALMAR GRASP (4½-6 mo.)
  Parent: Provides ample opportunities and materials which facilitate child's grasp

GENERAL GUIDELINES

The child begins to approach and grasp objects from the thumb-side of his hand. He uses his thumb as if it were another finger (i.e., his thumb does not oppose his fingers) to grasp an object with his index and middle fingers. He continues to hold the object close to his palm.

The child develops a radial palmar grasp through his experiences in handling a variety of toys, and through opportunities to bear his weight on his palms when he is in prone.

If the child's radial palmar grasp is delayed, toys can be presented toward the thumb-side of his hand to encourage this grasp.

MENTALLY RETARDED PARENT

May try to make her child hold things like an adult.

1. Hold a cube to demonstrate how children at this age hold a toy using a radial palmar grasp. Contrast this grasp with an adult grasp. Explain that children's thumb muscles at this age are not ready to hold toys the way we do. Review appropriate graspable toys and objects for her child to hold.

4.30

2. If the child's grasp is delayed:
   a. Explore through observation and questioning to assess if the child is having adequate experiences in prone.
   b. Demonstrate, and let the parent practice, presenting toys toward the child's thumb-side of his hand.
   c. Explain that we are trying to encourage him to hold toys on his thumb-side; he needs to be able to do this so he will be able to hold a spoon when he gets older.

BLIND PARENT

May not see how her child grasps objects.

1. Describe the child's grasp on a toy as the parent places her hand over her child's hand. The parent can encourage him to hold her finger to feel his grasp.
2. If the child is not demonstrating a radial palmar grasp, demonstrate and describe this grasp while the parent feels your palm and finger placement. Relate how offering toys to her child's thumb-side encourages him to use this grasp.

4.31 Child: **REGARDS TINY OBJECT**
(4½-5½ mo.)
Parent: Draws child's attention to tiny objects

GENERAL GUIDELINES

The child can clearly see an object in front of him that is as small as a raisin. He may reach for, swipe, or try to pat it, but cannot grasp it.

Parents can encourage their child's visual regard for tiny objects by pointing out small objects and detail in his environment. For example, parents can show their child pieces of food or a drop of juice that may have spilled, an insect crawling on a leaf, buttons on clothing, a fingernail with polish, an emblem on his shirt, or goldfish in a tank. Contrasting background colors may help the child visually discriminate a tiny object from its background.

The following activities assume the child is not visually impaired.

MENTALLY RETARDED PARENT

May expect her child to pick up tiny objects since he can pick up larger ones, and may not point out tiny objects to him during daily activities.

1. Explain to the parent that her child's eyes are just as good as ours are now; before, things needed to be about as large as our fist for him to see them clearly. Now he is learning to look at tiny things. Ask the parent if she can think of something tiny she has seen her child look at.
2. Demonstrate showing the child two or three tiny things, such as the parent's ring on her hand, an earring, or a Cheerio:
   a. Model a phrase to say as you tap one of the tiny objects to attract the child's attention, e.g., "Oh! See Mommy's ring? So shiny!"
   b. Ask the parent to think of something to tell her child about her earring (or other available object) to help attract his attention.
   c. Stress that we do not have to hold tiny things right next to her child's eyes for him to see it; he can see tiny objects from just about the same distance as us.
3. Sort through examples of children's toys, clothing, sheets, food boxes, and baby food jars. Let the parent find little pictures on them that her child may like to look at when they are being used.
4. Review that, since her child cannot move around a lot, he loves it when we show him things:
   a. Explain she can show him anything she happens to like or to be holding herself; e.g., a leaf she picks up, the baby on the pamper box, or a new necklace she got for a present.
   b. Relate that when she does this, she is letting him look at interesting things and showing him she cares enough to share the things she likes.
5. Describe the child's signs of attention when she shows him a tiny object, e.g., "He is looking at it so hard!" or "Look at that smile."
6. Explain that even though her child can pick up some toys, he usually cannot pick up things that are smaller than her finger yet because his finger muscles need more practice.
7. Stress to the parent that, since he is looking at tiny objects now and practicing picking things up, he will soon be able to figure out how to pick tiny things up:
   a. Explain that this is the time to start being careful to keep little things out of his reach unless she is right there because he could put it in his mouth and choke.
   b. List a few tiny objects to be careful of and let the parent think of some more, e.g., matches, buttons, pins, diaper pins, cigarettes, etc.
   c. Help identify places to keep tiny objects out of her child's reach unless the parent is supervising.
   d. Tell the parent to always check her child's crib, playpen, or other play area for tiny things he could choke on before putting him down.
8. Show the parent how much easier it is to see a tiny object that has a contrasting colored background. Put a Cheerio in one hand and a red Fruit Loop in the other. Relate how this applies to her child. Ask the parent which would be easier for her child to see on his white highchair tray, a tiny marshmallow or a raisin?

BLIND PARENT

May be unaware of her child's increasing visual capabilities.

1. Explain that, by four months of age, children can see as well as an adult:
   a. Contrast how earlier he could not see detail or tiny objects, such as a button, raisin, or picture of the baby on his baby food jar, as clearly as he can now.
   b. Relate that he can see tiny objects when they are one or two feet in front of him.
2. The parent can usually use auditory and tactual cues to help recognize when her child is looking at tiny objects. Let the parent present several tiny objects (helping, as needed, to assure it is within his visual field) one at a time and advise her when he is looking at it. The child may demonstrate a pattern of discriminating vocal sounds and/or gestural sounds by reaching, patting, or swiping.

3. Describe detail in the environment at which her child may be interested in looking, but does not provide tactual cues, e.g., pictures on food containers, the babies on diaper boxes, special pictures on his toys, emblems in his clothing, or even a bug!
4. Explain the importance of color contrasts for helping make small objects and detail more visually prominent if the parent is not familiar with this concept:
   a. Name contrasting colors and a few examples of tiny objects against them, e.g., her dark blue button on her white blouse is easier for him to see than the picture of the tiny yellow bunny on his white shirt, and drops of red juice on his white highchair tray will be easier to see than drops of white milk.
   b. This concept can be compared to texture contrasts, i.e., it is easier to identify things which feel completely different, such as honey and water, than things which feel similar, such as sand and salt.

4.32 Child: LOOKS AT DISTANT OBJECTS (5-6 mo.)
Parent: Draws child's attention to distant objects

GENERAL GUIDELINES

By four months of age, the child's visual accommodation, i.e., the adjustment of the eye for distance, is fully developed. The child can see as well as an adult at all distances.

Parents widen their child's visual experiences and motivate his interest in looking at distant objects by simply pointing them out, talking to him when walking into or around a room, and holding things up to give him a better view. The child often enjoys pictures on a wall, looking out of a window, and watching what others are doing across the room.

MENTALLY RETARDED PARENT

May restrict her child's visual experiences by keeping him in one place for most of the day.

1. Discuss how young children love to look at people and things all around him, such as pictures on the wall, happenings outside windows, and the refrigerator opening. Ask the parent to name other things at which her child would probably like to look.
2. Model pointing at, showing, and talking about various objects in the environment to the child. Ask the parent what she can talk about when she looks out the window with her child.
3. Review the importance of letting her child be in different rooms and positions throughout the day. Refer to 4.04 (Follows with eyes moving person while in supine).
4. Make a colorful poster with the parent to hang up in his room. Poster art can be an excellent parent group activity:
   a. Stress that perfect artwork is not important.
   b. Review how and where the poster will be hung.

BLIND PARENT

May be unaware of the distant objects in which her child shows interest.

1. Explain the child's ability to see objects at a distance. Name the various things he can now look at clearly from his highchair, the floor, his playpen, out the window, etc. Point out things that may obstruct his view from various angles.
2. Review how he is learning to anticipate what is going to happen next through visual and auditory cues. For example, when he hears his mother's voice from the next room, he starts to look for her to come in and pick him up; and when he sees her fixing his bottle, he knows he is going to eat soon.
3. Tell the parent the various things you observe her child to show a special interest in that are at a distance, e.g., the hanging plant, watching her when she walks to his toy box, and the kitty running by.
4. Describe various "showing" gestures that help attract her child's attention to things, e.g., holding things up so they are in clear view, such as showing him his shirt before putting it on, pointing, and shaking or tapping the object.

4.33 Child: DROPS OBJECT (5-6 mo.)
Parent: Provides ample opportunities for child to hold and drop objects, helps place them back in his hand

GENERAL GUIDELINES

The inhibition of the child's earlier grasp reflex enables him to practice moving his fingers when he is holding a toy. Consequently, he alternates between holding and dropping toys frequently. Continued grasping and dropping experiences help the child develop a more purposeful release later.

Parents can encourage their child's grasping and dropping schemes by giving him ample opportunities to hold a variety of interesting objects, such as teethers, rattles, a stick of celery, or a clothespin, during the day. He should have opportunities to hold and drop things with both hands. During this stage, the child may do more dropping than holding so the parent may feel like she is the one doing all the work!

MENTALLY RETARDED PARENT

May think her child does not want to hold a toy anymore if he drops it.

1. Give the child a teether or rattle to hold and explain to the parent in meaningful terms why her child seems to keep dropping a toy soon after we give it to him. The following phrases can help with this understanding:
   a. "When your child was younger, he held things in his hands automatically; if we put a rattle in his palm (demonstrate with your hand), he quickly closed his hand on it whether he wanted to or not."
   b. "Now he is learning to hold things on purpose because he has learned he can make his fingers move."

4.33

c. "Since he is doing a lot of practicing to move his fingers while he is holding something, he drops what he is holding by mistake; he does not always mean to drop the toy; it is just that he is trying out lots of new things with his hands."
d. "After he has had more holding and dropping practice, he will hold onto his toys longer."

2. Help the parent identify five interesting things that her child would like to hold; explain that children are interested in the way things look and how they feel:
   a. Demonstrate talking about and showing the child one of the toys before letting him hold it.
   b. Let the parent give it back to him after he drops it, explaining to wait a minute to see if he can pick it back up by himself.
   c. When the child drops the toy a second time, explain it is time to give his hands a rest.
   d. Remind her it is important to let her child practice holding and dropping with both hands, but only one hand at a time.

BLIND PARENT

May not be able to visually monitor when or where her child has dropped his toy.

1. Provide anticipatory guidance about the child's developmentally appropriate stage of dropping so the parent can check to see if her child is still holding a toy she gave him to hold.
2. Use squeak and shake toys, and ones with bells, so the parent can monitor the cessation of sounds and listen for her child's possible retrieval.
3. Use objects which do not roll away when dropped to help the parent locate them easily.
4. The parent can easily recognize when her child drops objects if she is holding him.

PHYSICALLY DISABLED PARENT

Who has limited mobility; may have difficulty retrieving toys which keep dropping to the floor.

1. The parent can tie elastic strings around little toys and attach them to her wheelchair, the child's changing area table, and crib. A smaller string could be lightly tied around the child's forearm. CAUTION: The child should never be left unsupervised with toys on strings.

4.34 Child: RECOVERS OBJECT (5-6 mo.)
Parent: Encourages child to recover objects dropped within easy reach

GENERAL GUIDELINES

The child's maturing eye-hand coordination and purposeful reach and grasp enable him to pick an object back up after he has dropped it. The toy must be within his reach and sight, or if out of sight, tactually available. He may begin to "work for" the object if it has dropped out of reach.

Parents can shake the dropped toy, bring it within his visual field, and/or touch their child's body with the dropped toy to help remind him that it is still there. They can also bring the toy back to his reaching range if it has dropped beyond his reach. If the child does not recover his toy, the parent can gently assist him by placing his hand back on the toy. A side-lying position may facilitate the child's toy recovery.

MENTALLY RETARDED PARENT

May expect her child to recover toys which are out of sight, reach, or touch.

1. Tell the parent when her child is ready to recover a dropped object:
   a. Stress that there are four things to remember about the dropped object in order for her child to be able to pick it back up: He must be able to see it, feel it, or hear it, and to reach for it.
   b. Demonstrate putting the toy where he can see it and reach it, feel it and reach for it, and hear it (squeak a toy) and reach it.
   c. Demonstrate putting the toy in a place where he cannot see, hear, or feel it and ask the parent why she thinks he cannot pick it back up.
2. Review appropriate attractive graspable toys appropriate for her child at this age as suggested in most of the previous fine motor skills.

BLIND PARENT

May be unaware of the visual cues her child uses at this age to recover dropped objects.

1. Relate how her child uses visual, auditory, and tactual cues to help him recover a dropped object; if he cannot hear, see, or feel the toy, he may forget that it is still around.
2. Describe several example situations that could occur in which her child would not be able to recover a dropped object because he could not see it, e.g., dropping a small lightweight teether on his chest or above his head when he is lying on his back, or dropping his rattle when he is in an infant seat and it drops into his lap which has a bulky towel used as a bib on it.
3. The parent can use squeak, rattle, and bell toys to monitor when her child drops and recovers toys.
4. The parent can position her child in side-lying to help assure dropped toys are in his reach and line of vision.
5. The parent can let her child play with toys on her hardwood, tile, or linoleum floor. She can then hear toys that drop to help determine their location and to help him pick it up, if needed.
6. Relate to the parent the methods her child may use to "work for" toys he has dropped out of reach.

4.35 Child: RETAINS SMALL OBJECT IN EACH HAND (5-6 mo.)
Parent: Encourages child to hold an object in each hand

GENERAL GUIDELINES

The child begins to be able to hold a small lightweight object, such as a rattle, in each hand for several seconds. This is the first step toward bilateral hand awareness and coordination. At this stage, he usually cannot reach for the second object; it must be offered to his hand. Initially, he forgets he is holding the first toy, and drops it when he takes the second toy.

MENTALLY RETARDED PARENT

May be unaware of this skill as a significant behavior.

1. Relate to the parent how learning to hold a toy in each hand will help her child when he gets older to do many things in which he needs to use two hands:
   a. Name examples of future two-handed skills, e.g., holding his paper down while he scribbles, and squeezing toothpaste on a toothbrush.
   b. Ask the parent to think of something she does for which she uses two hands. If the parent needs prompting, ask her how she peels a banana, cuts a sandwich, etc.
2. Demonstrate, and let the parent practice, offering her child two objects, one for each hand:
   a. Ask the parent to select three or four things she has seen her child hold.
   b. Stress the importance of giving her child the second toy rather than making him reach for it.
   c. Emphasize that it is okay if her child drops the first object; all children do this at first.
   d. Ask the parent what she can tell her child to let him know how pleased she is that he is trying to hold two toys.

BLIND PARENT

May be unaware if her child drops the first object to retain the second.

1. The parent can use squeak, rattle, or bell toys when encouraging her child to hold two toys.
2. The parent can hold her child on her lap when she offers him two toys, or can offer him the toys on a hard surface to hear if one drops.
3. Review the importance of showing him the second toy before giving it to him, if needed.

4.36 Child: WATCHES ADULT SCRIBBLE (5½-7 mo.)
Parent: Encourages child to watch her scribble on paper

GENERAL GUIDELINES

Although the child cannot actively participate, he enjoys watching intently as an adult scribbles or marks on paper in front of him. He is fascinated that new colors and designs can be created from seemingly out of nowhere.

Parents can encourage their child to watch them scribble by using bold colored crayons or markers (red, blue, green, or black) and keeping their markings simple. The child will be interested in watching his parent draw circles, angles, or simple happy faces. The parent should check to insure her child is positioned so he can see the markings being created. After the parent has finished her quick "artwork," her child may enjoy holding it and crumpling the paper.

MENTALLY RETARDED PARENT

May become too involved in her own coloring.

1. Explain to the parent that, although her child is not old enough to color, he is old enough to learn to watch other people color. Include the following concepts:
   a. When her child watches people color, he learns how crayons work, and sees that this interesting stick can make a plain piece of paper have color.
   b. The child is interested in watching his parent's hand move the crayon across the paper.
   c. When the parent lets her child watch her color, it will help him learn how to color as he gets older.
2. Model for the parent ways to encourage her child to watch coloring:
   a. Point out the color of crayons that are most attracting to her child. Ask the parent what her favorite color is and ask if she thinks her child has a favorite color.
   b. Demonstrate where to color so her child can see the paper, crayon, and adult hand. Ask the parent what her child could see if she were coloring at a table and he was on the floor; can she think of a better place to color so her child can see?
   c. Demonstrate making one or two simple shapes without spending the time to color them in or add detail. Explain that, at this age, her child likes to see very simple drawings or scribbles; he cannot wait for us to make a picture that takes too long to draw.
   d. Ask the parent to show you a simple scribble or drawing that her child would like to watch; prompt with a happy face, a few circles, or a few wavy lines.
   e. Demonstrate talking to the child about the scribbles or markings you make, e.g., "Round and round goes my crayon!" or "See my long line!"
3. Let the parent demonstrate scribbling for her child. Provide verbal prompts, as needed, to assure the concepts outlined in Activity No. 2 are implemented. Praise the parent's efforts concretely, e.g., "Great! You are really making sure your child can see the paper when you color."
4. Explain that her child may try to grab her crayon or the paper because he is so interested in what she is doing:
   a. Tell her to go ahead and let him have the paper so he can explore it by crumpling, waving, or mouthing it; she can color on another piece of paper while he is playing with the first one.
   b. Caution her that he may put the crayon in his mouth so he should not be left unsupervised; it is okay to let

him feel the crayon and "taste" it briefly, but then she needs to take it out of his mouth gently and say, "Yuk."

BLIND PARENT

May not be aware of her child's interest in watching people scribble or mark with crayons.

1. Acquaint the parent with each of the concepts outlined in the general guidelines, i.e.:
   a. Explain the child's interest in watching new lines, marks, and colors being produced on a blank piece of paper; what a surprise that is to see all the things a thin piece of wax can produce!
   b. Since he likes to watch the marks and scribbles produced, the crayon, paper, and adult hand need to be at or below his eye level.
   c. Dark colors are the best to use because they make the most contrast against white paper. (The parent will have her own marking system for identifying colors.)
   d. The artwork produced is not important! It is the creating process itself that is interesting to her child.
   e. Define what scribbling is: random circular strokes that do not necessarily take form, making scribbling marks often feels rhythmic, etc.

PHYSICALLY DISABLED PARENT

Who has limited wrist control or grasp; may have difficulty demonstrating scribbling to her child.

1. The parent may have adaptive equipment available which enables her to hold and control a crayon, e.g., a *universal cuff,** *elastic utensil holder,** or an *adaptive pencil holder.**
2. The parent may be able to use a large paint brush, stick in the dirt, fingerpaints, a built-up crayon, or her elbow or toe in dirt or sand to demonstrate strokes.

4.37 Child: REACHES FOR OBJECT UNILATERALLY (5½-7 mo.)
    Parent: Encourages child to reach unilaterally with each arm

GENERAL GUIDELINES

The child reaches for an object with only one arm. His shoulders are disassociating, and he can now roll in a segmental fashion which enable the independent arm movements needed for unilateral reaching. The child should be able to reach unilaterally with each arm. If the child displays a preference for reaching with only one arm, he should be provided with extra opportunities to encourage reaching with his non-preferred arm.

The child can be encouraged to reach for toys when he is supine and side-lying. If the child displays an arm preference, he can be positioned in side-lying on his preferred side to encourage him to reach with his non-preferred side. Parents can also gently tap his non-preferred hand with a toy to encourage his reach, while holding his preferred hand when he is supine or in supported sitting.

MENTALLY RETARDED PARENT

May expect her child to continue reaching for toys with both arms if bilateral reaching was recommended at an earlier age.

1. Advise the parent when her child can be expected to reach unilaterally if she was told earlier to encourage bilateral reaching:
   a. Explain that he is ready to do this because he has learned how to use each arm separately now.
   b. Remind her how he has learned to hold a toy in each hand, too.
   c. Point out that if he reaches for an object that is too big to hold in one hand (demonstrate examples), he will probably continue to use both arms to reach for it.
   d. Review appropriate toys or objects she can use to encourage her child to reach.
2. If the child displays asymmetries in reaching, refer to 4.26 (Reaches for object bilaterally).

BLIND PARENT

May not be able to recognize if and when her child demonstrates unilateral reaching.

1. Provide anticipatory guidance to the parent as to when to expect her child's unilateral reaching, and how he uses vision to help determine with which arm to reach. Include:
   a. Her child looks to see which arm is closest to the toy to decide with which arm to reach.
   b. Her child may use both arms to reach if he sees that the object is too big to hold with one hand.
2. Review positioning toys and objects within the child's slightly flexed arm reaching field.
3. If the child demonstrates a preferred arm during reaching, he can wear a wrist band with a bell on his non-preferred arm to help the parent monitor increased reaching.

4.38 Child: TRANSFERS OBJECT (5½-7 mo.)
    Parent: Provides safe toys which can be held with one hand

GENERAL GUIDELINES

The child transfers an object he is holding in one hand to his empty hand.

Initially, large ring-like objects, such as a small embroidery hoop or long handled toys, are the easiest for him to learn to transfer because transferring may occur accidentally during play. For example, if he is holding a plastic loop with one hand and brings his second hand up to help hold it, he may let go of it accidentally with his first hand during play and suddenly realize he has transferred the toy.

---

*See Glossary.

Parents can encourage this skill by providing their child toys which can be picked up and transferred by one hand and which are washable, since the child is probably doing a lot of mouthing at this stage. Rattles, teethers, squeak toys, toy keys on a loop, and canning jar rings are often favorites at this age and easy to transfer from hand to hand.

MENTALLY RETARDED PARENT

May be unaware of transferring as a positive developmental gain for her child.

1. Demonstrate moving an object from one hand to another as you explain transferring as an important new skill her child is learning. Relate that this shows us he is learning more control of his hands.
2. Help the parent discriminate which size toys are appropriate to help her child practice transferring. Explain that the toy must be small enough to hold in one hand, but big enough so it is not covered up by his hand when held. Show the parent a few appropriate toys:
   a. Demonstrate this concept with the parent. Ask her to transfer a beach ball from hand to hand. Ask her why she cannot do this.
   b. Demonstrate how objects which are very small are more difficult to transfer. Put a Cheerio in her child's fisted hand.
   c. Demonstrate, and let the parent practice, giving her child appropriately-sized toys.
3. Stress how all toys and objects her child holds should be clean and safe. Refer to 1.15 (Uses hands and mouth for sensory exploration of objects).

BLIND PARENT

May not see her child's transferring process.

1. The parent can hold her child in her lap facing outward. As he plays with small toys, she can feel his transferring attempts when her hands are lightly placed against his forearms. Sound toys will provide additional cues when the child shakes it with one hand, and then transfers and shakes it with his other hand.

4.39 Child: BANGS OBJECTS ON TABLE (5½-7 mo.)
   Parent: Allows child to bang objects on various surfaces; demonstrates how fun this can be

GENERAL GUIDELINES

The child purposefully bangs an object held in one hand during play. This skill demonstrates his maturing voluntary control of arm movements and his learning of a new way to interact with objects.

Parents can encourage their child to bang objects on hard surfaces by demonstrating how fun banging can be, e.g., banging objects makes fun sounds, lets him "make something happen," and attracts others to look at him.

MENTALLY RETARDED PARENT

May interpret her child's banging as "bad" or "mean."

1. Explain to the parent that banging objects on tables is one of the first steps her child uses to learn how to play with things. Point out what good arm control he is learning. Model praising the child's banging attempts as you admire this new skill to the parent.
2. If the parent is concerned about damage to table surfaces, help identify surfaces which are suitable for banging, e.g., highchair tray, floor, couch, etc.
3. Help the parent identify household items which are suitable for banging, e.g., banging his rattle on a coffee can, his squeak toy on the floor, and a spoon on a pot. Point out the interesting sounds they can make together.

DEAF PARENT

May be unaware of the positive auditory feedback her child receives when he bangs objects.

1. Explain that hard objects make sounds for the child when he hits them on tables, his highchair tray, and other hard surfaces. Encourage the parent to feel the vibrations as her child bangs objects on his tray.
2. Demonstrate banging a soft object (e.g., rolled up socks) and let the parent feel the absence of vibrations, explaining that soft objects (unless they are squeak toys) are not as fun for the child to bang since they are not as noisy.
3. Help the parent identify suitable household items which will be fun for her child to bang. Tapping and banging hands on a table with him provides auditory feedback for the child and tactual feedback for the parent.
4. Point out her child's physical behaviors in response to the sounds he is making, e.g., eye blinking or changes of facial expression.

4.40 Child: ATTEMPTS TO SECURE TINY OBJECT (5½-7 mo.)
   Parent: Encourages child to try to attain a tiny object

GENERAL GUIDELINES

The child's earlier visual regard and interest in tiny objects lead to a visually directed reach toward the object. At this age, he may overshoot his reach for tiny objects and since his grasp is immature, he cannot actually secure the object unless it happens to stick to his hand.

Parents can encourage their child to practice his visually directed reach toward tiny objects by attracting his attention to them and helping him swipe toward it, commenting how he made it move! Bits of cereal, a piece of carpet fuzzy, a cotton ball, a piece of a cookie, or a bead on Mom's necklace are often motivating objects for the child to reach toward.

4.40

MENTALLY RETARDED PARENT

May not anticipate safety considerations which arise when her child learns to approach tiny objects.

1. Praise the child's maturing visually directed reach as you present a Cheerio to him:
   a. Compare how now he is beginning to try to pick up tiny things, whereas earlier, they needed to be larger.
   b. Explain that her child needs more practice before he can actually pick it up.
   c. Relate how her child's swiping will lead to his ability to pick tiny things up.
2. Emphasize that, as with most new skills her child learns, she must think about new ways to make sure he is safe. Ask the parent what could happen now that her child is learning to pick up little objects, and has learned to put things in his mouth.
3. Show the parent a collection of common tiny objects that can be dangerous to have around children at this age:
   a. Include safety pins, paper clips, matches, cigarette butts, bottle caps, hair pins, pills, pennies, etc.
   b. Review each item and ask the parent where she can keep them out of reach.
   c. Encourage the parent to think of other tiny objects that can be dangerous.
4. Show the parent examples of tiny edible objects that she can let her child try to reach for.

BLIND PARENT

May have difficulty locating small objects after her child has swiped it.

1. The parent can encourage her child to reach for tiny edible objects which are placed on a tray with one- or two-inch sides, or in a shallow box or bowl.
2. The parent can string a bell or bead securely from the child's crib or playpen, or around her neck.
3. The parent can show her child the ring she is wearing or button on her blouse, and encourage him to feel it.

4.41 Child: MANIPULATES TOY ACTIVELY WITH WRIST MOVEMENTS (6-8 mo.)
   Parent: Provides safe toys and materials which encourage child's manipulating with wrist movement

GENERAL GUIDELINES

The child can rotate his forearm, palm facing down to palm facing sideways. This facilitates a more active rotational wrist movement when he is playing with a toy. He will not display complete forearm supination (palm facing up) or wrist extension for several months.

Children develop wrist rotation through their explorations with toys when they look at, bang, shake, and mouth them.

MENTALLY RETARDED PARENT

May not have a variety of appropriate toys with which her child can play.

1. Conduct a toy-making workshop with parents:
   a. Make rattle toys with empty juice cans and pill containers, filling them with popcorn. Cement the tops and wrap colorful plastic tape around them.
   b. Paint interesting designs on empty thread spools with non-toxic markers.
   c. Fill clear empty plastic trial-size shampoo bottles halfway with colored water. Cement and tape the tops so they are secure.
   d. Show parents a variety of common household objects that are fun for children to play with: metal spoons, wooden spoons, cups, butter tubs, measuring spoons, aerosol can tops, etc.
   e. Demonstrate the various great ways their children may play with each of the "toys": bang, mouth, wave, shake, and drop.
   f. Review the safety features of each "toy": no sharp edges, unbreakable, tops securely attached, and not small enough to swallow.
   g. Praise how much their children are learning when they play with these toys: moving their hands in different ways, learning how things look and feel, and learning about the sounds they make when dropped and banged.

BLIND PARENT

May not be able to see her child's active wrist movements when he plays with toys.

1. Describe and compare the child's earlier non-rotational hand movements in play with his new emerging active wrist movements:
   a. Demonstrate this comparison with the parent's hand.
   b. Explain that this lets him manipulate and look at objects from new perspectives, e.g., before, when he held his squeak toy, he could only see one side of it; now he can look at the bottom of it when he turns his wrist.
2. Review the various qualities of toys which encourage her child to look at and play with them: shiny, reflective, transparent or translucent, moving parts (rattles with spinning wheels), mirrored, etc.

4.42 Child: REACHES AND GRASPS OBJECT WITH EXTENDED ELBOW (7-8½ mo.)
   Parent: Encourages child to reach and grasp with extended elbow

GENERAL GUIDELINES

The child can reach out and obtain an object with a straight arm. Until now, he had reached for objects with a slightly flexed arm, but his maturing nervous system and movement experiences enable him to move out of flexor patterns and reach with an extended arm. This maturation is also demonstrated when he bears weight on his hands in prone and displays protective extension of arms downward.

Parents can encourage their child to reach for objects a few inches beyond his wrist when he is reaching with a flexed arm to encourage arm extension. Reaching for suspended balloons, floating soap bubbles, food, bottles, parent's hair and face, and his own image in a mirror can be motivating activities to encourage the child to reach with an extended arm.

The child can be encouraged to reach in prone, side-lying, or supported sitting. Reaching in unsupported sitting is not recommended due to his typically poor trunk control and immature protective responses in sitting at this stage.

MENTALLY RETARDED PARENT

May not encourage her child to reach for a toy with an extended arm, or may hold the toy too far away.

1. Explain to the parent that, as her child's arm muscles grow stronger, he is ready to learn to reach for things that are a little bit further away from his hand than before:
   a. Demonstrate holding an object at a distance from the child which does *not* encourage arm extension. Point out her child's bent arm.
   b. Move the toy to the child's fingertips and point out how his arm reaches further to grasp it because he can reach with a straight arm. Demonstrate how a straight arm is longer than a bent one.
   c. Let the parent practice a suitable distance from her child to offer objects. If she is having difficulty, use a concrete marker, such as the distance from her fingertips on his chest to her elbow.
2. Demonstrate for the parent how to encourage her child to reach in prone, side-lying, and supported sitting:
   a. Explain that it is hard to reach for things if he is sitting by himself on the middle of the floor because his muscles are working too hard to help him balance in sitting.
   b. Stress providing him chances to reach for things with each hand. Explain that, at this age, children usually are not left or right handed.
   c. Remind her never to pull his arm to make him reach.
3. Suggest daily activities for the parent to encourage her child to reach: let him reach for his bottle during feeding, for his shirt during dressing, for your nose when you lean over his crib, for his face in the mirror after his bath, and for bubbles during playtime.
4. Help the parent think of things to say to her child after he has worked so hard to get the toy, e.g., "Good reaching!", "Great! That was hard work," or "Look at what you got; your little doggie!"
5. Tell the parent to always give her child the toy after he has worked to reach it, even if he could not actually get it. Remind her that if she takes it away, he may cry and feel teased.

BLIND PARENT

May be unable to visually monitor her child's new reaching abilities.

1. Provide anticipatory guidance regarding the child's ability to reach for toys at increasing distances:
   a. Describe her child's extended elbow reach and compare it to when his arm was flexed.
   b. Provide initial assistance, as needed, to orient the parent to the increased distance she can hold objects away from her child in different positions.
2. Introduce blowing soap bubbles, using a straw-type blower, as a fun activity to encourage her child's reaching:
   a. Describe the interesting visual effects of bubbles which encourage her child to reach for them, e.g., they are shiny, transparent, move and sway in the air, and pop quickly when touched.
   b. The parent can blow the bubbles as she sits beside her child or from behind to help assure bubbles do not float into his eyes.
3. Refer to 4.27 (Reaches for toy followed by momentary grasp).

4.43 Child: USES RADIAL DIGITAL GRASP (7-9 mo.)
Parent: Provides materials which encourage child's radial digital grasp

GENERAL GUIDELINES

The child picks up small objects (approximately one square inch) with his thumb, index, and middle fingers. His thumb begins to move in opposition with his index finger and he no longer needs to use his palm to help pick the object up.

Parents can begin introducing more pliable materials for their child to manipulate, such as sand, playdough, yarn, and many types of fingerfoods, to encourage thumb opposition and finer finger movements. Placing small objects, such as cubes or thick pegs, in muffin tins or egg cartons can help the child practice picking things up with his fingers since he cannot place his whole hand around the object.

Demonstrate a radial digital grasp to parents and suggest materials which encourage their child to practice using his fingers to pick up objects.

4.44 Child: RAKES TINY OBJECT (7-8 mo.)
Parent: Provides opportunities for child to rake bits of food

GENERAL GUIDELINES

The child picks up tiny objects, the size of a raisin, by using his fingers in a raking motion toward his palm. He does not use his thumb.

Parents can give their child bits of fingerfoods and pieces of dry cereal to provide opportunities for him to practice raking up small objects. Since the child cannot usually discriminate between edible and inedible objects and may still

4.44

be mouthing objects, safety remains a concern. The child's play areas should be examined daily for tiny objects.

MENTALLY RETARDED PARENT

May not anticipate safety concerns for her child as he is learning to pick up tiny objects.

1. Refer to 4.40 (Attempts to secure tiny object).
2. Show the parent various pieces of fingerfoods which let her child practice his grasping skills, e.g., three pieces of dry cereal or tiny pieces of bread crust.
3. Stress that the parent needs to continue feeding her child most of his meal; if he does not try to pick up bits of food that is okay, try again at his next meal.

BLIND PARENT

May be unable to see how her child picks up tiny objects.

1. Describe the child's raking grasp. The parent can offer her child a piece of cereal from her hand and feel his grasp.
2. The parent can offer her child bits of food on a tray which has one or two inch edges to help contain the tiny pieces.

4.45 Child: USES INFERIOR PINCER GRASP (7½-10 mo.)
Parent: Presents tiny safe objects which encourage child to practice using an inferior pincer grasp

GENERAL GUIDELINES

The child's raking grasp matures to an inferior pincer grasp through maturation and experiences with securing small objects. He uses his thumb and index finger with his forearm supported to pick up tiny or thin objects, such as a Cheerio or shoestring. His thumb, however, does not oppose his index finger which is observed in his later neat pincer grasp. Instead, his thumb is positioned toward the lateral side of his index finger.

Parents can provide safe opportunities for their child to practice using his thumb and index finger to pick up tiny things by encouraging him to pick up bits of fingerfoods, strings on his pull toys, pieces of yarn, and straws, or pegs.

MENTALLY RETARDED PARENT

May be unaware of the developmental significance for encouraging her child to use a pincer grasp.

1. Demonstrate picking up a piece of cereal with a rake grasp and then using your thumb and index finger. Let the parent try it:
   a. Discuss how much easier it is to pick up tiny things with our thumbs and index fingers. Relate that her child's finger and thumb muscles are learning to do this now.
   b. Relate how a pincer grasp is also needed so her child can learn to pick up pencils, spoons, and strings.
2. Tell the parent that her child needs lots of practice picking up tiny things, but still needs to balance his forearm on a table to help his finger muscles work well. Demonstrate the arm position:
   a. List various tiny pieces of food to offer her child at each meal.
   b. Review safety concerns as outlined under 4.40 (Attempts to secure tiny object).

BLIND PARENT

May not be able to see how her child picks up tiny objects.

1. Describe the child's inferior pincer grasp. The parent can offer her child a tiny piece of food from her open palm to feel how he picks it up. She can lay her open hand toward the far end of his highchair tray to give him room to rest his forearm.

4.46 Child: BANGS TWO CUBES HELD IN HANDS (8½-12 mo.)
Parent: Encourages child to hit two objects together at midline during play

GENERAL GUIDELINES

The child is able to hit two objects, such as small blocks, together at midline when one is held in each hand. This skill demonstrates the child's increasing independent control of his arms and perceptual development which are important for his future bilateral coordination.

Parents encourage this skill by modeling how fun it is to bang objects together during play with their child. If he does not attempt to imitate them, they can physically prompt him through the motions.

Blocks, plastic butter cups, little squeak toys, aerosol can tops, and juice cans can be fun for the child to play with and practice banging together.

MENTALLY RETARDED PARENT

May try to over-manipulate her child's banging at midline skills if this skill is introduced as a teaching activity.

1. Introduce banging objects at midline as a new way to play "Pat-A-Cake":
   a. Demonstrate playing this game to the parent, explaining that it is okay if her child does not always copy us exactly during the game.
   b. Demonstrate some of the actions her child may want to do during the game, such as banging the table, trying to hit the object she is holding, or missing the "hit" at midline. Stress that this is okay.
   c. Play and sing "Pat-A-Cake" with the parent and child, keeping the game fun.
2. Suggest daily activities and materials to let her child play "Pat-A-Cake" with. For example, she can give him two rattles while she is changing his diaper, or let him play "Pat-A-Cake" with his shoes after she undresses him.

DEAF PARENT

May be unaware of the auditory reinforcement her child receives when he bangs two objects together.

1. Relate to the parent that when her child bangs two objects together, they make interesting sounds for him to hear; these sounds help make this skill fun and encourage him to keep practicing.
2. Point out that hard objects make louder sounds than soft materials. For example, when her child hits his cloth blocks together, they do not make a sound; but when he hits his wooden blocks, he hears a loud sound.

4.47 Child: REMOVES PEGS FROM PEGBOARD (8½-10 mo.)
Parent: Encourages child to remove "peg-like" objects from holes

GENERAL GUIDELINES

The child removes three or four thick pegs (¾" in diameter) from a pegboard. He *cannot* put them back in the board again.

Parents can encourage their child to pull out the "peg people" from commercial toys, or can make their own pegboard, using shoe boxes with holes punched in the top and unsharpened pencils for pegs. Parents can also let their child try to pull straws out of carryout drink containers which have tops with holes. The board (cup, box, etc.) can be slightly tilted or the parent can provide physical prompting if their child is having difficulty pulling out the pegs. When standard thick pegboards are used, a Cheerio can be placed under the peg to make it easier to pull out and to provide a motivating surprise for the child.

MENTALLY RETARDED PARENT

May expect her child to take all of the pegs out of a board and/or expect him to put them back in.

1. Explain to the parent that her child is ready to learn how to pull stick-like objects out of holes:
   a. Demonstrate this skill with a pegboard and other materials suggested in the general guidelines.
   b. Stress that he is *not* ready to put the pegs back into the hole and can only take out a few pegs at a time.
2. Demonstrate with the parent introducing a pegboard activity to the child:
   a. Point out an appropriate position for her child to sit so he can see and reach the pegs.
   b. Verbally prompt the parent to show her child how to pull out two pegs and then wait for him to try.
   c. Help her think of encouraging phrases to say to her child, e.g., "Come on, you can do it! Try pulling out the peg!"
   d. Ask the parent to think of things she can say to let her child know she is proud he is trying to pull out the pegs.
   e. Describe the child's signs which tell her it is time to stop or change the activity.

3. Make pegboard toys with the parent that she can let her child play with at home.

BLIND PARENT

May not be able to see when her child pulls out pegs, and it may be a nuisance to locate them as he drops them and they roll in numerous directions.

1. Pegboards can be placed in a shallow box which has edges to confine the peg's roll. The parent will be able to hear her child drop the pegs. The parent can also encourage her child to give her the peg when he pulls it by holding her open hand next to the board.

PHYSICALLY DISABLED PARENT

With poor hand coordination or limited grasp; may have difficulty placing pegs in the board and removing them for demonstration to her child.

1. If the parent does not have a functional grasp, she could use a *universal cuff** (adapted for peg size), her mouth, or a shortened reacher to put the pegs in the board. NOTE: If the parent uses her mouth to put the pegs in the board, recommend doing this out of her child's sight to prevent him from imitating this method.
2. If the parent has excessive hand tremors, she can try using both hands clasped together to pick up the pegs. The parent's arms can be held close to her body with her forearms supported on the table to help decrease tremor.

4.48 Child: TAKES OBJECTS OUT OF CONTAINERS (9-11 mo.)
Parent: Provides child containers and objects to play with

GENERAL GUIDELINES

The child begins to explore "container and contained" relationships. He removes objects from containers by taking them out one by one or by dumping the container over. Taking objects out of a container is easier than putting them in. Soon, however, the child develops both skills and may spend long periods of time repetitively putting objects in and out of their containers. Shallow containers are often easier for the child to learn this skill.

Parents can provide their child various types of household "container and contained" items to use during play. Pots, pans, butter tubs, Cool Whip tubs, plastic cups and bowls, and empty cans or boxes are suitable for safe containers. Plastic pop beads, empty thread spools, clothespins, blocks, poker chips, or plastic rollers can be used for objects. Parents can also let their child practice "container and contained" relationships during daily activities. They can let him eat fingerfoods from a bowl, take his new shirt out of the bag, and take his disposable diaper out of its box.

---

*See Glossary.

4.48

MENTALLY RETARDED PARENT

May expect her child to take all of the objects out of a container and put all of them back; she may also think he is being bad when he dumps containers over.

1. When you introduce container and contained activities, demonstrate the various things her child may do with the container and objects:
   a. Explain that he may only want to take out a few of the items and that is okay; he does not need to take them all out.
   b. Stress that he is not trying to be bad when he dumps things out of containers; he just loves to see how the objects fall out, roll around, and make sounds when they drop.
   c. Explain that taking objects out of things is easier for her child's finger muscles than putting them back in, i.e., "If he does not put them back in when you tell him, it is not because he does not want to; he just hasn't learned how yet."
2. Suggest safe household objects her child can use in play to practice dumping and taking things out. Review safety precautions when selecting the containers and the things to put in them for her child:
   a. Show the parent a few safe containers, pointing out that they are unbreakable and have no sharp edges.
   b. Show the parent a few unsafe containers (e.g., a coffee can with a sharp edge sticking out) and ask her if she can see why this is an unsafe container for her child to play with.
   c. Explain that the objects should be at least the size of her little finger so her child does not swallow them.
3. Explain to the parent that, when she tells her child what he is doing when he is playing with containers, she shows him she is interested. Model phrases to say to her child, e.g., "You are taking the blocks out; great!" or "Look how they all spilled out!"

BLIND PARENT

May have difficulty locating all of the objects her child dumps out of containers during play.

1. The parent can avoid giving her child round objects to dump, such as spools or thick pegs which are more likely to roll in a variety of obscure places when dumped.
2. The parent can count the number of objects she places in containers before and after her child's play.
3. The child can play with containers and objects on hard surfaces, such as his highchair tray or linoleum floor. The parent can then hear when her child drops or dumps objects and listen to where they roll.
4. Relate to the parent that, in addition to hearing the interesting sounds made when her child dumps objects, he likes to watch the way they fall, bounce, and slide when they are dumped.
5. Point out containers which are transparent:
   a. Explain how objects in transparent containers provide additional visual cues regarding "container and contained" relationships and he likes to watch objects drop through them.
   b. Relate how this can also be a bit confusing to her child at first so he may try to reach into the side of the container to obtain the object.

4.49 Child: EXTENDS WRIST (9-10 mo.)
Parent: Provides ample play materials and activities which promote child's wrist extension

GENERAL GUIDELINES

The child can bend his hands upwards at the wrist when he manipulates objects during play.

Parents help encourage their child to use wrist extension when they help him wave bye-bye, let him pat his image in a mirror and textured pictures on the wall, or show him how to squeeze squeak toys by pressing them with their palms.

The child's isolated wrist movements emerge with maturing gross and fine motor development. Bearing weight on one hand in prone, while propped with his hands and pushing himself into sitting, are gross motor milestones which encourage and use wrist extension. Refer to those skills in the gross motor section of this manual for applicable activities if the child is delayed in this area. Previously addressed fine motor activities which involve manipulation also provide experiences which promote the child's wrist extension.

4.50 Child: RELEASES OBJECTS VOLUNTARILY (9-11 mo.)
Parent: Provides child materials which encourages voluntary release

GENERAL GUIDELINES

The child is able to purposefully and intentionally let go of an object he is holding in a controlled manner. He can place his squeak toy on a table, drop a block in a large box, and drop his paper cup in the trash. His release continues to be somewhat clumsy with tiny objects and he usually does not have enough control to accurately release objects into small containers.

Parents can provide their child with materials which let him feel his control of grasp and release. For example, if encouraged to squeeze a squeak toy, playdough, or a wet sponge, he realizes he can control the sound or action of the object through his grasp and release. Parents can also give their child toys which encourage repetitive release, such as dropping blocks in plastic bowls. Dropping blocks in cans provides reinforcing auditory sounds which further encourage purposeful release.

MENTALLY RETARDED PARENT

May expect her child to release objects in a controlled manner before voluntary release develops.

1. If applicable, explain to the parent in meaningful terms why her child seems to always drop or fling objects instead of putting them in places she wants him to:

a. An example explanation could be: "Remember how you helped your child learn to hold things when he was younger? Now he can hold things real good. But, he can't always let go of them when he wants to, or when you want him to, because his fingers need more practice to know when to open at just the right time."
b. Relate that the games and activities you are going to show her will help her child's fingers practice letting go of things at just the right time.

2. Teach the parent a few "dropping games" that she can play with her child, e.g., drop the small ball in a basket, drop the block in a big can, or drop a spoon in a big pan:
a. Point out how each of these games make an interesting sound and sight for her child.
b. Demonstrate an exaggerated handspread upon release, explain that this helps her child see how to let go.
c. Explain to drop the object three times while her child is watching and then wait to let him try it.
d. Suggest saying "Drop!" each time she drops the object during the game and again when she gives her child his turn.
e. Provide anticipatory guidance and demonstrate how at first her child may just want to play with the toy or may keep his hand on it and lay it down instead of dropping it. Explain that is okay because he is just learning the game; after more practice he will be able to drop it better.
f. If the child has increased muscle tone, demonstrate and let the parent practice, gently rubbing the back of his head. Explain that this helps loosen his hand.

4.51 Child: POKES WITH INDEX FINGER
(9-12 mo.)
Parent: Provides materials which encourages child to "poke" with index finger

GENERAL GUIDELINES

The child is learning to isolate and use his index finger without using his other fingers. He uses this finger to poke, probe, and feel objects. His other fingers remain nearby in the same approximate plane as his index fingers. This is in contrast to his later pointing skills where he can extend his index finger and keep his remaining fingers held close to his palm.

Parents can encourage their child to use his index finger to poke and probe by giving him a variety of objects to examine which have holes and indentations to poke and explore. Busy boxes with buttons and dials, toy telephones, egg cartons, playdough, and eyes on dolls or stuffed animals are fun toys and materials which encourage the child to use an isolated index finger.

MENTALLY RETARDED PARENT

May try to manipulate her child's fingers when he probes toys with specific functions.

1. Anticipatory Guidance: The parent may over-stimulate or manipulate her child's play with busy box toys. These toys have multi-functions and activities which may encourage the parent to shift quickly from one activity to another which does not allow the child ample response time. The parent may also become too goal-oriented with toy telephone dials and physically manipulate her child's fingers to actually dial the phone rather than poke and probe it:
a. Stress to the parent that it is great to show her child how these toys work, but it is very important to only show one activity at a time and then let him have time to try to play with it all by himself.
b. Explain and demonstrate that young children learn by feeling, poking, and probing the various pieces on busy boxes; it is not important for them to do each activity just right.
c. Avoid busy boxes and toy telephones for encouraging the child's index finger probing if they present interaction problems. Use other items, such as egg cartons, pegboards, and finger puppets, or poking in the hole of a fisted hand.
d. Relate how these poking activities will help her child learn to point with his finger.

2. Help the parent anticipate new safety hazards now that her child is beginning to use his index finger:
a. Ask the parent what her child may try to do at an electrical outlet now that he likes to poke with his finger. Help identify and cover all unused outlets at home.
b. Help sand down any places in the child's play area that have peeling paint, explaining that her child may begin to pick at the paint and swallow pieces which can be poisonous.
c. Check for toys with button eyes or small pieces, such as tiny cars with wheels that can break off.

4.52 Child: USES NEAT PINCER GRASP
(10-12 mo.)
Parent: Presents tiny safe objects which encourage child to pick up with a pincer grasp

GENERAL GUIDELINES

The child picks up tiny objects using his thumb and index finger in opposition. He no longer needs to support his forearm on the table. The general guidelines and activities for 4.45 (Uses inferior pincer grasp) are applicable to this skill. In addition, parents can put little goodies, such as Cheerios, in empty egg cartons to encourage their child's pincer grasp without supporting his forearm.

4.53 Child: TRIES TO IMITATE SCRIBBLE
(10½-12 mo.)
Parent: Demonstrates scribbling and encourages child to imitate in any way

GENERAL GUIDELINES

The child watches an adult scribble and then tries to make his own marks on the paper. Initially, he is not always successful. His initial markings may happen by accident and are then

4.53

made hesitantly as he discovers he can control and produce marks with a crayon. Scribbling helps the child practice his fine motor coordination and test his creativity.

Parents can help their child learn to scribble by demonstrating how crayons can produce interesting strokes of color on paper and then letting him have the crayon to explore and practice this new discovery on his own. Large pieces of sturdy paper can be taped to the table to prevent it from slipping. Oversized kindergarten crayons or felt tip non-toxic washable markers are recommended to accommodate the child's grasp and initial light markings.

MENTALLY RETARDED PARENT

May try to over-control her child's scribbling attempts.

1. Before introducing paper and crayon activities, provide the parent with anticipatory guidance regarding developmental expectations at this age. Demonstrate and include the following concepts:
   a. At first, her child may want to taste the crayon; that is okay; do not scold him; just say "Yuk!" and show him how crayons are for marking.
   b. Young children cannot hold crayons like adults; they hold them in their fist.
   c. At first, he may not be able to make any marks; that is okay; he will be able to with more practice.
   d. He may not want to sit at the table for very long; at this age, many children can only sit with this activity for two or three minutes. When he wants to get down, that is fine.
   e. It does not matter which hand her child uses to scribble; she can let him decide which hand to use.
2. Give the parent lots of discarded computer paper to keep for coloring activities. Show her how the insides of flat boxes or bags can also be used for coloring.
3. Provide a few thick crayons. Demonstrate how easily thin crayons can break and point out that her child could swallow these pieces and choke. Advise the parent not to let her child use pens or pencils because they are harder to scribble with and have sharp points which are dangerous for young children.
4. Demonstrate how easily paper slips if you do not hold it down with one hand when coloring:
   a. Let the parent put one hand in her lap and try to write her name on the paper without holding it.
   b. Explain that her child is not old enough yet to learn how to always hold his paper down.
   c. Show the parent how taping or weighting the paper down at the corners can help keep the paper from slipping.
5. Enjoy a scribbling activity with the parent and child, reminding the parent, as needed, about developmental expectations at this age to prevent over-control (see Activity No. 1).

BLIND PARENT

May not be able to see her child's markings on paper.

1. Use crayons rather than felt tip markers and use slick paper, such as the shiny paper used in copy machines. The parent will be able to feel her child's markings. (Crayon marks are not as easily identifiable on standard paper, such as newsprint or bond paper.)
2. Explain that children's initial markings are usually light, brief, and often missed. Describe the child's markings as he produces them.
3. Refer to 4.36 (Watches adult scribble) for activities relating to the introduction of scribbling and the visual effects for children.
4. The parent and child can enjoy making markings in the sand with their fingers or with a dowel.

4.54 Child: USES BOTH HANDS FREELY (11-13 mo.)
Parent: Does not force child's hand preference

GENERAL GUIDELINES

The child's gain in gross motor development, such as standing and sitting without support, frees his hands to play and enable him to develop further fine motor skills. He uses both hands during play and may begin to separate assignments for each. For example, he may use his left hand for carrying or holding and his right for manipulating. He may show a preference for one hand during manipulative play; however, grasp patterns should be consistent for each hand. Hand dominence in children is not firmly established until they approach preschool age.

Parents should avoid encouraging their child's hand preference at this age. Instead of offering their child a toy, crayon, or spoon to one hand, they can offer toys at their child's midline and let him choose with which hand to pick it up.

If, however, the child demonstrates asymmetrical grasp patterns, such as the lack of a mature pincer grasp with one hand, parents should encourage the use of that hand by presenting objects to that side.

MENTALLY RETARDED PARENT

May try to make her child use only one hand during manual activities, expecting him to have hand dominence.

1. Explain to the parent that, at this age, her child still needs lots of practice using both of his hands because his hand and arm muscles are still developing:
   a. Relate how using both hands now will help him button his shirt and tie his shoes when he is older.
   b. Explain that, for the next year or so, her child will experiment with which hand he uses; one day he may hold his crayon with his left hand and the next day use his right hand. Relate how this helps him learn which hand he likes best.
   c. Point out pictures of children in magazines or childcare books holding toys, utensils, crayons, etc. in different hands.
2. Demonstrate to the parent how to present various materials to her child at his midline; point out how this lets him choose which hand to use. Advise her not to take an object out of his hand and try to make him hold it with the other one.

3. If the child has grasp asymmetries, omit Activity Nos. 1 and 2. Instead:
   a. Explain that her child uses one hand more than the other, not because he is right-handed (or left-handed, if applicable), but because the muscles in his other hand cannot hold things as well.
   b. Explain that he needs more practice using the hand he does not use very much to help his hand muscles hold things better.
   c. Demonstrate offering a toy to the child's non-preferred hand.
   d. Suggest a concrete marker to help the parent remember which of her child's hands to offer materials, e.g., a certain freckle or wrist band.
   e. Let the parent practice offering her child a toy to his non-preferred hand. Reinforce how she is helping him to learn to use that hand better.
   f. Name common materials for the parent to offer to her child's non-preferred hand during daily activities: his spoon during feeding, his cookies, his crayon, fingerfoods, and his toys.
   g. Ask her to show you where to place his fingerfoods on his highchair tray to encourage him to pick them up with his non-preferred hand.
4. Review and demonstrate toys which encourage the child to use both hands: spoon and a cup for stirring, large ball, rings on a stick, playing "Pat-A-Cake" with blocks or butter tubs, and holding a book and flipping the pages.

4.55 Child: **GRASPS CRAYON ADAPTIVELY** (11-12 mo.)
Parent: Provides crayons which facilitate child's grasp

GENERAL GUIDELINES

The child holds crayons and markers using a primitive palmar grasp, i.e., in his fist, until a more mature finger grasp develops, often a year later. Thick hexagonal or kindergarten crayons are recommended to accommodate this immature grasp.

Children who have motor impairments and limited grasping abilities may be able to hold crayons which are made thicker with putty or foam rubber.

MENTALLY RETARDED PARENT

May expect her child to hold crayons with a mature grasp like her own.

1. Demonstrate how young children hold their crayons:
   a. Explain that her child cannot hold his crayon the way we do because his finger muscles are not ready to control the crayon as well as his fist can.
   b. Relate that, as her child gets older, he will hold his crayon like us. He learns this from practicing marking with crayons and by watching how others hold their crayons.
   c. Show her pictures of young children coloring and holding crayons with their fist.

2. Provide the parent with a few thick crayons for her child, explaining that thick crayons are easier for him to hold and mark with. Demonstrate how thin crayons can break easily. Suggest storing them in an empty coffee can with a top. Ask the parent where she can keep them out of her child's reach when she is not supervising or coloring with her child.

4.56 Child: **PUTS OBJECTS INTO CONTAINER** (11-12 mo.)
Parent: Provides child containers and objects to play with

GENERAL GUIDELINES

The child's continuing interest in "container and contained" relationships, and his more controlled eye-hand coordination skills enable him to put a variety of small objects into a variety of containers which have large openings.

The general guidelines and parent activities for 4.48 (Takes objects out of container) and 4.50 (Releases object voluntarily) are applicable to this skill.

4.57 Child: **SUPINATES FOREARM** (11-12 mo.)
Parent: Introduces gestures and materials which encourage child's forearm supination

GENERAL GUIDELINES

The child can turn his hand so that his palm faces upward through his rotational forearm movement, or "forearm supination." Forearm supination is not developed until the child is able to rotate his trunk. The development of forearm supination also enables the child to reach and grasp objects with his thumb side upward and palm side facing the object, or midsupination.

Gesture games, such as "Pat-A-Cake," "So Big," "All Gone!", "Open, Shut Them," "Twinkle, Twinkle Little Star," and "Give Me Five" encourage the child's supination and midsupination forearm skills. Manipulating toys can also encourage the child's forearm rotations. For example, the child can play with a telephone and rotate his arm when he brings the receiver to his ear, beat a drum on its side, or hit a tamborine with his hand.

MENTALLY RETARDED PARENT

May not use gestures or have toys which encourage her child's forearm supination.

1. Play gesture song games as suggested in the general guidelines with the parent and child. Lend a cassette recorder with the songs on tape for the parent to play with her child.
2. Show the parent the "All Gone" gesture, pointing out how your forearms are rotated:
   a. Tell her when she gestures and says "all gone" to her child, she is teaching him what "all gone" means and showing him a new way to use his arm muscles.

4.57

b. Suggest times to say and gesture "all gone," e.g., when he is finished with his bottle, his cookie, or his meal; when he is finished with his bath and the water is drained; and when she wipes up some juice that spilled.
3. Show the parent new toys or materials she can begin introducing to her child now that he is learning to use his hands so well:
    a. Show her how cylindrical oatmeal boxes and coffee cans can be used as drums. Help think of phrases she can say to the beat of the music, e.g., "boom, boom, boom, boom."
    b. Demonstrate how fun cardboard paper towel and toilet paper inserts can be. Her child can roll them, hit the tops and sides of his coffee can with them, and use them as a megaphone to make his special sounds.

BLIND PARENT

May be unfamiliar with young children's gestures used in songs or communicative interactions, and may be unaware of the visual cues her child uses to determine how he will approach and grasp objects.

1. Describe and physically assist the parent, as needed, to understand the common gestures children like to watch and imitate: "All gone," "So big," "Come here," and extending arms for the reaching gesture.
2. Explain how children adapt their hand and arm approach to objects, dependent upon seeing how large the object is and the position in which it is offered. For example:
    a. If she offers him a beach ball, her child reaches with both arms; but if she holds out a small block, he sees he only needs to reach with one hand.
    b. If she presents a tennis ball using an overhand grasp, her child is more likely to rotate his forearm and grasp it underhand.
    c. If she holds out a cylindrical object horizontally, her child is likely to approach it overhand; but if she holds it vertically or pointed toward him, he is more likely to approach it in mid-supination.

4.58 **Child:** **PLACES ONE BLOCK ON TOP OF ANOTHER WITHOUT BALANCING (11-12 mo.)**
Parent: Provides materials suitable for child's stacking efforts

GENERAL GUIDELINES

The child is learning how objects relate to one another in equilibrium. His initial attempts at putting blocks on top of each other are hesitant because he is unsure about the precise timing needed to release the second block for stacking. His level of eye-hand coordination also makes it difficult for him to accurately line up a second block on top of the first to insure balance. Consequently, the child usually holds onto his block when he places it on top of another one or it topples over upon release.

Parents can introduce materials which may be easier than blocks for the child to practice stacking and help him learn the concept of equilibrium and balance. For example, parents can demonstrate and let their child practice stacking butter tubs with tops, cans, tissue boxes, books, wooden stacking rings, sponges, bean bags, round flat cookies, or squares of toast.

MENTALLY RETARDED PARENT

May not have blocks for her child to play with, or may expect her child to stack blocks accurately.

1. Make homemade blocks with the parent using small single serving cereal boxes and colorful contact paper. Weight the boxes with dried beans or sand.
2. Demonstrate how sponges, cans, and other boxes can be used as blocks.
3. Before introducing blocks to the child, stress that, at first, he will not know how to build with them, but he will learn with practice:
    a. Demonstrate how young children hold a block on top of another without release and how, sometimes, they release the block, but cannot make it balance yet.
    b. Explain that if she tries to make him stack his blocks, he may get frustrated and not want to play with the blocks; at this age, children like to see what they can do with them all by themselves.
    c. Role-play how to respond if her child begins to throw the blocks.
4. Demonstrate giving the child three blocks, one at a time, while the parent also has three blocks:
    a. Tell the parent it is great if she builds with her blocks next to him, but let him practice building with his blocks by himself.
    b. Relate how discouraging it can be for her child when he tries to build, but the block falls off. Ask her if she can think of something to do or say to him to show him she cares and is happy he is trying.
    c. Relate how he likes her approval when his block does not fall down; ask the parent what she can say to let him know she is pleased.

BLIND PARENT

May not be able to see her child's attempts and successes in block-stacking.

1. Describe the child's block-stacking efforts as the parent demonstrates this skill to her child. Does he hold onto the block, stack without regard to alignment, or stack with regard to size and balance (i.e., he knows it is easier to place smaller blocks on top of larger ones)?
2. The parent can hear blocks topple over and provide reinforcement to her child that it is okay:
    a. When she hears cessation of activity, she can tell her child she wants to see what he made and proceed to feel his block placement.
    b. The child will begin to expect his parent to periodically "check" how he is doing, eagerly awaiting her praise.
    c. Larger heavy blocks and unopened canned goods may be easier for the parent to tactually monitor without knocking them down.

d. If cubes topple over when the parent approaches them, she can determine how many her child stacked and return the tower to its original form.

PHYSICALLY DISABLED PARENT

With limited upper extremity or hand control; may have difficulty modeling block stacking for her child.

1. The parent may be able to demonstrate the concept of stacking using larger items, such as tissue boxes, while the child practices with smaller blocks.
2. The parent can provide pictures of blocks stacked as a model.
3. The parent can provide verbal directions and prompts to her child while tapping the bottom block to encourage him to try stacking.

4.59 Child: MARKS PAPER WITH CRAYON (12-13 mo.)
   Parent: Demonstrates making simple strokes and scribbles on paper; encourages child to make marks

GENERAL GUIDELINES

The child has learned that if he maneuvers a crayon or marker in a certain way, he can make marks on paper. Early marks with crayons are often short wavy lines produced by his backward and forward hand and arm motion.

Parents encourage their child's early attempts with marking by providing him with opportunities to practice with crayons and paper, demonstrating how to make marks, and praising his "artistic" works.

Refer to 4.36 (Watches adult scribble), 4.53 (Tries to imitate scribble), and 4.55 (Grasps crayon adaptively) for prerequisite parent training activities.

MENTALLY RETARDED PARENT

May not reinforce her child's marks on paper.

1. Engage the parent and child in paper and crayon play. When you observe the child making marks on paper, praise the parent for helping him learn how to do this. Relate how he has learned to do this from watching her making crayon marks and seeing how much fun this can be.
2. Tell the parent that when her child makes marks on his paper, he likes to hear her talk about them; this makes him feel good because he knows she thinks his work is special:
    a. Model example phrases she can say to her child, e.g., "Look at that beautiful line!", "I like that mark you made; I am going to make one," or "You made that mark just where you wanted it."
    b. Prompt the parent to say reinforcing phrases while her child is coloring by saying, "Tell him about the marks he is making" and "What can you say to tell him you like his coloring?"
    c. Interpret the child's positive reactions to her phrases, e.g., "See how he smiled when you said that" and "Look how he started scribbling more when you told him you liked it!"

BLIND PARENT

May not be able to see her child's marks on paper.

1. The parent can hear her child mark with chalk on the blackboard; she can feel the waxed markings from crayons on shiny smooth paper.
2. Relate how children like to color on anything, such as walls, shoes, themselves, and tables, and thus her child should always be closely supervised with crayons.

4.60 Child: PUTS THREE OR MORE OBJECTS INTO CONTAINER (12-13 mo.)
   Parent: Encourages child to put at least three objects into small containers

GENERAL GUIDELINES

The child's maturing purposeful release skills enable him to accurately put small objects, such as cubes, into containers the size of a cup or a bowl. His persistence and interest in this activity is also displayed as he puts at least three objects consecutively into the container before moving on to another activity or removing them.

Parents can encourage their child to practice his more precise release skills during daily activities, such as letting him put away his crayons in a juice can, letting him put his cubes of cheese in a bowl, and giving him a plastic cup to put a piece of ice in for a drink.

Parent training activities for 4.48 (Takes objects out of containers) are applicable to this skill. If the child is having difficulties with release, refer to 4.50 (Releases object voluntarily) and continue to use larger containers, such as coffee cans or boxes.

4.61 Child: BUILDS TOWER USING TWO CUBES (12-16 mo.)
   Parent: Provides materials which encourage child to build a tower of two cubes

GENERAL GUIDELINES

The child's maturing eye-hand control and more precise accurately timed release enable him to build a tower of two, using one-inch cubes. Refer to 4.58 (Places one block on top of another without balancing) for alternative stacking of materials and parent activities which encourage the child's stacking.

4.62 Child: PLACES ONE ROUND PEG IN PEGBOARD (12-15 mo.)
Parent: Demonstrates and encourages child to place peg in pegboard

GENERAL GUIDELINES

The child's maturing eye-hand coordination and voluntary release enable him to place at least one thick peg (three-fourths inch in diameter) into a pegboard. Initially, he may overshoot the hole and then like to place and remove the peg repetitively to practice and gain confidence with this task.

Parents can make their own pegboards using a shoebox or the bottom of a Velveeta cheese box by punching four or five holes in it. Pegs can be small plastic hair rollers, unsharpened pencils, thick straws cut in half, or thick crayons.

MENTALLY RETARDED PARENT

May expect her child to place all of the pegs in the board without exploration and practice time, and may present the board in positions which are difficult for her child to practice this skill.

1. Do not introduce more than four to six pegs at a time. Provide parent anticipatory guidance regarding how many pegs young children can be expected to try to place in the board. Show the parent two positions for her child during pegboard activities to insure his stability and facilitate eye-hand coordination, e.g., at a highchair, or on the floor sitting with a sturdy box or stable lap tray:
   a. Point out how the board needs to be within reach of the child and below his eyes.
   b. Demonstrate how difficult it is to try to put a peg in the board if you are not positioned well, e.g., stand on one foot while trying to put a peg in a board which is on top of the refrigerator. Let the parent try this awkward position.
2. Explain that children often need to practice all by themselves before they can figure out how to put the pegs in the holes. Demonstrate how they may roll the peg, poke at the board, and miss inserting it a few times. Stress that this is okay because that is how children learn.
3. Explain that her child should practice using only one peg at a time so he does not get confused or start throwing them.
4. Model demonstrating this skill for the child while verbally encouraging and allowing him to explore the pegs and board without demands. Let the parent practice demonstrating and verbally encouraging her child to put the peg in, with your reinforcement. Switch activities if the parent becomes too manipulative and re-introduce at a later time.
5. Help the parent make a pegboard crayon box out of a shoebox. The child can help put his crayons away after a coloring activity.

BLIND PARENT

May not be able to see if and when her child puts a peg in the hole.

1. Help make pegboards with boxes. When the child inserts the pegs, the parent can hear them drop.
2. Refer to 4.47 (Removes pegs from pegboard).

4.63 Child: POINTS WITH INDEX FINGER (12-16 mo.)
Parent: Models pointing; encourages child to point for communication and fine motor skills

GENERAL GUIDELINES

The child isolates his index finger to point, keeping his remaining fingers held close to his palm. Refer to the general guidelines and activities for 4.51 (Pokes with index finger) if the child is having difficulty isolating his index finger.

Pointing is also a powerful communicative tool for the child which is addressed in 1.73 (Understands pointing).

4.64 Child: INVERTS SMALL CONTAINER TO OBTAIN TINY OBJECT AFTER DEMONSTRATION (12½-18 mo.)
Parent: Shows child how to obtain object from narrow-necked containers

GENERAL GUIDELINES

Inverting a small container to obtain an object requires the child's fine motor ability to rotate his forearm. In addition, this skill also tests the child's cognitive ability to solve the problem of how to get an object out of a container when his hands will not fit in it.

The container's opening should be small so the child cannot place his hand in it to retrieve the object. Small plastic pill containers or clear plastic trial-size shampoo bottles are suitable. Objects could be a piece of dry cereal (e.g., Trix or Cheerios), a breath mint pellet (e.g., Tic Tacs), a bell, or a bead. Bells and beads should not be used if the child is prone to mouthing or if he is left unsupervised.

Parents can encourage their child's problem-solving and manipulative skills required for inverting containers by showing him how and letting him practice: emptying sand from containers in his sand box, getting a tennis ball out of its cylindrical container, squeezing catsup out of a squeeze bottle, or dumping his small block or peg toy out of his empty bottle.

At this stage, the child usually requires clear demonstration and sometimes physical guidance through the motions. Initially, the child may poke his finger into the container or shake it in his attempt to retrieve the object.

MENTALLY RETARDED PARENT

May not understand the problem-solving process involved to obtain objects from narrow-necked containers.

1. Present a narrow-necked container with a piece of cereal in it and ask the parent how she would get it out:
   a. Point out how she automatically knew that all she needed to do was turn it over.
   b. Demonstrate the task slowly and point out how you also need to be able to turn your wrist in just the right way.
   c. Relate that her child is ready to learn how to do this, but since he is so young, it will take him time and practice.
2. Demonstrate the way many young children initially try to get things out of containers, i.e., poking their finger in the hole and/or shaking it:
   a. Stress that this is okay because it shows he is really trying.
   b. Explain that with more practice he will learn to figure it out since shaking or poking does not always work.
   c. Review that her child learns by watching her so she can show him how to do it and then let him try it all by himself.
3. Help the parent collect suitable containers to use with her child. Limit the objects to edible items.

BLIND PARENT

May have difficulty locating tiny dumped objects and assuring that her child does not swallow them.

1. Identify transparent from non-transparent containers, as needed. If tiny objects are used, they could always be edible to insure the child does not choke.
2. Suggest working within a contained area, such as "work-play" tray or cookie sheet. This will confine the area in which the tiny object would drop when the container is inverted.
3. The parent can encourage her child to dump out the object in her hand.
4. Review how her child relies upon watching her to learn how to obtain the object. Emphasize showing him the object first and then slowly turning it over within his view.

4.65 Child: SCRIBBLES SPONTANEOUSLY (13-18 mo.)
Parent: Provides ample opportunities for child to scribble

GENERAL GUIDELINES

The child's light wavy lines and sometimes hesitant marks emerge into endless scribbling, sometimes taking up the entire page. His brief lines take on repetitive circular patterns of spirals with increasing force. Later he begins to mix his circular patterns with lines. His maturing eye-hand control enables him to repeat his own markings over and over.

Parents should continue to give their child the freedom and experiences to scribble without regard to form or design. They will need to set limits, however, that crayons are for marking on paper, not walls, tables, or floors.

Refer to 4.36 (Watches adult scribble), 4.53 (Tries to imitate scribble), 4.55 (Grasps crayon adaptively), and 4.59 (Marks paper with crayon) for prerequisite parent training activities.

MENTALLY RETARDED PARENT

May have unrealistic coloring expectations for her child.

1. Praise the parent for her child's progress in scribbling, remarking that he has learned to scribble like that because she has been giving him chances to practice.
2. Advise the parent that her child will not be ready to draw actual pictures or color within the lines of coloring books until he is much older.
3. Model and encourage the parent to say phrases to her child, such as "Round and round, you are making the crayons make circles!"
4. Explain that young children often scribble on walls, tables, floors, etc. They are not being bad; they just do not know better yet:
   a. Ask the parent if she can think of ways to prevent his coloring on walls (i.e., close supervision).
   b. Role-play how to respond just in case her child happens to scribble on the floor.
5. Suggest hanging her child's pictures on the refrigerator to show him she thinks his artwork is terrific.

4.66 Child: INVERTS SMALL CONTAINER SPONTANEOUSLY TO OBTAIN TINY OBJECT (13½-19 mo.)
Parent: Anticipates and accommodates for child's new problem-solving and fine motor skills

GENERAL GUIDELINES

The child spontaneously turns over a bottle to obtain a tiny object. He no longer needs a demonstration to solve this problem. If the child does not spontaneously invert the bottle, refer to the general guidelines and parent activities for 4.64 (Inverts small container to obtain tiny object after demonstration).

If the child spontaneously inverts the bottle, his level of active wrist rotation and problem-solving skills enable him to begin learning to activate mechanical or wind-up toys and open door knobs.

MENTALLY RETARDED PARENT

May not anticipate new safety concerns which arise with her child's developing fine motor and problem-solving skills.

1. Praise the parent for her child's rapidly developing fine motor and problem-solving skills when he solves the problem of how to get the object out of the bottle. Point out how well her child's wrist turns now.

4.66

2. Remind the parent how each new developmental milestone for her child usually also means there are new safety concerns:
   a. Point out that, since he can turn his wrist now and is learning to figure things out, he is ready to turn knobs to open things or turn them on.
   b. Ask the parent to think of things that might be dangerous to her child now that he is ready to turn bottle caps to open things up. Prompt, as needed, concerning medicine bottles, toxic cleaners, etc.
   c. Concretely show and tell the parent how to prevent her child from opening up dangerous things, e.g., place out of reach or use safety caps.
   d. Ask the parent what her child could do that would be dangerous now that he can turn knows, e.g., knobs of stoves, hot curlers, fans, heaters, and doors leading to stairways or outdoors.
   e. Show the parent how to prevent her child from turning dangerous knobs, e.g., putting safety chains on doors, placing things out of reach, removing the knobs.
3. Refer to 1.98 (Attempts and then succeeds in activating mechanical toy) to help the parent teach her child to activate mechanical toys.

BLIND PARENT

May not be able to see when her child turns various knobs.

1. Provide developmental anticipatory guidance when the child begins to demonstrate wrist rotation. Relate how he may start opening doors, turning on the stove or heater, etc. The parent can child-proof accordingly.

4.67 Child: PUTS MANY OBJECTS INTO CONTAINER WITHOUT REMOVING ANY (14-15 mo.)
Parent: Demonstrates and encourages child to put various objects into a variety of containers

GENERAL GUIDELINES

Putting small things into containers and emptying them out is a favorite activity for the child. His persistence, interest in finishing a task, and competence with spacial awareness and release enable him to put at least eight objects into a container without removing any in the process. Filling containers offers the child an immediate concrete sense of achievement and helps build his self-esteem.

Parents can encourage their child to put many small objects into a container through activities, such as:
1. Offer the child containers to put things in which are difficult for him to take them back out of, e.g., a coffee can with a hole cut in the lid to drop spoons through.
2. Use lots of verbal encouragement: "Put them all in!" and "Make them all gone!"
3. Give him only a few objects at a time and then quickly give him another one before he has time to remove any.
4. Encourage him to put them all back before he gets to play with another toy; help, as needed, to get this concept across.

Paper bags, bowls, pocketbooks, pots and pans, washtubs, and boxes can be used as containers.

MENTALLY RETARDED PARENT

May not generalize structured "container and contained" activities to her child's daily activities and play.

1. Praise the parent on her child's progress with putting objects into containers:
   a. Name the actual objects and containers you have observed him use during play activities.
   b. Relate how this helps him learn to put his things away as he gets older.
2. Make a special container with the parent for her child in which to keep his blocks or crayons:
   a. Use a large coffee can and cut out an appropriate-sized hole in the lid.
   b. Show the parent two cans, one with smooth edges and one with sharp edges sticking out. Ask her which container she should use and help identify why.
3. Help collect old household items for the child to use as bath toys and find a special box or plastic washtub basin to store them in when not in use:
   a. Plastic cups, empty shampoo bottles, funnels, and sponges can be fun bath-time toys. Show the parent the different things she can show her child to do with them while taking a bath or to use in a dish tub for water play outdoors.
   b. Suggest letting her child take his own bath "toys" out of the bath toybox and let him drop them in the tub. Suggest also letting him help put them back when he is finished. Remark, "Think how proud he will feel helping you during bath-time!"
   c. Caution the parent never to leave her child alone in the bathtub or children's pool. Explain that, even though he is bigger now, a child this age can drown when there is only a little water in the tub (gesture how much).
   d. Ask the parent what she could do if the phone rang while her child was in the bathtub playing with his toys.
4. Suggest and encourage the parent to think of safe "goodies" to put in an old pocketbook for her child to play with, e.g., comb, brush, toy keys, peg dolls, and blocks.
5. Stress how hard it is for her child to put *all* of the objects he has emptied out back into their containers (purse, bath toybox, etc.):
   a. Explain that, he is so curious about everything, it is hard for him to stay with one task for a long time.
   b. Ask the parent what she can tell her child to let him know she is proud of him when he can put all of his blocks back into the can (toys in box, etc.).
   c. Help think of things to tell her child to encourage him to put all the things back in the container, e.g., "Here you go; try another one; great!"
6. Role-play possible parental responses to situations where the child empties out containers he should not, e.g., he empties out the trash on the floor or empties out his bottom drawer of clothes.

BLIND PARENT

May benefit from anticipatory guidance regarding young children's favorite pasttime of transporting objects from containers and "stashing them away."

1. Advise the parent that her child's interest in filling and emptying containers may lead to antics, such as stuffing things under his bed, and dropping his toys or other household objects in the trash or even the toilet!

4.68 Child: USES BOTH HANDS IN MIDLINE — ONE HOLDS, OTHER MANIPULATES (16-18 mo.)
    Parent: Introduces child to toys and activities which encourage him to use two hands cooperatively

GENERAL GUIDELINES

The child demonstrates his maturing bilateral coordination skills when he uses both hands at the same time, but for different roles. At this age, he uses one hand as the "holder" or stabilizer of an object and the other hand as the "manipulator" or explorer of the object. Hand preference usually becomes more pronounced during this period. The child uses his dominant hand as the manipulator and explorer while he uses his non-dominant hand as the holder or stabilizer.

Parents can encourage their child's bilateral hand coordination with any of the following toys or activities:

1. Stirring with a spoon and cup or pouring sand from one cup to another.
2. Pounding boards and hammers or ring stacks and rings.
3. Holding a pinwheel and spinning it with the other hand.
4. Squeezing toothpaste onto a toothbrush.
5. Holding a doll and brushing its hair.
6. Holding a container and putting things in or taking them out.
7. Opening a plastic egg carton.
8. Any toy or activity which requires two hands.

MENTALLY RETARDED PARENT

May be unaware of new activities or toys to introduce to her child as his developmental skills advance.

1. Point out to the parent how her child is learning to use both of his hands at the same time, and each hand can be doing a different thing. Concretely describe this concept, dependent upon the particular toy or activity the child is engaged in, e.g., "See how he holds his paper when he colors now. You don't need to keep taping it down."
2. Help the parent identify new toys that her child can begin to learn how to play with, and activities he can participate in now that he is learning to use two hands:
   a. Refer to the general guidelines for suggested toys and activities.
   b. Help make a special toybox in which to put a few of his toys. Identify low shelves and drawers in various rooms that can also be used to hold his favorite toys and household objects.
   c. Review the child's current toy assortment. Point out toys which her child is too old for now and explain why.
   d. Post pictures of children engaged in two-handed activities as a reminder.

4.69 Child: BUILDS TOWER USING THREE CUBES (16-18 mo.)
    Parent: Reinforces child's continuing stacking efforts

GENERAL GUIDELINES

The child can build a tower of three or four cubes as evidence of continuing improved eye-hand coordination. He enjoys being able to direct his own actions as he modulates and times his release to match his intentions. He may also begin to enjoy knocking down his towers so he can watch and listen to the effects of blocks toppling.

Refer to 4.58 (Places one block on top of another without balancing) for alternative fun stacking materials and prerequisite parent activities. Parents can also begin to introduce thread spools and nesting toys for their child to practice stacking.

4.70 Child: PLACES SIX ROUND PEGS IN PEGBOARD (16-19 mo.)
    Parent: Encourages child to place at least six pegs in a board

GENERAL GUIDELINES

The child's increasing confidence with pegs, and his ability to attend to and persist with a task for a longer period of time, enables him to place at least six pegs in a board.

Parents can encourage their child's persistence and confidence by keeping distractions at a minimum and providing verbal encouragement and praise.

Refer to the general guidelines under 4.62 (Places one round peg in pegboard) for alternative homemade pegboard toys. The parent activities for that skill are also applicable to placing six round pegs in a pegboard.

4.71 Child: IMITATES VERTICAL STROKE (18-24 mo.)
    Parent: Encourages child to imitate her vertical stroke with a crayon

GENERAL GUIDELINES

The child has learned to repeat his own lines in scribbling and now is beginning to try to imitate strokes other people make. A vertical stroke is usually the first controlled line the child learns to imitate, but he must observe the stroke being drawn in order to imitate it. His vertical stroke should be drawn in a general vertical direction with a beginning and an end, but does not need to be drawn exactly like the model he

4.71

is imitating. The child's line may be longer, shorter, and tilt somewhat within a thirty-degree angle of the demonstrated line.

Parents can encourage their child to imitate their vertical crayon strokes by giving him ample opportunities to test his control with crayons, and giving visual, tactual, and verbal cues during the imitation process. For example, parents can say, "Down," when they draw their dark bold vertical stroke in clear view of their child and then encourage him to trace his finger down it. Parents can also demonstrate making vertical strokes during fingerpainting, and in the sand or dirt with their finger or a stick.

MENTALLY RETARDED PARENT

May try to make her child draw vertical strokes exactly right.

1. Introduce imitating vertical strokes subtly during paper and crayon activities rather than stressing this as a specific skill:
   a. Emphasize creativity; explain when she lets her child scribble the way he wants, he is learning how to create his own forms.
   b. Explain that he likes to watch her make marks on the paper and sometimes may want to try making the same mark; a line going up and down is the easiest type of line for her child to make at this age.
   c. Demonstrate making a vertical line while saying "down." Encourage the parent to try this while her child is watching.
   d. Relate how good she makes her child feel when she tells him she likes whatever marks or scribbles he makes.
   e. Let the parent and child have separate pieces of paper to "draw" on to help prevent interference.
2. Suggest unconventional fun places to draw vertical lines with her child and say "down," e.g., in the dirt outside, on a steamy window, or on a mirror with your finger; and with a sponge on the table.

BLIND PARENT

May not be able to see if her child can imitate her vertical strokes.

1. Use chalk and a chalkboard. The parent can discriminate the sound of a scribble versus lines.
2. The parent may feel her child's crayon markings on slick paper, such as ones used in "wet" copier machines.
3. Emphasize to the parent how her child watches her hand movements when she draws lines to help him learn to copy making the same lines; he uses these visual cues as well as her verbal directions and practice in feeling the up and down movements.

SOCIAL-EMOTIONAL DEVELOPMENT

5.01 **Child:** ENJOYS AND NEEDS A GREAT DEAL OF PHYSICAL CONTACT AND TACTILE STIMULATION (0-3 mo.)
  Parent: Provides child with adequate and appropriate physical contact and tactile stimulation

MENTALLY RETARDED PARENT

May physically over- or under-stimulate child.

1. Observe the parent's positions when she's holding her child to assure they are each comfortably positioned:
   a. If the parent or child are not positioned comfortably, describe why and demonstrate alternate positions, e.g., "He likes to look at you when you hold him but his head is down too low for him to see you. He can't lift his head up by himself yet" or "When you hold him like that, it looks uncomfortable for you because you have to lean way over to the side."
   b. Reinforce the parent when you see her positioned comfortably with her child. Describe the child's positions and his signs of comfort, e.g., "See how his body cuddles into yours and he stopped fussing."
2. Name specific times for the parent to hold her child during feeding, when he's crying, when she's showing him a new toy, and after bathing while he is wrapped in a towel.
3. Tell the parent how much her child likes to be held. Relate how this lets him know she loves him and makes him feel safe. Stress she will not spoil him by holding him.
4. Turn on a music box and model gentle rocking with her child. Let the parent practice as you comment about the child's expressions that tell her she's rocking him gently.
5. Observe the parent's interactions when she's holding her child. If over-stimulation is observed, via tickling, jiggling, shaking, face prodding, or poking, describe the child's signals which tell us he doesn't like it, e.g., face turning red, crying, fussing, body stiffening, or turning away.
6. If the parent swaddles her child in a blanket, or does not but the child could benefit from swaddling, demonstrate and help the parent:
   a. Select suitable swaddling blankets, i.e., small and light.
   b. Determine appropriate wrapping techniques, not too tight or loose.
   c. Determine when to swaddle; caution not to keep him swaddled all day.
   d. Know at what age she should stop swaddling, i.e., when he's two to three months old.

BLIND PARENT

May be unaware of her child's visible signs of enjoyment during physical contact and tactile stimulation.

1. Monitor and describe the child's facial expressions while the parent holds and cuddles him, e.g., "His eyes widen when you rock him" and "He looks at you when you stroke his arm."

PHYSICALLY DISABLED PARENT

Who has decreased mobility, coordination, or strength; may have difficulty providing comfortable close physical contact with her child.

1. Encourage household members and others who may help out in the home to position the child in his parent's lap or with her in bed often during each day. If the parent cannot hold her child, she may be able to nuzzle and transmit other important feelings of closeness through facial contact, smiling, and soothing voices.
2. The child can be placed in a *snuggly vest** around the parent's chest.
3. Refer to 1.01 (Quiets when picked up) for adaptive techniques to help the parent pick her child up.

5.02 **Child:** REGARDS FACE (0-1 mo.)
  Parent: Offers child sufficient face-to-face contact

GENERAL GUIDELINES

Face-to-face contact with others is one of the child's first social interactions. His stare is usually momentary and solemn, but he looks intently as if he is "studying" and understanding the facial patterns and expressions he sees. During his first month, face-to-face contact with others is usually the most comfortable and visually clear at eight to twelve inches away; interestingly, just the right distance from his parent in a cradled feeding position!

MENTALLY RETARDED PARENT

May not offer frequent face-to-face positions with her child, or may position her face too closely to his.

1. Demonstrate and let the parent practice face-to-face positioning with her child while holding him cradled, and while he's lying down:
   a. Model the appropriate distance between faces. Use an exaggerated handspread from your nose to the child's chest as a concrete marker, if needed.
   b. Describe and explain why her child alternates looking with looking away. Relate that, at this age, he can't look at anyone for more than a few seconds; his eyes get tired so he takes a break and then returns to look back at the parent.
   c. Stress talking softly to her child when she looks at him. Suggest specific short phrases to say, e.g., "You're so pretty today" and "I see you looking at me."
   d. Name specific behaviors which tell us her child is too tired to look anymore, i.e., when he twists, continues to look the other way, or closes his eyes.

---

*See Glossary.

5.02

2. Name specific daily activities for the parent to look at her child and talk gently to him, e.g., lean over and face him before picking him up from the crib, while feeding him, before and after each diaper change, whenever you hold him for pleasure, or when he starts crying.

BLIND PARENT

May not provide face-to-face interactions, especially if congenitally blind, and may be unaware when her child looks at her.

1. Anticipatory Guidance: If the parent does not spontaneously incorporate face-to-face contact during interactions, these positions could be uncomfortable for her and the child:
   a. The child will have numerous opportunities to receive face to-face contact with others while maintaining close tactile and vocal contact with his parent.
   b. The parent and child can enjoy positions which maintain close tactile contact, while allowing the child to look at his parent's profile, hear her soothing voice, and look at other things around him.
   c. A favored position may be for the child to face outward with his back supported against the parent's chest and abdomen.
2. Describe to the parent the changes in her child's facial expressions when she talks to and cuddles him.
3. The parent can recognize when her child is facing her by monitoring the direction of his breathing.

5.03 Child: SMILES REFLEXIVELY (0-1½ mo.)
Parent: Recognizes child's reflexive smiles

GENERAL GUIDELINES

The child's initial smiles are brief and usually a reflexive response.

MENTALLY RETARDED PARENT

May try to force her child to smile.

1. If the parent is observed to tickle or poke her child's cheek explain that, at this age, her child can only smile briefly and she shouldn't try to make him smile. Relate that he will start to smile more often in a few weeks and he learns to smile by watching us smile.
2. Explain that, at this age, her child shows us he's happy by looking at us, making soft sounds, and cuddling.
3. Model head nodding, smiling, and gently talking to the child often. Reinforce the parent's similar interactions saying, "Look at that special look he gives you when you smile."

BLIND PARENT

May be unaware of her child's reflexive smiles.

1. Describe the child's smiles as they occur, e.g., brief smile, eyebrows raise, mouth opens, mouth closes, etc.
2. Describe the child's reactions to his parent's smile.

5.04 Child: ESTABLISHES EYE CONTACT (0-2 mo.)
Parent: Encourages child's eye contact via compatible interactions

GENERAL GUIDELINES

The child consistently looks into the eyes of adults when approached slowly and within a compatible distance of 8-12 inches.

If the child displays gaze aversion he may be over-stimulated, or may be reacting to a stressful situation.

If he displays consistent gaze aversion and resists physical contact, professional consultation is recommended.

MENTALLY RETARDED PARENT

May not respond to child's eye contact, or may try to force child's eye contact.

1. As the situation arises, describe the child's eye contact, e.g., "See how he's looking at you? He's waiting for a smile." Reinforce the parent's eye contact with her child.
2. If the child averts his gaze often while the parent is interacting with him, point this out and explore possible reasons and suggest alternative responses:
   a. Is the parent's face too close? Change positions.
   b. Is the parent's voice too loud? Try gentle sounds or coos.
   c. Is he tired? Let him rest.
   d. Are there too many things to look at, feel, and listen to at one time (bright lights, loud music, too much bouncing, too many people looking at him at one time)? Adjust lights, turn down music, hold gently without bouncing, etc.
3. Tell the parent not to turn her child's head or make him look at her when he looks the other way.
4. Explain that her child likes to look at faces the most when we're smiling, nodding, and talking gently to him.

BLIND PARENT

May be unaware of her child's eye contact and its relation to social and communicative development.

1. Anticipatory Guidance: The child may establish gaze aversion toward his parent, with only fleeting moments of eye contact. As long as he establishes eye contact with others, there is no reason to stress the issue. He may be using this as an adaptive method to interact with his parent. The important issue is for the parent and child to be comfortable in their own style of interactions. In a few months, the intensity of the child's gaze aversion will probably gradually decline.

    Parents, however, should be given the opportunity to understand their child's eye contact and its meaning for him and others.
2. Explain the child's eye contact behaviors and their social and communicative role at this age. An example descriptive explanation could be: "Your child is learning to use eye contact, i.e., look at us directly in the eyes, as a way to get attention from others in much the same way he's

learning that when he cries, someone will feed him or hold him. His eye contact says 'I'm ready to interact.' His eye contact also lets us know when he is responding to our efforts of interacting; for example, when we talk to him and he looks back, he tells us he's interested. When he looks away he lets us know he's tired of watching us or listening to us. At first, a child only gives momentary eye contact, i.e., 4-10 seconds. Then he'll stop looking for a second and look again."
3. The child may develop his own alternative to eye contact when communicating with his parent. She can in turn monitor her child's auditory and movement signals which say "I'm ready to interact," "I'm interested," or "I've had enough."

5.05 Child: MOLDS AND RELAXES BODY WHEN HELD: CUDDLES (0-3 mo.)
Parent: Holds child in a manner which is conducive for cuddling and molding

GENERAL GUIDELINES

The child's body molds or snuggles into his parent's when he is held. The parent and child appear comfortable and relaxed.

Some children who are hypersensitive, tactually defensive, and/or have abnormal muscle tone appear to actively resist being held and do not mold their body to their parents'. This can easily be misinterpreted by parents as meaning their child does not want to be held or that he does not need closeness. It is critical to consult with an occupational or physical therapist to help determine individual handling and positioning techniques which are comfortable for the parent and child. Refer to the early skills in the gross motor section of this manual for parent training activities if special positions have been prescribed

The following activities also supplement 5.01 (Enjoys and needs a great deal of physical contact and tactile stimulation).

MENTALLY RETARDED PARENT

May not position her child comfortably, and may interpret her child's resulting signs of distress as not wanting to be held or as being bad.

1. Observe the parent and child's positions when she is holding him at various times during daily activities:
   a. If the parent or child appear "strained," demonstrate alternative positions. Point out important features of the position and the reason, e.g., "When you cradle the back of his head in your arm, he feels safe and he can see your face" or "When you hold him with both arms at your shoulder, he can relax."
   b. Reinforce the positions the parent is using which allow her child to mold to her during holding with a relaxed body. Describe what makes it a good position and the child's responses.
   c. Take a picture of the parent and child in various comfortable positions to leave at home.

2. Describe and interpret the child's signs of resistance when he is being held:
   a. The child's resistance signs may include stiffening, twisting, and/or crying.
   b. Explain that these behaviors show us that her child's body is uncomfortable. Stress that they do not mean he does not like her closeness or does not love her.
   c. If special handling and positioning techniques have been prescribed, contrast and stress how these techniques do not cause her child to stiffen, twist, and/or cry.

5.06 Child: DRAWS ATTENTION TO SELF WHEN IN DISTRESS (0-3 mo.)
Parent: Recognizes and responds appropriately to child's signs of distress

GENERAL GUIDELINES

The child cries or fusses when he is distressed. At this age, he may become distressed at over-stimulation, under-stimulation, hunger, and/or pain.

MENTALLY RETARDED PARENT

May not recognize the cause of her child's distress, may interpret his distress as "being bad," and may think she will spoil him if she always picks him up.

1. Facilitate a discussion with the parent about why children cry. Use pictures of babies crying to facilitate the discussion and help the parent think of why they are crying.
2. Emphasize that, at this age, since her child cannot talk, he may fuss, cry, or scream to tell us when something bothers him. He is not being "bad":
   a. Probe with the parent the different things that can make her child cry: tired, hungry, lonely, something hurts, or something is too loud or bright.
   b. Role-play the various responses that the parent can make when her child cries, dependent on the cause. Use situations, such as "What if he's crying because the music is too loud?", "What if he's crying because he hasn't eaten in three hours?", "What if he's crying and you don't know why; what are things to check?"
3. As the child's distress situations arise, verbally prompt the parent to check for the various possible causes:
   a. Reinforce the parent's attention and calming techniques; refer to 5.08 (Stops unexplained crying).
   b. Comment how her baby feels loved and learns he can trust people when she attends to his distress.

DEAF PARENT

May be unaware of her child's various distress vocalizations and be unaware when he is in distress if out of sight.

1. Explain that her child expresses his distress through various vocal sounds, e.g., fussing, where he's not actually crying, but making crying-like sounds; crying; and screaming, which is usually one very loud "ah" sound.

2. The parent can visually discriminate her child's facial and bodily movements which accompany his distress sounds. Refer to Activity Nos. 1-4, 1.01 (Quiets when picked up) to help the parent recognize when her child is in distress if he is out of her sight.

5.07 Child: RESPONDS WITH SMILE (1½-4 mo.)
Parent: Enjoys compatible doses of social play with child, reinforcing child's smile

GENERAL GUIDELINES

The child's smile becomes socially intentional. He smiles easily when he is not in distress, especially to his parents' playful and comforting interactions.

MENTALLY RETARDED PARENT

May over-stimulate her child in an effort to make him smile.

1. If the parent is observed to poke, tickle, shake, or jiggle her child to try to make him smile, explain that, although this may make us smile, these things don't feel good to children at this age.
2. Name and demonstrate several things that usually make children smile at this age. These may include making a silly face, smiling, tongue clicks, and a gentle tummy touch. Ask the parent to think of things she's seen that seem to make her child smile.
3. Name specific times for the parent to give her child a special smile and gentle tummy touch, e.g., before picking him up, and during diapering, bathing, and feeding. Ask the parent to think of some other good times to make special smiles.
4. When you see the child smile, relate to the parent what seemed to cause it, such as his special music box, the parent talking in a high pitched voice, or her gently rocking him.
5. Leave pictures posted in various places of the home which depict the parent and child engaged in pleasurable interactions. These may help the parent remember their pleasurable times and interactions during stressful times.
6. Comment how sometimes children just don't feel like smiling, even when we do things they like. This does not mean they don't like us to talk, to smile at, kiss, or hold them.

BLIND PARENT

May not be able to visually monitor her child's smiles.

1. Describe the child's smiles to the parent as they occur in response to various visual, auditory, and touch stimuli. Relate how her child's smiles are no longer reflexive but responsive to what he sees, hears, or feels in his environment.

5.08 Child: STOPS UNEXPLAINED CRYING (3-6 mo.)
Parent: Utilizes soothing techniques if child has not stopped unexplained crying

GENERAL GUIDELINES

Long periods of fretful, colicky crying usually end after the first three months. Some children, however, may continue "bouts" of irritable crying for several more months.

Soothing techniques to help calm the child during this period include:
1. Rhythmic movement or motion, such as gently rocking, walking, car rides, and infant swings (at slow speed).
2. Gently but firmly placing a hand on the child's abdomen, or holding the child's hands on his abdomen.
3. Continuous monotonous sounds, such as quiet music, humming, or a clock ticking.
4. Reducing stimulation, such as dimming lights, removing excessive visual targets, and auditory stimulation.

Soothing techniques must be individualized according to the child. Some may be more appropriate than others.

It is natural for parents to feel helpless, angry, and distraught during these trying periods. Whenever possible, respite times should be encouraged via other family members, friends, sitters, or neighbors. Parental tension is transmitted to the child which can compound the crying. There may be times when the parent and child will benefit from having the parent take a few minutes break in another room to relax, take a few deep breaths, and put the situation into perspective.

The child's physician should be advised of excessive irritability to rule out any medical causes.

MENTALLY RETARDED PARENT

May interpret her child's continuing irritability as "mean," that he doesn't love her, that he needs more food, or that he needs more stimulation.

1. If the child's crying is excessive, rule out any physical or medical precipitants:
   a. Ask the parent if it's okay if you talk to her child's doctor, or accompany them on their next doctor visit, to help describe the intensity, duration, and frequency of the child's crying.
   b. Explore feeding, sleeping, and bowel patterns, e.g., is her child getting too much air sucking? not enough food? not enough rest? constipated? not burping after feeding?
2. Emphasize the child's cries as his only way to tell us he feels bad. Relate that crying never means her child is bad or doesn't love or appreciate his parent's hard work in caring for him. Empathize how frustrating this can be for parents. Let her know her child is not the only one who cries a lot.
3. Observe the parent's interactions during her child's irritable crying. If she is rough or abrupt (e.g., too much bouncing, loud talking, etc.), do not say she is handling him wrong, but suggest alternative interactions with verbal "coaching from the sidelines," e.g., "Try humming instead

of talking; he likes to hear you hum" or "Try rocking instead of bouncing; he likes soft touches and gentle motion."
4. Explore various calming techniques with the child. Teach the parent techniques which seem to work through demonstration and verbal prompts.

BLIND PARENT

May be unaware of visual stimuli which may be contributing to her child's distress.

1. If the parent relates periods of unexplained crying, explore if this occurs at predictable times or places. If so, check the area for visual stimuli that may be adversive to her child, e.g., bright sunlight streaming in his window directly on his crib or playpen, unshaded light, or harsh overhead lighting.

5.09 Child: **VOCALIZES IN RESPONSE TO ADULT TALK AND SMILE (3-5 mo.)**
Parent: Initiates communicative interaction with child and encourages his responsive vocalizations

GENERAL GUIDELINES

The child is learning his role as a responder in social interactions. He vocalizes, coos, or makes other happy sounds in response to social interactions.

MENTALLY RETARDED PARENT

May not talk to her child as a means of social interaction.

1. Explain that, at this age, one of children's favorite things to play is a game of turn-taking with sounds, i.e., "First you say something about the child, like 'Hi there, what ya doing?', smile, and wait for him to make a sound; when he makes a sound, say it back to him and wait again. He likes to do this two or three times":
   a. If the parent is comfortable in role-play, practice this game a few times, switching roles of parent and child. Keep it fun. Model and encourage animated facial expressions and voice tone.
   b. Demonstrate, and let the parent practice, playing this game with her child.
   c. Define the waiting period to give her child, e.g., silent count of five.
   d. Name, and encourage the parent to suggest, times during daily activities to play this game with her child, e.g., diapering or bathing.

DEAF PARENT

May be unaware of her child's sounds, and may thus not "wait" for his vocal responses.

1. Relate to the parent the sounds her child is making and their social meaning at this age, e.g., "He's learning to make sounds after you gesture or talk to him. He does this as a turn-taking partner to your interactions to tell you he likes the interaction and wants more." Explain the importance of watching his face for a vocal response to her interactions:
   a. Demonstrate talking to the child for a few seconds with animated facial expressions and then waiting for a response without gesture or voice. When the child vocalizes, unobtrusively cue the parent while you listen attentively to the child. Repeat one more time.
   b. Let the parent practice this game using her facial expressions and speech, if possible. Remind the parent to withhold her gestures, except for her eye contact and a smile, until she has seen her child finish talking or five seconds have elapsed.

5.10 Child: **DISCRIMINATES STRANGERS (3-6 mo.)**
Parent: Recognizes and understands child's discriminatory behaviors toward strangers

GENERAL GUIDELINES

The child, if cared for and surrounded by consistent people, learns to discriminate unfamiliar people. He demonstrates this discrimination by decreasing his movement, quieting, staring wide eyed, or initially refusing to smile.

MENTALLY RETARDED PARENT

May be confused by her child's behaviors toward strangers.

1. Provide the parent with anticipatory guidance regarding her child's awareness of strangers:
   a. Discuss the various people her child sees everyday and seems to know.
   b. Ask the parent to name some relatives or friends that she knows but that her child hasn't met yet or has only met a few times.
   c. Explain that, even though she knows them, her child at this age needs to be around them many times before he knows them; this is because his memory isn't that long yet.
   d. Relate that when people are unfamiliar or new to him, he realizes he doesn't know them and may act differently.
   e. Describe the things he may do, and ask the parent if she's ever noticed him doing those or other things in response to strangers.
2. If the child has only seen you a few times and displays discriminating behaviors, point them out to the parent and praise how her child is showing us he knows familiar from unfamiliar people.
3. Stress to the parent that her child learns that people whom he doesn't know are okay if:
   a. She doesn't make him smile or go to them right away.
   b. He sees his parent talking and smiling to unfamiliar people.
4. If the parent and child are socially isolated, suggest taking her child for walks, to the store, to parks, to neighbors, and to the mailbox to meet the mail carrier.

5.10

BLIND PARENT

May be unaware of her child's non-audible signs which indicate he discriminates strangers.

1. Explain to the parent that her child is beginning to recognize familiar from unfamiliar people and shows us he knows the difference by acting different. Relate how he may stare, refuse to smile, or not move.
2. Point out that her child knows familiar from unfamiliar people mostly by remembering how they look. Explain that, if a familiar person changes their appearance significantly, such as cutting their long hair or shaving a beard or mustache, her child may act differently because they seem unfamiliar; as he realizes they move, sound, and smell the same, he refamiliarizes himself.

5.11 Child: **SOCIALIZES WITH STRANGERS/ANYONE (3-5 mo.)**
Parent: Exposes child to strangers in a supportive environment

GENERAL GUIDELINES

During this stage, although the child discriminates strangers, he usually responds well and socializes after a few movements of warming up. Some children may resist and display anxiety. They should not be forced to separate and play or interact with a stranger. Strangers should be introduced gradually while held by the parent or other familiar person.

MENTALLY RETARDED PARENT

May expect her child to play and respond positively to strangers.

1. Explain the child's emerging awareness of unfamiliar people. Refer to 5.10 (Discriminates strangers).
2. If you are unfamiliar to the child, use your entry situation to demonstrate gradual introductions, talking aloud for the child, e.g., "He's not ready for me to hold him; see how he's cuddled close to you?"
3. Name example situations that could arise and the behaviors her child may display toward unfamiliar people. Explore with the parent ways to gradually introduce her child to strangers in these situations.

5.12 Child: **DEMANDS SOCIAL ATTENTION (3-8 mo.)**
Parent: Recognizes and responds to child's demands for social attention

GENERAL GUIDELINES

The child is learning the value and benefits of social attention and will thus cry or fuss when left alone to attract attention. This is a positive social behavior.

Children should *not* be left alone to be taught independence at this age. They should, however, learn to entertain themselves for short periods without constant direct attention.

MENTALLY RETARDED PARENT

May not recognize her child's fretfulness as a sign of wanting attention, or may be angry and think he is spoiled.

1. Praise the child's emerging need for social interaction:
   a. Relate to the parent how her child's cries for attention compare to our need to be around people. Discuss how boring it can be if we are alone for a long time and have no one to talk to.
   b. Contrast how, at this age, however, her child cannot call someone on the phone or go out for a visit to have company. The only way he knows how to get the attention he needs is to fret or cry.
   c. Stress that he is not spoiled when he fusses for attention.
   d. Praise the parent for helping him learn that it is more fun to be with her than to be alone.
2. Tell the parent not to ignore her child's crying when he wants attention. Explain that, if she is busy, she can move him in the same room with her and give him toys to play with.

5.13 Child: **VOCALIZES ATTITUDES – PLEASURE AND DISPLEASURE (3-6 mo.)**
Parent: Discriminates and responds appropriately to child's vocalized attitudes of pleasure and displeasure

GENERAL GUIDELINES

The child is learning to express his different feelings more clearly through vocalizations. Displeasure is no longer only expressed through crying; he may now grunt, whine, or make other unhappy sounds. Feelings of pleasure are also no longer limited to cooing; he begins chuckling, laughing, and making high pitched happy sounds. These sounds, especially of displeasure, are not very consistent yet.

MENTALLY RETARDED PARENT

May not be able to differentiate her child's new subtle expressions of displeasure.

1. Explain that her child is learning new ways to tell us he's unhappy. Ask the parent if she's seen new ways her child tells us he's unhappy. If needed to facilitate discussion, use probes, such as "Does he stick his lower lip out, or whine?"
2. Describe and point out, as they occur, the child's new vocal and gestural behaviors which indicate that he is unhappy. Explain that, if we attend to him when he makes those sounds, he is learning he doesn't always have to cry.
3. Model for the parent and suggest ways of responding to her child's vocalized attitudes of displeasure, e.g., talking in a soothing voice or gently rubbing the child's tummy.
4. Monitor the parent's interactions with her child frequently to assure she interprets her child's attitudes correctly. When needed, interpret the child's vocalized attitudes and relate the situation which may have caused it.

DEAF PARENT

May not be able to discriminate her child's vocal attitudes, and thus may have difficulty responding to them or pacing her interactions accordingly.

1. Relate to the parent when her child is developing new vocal abilities to express his feelings. Describe how he vocalizes his attitudes:
   a. When he is happy or enjoying a particular activity, he may coo, which is a rhythmic vowel sound; squeal, which is a loud sudden burst of vowel sounds; laugh and chuckle, or talk to people or his toys.
   b. When he is feeling angry, upset, or wants something, he may grunt, which is a deep sound coming from his chest and throat; or whine, which is a higher pitched sound coming from his nasal area.
2. Alert the parent when her child is vocalizing various attitudes:
   a. She can discriminate his corresponding facial and bodily changes and gesturing.
   b. Emphasize looking for these cues before interacting or changing a toy to help insure contingent pacing.

5.14 Child: BECOMES AWARE OF STRANGE SITUATIONS (3-6 mo.)
Parent: Provides supportive experiences for child to become aware of unfamiliar places and people

GENERAL GUIDELINES

Exposing children to new people and places provides them with rich experiences for varied sights, sounds, smells, textures, and interactions.

If it appears that a parent's disability is limiting the child's exposure to unfamiliar experiences, plan special outings with the parent and child to nearby stores, libraries, beaches, parks, etc. Determine accessibility needs and facility accommodations during your planning.

Setting up a special safe play area in the yard, on the porch, or on the balcony during nice weather can also provide new or varied experiences to the child.

5.15 Child: ENJOYS SOCIAL PLAY (3-6 mo.)
Parent: Plays interactive games with child

GENERAL GUIDELINES

Interaction "games" with people are a child's primary mode for social play during this developmental stage. These "games" do not require props or toys, just an interested adult who initiates an action (eye contact, smile, gesture, phrase), waits for response from the child (eye contact, smile gesture, vocalization), and then makes another interesting action. Through this "game," the child is learning to be a social receiver and responder and is learning he can affect others' interactions.

To play these games, parents often:
1. Speak the same language (high pitch, slower phrasing, simplified grammar).
2. Take turns with the child according to his pace (e.g., she talks and pauses, he chuckles or vocalizes and pauses, she chuckles, etc.).
3. Watches for and accommodates the child's signals or cues of attention (eye contact), arousal (laugh, vocalization), or fatigue (squirming, gaze aversion, yawning).

Social games can include rituals, such as "Peek-a-boo," "Pat-A-Cake," or "This Little Piggy." However, it is the increased inflection, turn-taking, and interaction exchange that make the "game," not the words. "Homemade" games arising spontaneously from any parent or child sound or action can be just as effective as the classic "Peek-a-boo" ones.

Higher arousal techniques to the child, such as larger movements and higher voice variability, may be helpful for the less responsive infant. In contrast, these techniques may precipitate over-stimulation and overload for the hypersensitive child.

High risk, handicapped, or developmentally delayed infants' signals may be either less responsive and/or hypersensitive to stimulation which can make game playing difficult. Parents will need to be especially sensitive to his more subtle or excitable signals and modulate their own responses accordingly to prevent over-stimulation, or to bring their child to an interactive and alert state.

MENTALLY RETARDED PARENT

May not pace her interactions with her child's signals, or may be too rough or abrupt during interactive play.

1. Help sensitize the parent to her child's interaction signals. Teach her to play a "Copy Tommy" game (substituting child's name):
   a. Demonstrate comfortable en face positioning with the child on your lap.
   b. Demonstrate and explain that you are waiting for him to smile, look at you, or make a sound and until then, just watch him and smile.
   c. Copy each sound, smile, or vocalization exactly like the child's.
   d. When the child stops the game, name the behaviors he used to tell you it was time to stop.
   e. Let the parent practice this game while you "coach from the sidelines." Point out and reinforce all subtle movements as they occur.
   f. Discuss that, at this age, her child thinks this is a great game and likes it better than playing with toys.
2. Teach the parent a turn-taking game where the parent initiates an action and waits for her child to make a response. Teach through demonstration and "coaching from the sidelines" as described in Activity No. 1. Stress:
   a. Getting the child's attention.
   b. Using smooth quiet movements or sounds.
   c. "Reading" when her child is ready to stop.
3. Name daily caretaking activities in which these games can be incorporated.
4. Continue to interpret the child's initiating, responding, and "all done" signals aloud to the parent during all of your contacts with the parent and child, e.g., "See that special smile he's giving you!"

5.15

DEAF PARENT

May be unable to monitor her child's vocal signals which indicate he's initiating or responding during interactive games.

1. The parent can pay special attention to her child's visual and touch cues of "game playing." It is important for her to watch for his signs of vocalizing so that she does not interrupt or prevent them. Explain the role of her child's vocalizations in interactive games so she can pay special attention to them and reinforce and pace herself accordingly.
2. Encourage the parent to make initiating vocal sounds, e.g., tongue click, hum, or voice, if possible, to her child during game-playing and watch for his response.

BLIND PARENT

May not be able to see her child's interactive cues to initiate or maintain game playing.

1. Anticipatory Guidance: Although the parent may be unaware of her child's visual cues of affect and attention, and may not convey visual affective information to her child, they can enjoy rich vocal and tactile games which provide mutual enjoyment and reciprocal patterns of interaction. If vocal and tactile interactive games are not observed to be spontaneously incorporated into their interaction because the child is less responsive, interventions can be beneficial to help the parent detect her child's more subtle cues.
2. If en face positions are not spontaneous, a favored position may be for the child to face outward on the parent's lap with his back supported against her chest and stomach. The parent can maintain tactile contact while playing games with her child's fingers or by patting him and rhythmically exploring his body in response to his cues. The parent can play:
   a. "You wiggle, I wiggle" game with her child.
   b. "You make a sound, I'll make a sound" game.
3. The parent can play a "water trickle" game with her child during bathing, e.g., the parent says, "Here comes the water," while gently squeezing water on his arm or leg and pausing for a reinitiating response from her child.

5.16 Child: MAKES APPROACH MOVEMENTS TO MIRROR (3-5½ mo.)
Parent: Provides opportunities for child to look at himself in a mirror

GENERAL GUIDELINES

The child stares, waves, or moves slightly toward a mirror when he is held in front of it. He is not aware that the reflection he sees is himself.

MENTALLY RETARDED PARENT

May not recognize mirrors as a play and learning vehicle for her child.

1. Demonstrate, and let the parent practice, presenting a mirror to her child:
   a. Model attracting the child's attention by tapping the mirror.
   b. Describe his responses, e.g., "His eyes got wider" or "Look at that smile!"
   c. Explain that children enjoy looking into mirrors and they are also learning what they look like.
2. Attach a safe mirror to the child's crib, playpen, or other play area. Stress:
   a. The safe features of the mirror.
   b. Appropriate mirror placement so her child can see it since he cannot move around yet very much.
3. Ask the parent where mirrors are located in their home:
   a. Name specific times she can let her child look at himself in various mirrors, e.g., "When you're holding him and are walking into the bathroom to get something, stop for a minute and let him look in the mirror."
   b. Demonstrate appropriate handling and positioning, as needed, to assure the mirror is in her child's visual field.

BLIND PARENT

May be unaware of the visual benefits mirrors play for her child, and may not have mirrors visually available to him.

1. Refer to 1.90 (Identifies self in mirror).
2. Demonstrate and describe attracting her child's attention to the mirror by tapping it and calling his name.
3. Physically assist the parent with positions which assure mirrors are in her child's visual field.
4. Describe her child's facial responses to the mirror, such as eyes brightening, staring, smiling, etc. The parent can feel his approach movements toward the mirror. Explain that, at this age, his reflection is new to him and thus unfamiliar; he reacts with staring and intense expression because he is not sure who he sees.

PHYSICALLY DISABLED PARENT

May be unable to lift her child up to mirrors in the home.

1. Suggest a floor-length mirror on the back of an accessible door.
2. Safe mirrors can be attached to the child's crib and play areas.
3. Parents who use a wheelchair may have had mirrors adjusted to wheelchair height. The child can look at them held upright against the parent's chest.

5.17 Child: RECOGNIZES MOTHER VISUALLY (4-8 mo.)
Parent: Maintains primary caregiving and interaction roles with child; responds positively to his signs of recognition

GENERAL GUIDELINES

The child displays overt signs of recognizing his mother or primary caregiver. He may smile, excite, and fuss to obtain her attention when he sees her. In addition, he recognizes her touch, smell, and voice. If the parent's visual or voice appearance changes, he may display a facial expression of confusion.

The child's special recognition to his parents reinforces their feelings of importance and competence as parents.

A parental disability may necessitate extended family members or others to carry out primary caregiving activities with the child during his first few months of life. If so, extra effort should be extended to include parents in these and extra play activities.

MENTALLY RETARDED PARENT

May be unaware of her child's discriminating behaviors toward her.

1. Frequently describe the child's special signs of parent recognition as they occur to promote parental self-esteem and awareness of her importance to her child, e.g., "See that special look he gave you!"

BLIND PARENT

May be unaware of her child's visual signs of recognition toward her.

1. Frequently describe the child's inaudible special signs of recognition toward the parent, e.g., "He really started waving his hands when you came in the room!" If the child demonstrated gaze aversion with the parent during the first few months, he may begin to start looking toward the parent more frequently during this period. Describe his new looks as they occur, e.g., "He really watched you smile."

5.18 Child: ENJOYS FROLIC PLAY (4-8 mo.)
Parent: Engages child in frolic play, monitoring over-stimulation

MENTALLY RETARDED PARENT

May be too rough or abrupt during frolic play activities, or may restrict her child's experiences to a crib for extended periods.

1. Many "frolic play" activities described in early childhood curricula (e.g., "lift child up high," swinging in a blanket, tickle, etc.) may be inappropriate if the parent displays a rough or abrupt interaction style. Instead, introduce activities which are "smoother" and do not over-stimulate the parent or child. These may include dancing or bouncing to music, splashing water in a shallow tub, and/or getting down on the floor and crawling around with the child.
2. Remind the parent that, as her child is getting older, he should spend lots of time out of his crib and infant seat. Suggest times during the day for him to be on the floor, in a playpen, or in her lap. Relate these to specific daily events, e.g., "After his nap, play games with him on the floor."
3. If you observe unsafe or rough play, clearly point out why it is rough and the child's consequential behaviors, and offer an alternative technique. For example, "When you tickle him under his arms so hard, it doesn't feel good at

this age; see how he's trying to move away by turning? Try tickling him gently, like this on his tummy."

BLIND PARENT

May be anxious about excessive frolic play if she cannot see her child's responses.

1. Describe your frolic play activities to the parent before engaging in them with her child.
2. The parent can play body-on-body frolic play games, such as gentle swinging, or bouncing, and monitor her child's safety and reactions easily.

PHYSICALLY DISABLED PARENT

With limited mobility or control; may have difficulty engaging her child in frolic play activities.

1. The parent may be able to bounce her child by pushing up and down on her mattress with her body while he is on the bed and she's singing playful songs. CAUTION: Parents with arthritis should *not* be doing heavy lifting, shaking, or bouncing due to possible joint damage. This activity would thus not be suitable unless it is a waterbed.
2. Wind-up infant swings provide excellent stimulation for children who do not have extended frolic play opportunities. The parent can sing, tickle her child, and play "Peek-a-boo" while he's in the swing.
3. The parent may be able to lie supine with her child on her chest and include rolling or bouncing together in their play.

5.19 Child: REPEATS ENJOYABLE ACTIVITIES (4-8 mo.)
Parent: Initiates and repeats activities and games with child which are likely to encourage him to repeat and enjoy

GENERAL GUIDELINES

The child's interactive play is expanding to include attempts at and successes in repeating enjoyable activities. He loves repetitive interactions with adults and objects. Interaction games, such as "Pat-A-Cake" and "Row Row Row Your Boat," have repetitive actions and sounds for the child to enjoy and try to repeat. Hitting mobiles, chime balls, and bells on strings also provide interesting repetitive visual and sound stimulation which encourage him to repeat the action. The child may frequently "check-in" with his parent for approval by looking at her during his repetitive interactions with toys.

The importance of pacing in repetitive interaction games with adults follow the same guidelines under 5.15 (Enjoys social play). That skill is a prerequisite for the parent and child to carry out activities under this skill.

5.19

MENTALLY RETARDED PARENT

May need direct context cues to help her identify when and which activities her child enjoys repeating.

1. Observe or explore which activities or "games" the child enjoys and repeats, or attempts to repeat. Make a picture list of two or three of these games for the parent, e.g., "Pat-A-Cake" and "Peek-a-boo":
   a. Explain that these are games which her child seems to like; he learns them by doing them over and over again.
   b. Demonstrate with the parent how to "start" these "games" and repeat them with their child.
   c. Name concrete times to "start" these games each day. For example, "After every diaper change, start 'Pat-A-Cake,' and when watching television, start 'knee bouncing'."
   d. Tell the parent to stop the game if her child is not interested, helping her identify her child's "uninterested" cues, if needed (e.g., wiggling, crying, wandering gaze, pushing away, etc.).
   e. Change this game list for the parent as the child's interest and/or development demands.
2. Describe and point out the child's signals which indicate he is repeating or attempting to repeat a game or activity, as they occur.
3. Stress to the parent that her child is not ready to repeat games exactly like us yet. Demonstrate the crude actions young children often make to play "Pat-A-Cake" or "Peek-a-boo."

DEAF PARENT

May not be aware that her child uses objects to repeat sounds.

1. Refer to 1.66 (Initiates several new gestures).

BLIND PARENT

May not be able to detect her child's attempts to repeat games which do not produce sound or movement cues.

1. Anticipatory Guidance: If the child avoided eye contact or en face positions with his parent during his first few months, he may begin to initiate and maintain activities with en face positioning now, especially with the introduction of play materials.
2. Suggest playing with objects which produce sounds, e.g., chime balls, bells, or drums.
3. Suggest playing games which involve clapping, or provide wrist bells so the parent can detect sounds produced by the child's movement.
4. Suggest playing "body-on-body" games which will provide immediate cues when the child repeats movements.
5. If the child is on his parent's lap facing outward to play repetitive actions with toys, the parent will recognize when he turns to "visually check-in" with her.

5.20 **Child:** DISPLAYS STRANGER ANXIETY (5-8 mo.)
Parent: Understands and adapts for child's stranger anxiety

GENERAL GUIDELINES

The child, in addition to being able to discriminate strangers, is now actively frightened by them. He may suddenly cry and protest their interactions or handling. Although certainly a very trying time for parents and the "stranger," the child's anxiety actually represents a very positive emotional growth. He is demonstrating that he will offer his affection and attention discriminately to those who are familiar.

Parents can adapt for their child's stranger anxiety during this stage by introducing him to strangers within the safety of their own homes and by holding him during introductions. They can also ask others to gradually introduce themselves and not interact with their child until he makes the initial move. As children become acquainted with strangers, they will continue to "touch base" with the parent. The parent can offer a supportive nod and reassurance that everything is fine.

Stranger anxiety may never evidence itself if the child has had numerous positive frequent experiences with strangers and caregivers. The child should, however, demonstrate a positive discriminatory attachment to his primary caregivers.

MENTALLY RETARDED PARENT

May assume that, since she's not fearful of someone, her child should not be anxious.

1. If the child is demonstrating stranger anxiety and the parent is interpreting this as "bad" or forcing her child to interact with strangers, explain this developmental stage and its rationale to illustrate the child's positive emotional growth.
2. Discuss how some people, who are not strangers to her, may still be strangers to her child because he hasn't seen them in awhile or has not had as much time to get to know them. Have the parent name people and relatives she knows that her child doesn't really know yet.
3. Stress the importance of holding her child during this age when she introduces him to others because, "he will feel safe with you; meeting new people is scary!"
4. If the child displays stranger anxiety toward you, take the opportunity to verbally prompt the parent to hold her child and *not* let go until he's ready. Talk for the child, e.g., "I don't know her yet, Mom, I'm not ready to play."
5. Help the parent anticipate situations that may trigger her child's stranger anxiety at the grocery store, laundromat, on walks, and when people come to visit.

5.21 **Child:** LIFTS ARMS TO MOTHER (5-6 mo.)
Parent: Encourages child to lift arms before picking up

GENERAL GUIDELINES

The child lifts his arms toward his mother and other primary caregivers to indicate he wants to be picked up. This skill demonstrates the child's display of preferential social interaction toward familiar loved ones.

Parents encourage their child to lift his arms by holding their own arms out, saying "Up" invitingly, and then waiting a few seconds for him to make a similar gesture before picking him up. The child soon learns that this gesture is an effective social communicative method to say he "wants to get up."

If the child's motor limitations prevent his actual arm-lifting, parents can watch for and reinforce other preferential gestures which may indicate that he wants to get up or go to the parent.

MENTALLY RETARDED PARENT

May pick her child up abruptly during daily activities, without gesturing and allowing him any response time.

1. If the child is not motor impaired, show a picture of a child raising his arms to an adult. Ask the parent what the child is saying with his arms. Relate how her child is learning to do this, too.
2. Demonstrate putting your arms out before picking up the child; emphasize getting his attention by calling his name and giving him time to respond.
3. Point out, as they occur, the child's various gestural movements which indicate he wants to be picked up, especially if the child is motor impaired. Emphasize that, while he is learning this new skill, he may not always lift his arms directly out.
4. Help the parent think of specific times to hold her arms out before picking her child up, e.g., from his highchair, crib, playpen, and floor.
5. Caution the parent never to pick her child up by his arms. Explain that she could pull his arms out of his shoulder joint as you point to the shoulder joint on her child. Demonstrate picking the child up with both of your hands under his arms, while supporting his trunk (unless different handling techniques have been described). Have the parent practice picking her child up from various places, e.g., his highchair, crib, or playpen.

BLIND PARENT

May be unaware that her child is learning to use a reaching gesture.

1. Provide anticipatory guidance regarding this gesture as described in the general guidelines. The parent can then anticipate and wait to feel her child's response after she extends her arms within his reaching range.

5.22 Child: **EXPLORES ADULT FEATURES**
(5-7 mo.)
Parent: Encourages child to explore adult features

GENERAL GUIDELINES

The child touches and explores adults' facial features. In addition to the pleasurable social interaction underlying this skill, this activity also helps him learn that adults are separate from himself.

Parents can encourage their child's exploration of their faces by making fun and inviting facial expressions, such as puckering lips, raising eyebrows, or wrinkling their noses. If the child pulls an adult's hair, he may not have the voluntary release to let go. Parents can bend his wrist down to help him release their hair. The child should not be scolded for his unintentional hair-pulling.

MENTALLY RETARDED PARENT

May interpret her child's exploration of her face as "mean," especially if he scratches her face or pulls her hair.

1. Ask the parent if her child ever tries to touch her face or poke her nose and cheeks. Interpret this positive interaction, i.e., "When he touches your face, he's learning about you and the movements you can make with your face, like wiggling your nose." Help the parent think of other ways to move her facial parts that would be fun for her child to watch.
2. Provide anticipatory guidance regarding hair pulling and scratching:
   a. Explain that her child pulls hair by accident and that he hasn't learned to let go of it yet. Demonstrate with the parent how to bend her child's wrist to promote release. Let her practice with you.
   b. Explain that her child doesn't know his nails can scratch, so be sure to keep them trimmed.

5.23 Child: **SMILES AT MIRROR IMAGE**
(5½-8½ mo.)
Parent: Encourages child to smile at his image in a mirror

GENERAL GUIDELINES

The child recognizes his mirror image as familiar and smiles. The following activities supplement 5.16 (Makes approach movements to mirror) which is a prerequisite to this skill.

MENTALLY RETARDED PARENT

May not play with her child in front of a mirror, or may not position him so he can see his own image.

1. Demonstrate for the parent the appropriate distance and placement of the mirror when playing with her child to assure that it is within his visual field and reach. Let the parent experience how difficult it is to see herself if the mirror is too high or too low.
2. Demonstrate specific games, such as "Peek-a-boo" or making silly faces with her child in front of a mirror:
   a. After demonstrating, encourage the parent to practice playing this game with her child.
   b. Reinforce by specifically naming the positive things they are doing, e.g., "Great; you're holding Susie so she can see you both in the mirror" or "Look how Susie smiled when you said 'Peek-a-boo' and smiled."
3. Ask the parent if she can think of stores she goes to which have mirrors hanging up, e.g., dressing rooms at department stores or meat department at grocery stores. Suggest letting her child look at them while they are there.

5.23

BLIND PARENT

May be unaware of her child's smiles in front of a mirror.

1. If mirrors are not visually available for the child, refer to 1.90 (Identifies self in mirror).
2. Explain to the parent that, as her child begins to recognize his own reflection in a mirror as a familiar person, he will begin to smile; his earlier stares of confusion or intensity change with this familiarity.

5.24 Child: **DISTINGUISHES SELF AS SEPARATE FROM MOTHER (6-9 mo.)**
Parent: Facilitates child's awareness of self as separate from parent and the environment

GENERAL GUIDELINES

During the first few months of life, infants are not aware of themselves as separate "beings" from their parents or the environment. Many of their responses are reflexive and their emotions are not directed at anyone. Experiences with the environment and the development of motor and mental skills enable him to differentiate himself as separate from others and his environment.

The child's ability to distinguish himself as separate from his environment is thus a culmination of the developmental skills listed in this manual from 0-6 months. For example, his purposeful movements and motor abilities provide him with the opportunity to move away, make something else move, and explore the separate parts of his body. His early social interactions with others also help him realize his separateness as he learns to cooperate in reciprocal "game-playing" and affect other responses. Cognitively the child is learning he can control his actions to "make something happen," and communicatively he is realizing his power to receive and send thoughts and feelings.

Parent training activities suggested under each area of development for child skills within the 0-6 month range are, therefore, applicable to facilitate the child's awareness and understanding of himself as a distinct person.

5.25 Child: **SHOWS ANXIETY OVER SEPARATION FROM MOTHER (6-9 mo.)**
Parent: Gradually helps child "work through" separation anxiety

GENERAL GUIDELINES

Separation anxiety reflects the child's recognition that he feels safer and is greatly dependent upon his parents. Working through the child's anxiety over separation is a gradual process which may last through the preschool years.

Initial separations should be short. When they occur, the child should always be with a familiar supportive person and, when possible, within his own environment. Parents should always reassure their child that they will return.

The social and emotional issues and interventions for separation anxiety are numerous. The reader can refer to this skill in the *Hawaii Early Learning Profile Activity Guide* or other early childhood curricula for detailed sequential steps toward successful separation.

Parents can benefit from supportive counseling and empathy during this "trying" period. They too may have separation anxieties when leaving their child.

MENTALLY RETARDED PARENT

May force abrupt separations with her child and interpret her child's anxieties as "bad."

1. Ask the parent how her child reacts when she leaves him with someone else. If necessary, probe with "Does he cry?" and "Does he try to hold onto you?":
   a. Name a specific situation you are aware of in which the parent leaves her child with someone else and explore how the parent and child react to the separation, e.g., "When you go to the Activity Center, does Jimmy cry?"
   b. Facilitate further exploration with prompts, such as "Does he see you leave?", "Why do you think he's crying?", "What do you say to him?", and "Who does he stay with?"
   c. Try to establish if there is a pattern of separation anxiety for the child. Name additional separation situations you are aware of, exploring again the parent and child reactions.
   d. If there are other primary caregivers, explore his separation reactions with them along the same lines.
2. If the child has separation anxiety, help the parent understand why he becomes upset:
   a. Provide a meaningful interpretation of separation anxiety, e.g., "You are the most important person to your child. He knows he needs you to grow up and knows how much you love him. When you leave, he is afraid you won't come back. He's not old enough to know that you'll be coming back soon, so he's worried. At this age, he can't tell us his feelings with words so he tells us by crying."
   b. Relate that many children act like this at this age; their crying is not bad, it's just a sign of loving their parent.
   c. Explain that it sometimes takes two years for children to get over this worried feeling.
3. Suggest and prompt the parent to think of ways to help make separation easier. Prompt with questions, such as:
   a. "Before you leave what can you tell your child to let him know you'll be back?"
   b. "Is there someone who he doesn't seem to cry as much with?"
   c. "If you take him to daycare or to someone's house, does he have a special toy or blanket he can take with him?"
4. Let the parent practice gradual separation from her child within your center, clinic, etc. and/or during your home visit after the child has become familiar with you:
   a. Prompt the parent, as needed, to tell her child she'll be back.
   b. Initially start with a five-minute separation, gradually increasing this time each visit.

c. Reinforce all of the parent's empathetic supportive responses to her child.
d. Talk for the child to explain his feelings, e.g., "Boy, I'm glad to see you," "Tell me when you'll be back, Mom," and "I worry when you leave, but I'll be fine."
5. Use "separation anxiety" as a topic for a parent group. Parents can share their frustration and experiences within a supportive environment.

5.26 Child: COOPERATES IN GAMES (6-10 mo.)
Parent: Plays simple "give and take" games with child

GENERAL GUIDELINES

The child's social play is expanding from simple turn-taking and repetition attempts to keep an activity going, to purposeful cooperative "give and take" games. He is learning to attach specific "give and take" responses, depending upon the game, as a means to keep the activity going.

Cooperative games at this age include putting objects in and out of containers together, playing "Hide-and-seek" with a toy under a cloth, playing "Peek-a-boo" with a cloth, playing "Pat-A-Cake," and giving toys back and forth to each other during "pick up the toy I drop" game.

Parents encourage their child's cooperative game playing by initiating "give and take" games; recognizing and responding when their child initiates a game; giving their child ample response time during give and take games; providing verbal and physical prompts, as needed; and, most importantly, by keeping the game fun.

MENTALLY RETARDED PARENT

May try to "make" her child cooperate in games and may choose games which are too difficult for her child to play.

1. Demonstrate for the parent cooperative games to play with her child which are likely to be successful for both parent and child. Name cooperative responses we can expect and those which we cannot expect because her child is not old enough, e.g., during "Peek-a-boo," we can expect him to pull a cloth off our face, but he needs help putting the cloth back on.
2. Explain to the parent that young children do not always play games the way we may want them to play, and that is okay. Tell her to stop the game rather than to make her child play after a couple of unsuccessful attempts. Describe concrete examples.
3. If the parent becomes impatient and tries to manipulate or hurry her child's correct response during a game:
   a. Emphasize that children need more time to do things at this age.
   b. Model appropriate verbal reinforcement to the child, i.e., "You can do it" or "That's right; put it in."
   c. Point out to the parent how hard her child is trying to do the activity. Praise the parent for being patient, empathizing how difficult it is sometimes to wait for children to "figure things out."
4. The parent should never be placed in a position where she feels it is important to force her child to play or cooperate in a game for the sake of accomplishing the goal.
5. When playing "give and take" games, if the child's release is immature:
   a. Explain the child's unintentional throwing behaviors.
   b. Use materials that are suitable for throwing, e.g., balls, bean bags, and crumpled up paper.
6. Point out, describe, and praise the child's cooperative behaviors to the parent as they occur. Praise and describe the parent's appropriate responses, e.g., "Great; you knew he wanted to play 'Peek-a-boo'."

BLIND PARENT

May be unaware of her child's gestural responses to initiate or continue cooperative games.

1. Describe "give and take" responses the parent can begin to expect her child to incorporate into his games. The parent can then anticipate, encourage, and monitor them through touch and audible cues. "Body on body" games, hand to hand games, and using objects which make sounds during cooperative games provide extra touch and sound cues to help the parent accurately monitor and pace cooperative play, e.g., hide squeak toys, drop blocks in a can, and play "Pat-A-Cake" on lap.

5.27 Child: STRUGGLES AGAINST SUPINE POSITION (6-12 mo.)
Parent: Understands and adapts for child's resistance to supine positions

GENERAL GUIDELINES

The child's interest in the environment, mastery of motor skills, and enjoyment of upright positions may cause him to actively resist confinement, especially lying on his back. He may twist, turn, squirm, whine, and roll over when someone tries to make him lie down. Changing diapers and dressing their child can thus become quite a task for parents! Many parents learn to change their child while he's "on the run" or standing up at a couch or his crib railings. Others may find it helpful to offer him a toy, sing a special song, or play a "footsie" game during changing to help distract him from his urge to move or be upright. Disposal diapers with tape tabs for fastening may also be recommended to prevent inevitable pin sticks to both parent and child.

MENTALLY RETARDED PARENT

May scold her child for resisting her when she changes his diapers or clothes.

1. Interpret the child's resistance to supine positions for the parent in meaningful terms. Include the following concepts:
   a. "You have helped your child learn so much that he always wants to move around now so he can see what's happening around him."

5.0 SOCIAL-EMOTIONAL

b. "When you change his diaper or clothes when he's lying down, he doesn't like it because he'd rather move around."
c. "He's not wiggling or trying to move away from you to be mean; he's just so proud of being able to move around; it's hard to stay still!"
d. "He gets bored lying on his back; imagine if someone made you lie down to change your clothes and you would much rather be watching TV or playing cards."

2. Demonstrate for the parent how to change her child's diaper or clothes while he is standing at a support, if appropriate:
   a. Help identify various suitable places in the home where the parent can change her child while he is standing up, e.g., crib railings, cocktail table, chairs, and next to a window.
   b. Let the parent practice this with your encouragement and empathetic responses regarding how frustrating this can be.
3. Show the parent how to distract her child with a toy or game during changing if he is lying on his back:
   a. Relate how this helps make him forget that he doesn't like lying down because he is too busy playing.
   b. Stress the importance of selecting a toy for him to play with *before* she lays him down.
   c. Help identify interesting toys or household objects which are suitable for the child to play with in a supine position. Suggest keeping a few next to his changing area.

PHYSICALLY DISABLED PARENT

Who has limited ambulatory skills; may have difficulty keeping up with her child if he moves away during changing.

1. Suggest giving the child a special toy or household object to play with during changing times. The parent can only let him play with it during changing times to insure the toy's novelty and help insure the child's interest.
2. The parent may be able to change her child while he is standing up if she can:
   a. Change him while she is sitting on the couch and he is standing next to her holding onto the back of the couch.
   b. Sit on the floor and change him while he is standing at the couch or low table.

5.28 Child: RESPONDS PLAYFULLY TO MIRROR (6-9 mo.)
Parent: Plays with child in front of a mirror

GENERAL GUIDELINES

As the child becomes accustomed to seeing his image in a mirror, his responses go beyond looking and smiling; he laughs, pats, makes faces, and talks to his mirror images.

Rattle toys and "Peek-a-boo" games encourage the child's playful responses and produce interesting visual spectacles for him to watch.

The parent training activities for 5.16 (Makes approach movements to mirror), 5.23 (Smiles at mirror image), and 1.90 (Identifies self in mirror) are applicable to this skill.

5.29 Child: MAY SHOW FEAR AND INSECURITY WITH PREVIOUSLY ACCEPTED SITUATIONS (6-18 mo.)
Parent: Offers a sympathetic but casual and supportive approach to child's fears and insecurities with previously accepted situations

GENERAL GUIDELINES

As the child's awareness of his "separateness" and dependency on others to protect him increases, fears and insecurities frequently develop. Each developmental stage may bring new fears and insecurities but may also bring resolutions of old fears.

The child's earliest fears are often to loud sudden sounds, such as vacuum cleaners, garbage disposals, sirens, airplanes, or pans dropping. Large animals and a fear of falling can also provoke his fears. Sometime after he is a year old, the child may become suddenly afraid of bathing, dark places, and things breaking (he fears "if an object can break, maybe I can, too!"). As the child approaches two years of age, he may develop fears of thunder and lightning, doctors, and losing his parents' love if he does something bad.

Parents can help their child "work through" some of their fears by providing calm and friendly reassurance. When possible, the environment can be adapted during specific fear stages. For example, parents can leave a nightlight on if the child becomes fearful at night; hold and reassure the child when animals are nearby; and make bathtime especially fun or revert to sponge baths if his fear of tubs is extreme, gradually reintroducing the tub. As the child gets older, parents can help their child "work through" fears through play. They can read stories about fire engine sirens and use dolls to act out fearful situations which turn out just fine.

MENTALLY RETARDED PARENT

May not understand "child-size" fears, and may try to make her child "be brave" in fearful situations.

1. Name things that children are frequently afraid of with each developmental stage. Ask the parent if she can think of things of which her child seems to be afraid. As you recognize the child's fearful reactions, name them and interpret why he is afraid, e.g., "He's afraid of that chair now because he thinks he might fall. Let him sit here instead."
2. Help the parent understand her child's fears:
   a. Explain that "adults are not afraid of lots of the things that children are afraid of because we know better at this age. Children don't understand that things won't hurt them."
   b. Give concrete examples, e.g., "We know a vacuum cleaner won't 'eat us up' but a child doesn't know that yet."

c. Explain how the child's small size can make things scarier, e.g., "When your child sees a dog that may be twice as big as him, just think of how we would feel if we saw a bear moving toward us that was twice as big as us!"
3. Demonstrate ways to help her child be less afraid as you and the parent identify his fears:
   a. Use a nightlight, give sponge baths, etc. (depending upon the fear).
   b. Tell the parent never to make him "be brave." Explain we can't teach him to be brave at this age. Reassure her that he will soon forget some of his fears we think are silly.
   c. Suggest reassuring phrases the parent can say to her child when he is afraid.

DEAF PARENT

May be unaware of environmental sounds which may trigger her child's fears.

1. Provide anticipatory guidance regarding environmental sounds which may suddenly scare her child so that the parent can reassure him:
   a. Point out things in the home which may make sounds that frighten her child: appliances, toilet flushing, and bathtub water running.
   b. Point out the things outdoors which make sounds that may scare her child: airplanes, sirens, car horns, and dogs growling or barking.

BLIND PARENT

May be unaware of the visual stimuli which precipitate her child's fears in insecurities.

1. Review the general guidelines under this skill with the parent:
   a. Help select nightlights if indicated for her child to help alleviate his fear of the dark.
   b. Anticipatory guidance regarding her child's sudden crying to loud noises, the bathtub, etc. can help alleviate parental anxiety that her child has been physically hurt.
2. If the parent has a seeing eye dog or attains one during this period which her child becomes fearful toward, assure her that any fears her child displays are probably temporary. She can help him by exposing him to the dog gradually within the safety and assurance of being held in her arms.

5.30 Child: SHOWS LIKE/DISLIKE FOR CERTAIN PEOPLE, OBJECTS, PLACES (7-12 mo.)
Parent: Recognizes and respects child's likes and dislikes for certain people, objects, places

MENTALLY RETARDED PARENT

May expect her child to have the same likes and dislikes as hers.

1. Remark about the child's preferences to people, objects, and places when you observe them, e.g., "He doesn't like this stuffed bear; he keeps putting it down when I give it to him"; "He really likes to go to the porch so he can watch cars go by; see how he's watching and smiling."
2. Facilitate a discussion about children's individual likes and dislikes. Explain that, although children like and dislike lots of the same things their parents do, they also have their own special likes and dislikes:
   a. Ask the parent what foods, places, toys, and people her child seems to like; are there any he seems to like that she doesn't? Are there any he does not like that she likes? How can she tell?
   b. As the child's likes and dislikes are identified, help interpret why he may like or dislike certain things.
3. Model offering the child choices without forcing him to take something he doesn't want, e.g., "Oh, you'd rather sit there? That's okay" and "Do you want to play with the blocks or the book?" Ask the parent if she can think of situations to let her child make choices during eating and playing.

DEAF PARENT

May be unaware of her child's sound preferences.

1. Describe the child's expanding attraction to different sounds as you notice them, e.g., "He seems to like this record the most; it makes animal sounds" and "When you're cleaning, he doesn't like the sound of the vacuum cleaner."

BLIND PARENT

May be unaware of her child's expanding visual preferences at this age.

1. Describe the child's expanding visual preferences and dislikes as they occur, e.g., "He seems to like drinking from this cup the best because it has a little picture of a bunny on it," "He seems to turn away from people with beards," and "He likes looking at pictures of animals."

5.31 Child: LETS ONLY MOTHER MEET HIS NEEDS (8-12 mo.)
Parent: Recognizes and respects child's need to let only mother meet his needs

GENERAL GUIDELINES

The child, now an expert at discriminating strangers and recognizing his need and dependency for his parent, actively rejects other people's attention and caregiving attempts. He may refuse to eat, cry, fuss, and reach for the parent when others intervene.

He may be more accepting of others' caregiving if the parent is out of sight.

If a parent's disability prevents her from carrying out full caregiving responsibilities, the child may have become quite accustomed to others helping out and may not display these reactions.

5.31

MENTALLY RETARDED PARENT

May interpret her child's reactions to others' caregiving as "mean."

1. Explain the child's reactions to others' caregiving attempts as a normal "stage" he'll get over. Reinforce how important she is to her child.
2. During your visits with the parent and child, reinforce the parent to assume the caregiving activities with her child, i.e., "He wants you to help him with his cup" or "He feels better when it's you who changes him."

5.32 **Child: EXTENDS TOY TO SHOW OTHERS (9-12 mo.)**
Parent: Encourages child to show toy to others; understands that the child is not ready to release it

GENERAL GUIDELINES

The child is ready to show others his toys as a means of socializing; he is not ready to let them actually take it. His "showing" gestures include extending his arm toward another person or simply holding the toy up.

Parents encourage this skill by asking their child to show themselves and others toys he is holding. He is more likely to "show" his toys to others as he learns that people enjoy this and do not take them away. If a toy is accidentally released, it should be promptly returned.

MENTALLY RETARDED PARENT

May expect her child to hand the toy over to the person he is showing it to, or may not recognize his "showing" gesture as an attempt to socialize with her.

1. Provide anticipatory guidance that her child may start showing people his toys but this does not mean he wants us to take them:
    a. Demonstrate the possible "showing" gestures her child may use.
    b. Explain the meaning of his showing toys in a positive manner, e.g., "When he shows a toy to someone, he's saying 'I like you so I'm going to let you look at this'."
    c. Stress that he is not old enough to share his toys by letting others hold them yet; this takes time.
2. Model, and let the parent practice, encouraging her child to "show" a toy he is holding. Emphasize how to:
    a. Encourage her child to show her the toy using inviting facial and verbal inflections.
    b. Talk about the special toy the child is holding but don't take it away from him.
    c. Return the toy to her child immediately if he accidentally drops it.

BLIND PARENT

May be unaware of her child's "showing" gesture.

1. Describe the child's "showing" gesture and its meaning. The parent can then be sensitive to listening for her child's associated vocal sounds which accompany the gesture.
2. The parent can recognize which toy her child is showing her by the sound it makes or by feeling it while it remains in the child's hand.

5.33 **Child: TESTS PARENTAL REACTIONS DURING FEEDING (9-12 mo.)**
Parent: Understands and responds appropriately to child's "testing" during feeding

GENERAL GUIDELINES

As a child's feeling of independence grows, he begins testing his newly realized power to refuse and make his parents angry. During feeding, the child may refuse to eat, insist on feeding himself, refuse to feed himself, throw or drop food and utensils, or spit food purposely.

He knows that mealtimes are an excellent time to test his limits to discover how much "naughtiness" can he get away with. When his parent has to continuously pick up thrown food or utensils, he may even find this quite humorous.

To help parents "weather" this stage and respond effectively to their child's testing behaviors, the following technique and information may be helpful for them:

1. Do not force feed; this can lead to more severe feeding problems. A healthy child of this age will not be nutritionally hurt by missing periodic meals. One good meal a day is usually adequate.
2. Let him stick to his favorite foods; substitute foods within the basic food groups if he refuses some.
3. If he refuses parental help during feeding, consider serving only fingerfoods or let him also have a spoon. Expect and allow reasonable messiness during this period.
4. If he refuses to try to feed himself and wants his parent to, go ahead and feed him, he must just want to make sure "Mom" will always take care of his needs.
5. If the child throws, spits, or becomes excessively messy, the parent can remove the food, utensil, or the child and calmly but firmly respond, "No throwing," "No spitting," etc.

MENTALLY RETARDED PARENT

May force feed, stop feeding, or scold her child during feeding if he tests her reactions with misbehaviors.

1. Periodically schedule home visits during feeding times to observe the child's and parent's behavior during mealtimes.
2. Help interpret the child's various testing behaviors during feeding, i.e., "When he throws food (or whatever behavior her child actually displays), he is just trying to see what you will do; lots of children do this":
    a. Ask the parent what she thinks would happen if she laughed when he did this (i.e., he will continue to misbehave because he likes to see her laugh).
    b. Stress that, although misbehavior makes us angry, she should not hit her child, or stop letting him have chances to eat by himself. Instead, explain she should tell him, "No throwing" (spitting, etc.), take the food away, and try again in a few minutes.

c. When possible, model appropriate responses to the child's testing behaviors and verbally prompt the parent's responses as other testing situations arise.
3. If the child is reportedly refusing foods, help identify causes and alternatives with the parent:
   a. If there is concern about the child receiving adequate nutrition, ask the parent to keep a list of everything he eats for one day. If the parent doesn't write, lend a tape recorder for a day or two.
   b. Help identify which foods her child will eat as alternatives to try for foods he is refusing.
   c. Tell the parent not to make her child eat. Explain if she makes him eat, he may refuse foods for a longer period of time.
   d. Explain that her child is not as hungry as he used to be because he is not growing as fast as he did during the first year.
   e. Explain that her child may be hungry at different times than the parent. Help establish a suitable feeding schedule and suggested foods for the child. Leave picture menus with corresponding times illustrated by a clock which recognizes the child's decreased appetite and need for only one larger meal per day.
4. If the child is resisting his parent's help during feeding, explain he's just trying to show us he's a "big boy." Suggest foods he can manage by himself without too much of a mess.
5. If the child is refusing to feed himself things he is capable of:
   a. Explain, "He still wants to make sure you're there to help."
   b. Assure the parent that it's okay to feed him if that's what he wants right now; she won't spoil him and he'll still learn to eat by himself later.
6. Incorporate "testing" behaviors at mealtime as a parent group topic:
   a. Play videotape or role-play situations of various testing behaviors with young children.
   b. Facilitate group discussions about appropriate ways to respond to each "testing" behavior.
   c. After the parent group, join the parents with their children for snack time. Model appropriate responses to testing behaviors as they occur.

BLIND PARENT

Who cannot visually monitor her child's food and utensil throwing; may have an especially difficult time with her child's "testing" during mealtimes.

1. Suggest offering only small amounts of fingerfood at a time.
2. Suggest offering only soft plastic utensils to avoid parental injury if they are thrown.
3. Review the general guidelines and suggestions with the parent, as needed, to help reassure her that it's okay if her child refuses her feeding attempts or does not finish meals.

5.34 Child: TESTS PARENTAL REACTIONS AT BEDTIME (9-12 mo.)
Parent: Understands and responds appropriately to child's testing at bedtime

GENERAL GUIDELINES

In addition to testing his limits and powers to make parents angry at mealtime, the child may try to use bedtime as another "testing ground." He may scream, cry, throw his bottle or other toys across the room and call for "Mama" helplessly. He may interrupt these behaviors periodically to listen for his parent's responding footsteps.

Separation anxieties and fear of the dark can also complicate the child's bedtime behaviors.

The following suggestions may help parents respond effectively to their child's "testing" and their own concurrent anxieties at the child's bedtime:
1. Provide a consistent bedtime routine, such as reading a story, rocking in a chair while singing a lullabye, or playing a special music box.
2. Do not engage the child in active frolic play before bedtime.
3. Keep a nightlight on and remain cheerful when putting the child to bed.
4. Ignore toy throwing, crib rocking, and screaming.
5. Do not re-enter his room in response to crying; instead, tiptoe near the door and peek in if concerned, or call to him to reassure him you are still there and everything will be okay.

MENTALLY RETARDED PARENT

May not have a consistent bedtime or routine for child, may give in to many of the child's pleas, or may punish her child for being "mean" at bedtime.

1. Facilitate a discussion to determine the child's sleep habits, routines, and behaviors at bedtime. The following place, time, and behavior questions may help establish the child's patterns:
   a. "Where does your child sleep at nighttime? Does he sleep alone? Does he sleep in a crib? Does he have a light on when he sleeps? Does he sleep with any special toys or blankets?"
   b. "What time did he go to sleep last night?" If the parent does not know what time, use other reference points, such as "Was it dark? What T.V. show was on? Is that when you go to bed? Does he go to bed around the same time each night? How do you know when it's time for him to go to bed?"
   c. "What was he doing before you put him in bed last night? Playing with toys? Listening to a story?"
   d. "When you put him to bed, what does he do? Go straight to sleep? Does he cry? Play? Fuss? Scream?"
   e. "If he cries or calls to you, what do you do?"
2. If the child's bedtime is irregular, too early, or too late, explain the importance of consistent bedtimes including the following points as applicable to the situation:
   a. Children have different sleep needs than adults.

5.0 SOCIAL-EMOTIONAL

5.34

b. When possible, children need to go to bed around the same time each night so they don't get confused.
c. As children get older, they don't need to go to bed so early (if the parent is putting her child to bed too early and he is upset).
3. Help the parent think of a suitable consistent bedtime according to the parent's and child's schedules.
4. Suggest a specific calming activity to implement with her child before bedtime.
5. If the child reportedly cries or fusses at bedtime, explain:
   a. Crying at bedtime is normal: "He is not being mean; children cry at bedtime because they don't want to be alone, are afraid, or just want to see what you will do."
   b. (If applicable) "If you spank him, he may just cry more and his feelings will be very hurt; he'll feel bad about himself and worry a lot."
   c. (If applicable) "If you go to him each time he calls or cries, he'll keep doing that because he learns that this is a great way to get your attention."
6. Explain how to handle her child's testing behaviors; include:
   a. "Do not go into his room; think about something else or go about your other activities."
   b. "You must ignore him *every* night; if one night you go to him and the next night you pretend you don't hear him, he gets confused and will keep on crying."
   c. "It's okay to call his name from outside his door to let him know you're still there and love him."
7. Suggest ways to make the child's environment more conducive for bedtime, if needed, e.g., nightlights or moving crib to a quieter place (away from the window, out of living room, etc.).
8. Ask the parent to name times when she *should* go into his room if he cries; prompt, as needed, when he's been sick, if she hears him fall, if he cries for longer than thirty minutes (or the length of a T.V. show), and if she realizes he did not have his bottle or his diaper changed before bedtime.

DEAF PARENT

May have established a pattern of quickly responding to all of her child's sounds via her sound receiver box* and thus reinforce his testing behaviors.

1. Provide parent anticipatory guidance according to the above general guidelines.
2. The parent can peek into her child's room, if necessary, to check on her child. Explain that her child will listen very carefully to hear her footsteps, so she should remove her shoes and tiptoe when nearing his room.
3. If the parent uses speech, she can call to the child for reassurance when the *sound receiver box** indicates he is fussing or crying.

---

*See Glossary.

BLIND PARENT

May be unable to visually monitor her child's safety and thus establish patterns for responding to all of child's calls at bedtime.

1. Provide anticipatory guidance and reassurance that children's crying at bedtime is typical. The parent can assure her child's safety by listening to his crying patterns.
2. If the parent "checks on" her child after putting him to bed by listening near his door, explain how he may watch for her shadow or figure even through a small crack in the door. Relate that if he sees her, he may start crying again.
3. Help select appropriate nightlights, if indicated.

5.35 **Child:** ENGAGES IN SIMPLE IMITATIVE PLAY (9-12 mo.)
Parent: Encourages, and facilitates when necessary, child's engaging in simple imitative play

GENERAL GUIDELINES

The child's expanding memory and association skills help him incorporate actions he has seen others perform into his play. He remembers simple "Pat-A-Cake" games from the day before and will start the game by himself; when he sees a comb or a washcloth, he tries to comb his hair or dab his face with the cloth; and when he sees a spoon, he "feeds" himself in play or he may try to feed Mom.

The child's imitative play at this age is brief and usually only an approximation of the actual behavior. For example, he may bang the comb to his head briefly rather than combing his hair. This "play" is preparing him for his later daily living and learning skills.

Parents can encourage their child's imitative play by acknowledging it as "play" and not try to make him do it the "right way." When parents smile, praise their child, and tell him what he is doing, he is more likely to continue. Parents can also encourage imitative play by giving him some of the real-life "tools" to use as toys, e.g., extra washcloth during bath, extra spoon during feeding, plastic cups, combs and brushes, etc. Playing simple "give and take" games with children also encourage their imitative play. Refer to 5.26 (Cooperates in games) for parent training methods to play "give and take" games with their child to supplement the following activities.

MENTALLY RETARDED PARENT

May not recognize her child's imitative behaviors as play, and may try to "make him do it right."

1. Ask the parent if she has ever seen her child play with a comb (cloth, spoon, etc.) and ask what he does with it. Explain his actions as trying to be "just like Mom."
2. Suggest household objects to let her child use for toys and let the parent select a special drawer or box in which to keep them:
   a. Explain that children at this age like to play with these objects just as much as toys.

b. Stress that her child may try to use these objects just like he sees other people using them, but can't copy us exactly at this age.
c. Relate that if we try to make him copy us exactly, then it's not play for him anymore and he may stop trying to copy us.
3. Help the parent think of special phrases to say to her child when she sees him trying to copy her. Explain that these phrases let him know she thinks he is doing a great job which makes him feel good.

BLIND PARENT

May be unaware of her child's imitative play gestures.

1. Provide the parent anticipatory guidance regarding children's imitative play at this age as described under the general guidelines:
   a. Explain how her child is learning these play behaviors from watching others.
   b. Refer to Activity No. 1, 1.42 (Imitates familiar then new gestures), for a perceptual analogy statement, if needed.

5.36 Child: **EXPLORES ENVIRONMENT ENTHUSIASTICALLY – SAFETY PRECAUTIONS IMPORTANT (9-12 mo.)**
Parent: Allows child to safely explore the environment

MENTALLY RETARDED PARENT

May discourage her child's active exploration, and/or may not be aware of safety precautions in the home.

1. Praise the child's new abilities to move around:
   a. Reinforce the parent's hard work with helping her child's motor development.
   b. Explain that it is important to let her child use his new creeping, crawling, and cruising skills to move around and play with things in the house so he can keep learning even more.
2. Always point out and correct hazardous conditions in the environment with the parent:
   a. Directly tell the parent that the danger needs to be eliminated. DON'T say, "It would be safer if you move the heater." DO say "You need to move the heater so your child does not get burned!"
   b. Make a home visit and pay particular attention to the child's play and sleep areas with the parent. Identify potentially dangerous situations and, again, be specific about telling the parent how to make it safer.
   c. Involve the parent in changing the hazardous situation, e.g., "Where do you think a safe place for the iron would be?"
3. Put "Mr. Yuk" stickers on all potentially dangerous items. Explain that they are to help remind the parent, not the child, because the child is too young to know what the stickers mean.

4. Provide a safety kit for the parent which includes foam covering for sharp corners of furniture, plug covers, and cabinet closures.
5. Explain that, if her child is in danger, saying "no" is not good enough. The parent must physically stop her child. Give concrete examples.
6. Role-play calling the poison control center. The parent should be able to give the following information: her name; address; age of child; and description of what the child ingested, and how much.
7. Review various potentially dangerous situations, asking "What could happen" questions followed by "How can you keep that from happening?", e.g., "What could happen if you leave Bobby in the bathtub by himself?", "How can you keep that from happening?"; and "What could happen if you leave the door to the basement open?", "How can you keep that from happening?"

BLIND PARENT

May be unaware of subtle safety hazards in the home, and may be especially anxious about her child's enthusiastic explorations.

1. The parent can child-proof the home for obvious safety hazards, such as poisons, plastic bags, heaters, safety gates, etc. Offer to help child-proof the home for more subtle safety hazards. For example, check for:
   a. Electrical outlets which are not used and of which the parent may be unaware.
   b. Windows with cracks.
   c. Appliance and lamp cords which are hanging down or frayed.
   d. Poisonous plants in the yard.
   e. Sliding glass doors; mark with tape at the child's eye level.
   f. Nails or screws protruding under tables or chairs, carpet tacks, and small buttons on the floor or cushions.
   g. Toys with small parts.

PHYSICALLY DISABLED PARENT

May need to keep potentially dangerous things within her child's reach in order to keep them accessible to her needs, and may be unable to quickly rescue her child from a hazard.

1. The parent can use special lock boxes for medicines, flammables, and toxic substances.
2. Situations may arise where a parent's impaired mobility prevents her from reaching the child quickly to prevent an accident. At this age, saying "no" may stop the child momentarily, but he is likely to continue (e.g., the parent notices he is crawling quickly toward an open door to the basement):
   a. The parent could wear a loud whistle around her neck to be reserved only for extreme situations. (The child should not get used to hearing it too often or he will begin to ignore it.) When the parent blows it quickly, the shocking quality will stop the child and, although perhaps only briefly, give the parent the few extra seconds needed to reach him in time.

b. CAUTION: The whistle should never be blown if the child is climbing on something or at the edge of a stairwell. In this case, a calm parent approach is advised.
3. Help child-proof the home, as needed, with safety gates, locks, etc.

5.37 Child: LIKES TO BE IN CONSTANT SIGHT AND HEARING OF AN ADULT (12-13 mo.)
Parent: Recognizes and accommodates for the child's need to be in constant sight and hearing of an adult

GENERAL GUIDELINES

The child, although enjoying his new feelings of independence through mobility, also recognizes his great dependency on his parents. He wants to explore his environment but often needs his parent as a secure base from which to explore at this age.

Parents can help their child during this stage by allowing him to follow them around when possible and by setting up safe play areas in various rooms.

MENTALLY RETARDED PARENT

May scold her child for demanding close proximity or may isolate him to get her chores done.

1. Provide the parent with a meaningful interpretation for why her child wants to be near her all the time. Include:
   a. All children go through this stage.
   b. Her child feels safer when he can see or hear her.
   c. He worries about where she is if he can't see or hear her.
   d. We cannot teach him how to be alone at this age.
2. During a home visit, show the parent specific ways to "set up" or adapt the home so that her child can be safely within the parent's sight or hearing, e.g., playing in a playpen in a hallway, placing a safety gate at a hallway entrance, playing in a room or area that has been child-proofed, and having special drawers in different rooms for her child's toys.
3. Help the parent think of activities for her child which enable him to be near her while she is involved in various daily activities:
   a. Prompt the parent with specific activity related questions, such as "When you are cooking, what can he play with in the kitchen?"
   b. Help the parent select developmentally appropriate toys and household objects for her child to play with. Associate when her child can play with them to specific times of the day and parent activities.

5.38 Child: GIVES TOY TO A FAMILIAR ADULT SPONTANEOUSLY AND UPON REQUEST (12-15 mo.)
Parent: Reinforces child's "sharing"

GENERAL GUIDELINES

Parents are becoming more than just a secure "home base" to the child. He wants to share everything with them and may constantly bring "priceless treasures" (which may seem quite unimportant to the parent) over to share his enjoyment and discoveries.

Parents promote their child's enjoyment and sense of social sharing by showing lots of interest in the things he brings to them, and help develop his sense of trust by always returning the toy to him.

MENTALLY RETARDED PARENT

May "tease" her child by withholding toys he had only intended to share.

1. As situations occur, interpret the child's "giving a toy" as a positive sign of wanting to share his fun with the parent. Stress:
   a. "If you show him how pleased you are, he'll learn sharing is a good thing."
   b. It is important to give toys back as soon as her child reaches or gestures for it back.
   c. If we don't give toys back, her child will feel teased and stop wanting to share.
2. Role-play possible positive responses to specific situations. Ask "What can you say to Sarah when she brings you her stuffed dog to let her know you like her sharing with you?"

5.39 Child: DISPLAYS INDEPENDENT BEHAVIOR; IS DIFFICULT TO DISCIPLINE; THE "NO" STAGE (12-15 mo.)
Parent: Understands, allows, and responds effectively to child's independent behavior

GENERAL GUIDELINES

The child's continuing strive toward independence and positive self-image expands as he tests his power to say "no" and influence others' behavior. He says "no" gesturally and/or verbally to most suggestions or requests, even if he means "yes"! This is an important time for the child as he learns that he can make decisions as an independent individual and continues to learn his behavioral limits.

Parents can set appropriate limits and foster their child's self-image and independence while avoiding power struggles by:
1. Reinforcing the child's positive behaviors while ignoring his negative reactions, when possible.
2. Providing clear, consistent, and developmentally reasonable limits.

3. Not asking "Do you want. . ." questions unless the child really has a choice.
4. Respecting the child's "no's," when possible.
5. Avoiding over-use of "no's" to the child by modifying the environment to prevent "no" situations.
6. Redirecting him toward a more appropriate activity when he is displaying inappropriate behaviors.

Anticipatory Guidance: Most parents, with or without disabilities, can benefit from behavioral management guidelines, reassurance, and support during the child's "no" stage. Parents who happen to be deaf, blind, or physically disabled will probably not require adapted training techniques. Mentally retarded parents, however, may need intensive intervention to help them understand their children's behavior from a "new" point of view. They may also have only experienced or been exposed to punishment as a means for responding to misbehaviors. The following parent training activities can be incorporated into individual or group sessions over a four- to six-week period. Each training concept must then, however, continue to be an integral part of your future interventions with the parent and child when dealing with all areas (i.e., cognition, motor, and language) of the child's developmental program.

MENTALLY RETARDED PARENT

May not reinforce her child's positive behaviors, may place unreasonable demands on her child, and may be unaware of discipline techniques which do not require physical punishment.

1. Help the parent identify and reinforce her child's positive behaviors:
   a. Within a discussion and demonstration framework, list her child's behaviors which the parent thinks are positive:
      (1) Introduce the activity concretely, for example: "Sometimes it's hard to think of or remember things our children do that we like at this age. We're often too busy watching and stopping things the child does that we *don't* like! For example, when a child is moving around the house, we may be so busy watching to make sure he doesn't mess up, break something, or hurt himself, we don't notice the nice things he does.
      "It takes practice to help remember to watch for the nice things. Today we are going to watch him while he's playing with his toys and name only the things he does that we like when he plays. I'll write them down and make a list to look at later."
      (2) If videotapes are available, play back a previous play session. If not, set up play materials for the child to interact with during a three- to five-minute period.
      (3) Encourage the parent to identify three positive behaviors she sees her child exhibit, such as smiling, showing her toy, making sounds, exploring the toy, etc.
      (4) As various positive child behaviors occur, prompt the parent to name them by asking "What's he doing? Do you like that?"
      (5) If the parent cannot label her child's positive behaviors when asked, name them for her and remark "That's a good thing; let's write it down."
      (6) If the parent names negative behaviors, agree but remind her you're only writing down the things we like this time.
   b. Review with the parent her child's list of positive behaviors which were generated during the play session. Explain that he learns these are good behaviors or good ways to act by being told these actions are good; at this age, he is trying to figure out what is good and what is not good.
   c. Facilitate a discussion about the ways to let her child know when we like the things he is doing:
      (1) Explain we can tell him we like his good behavior with our words or our actions.
      (2) Give examples of verbal "I like" statements, such as "Good playing" or "I like the way you put the block in the can."
      (3) Prompt the parent to think of things to tell her child that she likes the way he is looking at his book, used his cup to drink juice, and showed her his toy.
      (4) Give examples of showing her child she likes what he did without using words, such as clapping, patting, kissing, or smiling.
      (5) Review each positive behavior listed from Activity Nos. 1 and 2. Help the parent think of a way she can tell him she likes each behavior. Stress that, when she lets him know she likes it, she is teaching him good ways to act.
   d. Reinitiate a five-minute play session. During the first two minutes, model reinforcing one or two of the child's positive behaviors. Let the parent practice reinforcing his positive behaviors for the remaining time. "Coach from the sidelines," as needed, with verbal prompts.
   e. Post the generated list of the child's positive behaviors with corresponding positive parent responses next to one of his play areas. Draw a happy face on the top. Keep the list simple.
   f. Reinforce and prompt the parent's continued positive identification and reinforcement of her child's positive play behaviors during all of your interventions with the parent and child.
   g. Repeat similar procedures as described in Activity Nos. 1-6 for training the parent to identify and reinforce her child's positive behaviors during eating and dressing. These controlled activities should be spread out over a period of four to six sessions, and continue to be reinforced by the facilitator during all future involvement.
   h. Interpret to the parent the positive aspects of her child's behavior which may be easily misinterpreted as "mean" or "bad," e.g., "When he says 'no' to you, it shows he is learning to make decisions on his own"; "When he pulls the spoon out of your hand, he wants to show you he's trying to learn how he can eat all by himself."

5.39

2. Teach the parent how to make requests and ask questions appropriate to her child's developmental level:
   a. Explain, "It's easy to use too many words with children that they don't understand; if we want them to do what we ask, they need to understand what we say before they can do it":
      (1) Review the child's receptive vocabulary words and phrases.
      (2) Role-play developmentally appropriate and inappropriate requests that could be made to her child. Specify what makes it a "good" request and what makes it an inappropriate request because he cannot understand what we are asking.
   b. Practice changing unclear requests for young children into clear requests with the parent:
      (1) Role-play common situations, such as "Lisa is getting into your purse and you don't want her to; What can you say and do to tell her that?"
      (2) Name common unclear phrases we might use in example situations. Help the parent think of ways to make the statement clearer, e.g., change "Don't do that" to "No throwing food."
      (3) Tell the parent that, at this age, children don't understand and cannot answer "why" questions and give concrete examples.
      (4) During naturally occurring situations with her child, point out when the parent's statements are not clear, supplying the "clear statement" the parent could use instead.
   c. Stress to the parent the importance of not over-using "no" with her child:
      (1) Explain that if we say "no" to children too many times, they can feel bad. They feel bad because they are interested in trying things out and learning about everything. When they hear "no," they feel bad because they think we don't want him to try things out for himself.
      (2) Give an example of an experience you had (e.g., in school, at home as a child) when someone kept telling you "no." Relate how you felt and why. Ask the parent if she can remember times when someone kept telling her "no" and how she felt.
      (3) Explain that if we say "no" to children too many times, they may also stop listening; the word "no" begins to sound like any other word.
      (4) Name times when the parent should say "no" to her child, i.e., when he is hurting himself, hurting someone else, or can hurt or break something. Give an example of each situation and prompt the parent to name times she should say "no," e.g., pulling hair, biting, going near the street, and playing with matches. Stress that she must stop these activities in addition to saying "no."
      (5) Name concrete example situations when we might be tempted to say "no" to her child, but since he is not hurting himself or anyone else, we should say something else or nothing. Situations could include playing with his food by spreading it a little on the tray, crumpling his paper instead of coloring on it, dumping his blocks out of their box instead of building with them, and misarticulating a word. Encourage the parent to think of a time she said "no" to her child when she probably could have "saved" it.
      (6) List a variety of potential "no" situations on separate index cards. Alternate selecting cards and decide with the parent which situations warrant a "no" and in which situations "no's" can be saved, as you sort them into two piles.
      (7) Review how to say "no" to make it meaningful to her child. Refer to 1.56 (Knows what no-no means and reacts).
      (8) Explain that when she says "no," at this age, her child thinks "no" means "not now"; he does not understand that "no" means "never." Relate that, even though the parent said "no" when her child pulled her hair (name various examples), he may pull her hair again tomorrow.
   d. Stress to the parent the importance of only asking her child "yes" or "no" questions if he really has a choice:
      (1) Explain that "if we ask your child if he wants to do something and he really doesn't have a choice, it's not fair to ask the question. Only ask him questions if he has a choice." Follow with several concrete examples, e.g., "If you ask him if he wants to go to bed and it's his bedtime, what happens if he says no? It's better just to tell him it's time to go to bed."
      (2) Help the parent think of daily activities and situations where she should tell him what is going to happen but *not* ask him if he does not have a choice, e.g., "It's time to take a bath," *not* "do you want to take a bath?"
      (3) Name situations which are good to give her child a chance to choose to say "no," explaining this lets him know we respect his feelings and decisions.
3. Show the parent how to modify the environment to foster her child's independence and decrease excessive demand:
   a. Introduce this activity by explaining, "At this age, children spend a lot of time exploring things around the house. This is good because they learn this way. But, at this age, children are naturally tempted to get into things they shouldn't which makes us get angry or say "no" too much. We can help him explore and learn without getting into trouble by moving things that are tempting to different places in the house, and keeping things that are okay for him to play with nearby."
   b. Explore each room in the household with the parent. Help make changes, as needed, which are agreeable with the parent. Explain the reasons for each change:
      (1) Set up a box of toys in various rooms explaining, if her child has things he is allowed to play with, he is less likely to play with things he should not get into.
      (2) Set up special low drawers or shelves that have things with which the child is allowed to play.

(3) Put televisions and stereos out of reach, if possible, explaining this keeps him from temptation and prevents her from having to say "no" all of the time.
   (4) Put breakable items out of reach to prevent breaking and saying "no."
   (5) Suggest restricting her child's eating to kitchen and dining areas to keep his food mess in one area.
   (6) Put garbage cans under a safely-locked cupboard.
   (7) Move cleaning supplies, medicine, and toxic substances to high cupboards.
   (8) Rearrange chairs or end tables to provide extra play space.
4. Teach the parent how and when to use "ignoring" and "distracting" as discipline techniques with her child:
   a. Facilitate a discussion about children's undesirable behaviors at this age:
      (1) Explain that some things children do can hurt themselves, other people, or things. Name a few examples, such as hitting, breaking, or biting. Ask the parent to think of things a child might do which could hurt himself, others, or things. Make a list of these behaviors and label them as "hurting actions."
      (2) Explain there are also things a child may do that we don't like but he isn't hurting anyone or anything by doing them. Help the parent name some of these behaviors (e.g., whining, not listening, stomping his feet, pounding his highchair tray). Make a list of these behaviors and label them as "annoying actions."
      (3) Review the picture chart or list of children's "hurting actions" and "annoying actions." Introduce teaching the parent ignoring and distracting as discipline techniques to use with her child through an explanation, such as "When children do these things, there are better ways to teach him how to act besides spanking and yelling. Since spanking and yelling hurt children and do not always work, I will be teaching you some new ways to help stop your child when he misbehaves. First, we will be working on learning ways to handle your child's 'annoying actions' by ways called 'ignoring' and 'distracting'."
   b. Teach the parent how to ignore her child's "annoying actions":
      (1) Review with the parent the list of her child's identified annoying behaviors and help identify which child behaviors can be ignored, e.g., whining, foot stomping, and crying for no reason.
      (2) Clearly explain the rules for ignoring: Do not look at, touch, or talk to the child while he is being annoying; when he stops the action, smile, look at him, and talk to him.
      (3) Role-play ignoring several annoying behavior situations with the parent.
   c. Teach the parent ways to distract her child when he is displaying "annoying actions":
      (1) Explain that we can also stop her child's annoying actions by distracting him with another activity. Give an example, such as "If you are trying to cook and Bobby keeps pulling on your legs and whining for you to play with him, give him some pots, pans, and spoons to play with. This way, he will forget about wanting to play with you and whining because he'll be too busy playing with the pans."
      (2) Illustrate several more situations that can be annoying and help the parent think of ways to distract her child. Sample annoying situations and distractions could be:
         (a) Child interrupts Mom when she is trying to talk to a friend on the telephone: give the child his toy telephone.
         (b) Child kicks and screams when he is getting his diaper changed: give the child his stuffed dog to play with.
         (c) Child starts throwing his wind-up toy because he can't make it work: give the child another toy that he does know how to use.
      (3) Review the child's list of annoying behaviors and help decide which actions can be stopped by distracting him with another toy from behaviors which can be ignored.
   d. Whenever you are with the parent and child, model and prompt her to use the "ignoring" and "distraction" methods she has learned. Reinforce all of the parent's efforts enthusiastically and point out how she is helping her child behave.
   e. Refer to Activity No. 2.e, 5.40 (Acts impulsively, unable to recognize rules) to help the parent redirect her child's inappropriate behaviors.

5.40 **Child:** ACTS IMPULSIVELY, UNABLE TO RECOGNIZE RULES (12-15 mo.)
   Parent: Understands and responds effectively to child's impulsive behaviors

GENERAL GUIDELINES

Rules for children at this age should not be above their developmental capabilities. For example, children at this age are naturally messy and should not have strict rules for complete neatness. Children's high activity level and short attention span at this age also prohibit rules, such as sitting quietly at the dinner table or looking at a book for more than a few minutes.

Necessary rules at this age should, however, include health, safety, respect for other's property (within reason!), and simple mealtime manners, such as no excessive throwing of food or utensils. A child should not be allowed to hurt himself, hurt others, or break important things.

At this age, a child usually cannot stop his undesirable behaviors, and saying "no" is not enough. He needs an adult to help him comply. Parents can help him comply by: 1) telling him the behavior is wrong ("No pinching; that hurts),

5.40

2) stopping the behavior (removing his hands), and then 3) redirecting him to a more appropriate behavior ("It's okay to rub my arm").

All parents may benefit from anticipatory guidance, management techniques, and reassurance during this stage of their child's development.

MENTALLY RETARDED PARENT

May expect her child to understand and comply with unrealistic rules or may not have set any limits for her child.

1. Help the parent identify and understand developmentally appropriate rules or limits for her child:
   a. Identify through observations and discussions what rules, limits, or expectations the parent has for her child and how she enforces these rules. Explore the parent's rules for her child at bedtime, mealtime, playtime, when visiting friends, when going out to dinner, and regarding being neat and treating people nicely. Use probing questions, such as:
      (1) Bedtime Rules: Does he have a set bedtime? Is he allowed to get up for a drink?
      (2) Mealtime Rules: Does he have to wait for everyone to finish eating before he gets down? Does he have to eat all of his food? What happens if he doesn't finish his dinner? Is he allowed to throw his food? What happens if he throws his food?
      (3) Playtime Rules: Is her child allowed to play with her jewelry? Is he allowed to play with the things she has on her coffee table? Is he allowed to throw his blocks? What does she do if he throws his blocks? Is he allowed to color on walls? Is he allowed to color on paper? Does she expect him to color in a certain way (e.g., can he scribble or does Mom expect him to make a picture)?
      (4) Neatness Rules: What happens if her child gets his clothes dirty? What happens if he spills food on his tray? Is he allowed to empty drawers? Does she expect him to put all of his toys away?
   b. Make a list of all of the rules the parent appears to have for her child that were generated from Activity No. 1.a. Keep the list simple and in categories, such as mealtime, playtime, and bedtime rules.
   c. Identify the listed rules which are developmentally inappropriate, too harsh, or too lenient for the child:
      (1) Review each of the child's rules separately and explain why it is inappropriate, when applicable. Use rationale statements, such as: "At his age, children:
         (a) "Can't stay interested in an activity very long."
         (b) "Don't have as much patience as adults."
         (c) "Don't eat as much as older children."
         (d) "Are messy; they have a hard time being too neat."
         (e) "Don't need as much sleep as when they were young."
         (f) "Like to try to experiment with their toys so they don't always play with them exactly the way we think they should be played with."
         (g) "Want to try to do things by themselves."
      (2) Suggest alternatives to the parent's current unrealistic rules, such as let him play with his toys if he finishes dinner before everyone else, let him wear old clothes when he's playing with messy things, and change his bed or nap times.
      (3) Cross out the rules on the child's list which have been identified as inappropriate.
   d. Explain and define what rules young children should have at this age. Generate a list of primary things her child should *not* be allowed to do: He should not be allowed to hurt himself, other people, or animals; and he should not be allowed to ruin or break other people's belongings.
   e. Name specific examples for each of the primary things her child should not do and prompt the parent to name more. For example:
      (1) Her child should not be allowed to walk in the street, play with matches, or play in cabinets that have dangerous things in them, because these things can hurt him.
      (2) He should not be allowed to hit, bite, pull hair, or kick because these things hurt other people.
      (3) He should not be allowed to throw dishes or food, throw his blocks at the TV, play with the stereo, mess with Mom's makeup or play with her important things, because he can ruin or break other people's things.
   f. Make a more permanent chart of the child's realistic rules and limits to post where all family members can see it. Make pictured captions next to each rule to help the parent identify if she does not read. Remind the parent that this chart is for her, not her child; he can only learn these rules from her.
2. Teach the parent how to teach her child his rules and what to do when he breaks them:
   a. Review the child's chart of rules with the parent. Explain that her child *cannot* learn what his rules are by looking at the chart or be being told what they are, i.e., she cannot sit down with him and tell him what the rules are!:
      (1) Explain that her child learns what his rules are by breaking them and then being told and shown that he is not to do that. Provide a concrete example situation.
      (2) Relate how, if we went to a new school or job, we probably wouldn't know what all the rules were until we broke them. For example, if the school had a rule that there was no chewing gum and we chewed gum, we'd learn that rule because someone would tell us to stop.
   b. Explore through observations and discussions how the parent reacts or stops her child if he breaks any of these rules:
      (1) Explain that spanking and yelling hurt her child and are not good ways to teach him to learn the rules because spanking and yelling don't show him what he should do. Point out that spanking does teach him to hit.

(2) If appropriate, facilitate a discussion about yours and the parent's memories and feelings from childhood about how you were disciplined.
c. Provide the parent a meaningful rationale for using the "showing him the right way" technique when her child breaks rules:
  (1) Use an explanation, such as "Your child learns what he can do and what he *cannot* do from you; that's because you are his most important teacher. If you tell him 'no' or tell him he can't do something, then you need to show him what he *can* do instead."
  (2) Relate a personal experience of how you needed to be shown how to do something the right way, not just told you were wrong, e.g., "Everytime you cooked pudding, it came out too watery. Your Mom needed to show you how to cook it on a higher heat with less water. If she had told you 'no, you cooked it wrong' and told you to stop making pudding, you never would have learned how to do it the right way."
  (3) Ask the parent if she can think of a time someone told her "no" but then showed her the right way.
d. Explain why young children break rules. Include the following concepts:
  (1) Young children don't know what the rules are.
  (2) They may forget what the rules are.
  (3) They may break a rule several times just to keep checking that it's still a rule.
  (4) When children break rules, they are not always trying to annoy their parents or act "bad"; it's just their way of learning what the rules are!
e. Teach the parent how to redirect her child's inappropriate behavior or activity to an appropriate one, i.e., "Showing him the right way":
  (1) Explain to the parent that, when her child breaks a rule, there are three steps to "showing him the right way." First, tell him what he did wrong; second, stop him from what he is doing; and third, show him what he can do instead.
  (2) Illustrate these steps with a specific example, preferably one you have observed with the child. An example could be: "If your child tore pages out of your important book, he would be breaking a rule because he is hurting someone else's belongings. Therefore, tell him 'No tearing Mommy's book', then take your book away, and show him what he can do instead of tearing your book. This could be letting him tear pieces of scrap paper or giving him an old magazine especially for him to tear."
  (3) Rehearse numerous possible situations in which the child may break a rule and practice anticipating the steps the parent can use to redirect his behavior or "show him the right way."
  (4) Example situations for rehearsal or role-play could be redirecting the child from pulling hair to patting hair, pinching Mom's arm to rubbing her arm, dumping out Mom's purse to dumping out his blocks from his can, biting someone to patting them, playing with Mom's glass vase to playing with his plastic cups, climbing on the table to climbing on his chair, climbing in the fireplace to climbing in a big box, and throwing blocks to throwing balls.
  (5) Add to the child's "Rule chart" pictures of behaviors or activities to redirect her child to when he breaks a rule.
f. Whenever possible, schedule extra sessions with the parent and child to help insure carry-over of new behavior management techniques and to provide extra reinforcement for the parent. During all of your sessions, model appropriate redirecting techniques as the child's behavior demands and help the parent practice with your verbal leads and prompts.
g. When undesirable child actions occur, help the parent choose the best way to stop it:
  (1) Remind her to ask herself "Is this an annoying action, or is he hurting himself, others, or other people's belongings?"
  (2) If it's an annoying action, remind her she can "ignore" or "distract" her child. Refer to 5.39 (Displays independent behavior; is difficult to discipline; the no stage).
  (3) If it's a "hurting action," remind her she needs to stop him and show him the right way.
h. Emphasize the importance of being consistent when her child breaks rules. Use examples of situations that could occur where it's easy not to be consistent because the parent is busy. Explain how confusing this is to the child. Stress that he cannot learn his rules unless she always stops his misbehavior and shows him the right way.

5.41 Child: ATTEMPTS SELF-DIRECTION; RESISTS ADULT CONTROL (12-15 mo.)
Parent: Understands child's resistance to adult control and allows opportunity for his self-direction within safe limits

GENERAL GUIDELINES

Resisting parental control is another sign of the child's emerging sense of autonomy and independence. He has learned he can do things for himself and will want to make his own decisions about things, such as what toys to play with and what foods he'll eat.

Parents can facilitate their child's independence by fostering self-direction in positive ways. For example, they can let him feed himself according to his own abilities, let him choose when he's finished with things (toys, food, etc.) when possible, and allow him the freedom to safely explore his environment. The child's urge to climb and explore to satisfy his curiosity and his strive for independence often requires new child-proofing at home.

Parents should express their natural feelings of displeasure and anger when their child openly defies them; however, physical punishment will leave him feeling powerless and can hinder his social and emotional growth.

5.41

MENTALLY RETARDED PARENT

May interpret her child's attempts for self-direction as "mean or bad," and may be unaware of ways to release her angry feelings.

1. Prepare the parents for this normal behavior well in advance of this stage:
   a. Expose the parent to other children at this age (in person, through pictures, video, etc.), explaining their self-direction as a positive indication of learning.
   b. Role-play situations with the parent which illustrate how to handle the child's self-directed behavior with appropriate limits.
2. Explain the importance of allowing children to have choices at this developmental age:
   a. Provide the parent with specific situations in which she can offer choices to her child, e.g., which foods to eat, which toy to play with, and which pants to wear. Ask her to think of additional things about which she can let her child make decisions.
   b. Name specific situations that the child should *NOT* have choices in at that age, e.g., her child should not have the choice of summer and winter clothes when it is cold out, or a choice of toys when one is dangerous.
3. If the parent is confused or frustrated when her child suddenly refuses her help or resists adult control, explain that he is trying to do it all by himself and that is great:
   a. Model saying to the child, "Okay, you want to show us how you can try and do it all by yourself."
   b. Describe the child's behaviors which indicate he needs some adult help explaining that, although it is important that he try things on his own, he may sometimes need help.
   c. Model unobtrusively holding out your hand saying "Do you need some help?" If the child doesn't give the toy, model, "That is okay; maybe you want some more time."
   d. Have the parent practice a, b, and c above with you, providing her any needed verbal or physical guidance and lots of reinforcement.
4. Explain, at this age, children are so active and curious, they often don't like to finish things they have started:
   a. Give examples, such as meals and toys. Ask the parent to name additional things her child may not want to finish.
   b. Help anticipate what may happen if the parent tries to make her child finish an activity at this age.
5. Discuss that it is natural for parents to have feelings of anger and frustration when children misbehave. Emphasize that it is not okay to express those feelings in a way that will harm her child:
   a. Give, and prompt the parent to name, examples of child behaviors which can cause parents to feel angry and frustrated.
   b. Name reactions parents should never use to express their anger to children: spanking hard, hitting, kicking, slapping, burning, or shaking.
   c. Discuss better ways to release feelings of anger and frustration: leave another adult in charge and go out for a walk, go to another room and do exercise, pound a pillow, or take a few deep breaths.
   d. Review better ways to respond to her child's misbehaviors as outlined in 5.39 (Displays independent behavior) and 5.40 (Acts impulsively).
6. Behavior management and "controlling anger" should be extended parent group topics to cover over a period of four to six weeks and continued to be reinforced throughout all of your interventions with the parent.

BLIND PARENT

May not be able to visually monitor the safety of her child's self-directive behaviors.

PHYSICALLY DISABLED PARENT

With limited mobility; may not be able to respond quickly to hazardous situations which could arise with her child's new self-directive behaviors.

1. As the child's mobility increases, additional environmental modifications should be examined:
   a. There may be furnishings which invite the child's urge to climb. Bookcases could be turned around, chairs should be moved away from potentially dangerous situations (windows, cabinets), and table lamps can be secured with *dycem*.*
   b. Play areas outdoors should be securely fenced off and the yard inspected for yard tools, poisonous plants, holes, etc.
   c. Safety gates may need readapting because the child may now be able to manipulate the lock or climb over them.
   d. Assure that the child's toys are within his safe reach.
2. Refer to 5.36 (Explores environment enthusiastically) for additional environmental safety checks.

5.42 **Child: DISPLAYS FREQUENT TANTRUM BEHAVIORS (12-18 mo.)**
Parent: Understands, anticipates, and responds effectively to child's tantrum behaviors

GENERAL GUIDELINES

Temper tantrum behaviors include screaming, kicking, hitting, falling to the floor, and/or head-banging. They may range from short outbursts of only a minute, to major seemingly hysterical screams lasting up to forty-five minutes.

A child uses temper tantrums as a vehicle to express and release anger, frustration, and, in some cases, as a way to attract attention. He becomes angry when his independence is blocked or restricted and realizes he does not have the power to change this reality. His desire to do something also frequently surpasses his cognitive and manipulative abilities and thus he becomes easily frustrated. To make matters worse, he does not have the verbal abilities to express his feelings of frustration and anger, and does not have the inner controls or

---

*See Glossary.

capabilities for redirecting or resolving these feelings. A child who is over-tired, over-stimulated, over-excited, and over-restricted is especially vulnerable to tantrums.

Parents can help their child during this period through prevention and consistency, and by maintaining their own control. Some tantrums may be prevented if parents can identify a trend of events or situations which seem to lead up to, or trigger, a tantrum. They can then eliminate or modify these precipitants. When a child is angry or frustrated, parents can verbally express those feelings for the child and let him know they understand. Frustrating situations, such as developmentally inappropriate toys or behavior expectations, should be avoided.

If a child is not hurting himself or others, his tantrum should be completely ignored throughout its duration. Consistency is critical. Tantrums may increase in intensity and duration before diminishing when ignoring techniques are initiated. If the parent "gives in," the child's tantrum behavior will continue and be used often.

Parents should maintain an air of calmness and control during their child's tantrum. This provides the child the sense of security needed to let him know he can regain control of his behavior.

If a child is hurting himself during a tantrum, he cannot be ignored. He needs to be held firmly and calmly to prevent harm to himself or others, and to let him know there is someone who will not let him hurt others when he cannot control himself.

All parents may benefit from guidance to help them understand and respond to their child's tantrums effectively.

MENTALLY RETARDED PARENT

May be unaware of the cause-effect issues precipitating her child's tantrum, and may react impulsively with punitive measures.

1. Determine if the child is having tantrums and how they are responded to through observation and conversation with the parent. Ask if her child hits, falls to the floor, holds breath, etc., and ask what she does when he acts like that.
2. Explore the parent's understanding of the cause or reasons for his tantrums, i.e., "Why do you think he hits?"
3. Try to determine if there are trends which seem to precipitate his tantrum by asking the parent to think of what happened right before he screamed, hit, etc.
4. Interpret the causes of children's tantrums at this age. Compare how adults can tell people what is wrong or why they are angry, but children cannot tell others so his (name child's specific behaviors) is the only way they know how to express their feelings.
5. Review the importance of never physically punishing her child but, instead, using her technique of "ignoring" (as outlined in 5.39, 5.40, and 5.41):
   a. Role-play ignoring techniques during a child's tantrum.
   b. Stress not looking, talking, or touching the child in any way until the tantrum stops.
6. Tell the parent she cannot ignore her child if he is hurting himself or others during tantrums:
   a. Name specific behaviors which cannot be ignored: head-banging, biting, and hitting.
   b. Demonstrate with a doll, and video clip, if available, firm holding to prevent her child's arms and legs from moving, gradually decreasing the hold as the child resumes control.
7. Expose the parent to effective models of responding to tantrums via videotapes and situations with her child that arise during children's play groups.

5.43 Child: NEEDS AND EXPECTS RITUALS AND ROUTINES (12-18 mo.)
Parent: Respects and accommodates child's need for rituals and routines within appropriate limits

GENERAL GUIDELINES

The child begins to expect and demand consistency through familiar routines during daily activities. For example, at mealtime he may only eat from a certain plate or may expect to wear only a certain bib. At bedtime he may refuse to go to bed unless he has had his drink, kissed everyone goodnight, and has his door left open at exactly the correct angle.

Simple consistent routines help provide the child with needed predictable order during this period of emerging conflicts between dependency and autonomy. An excessive need for rituals and environmental sameness, however, should *not* occupy much of the child's day, and may be indicative of attachment or other emotional conflict which requires professional consultation.

MENTALLY RETARDED PARENT

May provide an inconsistent environment, or misinterpret her child's behavior if a routine is changed.

1. Explain the child's development need for certain routines using examples from the general guidelines.
2. Through observation and discussion with the parent, help identify and clarify any favorite routines her child may have during various daily activities, such as bath, bed, and mealtime:
   a. Explain that her child may refuse to eat, sleep, etc. if she doesn't follow these routines each time.
   b. Stress that her child is not being mean when this happens; he just gets worried when things don't go the way he expects.
3. If there are no clear consistent rituals or routines for the child, help the parent think of some simple routines to use each day. Make a picture list to post over his bed, highchair, or bath as a reminder. For example, a bedtime routine could be: first put on pajamas, then let him kiss family members and a favorite stuffed animal goodnight, and finally turn on his favorite music box each night after putting him in bed. The picture chart would have pictures of pajamas, kissing, and the music box in matching order.

5.44 Child: BEGINS TO SHOW A SENSE OF HUMOR – LAUGHS AT INCONGRUITIES (12-18 mo.)
Parent: Reinforces and encourages child's sense of humor

GENERAL GUIDELINES

The child has developed a strong sense of social expectations from his environment through his daily experiences. During his first year, he may have looked confused or upset when faced with environmental incongruities, such as seeing a talking dog on a television commercial or watching mom put a hat on their pet dog; now he laughs aloud.

At the same time, the child is learning he can be the cause for making others laugh by acting silly or "performing." He may even tease an adult by hiding under his covers or the table thinking no one can see him. He likes to repeat and have the funny situation repeated many times, laughing each time as if it were the first.

Parents encourage their child's budding sense of humor and self-esteem by attending to his antics in his effort to become the center of attention, and by continuing to laugh and attend as he repeats it over and over again (even though it was really only funny the first time). Parents can also "set up" funny situations, such as putting a sock on the child's or her own hand and laugh to help him see the humor in incongruities.

MENTALLY RETARDED PARENT

May not recognize her child's sense of humor and antics as an effort to make others laugh.

1. Interpret the child's behaviors positively when he is trying to tease and be silly with the parent. For example: "When he dances, he's looking at you to see if you'll laugh or clap; he's trying to do things that he thinks you'll find funny."
2. Relate some of the things that children think are funny at this age. Help the parent think of some activities that might be funny to do with her child during daily activities, such as putting diapers on her head and laughing.

5.45 Child: ENJOYS IMITATING ADULT BEHAVIOR; RESPONDS WELL TO THE INTRODUCTION OF NEW TASKS (12-18 mo.)
Parent: Introduces and encourages child to imitate appropriate new tasks and adult behaviors

GENERAL GUIDELINES

The child watches and tries to copy the actions of older siblings and adults during daily activities. At first, he may try to wipe off his highchair tray, wipe his face, feed others, or stir vigorously with spoons and cups. Within a few months, the child becomes especially interested in the "tools" his parents and siblings use. He watches them use lipstick, keys, wallets, screwdrivers, pens, or watches while waiting impatiently to try these things out.

The child's imitation of adult behaviors is often brief and only an approximation of the actual behavior. He uses imitation as a way of learning to understand and incorporate social interactions in his environment, and as a form of play for entertainment and expression of self.

Parents can capitalize on their child's interest in imitation as a valuable teaching tool. They can let him play with actual household items, such as dusting cloths, spoons, old wallets, purses, and combs, during daily activities when they are using similar items. Parents can reinforce and help their child learn from his imitative play by praising him and talking about the activity in a fun way without expecting completion of a task or perfect imitation.

MENTALLY RETARDED PARENT

May expect her child to copy behaviors exactly, and may not provide safe opportunities for him to use adult objects as play materials.

1. Explain that, at this age, much of her child's learning and play involves trying to copy what other people do. Describe a few common examples and ask the parent if she has seen her child copy things she does.
2. Clearly explain the limits of children's imitative play at this age:
   a. Name specific adult activities (wiping tables, washing faces, cooking) and compare how her child may try to imitate the activity, i.e., not exactly and only briefly.
   b. Name additional activities the parent may do (e.g., combing hair, brushing teeth) and ask her to show how her child may try to copy her. Again, stress that he is not expected to imitate her exactly.
3. Help identify adult "tools" or materials that the parent can let her child play with to encourage imitation:
   a. Name several specific situations and ask the parent what she could give her child to use so he can try to do the same thing, e.g., "When you are dusting, what can you give your child to dust with?"
   b. Help collect adult "tools" or materials to let her child play with and put them in special drawers or boxes in various rooms.
4. Name imitative play situations and help the parent think of things she can tell her child to let him know she's proud of him, e.g., "You're wiping the table; good job!"
5. Help identify and anticipate potentially dangerous situations her child may try to copy. Provide examples, such as playing with matches, turning on stoves, getting into makeup, or playing with scissors or knives. Ask the parent if she can think of other things that could be dangerous that her child may try to copy:
   a. Stress that her child is not trying to be bad or get into trouble; he is only trying to learn to do what he sees others do.
   b. Specifically show the parent how to avoid these situations, e.g., keep matches, knives, etc. out of reach; and always watch him when he is in the kitchen, etc.

BLIND PARENT

May be unable to discern her child's inaudible imitative adult behaviors.

1. Describe common adult behaviors and materials children often try to imitate. The parent can then pay special attention to letting her child watch her during these activities and give him similar adult materials to use.
2. Describe the child's imitative behaviors and concurrent facial expressions as they occur.

5.46 Child: PLAYS BALL COOPERATIVELY (12-15 mo.)
Parent: Plays ball with child

GENERAL GUIDELINES

The child is now enjoying cooperative game-playing and can keep an activity going through purposeful "give and take" cooperation.

He is willing to give the ball up during play because he knows it will be returned. At this age, he can rarely catch a ball with his hands, but may try to trap it between his legs and enjoys a game of chasing and throwing it.

Parents can encourage ball play by initiating ball games or responding to the child's initiation; allowing the child ample time to respond; providing verbal and physical prompts, as needed; and, most importantly, by keeping the game fun.

Soft rubber balls, rolled up socks, clutch balls, and small beach balls are fun to toss and chase after.

MENTALLY RETARDED PARENT

May expect developmentally higher ball-playing skills from her child.

1. Engage the parent and child in a game of ball play, setting the pace for keeping the game fun. Explain that, at this age, the most important thing is to keep the game fun; it does not matter how far or how fast her child throws the ball:
    a. Explain that we cannot expect her child to throw or catch balls well at this age.
    b. Model accepting and praising each of the child's attemps to toss the ball or retain it.
    c. Stress promptly returning the ball so he won't be afraid to give the ball up.
    d. Emphasize gentle rolling and throwing.
2. Help the parent discriminate safe from unsafe areas to play ball with her child:
    a. Point out safe areas in the child's home and explain why they are suitable.
    b. Anticipate dangerous areas and ask the parent to think of what could happen if she and her child played ball there, e.g., playing ball on a bed, next to a lamp, or in the front yard without a fence.
3. Help collect suitable balls or objects for ball play:
    a. Point out the appropriate features of balls at this age for her child to play with, i.e., soft and easy to handle.
    b. Demonstrate using soft round sponges or rolled up socks for ball play.

4. Identify and describe the child's behaviors which indicate it is time to stop the game, such as crying, going to another toy, or refusing to get the ball anymore. Describe his behaviors if he becomes over-stimulated and demonstrate changing the activity to a quieter one, such as playing with his stuffed animals, dolls, or musical radio.

BLIND PARENT

May have difficulty knowing where the ball is during play.

1. The parent can play ball in a narrow hallway with her child to physically limit the amount of space that a ball can travel during ball play. The space may be further confined by putting a child safety gate at each end of the play space.
2. Parents can use balls which provide extra auditory cues. For example, a bell could be inserted into hollow plastic balls, or use a *beeper ball** which emits an audible signal.

PHYSICALLY DISABLED PARENT

Who uses a wheelchair, or who has limited upper extremity control; may have difficulty playing ball with her child.

1. Parents who use a wheelchair can toss light balls to her child from a chair and verbally encourage her child to return it to her lap, or use an object (e.g., cardboard insert from wrapping paper, or a broom) to bat the ball gently back to her child during play.
2. Parents with limited grasp or upper extremity control may be able to hold and control clutch balls, foam rubber balls, or partially inflated beach balls and balloons.

5.47 Child: SHOWS TOY PREFERENCES (12-18 mo.)
Parent: Recognizes, understands, and respects child's individual toy preferences

GENERAL GUIDELINES

One of the first signs of a child's developing individuality is his desire to make his own decisions. He begins to show preferences toward things, such as foods and toys, based on their appeal to him. Certain toys will appeal to him, others will not, even though they may be favorites of his peers. He may also develop a special attachment to a favorite doll, stuffed animal, or car, insisting that he take it wherever he may go.

Parents can encourage and respect their child's individuality by exposing him to a variety of appropriate toys and allowing him to make choices.

The following toys and materials are often attracting materials for children to play with during this developmental age: books, empty boxes, kitchen utensils, clothes pins or spools and containers, balls, rolling toys, stacking rings, dolls, cars, musical toys (xylophone, bells, shakers), play telephones, adult tools (combs, brushes, purses, big shoes), and later, push and pull toys.

---

*See Glossary.

5.47

Too many toys can overwhelm a child and inhibit creative play and preferences. Toys can be rotated on a weekly basis to extend interest and prevent the child from being overwhelmed.

MENTALLY RETARDED PARENT

May not provide developmentally appropriate play materials for her child, or may expect him to prefer toys that she thinks are attractive.

1. Ask the parent to show or tell you the toys her child likes to play with. Help identify common features of the toys which make them attractive to her child, such as color, toys that fit together, or toys he can push.
2. Remark and laugh about how many times children's favorite playthings are not toys we'd think of as pretty, exciting, or fun:
   a. Ask the parent if she can think of any favorite toys or materials her child plays with that she doesn't think are particularly interesting or fun.
   b. Praise how her child is learning to make his own decisions and choose his own favorite toys.
   c. Discuss and compare how we as adults also have individual preferences toward foods, clothes, television shows, etc. Comment, "Think how awful it would be if we were expected to like the same things everyone else did!"
3. Periodically review the child's available play materials:
   a. Every few months make a picture list of developmentally appropriate play materials and toys.
   b. Help the parent collect suitable household objects for play and lend toys via a toy lending library, if possible.
   c. Point out why the listed toys are fun for her child, name his possible interactions with them, and suggest special areas to keep them easily accessible.
   d. Review safety precautions with each play material and identify which materials need close supervision by the parent.

BLIND PARENT

May be unaware of the visual qualities of toys her child displays a preference toward.

1. Describe the various visual qualities of any toys or materials toward which you observe the child shows preference. For example, he may prefer cartoon-type pictures in storybooks to picture drawings, or may prefer his blocks with pictures on them to his blocks that have solid colors.

5.48 Child: DISPLAYS DISTRACTIBLE BEHAVIOR (12-15 mo.)
Parent: Understands and adapts for child's distractible behavior

GENERAL GUIDELINES

The child's short attention span, relentless energy, and interest in exploring his entire environment prevent him from attending to any one toy or activity for very long. He may empty out his drawer of toys in less than a few minutes and then quickly move on to a new book or toy in another area of the room, again only playing with it for a few moments.

The child should, however, be able to attend to interesting play activities without being overly distracted for at least five minutes several times during the day. A chaotic unstructured environment can hinder the child's ability to attend for even short periods. Children who are easily distracted by common environmental sights or sounds, or children who are hyperexcitable, often need extra structure and an adapted environment during learning and play activities.

Parents may benefit from anticipatory guidance to help accommodate their child's typical distractible behaviors. Discuss the following guidelines or "hints," as needed:

1. Keep a special bag of activities to take along to restaurants, doctor appointments, and on long car rides.
2. Do not expect the child to sit at the dinner table, listen to stories, or interact with play materials for very long.
3. Children often attend longer to activities when adults participate and add variety to the activity.
4. Provide special quiet play times with the child in areas free from day-to-day distractions to help him attend to activities (e.g., reading, books, mirror play, coloring).

MENTALLY RETARDED PARENT

May interpret her child's distractible behavior as being "bad."

1. Always stress throughout your interventions with the parent and child that young children *cannot* attend to activities for as long a time as adults and they are not trying to be "bad":
   a. Help anticipate how long her child can be expected to play with a toy or attend to an activity before you introduce the toy or activity to the parent and child, e.g., "He may only want to play with his ring stack long enough to take the rings off, and that is fine at this age."
   b. Point out the child's specific behaviors or "signs" which indicate he is distracted, e.g., looking the other way, throwing the toy, whining, and body twisting. Explain that when we see these signs, it is time to change the activity rather than making him continue with the same toy.
2. Help the parent make up a "goody bag" with special interesting toys and activities to use only in special situations, such as when going to a restaurant, a friend's house, and on long car rides.
3. Role-play common situations to help the parent anticipate how to handle her child's distractible behaviors. Possible situations could include:
   a. The parent is at the doctor's office with her child but four others are ahead of her; her child starts fussing, throwing toys, and tugging at her arm.
   b. The parent is reading a story to her child; halfway through the story he twists in the chair and tries to get down.
   c. During dinner time, the parent and siblings have not finished dinner but the child is finished and starts throwing food and trying to climb out of his chair.

4. Help the parent choose a quiet time and place at home for at least one special quiet time activity with the child each day:
   a. Make a simple picture list with three or four quiet activities for the parent to choose from.
   b. Dependent upon the child's activity level and attention span, provide a concrete guideline for how long she can expect her child to attend to each activity on the list.

5.49 Child: TENDS TO BE QUITE MESSY (12-18 mo.)
Parent: Understands and allows, within limits, child's messiness

GENERAL GUIDELINES

The child's insatiable desire to explore and touch everything takes priority over his concern for neatness or order. Although understandably frustrating for parents, if they allow their child to be somewhat messy without undue concern, they encourage him to explore and discover his world.

Parents can allow their child's messy play while providing reasonable limits. For example, parents can show their child it is fun and okay to play with mud pies, but hands need to be washed afterwards; or it is okay to wipe a little pudding or food on his highchair tray, but it is not okay to wipe food in other places. Parents can also set up special times and areas to play with dough, sand, water, and clay; or to dig in dirt. Old play clothes, buckets of water, and old towels can help minimize parental concern with messiness so that energies can be directed toward the joy of discovery.

Children who hesitate to explore new textures and messy activities should be gradually introduced to them, as the parent models that being a little messy is okay and fun.

MENTALLY RETARDED PARENT

May interpret her child's messiness as being "bad," and may thus prevent his messy explorations.

1. Discuss how most children tend to be quite messy at this age; they are not being messy to be "bad"; they are just too young to know how to keep clean all the time.
2. Introduce structured messy play activities within a parent-child play group situation:
   a. Let each parent bring in an old shirt for herself and old play clothes for the child.
   b. Provide materials, such as water basins, towels, and newspapers, to facilitate easy clean up.
   c. Make positive remarks throughout the activity. Stress how the fun and learning of the activity outweighs a little mess which can be cleaned up.
3. During a home visit, help the parent think of specific ways to accommodate her child's messy behaviors:
   a. Place a stool or wooden box near the sink to help her child wash up.
   b. Sort through the child's clothing with the parent to help discriminate which clothes to dress her child in for play activities and which clothes to save for special outings.
   c. Help make a few toyboxes for the child's room and living areas to facilitate easy toy pick-up. Remind the parent that, at this age, her child can help put a few toys away, but still needs help from her.
4. Provide anticipatory guidance that her child may play with his bowel movement. Role-play how to respond if this occurs. Stress that she should not scold or spank her child because he does not know this is wrong.
5. Name additional various potential messy situations with young children. Help the parent discriminate when she should intervene and stop her child from being messy, and when she should not make a big deal about it.

BLIND PARENT

May have realistic concerns about her child's messiness as she may rely upon environmental order for mobility.

1. Explain that children at this age usually do not return things to their proper places; they may move chairs, empty drawers on the floor, and leave their playthings everywhere:
   a. Suggest keeping extra cardboard boxes accessible to her child to encourage him to "stash" his stray toys and other collected household items after play.
   b. At the end of the day, she can sort through the boxes and return the various items to their proper place.
2. The parent can encourage her child to become accustomed to giving her things when he is finished with them by frequently saying, "All done? Give it to Mommy."
3. Refer to 1.68 (Enjoys messy activities such as fingerpainting) for adaptations during messy play activities.

5.50 Child: ENJOYS BEING CENTER OF ATTENTION IN FAMILY GROUPS (12-18 mo.)
Parent: Provides sufficient opportunities for child to be the center of attention

GENERAL GUIDELINES

As the child's self-awareness and understanding of his effect upon others grows, he realizes he can become the center of attention.

The child tests out his role, worth, and power in the family when he acts silly or performs a new skill in his effort to become the focus of attention. Applause, smiles, and laughter from his family help build his sense of self-esteem and competence. He sees that what he does is important and he holds an important and worthwhile place in the family. If he is unsuccessful, he may shout, purposefully misbehave, or become disruptive.

MENTALLY RETARDED PARENT

May attend more to her child's negative behaviors than to his positive behaviors.

1. Help the parent identify and praise her child's positive behaviors to help make him feel important; refer to Activities a-h under No. 1, 5.39 (Displays independent behavior).

5.50

2. Interpret each of her child's behaviors which are attempts to gain attention as they occur during each of your sessions:
   a. When you are talking with the parent, the child may try to perform or misbehave. Use this opportunity to interpret that he acts like this because he does not like to feel left out. Help the parent think of things to say and do to show him he is important, e.g., say, "I know you're there," and give him a hug.
   b. When the child repeats adult gestures, dances, or "performs," remark, "He is trying to do things he thinks you'll like."
   c. Ask the parent how she can let him know she liked what he did, e.g., smile, hug, verbal praise, or laugh.
3. Discuss the importance of letting the child have opportunities to "show off" to the whole family so he feels important:
   a. Name possible things her child may do to try to show off, dependent upon your experiences with the child's individual methods for "showing off," e.g., the child may "dance," put on the parent's shoes, talk on a toy phone, or copy someone else coughing or sneezing.
   b. Suggest ways she can let her child know she likes watching what he is doing; these may include clapping, laughing, and calling others to come and watch him.
   c. Name "show off" situations which should *not* be laughed at or receive too much attention, such as throwing food, biting, or tearing things up.

5.51 Child: HUGS AND KISSES PARENT (14-15½ mo.)
Parent: Encourages and reinforces child's hugs and kisses

GENERAL GUIDELINES

As the child becomes more social and adept with imitating adult behaviors, he begins to express his affection with hugs and kisses to his parents.

Displays of affection are a vital ingredient to a child's healthy emotional development and should be fostered. A child who is never hugged or kissed will have difficulty learning to express affection. On the other hand, children who are hugged and kissed constantly or who are encouraged to kiss everyone, may lose the value of the experience.

Parents encourage their child's expressions of affection by hugging and kissing him and unconditionally accepting his displays of affection, drooling mouth and all!

MENTALLY RETARDED PARENT

May not overtly display affection toward her child.

1. Model affectionate behavior toward the child during all interventions with the parent and child.
2. Discuss the positive feelings people have when they are hugged and kissed, e.g., they feel loved, special, and good about themselves. Relate that, since the parent is the most important person to her child, her hugs and kisses to him are the most important.

3. Name specific special times that the parent can hug and kiss her child, e.g., after a bath, when waking up or going to sleep, and when he gets hurt. Ask the parent to name additional times she can kiss and hug her child to make him feel good. Emphasize the best times are anytime the parent feels like it!
4. Take pictures of the parent and child enjoying affectionate behaviors together. Encourage the parent to hang them up at home for reminders of the good feelings they each have when they hug and kiss. Give the parent a "Have You Hugged Your Kid Today?" bumper sticker to put on her refrigerator.
5. Reinforce all of the parent's expressions of affection with her child when you observe them, e.g., "See that special smile he made when you hugged him (patted, kissed, etc.)?"
6. Interpret and praise the child's affectionate behavior toward others or yourself, as a sign that the parent has made him feel loved and that is why he is able to be affectionate with others. This may help prevent the parent's possible feelings of jealousy.
7. Point out that, just like us, there may be times when her child does not feel like hugging or kissing. Emphasize that this does not mean he does not love her; he may just not feel like hugging or kissing right then. Explain that she should never make him hug and kiss her or others because then he will think this is a chore.

5.52 Child: IMITATES DOING HOUSEWORK (15-18 mo.)
Parent: Encourages child to imitate simple household chores

GENERAL GUIDELINES

The child imitates various housework activities, such as dusting with cloths, wiping with sponges, and sweeping with toy brooms. He practices these grown-up behaviors in an effort to be like his parents, gain a feeling of control, and for the pure enjoyment of it.

Refer to guidelines and activities under 5.45 (Enjoys imitating adult behavior) which are applicable for encouraging the child to imitate housework.

5.53 Child: EXPRESSES AFFECTION (18-24 mo.)
Parent: Encourages child's expressions of affection

GENERAL GUIDELINES

The child's expressions of affection go beyond hugging and kissing his parents as he learns additional ways to express his affectionate feelings. He may pat, hug, and want to carry around real and stuffed animals; initiate fun games with others; and simply rest his head on others when he feels affectionate toward them. His experiences from a warm and loving relationship with his parents enable him to reciprocate and express his own positive feelings.

MENTALLY RETARDED PARENT

May not display affectionate behaviors.

1. Verbally prompt the parent to provide a wide variety of affectionate behaviors to her child throughout all of your interventions with the parent and child. Prompt with phrases, such as:
   a. "He's not feeling good; gently rub his back to show him you understand how he feels and want to make him feel better."
   b. "Tell him how great you think he is."
   c. "Let's give him a clap to show him how proud you are of him."
2. Interpret and praise all of the child's subtle displays of affection as they occur, e.g., "He's showing you his toy as a way of saying 'I love you and want to share'," or "When he hugs his doll, he's telling us he has learned that hugging feels good."
3. Refer to 5.51 (Hugs and kisses parents).
4. Anticipatory Guidance: The parent may have experienced minimal affection as she was growing up. Your expressions of respect, caring, and interest toward the parent can provide her with an affectionate base for being nuturing and affectionate toward her child:
   a. Periodically compliment the parent's appearance, cooking, housekeeping, etc.
   b. Provide ample verbal praise to the parent during your sessions.
   c. Demonstrate your interest and concern about the parent's well-being as well as the child's.
   d. Periodically give the parent warm handshakes and pats on the back.

5.54 Child: SHOWS JEALOUSY AT ATTENTION GIVEN TO OTHERS, ESPECIALLY OTHER FAMILY MEMBERS (18-24 mo.)
Parent: Understands and responds supportively to child's signs of jealousy

GENERAL GUIDELINES

The child is very possessive of his parents and has difficulty sharing them with anyone, especially with a new baby. His feelings of jealousy arise from his sense of loss when his parent's love and attention are devoted beyond him. His realization that he must share their attention and love is a difficult and fearful feeling.

The child may exhibit his jealous feelings through either aggressive or regressive behaviors. He may whine, hit, become more clinging to parents, revert to baby-talk, and give up any interest in toilet training. Eating and sleeping problems may also arise in an attempt to "win" attention and concern.

Jealousy is a normal but difficult emotion for children which should be dealt with in a supportive and understanding environment. The child cannot be talked out of these feelings, and telling him to "Stop being a baby" can make his self-esteem diminish further.

Parents can help their child through his helpless feelings of jealousy by:
1. Recognizing the child's behavior changes as a symptom of jealousy and need for extra attention.
2. Letting him know they understand his feelings and love him no matter what attention they need to give to others.
3. Minimizing or avoiding situations, when possible, which make him jealous, e.g., avoiding too much affection toward a neighbor's child when he is feeling especially vulnerable.
4. Acknowledging his often irritating interruptions when talking to other adults by firmly, but gently, telling him she's in the middle of something but will talk to him in a minute.
5. Letting the child help out with a new baby and giving him dolls to role-play his feelings.
6. Admiring his big-boy abilities and ignoring his regressive behaviors.
7. Providing special times alone together.
8. Implementing special self-esteem building activities, such as hanging up his latest drawings and taking pictures of him to hang up around the house.

MENTALLY RETARDED PARENT

May not interpret her child's symptoms of jealousy.

1. Facilitate a discussion about the feelings associated with jealousy, within a parent support group, if available:
   a. Generate a list of situations which can make people feel jealous, such as: seeing a boyfriend with another girl, having a parent give your sister a present but not you, or seeing your girlfriend with a new dress.
   b. Name times you have felt jealous, and describe the feelings.
   c. Ask the parent to think of times she has felt jealous and help her describe the feelings.
   d. Develop a concrete definition of the term "jealousy" from the feelings and situations discussed. For example: "Jealousy is a terrible feeling of hurt and anger we may have when we think we are going to lose something (love or attention) from someone we care about, or a feeling we have when we want something we do not have."
   e. Explore how we act when we feel jealous using the specific situations discussed above, e.g., cry, being unable to think about anything else, trying to get "back" at the person, etc.
2. Compare and contrast how young children have feelings of jealousy just like adults:
   a. Ask the parent to think of times her child seemed to be jealous, why, and how did he act.
   b. List things that make young children feel jealous, e.g., mother bringing home a new baby, the parent talking to someone else, or the parent playing with another child. Relate that children's feelings of jealousy usually center around worrying about the loss of attention and love from a parent.

5.54

3. Describe the ways children tell us they are feeling jealous. Explain that, since they do not have the words to tell us how they feel, they act like that. Ask the parent if she can think of times she has seen her child act jealous.
4. Role-play several jealousy situations that could arise with the child and effective parental responses to help the child feel better:
    a. Name a situation and two possible parental responses, e.g., a parent feeding her new baby and the older child hits the parent; the parent could either hit the child back and tell him to go away, or give him a kiss and tell him she loves him.
    b. Discuss why the child acted like that, and how he would feel with each of the contrasting parental responses.
    c. Name additional situations and prompt the parent to think of an effective response.
5. Suggest and encourage the parent to think of ways to help her child feel special:
    a. Suggest phrases to say, "I love you" and "What a nice job you did."
    b. Name phrases to avoid saying because they make the child feel worse: "Stop being a baby" or "Go away; I'm busy."
    c. List special one-on-one activities and times to devote to her child.
6. If there is a new baby in the home, screen for problems that may arise:
    a. Ask specific questions about any changes in the child's behavior.
    b. Help interpret the child's jealous behaviors, if indicated.
    c. Demonstrate and discuss effective responses.

SELF HELP

6.01 **Child:** OPENS AND CLOSES MOUTH IN RESPONSE TO FOOD STIMULUS (0-1 mo.)
Parent: Feeds child in an appropriate and comfortable position

GENERAL GUIDELINES

The child turns his head and opens his mouth toward a stimulus touching his cheek or the area around his mouth. This automatic response, known as the "rooting reflex," helps him find the breast or bottle for feeding and a suck reflex follows. Around four to six months, this automatic response diminishes and the child's suck becomes voluntary.

During feeding, the child can be encouraged to turn his head toward the nipple and open his mouth for sucking by touching one side of his mouth (side closest to the parent when held) with the nipple. The child's mouth should not be stimulated on both sides.

Proper positioning for both parent and child is critical during feeding, with breast or bottle. The child should be positioned with his head and arms forward, and his shoulders slightly rounded. If the child is also positioned with his hips slightly flexed, his extensor thrust reflex, which causes his legs to extend, can be inhibited and a stronger suck encouraged.

When possible, the child should be positioned cradled in his parent's arms. The parent should hold and feed her child in alternating arms to prevent his neck asymmetries.

The child can also be positioned in a semi-reclined infant seat or held semi-reclined on a wedge leaning against a table top. These later positions may be more suitable if the child has motor abnormalities. Direct consultation with an occupational, speech, or physical therapist is critical for additional handling techniques and specific individualized positioning during feeding if the child has abnormal tone, postures, and/or reflexes.

The parent should also be positioned comfortably in relation to her child during feeding. A chair with a back and armrests may be the most comfortable place for feeding. In addition, the environment should be calm and quiet. Face-to-face positioning and close, relaxed contact help facilitate enjoyable feeding experiences and interactions for the parent and child.

MENTALLY RETARDED PARENT

May feed her child in inappropriate positions.

1. Schedule several of your sessions during the child's feeding time to observe how the parent is feeding her child, and how he responds. Observe:
   a. How the parent positions herself in relation to her child; physical contact and face-to-face positioning?
   b. The child's position; hips flexed, head and arms forward?
   c. How the parent introduces the bottle or her breast, i.e., does not over-stimulate the child's rooting reflex; introduces nipple slowly?
   d. The child's environment during feeding; calm, quiet, parent does not over-stimulate during feeding?
   e. If the parent initiates and stops feeding according to the child's hunger, satiation, and distress cues.
2. Anticipatory Guidance: Feeding can be a very sensitive area when providing intervention for the parent. The parent often measures her ability to parent by how well she feeds her child. Intervention efforts should be positive, non-critical, and unobtrusive. The parent's strengths and confidence during feeding should be reinforced frequently.
3. If the parent and child's positions during feeding are awkward or inappropriate:
   a. Model proper positioning while the parent holds her child and you demonstrate with a child-size doll.
   b. Emphasize that her child's head should be higher than his bottom and his arms positioned forward.
   c. Let the parent try to take a drink with her head leaning backwards to experience how difficult it would be for her child to drink in this position.
   d. Help identify chairs in their home in which it would be comfortable for her to feed her child.
   e. Take a Polaroid picture of the parent and child enjoying comfortable positions together during feeding and post it above the chair the parent usually sits in to feed her child.
4. Discourage the parent from propping a bottle next to her child to feed him:
   a. Discuss how feeding time is a very important time for her child to feel warm and loved; she makes him feel that way when she holds him during feeding.
   b. Explain that her child can choke or vomit if he drinks from a bottle propped next to him.
5. Assess how often and how much the parent feeds her child. If the parent is unclear or does not appear to have a suitable method for scheduling feedings (e.g., she feeds him when she eats, or feeds him everytime he cries), help set up a concrete guide to help the parent recognize when to feed her child:
   a. Construct a clockface using cardboard and moveable hands.
   b. Demonstrate moving the hour hand on the clock three numbers (hours) forward from the time of her child's last feeding.
   c. The parent can use this time as a reference point to help recognize when to feed her child, i.e., she can feed him anytime he starts crying after this time, but if he does not cry and it is an hour past the marked time, the parent can go ahead and try to feed him.
   d. Rehearse using the homemade clock several times, giving examples of when her child may have finished eating and let the parent set the hands for his next potential feeding time.
   e. Explain and demonstrate that after each feeding, the parent should match the homemade clock to the actual time, and then move the hour hand forward three hours.

6.01

    f. Tell the parent she does not need to wake her child up to feed him (unless recommended).

    g. NOTE: Three to four hours is a typical timeframe interval for feeding infants. If the child was premature or has special feeding needs, check with the child's physician regarding feeding intervals.

    h. As the child gets older and feeding intervals increase, be sure to change the clock interval time with the parent accordingly.

6. Help the parent identify her child's behaviors which indicate he is finished feeding or needs to take a break:

    a. Ask the parent how she can tell when her child has had enough.

    b. Tell the parent behaviors which usually indicate the child has had enough, e.g., he falls asleep, turns his head and fusses, or spits out the nipple three times.

    c. Describe the child's signals to stop as they occur during feeding, e.g., "He's really turning his head away from the bottle; since his bottle is almost empty he must be telling us he is finished."

    d. Periodically ask the parent when she is feeding her child what he is telling us when he spits out his nipple, cries, etc.

7. Help find a quiet place in their home to feed the child if the household is large or very busy. Suggest playing a soft music box during feeding.

8. Stress gentle handling during feeding. Explain that too much rocking or jiggling can make her child spit up.

BLIND PARENT

May unintentionally over-stimulate her child's rooting reflex by touching his mouth area frequently to monitor his feeding.

1. Explain and describe to the parent her child's automatic rooting reflex in response to being touched in the oral area:

    a. Relate that any touch to the oral area is interpreted as a food stimulus by her child so over-stimulation of the reflex may be confusing to him.

    b. If the parent is having difficulty locating her child's mouth without over-stimulating his rooting reflex, help her find another method to locate his mouth. For example, she could gently follow the outside curve of her child's head by his ear, under his chin and then move the nipple to his mouth.

2. If the parent reports difficulties with her child's feeding, observe the parent as she positions and feeds her child, noting with her any difficulties she may encounter. Use physical cues, if needed, to assist her in proper positioning:

    a. The parent will be able to determine when the bottle is empty by its weight or by gently shaking the bottle.

    b. The parent can determine when her child needs a break or has had enough feeding by feeling and listening to his sucking movements stop or feeling his head turn.

PHYSICALLY DISABLED PARENT

With limited upper extremity control or strength; may have difficulty holding her child during feeding.

1. The parent can sit at a table with her child on her lap (face-to-face) in a semi-reclined position on a wedge or firm pillow against the table as illustrated.

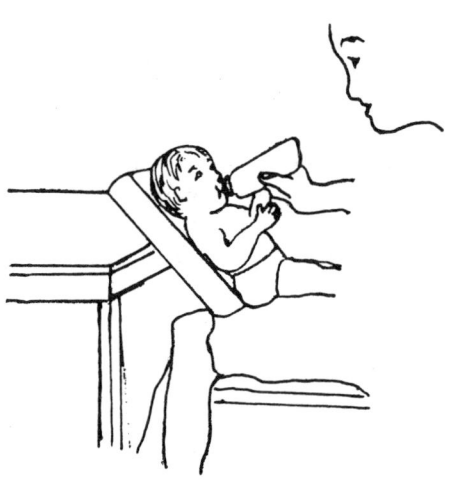

2. The parent could feed her child positioned in an infant seat, placed next to her in bed, on a couch, or on her lap.

6.02 Child: COORDINATES SUCKING, SWALLOWING AND BREATHING (1-5 mo.)
Parent: Feeds child in pace with his sucking, swallowing, and breathing

GENERAL GUIDELINES

The child develops a pattern of "bursts and pauses" when he sucks on a nipple during feeding. This allows him to coordinate his sucking and swallowing with his breathing.

During the first few months, he demonstrates a "lick-type" sucking pattern, with minimal lip closure around the nipple. He retracts his tongue during his suck and then protrudes it somewhat during swallowing. This pattern of sucking is often referred to as "suckling" and usually lasts for four to six months. A more mature suck should then develop as the child's lip and tongue pressure on the nipple increases, forming true negative pressure with an up and down tongue movement.

Proper positioning, nipple hole size, and a quiet environment during feeding help the child coordinate his sucking and swallowing with breathing. The child needs to be burped once or twice during feeding and when he is finished to allow his swallowed air to escape.

If the child displays poor oral-motor patterns or if he has been tube-fed for a long period, consult with an occupational or speech therapist. Special oral-motor facilitation techniques and nipples may be prescribed.

MENTALLY RETARDED PARENT

May be too rough or abrupt when feeding her child, and may have difficulty with formula preparation and using suitable bottle nipples.

1. If the parent uses a bottle during feeding for her child, observe her bottle and formula preparation and their storage during a home visit. Assess the following:
   a. Does the parent buy one consistent type of formula?
   b. If the formula is not "ready to serve," is it mixed in proper proportions?
   c. Are the bottles and nipples thoroughly cleaned?
   d. Are prepared bottles stored in the refrigerator, and if so, how long do they stay there before feeding?
   e. What is the expiration date on the formula?
   f. Does the nipple hole allow the formula to drip consistently (approximately one or two drops per second) if the bottle is held upside down?
   g. Is the temperature of the formula suitable for the child?
2. Show the parent how to check the expiration dates on formula cans. If the month is identified numerically, interpret, as needed, and tell the parent which number month it is during each of the next few months while the child is on formula. Let the parent practice discriminating expiration dates that you write down and decide if that date is okay for buying the formula.
3. If the parent has several brands of formula, check with the child's physician to see which type of formula has been recommended:
   a. Explain to the parent that each type of formula has different ingredients; it is important to buy the same brand each time so her child does not get a stomachache.
   b. Formula preparations with iron can be very irritating for some infants. Commercial brands often sell regular formula and formula prepared with iron. Help the parent discriminate and buy the proper type as recommended by the child's doctor. Although the formulas have the same name, the cans are usually different colors.
4. If the parent is not mixing the formula in appropriate proportions:
   a. Practice mixing ingredients with the parent. Special cups and pitchers can be used specifically for mixing formula. Permanently mark the cup or pitcher to show the parent how high to fill it with water in proportion to a can of concentrated or powdered formula. Leave step-by-step picture instructions.
   b. Point out the differences between "ready-made" formula and formula which needs mixing to prevent the parent from diluting ready-made formula.
   c. If the parent has difficulty mixing formula properly, recommend "ready-made" formula, if financially feasible.
5. Demonstrate proper cleaning of bottles and nipples, as needed. Explain that only hot water can kill germs. Disposable liner bottles may be preferable.
6. Explain that her child needs a fresh bottle with each feeding and not to give her child a bottle that has been unrefrigerated more than an hour:
   a. Explain that germs start growing in the formula when bottles have been left out of the refrigerator for more than an hour; these germs can make her child have a stomachache or spit up a lot.
   b. Give examples of hypothetical situations to assure the parent understands, e.g., "If your child fell asleep after a few sips of his bottle and wakes up two hours later, can he drink the same bottle if you left it out on the table?"
7. Demonstrate checking the nipple hole to insure proper milk flow:
   a. Hold the bottle upside down and explain the milk should drop one or two times with each number counted aloud.
   b. Have the parent practice checking each of her child's bottle nipples.
   c. Explain that she should also check the nipple each time before feeding.
   d. If the child is using a "preemie" nipple, alert the parent when it is time to switch to regular nipples.
8. Practice testing for appropriate temperatures of formula by using several bottles of water with varying temperature:
   a. Demonstrate and have the parent practice test the temperature by letting a few drops drip on her inner forearm.
   b. Show the parent how to warm up formula which may be too cold, and has to cool down the bottle which is too hot by running tap water in a pan for a few minutes.
   c. Tell the parent to check the bottle's temperature each time before she feeds her child.
9. Demonstrate how and when to burp her child during feeding:
   a. Stress *gently* patting or rubbing the child's back when he is upright at the parent's shoulder.
   b. If the parent pats or bounces the child too abruptly, encourage her to only hold him at her shoulder without patting.
   c. Put a permanent mark at three-ounce intervals on the bottle to cue the parent when it is time to burp her child.
10. If you observe the parent teasing her child with the bottle or forcing the nipple in and out of his mouth:
    a. Interpret the child's feelings aloud, e.g., "Mom, I'm still drinking; don't pull the bottle away; I get upset" or "Mom, I need a break; see how I'm fussing; don't make me drink now."
    b. Discuss how her child will feel teased if we pull the bottle away before he is ready to stop sucking.
    c. Demonstrate "feeling" for the child to release the nipple with his mouth and gently taking it out.

6.02

11. Suggest things to say or simple songs to sing while the parent is feeding her child, e.g., "Mmm, that tastes good," "I love you," "You're looking at me," and "You're drinking your bottle."
12. Check local health departments and social services for the availability of parent aides or home health aides if the parent needs extensive help with feeding her child.
13. Suggest checking and changing her child's diaper after each feeding if he does not fall asleep.
14. Refer to 6.01 (Opens and closes mouth in response to food stimulus) for activities relating to positioning and scheduling feedings.
15. Advise the parent to give her child extra breaks during feeding time if he has a stuffy nose, and if he is having trouble drinking his bottle to take him to the doctor.

BLIND PARENT

May not be able to visually monitor if air is getting into the nipple of a bottle.

1. The parent will usually be able to monitor milk flow by listening to her child's sucking and feeling the position of the bottle in relation to the quantity of liquid left.
2. When the parent holds her child to her breast or bottle, she will be aware of her child's hand, arm, and head movements to recognize his sucking and swallowing patterns. The child will turn his head, push with an arm or hand, or open his mouth for a rest during his sucking, swallowing, and breathing. The parent will be able to interpret additional tactual and auditory cues from her child as they develop together as a feeding couple.

PHYSICALLY DISABLED PARENT

With upper extremity weakness or grasp; may have difficulty holding the bottle during formula preparation and feeding.

1. The parent may be able to hold the bottle by attaching a *Sure Grip* or *bilateral glass holder** to it.

6.03 Child: SLEEPS NIGHTS FOUR-TEN HOUR INTERVALS (1-3 mo.)
Parent: Accommodates child's individual sleeping patterns and needs

GENERAL GUIDELINES

Children's sleep patterns vary greatly from child to child and from day to day. Many children combine two of their earlier four-hour sleep cycles during the night by the second or third month and thus sleep through the night.

The child's sleeping cycle consists of moving in and out of light or restless sleep to a deep sleep. During deep sleep, the child displays little movement, a reposed face, and regular breathing patterns. He demonstrates little response to outside stimuli and keeps his eyes closed tightly. He becomes more susceptible to inner and outer stimuli when he moves into light sleep, and may squirm around and display numerous facial grimaces until either waking up or moving back into a deep sleep.

Parents usually do not need to awaken their child to feed him and should wait to see if he moves back into a deep sleep instead of waking him up at his first signs of restlessness.

Activities for 1.01 (Quiets when picked up) and 1.18 (Awakens or quiets to mother's voice) are also applicable to this skill item.

MENTALLY RETARDED PARENT

May expect her child to always sleep through the night, and may not anticipate safety considerations.

1. Facilitate a discussion about children's sleep patterns during the first year:
   a. Empathize how tiring it can be to have to get up in the middle of the night if her child wakes up.
   b. Explain how children do not know the difference between daytime and nighttime; when they wake up in the middle of the night, they do not understand that adults are sleeping.
   c. Point out that since her child is so small, his stomach is smaller so he can only drink one bottle at a time. This can make him get hungry in the middle of the night.
   d. Help the parent identify a time during the day that she can take a nap if she has to get up in the middle of the night.
   e. Stress that her child will not nap when she wants him to because he is too young for that; she will need to schedule her naps when he is asleep.
2. Advise the parent never to leave her child unattended at home even if he is sleeping:
   a. Anticipate situations which could arise if the child was unattended and ask the parent what could happen, e.g., "The child could wake up and cry; since no one could pick him up, how would he feel?", "A fire could start; since no one would be there to stop the fire and take the child out of the house, what could happen?", and "Her child could get very sick or throw up in his sleep; what could happen if no one was there to help him?"
   b. Help the parent identify alternatives to leaving her child alone if she needs to go out, e.g., take him with her or ask a friend or relative to stay with the child.
3. Explain that the parent does not need to wake her child up to feed him.
4. Help the parent identify quiet safe areas in the home for her child to sleep within hearing range of her room:
   a. Caution the parent never to let him sleep on a regular bed unattended because even though he is very little, he can squirm around and fall off.
   b. Check the distance between crib railings or other bedding sides to ensure the child's head cannot get stuck.
   c. Tell the parent not to leave hard, sharp, or small objects in his sleep areas. Show the parent appropriate soft toys which are okay to leave with her child.

---

*See Glossary.

d. Explain that her child does not need a pillow at this age and that it could smother his face; his blanket should be small and light.
5. Help identify and interpret the child's sleepy signs, such as excessive fussing, dropping eyelids, and face rubbing.
6. <u>Ask the baby's doctor what position is best for the baby when sleeping.</u> The American Academy of Pediatrics recommends that healthy babies be placed on their back for sleeping in order to reduce the incidence of SIDS.
7. Refer to 5.08 (Stops unexplained crying) if the child has difficulty calming before sleep.

BLIND PARENT

May not be able to monitor her child's visual cues when he is sleepy.

1. Explain the natural rhythms of sleep to the parent emphasizing that these patterns may change from day to day. Point out that he may make sounds and movements when he is in a "light" sleep.
2. Describe signs the parent can use to help recognize when her child is sleepy:
   a. The parent may tactually feel her child's droopy bobbing head is it bumps her shoulder, arm, etc.
   b. Her child may begin to feel limp or may begin to thrash and cry in any position when held because he is tired.
   c. Her child's breathing may become deeper and very regular which may indicate he is sleepy or nearing sleep.
   d. He may rub his face in her shoulders.
3. Remind the parent, if needed, to close the blinds and turn off lights. Help identify a suitable dim nightlight and safe soft toys for him to look at when he awakens.

6.04 Child: STAYS AWAKE FOR LONGER PERIODS WITHOUT CRYING (1-3 mo.)
Parent: Provides a responsive environment during child's waking hours

GENERAL GUIDELINES

The child cries less as his feeding and sleeping patterns become more established. He stays awake longer and is more alert and responsive between his naps. There may continue to be some fussy periods during the day (often occurring during adult dinner-time) and periodic "off" days when nothing seems to please him.

Social interactions and a rich visual and auditory environment can encourage the child's optimal level of arousal and learning. If there are little or no opportunities for pleasing interactions with the environment, the child may "shut" out his world and sleep excessively. Children who remain on medications may also have fewer alert or responsive periods. Controlled social interactions and auditory and visual stimuli will be especially important to facilitate optimal arousal and learning.

If the child cries excessively, refer to 5.08 (Stops unexplained crying). Refer to developmentally age appropriate activities under the Cognitive, Language, Social-Emotional and Fine Motor sections of this manual to help parents capitalize and encourage their child's responsiveness during awake periods.

6.05 Child: NAPS FREQUENTLY (1-3 mo.)
Parent: Accommodates child's individual sleeping patterns and needs

GENERAL GUIDELINES

The frequency and duration of children's naps vary from child to child. The child may take a twenty-minute nap every two hours, or may take a two-hour nap in the morning and another one in the late afternoon. During the first few months, four or five short naps per day is quite common.

Usually, the child will have become accustomed to normal environmental sounds. Parents, therefore, usually do not need to worry about keeping the household completely quiet.

Parent activities under 6.03 (Sleeps nights four-ten hour interval) are applicable to this item.

6.06 Child: SUCK AND SWALLOW REFLEX INHIBITED (2-5 mo.)
Parent: Continues to position child appropriately during feeding; if bottle fed, assures suitable nipple hole size and proper formula preparation

GENERAL GUIDELINES

The child's sucking develops a more voluntary suck and swallow pattern as his sucking reflex diminishes. He displays a more coordinated up and down tongue movement during sucking and maintains better lip closure around the nipple.

Proper positioning, nipple size, and burping continue to be important. Refer to activities for 6.01 (Opens and closes mouth in response to food stimulus) and 6.02 (Coordinates sucking, swallowing, and breathing).

6.07 Child: BRINGS HAND TO MOUTH (2-4 mo.)
Parent: Allows child to bring hands to mouth for oral stimulation and exploration; facilitates when necessary

GENERAL GUIDELINES

The child voluntarily brings his fingers or whole hand to his mouth for oral stimulation and exploration. Hand-to-mouth exploration is the child's first step toward looking at and playing with his hands and later finger feeding.

If the child does not spontaneously bring his hands to his mouth or has muscle tone abnormalities, holding him in a cradled position or placing him in side-lying can help facilitate this skill. Refer to activities under 3.12 (Extensor thrust inhibited) to help parents position their child in side-lying.

6.07

Parents can also encourage their child's hand-to-mouth explorations by putting strained applesauce on his fingers and by gently guiding his hands toward his mouth.

MENTALLY RETARDED PARENT

May think that it is bad for her child to stick his fingers in his mouth.

1. Provide parent with anticipatory guidance regarding the "okayness" of letting her child put his hand to his mouth. Relate how this will help him learn to feed himself when he gets older.

BLIND PARENT

May not be able to visually monitor her child's hand-to-mouth activity.

1. Describe to the parent her child's hand-to-mouth activity. Explain that in addition to his enjoying the tactual feelings, this will soon lead to hand-watching in preparation for reach and play.
2. The parent will be able to hear her child's sucking and other mouthing sounds as he puts his hand to his mouth.
3. Remind the parent to check to be sure that both of her child's arms are forward when she is cradling him or when he is lying on his side.

6.08 Child: SWALLOWS STRAINED OR PUREED FOODS (3-6 mo.)
Parent: Introduces strained foods to child as recommended, and encourages mature lip closure and tongue movements

GENERAL GUIDELINES

The age at which a child is introduced to strained foods will vary with each child according to his needs and the pediatrician. Foods should be introduced gradually, one at a time with at least a week's interval between a new food. This will give the child time to become accustomed to the new taste and texture of the food and alert the parent to any food sensitivities or allergies which could result.

Initially, the child sucks the food off the spoon and may push some of it back out with his tongue. Parents can facilitate their child's more mature lip closure and tongue movements by placing the tip of the spoon on his tongue and encouraging him to remove the food from the spoon with his lips, rather than raking it off on his gums and lips. Parents should use small shallow spoons, or rubber coated spoons if the child has a strong bite reflex.

Jaw control may be recommended if the child needs help to actively remove food from the spoon. Parents can apply jaw control by: a) placing their thumb on their child's chin directly below his lip, b) placing their index finger of the same hand along his jawline while, c) placing their middle finger under his chin for stability. The parent uses her thumb to control her child's jaw movements while presenting the spoon to him with her dominant hand as illustrated. Jaw control should be supervised by an occupational or speech therapist.

The child should always be positioned upright during feeding.

MENTALLY RETARDED PARENT

May try to feed her child solids while he is lying down, through a bottle, or with an inappropriate spoon.

1. Help identify with the parent suitable feeding positions to introduce strained foods to her child. Help position him upright when sitting in the parent's lap or in an infant seat facing her:
   a. Advise, and demonstrate with your neck, never to let her child's head fall backwards or feed him laying down. Explain how difficult it is to swallow that way. Let the parent try or imagine swallowing some applesauce lying down or with her head extended back.
   b. Caution the parent never to leave her child unattended in his infant seat. Ask her what she could do if the doorbell or phone rang while she was feeding her child.
2. Show the parent appropriate spoons to use when feeding her child. Relate the need for the spoon's small size to her child's small mouth.
3. Check with the child's pediatrician or public health nurse to confirm when and which foods are to be introduced to the child. Clarify, as needed, specific foods with the parent:
   a. If cereals have been recommended, point out the difference between adult and infant cereals and check to make sure the parent can mix it properly.
   b. If fruits have been recommended, check to make sure the parent knows which fruits she can give him.
4. Help the parent recognize appropriate baby foods to buy if she is using commercial ones and cannot read labels:
   a. Give her used labels to take with her to the store for matching.
   b. The parent can select brands which have pictures of the food on the label. Advise her initially not to buy mixed fruits (the labels will identify with two pictures of fruit) until food sensitivities have been ruled out.

c. Demonstrate how to check that the jar's seal has not been broken and how to check for the expiration date.
d. Advise storing opened jars in the refrigerator.
5. Monitor the introduction of new foods to insure the parent does not introduce more than one new food per week. Ask the parent weekly if she noticed any rashes on her child, diarrhea, or vomiting.
6. Demonstrate the difference between feeding the child by scaping the food off with his upper gums and the more appropriate method of letting the child use his lips to remove the food:
   a. Point out how the second method is better because her child has to use his mouth muscles which will help him learn to eat better.
   b. Let the parent practice several times, giving her verbal prompts and praise.
7. If jaw control has been prescribed for the child, demonstrate appropriate finger positions and explain the purpose in meaningful terms:
   a. Contrast current feeding methods to using jaw control with the child. Point out how the child does not lose as much food out of his mouth and he uses his lips better with jaw control.
   b. Let the parent practice jaw control with you several times.
   c. Provide verbal and physical assistance as the parent practices the technique with her child.
   d. Post a Polaroid picture of the parent's hand positioned properly with her child for jaw control above his feeding area.

BLIND PARENT

May not be able to visually monitor her child's feeding responses to strained foods.

1. Review with the parent the importance of keeping her child's food in front of him so he can see it. Explain children respond to the color of food as well as its smell and texture; her child will soon learn to anticipate what he will be eating by the food's appearance and smell.
2. Explain to the parent that, at this age, much of her child's food will dribble out of his mouth and he is likely to smear food over his face, hands, and hair:
   a. The parent can then articulate the need to check him thoroughly after eating for clean-up.
   b. A vinyl mat can facilitate clean-up.
   c. A *dycem pad** may be helpful to keep the feeding bowl in place.
3. Help orient the parent to feeding positions which facilitate the feeding process. The parent can tactually check to insure her child's arms are forward and head and trunk upright.
4. The parent can introduce new foods to her child by placing a little bit on her index finger and letting him taste it, while she uses her other hand to touch the side of his neck as a reference point to his mouth. She can then detect her child's reactions to new foods and proceed with the spoon more easily.
5. The parent can hold one side of her child's face on his jawline with her non-dominant hand, and hold the spoon in her dominant hand to feed her child. The parent's non-dominant hand placement will allow her to monitor her child's movements and facilitate accurate spoon presentation.
6. If jaw control has been prescribed:
   a. Orient the parent to proper hand placement on her child's face during a non-feeding time.
   b. Provide jaw control to the parent so she can feel hand placement and experience the effects.
   c. Let the parent practice jaw control with you.
   d. Describe her child's lip movements while the parent uses jaw control and feeds him. She can become familiar with the pressure her child's lips exert on the spoon to monitor his lip closure.
   e. Advise the parent to wait until she feels him swallow (with her middle finger which she uses under his chin for stability) before introducing the next spoonful.
7. Explain the visual cues and reinforcement she can provide her child during feeding, e.g., opening her mouth, making exaggerated chewing and tasting movements, smiling of delight, and a happy face.
8. Anticipatory Guidance: The parent will have her own marking system for identifying various baby foods. Demonstrate broken and unbroken seals on baby food jars (via the raised center on the jar top), if needed.
9. The parent can watch for any food sensitivities her child may have by noticing if he spits up more or if he has diarrhea.

PHYSICALLY DISABLED PARENT

Who has a limited grasp; may have difficulty holding her child's spoon during feeding.

1. The parent can use assistive devices for spoons which she uses with herself when she feeds her child. These may include built-up spoons, weighted spoons, or scoop plates.

6.09 Child: BRINGS HAND TO MOUTH WITH TOY OR OBJECT (3-5 mo.)
Parent: Allows and facilitates, if necessary, child's safe exploration of toys with his mouth

GENERAL GUIDELINES

The child holds and mouths toys and objects as his method for exploration and learning. His hand-to-mouth activity helps prepare him for his later finger feeding skills.

Refer to 1.15 (Uses hands and mouth for sensory exploration of objects), general guidelines, and parent training activities to encourage the child's mouthing.

Side-lying positions may help facilitate the child to bring toys to his mouth, especially if he has increased or decreased muscle tone. Refer to 3.12 (Extensor thrust inhibited) to help parents position their child in side-lying.

---

*See Glossary.

6.10 Child: RECOGNIZES BOTTLE VISUALLY (3½-4½ mo.)
Parent: Provides ample opportunity for child to visually observe his bottle

GENERAL GUIDELINES

The child recognizes his bottle or mother's breast and associates it with feeding time. He demonstrates this recognition through anticipatory excitement, such as waving his arms, smiling, making sucking motions, or opening his mouth.

BLIND PARENT

May be unaware of the importance of showing her child his bottle before feeding him.

1. Provide parent anticipatory guidance. Explain how her child is learning to associate and anticipate what his bottle is before he actually tastes it; when he sees it, he knows his hunger will be satisfied soon:
   a. Advise the parent to hold the bottle upright in front of her child's face, about one or two feet away, before feeding him.
   b. Tell the parent to listen for her child's anticipatory excitement when she holds the bottle in front of him. His breathing may become audible, his hands may hit his infant seat as he waves them, or his vocalizations may increase. The parent can feel the changes in his body movements as he becomes excited while cradled in her arms for feeding.
2. Explain that plastic baby bottles come in various pale colors, such as yellow, pink, and blue, and some have pictures of clown faces or other pictures. Relate how colors and pictures on the bottle are often attractive to children. Describe the bottles her child has and help the parent pick out bottles with pictures on them, if she is interested. Bottles with pictures on them are usually tactually discriminating.

6.11 Child: USES TONGUE TO MOVE FOOD IN MOUTH (4-8½ mo.)
Parent: Introduces foods to child with lumpy textures

GENERAL GUIDELINES

The child's earlier sucking patterns to remove food from a spoon diminish as he learns to move food with his tongue moving forward and backwards. Some lateral tongue movements begin to emerge with continued experience and maturation. The child's lower lip also becomes more active and he draws it in when the spoon is removed, especially if there is some food left on it.

Parents can encourage their child's increased tongue movements by introducing foods which have a lumpy texture. Mashed bananas, thickened baby cereal, cottage cheese, yogurt with fruit, and mashed pears or peaches are examples of appropriate foods which provide textures and encourage the child to actively move his tongue. The child should *not* be fed foods with different textures in the same spoonful, e.g., soup broth with vegetables or mashed peaches with their canned liquid.

MENTALLY RETARDED PARENT

May need concrete examples before introducing lumpy textured foods to her child.

1. Help the parent mash bananas or another food item as suggested in the general guidelines. This can make an excellent parent group activity; let the parents feed their children after preparing various fruits and cereals to a lumpy consistency.
2. Stress through demonstration and parent practice, placing the spoon on the child's lips and tongue and waiting for him to use his lips to clean the spoon.
3. Empathize how messy feeding can be and point out the positive aspects which make the messiness worthwhile, e.g., he is learning to use his tongue and lips, he is learning about different tastes and feelings in his mouth, and it is preparing him for eating all by himself later. Suggest methods to help make clean-up easier (vinyl placemats, wet cloth, bib).
4. Help the parent plan nutritious menus for her child during the next week. Look through magazines and newspapers together to find food coupons.
5. Suggest phrases the parent can say to her child while she is feeding him. Explain how her child likes it when we tell him what he is eating because he does not know the names for different foods yet. Relate how if we say "Mmm!" he learns it must be pretty good!
6. Explain that new foods, especially lumpy ones, feel and taste different to her child so, at first, he may refuse to eat it. Stress that this is okay and never to make him eat something; she can try letting him taste it another time. Ask the parent if she can remember someone trying to make her eat something and how that made her feel.
7. Emphasize to the parent to watch and wait for her child to swallow his food before giving him another spoonful.

BLIND PARENT

May not be able to visually monitor her child's oral-motor patterns when eating.

1. Describe the child's tongue and lip movements when the parent feeds her child. Describe his facial expressions which help define his reactions to new food:
   a. The parent can listen for her child's sounds of lip and tongue smacking, licking, food spitting, etc.
   b. She can recognize his food likes and dislikes when he pushes out foods with his tongue, closes his mouth tightly during feeding, or turns his head.
   c. Periodically, the parent can tactually monitor her child's tongue and lip movements. She can place her hands on his jaws so that her pinky fingers are resting at the corners of his upper and lower lips while her remaining fingers rest and circle down under his jaw and chin.
2. Provide samples of the proper consistency for mashed foods which provide her child a lumpy texture. The parent can taste her food preparation before feeding her child to check its consistency.

6.12 Child: ROOTING REFLEX INHIBITED (4-6 mo.)
Parent: Helps inhibit child's rooting reflex if prescribed

GENERAL GUIDELINES

The child's rooting reflex, which has been present since birth, begins to diminish. During his first few months, if the side of his mouth was touched, he automatically turned his head and opened his mouth toward the stimulus. Children who are breast-fed may exhibit a rooting reflex longer than children who are bottle-fed.

A persistent rooting reflex can interfere with feeding. If the child's rooting reflex has not diminished, parents should feed their child in a face-to-face position and avoid contact with the side of their child's mouth or cheek. Light tactile stimulation to the area around the child's mouth should also be avoided. Firmly patting or rubbing with deep pressure around the child's lips may be prescribed to help inhibit this reflex in the older delayed child. This stimulation should only be carried out in consultation with a speech or occupational therapist and be applied when the child is not hungry.

The following parent training activities assume the older delayed child continues to have the rooting reflex.

MENTALLY RETARDED PARENT

May misinterpret her child's rooting reflex, and may have difficulty judging the appropriate amount of pressure to apply to her child's mouth area if firm patting or rubbing has been prescribed.

1. Demonstrate the child's rooting reflex:
    a. Explain that he turns his head and opens his mouth automatically; he is not doing this on purpose.
    b. Relate that this can interfere with her child being able to eat well and that is why special feeding positions and activities are being recommended.
    c. Stress that, although you lightly touched the side of his mouth, she should not do that; explain you only did that to show her why special activities were being recommended.
2. Demonstrate face-to-face feeding positions with the child in his infant seat. Explain that when we feed him by facing him, his cheek area is not touched, which is good because that way he will not automatically turn his head.
3. Demonstrate applying firm pressure around the child's mouth area and cheeks with rubbing or patting as prescribed:
    a. Demonstrate this procedure on the parent so she can feel the amount of pressure to apply.
    b. Let her practice the procedure on you.
    c. Have the parent practice this with her child while you observe on several different occasions before recommending this activity at home.
    d. Tell the parent to do this with her child after every feeding when she demonstrates proficiency.
4. Demonstrate, and let the parent practice, washing her child's face using firm pressure with the washcloth around his mouth area and cheeks.

BLIND PARENT

May over-stimulate her child's rooting reflex if she feels her child's mouth area often during feeding to insure proper spoon presentation.

1. Observe the parent as she feeds her child. If she stimulates her child's rooting reflex by touching his mouth or cheek during feeding, explain her child's rooting reflex in response to touch in his mouth area. Suggest alternative methods for feeding. For example, she could approach his face from the side of his neck and move her hand to hold his chin or jawline lightly during feeding.
2. If patting and firm pressure have been recommended for the child around his mouth area:
    a. Demonstrate on the parent so she can feel the exact locations and amount of pressure to use with her child.
    b. Let her practice on your mouth giving her initial hand-over-hand guidance.
    c. Let her practice with her child while you provide verbal and physical assistance until she is comfortable with the technique.

6.13 Child: PATS BOTTLE (4-5 mo.)
Parent: Encourages child to pat bottle

GENERAL GUIDELINES

The child periodically pats his bottle with both hands while he is being fed. The child at this age does not have a voluntary grasp and thus cannot hold his bottle independently.

The child must be able to bring his arms to midline and be able to reach toward objects before he can be expected to pat his bottle.

Parents can encourage their child to pat his bottle by holding him during feeding with his shoulders rounded and both arms drawn forward. Bottles with pictured designs, wrapped in a special texture, such as a sock or wash cloth, and bottles which are not too cold can also encourage the child to pat it. The child's hands can be gently guided to touch his bottle if he needs extra help.

MENTALLY RETARDED PARENT

May expect her child to hold his own bottle.

1. Explain to the parent that, although she may see her child start to pat his bottle (demonstrate), he is not strong enough to hold the bottle all by himself:
    a. Explain that it is great for her child to pat his bottle while she holds it because it helps him learn how to hold it later on.
    b. Point out that if her child's arms are tucked behind him or around her back when cradled, he will not be able to pat his bottle.
    c. Ask the parent to show you a good way to hold her child which lets him try to touch his bottle.
2. Review the importance of never propping a bottle next to her child to feed him. Remind the parent that he could choke or vomit if he eats this way. Reinforce how good she makes him feel when she holds him to give him his bottle.

6.13

PHYSICALLY DISABLED PARENT

With upper extremity weakness; may have difficulty holding her child's bottle.

1. The parent may be able to use a *Sure Grip* or *bilateral glass holder** attached to her child's bottle. The holder should be adjusted toward the end of the bottle as the child begins to pat his bottle.

6.14 Child: **SLEEPS NIGHTS TEN-TWELVE HOURS WITH NIGHT AWAKENING (4-8 mo.)**
    Parent: Attends to, without reinforcing, child's fussing during nighttime sleep

GENERAL GUIDELINES

The child's sleeping patterns at night become more regulated to conventional sleeping times. He may sleep ten to twelve hours at a time with a brief awakening during that period. Some children may wake up to play for a few minutes while others fuss and require reassurance that his parents are nearby.

Parents should attend to their child's cries with a reassuring pat or diaper change. They should not, however, play with him nor make middle of the night wake-ups too fun for the child as he may turn this into a frustrating and habit forming event.

The general guidelines and activities for 6.03 (Sleeps nights four-ten hour intervals) are applicable for this behavior.

6.15 Child: **NAPS TWO-THREE TIMES EACH DAY, ONE-FOUR HOURS (4-8 mo.)**
    Parent: Recognizes and responds appropriately to child's individual sleeping patterns

GENERAL GUIDELINES

Many children who took frequent short naps during their first three months begin to combine two short naps into one longer one. Children often take a two-hour morning nap and then a one- or two-hour afternoon nap. Parent training activities under 6.03 (Sleeps nights four-ten hour intervals) are applicable to this item.

6.16 Child: **PLACES BOTH HANDS ON BOTTLE (4½-5½ mo.)**
    Parent: Encourages child to hold his bottle with both hands when it is held for him during feeding

GENERAL GUIDELINES

The child holds his bottle with both hands during feeding if it is held for him. He may also continue to periodically pat it or simply rub and feel it with his fingertips.

*See Glossary.

The general guidelines and parent activities for 6.13 (Pats bottle) are appropriate for this skill.

6.17 Child: **MOUTHS AND GUMS SOLID FOODS (5-8 mo.)**
    Parent: Introduces child to foods which encourage mouthing and gumming; demonstrates first aid for possible choking

GENERAL GUIDELINES

The child mouths and gums foods which are of a solid texture. His tongue does most of the work moving the food against his gums. Children do not need teeth to "gum" foods.

At this age, children can usually grasp and bring teething biscuits to their mouths which is their first step toward self-feeding. Parents can also encourage self feeding at this age with dried toast, graham crackers, melon strips, and cooked carrot strips. Lumpy textured spoon foods, such as cottage cheese and mashed fruit, help the child practice mouthing and gumming various textures.

The child should *not* be introduced to hot dogs (and other meat sticks with slippery sides), bacon, raw carrots, nuts, or popcorn. These food items can be very dangerous as they have been found to be more easily inhaled which causes choking. Shredded meats should also be avoided until the child develops more mature chewing patterns.

The child should not be left unattended when solid foods are introduced in case the child begins to choke. Children who have difficulty coordinating sucking and swallowing can be more vulnerable to choking. All parents should be encouraged to receive training in basic first aid for infants and small children. Free or nominal cost training is available through local Red Cross Chapters. Parents who have a disability may need alternative training considerations. The following activities include these considerations which could be forwarded to the first aid trainer or parent facilitator, if applicable.

MENTALLY RETARDED PARENT

May not be able to respond appropriately if her child chokes.

1. Make a picture list of foods the parent can begin introducing to her child and another list of foods to avoid, marking a big X across this list:
    a. Cut coupons and pictures with the parent from magazines and food labels to make the picture list.
    b. Suggest taking the list with her when shopping.
    c. Identify next to each picture how much she can anticipate her child to eat at one time, e.g., a drawing of two teaspoons, one half of a graham cracker, etc.
2. Demonstrate feeding the child in an upright sitting position. Let the parent experience the importance of proper positioning by letting her try to eat a cookie in an awkward position, e.g., chin tucked down to neck, neck hyperextended, or lying down.
3. Facilitate arranging first aid training for choking. Accompany the parent to this training session or, if possible,

arrange for the trainer to implement training during a series of your parent groups. Help make a concrete first aid notebook:

a. Stress not doing anything if the child is actively coughing and *never* pat his back if he is sitting up. Use a picture diagram to demonstrate how patting someone's back can push the object further into their airway. Put the picture of someone hitting the cougher's back in the parent notebook marking a big X through it.

b. The trainer should list and demonstrate the signs of a blocked airway which require immediate first aid. Help make a picture list for the parent's notebook of these signs, e.g., the child does not make any sounds, cry, or breathe. Include a picture of an adult with her ear near the child's mouth listening for sounds.

c. The trainer should demonstrate the steps of choking first aid at least three times using a doll.

d. Markers could initially be placed on the doll to help the parent identify where to apply the back blow and chest thrust. Have the parent identify these areas with her own child.

e. Demonstrate the amount of pressure to apply during back blows or chest thrusts by applying them to the parent. Let her try to use the same amount of pressure with you.

f. Provide a picture chart of these steps and let the parent practice this procedure with the doll several times. Include the pictured steps in the parent's notebook. Give her an extra copy to post above his highchair.

g. Role-play choking situations with a doll describing the doll's symptoms.

h. Demonstrate, and let the parent practice, proper positioning to apply choking first aid with her child, but without actually applying blows or thrusts. Stress that the child's head is lower than his chest.

i. Demonstrate and let the parent practice applying back blows to the child as he straddles the parent's arm or leg. Let the parent practice turning the child over for the chest thrust but do not have her actually apply them. Instead, ask her to tell you what she would do.

j. Emphasize when to stop the procedure, i.e., when the child begins to breathe, cry, or cough. Include a picture of a stop sign over a picture of a child who is making sounds with the adult watching to make sure he does not choke again.

k. Role-play calling a doctor or ambulance to explain the incident. Stress to wait for the other person to hang up first in case they have another question to ask.

4. If the parent *cannot* demonstrate proficiency in responding to choking:

a. Assure her that many people have difficulty knowing how to do this.

b. Explain, however, that since a child could die from choking, it is important to have someone nearby to help if he chokes. Explore the possibilities of close neighbors or others in the household who can apply first aid for choking.

c. If there are no immediate people who are available, and the child is prone to choking, advise the parent to wait to give her child textured foods unless you are present. Explain he can still receive the nutrition he needs from pureed foods.

5. Tell the parent how to respond if her child swallows a foreign object, but does not choke, i.e., do not give him anything to eat or drink and call the clinic or doctor.

6. Review preventative measures to prevent small children from choking. Make a picture list of do's and don'ts, again marking the don'ts with an X. Include:

a. Keep small objects out of reach, such as pins, coins, paper clips, and nails (ask the parent to think of additional examples).

b. Tell your other children never to put anything into baby's mouth.

c. Do not put diaper pins in your mouth when changing your child (explain this may teach him that it is a good thing to do, and the pin could also drop out and fall into his mouth).

d. Do not give him nuts, candy with nuts, raw carrots, fruits that need chewing, unchopped meats, or any food with seeds or pits (name different types).

e. Do not do anything that could make him laugh or cry if he has food or drink in his mouth (name concrete examples and let the parent think of some).

f. Do not let the child walk around or lie down when eating or drinking.

g. Check food for bones, shells, foil, or paper before letting her child eat it.

h. Do not let her child play with large seeds or dried beans and peas.

i. Do not let her child play with toys with small pieces (demonstrate several types).

DEAF PARENT

May not be able to hear if her child can make a sound to determine if his airway is obstructed during choking.

1. The first aid trainer should emphasize discriminating facial grimaces, skin color, gesturing at the throat, and watching for cessation of breathing. These signs should continue to be watched.

BLIND PARENT

May be unable to visually monitor her child's mouthing and gumming patterns, or visible signs of choking.

1. Describe to the parent how her child mouths and gums his teething biscuit. The parent can feel his movements by placing her thumb under his chin. She can also listen to his various mouthing and gumming sounds.

2. Demonstrate and let the parent become tactually familiar with appropriate food textures and consistencies for her child at this age.

3. The first aid trainer should emphasize feeling for the cessation of breathing, listening for gasping, and then the cessation of sounds to help determine if her child is choking:

a. Advise the parent to do nothing if she hears her child coughing. Assure her that coughing in itself is the best

6.17

treatment for choking; she should only remain calm and listen to assure his breathing or sounds have not stopped.

b. The parent can also feel if her child is struggling. The choking child struggles while the child who is gasping or holding his breath for attention does not.

c. If the parent is in doubt, advise her to go ahead and apply the first aid procedure; the worst that can happen is that her child may vomit.

4. Procedures for choking first aid can be demonstrated with a doll using the following steps:
   a. The parent practices the procedure with her hand over the trainer's hand who emphasizes hand position in relation to specific bones and muscles.
   b. The parent practices the procedure with physical and verbal prompting with her hands directly on the doll, gradually reducing prompts.
   c. The parent practices without prompts on the doll.
   d. The parent goes through the positions and motions with her own child without actual firm back blows or chest thrusts.
   e. Provide the parent a Red Cross poster with the first aid procedures in braille.
5. Advise the parent to check her child's hands after he had a biscuit or cookie for small pieces which have broken off.

6.18 Child: HOLDS OWN BOTTLE (5½-9 mo.)
Parent: Uses bottles which are easy for child to hold

GENERAL GUIDELINES

The child's increasing coordination and voluntary grasping abilities enable him to hold his own bottle. Plastic bottles are recommended because they are lighter and thus easier for the child to hold. They also will not break if the child decides to drop it on the floor. Children often adjust their own bottles if they are getting too much air. Bottles with disposable liners, however, can help him drink in a more upright position without having to raise his bottle.

Although the child may be quite adept with a bottle, parents should continue to provide him opportunities to be held during feeding. Some children, although quite able to hold their own bottle, may refuse to do so because they prefer the close contact and intimacy during feeding. This child should not be forced to drink it independently.

Parents should not put their child to bed with a bottle of milk or juice. This can easily lead to tooth decay. If the child uses a bottle at night, it should only be water.

MENTALLY RETARDED PARENT

May stop holding her child during bottle feeding.

1. Explain that, although her child can drink from his bottle all by himself, he still enjoys being held by his parent during feeding. Discuss the pleasant close times they have shared when she has held him during feeding in the past.
2. Advise the parent to always remember to look for her child's bottle after he has been drinking one alone. Explain he may drop it behind a chair or cushion; if he finds it later, his milk will be spoiled and he will get sick.
3. Tell the parent to only let her child have water in his bottle if he takes a bottle to bed. Explain that all other liquids, even milk, have lots of sugars which will stay on his gums and teeth while he sleeps and can cause him to have holes in his teeth.
4. If the parent uses glass bottles, suggest switching to plastic ones. Point out that these are lighter and easier for her child to hold. Ask her what would happen if he dropped a glass bottle on the hard floor by mistake.

6.19 Child: BITES FOOD VOLUNTARILY (6-8 mo.)
Parent: Offers and presents food which facilitates child's biting

GENERAL GUIDELINES

The child's bite reflex, which is a strong uncontrolled closure of the jaw in response to gum or teeth stimulation, should be diminished. At this age, the child uses a controlled voluntary vertical jaw movement to bite off a piece of food. He usually cannot, however, judge how much food to bite off.

Parents can facilitate their child's emerging voluntary biting skills by presenting him with strips of graham crackers, soft cookies, or dried toast. The food should be able to dissolve in the child's mouth through mouthing and gumming. The parent should hold the end of the cookie while presenting a small portion to the child's mouth to prevent him from biting off a piece which is too big to mouth or gum.

If the child has a persisting bite reflex, or hypersensitivities around his mouth area, consult with an occupational or speech therapist for individualized treatment techniques. The child's bite reflex can be released by applying firm pressure on his jaw bone and rocking him gently to decrease hypertonicity.

MENTALLY RETARDED PARENT

May not give her child opportunities to bite foods, or may give him foods which are not suitable for him to bite independently.

1. Demonstrate with yourself and then the child the difference between biting a piece of cookie off from breaking a piece off and putting it directly in the mouth:
   a. Stress the importance of holding onto the end of the cookie since her child does not know how much to bite off yet.
   b. Let the parent practice encouraging her child to bite a piece of cookie.
2. Make a picture list of foods which are suitable for her child to practice biting off pieces:
   a. Point out that each of these foods can dissolve in her child's mouth without chewing.
   b. Ask the parent what could happen if he bit off a piece of raw carrot or apple and then could not chew it up.
3. If the child has a persisting bite reflex, explain that he is not doing this on purpose; his mouth muscles need extra help to let go. Demonstrate applying pressure on the

child's jaw bone with your hand over the parent's while rocking him to help release his bite.
4. If special oral-motor activities have been prescribed, concretely specify the frequency and duration of each activity. Do not recommend carry-over at home until the parent has demonstrated proficiency several times on different occasions.

6.20 Child: **DRINKS FROM CUP HELD FOR HIM**
(6-12 mo.)
Parent: Helps child drink from a cup

GENERAL GUIDELINES

The child is able to drink small amounts of liquid from a cup for held for him. Cup drinking helps him learn mature drinking and swallowing patterns. Initially, the child may bite the rim of his cup and spill from the corners of his mouth. He may also choke easily, but quickly adjusts without intervention.

Proper head and trunk positions are critical when introducing the child to cup drinking. He should be in an upright sitting position. The cup should be tilted at the child's mouth to prevent his head from leaning backwards or hyperextending. Small short cups require only slight tilting without encouraging the child to tilt his head backwards. A *Nosey Cut-out Cup** is also recommended because it enables the cup to be tilted without the child's nose interfering which often encourages him to lean his head back. The child's lip closure on the cup rim can be monitored by looking through the cut-out portion of the cup.

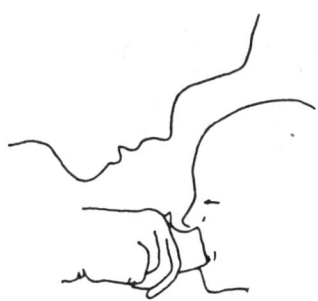

Parents should place the rim of the cup between their child's lips rather than his teeth or gums, offering only one sip at a time and waiting for him to swallow before offering more. Children's cups with spouts should be avoided because they encourage the child's less mature sucking patterns.

Children with oral-motor abnormalities usually require individualized jaw control or muscle facilitation techniques prescribed by an occupational or speech therapist.

---

*See Glossary.

MENTALLY RETARDED PARENT

May not offer her child opportunities to drink from a cup, or may encourage him to hyperextend his neck during drinking.

1. Advise the parent when her child is ready to begin learning how to drink from a cup and help her select appropriate cups to use:
   a. Show the parent suitable sized cups to let her child learn to drink from.
   b. Explain that plastic cups are the best and glassware and paper cups should not be used. Ask the parent if she can think of reasons why glasses and paper cups would not be good for her child at this age.
   c. Point out that small cups are better for her child's small mouth and small hands.
   d. Suggest letting her child have a plastic cup to play with during non-feeding times of the day.
2. Stress to the parent the importance of making sure her child's head is upright when he drinks out of a cup:
   a. Demonstrate taking a drink with your neck hyperextended. Tell the parent how awful this position is because it is too hard to swallow.
   b. Encourage the parent to try taking a sip of liquid with her head leaning backwards. Then let her take a sip with her head upright. Discuss which position was easier.
   c. Leave a simple drawing of a child drinking from a cup with his neck hyperextended. Mark a big X through it. Post this next to a Polaroid picture of her child taking a drink with his head properly aligned.
3. Give the parent a Nosey Cut-out Cup to use with her child if she is having difficulty presenting regular cups to her child without encouraging his neck to hyperextend:
   a. Draw lips on the rim where her child's lips should be placed with a permanent non-toxic marker.
   b. Cut-out cups can also be homemade using small soft plastic cups or yogurt cups.
4. Demonstrate, and let the parent practice, holding the cup while her child takes a drink. Emphasize how to:
   a. Place the rim of the cup on her child's lips, *not* his tongue or gums.
   b. Give him one sip at a time and watch for him to swallow before giving him more.
   c. Only tilt the cup slightly so his head will not fall back.
5. Draw a line on the child's cup with a non-toxic marker to help the parent judge how high to fill it.

BLIND PARENT

May benefit from tactual cues to facilitate the child's cup drinking.

1. The parent can use special positioning to help assure her child's proper head alignment when presenting him his cup. She can:
   a. Hold her non-dominant hand behind the child's neck when feeding him in a face-to-face position. Her thumb

6.20

can be extended to the front of his face and placed on the side of his lips as a reference point to present the cup.

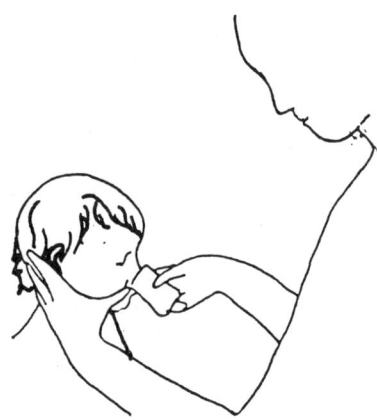

b. Hold her child in her lap facing outward with his head supported against her chest. She can use her non-dominant hand to apply jaw control or to place her finger next to his mouth as a reference point to present the cup.
c. Use a cut-out cup to discourage neck-hyperextension.
2. The parent can leave her finger placed lightly to the side of the child's lower lip to monitor his lip closure and the amount of liquid being lost, swallowed, or dripped.
3. The parent will be able to reduce her need for tactual cues with experience and through kinesthetic memory, and as the child becomes more proficient with independent cup drinking.
4. Provide anticipatory guidance that children frequently choke when liquids are initially introduced with a cup. Advise her that all she needs to do is remain calm and wait for him to stop coughing.
5. Let the parent become familiar with various bibs and cups commercially available. Demonstrate how some bibs are made with pockets or extended plastic edges to help catch excess drippings.
6. Describe to the parent her child's method of releasing his cup as he begins to drink independently. Discuss how many children like to toss, drop, or play with their cups when finished, even if there is still liquid in them. The parent can offer less liquid and provide physical or verbal prompts, as needed, to encourage him to return his cup to her or the table.

PHYSICALLY DISABLED PARENT

With a limited grasp; may have difficulty holding a cup to help her child drink.

1. The parent may have adapted cup holders to use when she drinks from glasses. These can be adapted to fit her child's smaller cup.
2. Weighted cups or cut-out cups may help the parent hold and control the child's cup during feeding.

6.21 Child: FEEDS SELF A CRACKER
(6½-8½ mo.)
Parent: Provides ample opportunities for child to feed himself appropriate crackers with supervision

GENERAL GUIDELINES

The child holds and feeds himself a piece of cracker, cookie, or toast. He approaches a cookie by closing his palm around it and bringing it to his face, often licking or sucking on it before managing a bite. Small pieces of food are usually too difficult for him to pick up; since his grasp is not controlled, he may keep bits of crackers stored in his hands until removed by his parent.

Teething biscuits, a quarter piece of dried toast, a section of a graham cracker, and Vanilla Wafers are examples of graspable sizes of crackers for the child to feed himself. Parents should continue to supervise his self-feeding because the child may take bites which are too large to manage.

MENTALLY RETARDED PARENT

May not anticipate safety concerns when her child feeds himself a cracker.

1. Suggest appropriate cracker-type foods to let her child try to feed himself. Give examples of both appropriate and inappropriate crackers to use; point out distinguishing features of each, e.g., too crumbly, too hard, or too small to pick up.
2. Caution the parent never to offer her child a cracker while he is lying down. Explain it is too hard for him to swallow lying down and he can choke. Tell her to always be nearby while he is eating cookies or crackers because he cannot always take the right sized bite and can choke. Ask the parent what she should do if her child bites off a big piece of cookie.
3. Help the parent find appropriate cookie and cracker coupons in magazines; baby magazines usually have an abundance.

BLIND PARENT

May not be able to visually monitor her child when he feeds himself cookies or crackers.

1. Advise the parent that her child may bite off pieces of cookies or crackers which are too large for him to manage. She can listen for her child's munching, sucking, and lip smacking sounds which can help her discern if he has bitten off too much.
2. Provide the parent anticipatory guidance to check her child's hands for remaining cracker pieces which he was unable to release.

6.22 Child: **BITES AND CHEWS TOYS** (7-8 mo.)
      Parent: Provides child safe toys to bite and chew

GENERAL GUIDELINES

The child begins to bite and chew toys for sensory exploration and to help soothe his gums during teething. Parents can provide their child teething rings and safe flexible small rubber toys during this period. If the parent sees her child biting objects which are unsafe, she should replace it with his teething ring or a safe toy.

Refer to activities for 1.15 (Uses hands and mouth for sensory exploration of objects). Squeak toys should be checked to assure that the squeak mechanisms are secure to prevent possible dislodging during the child's chewing.

6.23 Child: **DROOLS LESS EXCEPT WHEN TEETHING** (7-12 mo.)
      Parent: Implements "drool control" techniques with child if prescribed

GENERAL GUIDELINES

The child's earlier drooling should be substantially decreased unless the child is teething, congested, or concentrating on a task.

Poor lip, tongue, or jaw control, or hypersensitivity around the mouth area may be the cause for persistent excessive drooling.

The following activities are often prescribed by therapists for parents to help their child decrease drooling:
1. Play imitation games, such as smacking and puckering lips and making "mmm" sounds. Play these in front of a mirror and gently pinch the child's lips together with your index finger and thumb.
2. Gently push the child's lower lip up and in with your thumb while gently pushing his upper lip in with your index finger to encourage him to close his mouth. Praise his "good mouth closing."
3. Encourage the child to swallow his saliva while his mouth is closed by stroking downward on his throat with your index and middle fingers.
4. Help the child develop an awareness of having dry lips and a dry chin. Wipe his drool away frequently and comment how nice it feels to be dry. Never scold a child for drooling.
5. Wipe the child's mouth with a napkin or cloth using firm outward strokes, wiping from the center to the corners of his mouth.
6. Avoid excessive sugars, such as soda and commercial popsicles, which increase drooling.

Jaw control may also be prescribed; refer to 6.08 (Swallows strained or pureed foods), if applicable. The following parent training guidelines assume drool control activities have been prescribed.

MENTALLY RETARDED PARENT

May have difficulty implementing prescribed drool control techniques.

1. Concretely explain to the parent the rationale for prescribing drool control activities for her child.
2. Demonstrate, and let the parent practice, only one recommended drool activity per session. Have the parent practice in your presence until proficient before recommending carry-over at home.
3. Point out how her child cannot drool if his mouth is closed when teaching the parent to encourage lip closure (Activity No. 2 under the general guidelines):
   a. Demonstrate this activity on the parent's mouth and let her practice with you so she can feel and practice applying gentle handling.
   b. Do not describe this technique as "pinching his lips together" to help prevent rough handling; instead, use terminology, such as "gently push his lips together."
   c. Clearly name times when to implement each activity in association with specific daily activities.
4. Explain that her child cannot help it when he drools a lot and should never be scolded for this.
5. Help the parent think of positive phrases to say to her child when his mouth is closed and when she is wiping his mouth.
6. Demonstrate how to wipe the child's mouth, outwards toward his cheek. Let the parent practice as you monitor the degree of pressure she uses.

BLIND PARENT

May not be able to visually monitor your demonstration of drool control techniques.

1. Demonstrate the techniques on the parent as you describe the process. Let her practice with you as you provide feedback regarding the amount of pressure, firmness, and positioning.
2. The parent should approach her child's mouth for drool control with a loosely held fist or the back of her hand to prevent poking.
3. Emphasize to the parent the importance of letting her child watch her mouth during lip smacking and puckering games to help him learn to imitate her movements.

6.24 Child: **CHEWS FOOD WITH A MUNCHING PATTERN** (8-13½ mo.)
      Parent: Offers child a variety of textured foods

GENERAL GUIDELINES

The child's earlier gumming and mouthing of textured foods matures into a munching pattern. His jaw moves up and down while his tongue moves the food in a lateral direction.

Parents encourage their child's munching patterns by offering him a variety of textured foods. New foods should be introduced gradually and positively. The parent can model exaggerated chewing motions while her child is eating and offer encouraging comments, such as "Mmm, so good!" and

6.24

"What a good job you're doing chewing that up!" Parents can also present foods to the side of their child's mouth or over his molar area to encourage tongue lateralization.

Although the child can eat many mashed table foods, foods which require a great deal of chewing and small hard items, such as hard candies, raw carrots, and popcorn, must be avoided to prevent choking.

Recommended foods include commercial junior foods; mashed fruits; cooked vegetables; chopped foods, such as chicken, tuna, or turkey; well cooked pasta, such as macaroni, rice, and spagetti pieces; and soft cheeses.

If the child has oral-motor difficulties, consult with an occupational or speech therapist. If jaw control has been prescribed refer to 6.08 (Swallows strained or pureed food).

MENTALLY RETARDED PARENT

May not offer her child foods which encourage munching patterns, and may be unaware of nutritional and food safety considerations.

1. Ask the parent to keep a diary of everything her child eats for three days. This can help assess quantity and types of foods her child is eating to determine intervention needs. The diary can be written or tape recorded.
2. Teach the parent about the four basic food groups. Use commercially available food group charts as an introduction, then use magazine pictures to make an individual food picture booklet for the child:
   a. Explain that her child needs foods from each group everyday to help him grow and stay healthy.
   b. Consult with the child's health care provider to confirm how much of each food group has been recommended to meet the child's individual needs.
   c. Name recommended foods for her child from each food group. Help cut out and paste pictures of these foods for the child's food booklet, one food group per page.
   d. Review each food group page and explain why each group is important for her child. For example: The protein group helps her child feel strong enough to move, run, play and be healthy; the fruits and vegetables group has vitamins which help his skin stay healthy; and the milk group helps keep his teeth and bones strong.
   e. At the bottom of each food group page, identify how much her child should eat from each group everyday. Use concrete labels or diagrams, such as a picture of a cup filled halfway with orange juice rather than saying four ounces of vitamin C.
   f. Insert a picture list of foods *not* to feed her child at this age because he can choke. Mark a big X across the page.
   g. If the child has food sensitivities, add a picture page of these foods to the booklet with an X also marked across the page.
3. Help the parent plan a week of meals for her child with the recommended foods from the four basic food groups:
   a. Discuss the importance of varying the texture, color, and taste of foods.
   b. Make a picture menu with one page per day, three meals per page to include in the child's food notebook from Activity No. 2.
   c. Make a picture page of low cost nutritious snacks for the child.
   d. Help cut out coupons of foods listed in the child's menus.
   e. Develop a purchasing list around the planned menu and snack list.
   f. Plan a shopping trip together, if possible.
4. Devote a session toward food storage and safety. Explain that some foods can become dangerous for people to eat if they are not stored or cooked properly:
   a. List the three primary rules to keep in mind to prevent germs from growing in foods, i.e., keep hot foods hot, keep cold foods cold, and keep food clean.
   b. Explain that germs grow in hot or cold foods that have been left out for two hours and, if it is a hot day, germs grow more quickly in cold foods, sometimes in twenty minutes. Point out that we cannot see the germs.
   c. Give examples of hot and cold foods to keep hot or cold, e.g., stews hot and pudding cold. Review the child's weekly menus and ask the parent which foods should not be fed to her child after they have been left out two hours (twenty minutes if it is a cold item eaten on a hot day).
   d. Relate that, if our hands or utensils have germs on them and we touch food with them, the food will then have germs. Since we cannot see germs, it is hard to know when our hands, spoons, or dishes have germs on them. Advise the parent to, therefore, always wash her hands and utensils thoroughly before preparing food.
   e. Demonstrate washing fruits and vegetables properly before serving.
   f. Describe how to store leftovers using examples from the child's planned menu. Remind the parent to throw the leftovers away if they were left out for more than two hours.
   g. Explain how long each food on her child's food list can stay fresh in the refrigerator.
   h. Demonstrate how to find "dates of freshness" on food packages.
   i. Caution the parent to always cook meat completely. Explain that cooking kills germs.
   j. Caution the parent never to buy or use canned foods which are leaking, cracked, or severely dented because they may have poisonous germs in them. If available, show examples of these types of cans.
5. Model, and let the parent practice, presenting foods to each side of her child's mouth to "help his tongue learn to move the food around better."
6. Refer to 5.33 (Tests parental reactions during feeding) to help the parent with behavioral issues during feeding.
7. Model, and help the parent think of, pleasant phrases to say to her child during mealtimes. Explain this makes mealtime more interesting and fun.

BLIND PARENT

May be unaware of visual reinforcement which encourages her child to eat various foods and practice munching.

1. Explain that, in addition to food textures and tastes, food appearance is important to children. Relate food colors which appear to appeal to her child and explain, as needed, how colors change when foods are mixed together or catsup and sauces are added.
2. Point out that when we model exaggerated chewing motions, her child watches and this helps encourage him to practice chewing.
3. The parent can monitor her child's munching patterns by placing her index and middle finger on the side of her child's chin.

6.25   Child: FINGER FEEDS SELF (9-12 mo.)
Parent: Provides ample opportunities and foods which encourage child to finger feed himself

GENERAL GUIDELINES

The child's fine motor and hand-to-mouth skills enable him to feed himself most of a meal using his hands and fingers. He is also now able to bite off the correct amount from larger pieces of fingerfoods. Messy mealtimes continue to be unavoidable.

Examples of appropriate fingerfoods include cooked whole string beans, cooked diced carrots or potatoes, chopped fresh ripe fruits, toast, cheese strips, diced cooked chicken, and cooked beets or broccoli.

The child with gross or fine motor delays may need special seating to insure proper head and trunk alignment and support. Fingerfoods can be placed in the child's hand if he has not developed grasping skills.

MENTALLY RETARDED PARENT

May not provide foods which are appropriate for her child to finger feed, or may not let him finger feed because it is too messy.

1. Demonstrate to the parent the suitable size for foods to be cut up according to the child's grasping abilities.
2. Discriminate spoon foods from finger feeding foods. Let the parent sort pictures of foods accordingly. Star (*) the foods on her child's weekly menu to let him finger feed.
3. If the parent is hesitant to let her child finger feed himself:
    a. Plan a finger feeding meal for a parent-child group session. Discuss the positive aspects of finger feeding during the group even though it can be quite messy.
    b. Introduce fingerfoods gradually, encouraging the parent to include one fingerfood for her child at each meal. Initially suggest fingerfoods which are the least messy, such as a diced apple.
    c. Suggest giving her child only four pieces at a time.
    d. Help identify a place at home to let her child eat where his messiness can be easily wiped up.
    e. Suggest the use of vinyl placemats and newspapers on the floor to facilitate easy clean-up.
    f. Reinforce how nice it will be when her child will be able to feed himself his entire meal; that way she will be able to eat without too much interruption during mealtime. Stress that her child's messy finger feeding now helps him learn to eat better later.
    g. Point out how the child is eating more and is happier when he feeds himself.

BLIND PARENT

May not be able to visually monitor how much food her child is putting in his mouth at one time.

1. The parent can offer her child only a few pieces of chopped foods at a time. If you observe the child having difficulties grasping the foods, describe his difficulties and suggest larger sizes for foods. The parent can monitor her child's grasp and finger feeding by periodically offering him foods from her hand.

6.26   Child: HOLDS SPOON (9-12 mo.)
Parent: Helps child hold spoon when needed; allows child to hold spoon during feeding and play

GENERAL GUIDELINES

The child holds a spoon with a fisted hand. His initial independent spoon feeding attempts are usually quite awkward as he attempts to figure out how to rotate his wrist and insert the bowl of the spoon into his mouth. He usually cannot dip his spoon to fill it with food.

The following suggestions may help parents encourage their child's initial spoon handling attempts:
1. Let the child place his hand on the parent's hand as she feeds him.
2. Give him a spoon which already has some sticky food on it (pudding, mashed potatoes, applesauce, yogurt, cream of wheat).
3. Give the child spoons and cups to use during play.
4. Help the child hold his spoon and guide his hand to his mouth.
5. Give the child an extra spoon to practice with while the parent uses another one during feeding.

Adaptive spoons may be prescribed by a therapist for children with limited grasping abilities.

MENTALLY RETARDED PARENT

May expect her child to use developmentally higher spoon feeding skills.

1. Demonstrate how young children hold their spoons and try to feed themselves.
2. Show the parent spoons which are suitable for her child to practice feeding himself. Advise her not to let her child use plastic spoons because they can break too easily. Ask the parent what could happen if it broke in her child's mouth.

6.26

3. Name foods that are good with which to let her child practice independent spoon feeding:
   a. Demonstrate how these foods stick to the spoon somewhat which helps them stay on the spoon when her child brings the spoon to his mouth.
   b. Ask her what would happen if her child tried to eat Jello or soup by himself with a spoon.
   c. Stress that, at this age, she needs to put the food on the spoon for her child.
4. Suggest putting a spoon and cup with her child's playthings.

BLIND PARENT

May not be able to visually monitor her child's independent spoon feeding attempts.

1. Describe to the parent her child's independent feeding attempts with a spoon. Relate the child's grasp, facial expressions, how he turns his spoon over, how much food he gets to his mouth, and how he brings it to his mouth, e.g., "He misses his mouth and the food gets on his cheeks and hair; he feels the food with his other hand first and then waves the spoon."
2. Advise the parent that she can expect a lot of food to spill on her child's hands, arms, hair, face, and even his ears sometimes.
3. Stress the importance of letting her child become acquainted with the spoon visually. Explain that he watches her use a spoon to help learn how to feed himself.
4. The parent can help guide her child's hand to his mouth with the spoon by placing her hand over his and placing a finger from her other hand beneath her child's lower lip as a reference point.
5. Suggest placing the child's non-breakable dish on *dycem** when the child begins to dip his spoon into the dish.

6.27 **Child: SLEEPS NIGHTS TWELVE-FOURTEEN HOURS (9-12 mo.)**
6.28 **Child: NAPS ONCE OR TWICE EACH DAY ONE-FOUR HOURS, MAY REFUSE MORNING NAP (9-12 mo.)**
   Parent: Allows child to get as much sleep as he needs; does not reinforce child's "testing" at bedtime

GENERAL GUIDELINES

The child's evening sleeping pattern is usually regular. At this age, children often sleep twelve to fourteen hours through the night.

Around this time, the child may also begin to refuse his morning nap. Adjusting his lunch and afternoon nap to an earlier time may help avoid midday irritability.

Explore the child's sleeping patterns with the parents and provide anticipatory guidance about typical sleeping patterns, as needed.

---

*See Glossary.

Refer to parent activities and general guidelines for 6.03 (Sleeps nights four-ten hour intervals) and 5.34 (Tests parental reactions at bedtime). These are applicable for most children's sleeping patterns.

6.29 **Child: COOPERATES WITH DRESSING BY EXTENDING ARM OR LEG (10½-12 mo.)**
   Parent: Encourages child to help during dressing

GENERAL GUIDELINES

The child purposefully extends his arm to help put on his shirt and sticks out his leg to help put on his pants, shoes, and socks.

Although it is easier and quicker to dress their child themselves, parents can help encourage this skill by dressing their child slowly and prompting him to help. Parents can help make dressing a fun learning experience by singing made up songs and talking about body parts and clothing articles; playing dress-up with big shoes and hats; and dressing him in front of a floor-length mirror.

MENTALLY RETARDED PARENT

May not encourage her child's participation during dressing.

1. Demonstrate dressing the child and encouraging him to "help":
   a. Relate that waiting for her child to help put his arm in his shirt and his legs in his pants is his first step toward learning how to dress by himself.
   b. Empathize how much longer it takes to wait for him to help, but "just think how nice it will be when he can dress all by himself."
   c. Model describing to the child interesting things about his clothing and praising his hard work.
   d. Let the parent practice encouraging her child to stick his legs out for his shoes after you have demonstrated encouraging him to help put on his shirt and pants.

BLIND PARENT

May be unaware of visual cues which encourage her child to help during dressing.

1. Stress the importance of holding her child's clothes up in front of him before dressing him:
   a. Explain how this helps her child associate clothing articles with their word labels and the body parts they go on.
   b. The parent will have her own system for identifying clothing colors, solids, and prints. Describe any special embroidered pictures or decals on the child's clothing.
2. The parent can feel her child's attempts to help dress as his arms or legs approach the clothing item, or by lightly placing her hand on his arm or leg while verbally prompting him to help.

6.30 Child: MAY REFUSE FOODS — APPETITE DECREASES (12-18 mo.)
Parent: Understands child's "stage" of refusing foods; continues to encourage and monitor adequate nutritional intake

GENERAL GUIDELINES

The child may begin to refuse foods or entire meals as his appetite decreases to accommodate his slowed down growth, and to test his power to refuse foods. He may play with his food, throw it, spit it out, or defiantly shake his head "no" with his lips tightly sealed. These behaviors may be inconsistent from meal to meal and last throughout toddlerhood. A skipped meal and decreased appetite should not be a cause for alarm. If a food diary were kept and analyzed for a two-week period it would reveal that most children end up consuming a well-balanced diet if a variety of foods were available to him. Pressuring the child to eat, however, can cause long-term eating problems and be used as a weapon against parents.

If the child has special nutritional or caloric needs, consult with a nutritionist. Egg milkshakes and other appealing high caloric boosters may be suggested.

Some children may be especially finicky about certain textures, tastes, colors, spices, or mixtures, such as casseroles. Parents can watch for their child's individual food preferences and serve him accordingly. Sometimes letting the child dip his food into a little catsup helps make eating more fun and tasty.

All parents may benefit from the following helpful hints if their child is a "choosy" eater:

1. Do not use food as a reward or punishment with children.
2. Introduce a variety of new foods one at a time and allow him plenty of time to look at, feel, smell, and taste it without coaxing.
3. Do not comment about how much food the child eats or whether he is a "good" or "bad" eater.
4. If the child spits or throws food, remove the food and try it at a later time.
5. Refrain from modeling (via verbal comments or facial expression) personal likes and dislikes.
6. Offer the child small amounts of a variety of foods. Let him select what he wants to eat from his plate or tray. Never force him to eat something.

MENTALLY RETARDED PARENT

May try to make her child eat foods, punish him for not eating, or stop feeding her child if he refused food.

1. Help the parent anticipate, understand, and respond effectively to possible feeding problems that may arise with her child. Use the following common problem situations for rehearsal and discussion:
   a. Problem situation: The child will not try a new food you want him to eat. Ask the parent to name a new food he would not eat or one she might try:
      (1) Possible reasons: He is afraid of something new; he saw someone make a face that told him it must taste terrible.
      (2) Good parent responses: Give him only one new food at a time; mix it with something he likes, such as catsup; let him have lots of time to look at, touch, and smell it; offer foods you know he likes at the same meal and if he refuses, that is okay, try it again in a few days.
   b. Problem situation: There are some important foods we think a child must eat, but he refuses. Ask the parent to name a food she thinks is important that her child will not eat:
      (1) Possible reasons: He dislikes the taste; he dislikes the way it feels in his mouth (e.g., too sticky, mushy, chewy); he wants to show us he is big enough to make his own decisions about food.
      (2) Good parent responses: Prepare the food in a different way (make specific suggestions depending upon the food, such as mixing an egg in his milk if he will not eat eggs); offer different types of food from the same food group (name specific alternatives according to the child's dislikes); stop trying to make him eat it.
   c. Problem situation: The child refuses to eat something during one of his mealtimes. Ask the parent if her child ever does this; if so, how often. Every day? Every night?
      (1) Possible reasons: He is not hungry; he does not feel good; now that he has stopped growing so fast, he does not need as much food; he wants to see how we will react; he had too many snacks between meals.
      (2) Good parent response: Check to see if he is sick; remove the food and try again in a few hours; stop giving him in-between meal snacks.
   d. Problem situation: The child plays with his food or takes too long to eat it:
      (1) Possible reasons: He is not hungry; he would rather play; he wants you to give him some attention; the food is too difficult to eat (e.g., soup, tough meat).
      (2) Good parent responses: Give him attention when he is *not* playing with his food; allow him five minutes to begin eating and if he does not, remove his food and do not give him snacks until the next meal.
   e. Problem situation: The child will only eat one or two types of food. Ask the parent if there are only certain foods her child will eat and, if so, which ones:
      (1) Possible reasons: That is just the way some children are; they have strong food likes and dislikes.
      (2) Good parent responses: Continue to put additional types of foods on the child's plate; do not worry if the child only eats one or two types of foods for a few days; when he sees you are not upset, he will probably start eating other foods again.
2. Monitor the child's eating habits on a regular basis to insure he is getting an adequate nutritional intake. Refer to 6.25 (Finger feeds self), Activity No. 1.

6.30

3. Make a chart with "Do's and Don'ts" during feeding to post in the child's dining area. Refer to the general guidelines, if needed, to develop this chart.
4. Facilitate a discussion about individual differences and food preferences:
   a. Name some of the foods you like and some you don't like and compare them with the parent's food likes and dislikes.
   b. Relate how her child also has his own food likes and dislikes; he may like something she does not like, and not like something she does like.
   c. Explain that if she gives him a chance to try only foods she likes, there may be other things he likes that we do not know about.
   d. Caution the parent not to "let on" when she gives her child a food she does not particularly like because he may automatically not want to try it.
   e. Demonstrate facial and vocal expressions that could let her child know we do not like a particular food.

BLIND PARENT

May be unaware of her child's food likes and dislikes based upon the food's appearance.

1. Explain that children sometimes base their food preferences on the food's color, form, and texture as well as its taste. Point out that some children refuse to eat if they see too much on their plates or if the foods are mixed together:
   a. The parent can keep track of the foods her child refuses to help determine if there are any trends.
   b. Suggest using children's dishes which have separate compartments.
   c. Point out that many commercial baby foods and blenderized foods, especially meats, vegetables, and mixed foods, are often visually unattractive.
2. Suggest talking about the food's color, taste, and texture during the meal.
3. Advise the parent that her child will be watching her facial expressions as she prepares and serves his food:
   a. Explain that if her child sees her "make a face," he will know she does not like it and may refuse it.
   b. Point out if she shows him she is worried when he does not eat, he may refuse foods just to get attention.

6.31 **Child: BRINGS SPOON TO MOUTH – TURNS SPOON OVER (12-15 mo.)**
Parent: Lets child practice feeding himself with a spoon; accommodates his crude spoon handling

GENERAL GUIDELINES

The child can feed himself with a spoon, but turns it upside down before it reaches his mouth. He continues to hold his spoon with a fist and has difficulty rotating his wrist to prevent the spoon from turning over. He may be able to dip the spoon in his dish to refill it, but does so quite crudely.

Refer to the general guidelines and activities for 6.26 (Holds spoon) which are also applicable to this skill. Advise parents to allow their child to grasp his spoon with either hand and to continue to let him finger feed during much of the meal.

6.32 **Child: HOLDS AND DRINKS FROM CUP WITH SOME SPILLING (12-18 mo.)**
Parent: Lets child drink from a cup independently, understanding inevitable spills

GENERAL GUIDELINES

The child drinks from his cup alone, usually holding it with both hands. He may spill some of the liquid during the learning process because of his lack of experience in coordinating the cup tilt with his drinking and swallowing. He may also spill as he places it back on his tray or drops it. Small cups with only a small amount of liquid can help decrease spilling. Parents can help their child guide his cup back to the try, if needed.

Refer to 6.20 (Drinks from cup held for him) for guidelines and activities relating to appropriate cups and positioning.

6.33 **Child: HOLDS CUP HANDLE (12-15½ mo.)**
Parent: Provides experiences for child to hold appropriate cup by its handles

GENERAL GUIDELINES

The child's increasing hand and finger control enables him to hold a children's cup by its handle or handles using his fingers.

Parents can encourage this skill by providing their child plastic cups with handles during play and feeding. For example, the child can be encouraged to hold cups or small sand pails by their handles while filling and dumping them during sand and water play. During feeding, parents can model holding cups by their handles to drink from and verbally prompt their child to try it. Initially, the child may need adult support on the cup to help facilitate accurate cup tilting.

MENTALLY RETARDED PARENT

May try to make her child always hold his cup by the handles.

1. Assure the parent that although some children's cups have handles, it is okay for her child to take a drink without holding them.

BLIND PARENT

May not be able to visually monitor if her child holds cups by their handles.

1. Let the parent become tactually familiar with several commercially available children's cups which have handles.
2. Describe how the child manipulates cups with handles. The parent can offer her child the cup by holding the lower portion of the handles and feeling if he takes it by holding the handle.

6.34 Child: SHOWS BOWEL AND BLADDER CONTROL PATTERNS (12-18 mo.)
Parent: Recognizes child's more regular elimination patterns; understands this does not mean he is ready for training

GENERAL GUIDELINES

The child begins to show a pattern of regularity with his urination and bowel movements. His diapers remain dry for longer intervals, sometimes up to two hours, and his two daily bowel movements usually occur at the same time each day. Some children have a predictable bowel movement after each meal. Although the child is developing more regularity, his pattern of elimination is automatic; he is not physically ready for voluntary toilet training.

Parents usually recognize when their child has begun to show a pattern of regularity as they find he needs to be changed less frequently and often at predictable times. Later, when deciding if their child is ready for toilet training, parents can confirm a pattern of regularity has been established by keeping a record of their child's elimination patterns over a week's time.

MENTALLY RETARDED PARENT

May try to toilet train her child, or may have difficulty recognizing her child's bowel and bladder problems.

1. Provide anticipatory guidance to the parent about toilet training. Explain that her child's body is not ready to know when it is time to go to the bathroom; he still wets and has a bowel movement (use parent's terminology) automatically; he cannot decide when to go to the bathroom.
2. Empathize with the parent's anxiousness to have her child toilet trained. If cloth diapers are used, they can be a lot of work and, if disposable diapers are used, they can be very expensive:
   a. Explain that if she tries to train her child too early, it may take a lot longer to train him than if she waits until his body is ready for training.
   b. Point out that if it takes longer to train her child, she will have to deal with diapers for a longer period of time than if she waits until he is ready.
   c. Offer to help let her know when her child is ready for toilet training.
   d. Review the skills and conditions necessary before children are ready for toilet training, e.g., control of his rectal muscles (usually not until twenty months) and awareness that he needs to go ahead of time.
2. During the next several months, help the parent recognize if her child has established regular elimination patterns to help discern his future training readiness. If the parent has difficulty judging or relating time intervals or elimination patterns:
   a. Check the child's diaper at the beginning and end of each of your sessions with the parent and child.
   b. Show the parent how to keep a tally of how many diapers she uses each day. She can make a mark on a sheet posted next to her child's diaper changing area, or save the diaper tabs if using disposable diapers in a jar.
   c. Use typical daily activities as a basis for questioning when and how often the parent needed to change her child's diaper. For example: Did he have a bowel movement after his breakfast, lunch, and dinner? Was he wet when he woke up from his nap? Did she have to change him again before supper?

6.35 Child: INDICATES DISCOMFORT OVER SOILED PANTS VERBALLY OR BY GESTURE (12-18 mo.)
Parent: Recognizes and responds to child's signals which indicate he has soiled or wet pants

GENERAL GUIDELINES

The child demonstrates he knows when he has wet or soiled his pants and wants to be changed through his gestures and/or by verbally telling us. He may point toward, tug at, or remove his diaper; stop his activity; have an awkward or strained facial expression; squat; hide his face; or say his word label for elimination. The child is usually unaware of his need to eliminate in advance and is not ready for voluntary toilet training. His awareness of, and discomfort over, wet or messy diapers is, however, a positive sign for future training.

Parents can watch for and reinforce their child's indicators of elimination to help prepare him for his future more formal toilet training. They should label his bowel movement and urination with consistent family words and promptly change him. Prompt changing prevents him from becoming too accustomed to soiled pants and reinforces the child to continue indicating the need for a change.

MENTALLY RETARDED PARENT

May not recognize her child's signals of elimination awareness.

1. Ask the parent if her child ever tells her or shows her when he has wet or messed in his pants and, if so, ask what he does.
2. If the parent does not know how or whether her child indicates wet or soiled pants, describe some typical indicators children often display. Point out and describe her child's signals that you observe as they occur in your presence.
3. Ask the parent if she has any special words she uses to label urination and bowel movements. Suggest consistent terms to say with her child, if needed.
4. Encourage the parent to check her child's diaper frequently, especially after he has gestured or told her he has wet or soiled his diapers. Explain that, if he gets used to being wet or soiled, he will not be very interested in learning to sit on a toilet because he will not mind messy diapers.
5. If the parent is initiating toilet training prematurely, refer to 6.34 (Shows bladder and bowel control pattern).

6.35

BLIND PARENT

May be unaware of her child's visible gestures which signal discomfort over soiled or wet diapers.

1. Describe audible and inaudible behaviors children typically display to indicate soiled or wet diapers. Advise the parent when you observe her child displaying any of those signs:
   a. The parent can listen for her child's audible cues, such as straining, grunting, ceasing his activity, expelling gas, or pulling at his rubber pants.
   b. She can encourage him to let her know verbally when he needs a change by modeling verbal labels for his elimination when she hears his audible signs.
   c. The parent can pay special attention and listen for her child's indicators of messy diapers during the times he has displayed a pattern for eliminating.

6.36 Child: **SLEEPS NIGHTS TEN-TWELVE HOURS (13-18 mo.)**
6.37 Child: **NAPS ONCE IN AFTERNOON ONE-THREE HOURS (13-18 mo.)**
    Parent: Allows child to get as much sleep as he needs

GENERAL GUIDELINES

The child may reduce his nighttime sleep to ten or twelve hours during his second year rather than the twelve to fourteen hour sleep he may have demonstrated at one year. A morning nap is rare and the duration of his afternoon naptime may decrease.

Children continue to display varied sleep patterns dependent upon the child's individual sleep needs, biological make-up, and environmental conditions. Medication can also influence the duration and intensity of a child's sleeping patterns.

Explore the child's sleep patterns with parents and provide anticipatory guidance regarding typical child sleeping patterns at this age. Parent activities for 6.03 (Sleeps nights four-ten hour intervals) and 5.34 (Tests parental reactions at bedtime) are applicable for most children's sleeping patterns.

6.38 Child: **SCOOPS FOOD, FEEDS SELF WITH SPOON WITH SOME SPILLING (15-24 mo.)**
    Parent: Uses dishes and foods which help child feed himself with a spoon

GENERAL GUIDELINES

The child is able to dip his spoon in a dish to scoop food and bring it to his mouth. He continues to invert the spoon as it enters his mouth and thus continues to spill or lose some of his food.

To help encourage their child's independent spoon feeding, parents can:

1. Provide foods which stick to the spoon while it travels from the child's dish to mouth, e.g., mashed potatoes, cream of wheat, and thick pudding.
2. Use plates or bowls with at least one raised edge for the child to scoop his spoon against (positioning the highest edged side on the side toward which the child is scooping).
3. Use bowls with non-skid bottoms or place them on *dycem** or a piece of rubber, such as a rubber ring from a canning jar.
4. Show minimal concern over the child's unavoidable messes.
5. Allow the child to also fingerfeed during meals.

Parents can also help guide their child's hand through the "scooping to mouth" process if he is having difficulty. Letting the child use various spoons and bowls or pails during sand or uncooked rice play provides him additional fun scooping practice.

The following activities supplement and are additive to the general guidelines and parent activities for 6.26 (Holds spoon) and 6.31 (Brings spoon to mouth — turns spoon over).

MENTALLY RETARDED PARENT

May use dishes which are difficult for her child to scoop from, and may try to make him scoop his food up "just right."

1. Show the parent samples of appropriate and inappropriate dishes to let her child eat from. Point out the discriminating features of each dish which make it either appropriate or inappropriate:
   a. Contrast plastic dishes with glass or ceramic dishes and ask the parent what could happen if the dish fell on the floor.
   b. Demonstrate how much easier it is to scoop up food if there is a rim on the dish. Let the parent try this, too.
   c. Ask the parent to show you a dish she has that would be good for her child to eat from.
2. Give the parent a rubber ring from a canning jar to place under her child's dish during feeding. Demonstrate how the ring helps keep the dish from sliding around.
3. Demonstrate various ways young children usually scoop food from dishes including their typical spilling:
   a. Explain that children's hand muscles at this age are not developed enough to be neat with a spoon.
   b. Empathize how frustrating the mess can be.
   c. Relate that, when she lets him practice all by himself, even though it is messy, she is helping him learn how to feed himself.
   d. If the child needs physical guidance to scoop up the food, remind the parent to let go of his hand once the food is on his spoon.
   e. Stress that it is still okay to let her child finger feed, and okay for her to feed him parts of his meal when he wants.

---

*See Glossary.

BLIND PARENT

May be unable to visually monitor her child's self-feeding attempts with a dish and spoon.

1. Show the parent various commercial dishes that are available specifically for young children. Point out the non-skid features and raised edges. Show her children's spoons which have a bent stem to help prevent the spoon from turning over.
2. Help the parent identify an appropriate position to place her child's dish in relation to the edges of his highchair tray or his flexed arm's length.
3. Describe the child's scooping and spoon-to-mouth movements during a meal or applesauce snack. The parent can listen for his spoon hitting the dish and his lip-smacking sounds.
4. If the child needs physical assistance to help scoop or guide his spoon to his mouth, advise the parent to remain seated when she helps him. Explain that if she stands her child may tilt his head back to look at her which makes it more difficult to chew and swallow.
5. Relate that her child's independent spoon feeding attemps are likely to increase the amount of spillage and increase the area in which his food will splatter. She can start checking the floor, chair, and nearby walls after each mealtime for clean-up.

6.39   Child: REMOVES SOCKS (15-18 mo.)
Parent: Encourages child to remove his socks independently

GENERAL GUIDELINES

The child pulls socks off his feet when he is lying or sitting down. He takes delight in his expanded self-help abilities and may take them off just as soon as his parent dresses him!

Parents can help their child learn to pull off his own socks by letting him practice with loose or slightly larger sized socks. Socks without heels, cotton socks, and short cuffed socks are the easiest to handle. If the child needs physical assistance, parents can help position their child in sitting (supported, if necessary), flex one of his legs, and slowly demonstrate the motions involved in pulling off the sock. Initially, the child's socks can be partially removed to facilitate the child's efforts.

MENTALLY RETARDED PARENT

May not provide opportunities for her child to try pulling off his socks, or may be angry if he keeps pulling them off and she wants them to stay on.

1. If it appears that the parent pulls off her child's socks before giving him a chance to try it himself:
   a. Explain that it is good to encourage her child to take off his own socks even though it is quicker and easier for her to do it.
   b. Point out how this helps her child practice and get ready for harder dressing skills, such as taking off his own pants when he gets older.

2. Advise the parent to check the size of her child's socks frequently:
   a. Explain and demonstrate how socks which are too tight make her child curl his toes, can hurt, and make walking harder.
   b. Demonstrate checking for the correct fit of socks by gently wiggling her child's toes; if she can wiggle his toes, they fit okay.
3. If the child needs help with learning to take off his own socks:
   a. Demonstrate leaving the child's sock slightly on his foot and prompting him to pull it off the rest of the way. Let the parent practice and encourage her to let him try this each day when she undresses him for his bath.
   b. Demonstrate leaving the child's sock on his foot a little higher with each of your visits.
   c. Explain that her child needs to be sitting or lying down to pull off his sock. Relate how difficult it is, even for adults, to take off socks if we are standing up.
4. If the child can pull off his socks and the parent is frustrated because she has to keep putting them back on again:
   a. Explain that her child is not trying to be mean when he keeps pulling off his socks; he is just so happy that he has learned this, he likes to keep doing it.
   b. Assure her that once he gets used to taking them off and learns other new skills, he will stop doing this at the wrong times.

BLIND PARENT

May have difficulty finding her child's socks if he likes to take them off in various places throughout the house.

1. The parent can encourage her child to give her his socks whenever he takes them off:
   a. As soon as the child begins to take off his socks, he can be taught to follow the parent's simple request, "Give me your socks."
   b. The parent can give him extra praise for following this request to encourage him to automatically hand them to her in the future.

6.40   Child: REMOVES HAT (15-16½ mo.)
6.41   Child: PLACES HAT ON HEAD (16½-18½ mo.)
Parent: Encourages child to take off and later put on his own hat

GENERAL GUIDELINES

The child learns to take off his own hat (as long as there are no chin straps to unfasten) before learning to put it on.

Parents can encourage their child to take off his own hat and then learn to put it on by letting him practice in front of a mirror; giving him fun hats, such as cowboy or fireman hats. to play with; and encouraging him to take off, and later put on, hats which are on the parent or a favorite doll.

6.41

Provide anticipatory guidance, as needed, for encouraging these self-help skills. Suggest making paper hats with newspapers or pretend helmets with large plastic Cool Whip or butter tubs as an additional fun hat for the child to practice with.

6.42 Child: GIVES EMPTY DISH TO ADULT (18-19 mo.)
Parent: Encourages child to give her his dish when finished or wants more

GENERAL GUIDELINES

The child gives his empty dish to an adult when he is finished eating or wants some more food. He may also drop it on the floor if there is no one to whom to hand it to gain attention.

Parents can encourage their child to hand them their dish by using verbal and gestural prompts when he is finished eating or indicates he wants more. If the child uses a dish with a suctioned bottom, the parent can encourage him to give her his dish after she has released the plate and/or encourage him to giver her his cup when he is finished.

MENTALLY RETARDED PARENT

May not model verbal or gestural prompts when encouraging her child to hand her his dish.

1. Demonstrate gesturing and saying, "All done?", "Want more?", and "Give Mama your dish" to the child during your feeding interventions. Encourage the parent to start saying these phrases with gestures, verbally prompting her, as needed, e.g., "He just asked for 'more'; what can you say so he will give you his dish?"
2. Provide anticipatory guidance that her child may throw his dish on the floor if no one is around to take it from him. Explain that he is not trying to be mean; he is just trying to get someone's attention so he can have more or let someone know he is finished.
3. Explain to the parent that her child may be telling her he wants more food, or that he is all done, when he hands her his dish. Help the parent interpret which meaning her child is intending by pointing out additional available cues (e.g., if dish is not empty, he probably does not want more).

6.43 Child: DISTINGUISHES BETWEEN EDIBLE AND INEDIBLE OBJECTS (18-23 mo.)
Parent: Prevents child from injesting inedible substances

GENERAL GUIDELINES

Although the child continues to sometimes "taste" inedible familiar objects, he knows they are not food and does not try to eat them. He does not know, however, if unfamiliar materials and liquids are inedible and thus the risk of accidental poisoning remains high.

Parents can help their child distinguish between edible and inedible objects by saying "Yuk" when he tastes an inedible object and demonstrating the object's appropriate function, e.g., "Yuk, crayons are for coloring, not for your mouth."

The child should not be left unsupervised to play with soap, paints, markers, or playdough. Toxic substances should be locked up or out of reach. Parents can begin teaching their child to never put things in their mouth that have a *Mr. Yuk sticker** on them by marking a few non-toxic substances, such as playdough, with the sticker.

MENTALLY RETARDED PARENT

May not anticipate new safety precautions which arise with her child's increasing motor abilities and curiosity about unfamiliar substances.

1. Caution the parent that one of the biggest causes of serious illness and death in children under five is accidental poisoning; this happens from eating or drinking something that is not meant for eating.
2. Explain why we have to be especially cautious about keeping things that are poisonous out of children's reach. Include the following concepts:
   a. Children are naturally curious about things and so they like to taste them.
   b. Children do not know which things are poisonous.
   c. At this age, children are learning to open bottle tops and other containers.
   d. Children figure out quickly how to climb to get things that are out of his immediate reach.
   e. Many adult medicines look like candy.
   f. Some poisonous liquids may look like an interesting drink.
3. Identify potentially dangerous substances that are commonly found in each room of a house. Include cleaning supplies, medicines, plants, paints, perfumes, and insecticides:
   a. Show the parent where to move each dangerous item so they are out of her child's reach.
   b. Point out that since her child can climb on things and sometimes even move chairs to reach something, there are many more places that she cannot store dangerous substances.
   c. Each time an item is moved to a safer place, ask the parent if she thinks her child could climb up to get it.
4. Help the parent place Mr. Yuk stickers on poisonous substances. Caution her that her child does not know what they mean yet. Explain she can put them on his box of crayons to help him learn what the sticker means later. Help identify a few more inedible, but non-toxic, common substances on which to place them.
5. Role-play calling the local poison control center. Post this number of the phone with a Mr. Yuk sticker. The parent should be able to identify what her child ingested and how much.

---

*See Glossary.

6. Model saying "Yuk" to the child when he tastes inedible objects and showing him the appropriate use of the object. Encourage the parent to do this at home to help teach her child better ways of learning about objects.

BLIND PARENT

May not be able to visually monitor what her child puts in his mouth.

1. The parent can place all toxic substances out of her child's reach; however, the parent may need help identifying poisonous plants outdoors and peeling paint in more obscure places.
2. The parent can listen for any signs that her child may be putting inedible items in his mouth (e.g., sucking, licking, chewing sounds) and inspect it accordingly.
3. Provide and describe Mr. Yuk stickers so the parent can begin familiarizing her child to them as a danger signal.
4. Help identify toxic from non-toxic materials that the child may be exposed to for play materials, e.g., crayons, markers, glue, paints, and soaps.

6.44 **Child: CHEWS COMPLETELY WITH ROTARY JAW MOVEMENTS (18-24 mo.)**
Parent: Gives child plenty of textured food experiences

GENERAL GUIDELINES

The child demonstrates adult-like chewing movements in response to textured foods. He chews by moving the food with his tongue sideways, forward, and backward, as he uses rotary jaw movements. He can thus now eat most table foods including most meats.

Usually, ample exposure to textured foods is enough to encourage the child to develop rotary chewing if he is developmentally ready. If the child is having difficulty with rotary chewing, textured foods can be presented to the side of his mouth, between his cheek and teeth. Refer to 6.24 (Chews food with a munching pattern) for activities and example food guidelines.

MENTALLY RETARDED PARENT

May be unaware when her child is ready for foods which require additional chewing.

1. Name new foods the parent can begin to introduce to her child:
   a. Explain and demonstrate through pantomine that her child is now chewing more like us which lets him chew more of the same types of foods that we eat.
   b. Demonstrate the size that meats will still need to be cut so he does not have to chew too long.
2. Encourage the parent to schedule her child's first dental appointment and spend a few sessions with teaching him to brush his teeth, if this has not been addressed:
   a. Help the parent identify an appropriate stool to keep by the bathroom sink and suggest that they brush their teeth together.

b. Caution the parent not to let her child put toothpaste tubes in his mouth because some tubes are coated with lead, which is poisonous.

BLIND PARENT

May be unaware when her child demonstrates rotary chewing.

1. Advise the parent when you observe her child using rotary chewing movements:
   a. Explain the movement as the same we use for chewing.
   b. The parent can feel her child's rotary chewing movements by placing her fingertips on his upper jawline.
2. Introduce cut-up meats to the child to observe and advise the parent of the suitable size for pieces to be presented.

6.45 **Child: GIVES UP BOTTLE (18-24 mo.)**
Parent: Encourages child to give up his bottle gradually

GENERAL GUIDELINES

Most children discard their bottles by the age of two years. Their independent cup drinking skills and strive toward autonomy facilitate this weaning. Some children may periodically ask for a bottle until they are three or four years, especially when they are feeling anxious or need a little extra comfort.

Parents can facilitate this transition, especially if the child is very attached to his bottle, by weaning him gradually.

MENTALLY RETARDED PARENT

May abruptly stop giving her child bottles, or start weaning him before he is ready.

1. Discuss the benefits and problems that can arise when a child is weaned from his bottle. A parent group can act as an excellent vehicle for discussion for parents to share their experiences:
   a. Benefits include: No more bottles to wash; not always having to drag a bottle around everytime you go out; less diapers to change because the child will probably drink less.
   b. Problems which might occur include: It may be harder to get the child to sleep; he may not drink as much milk; he may be upset for days and keep whining or crying for it.
2. Help the parent understand why it may be difficult for her child to give up his bottle. Include the following concepts:
   a. The child's first experiences of feeling good and loved center around being held and fed with his bottle.
   b. His bottle has made him feel better when he was hungry, tired, sick, or worried.
   c. He is used to having a bottle around ever since he was born; it has been something he could always count on.
   d. Ask the parent if she can think of other reasons why it may be difficult for a child to give up his bottle.

6.45

3. Explain that there is no specific age when a young child should be taken off his bottle. Include the following points:
   a. Each child is different.
   b. A certain age may be good for one child and not good for another child (give a concrete age example).
   c. We cannot decide when a child is ready to give up bottles by listening to what our friends say, or because a friend's child gave up his bottle at that age.
4. Help the parent plan a schedule to gradually reduce and eliminate her child's bottle:
   a. Explain that since his bottle is so important to him, it is often better not to stop giving him bottles in one day. Compare gradual elimination of the bottle to eliminating a favorite thing of the parent's, such as a favorite food, television, etc.
   b. Identify how many bottles the child is drinking each day, when he drinks them, and what they contain.
   c. Ask the parent to decide which bottles seem to be the most and the least important to him.
   d. Plan the weaning schedule over a two- to four-week period dependent upon the child, situation, etc. Eliminate the bottles that the parent feels are least important to her child first, explaining to give him his drink in a cup for those bottles instead.
   e. Tell her never to give him a bottle unless he asks for it, and never to tell him he cannot have a bottle because he has been bad.
   f. Help the parent find a place to keep the bottles out of sight during the weaning schedule. Point out that if he does not see them around, he will be more likely to think about other things.
   g. Discourage weaning her child from the bottle if the child has had a recent trauma, such as a hospitalization or loss of a family member; there is a new baby in the home; or the child is evidencing a severe attachment or separation problem.

6.46 Child: **REMOVES SHOES WHEN LACES UNDONE (18-24 mo.)**
Parent: Encourages child to take off his own shoes

GENERAL GUIDELINES

The child takes off shoes which are untied or unfastened, and loosened. High-topped shoes may be more difficult and need to be pulled slightly off his heel first.

Parents can physically guide their child through the process of pulling his shoe off at the heel and gradually reduce their prompts. They can also encourage him to try taking off slip-on shoes and adult shoes used in play.

If the child uses short-leg braces, the parent can also encourage him to remove them after their fastenings have been opened. The parent should hold the cuff of the brace or back of the shoe, if needed.

MENTALLY RETARDED PARENT

May not encourage her child to remove his own shoes.

1. Demonstrate encouraging the child to take off his own shoes if they need to be removed for an activity, e.g., therapy, water play, naptime:
   a. Praise the child's successes to the parent, pointing out the places he needs extra help.
   b. Empathize how it takes more time to let him take off his shoes, but relate how it is worth the extra time because it helps him learn to do things for himself.
   c. Stress that his shoestrings need to be loosened.
2. Monitor the child's shoe size:
   a. Demonstrate how to check her child's shoes for proper fit.
   b. Explain the importance of proper fitting shoes, i.e., if they do not fit, it is harder to walk and bad for her child's growing foot.
   c. Stress that expensive leather shoes are not important; sneakers bought at the grocery store are just fine.
3. If the child's shoes are frequently untied, demonstrate, and let the parent practice, tying and untying a double knot.

BLIND PARENT

May not be able to visually monitor when her child takes off his shoes.

1. The parent can ask her child to "give me your shoes" after he has loosened them for him. This will let her know if he is successful and help her keep track of little shoes which easily fall behind beds, cushions, etc. If she does not receive the shoes, or does not hear his shoes come off (shoestrings with bells may be recommended), she can provide him physical assistance.

6.47 Child: **UNZIPS, ZIPS LARGE ZIPPERS (18-21 mo.)**
Parent: Provides opportunities for child to try zipping and unzipping large zippers

GENERAL GUIDELINES

The child learns to first unzip and then later to zip a zipper. Heavy duty zippers and zippers with big tabs are recommended for the child to practice this skill. Strings, ribbons, or keyrings can be attached to zipper tabs to make them easier to manipulate. The parent can also hold the base of the zipper to facilitate her child's zipping.

MENTALLY RETARDED PARENT

May assume her child can zip and unzip all zippers if she sees he can unzip an easier type.

1. Demonstrate to the parent various types of zippers on clothing, purses, cushions, or zippered toys:
   a. Point out the discriminating features which make some zippers easier to zip than others.

b. Ask the parent to think of some things with zippers she or her child have which would be appropriate for him to practice zipping.
c. Ask the parent to identify a zipper that would probably be too difficult.
d. Explain that it is often easier to unzip than zip things; therefore, sometimes her child may unzip something but may need help zipping it back up.
2. Help attach ribbons or heavy strings with a securely tied bead to the child's zipper on his jacket or diaper bag.

BLIND PARENT

May not be able to visually monitor her child's zipping abilities.

1. Explain that children learn to zip and unzip things tactually and by watching others zip things.
2. The parent can encourage her child to practice zipping using metal zippers which are audible when zipped. She will be able to hear her child's zipping progress or lack of it if he runs into trouble.

6.48   Child: **SITS ON POTTY CHAIR OR ON ADAPTIVE SEAT OR TOILET WITH ASSISTANCE (18-24 mo.)**
Parent: Introduces child to toileting without pressure

GENERAL GUIDELINES

The child sits on a potty chair or adapted toilet seat, with or without eliminating. He begins to be aware of his need to eliminate and the function of potties.

The child should be allowed to see and explore his toilet seat or potty before having to sit on it. He should never be forced to sit on the seat, or scolded for being unsuccessful. Toilet training should not be pushed or rushed.

There are no absolute timetables for toilet training. However, most agree that training should not be initiated before the child has bowel or bladder control, awareness, motivation, and developed a secure sense of striving toward autonomy.

Training pants, secure seats, a friendly adult, relaxed atmosphere, and unconditional praise facilitate the toilet training process. Toilet training should be delayed if the child is undergoing an unusual or traumatic change in his life, such as a new sibling, new babysitter, or a move to a new home.

MENTALLY RETARDED PARENT

May expect her child to sit on the toilet or potty until he is successful.

1. If the parent is initiating toilet training too early, refer to 6.34 (Shows bowel and bladder control).

2. Provide the parent with concrete initial toileting expectations for her child, i.e., he will not eliminate every time she puts him on the potty, will still have accidents over the next year, and will still need a diaper at nighttime for another year.
3. If you observe the parent to be using the child's potty chair for other purposes, such as for punishment or simply as an extra seat around the house:
   a. Explain that her child will be confused about what he is supposed to do on his potty chair if it is used for things other than toileting.
   b. Relate that her child may start disliking his potty and not want to sit on it.
   c. Suggest keeping his potty in the bathroom to help him learn how it is really intended to be used.
   d. Point out the benefits of keeping the potty chair in the bathroom, e.g., easier to clean up, helps the child associate the proper room for bathroom needs, and offers him the privacy he likes just like adults.
4. Caution the parent never to make her child sit on the potty if he does not want to and never make him sit on a potty for more than five minutes:
   a. Suggest using an egg timer.
   b. Suggest letting him sit there for the amount of time it takes her to wash and dry her hands and talk to him about how proud she is of him.
   c. Point out that, if she makes him sit there or makes him sit there too long, he will dislike his potty and it may take longer to train him.
5. Role-play situations that may occur as the child is learning toilet training:
   a. Situations could include the child refusing to sit on the toilet, flushing the toilet in front of the child, having an accident, and waiting to get off the toilet and then wetting his pants.
   b. Rehearse appropriate and inappropriate responses.
   c. Explain that the inappropriate responses can make toilet training take even longer and make her child feel worried and scared.

BLIND PARENT

May not be able to visually monitor her child's toileting successes.

1. A potty seat may provide more consistent auditory cues while the child is eliminating. If she is in the next room, washing up, etc., she will always know when her child has eliminated.
2. If the child uses a toilet, explain that some children are fearful of watching their bowel movements being flushed away.

PARENT SKILLS REFERENCE LISTING

COGNITIVE

1.01 Helps quiet child by picking up and responding to any of the child's needs (0-1 mo.)
1.02 Handles and interacts with child in mutually satisfying manner (0-6 mo.)
1.03 Provides controlled opportunities for child to respond to sound (0-1 mo.)
1.04 Provides adequate vocal stimulation to child (0-2½ mo.)
1.05 Provides adequate opportunities for child to visually explore environment (1-2 mo.)
1.06 Encourages child to become actively interested in object or person for at least one minute (1-6 mo.)
1.07 Talks to child using modified "child-sized" language during daily activities (1-3 mo.)
1.08 Recognizes and provides opportunities which facilitate child's anticipatory excitement (1½-4 mo.)
1.09 Sets up opportunities for child to react to the disappearance of slowly moving objects if recommended by an educator or therapist (2-3 mo.)
1.10 Encourages child to search for sounds with eyes; sets up controlled sound stimulation activities if prescribed by educator or therapist (2-3½ mo.)
1.11 Encourages child to look at own hands; facilitates when recommended by a teacher or therapist (2-3 mo.)
1.12 Frequently assumes en face position with child when talking (2-3 mo.)
1.13 Places appropriate rattle toys in child's hand and encourages play (2½-4 mo.)
1.14 Provides opportunities for child to repeat newly learned activities (3-4 mo.)
1.15 Allows, and facilitates if necessary, child's safe exploration of toys with hands and mouth (3-6 mo.)
1.16 Talks to child from various locations during daily activities (3-7 mo.)
1.17 Encourages child to play with own hands, feet, fingers, and toes (3-5 mo.)
1.18 Uses a soothing voice to quiet or awaken the child (3-6 mo.)
1.19 Plays structured sound localization games with children when recommended (3½-5 mo.)
1.20 Encourages child to find partially hidden objects (4-6 mo.)
1.21 Starts, then stops, activities and waits for child to make an indication to continue (4-5 mo.)
1.22 Provides appropriate tactile stimulation to child; encourages child to localize if recommended (4-6 mo.)
1.23 Provides safe opportunities for child to play with paper (4½-7 mo.)
1.24 Restarts toy or activity when child touches her hand or toy (5-9 mo.)
1.25 Provides opportunities and encouragement for child to purposefully reach for a second object (5-6½ mo.)
1.26 Encourages child to "work" for toy out of reach (5-9 mo.)
1.27 Understands that child can distinguish between friendly and angry voices; avoids strong negative inflections (5-6½ mo.)
1.28 Recognizes excessive hand regard and provides an alternative interesting visual target (5-6 mo.)
1.29 Plays "footsie" games while encouraging child to bring feet to mouth and explore (5-6 mo.)
1.30 Demonstrates making different sounds with a single toy; encourages child to imitate (5½-8 mo.)
1.31 Sets up "disappearance games" which encourage child to anticipate where the object will reappear if recommended (5½-7½ mo.)
1.32 Hides attractive object under 1 screen and encourages child to find it; then hides object using 2 and then 3 screens as child's ability dictates (6-9 mo.)
1.33 Initiates "Peek-a-boo" games in a playful manner with the child (6-9 mo.)
1.34 Encourages child to smell different things in the environment (6-12 mo.)
1.35 Provides toys appropriate to child's developmental level and interests (6-9 mo.)

1.36 Demonstrates sliding different toys and objects on a variety of surfaces to child; encourages child to practice (6-11 mo.)

1.37 "Sets up" or uses naturally occurring experiences to encourage child to follow and find a rapidly moving or falling object after it passes behind obstacles (6-8 mo.)

1.38 Offers ample opportunity for child to hear names of family members, pets, and friends (6-8 mo.)

1.39 Uses a variety of facial expressions which *match* emotions or situations in front of the child (6-7 mo.)

1.40 Encourages child to obtain a third object while holding two (6½-7½ mo.)

1.41 Points out hidden sounds in the environment to child; sets up situations which encourage child to turn heads to sounds if recommended (7-10 mo.)

1.42 Plays imitation games with gestures (7-11 mo.)

1.43 Gives simple requests with gestures to child, encouraging his gestural responses (7-9 mo.)

1.44 Shows, and talks about, a variety of interesting pictures to child (8-9 mo.)

1.45 Provides opportunities for child to attain a third object while holding two (8-10 mo.)

1.46 Provides opportunities for child to successfully figure out how to overcome an obstacle (8-11 mo.)

1.47 Provides opportunities for child to successfully figure out how to obtain an object by pulling the support it is on (8-10 mo.)

1.48 Emphasizes labels for familiar words to the child during daily activities (8-12 mo.)

1.49 Encourages child to find an object he has seen hidden under three layers of screens placed one at a time (9-10 mo.)

1.50 Demonstrates action toy for child and encourages him to manually guide the toy when it has stopped (9-12 mo.)

1.51 Understands child's developmentally appropriate "throwing" of objects; provides experiences for suitable throwing activities (9-12 mo.)

1.52 Understands child's developmentally appropriate behavior of dropping objects systematically; provides appropriate opportunities for child to practice (9-12 mo.)

1.53 Encourages child to obtain an object moved out of reach (9-12 mo.)

1.54 Provides adequate opportunities to listen to speech without an excessively competing sound environment (9-11 mo.)

1.55 Says "no-no" to child using congruent facial and vocal expressions at appropriate times (9-12 mo.)

1.56 Gives child simple verbal requests, within context (9-14 mo.)

1.57 Encourages child to remove round piece from a shape puzzle (10-11 mo.)

1.58 Demonstrates and encourages child to take rings off a ring stack toy (10-11 mo.)

1.59 Gives child cups to play with; encourages "pretend" drinking games (10-15 mo.)

1.60 Provides child with interesting picture books (10-14 mo.)

1.61 Provides opportunities for child to obtain safe objects wrapped loosely in paper (10½-12 mo.)

1.62 Hides object from child with one displacement if recommended (11-13 mo.)

1.63 Demonstrates putting cylinders in matching holes of containers; encourages child to try (11-12 mo.)

1.64 Demonstrates and encourages child to put rings on a stick (11-12 mo.)

1.65 Provides opportunities for child to hear music and encourages him to move to rhythms (11-12 mo.)

1.66 Models and encourages child to initiate combining two familiar gestures (11-14 mo.)

1.67 Activates action toy and encourages child to give it back after it stops to reactivate (12-15 mo.)

1.68 Understands the importance of, and provides opportunities for, child to play with messy activities such as fingerpainting (12-18 mo.)

1.69 Exposes, and remarks to child about, various temperature and taste sensations; recognizes his reaction responses (12-18 mo.)

1.70 Emphasizes primary colors and contrasting size during daily activities (12-18 mo.)

1.71 Encourages child to place round piece in a formboard (12-15 mo.)

1.72 Provides various sized round containers, and encourages child to "nest" them; first two, then three containers (12-19 mo.)

1.73 Points to objects and interprets child's pointing (12-14 mo.)

1.74 Demonstrates, and provides opportunities for child to obtain objects and toys by pulling a string horizontally (12-13 mo.)

1.75 Sets up situations, and encourages child to make detours to retrieve objects (12-18 mo.)

1.76 Encourages child to look for the ball in the pace it rolled out of sight; helps him obtain it if needed (12-13 mo.)

1.77 Facilitates positive interaction between child and other adults beyond the immediate family (12-18 mo.)

1.78 Hides object from child by displacement using two screens, if recommended (13-14 mo.)

1.79 Demonstrates and encourages child to pull string vertically to obtain a toy (13-15 mo.)

1.80 Hides object from child by displacement using three screens, if recommended (14-15 mo.)

1.81 Hides an object by displacement, randomly under one of two screens if recommended (14-15 mo.)

1.82 Encourages child to pat pictures (14-15 mo.)

1.83 Encourages child to assist while turning pages of a book (14-15 mo.)

1.84 Imitates one of child's invisible gestures, encouraging him to imitate it again (14-17 mo.)

1.85 Points out familiar objects in the environment which match to child (15-19 mo.)

1.86 Encourages child to place square pieces in formboard (15-21 mo.)

1.87 Asks child to select two objects from a group of three to five familiar objects during daily activities (15-18 mo.)

1.88 Asks child to get a familiar object from another room (15-18 mo.)

1.89 Encourages child to turn pages of a book using his own methods (15-18 mo.)

1.90 Provides numerous opportunities for child to look at self and others playfully in the mirror (15-16 mo.)

1.91 Emphasizes "important" body parts for child on self, child, dolls, and others during daily activities (15-19 mo.)

1.92 Provides sufficient opportunities for child to see animals and animal pictures; emphasizes labeling animals when pointing them out to child (16-21 mo.)

1.93 Labels many noun objects for child throughout daily activities (16-19 mo.)

1.94 Hides objects by displacement under the third screen (17-18 mo.)

1.95 Sets up or uses naturally occurring situations which encourage her child to solve simple problems by using an unrelated object (17-24 mo.)

1.96 Imitates several of the child's invisible gestures on separate occasions, encouraging him to imitate them back (17-20 mo.)

1.97 Models pointing and calling child's attention to distant objects; acknowledges child's pointing by talking about the object pointed toward (17½-18½ mo.)

1.98 Activates a mechanical toy and encourages child to restart it after the action stops (18-22 mo.)

1.99 Provides opportunities for child to explore and manipulate playdough, and experience various painting activities (18-24 mo.)

1.100 Teaches child to apply paste on one side of shape and turn it over to stick on paper (18-24 mo.)

LANGUAGE

2.01 Interprets child's cry as his means of communicating his needs (0-1½ mo.)

2.02 Interprets child's cry as his means of communicating his needs (0-1 mo.)

2.03 Reinforces child's vocal sounds of comfort (0-2½ mo.)

2.04 Recognizes the child's nutritive and non-nutritive need for sucking (½-3 mo.)

2.05 Differentiates and responds appropriately to child's different cries (1-5 mo.)
2.06 Initiates social interactions with child which encourage him to laugh (1½-4 mo.)
2.07 Reinforces child's coos (2-7 mo.)
2.08 Encourages and reinforces child's vocalizations (2-3 mo.)
2.09 Differentiates and responds appropriately to child's different cries (2½-4½ mo.)
2.10 Encourages child's squealing (2½-5½ mo.)
2.11 Provides controlled sound and vocal stimulation to child (3-6 mo.)
2.12 Briefly and playfully covers child's head with a cloth (3½-4½ mo.)
2.13 Provides a meaningful and responsive language environment for child (4-6½ mo.)
2.14 Differentiates child's vocalized attitudes; responds accordingly (5-6 mo.)
2.15 Provides musical experiences which are pleasing to the child (5-6 mo.)
2.16 Vocalizes the child's name often during daily activities, reinforces his positive responses (5-7 mo.)
2.17 Includes double consonant words in her child's language environment (5-8 mo.)
2.18 Provides a meaningful and responsive language environment for child (5½-6½ mo.)
2.19 Encourages child to notice and respond to others' waves for "bye-bye," in context, during daily experiences (6-9 mo.)
2.20 Helps child associate his "dada" and "mama" vocalizations with corresponding parent (6½-11½ mo.)
2.21 Attends when child shouts for attention (6½-8 mo.)
2.22 Provides adequate vocal stimulation for child; reinforces child's vocalizations throughout day (7-15 mo.)
2.23 Exposes child to vocal interjectional patterns; reinforces child's interjections (7½-9 mo.)
2.24 Exposes child to speech with varied inflection; reinforces child's inflectional babbling (7½-12 mo.)
2.25 Reinforces and interprets child's single consonant vocalizations (8-12 mo.)
2.26 Interprets which words her child understands (9-14 mo.)
2.27 "Talks" to child meaningfully throughout day; reinforces child's vocal responses (11-15 mo.)
2.28 Provides time alone for child to babble to self and interesting toys (11-12 mo.)
2.29 Says "dada" or "mama" in meaningful context with child, and interprets his expanded meaning when he says "mama" or "dada" (11-14 mo.)
2.30 Laughs when appropriate at child's silly sounds or gestures (11-12½ mo.)
2.31 Understands that child's speech may plateau as child begins to learn to walk; continues appropriate vocal stimulation (11½-15 mo.)
2.32 Understands that child's speech may plateau as child begins to learn to walk; continues appropriate vocal stimulation (11½-15 mo.)
2.33 Understands child's developmentally appropriate omission of initial and/or final consonants; vocalizes correct speech to child in response (12-17 mo.)
2.34 Reinforces and responds to child's intricate vocal inflection patterns (12-18 mo.)
2.35 Recognizes child's experimentation with communication; interprets and replies when appropriate (12-17½ mo.)
2.36 Interprets and expands child's one word sentence into a complete sentence (12-14 mo.)
2.37 Exposes child to adequate speech and language activities; fosters and reinforces child's expressive vocabulary (12-15 mo.)
2.38 Correctly interprets child's vocalizations and gestures which indicate wants and responds appropriately (12-19 mo.)
2.39 Exposes child to varied opportunities to hear verbal greetings from others; encourages child's verbal greetings within an appropriate context (12-15 mo.)
2.40 Exposes child to exclamatory vocalizations (12½-14½ mo.)
2.41 Provides opportunities for child to say "no," abiding to his responses when possible (13-15 mo.)
2.42 Models correct pronunciation of object child named within a complete phrase (13-18 mo.)

2.43 Sings simple repetitive songs with child (13-16 mo.)
2.44 Interprets and responds to child's vocalizations and gestures (14-20 mo.)
2.45 Interprets and models correct pronunciation of words child says within a complete phrase (15-17½ mo.)
2.46 Encourages child to vocalize needs at mealtime (15-17½ mo.)
2.47 Does not expect child to pronounce his words perfectly; models correct pronunciation (15½-21 mo.)
2.48 Reinforces the value and usefulness of verbal communication with child (17-19 mo.)
2.49 Understands child's echoing can be a natural stage in language development (17-19 mo.)
2.50 Provides child a meaningful and responsive language environment (17½-20½ mo.)
2.51 Recognizes child's jargon as his way to practice sounds, inflections, and fluency (18-22 mo.)
2.52 Uses child's name during interactions and encourages him to refer to himself by name (18-24 mo.)
2.53 Models and encourages child to imitate environmental sounds (18-21 mo.)
2.54 Models "child-size" two-word phrases (18-21 mo.)
2.55 Exposes child to simple songs and finger plays (18-23 mo.)
2.56 Exposes child to a variety of meaningful pictures; encourages him to name a few (19-21½ mo.)
2.57 Encourages child to expand his single word sentences to two-word phrases (20½-24 mo.)

GROSS MOTOR

3.01 Understands child's neck righting reaction if tested (0-2 mo.)
3.02 Alternates stimuli and positions which encourage child to turn his head to both sides (0-2 mo.)
3.03 Provides ample opportunities for child to be on tummy; stimulates to lift head in prone (0-2 mo.)
3.04 Provides ample opportunities for child to be on tummy; stimulates to lift head in prone (0-2½ mo.)
3.05 Provides ample opportunities for child to be on tummy with interesting visual targets on each side of his head (0-2 mo.)
3.06 Supports child's head when held at shoulder and encourages him to lift his head (0-1 mo.)
3.07 Provides ample opportunities for child to be on tummy; stimulates to lift head in prone (1-3 mo.)
3.08 Lifts and carries child in a manner which facilitates his head control (1½-2½ mo.)
3.09 Provides opportunities for child to move out of a totally flexed posture into a more extended posture (1½-2½ mo.)
3.10 Encourages child to roll from side to supine (1½-2 mo.)
3.11 Does not restrict child's leg movements; carries out prescribed positioning if child's muscle tone interferes with reciprocal kicking (1½-2½ mo.)
3.12 Positions child in prone and side-lying if prescribed to help inhibit child's extensor thrust (2-4 mo.)
3.13 Positions child in prone and side-lying if prescribed to help inhibit flexor withdrawal (2-4 mo.)
3.14 If prescribed, implements positioning techniques to help normalize tone (2-3½ mo.)
3.15 Provides ample opportunities for child to play in prone; implements special positioning to help him lift his chest and bear some weight on forearms (2-4 mo.)
3.16 Encourages and if necessary, facilitates child's head extension and rotation in prone (2-3 mo.)
3.17 Encourages child to roll from prone to supine; facilitates through handling techniques if prescribed (2-5 mo.)
3.18 Lifts and carries child in a manner which facilitates his head control (2½-3½ mo.)

3.19 Implements prescribed positioning techniques which help inhibit child's asymmetrical tonic reflex if indicated (3-5 mo.)

3.20 Does not pull child up to sitting position, pulling his hands; implements prescribed handling techniques to accommodate poor head control if indicated (3-6½ mo.)

3.21 Provides necessary support and opportunities for child to develop head control in upright positions (3-5 mo.)

3.22 Places child in sitting, provides slight support at hips (3-5 mo.)

3.23 Does not encourage child to stand (3-5 mo.)

3.24 Inhibits moro reflex with gentle handling and adequate head support (4-5 mo.)

3.25 Understands child's protective extension responses; facilitates child's prone propping positions if recommended (4-6 mo.)

3.26 Provides ample opportunities for child to be on tummy; stimulates to lift head and chest in prone (4-6 mo.)

3.27 Implements prescribed handling techniques if indicated to improve child's head and trunk control (4-6 mo.)

3.28 Encourages child to roll from supine to side (4-5½ mo.)

3.29 Positions child in a manner which facilitates sitting momentarily while leaning on hands (4½-5½ mo.)

3.30 Provides ample opportunities for child to reach for toys in prone (5-6 mo.)

3.31 Provides ample opportunity for child to be in prone; encourages circular pivoting (5-6 mo.)

3.32 Assures adequate trunk support and environmental stimulation which promotes child's moving head actively in sitting (5-6 mo.)

3.33 Assures adequate trunk support and encourages child to hold head erect when leaning forward in sitting (5-6 mo.)

3.34 Carries out activites which facilitate child's sitting independently in a variety of appropriate positions (5-8 mo.)

3.35 Helps discourage child's supine "bridging" if it is prolonged or used as a form of locomotion (5-6½ mo.)

3.36 Does not encourage child to stand prematurely (5-6 mo.)

3.37 Holds child to sitting in a manner which encourages child to lift head and assist (5½-7½ mo.)

3.38 Encourages child to roll from supine to prone; facilitates segmental rolling when prescribed (5½-7½ mo.)

3.39 When indicated, carries out appropriate relaxation activites which promote child's body righting on body action (6-8 mo.)

3.40 Carries out activities which encourage child to demonstrate balance reactions in supine (6-7 mo.)

3.41 Carries out activities which promote child's protective extension of arms to side and front if prescribed (6-8 mo.)

3.42 Recognizes child's ability to lift head in supine as an indication of increasing head control (6-8 mo.)

3.43 Encourages child to reach for toys in prone (6-7½ mo.)

3.44 Helps child move into a sitting position if he is having difficulty (6-10 mo.)

3.45 Does *not* over-use weight bearing and bouncing activities with child (6-7 mo.)

3.46 Helps child stand at appropriate furnishings for short periods (6-10½ mo.)

3.47 Encourages child to pull up to standing; helps when necessary (6-10 mo.)

3.48 Implements prescribed handling techniques to help discourage child's trunk asymmetry if indicated (6-8 mo.)

3.49 Understands that child may crawl backwards as he experiments with moving (7-8 mo.)

3.50 Carries out activities which promote child's balance reaction on hands and knees if recommended (8-9 mo.)

3.51 Engages child in activities which encourage him to sit without hand support (8-9 mo.)

3.52 Provides ample opportunities for child in prone; encourages his forward movement (8-9½ mo.)

3.53 Does *not* encourage child to walk prematurely (8-10 mo.)

3.54 Helps child assume a hand-knee position if prescribed (8-9 mo.)

3.55 Implements balance activities with her child in sitting if prescribed (9-10 mo.)

3.56 Implements activities which help child develop backward protective extension if prescribed (9-11 mo.)

3.57 Encourages child to go from sitting to prone, facilitating through positioning if prescribed (9-10 mo.)

3.58 Encourages child to lower self safely to sitting from standing at furniture; assists as needed (9-10 mo.)

3.59 Encourages child to creep on hands and knees; implements weight-shifting activities if prescribed (9-11 mo.)

3.60 Provides opportunities for child to practice standing alone with an immediate support available (9½-11 mo.)

3.61 Encourages child to cruise around furniture (9½-13 mo.)

3.62 Implements prescribed handling techniques if prescribed to facilitate child's head and trunk control (10-11 mo.)

3.63 Encourages child to pivot in sitting (10-11 mo.)

3.64 Understands that some children creep on their hands and feet before gaining balance in an upright position (10-12 mo.)

3.65 Encourages child to walk three or four steps with adequate support (10-12 mo.)

3.66 Encourages child to stoop and pick up objects, insuring appropriate support as needed (10½-14 mo.)

3.67 Provides safe opportunities for child to pull up to standing (11-12 mo.)

3.68 Encourages child to stand alone 2-3 seconds after removing support (11-13 mo.)

3.69 Helps child assume and maintain an appropriate kneeling position (11-13 mo.)

3.70 Encourages child to walk a few steps while holding his hand (11-13 mo.)

3.71 Encourages child to stand alone; positions child in prone stander if prescribed (11½-14 mo.)

3.72 Encourages child to walk alone two to three steps, gradually reducing assistance as indicated (11½-13½ mo.)

3.73 "Sets up" opportunities which encourage child to develop balance reactions in kneeling when prescribed (12-15 mo.)

3.74 Provides safe opportunities for child to practice lowering himself from standing; responds positively when child falls to sitting (12-14 mo.)

3.75 Encourages child to stand up from supine independently (12½-15 mo.)

3.76 Understands that some children like to practice walking backward (12½-21 mo.)

3.77 Models throwing balls underhand in play; provides child physical assistance if needed (13-16 mo.)

3.78 Encourages and facilitates child's creeping or hitching upstairs (13½-15 mo.)

3.79 Provides child ample opportunities and encouragement to walk independently (13-15 mo.)

3.80 Sets up situations which encourage child to walk sideways (14-15 mo.)

3.81 Provides a safe environment which accommodates the child's early running (14-18 mo.)

3.82 Recognizes child's ability to bend over and look through his legs as a fun position which promotes his balance and flexibility (14½-15½ mo.)

3.83 Carries out activities which encourage child's balance reactions in standing if prescribed (15-18 mo.)

3.84 Demonstrates and encourages child to kick a ball using any methods (15-18 mo.)

3.85 Encourages child to throw balls while standing during play (15-18 mo.)

3.86 Helps child walk across an eight-inch board if recommended (15-17 mo.)

3.87 Demonstrates and encourages child to pull toys on strings while walking (15-18 mo.)

3.88 Plays ball with child aiming at targets; encourages his overhand throw (16-22 mo.)

3.89 Provides support for child in situations which encourage him to stand on one foot (16-17 mo.)

3.90 Holds child's hands and helps him walk upstairs (17-19 mo.)
3.91 Encourages child to independently carry large safe objects while walking (17-18½ mo.)
3.92 Sets up purposeful situations which encourage child to push and pull large toys or boxes around the floor (17-18½ mo.)
3.93 Sets up situations which encourage child to walk with a narrow base of support if needed (17-19½ mo.)
3.94 Provides support, if needed, as child is learning to bear weight on one foot (17½-18½ mo.)
3.95 Provides opportunities for child to seat himself in small chairs (17½-19 mo.)
3.96 Models, and encourages child to kick ball forward (18-24½ mo.)

FINE MOTOR

4.01 Presents colorful attracting objects at appropriate distances to child in a facilitating position (0-1 mo.)
4.02 Recognizes child's arm movements as a positive response to stimuli; implements special positioning if prescribed (0-2 mo.)
4.03 Presents colorful attracting objects at appropriate distances to child in a facilitating position (½-2½ mo.)
4.04 Provides opportunities for child to watch people during daily activities (½-1½ mo.)
4.05 Provides a visually stimulating environment for child (1-2 mo.)
4.06 Engages child in tracking activities which facilitate child's following an object with eyes to midline if prescribed (1-3 mo.)
4.07 Encourages child to bring hands to midline; facilitates through positioning when necessary (1-3½ mo.)
4.08 Presents toy which encourages child to activate arms on sight; facilitates arm movement as necessary (1-3 mo.)
4.09 Recognizes that the child blinks at sudden visual stimuli (2-3 mo.)
4.10 Engages child in tracking activities which encourage child to follow with eyes past midline if recommended (2-3 mo.)
4.11 Engages child in tracking activities which encourage him to follow an object downward (2-3 mo.)
4.12 When indicated, carries out activities and positioning techniques which discourages child's indwelling thumb (2-3 mo.)
4.13 Encourages child to actively grasp safe and appropriately sized objects (2-4 mo.)
4.14 Encourages child to look from one object to another (2½-3½ mo.)
4.15 Positions child in prone or side-lying to facilitate hand opening if indicated (2½-3½ mo.)
4.16 Encourages child to reach for toy (2½-4½ mo.)
4.17 Engages child in tracking activities which encourage him to follow an object with eyes 180° if recommended (3-5 mo.)
4.18 Provides opportunities for child to follow moving objects in supported sitting (3-4½ mo.)
4.19 Engages child in tracking activities which facilitate following objects upwards with eyes if recommended (3-4 mo.)
4.20 Provides ample opportunities for child to grasp object; places child in positions which help inhibit his grasp reflex if recommended (3-4 mo.)
4.21 Encourages and facilitates child bringing hands to midline and clasping them (3½-5 mo.)
4.22 Presents appropriately sized and shaped objects to child which facilitates child ulnar-palmar grasp (3½-4½ mo.)
4.23 Presents visual stimuli to child with his head in midline (4-5 mo.)
4.24 Recognizes child can look at things in his visual field without turning his head (4-6 mo.)
4.25 Positions child in prone or side-lying to facilitate hand opening if indicated (4-8 mo.)
4.26 Encourages child to reach with both arms (4-5 mo.)
4.27 Presents toys which encourage child to reach and grasp (4-5 mo.)

4.28	Provides graspable toys and objects within child's reach (4-5 mo.)
4.29	Provides ample opportunities and materials which facilitate child's grasp (4½-5½ mo.)
4.30	Provides ample opportunities and materials which facilitate child's grasp (4½-6 mo.)
4.31	Draws child's attention to tiny objects (4½-5½ mo.)
4.32	Draws child's attention to distant objects (5-6 mo.)
4.33	Provides ample opportunities for child to hold and drop objects; helps place them back in his hand (5-6 mo.)
4.34	Encourages child to recover objects dropped within easy reach (5-6 mo.)
4.35	Encourages child to hold an object in each hand (5-6 mo.)
4.36	Encourages child to watch her scribble on paper (5½-7 mo.)
4.37	Encourages child to reach unilaterally with each arm (5½-7 mo.)
4.38	Provides safe toys which can be held with one hand (5½-7 mo.)
4.39	Allows child to bang objects on various surfaces; demonstrates how fun this can be (5½-7 mo.)
4.40	Encourages child to try to attain a tiny object (5½-7 mo.)
4.41	Provides safe toys and materials which encourage child's manipulating with wrist movement (6-8 mo.)
4.42	Encourages child to reach and grasp with extended elbow (7-8½ mo.)
4.43	Provides materials which encourage child's radial-digital grasp (7-9 mo.)
4.44	Provides opportunities for child to rake bits of food (7-8 mo.)
4.45	Presents tiny safe objects which encourage child to practice using an inferior pincer grasp (7½-10 mo.)
4.46	Encourages child to hit two objects together at midline during play (8½-12 mo.)
4.47	Encourages child to remove "peg-like" objects from holes (8½-10 mo.)
4.48	Provides child containers and objects to play with (9-11 mo.)
4.49	Provides ample play materials and activities which promote child's wrist extension (9-10 mo.)
4.50	Provides child materials which encourages voluntary release (9-11 mo.)
4.51	Provides materials which encourage child to "poke" with index finger (9-12 mo.)
4.52	Presents tiny safe objects which encourage child to pick up with a pincer grasp (10-12 mo.)
4.53	Demonstrates scribbling and encourages child to imitate in any way (10½-12 mo.)
4.54	Does not force child hand preference (11-13 mo.)
4.55	Provides crayons which facilitate child's grasp (11-12 mo.)
4.56	Provides child containers and objects to play with (11-12 mo.)
4.57	Introduces gestures and materials which encourage child's forearm supination (11-12 mo.)
4.58	Provides materials suitable for child's stacking efforts (11-12 mo.)
4.59	Demonstrates making simple strokes and scribbles on paper; encourages child to make marks (12-13 mo.)
4.60	Encourages child to put at least three objects into small containers (12-13 mo.)
4.61	Provides materials which encourage child to build a tower of two cubes (12-16 mo.)
4.62	Demonstrates and encourages child to place peg in pegboard (12-15 mo.)
4.63	Models pointing, encourages child to point for communication and fine motor skills (12-16 mo.)
4.64	Shows child how to obtain object from narrow necked containers (12½-18 mo.)
4.65	Provides ample opportunities for child to scribble (13-18 mo.)
4.66	Anticipates and accommodates for child's new problem solving and fine motor skills (13½-19 mo.)
4.67	Demonstrates and encourages child to put various objects into a variety of containers (14-15 mo.)
4.68	Introduces child to toys and activities which encourage him to use two hands cooperatively (16-18 mo.)
4.69	Reinforces child's continuing stacking efforts (16-18 mo.)

4.70 Encourages child to place at least six pegs in a board (16-18 mo.)
4.71 Encourages child to imitate her vertical stroke with a crayon (18-24 mo.)

SOCIAL-EMOTIONAL

5.01 Provides child with adequate and appropriate physical contact and tactile stimulation (0-3 mo.)
5.02 Offers child sufficient face-to-face contact (0-1 mo.)
5.03 Recognizes child's reflexive smiles (0-1½ mo.)
5.04 Encourages child's eye contact via compatible interactions (0-2 mo.)
5.05 Holds child in a manner which is conducive to cuddling and molding (0-3 mo.)
5.06 Recognizes and responds to child's signs of distress (0-3 mo.)
5.07 Enjoys compatible doses of social play with child, reinforcing child's smile (1½-4 mo.)
5.08 Utilizes soothing techniques if child has not stopped unexplained crying (3-6 mo.)
5.09 Initiates communicative interaction with child; encourages his responsive vocalizations (3-5 mo.)
5.10 Recognizes and understands child's discriminatory behaviors toward strangers (3-6 mo.)
5.11 Exposes child to unfamiliar people in a supportive manner (3-5 mo.)
5.12 Recognizes and responds to child's demands for social attention (3-8 mo.)
5.13 Discriminates and responds appropriately to child's vocalized attitudes of pleasure and displeasure (3-6 mo.)
5.14 Provides supportive experiences for child to become aware of unfamiliar places/people (3-6 mo.)
5.15 Plays interactive games with child (3-6 mo.)
5.16 Provides opportunities for child to look at himself in a mirror (3-5½ mo.)
5.17 Maintains primary caregiving and interaction roles with child; responds to his signs of recognition (4-8 mo.)
5.18 Engages child in frolic play, monitoring over-stimulation (4-8 mo.)
5.19 Initiates and repeats activities and games with child which are likely to encourage child to repeat and enjoy (4-8 mo.)
5.20 Understands and adapts for child's stranger anxiety (5-8 mo.)
5.21 Encourages child to lift arms before picking up (5-6 mo.)
5.22 Encourages child to explore adult features (5-7 mo.)
5.23 Encourages child to smile at his image in a mirror (5½-8½ mo.)
5.24 Understands the importance of and facilitates child's distinguishing self as a separate person from parent (6-9 mo.)
5.25 Gradually helps child "work through" separation anxiety (6-9 mo.)
5.26 Plays simple "give and take" games with child (6-10 mo.)
5.27 Understands and adapts for child's resistance to supine position (6-12 mo.)
5.28 Plays with child in front of a mirror (6-9 mo.)
5.29 Offers a sympathetic, but casual and supportive, approach to child's fears and insecurity with previously accepted situations (6-18 mo.)
5.30 Recognizes and respects child's likes and dislikes (7-12 mo.)
5.31 Recognizes and respects, when possible, child's need to let only mother meet his needs (8-12 mo.)
5.32 Encourages child to show toy to others; understands that the child is not ready to release it (9-12 mo.)
5.33 Understands and responds appropriately to child's "testing" parental reactions during feeding (9-12 mo.)
5.34 Understands and responds appropriately to child's "testing" parental reactions at bedtime (9-12 mo.)
5.35 Encourages, and facilitates, when necessary, child's engaging in simple imitative play (9-12 mo.)

5.36 Allows child to safely explore the environment (9-12 mo.)
5.37 Recognizes and accommodates for their child's need to be in constant sight and hearing of an adult (12-13 mo.)
5.38 Reinforces child's sharing (12-15 mo.)
5.39 Understands, allows, and responds effectively to child's independent behavior (12-15 mo.)
5.40 Understands and responds effectively to child's "impulsive" behaviors (12-15 mo.)
5.41 Understands child's resistance to adult control and allows opportunity for his self-direction within safe limits (12-15 mo.)
5.42 Understands, anticipates, and responds effectively to child's tantrum behaviors (12-18 mo.)
5.43 Respects and accommodates child's need for rituals and routine within appropriate limits (12-18 mo.)
5.44 Reinforces and encourages child's sense of humor (12-18 mo.)
5.45 Introduces and encourages child to imitate appropriate new tasks and adult behaviors (12-18 mo.)
5.46 Plays ball with child (12-15 mo.)
5.47 Recognizes, understands, and respects child's individual toy preferences (12-18 mo.)
5.48 Understands and adapts for child's distractable behaviors (12-15 mo.)
5.49 Understands and allows within limits, child's messiness (12-18 mo.)
5.50 Provides sufficient opportunities for child to be the center of attention (12-18 mo.)
5.51 Encourages and reinforces child's hugs and kisses (14-15½ mo.)
5.52 Encourages child to imitate simple household chores (15-18 mo.)
5.53 Encourages and returns child's expressions of affection (18-24 mo.)
5.54 Understands and responds supportively to child's signs of jealousy (18-24 mo.)

SELF-HELP

6.01 Feeds child in an appropriate and comfortable position (0-1 mo.)
6.02 Feeds child in pace with his sucking, swallowing, and breathing (1-5 mo.)
6.03 Accommodates child's individual sleeping patterns and needs (1-3 mo.)
6.04 Provides a responsive environment during child's waking hours (1-3 mo.)
6.05 Accommodates child's individual sleeping patterns and needs (1-3 mo.)
6.06 Continues to position child appropriately during feeding; if bottle fed, assure suitable nipple hole size and proper formula preparation (2-5 mo.)
6.07 Allows child to bring hands to mouth for oral stimulation and exploration, facilitates when necessary (2-4 mo.)
6.08 Introduces strained foods to child as recommended, and encourages mature lip closure and tongue movements (3-6 mo.)
6.09 Allows and facilitates if necessary, child's safe exploration of toys with his mouth (3-5 mo.)
6.10 Provides ample opportunity for child to visually observe his bottle (3½-4½ mo.)
6.11 Introduces foods to child with lumpy textures (4-8½ mo.)
6.12 Helps inhibit child's rooting reflex if prescribed (4-6 mo.)
6.13 Encourages child to pat bottle (4-5 mo.)
6.14 Attends to, without reinforcing, child's fussing during nighttime sleep (4-8 mo.)
6.15 Recognizes and responds appropriately to child's individual sleeping patterns (4-8 mo.)
6.16 Encourages child to hold his bottle with both hands when it is held for him during feeding (4½-5½ mo.)
6.17 Introduces child to foods which encourage mouthing and gumming; demonstrates first aid for possible choking (5-8 mo.)
6.18 Uses bottles which are easy for child to hold (5½-9 mo.)
6.19 Offers and presents food which facilitates child's biting (6-8 mo.)
6.20 Helps child drink from a cup (6-12 mo.)

6.21   Provides ample opportunities for child to feed himself appropriate crackers (6½-8½ mo.)
6.22   Provides child safe toys to bite and chew (7-8 mo.)
6.23   Implements "drool control" techniques with child if prescribed (7-12 mo.)
6.24   Offers child a variety of textured foods (8-13½ mo.)
6.25   Provides ample opportunities and foods which encourage child to finger feed himself (9-12 mo.)
6.26   Helps child hold spoon when needed; allows child to hold spoon during feeding and play (9-12 mo.)
6.27   Allows child to get as much sleep as he needs; does not reinforce child's "testing" at bedtime (9-12 mo.)
6.28   Allows child to get as much sleep as he needs; does not reinforce child's "testing" at bedtime (9-12 mo.)
6.29   Encourages child to help during dressing (10½-12 mo.)
6.30   Understands child's "stage" of refusing foods; continues to encourage and monitor adequate nutritional intake (12-18 mo.)
6.31   Lets child practice feeding himself with a spoon; accommodates his crude spoon handling (12-15 mo.)
6.32   Lets child drink from a cup independently; understanding inevitable spilling (12-18 mo.)
6.33   Provides experiences for child to hold appropriate cup by its handles (12-15½ mo.)
6.34   Recognizes child's more regular elimination patterns; understands this does not mean he is ready for training (12-18 mo.)
6.35   Recognizes and responds to child's signals which indicate he has soiled or wet his pants (12-18 mo.)
6.36   Allows child to get as much sleep as he needs (13-18 mo.)
6.37   Allows child to get as much sleep as he needs (13-18 mo.)
6.38   Uses dishes and foods which help child feed himself with a spoon (15-24 mo.)
6.39   Encourages child to remove his socks independently (15-18 mo.)
6.40   Encourages child to take off and later put on his own hat (15-16½ mo.)
6.41   Encourages child to take off and later put on his own hat (16½-18½ mo.)
6.42   Encourages child to give her his dish when finished or wants more (18-19 mo.)
6.43   Prevents child from ingesting inedible substances (18-23 mo.)
6.44   Gives child plenty of textured food experiences (18-24 mo.)
6.45   Encourages child to give up his bottle gradually (18-24 mo.)
6.46   Encourages child to take off his own shoes (18-24 mo.)
6.47   Provides opportunities for child to try zipping and unzipping large zippers (18-21 mo.)
6.48   Introduces child to toileting without pressure (18-24 mo.)

GLOSSARY

Adapted cup holder — An adjustable glass or cup holder for people with limited grasp. Provides a handle which can be bent to fit over a person's hand.

Adaptive pencil holder — Holds a pencil or pen in the palm or fingertips of a person who has a weak grasp.

Adventitiously blind or deaf — an individual who was born with normal sight or hearing but lost it later in life through an accident or illness.

Asymmetrical tonic neck reflex (ATNR) — A primitive responds to head movement, where turning the head to one side causes the arm and leg of the face side to extend and the opposite arm and leg to flex.

Beeper ball — A ball which has an internal electronic beeper. Provides auditory cues for location to people without vision.

Bilateral — Pertaining to, affecting, or relating to two sides of the body.

Bilateral glass holder — An adapted cup holder with two handles. Helps people with limited hand control and grasps to lift a cup using both hands.

Book holder — A frame constructed from wood, acrylic, plastic, or wire which can hold a book at various angles. Helpful for people who have upper extremity limitations.

Braille paper — Heavy paper which is specially produced for use with braille producing instruments.

Congentially blind or deaf — An individual who is blind or deaf at birth.

Dycem® — A nonslip plastic which prevents plates, glasses, bowls, equipment, and machines from slipping and sliding.

Elastic utensil holder — see *Universal cuff*.

Expressive language — Expressing one's thoughts, ideas, and feelings through vocalizations, signs, gestures, and/or writing.

Extension — The straightening of any part of the body. Total extension is the straightening out of all joints of the body. The opposite of flexion.

Fingerspelling — The use of the manual alphabet to form words, titles, or personal names.

Fixing — Compensation for instability at a joint or joints resulting from weakness or hypotonia. It is characterized by hyperextension or "locking" of a joint, a widened base of support, or substitution by other muscle groups; e.g., elevated shoulders sometimes compensate for inadequate head control.

Flexion — Bending any part of the body at a joint. The opposite of extension.

Hyperextension — Too much extension; e.g., with neck hyperextension, the head is tilted too far back.

Hypertonia — Increased tension of muscles making movements difficult. Sometimes referred to as "tight" muscles.

Hypotonia — Decreased tension of muscles making upright postures difficult to hold. Sometimes referred to as "floppy" muscles.

Imitate – Repeating an activity after observing a demonstration.

Inflection – Pitch changes used in speech to add meaning to speech. For example, there is a rise in pitch at the end of questions, "Are you tired?"

Intonation – Changes in volume or quality used in speech to add meaning to speech.

Lap tray – A tray constructed from Masonite, plastic, or wood which can be attached to the armrests of a wheelchair.

Lipreading (speechreading) – To understand the spoken language through observation of the speaker's oral movements and facial expressions.

Log roll carrier – A heavy flat piece of canvas, leather, or vinyl which has handles attached to the ends. Firewood can be placed in the center and the ends drawn up in order to carry the wood. May be helpful to a parent in a wheelchair to lower her infant to the floor.

Midline – An imaginary line down the center of the body. This is the basic reference point for all body parts.

Model – To give an example to be imitated. To demonstrate how to do something.

Mr. Yuk sticker – Small round fluorescent sticker with a "Yuk" face and local poison control phone number.

Name sign – A manual sign which identifies and refers to an individual. Everyone has a different name sign which is unique to him or her.

Nosey cut-out cup – An unbreakable plastic cup which has a portion cut out for the nose. Helps a person drink without tipping their head back or extending their neck.

Orientation assistance – Provision of verbal explanation and tactile familiarization to help people without vision establish their position in relation to objects in an unfamiliar environment.

Page turning stick – To help people with upper extremity limitations turn pages of a book. Can be constructed by attaching a piece of rubber to one end of a dowel rod.

Pointer – A lightweight aluminum and plastic rod which can be worn around a person's head or held in a mouth as an aid for communication.

Port-a-play gym – Portable crib gym.

Prone – Lying on the stomach.

Reacher – A long handled aid which enables an individual with a limited reach or inability to bend at the knees, hips, or waist to pick up objects from shelves or the floor. Available commercially in various lengths, weights, and operating mechanism.

Receptive language – The ability to understand what is being communicated, usually through verbal communication.

Reciprocal – Moving one extremity at a time in alternation.

Residual vision – Many people who are blind have some degree of usable sight, often called *residual vision.*

Scoop plate – A plastic scoop dish with a high curved edge on one side and a low edge on the other side. Provides easy access to food and aids in filling the fork or spoon. It has a no-slip bottom.

Sign language — A manual language that uses signs and fingerspelling to represent ideas and concepts.

Snuggly vest — A carrier which is made of heavy fabric and worn on the front of an adult's chest to carry an infant.

Sound sensitive receiver box — Sound sensor box which receives sound waves and activates a visual stimulus, such as a light. Helpful to people without hearing to recognize when their child cries.

Stabiles, EMI nursery — Sets of three static-cling vinyl forms (face, checkerboard, and bull's eye patterns) printed in yellow, red, and blue. Attach without marring to glass and plastic surfaces and provide appropriate visual stimulation to neonates. The are reuseable and washable.

Supine — Lying on the back.

Symmetrical movements — Moving corresponding parts of the body simultaneously and in the same direction.

Tilt board — Platform on rockers which may be tilted to test child's balance reactions.

Total communication — A method of deaf education which employs any and all means of communication to develop language (speech training, amplification, lipreading, fingerspelling, signing, reading, writing, etc.).

Tri-wall — Thick sturdy cardboard which will not bend and can be cut with a carpet knife. Available at local hardware stores.

Twin vision books — Combines pages of print and braille so that blind and sighted readers can enjoy them together.

Universal cuff — A durable pouch attached to the palm of the hand by elastic. Enables a person with a poor grip to hold eating or writing utensils.

Upper extremity limitations — Any condition which interferes with a person's ability to move her arms through a functional range of motion. Conditions may include paralysis, arthritis, weakness, contractures, or amputations.

Velcro wrist cuff — See *Universal cuff*.

Wrist band bells — A wrist band made from soft ½-1 inch elastic with a jingle bell sewn on very securely.

REFERENCES

Materials

Adapted cup holder
Available at most local medical supply stores. Also available through most rehabilitation/medical supply catalogs. See examples below.

Adapted pencil holder
Available at most local medical supply stores. Also available through most rehabilitation/medical supply catalogs. See examples below.

Beeper Ball
Sammons Preston, Inc.,
P.O. Box 5071, Bolingbrook, IL 60440
(800) 323-5547

Bilateral Glass Holder
Available at most local medical supply stores. Also available through most rehabilitation/medical supply catalogs. See examples below.

Book Holder
Available at most local book stores. Also available through most rehabilitation/medical supply catalogs. See examples below.

Dycem
Available at most local medical supply stores. Also available through most rehabilitation/medical supply catalogs. See examples below.

Lap Tray
Available at most local medical supply stores. Also available through most rehabilitation/medical supply catalogs. See examples below.

Log Roll Carrier
Available at most local hardware stores

Mr. Yuk Stickers
Available through most local poison control centers

Nosey Cut-out Glass/cups
Available at most local medical supply stores. Also available through most rehabilitation/medical supply catalogs. See examples below.

Pointer
Available at most local medical supply stores. Also available through most rehabilitation/medical supply catalogs. See examples below.

Port-A-Play Gym
Commercially named, "Activity Links Gym" by Fisher Price
Available at major toy store chains.

Reacher
Available at most local medical supply stores and pharmacies which carry medical equipment. Also available through most rehabilitation/medical supply catalogs. See examples below.

Scoop Plate
Available at most local medical supply stores. Also available through most rehabilitation/medical supply catalogs. See examples below.

See-N-Say Toys
by Mattel
Available at major toy store chains.

Signed English Storybooks
Harris Communications, Inc.
Voice: 800-825-6758
TTY: 612-906-1198
http://www.harriscomm.com

Snugly Vest
Available in many baby departments of major Department store chains.

Sound Sensitive Receiver Box & Baby Cry Receiver
NFSS Communications
8120 Fenton St., Silver Spring, MD 20910
Voice: 888-589-6671
TTY: 888-589-6670
http://www.nfss.com

Hear-More Inc.
PO Box 3413
Farmingdale, NY 11735
Voice/TTY: 800-881-4327
http://www.hearmore.com

Twin Vision Books
National Library Service for the Blind and Physically Handicapped
Library of Congress
Washington, DC
202-707-5100
http://www.loc.gov/nls

Universal Cuff
Available at most local medical supply stores. Also available through most rehabilitation/medical supply catalogs. See examples below.

Rehabilitation Medical Supply Catalogs

The following are examples of a few companies but should not be considered exhaustive.

Sammons Preston, Inc.,
P.O. Box 5071, Bolingbrook, IL 60440
(800) 323-5547
http://www.sammonspreston.com

North Coast Medical Products
P.O Box 6070
San Jose, CA 95150
(800)235-7054
http://www.blvd.com/northcoa.htm

Yes I Can
1356 W. Valley Parkway - Suite J
Escondido, CA 92029
(619) 739-7900

Support Plus/FashionAble,
99 West St., Box 500, Medfield, MA 02052
(800) 229-2910

Additional Helpful Resouces and Organizations

General

ABLEDATA
8455 Colesville Road, Suite 935
Silver Spring, MD 20910
Voice: (301) 608-8998
TTY: (301) 608-8912
Voice/TTY: (800) 227-0216
WWW Home Page: http://www.abledata.com
Information and referral project that maintains a database of 20,000-plus assistive technology products.

Visually Impaired

AMERICAN PRINTING HOUSE FOR THE BLIND
1839 Frankfurt Avenue
P.O. Box 6085
Louisville, KY 40206
(800) 223-1839 or
(502) 895-2405
(502) 899-2292 FAX

NATIONAL FEDERATION OF THE BLIND
MATERIALS CENTER
1800 Johnson St., Baltimore, Md. 21230
410-659-5654
http://www.nfb.org

AMERICAN FOUNDATION FOR THE BLIND
Information Center
1-800-232-5463
http://www.afb.org/afb

Hearing Impaired

NATIONAL INFORMATION CENTER ON DEAFNESS
Gallaudet University
800 Florida Ave. NE
Washington, DC 20002-3695
Voice: (202) 651-5051
TTY: (202) 651-5052
FAX: (202) 651-5054
WWW Home Page: http://www.gallaudet.edu/~nicd/

REGISTRY OF INTERPRETERS OF THE DEAF, INC.
8630 Fenton Street, Suite 324
Silver Spring, MD 20910
Voice/TTY: (301) 608-0050
Certifies interpreters, provides information on interpreting to the general public, publishes a national directory of certified interpreters, and makes referrals to interpreter agencies.

BIBLIOGRAPHY

Adamson, L., et al. "The Development of Social Reciprocity Between a Sighted Infant and Her Blind Parents." *Journal of the American Academy of Child Psychiatry*, **16**, 1977: p. 194-207.

American Foundation for the Blind. *A step-by-step guide to personal management for the blind persons, second edition*. American Foundation for the Blind: New York, 1974.

American Red Cross. *Standard first aid and personal safety* (Second edition), 1979.

Bindt, J. *A handbook for the blind*. New York: Macmillan Co., 1952.

Blacha, S. "An Integrated Overview of the Development of Reach and Grasp." (Instructional Paper) *Neurodevelopmental treatment certification course*. Kingston, Ontario, May-June 1978.

Bobath, B. *Abnormal postural reflex activity caused by brain lesions*. London: Heinemann Medical Books Ltd., 1971.

Bobath, K., & Bobath, B. "The Facilitation of Normal Postural Reactions and Movements in the Treatment of Cerebral Palsy." *Physiotherapy*, **50**: 3-19.

Braun, M. A., Palmer, M. M., & Salek, B. *Early detection and treatment of the infant and young child with neuromuscular disorders*. New York: Therapeutic Media Inc., 1982.

Caplan, F. (Ed.). *The first twelve months of life*. New York: Grosset & Dunlap, 1978.

Caplan, F., & Caplan, T. *The second twelve months of life*. New York: Grosset & Dunlap, 1978.

Clark, G. N., & Seifer, R. "Facilitating Mother-Infant Communication: A Treatment Model for High Risk and Developmentally-Delayed Infants." *Infant Mental Health Journal*, **4**, 1983.

Cohen, J. "Disability Etiquette-Interating with People with Disabilities." New York: ACCESS Resources, 1993.

Crittenden, P. M., & Bonvillian, J.D. "The Relationship Between Maternal Risk Status and Maternal Sensitivity." Department of Psychology, University of Virginia, Charlottesville, Virginia, Photocopy.

Ferske, Robert (Ed.). *Mealtimes for the severely and profoundly handicapped*. Baltimore: University Park Press, 1977.

Finnie, N. R. *Handling the young cerebral palsied child at home*. New York: E. P. Dutton & Co., Inc. (Second Edition). 1975.

Furuno, S., et al. *Hawaii Early Learning Profile (HELP) Activity Guide*. Palo Alto, California: VORT Corporation, 1979.

Hopper, R., & Navemore, R. C. *Children's speech*. New York: Harper & Row, 1973.

Kukla, D., & Connolly, T. T. "Assessment of Auditory Functioning of Deaf-Blind/Multi-Handicapped Children." South Central Regional Center for Services to Deaf-Blind-Children. Dallas, Texas, 1978. Photocopy.

Lake, S. J. *The handbook*. Tucson, Arizona: Communication Skill Builders, Inc., 1976.

Luddington-Hoe, S. M. "What Can Newborns Really See?" *American Journal of Nursing* (Sept. 1983): 1286-1289.

McClowry, D. P. (Ed.). *Infant communication: development, assessment and intervention*. New York: Grune & Stratton, 1982.

McKenna, D. *Parent skills curriculum: a curriculum for mentally handicapped parents of young children*. Unpublished manuscript, Northwest Center Infant and Toddler Program. Seattle, Washington. Undated.

McLean, J. E., & Snyder-McLean, L. K. *A transactional approach to early language training*. Columbus, Ohio: Charles E. Merrill, 1978.

Meadows, K. P., et al. "Interactions of Deaf Mothers and Deaf Preschool Children: Comparisons with Three Other Groups of Deaf and Hearing Dyads." *American Annal for the Deaf*, **126**, June 1981: 454-467.

National Center for Access Unlimited. "Ten Commandments of Etiquette for Communicating with People with Disabilities." Chicago, Illinois, 1995.

Riekehog, L. *The joy of signing*. Springfield, Missouri: Gospel Publishing House, 1978.

Rosenberg, S.A., & McTate, G. A. "Intellectually Handicapped Mothers: Problems and Prospects." *Children Today* (II), 1982: 24-26.

Rosenberg, B. A. *Parentmaking*. Menlo Park, California: The Bannister Press, 1981.

SHHH. "Strategies for communication between hearing and the hearing-impaired", Bethesda, Maryland, 1995.

Wilson, J. M. (Ed.). *Oral-motor function and dysfunction in children*. University of North Carolina at Chapel Hill, North Carolina, 1978.

HELP – Hawaii Early Learning Profile Family of Products

#159–Inside HELP – Administration and Reference Manual for using HELP (0-3)
The essential resource to fully utilize HELP for IDEA Part C evaluation and assessment
This comprehensive reference manual shows you how to get started with HELP. It contains all the assessment guidelines and procedures for assessing each skill that you need to effectively use HELP 0-3. Provides procedures for curriculum- based assessment, planning, therapy, and intervention.

Supported by *Inside HELP*, following are the other HELP (birth-3) components for comprehensive assessment, planning, intervention, and family support

#157–HELP Family-Centered Interview
Facilitates your family interview and assessment process – a listing of 80 key open-ended questions and prompts based on over 400 sample questions from Inside HELP – in a simple format you can use directly with parents. Helps you focus on family-centered priorities and outcomes for more effective intervention.

#158–HELP Strands – Assessment record; skills grouped in hierarchical sequence
Developmental assessment booklet of 685 HELP skills grouped into 58 "concept-based" Strands for easier assessment and planning. Helps you meet IDEA, Part C regulations – in conjunction with Inside HELP, you can identify a child's level of development and interpret why a child may be having difficulty in a specific strand. Makes for easier identification and selection of target skills. Includes data columns for credit notes/dates/observations.

#151–HELP Checklist — Assessment booklet (option to the HELP Strands)
Covers the same six developmental areas of Cognitive, Language, Gross Motor, Fine Motor, Social and Self-Help as the HELP Strands, but the format is different – the skills are **not** arranged in hierarchical sequence. The Checklist groups the 685 skills by area and in age sequence with columns for easy recording of assessment dates, progress information, and comments.

#150–HELP Charts – Visually track progress
The Charts are a set of three different sheets that display 685 developmentally sequenced skills as a horizontal continuum for the six areas of Cognitive, Language, Gross Motor, Fine Motor, Social and Self-Help. Each sheet covers 2 areas. The clear format makes it easy to identify current mastery of skills, to target objectives, and to record and visually track progress. Ideal for communicating with and involving parents in their child's plan.

#156–HELP at Home – Best-selling resource in support of families
540 pages of unique, reproducible, ready- to-use parent handouts to help you make parent involvement easy and effective! Saves time – Practical and convenient format covers the 685 assessment skills from HELP – with each page formatted as a separate, reproducible activity sheet you annotate, copy and hand out directly to parents to facilitate their involvement. Interdisciplinary and comprehensive –Handouts for parents with children (developmentally) birth to three years, including disabled, delayed and at risk children. Provides thousands of activities in 6 major developmental areas. Written from the child's point of view – Parents definitely prefer this unique approach. Written in warm, simple and non-technical language. Easily individualized – With space for your notes.

#152–HELP Activity Guide– program curriculum
Comprehensive strategies and activities for intervention. This very popular and widely-used resource takes you easily beyond assessment to offer the important next step – thousands of task-analyzed, practical curriculum activities and intervention strategies indexed by the 685 HELP skills. Offering up to 10 activities per skill, this important tool includes definitions for each skill, illustrations and cross references to skills in other developmental areas, a glossary, and a list of commercial materials.